Lecture Notes in Computer Science 16867

The series Lecture Notes in Computer Science (LNCS), including its subseries Lecture Notes in Artificial Intelligence (LNAI) and Lecture Notes in Bioinformatics (LNBI), has established itself as a medium for the publication of new developments in computer science and information technology research, teaching, and education.

LNCS enjoys close cooperation with the computer science R & D community, the series counts many renowned academics among its volume editors and paper authors, and collaborates with prestigious societies. Its mission is to serve this international community by providing an invaluable service, mainly focused on the publication of conference and workshop proceedings and postproceedings. LNCS commenced publication in 1973.

Klaus Miesenberger · Helen Petrie · Petr Peňáz
Editors

Computers Helping People with Special Needs

20th International Conference, ICCHP 2026
Brno, Czech Republic, July 15–17, 2026
Proceedings, Part II

Springer

Editors
Klaus Miesenberger
Johannes Kepler University Linz
Linz, Austria

Helen Petrie
University of York
York, UK

Petr Peňáz
Masaryk University
Brno, Czechia

ISSN 0302-9743 ISSN 1611-3349 (electronic)
Lecture Notes in Computer Science
ISBN 978-3-032-31307-2 ISBN 978-3-032-31308-9 (eBook)
https://doi.org/10.1007/978-3-032-31308-9

This Springer imprint is published by the registered company Springer Nature Switzerland AG
The registered company address is: Gewerbestrasse 11, 6330 Cham, Switzerland

Preface

Welcome to the Proceedings of ICCHP 2026!

We are pleased to present the Proceedings of the 20th edition of the ICCHP conference. Since the first conference in 1989, nearly 40 years ago, ICCHP has become one of the largest and most respected scientific conferences on accessibility, assistive technologies and digital technology enhanced inclusion. Even if Artificial Intelligence (AI) is now the topic absorbing much scientific attention, ICCHP rightly keeps its highly user-centered focus on developments to support the integration and quality of life of people with disabilities and older people. The conference enables us to regularly meet and discuss the latest technical, political, legal and social developments in all topics relating to how technology can best support disabled and older people. It is also an opportunity to renew old friendships and make new ones, to network and collaborate with others in our field. This year's conference included sessions on technology to support people with dyslexia, blindness and low vision, people who are deaf or hard of hearing, people with motor disabilities, neurodivergent people, those with mental health issues and older people. Topics ranged from the perception of art, through plain language to web accessibility and of course the use of AI to support disabled and older people.

This year there were 258 submissions to the conference from more than 45 countries around the world. Naturally there was a highly competitive process for selecting contributions for presentation at the conference and publication in the proceedings. The Program Committee of 123 experts from across the field carefully assesses every proposal, with each one being reviewed in a double-blind process by three to five experts. Then the committee of 18 conference chairs assessed the reviews for each submission and led a discussion of it at the Program Committee Meeting. This selection procedure guaranteed the high scientific quality of the papers presented at the conference and included in the proceedings. 123 contributions were accepted for publication and you are able to read them in these Proceedings, organized into thematically grouped chapters. Several other contributions were presented at the conference in additional formats.

The chapters are based on the Special Thematic Sessions (STSs) proposed by researchers and experts on topics about which they are knowledgeable and which they believe are particularly timely and of interest to researchers and practitioners in the field. Each STS has an Introduction written by its organizers, to provide readers with context on both the scientific topic and the contributions which are included in that STS. With this approach, the ICCHP proceedings are highly readable and understandable, not only for our members of our own community, but also for researchers and practitioners in other fields who are interested in the topics. This makes them a key reference on the research and practice underpinning the development and implementation of a more open and accessible mainstream digital society.

This year ICCHP 2026 took place July 15–17, 2026, at Masaryk University in Brno, Czechia. It provided an exciting event open to everyone interested in new and original ways to put technology at the service of people living with disability.

Participants contributed to the conference in multiple ways:

- Scientific contributions, which underwent the rigorous peer review process and are now available in in two different publications:
  - These two *Springer Lecture Notes in Computer Science (LNCS)* volumes, which focus more on the development, engineering, and computer science perspective of Assistive Technology and Accessibility, and
  - the *Open Access Compendium "Assistive Technology, Accessibility and (e)Inclusion" (OAC)*, which focuses more on research related to the policy, education, implementation and social services perspective.

Papers accepted for both publication channels are presented in integrated thematic sessions which facilities a unique cross-disciplinary view and discussion in the specialized domains. The STS introductions included in these LNCS proceedings also reference and discuss the OAC contributions.

- Inclusion Area contributions, which provide a space for discussion, collaborations and participation of multiple stakeholders. Contributions to the Inclusion Area were reviewed by the program committee and were presented at the conference in different formats including workshops, tutorials, seminars, posters, and policy sessions with panel discussions. The conference also included a space for workshops, tutorials, seminars, posters, and policy sessions, where participants showcased projects, products, and services. Inclusion Area contributions are published in the digital Book of Abstracts, which collects short descriptions of all contributions to the conference.
- Students presented their ongoing research in The Young Researchers' Consortium.

We would like to thank the Panel of Chairs, the Young Researchers Committee, the Inclusion Area Committee, the International Scientific Committee, the Organizing Committee and the student volunteers who dedicated precious time and effort to the organization of this event. Many thanks to our sponsors and supporters who helped to make ICCHP a unique inclusive scientific experience.

Moreover, we want to thank all of the participants at the conference for furthering the mission of ICCHP, based on the belief that technology can contribute to breaking barriers, empowering people, and enhancing equity and inclusion for people with all abilities.

July 2026

Helen Petrie
Klaus Miesenberger
Petr Peňáz

Organization

ICCHP Committees

Our special thanks go to those contributing to put this conference in place

Conference Chair

Petrie, H.	University of York, UK

Publication Committee

Miesenberger, K.	Johannes Kepler University Linz, Austria
Peňáz, P.	Masaryk University, Czechia
Petz, A.	Johannes Kepler University Linz, Austria

Scientific Committee Chairs

Archambault, D.	Université Paris 8, France
Buehler, C.	Technical University Dortmund, Germany
Coughlan, J.	Smith-Kettlewell Eye Research Institute, USA
Covarrubias Rodriguez, M.	Politecnico di Milano, Italy
Debevc, M.	University of Maribor, Slovenia
Fels, D.	Toronto Metropolitan University, Canada
Janča, B.	Masaryk University, Czechia
Kobayashi, M.	Tsukuba University of Technology, Japan
Kouroupetroglou, G.	National and Kapodistrian University of Athens, Greece
Manduchi, R.	University of California at Santa Cruz, USA
Mavrou, K.	European University Cyprus, Cyprus
Weber, G.	Dresden University of Technology, Germany
Zagler, W.	TETRAGON Braille Systems GmbH, Austria
Zlatuška, J.	Masaryk University, Czechia

Young Researchers Committee

Archambault, D.	University of Paris 8, France
Chen, W.	University of Bergen, Norway
Fels, D.	Toronto Metropolitan University, Canada
Fitzpatrick, D.	National Disability Authority, Ireland
Kobayashi, M.	Tsukuba University of Technology, Japan
Morandell, M.	Smart In Life, Health University of Applied Sciences Tirol, Austria
Pagliara, S. M.	University of Cagliari, Italy
Plhák, J.	Masaryk University, Czechia
Pontelli, E.	New Mexico State University, USA
Prazak-Aram, B.	Ferdinand Porsche FERNFH, Austria
Ruh, D.	RuhGlobal, USA
Sik Lányi, C.	University of Pannonia, Hungary
Weber, G.	Dresden University of Technology, Germany
Zimmermann, G.	Stuttgart Media University, Germany

Inclusion Area Committee

Pavlíček, R.	Masaryk University, Czechia
Petz, A.	Johannes Kepler University Linz, Austria
Pühretmair, F.	KI-I, Austria

Scientific Committee

Abbott, C.	King's College London, UK
Abhayaratne, A.	University of Peradeniya, Sri Lanka
Abu Doush, I.	American University of Kuwait, Kuwait
Andreoni, G.	Politecnico di Milano, Italy
Andrich, R.	Global AT Information Network (EASTIN), Italy
Augstein, M.	University of Applied Sciences Upper Austria, Austria
Bernareggi, C.	Università degli Studi di Milano, Italy
Bosse, I.	University of Teacher Education in Special Needs, Switzerland
Boudy, J.	Télécom SudParis, France
Bu, J.	Zhejiang University, China
Chamberlain, H.	Helen Chamberlain Consulting, USA
Christensen, L. B.	Sensus, Denmark

Craddock, G.	Centre for Excellence in Universal Design, Ireland
Darvishy, A.	Zürcher Hochschule für Angewandte Wissenschaften, Switzerland
Desideri, L.	AIAS Bologna Onlus, Italy
Diaz del Campo, R.	Antarq Tecnosoluciones, Mexico
Dorabawila, S.	University of Perideniya, Sri Lanka
Draffan, E.A.	University of Southampton, UK
Dupire, J.	CNAM, France
Ebling, S.	University of Zurich, Switzerland
Encarnação, P.	Católica Lisbon School of Business and Economics, Portugal
Engelen, J.	Katholieke Universiteit Leuven, Belgium
Galinski, Ch.	InfoTerm, Austria
Gardner, J.	Oregon State University, USA
Grava Boland. S.	St. John of God Liffey Services, Ireland
Grinberg, M.	New Bulgarian University, Bulgaria
Hakkinen, M. T.	Educational Testing Service, USA
Hallewell-Haslwanter, J. D.	University of Applied Sciences Upper Austria, Austria
Haslwanter, T.	University of Applied Sciences Upper Austria, Austria
Heimgaertner, R.	Intercultural User Interface Consulting, Germany
Heumader, P.	Fabasoft, Austria
Hoeckner, K.	Hilfgemeinschaft der Blinden und Sehschwachen, Austria
Holone, H.	Østfold University College, Norway
Hoogerwerf, E. J.	AIAS Bologna, Italy
Hosono, N.	NPO Niimaru, Japan
Hoxha, M.	University of Tirana, Albania
Hruz, M.	University of West Bohemia in Pilsen, Czechia
Inoue, T.	National Rehabilitation Center for PwD, Japan
Isaksson-Daun, J.	Chalmers University of Technology, Sweden
Iversen, C. M.	U.S. Department of State (retired), USA
Jašková, L.	Comenius University in Bratislava, Slovakia
Jitngernmadan, P.	Burapha University, Thailand
Kastner, P.	University of Applied Sciences Upper Austria, Austria
Koumpis, A.	University of Passau, Germany
Koutny, R.	Johannes Kepler University Linz, Austria
Krainz, E.	University of Applied Sciences Joanneum, Austria
Kushalnagar, R.	Gallaudet University, USA
Lewis, C.	University of Colorado Boulder, USA

Lhotska, L.	Czech Technical University in Prague, Czechia
Macík, M.	Czech Technical University in Prague, Czechia
Magnusson, Ch.	Lund University, Sweden
Matamala Ripoll, A.	Universitat Autònoma de Barcelona, Spain
Matausch-Mahr, K.	Johannes Kepler University Linz, Austria
McSorley, J.	Pearson, USA
Míkovec, Z.	Czech Technical University in Prague, Czechia
Mohamad, Y.	Fraunhofer Institute for Applied Information Technology, Germany
Moreira Silva Dantas, P.	Universidade Federal do Rio Grande do Norte, Brasil
Mrochen, I.	MultiAccess Centre, Poland
Muratet, M.	INS HEA, France
Nussbaum, G.	KI-I, Austria
Osman, R.	Masaryk University, Czechia
Oswal, S.	University of Washington, USA
Øderud, T.	SINTEF Digital, Norway
Paciello, M.	Pearson, USA
Pagliara, S.	University of Cagliari, Italy
Panek, P.	Vienna University of Technology, Austria
Perez, E.	Constantine the Philosopher University in Nitra, Slovakia
Pino, A.	National and Kapodistrian University of Athens, Greece
Pissaloux, E.	University of Rouen Normandy, France
Plhák, J.	Masaryk University, Czechia
Pontelli, E.	New Mexico State University, USA
Rassmus-Groehn, K.	Lund University, Sweden
Raynal, M	University of Toulouse, France
Schaur, M.	Johannes Kepler University Linz, Austria
Scherer, M.	Institute for Matching Person & Technology, USA
Simsik, D.	University of Kosice, Slovakia
Slavik, P.	Czech Technical University in Prague, Czechia
Sloan, D.	The Paciello Group, UK
Soares Guedes, L.	Università della Svizzera Italiana, Switzerland
Stankovičová, M.	Comenius University in Bratislava, Slovakia
Stepankova, O.	Czech Technical University in Prague, Czechia
Stiefelhagen, R.	Karlsruhe Institute of Technology, Germany
Stoeger, B.	Johannes Kepler University Linz, Austria
Takahashi, Y.	Toyo University, Japan
Teixeira, A.	Universidade de Aveiro, Portugal
Teshima, Y.	Chiba Institute of Technology, Japan

Tjoa, A.M.	Technical University of Vienna, Austria
Tkáčik, M.	Braille Authority of Slovakia, Slovakia
Matej Hrebenda	Slovak Library for the Blind in Levoča
Velleman, E.	Accessibility Foundation, The Netherlands
Vigo, M.	University of Manchester, UK
Vigouroux, N.	IRIT Toulouse, France
Vogler, C.	Gallaudet University, USA
Vonen, M. A.	Oslo Metropolitan University, Norway
Wada, C.	Kyushu Institute of Technology, Japan
Wagner, G.	Upper Austria University of Applied Sciences, Austria
Wakatsuki, D.	Tsukuba University of Technology, Japan
Waller, A.	University of Dundee, UK
Waszkielewicz, A.	Foundation for Persons with Disabilities (FRONia), Poland
Watanabe, T.	University of Niigata, Japan
Weber, H.	ITA, University of Kaiserslautern, Germany
Wu, C. H.	National Taichung University of Education, Taiwan
Yamaguchi, K.	Nihon University, Japan
Yesilada, Y.	Middle East Technical University, Cyprus
Zbiejczuk Suchá, L.	Masaryk University, Czechia

Organization Committee

Aichinger, M.	IIS, Johannes Kepler University Linz, Austria
Bieber, R.	Austrian Computer Society, Austria
Bukovský, T.	Masaryk University, Czechia
Cincibus, Z.	Masaryk University, Czechia
Feichtenschlager, P.	IIS, Johannes Kepler University Linz, Austria
Miesenberger, K.	IIS, Johannes Kepler University Linz, Austria
Moravec, A.	Masaryk University, Czechia
Nuppenau, K.	IIS, Johannes Kepler University Linz, Austria
Ondra, S.	Masaryk University, Czechia
Pavlíček, R.	Masaryk University, Czechia
Penáz, P.	Masaryk University, Czechia
Petz, A.	IIS, Johannes Kepler University Linz, Austria
Schaumüller-Bichl, I.	Austrian Computer Society, Austria
Schult, C.	IIS, Johannes Kepler University Linz, Austria
Seyruck, W.	Austrian Computer Society, Austria
Wernerová, P.	Masaryk University, Czechia

ICCHP Roland Wagner Award Committee

Contents

Indoor and Outdoor Navigation for Disabled People: Challenges and Opportunities

Innovation, Accessibility, and Artificial Intelligence: Towards an Inclusive Technological Future

Design for Accessible/Inclusive Sports and Rehabilitation with Assistive Technologies

Design for Inclusive Sports and Rehabilitation with Assistive Technologies Introduction to the Special Thematic Session

Mario Covarrubias[1(✉)], Paolo Perego[2], Sara Arlati[3], and Giuseppe Andreoni[2]

[1] Department of Mechanical Engineering, Politecnico di Milano, Milan, Italy
mario.covarrubias@polimi.it
[2] Department of Design, Politecnico di Milano, Milan, Italy
{paolo.perego,giuseppe.andreoni}@polimi.it
[3] Institute of Intelligent Industrial Technologies and Systems for Advanced Manufacturing, Milan, Italy
sara.arlati@stiima.cnr.it

Abstract. The convergence of self-tracking technologies, Artificial Intelligence (AI), and eXtended Reality (XR) is rapidly transforming the design of assistive systems for inclusive sports and rehabilitation. The growing availability of low-cost wearable sensors, the maturation of deep-learning models for biosignal interpretation, and the diffusion of consumer-grade immersive hardware have created the conditions for a new generation of adaptive, personalized, and participatory solutions. This Special Thematic Session (STS) brings together multidisciplinary contributions addressing accessibility, adaptive training, and user-centered design across diverse contexts, from education to sport-specific applications.

This paper introduces a unifying framework for AI-driven XR ecosystems integrating multimodal sensing, virtual coaching, and inclusive interaction design. It further contextualizes the accepted contributions within the STS, highlighting their complementary roles: sensory substitution for inclusive sailing, accessible physical activity frameworks in primary education, AI-driven immersive training systems, and semantic interoperability between assistive technology standards.

Taken together, these works demonstrate how data-driven, adaptive, and inclusive technologies can support diverse users by enhancing participation, engagement, autonomy, and functional outcomes. The paper contributes a holistic perspective on the future of assistive technologies for sports and rehabilitation, emphasizing the importance of integrating technological innovation with human-centered design, clinical evidence, and standardized interoperability frameworks.

Keywords: Inclusive Design · Assistive Technologies · XR · AI · Rehabilitation · Adaptive Sports · Sensory Substitution

K. Miesenberger et al. (Eds.): ICCHP 2026, LNCS 16867, pp. 3–9, 2027.
https://doi.org/10.1007/978-3-032-31308-9_1

1 Introduction

The increasing availability and affordability of wearable sensors, mobile applications, and self-tracking technologies have enabled continuous monitoring of physical, cognitive, and behavioral parameters at a granularity that was until recently confined to specialized laboratories. Inertial measurement units, photoplethysmography, electromyography, electrodermal activity sensors, and smart textiles can now be deployed in daily life, in ecological environments, and for prolonged periods of time. These systems are reshaping how individuals understand and manage their health, while also providing valuable data for rehabilitation and adaptive training.

Beyond self-tracking, the integration of Artificial Intelligence (AI) and Extended Reality (XR) is enabling a qualitatively new generation of assistive technologies. AI-driven systems can analyze multimodal data streams—motion, physiology, voice, gaze, and context—to provide real-time, personalized feedback, thereby improving understanding of physiological and health data. At the same time, XR environments offer user interfaces for richer visualization, immersive training scenarios, and safe exploration of motor tasks that would otherwise be difficult, risky, or inaccessible. The combination of continuous sensing, machine learning, and immersive simulation is particularly relevant for inclusive sports and rehabilitation, where personalization, motivation, engagement, and accessibility are not desirable features but rather critical determinants of adherence and outcomes.

However, designing such systems requires a multidisciplinary approach that combines technological innovation with psychological, social, and design considerations. Purely technology-driven solutions tend to under-perform when deployed outside controlled settings, because they fail to account for the heterogeneity of users, the complexity of clinical and educational pathways, and the sociotechnical context in which assistive devices are actually used. The Design for Accessible/Inclusive Sports and Rehabilitation with Assistive Technologies STS addresses this need by bringing together contributions that explore different dimensions of this domain.

This paper provides a unifying perspective on the STS. It first proposes a conceptual framework for AI-driven XR ecosystems; it then situates the accepted contributions within a broader research landscape; and finally, it discusses open challenges and future directions for the community.

2 A Multidisciplinary Framework for Inclusive XR Systems

The design of inclusive assistive technologies for sports and rehabilitation can be structured around four key dimensions. These dimensions are not independent silos but rather tightly coupled layers of a single ecosystem, whose integration is the actual engineering challenge.

2.1 Multimodal Sensing and Data Integration

Modern assistive systems rely on heterogeneous data sources, including motion capture, wearable sensors, ambient and environmental sensors, and explicit user-given inputs such as perceived exertion or subjective well-being. These technologies enable detailed monitoring of motor performance, physiological states, cognitive load, and user interaction patterns, supporting data-driven adaptation and personalization.

2.2 AI-Driven Adaptive Feedback

Artificial Intelligence plays a central role in interpreting sensor data and generating meaningful, timely feedback. Virtual coaches built on machine learning and reinforcement-learning models can provide real-time guidance, adapting to user performance, cognitive load, affective state and fatigue. This allows for individualized training experiences that can evolve dynamically over time, thereby preventing users' boredom and frustration, and supporting optimal challange according to the user's current capability. Beyond performance optimization, AI also enables early detection of compensatory patterns, fall risk, or deterioration that may require clinical attention.

2.3 Immersive and Interactive XR Environments

XR technologies create engaging and controllable environments where users can safely perform tasks and receive immediate feedback. These environments allow full immersion and the reproduction of ecologically valid scenarios—urban cycling, sailing, alpine skiing, interactive playgrounds—without the corresponding physical risks; augmented and mixed reality overlay digital cues onto real environments, supporting wayfinding, motor learning, and social participation. Gamification mechanics (narrative, rewards, progression, cooperative play) transform repetitive rehabilitation protocols into meaningful experiences and are powerful levers for adherence, especially for children and young adults. Careful attention, however, must be devoted to cybersickness, sensory overload, and the risk of exclusion when XR hardware is designed around able-bodied, neurotypical users.

2.4 Inclusive and Human-Centered Design

Accessibility is a fundamental requirement for assistive technologies. Systems must be designed to accommodate diverse abilities, motor, and cognitive abilities minimizing cognitive load while maintaining engagement and autonomy. Key principles include simplicity, adaptability, multimodal feedback, and user participation in the design process. Co-design, living labs, and participatory research are key methodological tools to ensure that technology does not reproduce existing asymmetries of power between designers, clinicians, and users, but becomes instead a shared artifact that embodies the needs, values, and preferences of the communities it aims to serve.

3 Overview of the Special Thematic Session Contributions

The contributions included in this STS reflect complementary perspectives on inclusive sports and rehabilitation, addressing different user groups, technologies, and design challenges. They can be read as different entry points into the ecosystem described above: from the sensing and sonification of sport-specific parameters, to pedagogical frameworks for schools, to AI-powered immersive platforms, to the semantic scaffolding that allows heterogeneous systems to talk to each other.

3.1 Sensory Substitution and Inclusive Interaction

Sueda and Koh [4] present an innovative approach to inclusive sailing through auditory sensory substitution. Their system translates sail trim parameters—specifically the angle of attack between wind and sail—into real-time auditory feedback, enabling visually impaired sailors to perceive and optimize sailing performance without relying on sight. The sonification mapping is carefully designed to preserve the dynamic richness of the original signal while remaining cognitively manageable during the high-paced decisions typical of sail control.

This work highlights the importance of alternative sensory channels in assistive technologies and demonstrates how real-time sonification can support spatial awareness and fine motor control in highly dynamic outdoor environments. Beyond its specific sport application, the contribution represents a paradigmatic example of how sensory substitution can extend the accessibility of complex outdoor activities traditionally considered out of reach for blind or low-vision users, opening opportunities for competitive and recreational participation alike.

3.2 Accessibility Frameworks in Educational Contexts

Donno et al. [3] propose a framework for technology-enhanced physical activity in primary education, focusing on accessibility and inclusion for children with disabilities. Their approach emphasizes the integration of digital tools—wearable sensors, interactive surfaces, exergames—with evidence-based pedagogical strategies, in order to support genuine inclusive participation in physical education rather than mere physical co-presence.

The framework articulates requirements at multiple levels: the individual child, the classroom group, the teacher, and the institutional context. By doing so, it extends the domain of assistive technologies to early education, a stage in which motor, cognitive, and social development are tightly interleaved and in which inclusive experiences can have long-lasting effects on self-efficacy and social identity. This highlights the importance of designing systems that address developmental needs and promote inclusion from an early age. The contribution also underscores the role of educators and institutional contexts in shaping accessible interventions.

3.3 AI-Driven XR Training Systems

Covarrubias et al. [1] present an AI-driven virtual coaching system for immersive adaptive cycling training, tailored to young adults with disabilities. The system integrates XR environments, motion capture, and real-time feedback to support cognitive-motor development in a context—cycling—that combines aerobic benefits, balance training, and a strong recreational and social dimension.

This work exemplifies the integration of multimodal sensing, AI, and immersive interaction within a single platform. It demonstrates how adaptive XR systems can enhance engagement, improve motor performance, and support inclusive participation in sports, while also generating data that can inform individualized rehabilitation strategies.

3.4 Semantic Interoperability and Standardization

Criscuolo et al. [2] address the challenge of interoperability between assistive technology classifications by proposing a BERT-based semantic mapping between the International Classification of Functioning, Disability and Health (ICF) framework and the ISO 9999 standard in the context of vocational rehabilitation.

This contribution introduces a crucial infrastructural perspective, enabling better alignment among clinical, technical, and regulatory frameworks. It supports the scalability and integration of assistive technologies within broader ecosystems, facilitating data exchange and system interoperability across clinical, educational, and occupational settings, and ultimately reducing friction in the pathway from assessment to device provision and reimbursement.

4 Discussion

The contributions in this STS collectively illustrate the multidimensional nature of inclusive sports and rehabilitation technologies. From sensory substitution and enhancement, and educational frameworks to immersive XR systems and semantic interoperability, each work addresses a different layer of the ecosystem Read in isolation, each contribution provides a focused advancement within its sub-field; read together, they sketch the contours of an integrated pipeline in which data, algorithms, experiences, and institutional frameworks mutually reinforce each other.

A key insight emerging from these contributions is the importance of integration and of a multidisciplinary approach. Effective assistive systems require not only advanced technologies but also alignment between data, interaction design, user needs, and institutional contexts.

The combination of AI and XR enables highly adaptive and engaging experiences, while sensory substitution expands accessibility to new domains. At the same time, frameworks for inclusion and interoperability ensure that these technologies can be effectively deployed and scaled.

The living lab approach adopted in several contributions highlights the value of co-design and iterative development, involving users, educators, and researchers. This participatory approach is essential for ensuring that technologies are not only functional but also meaningful and usable in real-world contexts. It also helps to make explicit the trade-offs—between personalization and privacy, between automation and user agency, between novelty and robustness—that are intrinsic to this class of systems and that cannot be resolved at the purely technical level.

Several open challenges cut across the contributions. These include the long-term validation of outcomes beyond short pilot studies; the definition of meaningful benchmarks for inclusive XR and AI systems; the sustainability of infrastructures once research funding ends; and the ethical governance of the rich behavioral and physiological data generated by continuous monitoring. Addressing these challenges will require not only further research but also stronger dialogue with policy makers, industry, and user associations.

5 Conclusion

This Special Thematic Session highlights the transformative potential of AI-driven XR ecosystems for inclusive sports and rehabilitation. By integrating multimodal sensing, sensor data analysis, adaptive feedback, immersive interaction, and inclusive design principles, these systems can support diverse users in achieving improved participation, autonomy, and functional outcomes across educational, clinical, and recreational settings.

The contributions collected here demonstrate that accessibility is not a single feature but rather an emergent property of well-integrated systems that combine technological innovation, human-centered design, and standardized interoperability frameworks. Future research should focus on strengthening these integrations, expanding real-world deployment, beyond controlled pilot studies, consolidating shared evaluation methodologies, and ensuring the long-term sustainability and equity of impact of assistive technologies.

Acknowledgments. The authors thank all contributors to the Special Thematic Session and the participants involved in the experimental activities.

References

1. Covarrubias, M., Gandin, A., Riva, A., Butti, D., Stefanoni, L.: Ai-driven virtual coach for immersive adaptive cycling training in young people with disabilities. In: Miesenberger, K., Petrie, H., Penaz, P. (eds.): ICCHP 2026, 20th International Conference on Computers Helping People with Special Needs, Linz, Austria, Proceedings. Springer, Heidelberg (2026)
2. Criscuolo, S., Spolandore, D., Conti, E., Barbara, V.: Bridging ICF functioning and the iso classification of assistive products using bert-based semantic mapping. In: Miesenberger, K., Petrie, H., Penaz, P. (eds.) ICCHP 2026, 20th International

Conference on Computers Helping People with Special Needs, Linz, Austria, Proceedings. Springer, Heidelberg (2026)
3. Donno, L., et al.: Technology-enhanced physical activity in primary schools: a framework for accessibility and inclusion. In: Miesenberger, K., Petrie, H., Penaz, P. (eds.): ICCHP 2026, 20th International Conference on Computers Helping People with Special Needs, Linz, Austria, Proceedings. Springer, Heidelberg (2026)
4. Sueda, K.: Auditory sensory substitution for inclusive sailing: real-time sail trim feedback based on angle of attack. In: Miesenberger, K., Petrie, H., Penaz, P. (eds.): ICCHP 2026, 20th International Conference on Computers Helping People with Special Needs, Linz, Austria, Proceedings. Springer, Heidelberg (2026)

Auditory Sensory Substitution for Inclusive Sailing: Real-Time Sail Trim Feedback Based on Angle of Attack

Koh Sueda[1,2](✉) and Takahiro Miura[3]

[1] Hannan University, Osaka, Japan
apochang.jp@gmail.com
[2] SenseFoil PTE. LTD., Singapore, Singapore
[3] National Institute of Advanced Industrial Science and Technology (AIST), Kashiwa, Japan
miura-t@aist.go.jp

Abstract. Sailing is a highly visual sport in which performance-oriented sail trim is traditionally achieved by observing tell-tales on the sail. This dependence on visual cues creates a significant barrier for visually impaired sailors, especially in tasks requiring continuous fine-grained adjustment. This paper presents SoundTelltales, an auditory sensory substitution system that sonifies the sail's Angle of Attack (AoA) in real time to support non-visual sail trim control. Rather than attempting one-to-one visual replacement, the system re-encodes sail-state information into perceptually meaningful auditory structures. The design was shaped through co-design with blind accessibility researchers and blind sailors, followed by two pilot stages: a Wizard-of-Oz proof of concept in summer 2025 and a field deployment during a national blind sailing regatta in November 2025. These activities clarified design requirements related to cue contrast, cognitive load, learning differences across sensory backgrounds, and boat-specific audio identity. The paper also outlines a mixed-method comparative evaluation planned for 2026, focusing on performance, enjoyment, and sense of agency.

Keywords: Assistive Technology · Sensory Substitution · Inclusive Design · Sailing · Sonification · Sense of Agency

1 Introduction

Sailing is a sport in which motor action and environmental perception are tightly coupled. Efficient sail trim depends on reading fine-grained information about airflow across the sail, traditionally through visual inspection of tell-tales. For visually impaired (VI) sailors, this visual dependency creates a persistent barrier not only to performance but also to autonomy and embodied engagement with wind and boat motion. As a result, many blind sailors rely on verbal instructions

K. Miesenberger et al. (Eds.): ICCHP 2026, LNCS 16867, pp. 10–19, 2027.
https://doi.org/10.1007/978-3-032-31308-9_2

Fig. 1. Overview of the SoundTelltales platform, including the on-boat sensing setup and prototype hardware used for auditory feedback.

from sighted crewmates, which may support safety but can also fragment action, increase cognitive load, and reduce the feeling of directly controlling the boat.

This paper investigates whether auditory sensory substitution can support independent sail trim control while preserving enjoyment and a sense of agency. We present *SoundTelltales*, a system that converts sail-state information into non-speech auditory cues that can be interpreted during active sailing (Fig. 1). The purpose of the system is not to automate sail control, but to provide a perceptual interface through which sailors can directly regulate trim without relying exclusively on visual observation or continuous verbal mediation.

A central challenge in this problem is that auditory substitution cannot simply reproduce visual perception in another modality. Vision enables parallel, high-density spatial perception, whereas auditory spatial perception is coarser, more context-dependent, and unfolds over time. Accordingly, prior research on sensory substitution has emphasized that successful systems should not aim for literal visual replacement, but rather for the re-encoding of task-relevant information into perceptually meaningful structures [1]. SoundTelltales follows this principle by mapping the sail's Angle of Attack (AoA) to frequency-modulated auditory pulse rates that support continuous trim adjustment.

The current paper extends the earlier accepted abstract in three ways. First, it clarifies the participatory design process that shaped the sonification strategy. Second, it reports the iterative prototype development and 2025 field observations in greater methodological detail. Third, it reframes the planned 2026 study as a comparative evaluation of usability, performance, and agency rather than as a claim of direct equivalence with sighted visual sailing.

2 Related Work

2.1 Sensory Substitution and Perceptual Constraints

A fundamental challenge in auditory sensory substitution lies in the structural differences between visual and auditory perception. Vision supports broad, simultaneous access to spatially dense information, making it highly effective for dynamic monitoring tasks. By contrast, auditory spatial perception is typically characterized as coarser and more dependent on timing, context, and listening conditions. This difference has often been discussed through the Minimum Audible Angle (MAA), which measures the smallest angular difference between sound sources that a listener can discriminate [2,3]. Compared with visual resolution, auditory spatial discrimination is substantially less dense and not well suited to direct scene-by-scene substitution.

For this reason, effective sensory substitution systems do not attempt one-to-one visual replication. Instead, they selectively encode the subset of information most relevant for the task at hand [1]. SoundTelltales follows this approach. Rather than trying to recreate the visual appearance of tell-tales or airflow patterns, it translates deviations in AoA into changes in auditory pulse rate and pattern, thereby supporting immediate trim action.

2.2 Blind Mobility Beyond Obstacle Avoidance

A useful precedent is the Blind Driver Challenge, which explored how non-visual interfaces could allow blind users to directly control a vehicle rather than being displaced by full automation [4]. This line of work is relevant not because sailing and driving are identical, but because it foregrounds a design philosophy centered on agency. The question is not only whether the task can be completed safely, but whether the user remains meaningfully inside the control loop. SoundTelltales adopts the same principle: it is intended to support direct user control, not to replace the sailor with an automated trimming mechanism.

2.3 Performance-Oriented Audio in Fast Interaction Contexts

Accessible digital games and e-sports further demonstrate that non-speech audio can support rapid, action-oriented decision-making. For example, recent commercial game accessibility features have shown how audio can convey distance, state, and timing in ways that support high-tempo play without requiring full linguistic interpretation [5]. This is especially relevant in sailing, where conditions change continuously and support must remain timely, low-latency, and minimally intrusive. The implication is that auditory support is most effective when it communicates actionable structure, not when it attempts to mimic visual content in detail.

2.4 Existing Assistive Technology in Blind Sailing

Assistive technologies in blind sailing have primarily focused on macro-level navigation, such as course orientation and waypoint guidance. The Homerus project, for example, used acoustic buoys to support non-visual course keeping [6]. Such systems are essential for route-level assistance, but they do not address the micro-level control problem of sail trim. SoundTelltales occupies this gap by focusing specifically on the real-time control of sail state. In this sense, it complements rather than replaces navigation-oriented assistive technology.

Taken together, these bodies of work suggest that inclusive design for visually demanding sports should not be framed as a search for strict visual equivalence. A more productive framing is whether non-visual interfaces can support effective, enjoyable, and skill-based participation through task-specific perceptual redesign.

3 Participatory Design and Iterative Development

The development of SoundTelltales followed an iterative participatory design (PD) process involving blind researchers and blind sailors. Ethics approval was obtained for the participatory activities and pilot tests described in this section. The process was divided into an initial co-design phase and two iterative pilot tests.

3.1 Co-design Process

The initial design phase aimed to define the fundamental interaction model of SoundTelltales. We conducted a series of semi-structured interviews and brainstorming workshops with two congenitally blind accessibility researchers and one late-blind sailor. The two researchers did not have sailing experience, whereas the sailor had started sailing after vision loss.

A central design question was whether trim-state information should be communicated primarily through speech or through non-speech sonification using pitch and temporal patterns. During the discussions, participants generally favored non-speech cues for two primary reasons:

- **Responsiveness and cognitive load:** During active trim adjustment, continuously spoken information was expected to be slower to process and more cognitively intrusive than concise auditory patterns.
- **Perceptual contrast:** Under-trim and over-trim states needed to be immediately distinguishable, requiring a strong contrast in pitch and rhythmic structure.

Participants also suggested that when the sail is well trimmed, silence should be preferred over any confirmation sound. This would reduce cognitive load and allow the sailor to shift attention to steering, balance, and other environmental factors. The resulting rationale was therefore not to reproduce vision, but to provide a usable auditory control structure that minimizes unnecessary noise.

3.2 Iterative Prototype Testing

To validate these co-design outcomes, the concept was explored through two iterative pilot phases, moving from conceptual validation to environmental feasibility. Representative feedback from the participatory process and the corresponding design responses are summarized in Table 1.

Phase 1: Proof of Concept. The first test, conducted in summer 2025, functioned as a proof of concept. A late-blind sailor sailed together with an expert sailor who visually monitored the tell-tales and manually reproduced prospective sensory-substitution feedback using a whistle. This Wizard-of-Oz-style approach allowed rapid testing of the interaction concept before full device deployment. The blind sailor judged the feedback useful, supporting the decision to proceed with device implementation.

Phase 2: Field Testing under Realistic Conditions. The second test took place in November 2025 during a national blind sailing regatta to evaluate the feasibility and perceptual interpretability of the implemented prototype. The prototype was mounted on five boats. Participants included four late-blind sailors and one sighted sailor under blindfolded conditions. Among the blind participants, most had started sailing after vision loss, while one participant had prior sailing experience before becoming blind.

To capture objective data, one of the five boats was additionally equipped with a flight controller for GPS and sail-operation logging. This second phase did not aim to establish definitive effectiveness, but to evaluate feasibility, perceptual interpretability, and design implications under realistic sailing conditions.

3.3 Derived Design Requirements

These activities yielded four implementation priorities that directly informed the system described in the next section: non-speech corrective cues with silence at optimal trim, clear perceptual separation between under-trim and over-trim, sufficient audibility under maritime noise without causing fatigue, and low-latency feedback during active sail adjustment.

Table 1. Representative feedback and responses.

Feedback	Response
Continuous speech was intrusive during active trim adjustment	Non-speech sonification was used as the primary cue, with speech reserved for clarification and safety
Under-trim and over-trim had to be distinguishable immediately	Corrective direction was mapped to distinct auditory patterns
Participants preferred silence at efficient trim, but cues still had to remain audible under maritime noise	The optimal trim region was kept silent, and the sonification was tuned for salience without overload
Trim support alone did not address wider navigation and safety needs	The system retained verbal fallback and a monitoring architecture for safe operation

4 System Design and Implementation

SoundTelltales adopts a modular dual-unit architecture that separates navigation and logging from real-time sensory substitution. This design supports low-latency auditory feedback during sailing while preserving synchronized records for later analysis.

The navigation and logging unit, based on ArduPilot [7], records GPS, heading, and inertial data together with sail-related variables. This infrastructure supports post-session analysis of trim behavior and synchronization between environmental change and user action.

The sensory substitution unit, based on ESP32, processes wind-related data using a magnetic encoder attached to a custom vane mechanism. The system estimates the relative relationship between wind direction and sail position and derives an AoA-related control state. Rather than sonifying wind in a general sense, the system converts the functional role of visual tell-tales—namely, information about the sail's aerodynamic state relative to efficient trim—into auditory feedback.

To support fine-grained sail trim adjustment, the interface uses a frequency-modulated sonification strategy based on deviation from a target Angle of Attack (AoA), set to 38° as the default reference for the current rig. This reference value was measured on a Hansa 2.3 rig with full sails under a trimmed condition in which the tell-tales indicated optimal airflow. It may vary slightly with sail-profile conditions, including reefing status and draft depth. The mapping distinguishes the direction of correction: under-trim (AoA below the target) prompts the sailor to pull in the sheet, whereas over-trim (AoA above the target) prompts the sailor to ease it. These states are represented by distinct auditory patterns, enabling immediate corrective action (Fig. 2). In addition, the pulse rate increases as the sail approaches the target AoA, providing gradient feedback that helps the sailor perceive the efficient trim region without relying on physical tell-tales.

The sonification mapping was shaped by two design requirements identified through the participatory process. First, the direction of correction must be immediately legible, so that sailors can distinguish whether to pull in or ease the sheet without linguistic interpretation. Second, proximity to the target trim state should be perceived as a gradient rather than as a binary condition, enabling continuous adjustment rather than discrete correction only.

The system also incorporates a fail-safe mechanism. In the event of sensor-data communication loss, the device outputs a distinct warning tone and, outside racing contexts, can support switching the autopilot to Return-to-Home mode. The platform further includes an ArduPilot-based USV controller that provides GPS/IMU-based logging and telemetry of vessel position and attitude (Fig. 3). When coupled with actuators, this architecture can support autonomous or remote override in abnormal situations, as well as partial assistance with helm control and sail trimming. This is essential in maritime settings, where accessibility support must remain compatible with established safety procedures.

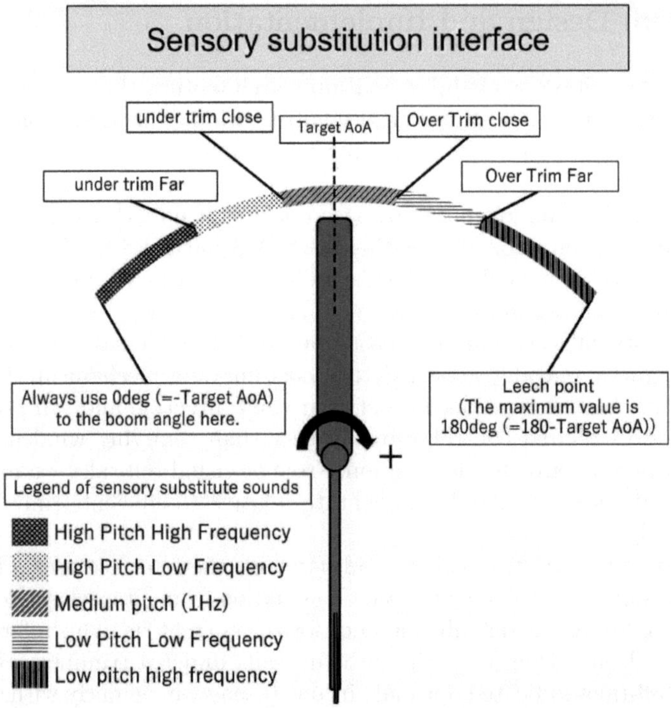

Fig. 2. Sensory substitution interface showing the AoA-based sonification mapping. The display distinguishes under-trim and over-trim relative to the target AoA, while pulse-rate changes indicate proximity to the efficient trim region.

5 Preliminary Field Evaluation (2025)

The November 2025 regatta deployment yielded several findings relevant to both design and evaluation.

First, the system was perceptible and usable after familiarization. Participants were able to interpret the auditory feedback sufficiently to engage with it during actual sailing. Consistent with the earlier co-design discussions, nonverbal cues were generally experienced as more immediate and less disruptive than continuous spoken guidance.

Second, the pilot revealed substantial variation in learning trajectory. Participants with prior visual experience of sailing appeared to connect the auditory cues more quickly to an existing mental model of sail behavior. Participants without such prior visual concepts required a longer initial learning period. Importantly, this was not interpreted as a failure of the system, but as evidence that sensory substitution in this context requires personalized onboarding and training rather than a uniform interface assumption.

Third, the pilot clarified that trim support and navigation support are related but distinct problems. The sighted sailor under blindfolded conditions had dif-

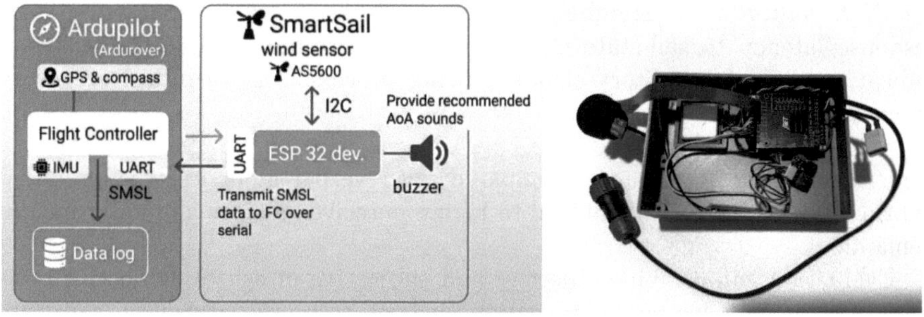

Fig. 3. System architecture showing the dual-unit configuration of SoundTelltales. The ESP32-based sensory substitution unit estimates the sail state and generates real-time auditory feedback, while the ArduPilot-based navigation/logging unit records GPS, heading, and sail-operation data for telemetry and post-session analysis.

ficulty maintaining heading, suggesting that non-visual trim support alone does not solve all control challenges in sailing. The presence of course-level audio navigation aids may therefore strongly affect user performance and should be considered when designing future comparative studies.

Fourth, participants and observers identified additional design requirements. In congested situations where multiple boats used the same sound timbre, it became cognitively demanding to distinguish the feedback of one's own boat from that of neighboring boats. This suggests that future iterations should provide boat-specific sound identities. More broadly, both blind and sighted sailors found tidal drift difficult to perceive, raising the possibility that future inclusive support systems may need to incorporate cues beyond sail trim alone.

Finally, the field deployment suggested broader inclusive value. For blind sailors, direct access to sail-state information appeared to support a stronger expectation of safe and independent sailing, especially in free-sailing contexts where route-support buoys are not always present. For less experienced sighted sailors, the system may also function as a learning aid that reduces the need for constant visual monitoring of the sail. These observations are consistent with the project's emphasis on sense of agency and with the idea that inclusive design can benefit mixed-ability sailing contexts rather than a single user group only.

6 Future Work: Planned Comparative Evaluation

Given the limited accessibility of the target user population, the next study will adopt a mixed-method comparative case-study design rather than a large-sample experimental design. The purpose is to evaluate whether the hybrid auditory approach improves trim-related interaction quality and agency relative to more speech-dominant support.

The study is guided by two hypotheses.

H1 (Internalization). Training with gradient-based sonification will reduce response latency to sail-state changes and support more stable trim control, indicating that the auditory signal is being processed as an intuitive sensory extension.

H2 (Agency and Workload). Compared with verbal guidance, the proposed hybrid auditory approach will lead to higher perceived agency and lower mental demand.

Evaluation will combine objective and subjective measures. Objective measures will include log-based indicators such as response latency to sail-state change and stability of AoA relative to the target range. Subjective measures will include Raw NASA-TLX for workload [8], UEQ-S for perceived interaction quality [9], and post-session semi-structured interviews focused on perceived control, enjoyment, and the relation between action and auditory effect. Particular attention will be paid to differences across sensory backgrounds, including congenitally blind, late-blind, and sighted-folded participants where appropriate. The interpretation of agency is informed by prior work on the sense of agency in human action [10].

Importantly, success in this study is not defined as perfect replication of sighted visual sailing. Rather, the key question is whether auditory sensory substitution can support a meaningful, skill-based, and enjoyable mode of participation in which the sailor remains actively in control.

7 Conclusion

SoundTelltales explores how auditory sensory substitution can support inclusive sailing by translating sail-state information into action-oriented auditory feedback. The system is grounded in a central insight from sensory substitution research: because hearing and vision differ structurally, effective auditory support should not attempt literal visual replacement. Instead, it should re-encode the information that matters most for action.

This paper extends the earlier abstract by clarifying the participatory design process, reporting iterative pilot development in greater detail, and articulating the practical lessons learned from the 2025 field deployment. These additions respond directly to the need for a stronger account of user involvement, methodology, and preliminary findings. The resulting contribution is therefore not only a technical proposal, but also an account of how inclusive sports technology can be shaped through co-design, real-world testing, and careful attention to agency, enjoyment, and learning.

Beyond its technical contribution, SoundTelltales may be framed as an inclusive redesign of sailing practice. Rather than simply replacing visual tell-tales with sound, the system re-encodes the tacit sensorimotor knowledge through which experienced sailors interpret wind conditions into a shareable form of embodied guidance that is not restricted by visual access. From this perspective, the significance of SoundTelltales lies not only in supporting blind sailing, but also in showing how visually dependent sports skills can be restructured into accessible and learnable forms of participation.

Acknowledgments. This work was supported by JSPS KAKENHI Grant Number 25K15203 and by the Tohoku University RIEC IT-21 Center. The authors would like to thank the blind sailors and their support teams, researchers from Tsukuba University of Technology and members of the Sailability community for their valuable contributions to the participatory design and pilot activities described in this paper.

Disclosure of Interests. The authors have no competing interests to declare that are relevant to the content of this article.

References

1. Maidenbaum, S., Abboud, S., Amedi, A.: Sensory substitution: closing the gap between basic research and widespread practical visual rehabilitation. Neurosci. Biobehav. Rev. **41**, 3–15 (2014)
2. Gori, M., Sandini, G., Martinoli, C., Burr, D.: Impairment of auditory spatial localization in congenitally blind human subjects. Brain **137**(1), 288–293 (2014)
3. Aggius-Vella, E., Jones, P.R., Bleau, J., Macpherson, E.A.: Minimum audible angle for frontal, lateral, and rear sound source positions. J. Acoust. Soc. Am. **147**(4), 2580–2592 (2020)
4. National Federation of the Blind: The NFB Blind Driver Challenge. https://nfb.org/programs-services/blind-driver-challenge. Accessed 12 Apr 2026
5. Capcom: Street Fighter 6 Sound Accessibility Features. https://www.streetfighter.com/6/accessibility. Accessed 12 Apr 2026
6. Blind Sailing International: The Homerus Project: Background information. https://www.blindsailinginternational.com/homerus-project-background-information/. Accessed 12 Apr 2026
7. ArduPilot Dev Team: ArduPilot documentation. https://ardupilot.org/. Accessed 12 Apr 2026
8. Hart, S.G., Staveland, L.E.: Development of NASA-TLX (Task Load Index): results of empirical and theoretical research. In: Hancock, P.A., Meshkati, N. (eds.) Human Mental Workload, pp. 139–183. North-Holland, Amsterdam (1988)
9. Schrepp, M., Hinderks, A., Thomaschewski, J.: Design and evaluation of a short version of the User Experience Questionnaire (UEQ-S). Int. J. Interact. Multimed. Artif. Intell. **4**(6), 103–108 (2017)
10. Haggard, P.: Sense of agency in the human brain. Nat. Rev. Neurosci. **18**, 196–207 (2017)

Technology-Enhanced Physical Activity in Primary Schools: A Framework for Accessibility and Inclusion

Lucia Donno[1,2(✉)], Samuele Ravazzani[1], Giorgia Palotti[1,2,4], Chiara Piazzalunga[1], Carlalberto Francia[1,2], Simona Ferrante[1,3], and Manuela Galli[1,2]

[1] Department of Electronics, Information and Bioengineering, Politecnico di Milano, Milan, Italy
lucia.donno@polimi.it
[2] Human Performance Lab (HPL)-E4Sport, Politecnico di Milano, Polo Territoriale di Lecco, Lecco, Italy
[3] LEARNLAB, Joint Research Platform, Fondazione IRCCS Istituto Neurologico Carlo Besta, Milan, Italy
[4] Department of Occupational and Environmental Medicine, Epidemiology and Hygiene, INAIL, Rome, Italy

Abstract. Physical activity is essential for children's development, yet those with disabilities often face barriers that limit their participation in school-based motor activities. The ActivE^3 project aimed to promote accessibility and inclusion in primary school physical education using technology. A multidisciplinary approach involving researchers, clinicians, and teachers was adopted to identify needs and design suitable solutions. Technological systems were implemented and tested in both controlled and real-world school settings. This paper focuses on the results obtained from the Nirvana interactive environment and collaborative exergames. The project involved approximately 760 children. Results showed high levels of engagement and positive feedback across all groups. No significant differences emerged be-tween typically developing children and those with cognitive or motor difficulties, suggesting that the proposed technologies can support inclusive participation. Although some limitations remain, including the small number of participants with motor disabilities and the use of a non-validated questionnaire, the findings highlight the potential of technology to encourage inclusive and engaging physical activity in primary schools.

Keywords: Primary education · Inclusive physical activities · Disability · Children · Accessibility

1 Introduction

Motor activities are essential for children's physical, behavioral, and social development. However, for children with fragilities, motor activities are often associated with dis-comfort and social exclusion [1]. According to United Nations Children's Fund

K. Miesenberger et al. (Eds.): ICCHP 2026, LNCS 16867, pp. 20–28, 2027.
https://doi.org/10.1007/978-3-032-31308-9_3

(UNICEF) 207.4 million (12.5%) children aged 5–17 years worldwide live with a moderate-to-severe disability [2] including physical, mental, intellectual or sensory difficulties, which may hinder full and equal participation in society. In fact, according to the biopsychosocial model [3], common limitations include attitudinal, communication, physical, and social barriers. In this context, if inclusivity addresses the social domain by fighting stereotypes and getting fair treatment, accessibility specifically refers to enabling individuals with disability to use services and products, for instance, through assistive technologies. In childhood and school settings, disability-related barriers are further compounded due to the heterogeneity of difficulties within class groups, including cognitive and neurodevelopmental fragilities or social communication and attention difficulties (Autism Spectrum Disorder (ASD) or Attention Deficit Hyperactivity Disorder (ADHD)), sensory and speech-language disorders and motor impairments (Cerebral Palsy (CP), muscular dystrophy, developmental coordination disorder). Although several tools support children with vulnerabilities in academic tasks, assistance for school-based physical education (PE) activities remain largely underexplored. However, in children and adolescents, physical activity improves cardiorespiratory, musculoskeletal, motor skills and academic performance, while reducing risk of obesity and depression [4]. Therefore, it is essential that also children with disabilities share these benefits with their peers. Hence, to prevent limitations and restrictions in participation, it is urgently needed to design tailored technologies addressing needs of both typically developing children and those with fragilities during PE activities at school.

2 State of the Art

Technology can promote social equity by enabling active participation and personalized, interactive learning suited to everyone's needs. Assistive technologies can support a wide range of disabilities [5]: for example, braille displays and speech synthesis for visual impairments, Interactive Whiteboards for cognitive support, Assistive Listening Devices and speech-to-text solutions for hearing impairments, Voice Output Communication Aids for communication disorders such as ASD, educational tools for Specific Learning Disorders, and adapted keyboards for children with motor disabilities. While assistive and educational technologies are widely used to support learning activities, considerably fewer tools have been developed for physical and motor activities. When available, such solutions are often limited to clinical settings, rather than being integrated into everyday school practices, and rarely address the combined physical, psychological, and social dimensions of wellbeing in an inclusive manner. This gap is particularly critical given the central role of motor activities in primary school, where children with fragilities are at greater risk of exclusion during PE activities, due to both functional limitations and contextual barriers, such as insufficient teacher training and adapted methodologies. PE activities at school should be an opportunity for participation and socialization with peers, rather than a source of frustration. Hence, the "ActivE^3–Everyone, Everywhere, Everyday" project aimed to develop new technological tools to promote accessible and inclusive physical activity of all children in primary school settings, including those with disabilities or other forms of fragility.

3 Methodology

The ActivE^3 project, conducted at the Lecco Campus of Politecnico di Milano (Italy), aimed to develop technological approaches to promote inclusive and accessible physical activity in primary schools, with a particular focus on children with disabilities. This project was conducted in collaboration with several partners from clinical and education sectors. The first step consisted of an analysis of barriers and needs, carried out through a multidisciplinary approach: clinical partners and primary school teachers were involved to ensure that both health-related and educational perspectives were considered. Their contribution ensured alignment between the proposed activities, educational goals, everyday school practices, and children's abilities and needs. Accordingly, technologies were identified or developed to implement the experimental environment, that, in addition to clinicians' and teachers' inputs, enable physical activity, even for children with fragilities and support both individual and group play activities.

The technologies included the Magic Room; the ACCEPT climbing wall; the Nirvana ® system (BTS Bioengineering, Milan, Italy); the D-Wall ® (Tecnobody, Bergamo, Italy); and custom sensor-based exergames. After identifying and developing such technologies, suitable spaces were selected in the university labs and the systems installed.

Among the previously described technologies implemented in the experimental technological environments, this study focuses on two in particular: the Nirvana system and the exergames. Nirvana consists of two projectors displaying the virtual environment onto walls or the floor, creating an interactive space, and two depth cameras detecting the user's movement. The system is equipped with an intuitive, web-based interface that allows the creation of personalized exercise sessions. Hence, Nirvana allowed children to move freely while interacting with the games in virtual scenarios, with integrated audio-visual feedback serving as support and encouragement. Tap the Mole, Balloon popping, Memory, alphabet and numerical games are examples of the activities implemented in the system and were among the most engaging for children. Each game was delivered in a team-based mode, enhancing cooperation among participants. Most teams included children with motor and/or cognitive difficulties as well as typically developing children. Through the software, the operator was able to ad-just the game difficulty in real-time making the activities more challenging for more active, typically developing children and easier for children with difficulties, without the teams being aware of these adjustments. The exergames module, called Elemental, is a collaborative real-time multiplayer exergame, that supports up to five simultaneous players. It includes 4 minigames: the Kitchen, in which children collaboratively select ingredients for breakfast, the Runner, a runner-style game where each player should catch or avoid a distinct obstacle, the Igloo, to assess reaction times to visual stimuli, and the Volcano which requires coordinated actions among players to escape from a volcano. Across all minigames, the system enables the collection of a wide range of gameplay data, with accuracy as the primary outcome measure (defined as the ratio between correctly responded stimuli and the total number of stimuli presented to a player). All minigames are designed to enhance collaboration and include configurable parameters to adapt the gameplay to players' abilities and needs. To promote accessibility and provide a shared, enjoyable experience for children with and without disabilities, the system integrates accessibility facilitators and multiple input devices. Facilitators are dynamic, individually configurable settings that address sensory, cognitive, and motor difficulties through features such as stimulus modulation, reduction of unnecessary distractions, and alternative interaction modes (e.g., seated play). The input modalities include pushing physical buttons Cosmo Switch ® (Filisia, Lon-don, UK), "iPad tablet tilting" (Apple, Cupertinto, USA), hand tracking via Leap Motion Controller ® (Ultraleap, San Francisco, USA), and full-body tracking using Homing ® (TecnoBody, Bergamo, Italy), enabling participation across a wide range of motor abilities.

The activities were conducted in compliance with the World Medical Association Declaration of Helsinki and approved by the Ethics Committee of Politecnico di Milano (protocol code n.19/2023). Parents or legal guardians of participants signed in-formed consent statements. After a pilot testing session involving 23 children to assess feasibility, 2-week trials were carried out involving 385 primary school children from two different schools: each day, half of the participants took part in 40-min sessions in each technological environment, followed by a lesson delivered by their teachers, and vice versa for the second half, simulating the typical alternation of activities in a school environment. At the end of each game activity, the children completed an appreciation 5-point Likert-scale questionnaire (1–5), provided in both standard text and Augmentative and Alternative Communication (AAC) format. Each questionnaire consisted of 6 items, designed to assess children's perceptions of the technology, their perceived abilities, and their engagement and interaction with peers: "Q1: Did you like the game? Q2: Would you like to play this game at your school? Q3: Did you understand how to play? Q4: Is it easy to play this game? Q5: Did you feel you did well? Q6: Did you play with the other children?". Then, the trial was extended, and further 6 days were conducted, involving an additional 172 primary school children.

After initial testing in a controlled environment, the technologies were adapted for deployment in primary schools to evaluate their use in real world settings. Four low-cost kits were developed, each including simplified versions of Nirvana and Homing. In this configuration, Nirvana used a single depth camera and projector for floor-based interaction, while Homing consisted of a camera and wall-mounted projector to deliver interactive games tailored to different school grades. The kits were designed to be affordable and feasible for autonomous school use. Through this deployment, approximately 200 additional primary school children were involved. Overall, the project reached about 760 children from 9 schools and engaged a multidisciplinary team, including 40 teachers, more than 10 master students, 5 technical-administrative staff, 20 researchers, and 10 clinicians, for a total of more than 150 h of technology use. Questionnaire responses relating to the Nirvana and exergames laboratory experience were collected for each participant and subsequently analyzed. Children, regardless of the school grade attended, were then categorized into two subgroups according to clinical condition: typically, developing (TD) and non-typically developing (NTD). The NTD group was further classified into children with cognitive-neurodevelopmental difficulties (CD) and children with motor difficulties (MD), to explore whether the type of disability could influence perceived usability and overall experience. Given the small number of participants in the MD subgroup (n = 3), respective results were presented and discussed through descriptive statistics, median and interquartile range (IQR), and excluded from statistical analyses for both Nirvana and exergames. The Anderson-Darling test verified that data had a non-normal distribution, hence the median and IQR were computed for each questionnaire item. To assess the inclusivity of the Nirvana technology, a 2-sample 2-tailed Mann-Whitney U test was used to compare the overall score between TD and CD children. To investigate whether the technology was suitable across different ages within primary school, the overall score of the most distant grades (1st vs 5th) within each subgroup (TD and CD) were compared, using 2-sample 2-tailed Mann-Whitney U tests. Significance level was set at $p < 0.05$. Regarding the exergames, to compare the accuracy between NTD children and TD peers, data normality was assessed using the Anderson-Darling test. Due to non-normal distributions, group comparisons between TD and NTD for the Runner minigame of the first 2-week trial were conducted using the 2-sample 2-tailed Mann–Whitney U test ($\alpha = 0.05$), and results were visualized using boxplots. Internal consistency of the questionnaire items was assessed using Cronbach's α index [6].

4 Results and Discussion

As regards the results obtained from the use of the Nirvana system, across all participants ($n = 557$), the median (IQR) rating for all questions was 5.00 (1.00). For each predefined subgroup (TD, NTD, CD and MD), Table 1 reports the sample size and the median (IQR) for each questionnaire item (Q), as well as the overall score (Score).

Table 1. Median (IQR) for each question (Q) and the overall score (Score) for the TD, NTD, CD and MD groups. # is the number of participants.

Group	#	Q1	Q2	Q3	Q4	Q5	Q6	Score
TD	503	5.00 (1.00)	5.00 (1.00)	5.00 (1.00)	5.00 (1.00)	5.00 (1.00)	5.00 (1.00)	5.00 (1.00)
NTD	54	5.00 (0.00)	5.00 (0.75)	5.00 (1.00)	5.00 (1.00)	5.00 (1.00)	5.00 (1.00)	5.00 (0.50)
CD	51	5.00 (0.00)	5.00 (1.00)	5.00 (1.00)	5.00 (1.00)	5.00 (1.00)	5.00 (1.00)	5.00 (0.50)
MD	3	5.00 (0.00)	5.00 (0.00)	5.00 (0.50)	5.00 (0.50)	5.00 (0.00)	5.00 (0.00)	5.00 (0.00)

No significant differences ($p = 0.108$) were found between TD and CD children, indicating comparable and positive perceptions across groups. In fact, both groups reported full positive ratings (median (IQR), number of subjects: TD = 5.00(1.00), 503; CD = 5.00(0.50), 51), supporting the inclusivity of the proposed technology.

Table 2 reports the median (IQR) questionnaire scores by primary school grade, allowing us to assess whether perceptions of Nirvana varied across grades or remained consistently positive across the age range. No significant differences were found between

1st- and 5th-grade children in either the TD or CD group ($p > 0.05$, with $p_{TD} = 0.118$ and $p_{CD} = 0.495$), indicating that the technology was perceived as similarly accessible and enjoyable for both younger and older children, regardless of the presence of cognitive or neurodevelopmental disorders ($TD_1 = 5.00(0.50)$, 91; $TD_5 = 5.00(1.00)$, 105; $CD_1 = 5.00(0.00)$, 9; $CD_5 = 5.00(0.88)$, 18).

Concerning the Cronbach's α, the overall sample showed $\alpha = 0.706$ ($n = 557$). Group-level values were $\alpha_{TD} = 0.708$ ($n = 503$), $\alpha_{NTD} = 0.674$ ($n = 54$), $\alpha_{CD} = 0.667$ ($n = 51$), and $\alpha_{MD} = 0.600$ ($n = 3$).

Table 2. Median (IQR) for each question (Q) ant the overall score (Score) for the 1st to 5th grade of primary school. # is the number of participants.

Grade	#	Q1	Q2	Q3	Q4	Q5	Q6	Score
1st	100	5.00 (0.00)	5.00 (1.00)	5.00 (1.00)	5.00 (1.00)	5.00 (0.25)	5.00 (1.00)	5.00 (0.50)
2nd	94	5.00 (0.00)	5.00 (1.00)	5.00 (1.00)	5.00 (1.00)	5.00 (1.00)	5.00 (1.00)	5.00 (0.50)
3rd	112	5.00 (1.00)	5.00 (1.00)	5.00 (1.00)	4.50 (2.00)	5.00 (1.00)	5.00 (1.00)	5.00 (1.00)
4th	128	5.00 (1.00)	5.00 (1.00)	5.00 (1.00)	4.00 (1.00)	5.00 (1.00)	5.00 (1.00)	5.00 (1.00)
5th	123	5.00 (0.00)	5.00 (0.00)	5.00 (0.50)	4.00 (0.00)	4.00 (0.00)	5.00 (0.00)	5.00 (1.00)

For each predefined subgroup, Table 3 reports the sample size and the median (IQR) for each questionnaire and the overall score. No significant differences ($p = 0.212$) emerged between TD and CD groups, indicating comparable positive perceptions across groups. Both groups reported full positive ratings, supporting the inclusivity of the exergames.

Table 4 reports the median (IQR) of the questionnaire scores, analyzed separately for the five primary school grades. This allowed us to determine whether perceptions of the exergames varied across grades or were consistently positive across the full age range of the primary school sample. No significant differences were found between 1st- and 5th-grade children in the TD group ($p_{TD} = 0.118$), whereas differences emerged within the CD group ($p_{CD} = 0.040$), with higher overall scores in younger children, based on a limited sample ($CD_1 = 10$, $CD_5 = 16$). Overall, the findings suggest that the technology was generally perceived as accessible and enjoyable across primary school ages ($TD_1 = 5.00(0.50)$, 91; $TD_5 = 5.00(1.00)$, 96; $CD_1 = 5.00(0.88)$, 10; $CD_5 = 5.00(0.00)$, 16).

As representative example, Fig. 1 reports the accuracy obtained by the NTD e TD groups in the Runner minigame from the two-week trial.

No statistically significant differences were observed between the two groups ($p_{week1} = 0.574$, $p_{week2} = 0.149$), indicating that an appropriate combination of facilitators and input devices allowed children with disabilities not only to participate but also

Table 3. Median (IQR) for each question (Q) and the overall score (Score) for the TD, NTD, CD and MD groups. # is the number of participants.

Group	#	Q1	Q2	Q3	Q4	Q5	Q6	Score
TD	521	5.00 (0.00)	5.00 (0.00)	5.00 (1.00)	4.00 (1.00)	5.00 (1.00)	5.00 (1.00)	5.00 (0.50)
NTD	63	5.00 (0.00)	5.00 (1.00)	5.00 (1.00)	5.00 (1.00)	5.00 (1.00)	5.00 (1.00)	5.00 (1.00)
CD	60	5.00 (0.00)	5.00 (1.00)	4.50 (1.25)	5.00 (1.00)	5.00 (1.00)	5.00 (1.00)	5.00 (1.00)
MD	3	5.00 (0.50)	4.00 (0.50)	5.00 (0.50)	5.00 (0.50)	5.00 (1.00)	5.00 (1.00)	5.00 (0.50)

Table 4. Median (IQR) for each question (Q) and the overall score (Score), for the 1st to 5th grade of primary school. # is the number of participants.

Grade	#	Q1	Q2	Q3	Q4	Q5	Q6	Score
1st	101	5.00 (0.00)	5.00 (1.00)	5.00 (1.00)	5.00 (1.00)	5.00 (1.00)	5.00 (1.00)	5.00 (1.00)
2nd	94	5.00 (0.00)	5.00 (0.75)	5.00 (1.00)	5.00 (1.00)	5.00 (1.00)	5.00 (1.00)	5.00 (0.50)
3rd	114	5.00 (0.00)	5.00 (0.00)	5.00 (1.00)	5.00 (1.00)	5.00 (1.00)	5.00 (1.00)	5.00 (0.50)
4th	163	5.00 (0.00)	5.00 (1.00)	4.00 (1.00)	4.00 (1.00)	5.00 (1.00)	5.00 (1.00)	4.50 (1.00)
5th	112	5.00 (0.00)	5.00 (0.00)	5.00 (0.50)	4.00 (1.00)	5.00 (1.00)	5.00 (1.00)	5.00 (1.00)

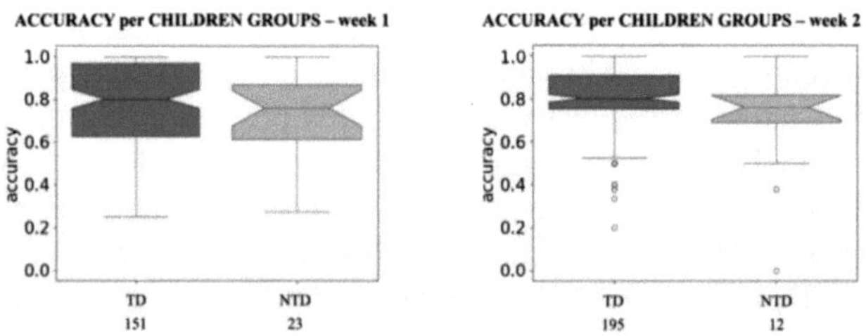

Fig. 1. Boxplots of the accuracy of the Runner minigame of the 2-week trial, divided between TD and NTD.

to achieve accuracy levels comparable to TD peers. For NTD children, appropriate facilitators were applied: in week 1, device usage was highest for Leap Motion (22), Homing (21), and Buttons (19), while Tablet was least used (9); in week 2, usage was more evenly distributed across Buttons (12), Homing (11), and Leap Motion (11), with Tablet still the least used (8). Concerning the internal consistency of the exergames questionnaire, group-level Cronbach's α resulted 0.783 for TD ($n = 521$), 0.827 for NTD ($n = 63$), and 0.831 for CD ($n = 60$). A lower value resulted for the MD subgroup ($\alpha = 0.695$; $n = 3$). These results support Nirvana and exergames as inclusive technologies promoting shared gameplay among children with different abilities across all primary school grades. Teachers using low-cost kits regularly reported high student enthusiasm and engagement. Although the questionnaire's affirmative Likert-scale format may have influenced responses, Cronbach's α values indicated generally good consistency across TD, NTD, and CD groups. The lower value in the MD group is likely due to the very small number of participants and should be interpreted with caution. Most responses clustered at the higher end, suggesting the questionnaire was easy to understand and captured differences in opinions [7].

In conclusion, the ActivE^3 project created technological spaces and provided training and awareness activities for children, families, and teachers. It also developed age-appropriate protocols to support inclusive physical activities in primary schools. By supporting schools and teachers, ActivE^3 helped promote a more equitable and health-promoting educational environment. Future work should include a larger number of children with motor disabilities and further refine the questionnaire with the support of educators and clinical staff. Building on this experience, a new project ("INSIEME", funded by Fondazione Cariplo) has been developed as a complementary initiative, promoting inclusion among children while shifting the focus beyond disability to address socio-economic vulnerabilities.

Acknowledgments. This research was conducted within ActivE^3 project funded by Cariplo Foundation and Regione Lombardia.

Disclosure of Interests. The authors have no competing interests to declare that are relevant to the content of this article.

References

1. Dubon, M.E., Tow, S., Rabatin, A.E.: Physical activity and sports participation among children and adolescents with disabilities. Pediatr. Clin. North Am. **70**, 603–614 (2023). https://doi.org/10.1016/j.pcl.2023.01.009
2. Olusanya, B.O., Kancherla, V., Shaheen, A., Ogbo, F.A., Davis, A.C.: Global and regional prevalence of disabilities among children and adolescents: analysis of findings from global health databases. Front. Public Health **10**, 977453 (2022). https://doi.org/10.3389/fpubh.2022.977453
3. Engel, G.L.: The need for a new medical model: a challenge for biomedicine. Science **196**, 129–136 (1977). https://doi.org/10.1126/science.847460
4. Bishop, J.C., Pangelinan, M.: Motor skills intervention research of children with disabilities. Res. Dev. Disabil. **74**, 14–30 (2018). https://doi.org/10.1016/j.ridd.2017.11.002
5. Francia, C., et al.: Validation of a MediaPipe system for markerless motion analysis during virtual reality rehabilitation. In: De Paolis, L.T., Arpaia, P., and Sacco, M. (eds.) Extended Reality. pp. 40–49. Springer Nature Switzerland, Cham (2024). https://doi.org/10.1007/978-3-031-71710-9_3

6. Heo, M., Kim, N., Faith, M.S.: Statistical power as a function of Cronbach alpha of instrument questionnaire items. BMC Med. Res. Methodol. **15**, 86 (2015). https://doi.org/10.1186/s12874-015-0070-6
7. Lubiano, M.A., Montenegro, M., Pérez-Fernández, S., Gil, M.Á.: Analyzing the influence of the rating scale for items in a questionnaire on cronbach coefficient alpha. In: Balakrishnan, N., Gil, M.Á., Martín, N., Morales, D., and Pardo, M.D.C. (eds.) Trends in Mathematical, Information and Data Sciences, pp. 377–388. Springer International Publishing, Cham (2023). https://doi.org/10.1007/978-3-031-04137-2_32

AI-Driven Virtual Coach for Immersive Adaptive VR Cycling Training in Young Students with Disabilities

Mario Covarrubias(✉), Alessandro Gandin, Alessandro Riva, Davide Butti, and Luca Stefanoni

Department of Mechanical Engineering, Politecnico di Milano, Milan, Italy
mario.covarrubias@polimi.it, {alessandro.gandin,alessandro.riva, davide.butti,luca.stefanoni}@mail.polimi.it

Abstract. This paper presents an AI-driven Virtual Coach system for inclusive adaptive cycling training in young adults with disabilities (18–34 years old). The platform combines a physical stationary bicycle, a Unity-based Virtual Reality (VR) cycling environment, and real-time markerless motion capture using The Captury Live. Full-body kinematic data are streamed to a digital avatar, while virtual terrain changes are synchronized with dynamic bicycle resistance to simulate uphill and downhill riding in a safe and controlled setting.

The AI-driven coach monitors cadence, trunk alignment, pedaling symmetry, and fatigue-related indicators, providing simplified visual and audio feedback adapted to users' cognitive and motor abilities. The system was evaluated in a university living-lab context with 66 participants from local associations, supported by educators. Usability, tolerability, and functional changes were assessed through the System Usability Scale (SUS), an adapted cybersickness questionnaire based on the SSQ, and the International Classification of Functioning, Disability and Health (ICF).

Results showed high usability, low cybersickness symptoms, and short-term improvements in attention, coordination, and engagement. The proposed framework demonstrates a scalable and accessible approach for inclusive sport training and cognitive-motor empowerment through immersive VR cycling.

Keywords: Adaptive Sports · Inclusion · Disabilities · Rehabilitation · Virtual Reality · Unity · Cycling

1 Introduction

Young adults with cognitive disabilities often experience difficulties in attention regulation, working memory, executive control, and motor coordination, affecting autonomy, learning, and participation in daily life. Conventional rehabilitation and training approaches provide structured support, but they may lack the engagement, adaptability, and motivational value needed for sustained

K. Miesenberger et al. (Eds.): ICCHP 2026, LNCS 16867, pp. 29–36, 2027.
https://doi.org/10.1007/978-3-032-31308-9_4

participation. In this context, Virtual Reality (VR) offers an effective alternative by enabling safe, immersive, and customizable environments for cognitive-motor training [6,10].

Cycling is particularly suitable for this purpose because it combines rhythmic bilateral movement, postural control, endurance, and sustained attention. When integrated with VR, cycling can become a multisensory activity that stimulates both physical and cognitive processes within a controlled environment. In addition, adaptive VR systems can personalize difficulty, provide real-time feedback, and increase motivation through interactive scenarios.

This paper presents a VR cycling platform that integrates a physical stationary bicycle, a Unity-based immersive environment, dynamic resistance control, and full-body markerless motion capture using The Captury Live. A key element of the system is an AI-driven Virtual Coach, developed from expert cyclist motion data, which provides visual guidance and simplified corrective feedback during training [3]. The system also synchronizes virtual slopes with bicycle resistance, strengthening embodiment and sensorimotor coherence.

The intervention was conducted in collaboration with local associations supporting young adults with disabilities. A total of 66 students and 14 educators participated. The study evaluated usability, cybersickness, and short-term functional impact through SUS, an adapted SSQ, and the ICF framework. By combining immersive simulation, adaptive mechanics, and intelligent feedback, the proposed approach contributes to research on inclusive XR-based training and rehabilitation [1,5,7,8].

2 Methodology

The study evaluated the cognitive, motor, and usability effects of an immersive adaptive cycling intervention based on synchronized physical–virtual interaction. The system combined a VR cycling simulator, a stationary bicycle with dynamic resistance control, real-time full-body motion capture, and an AI-driven virtual coach.

2.1 Participants

The intervention involved 66 young adults with disabilities, supported by 14 educators, for a total of 80 participants. The collaborating groups were Progetto InAUT (18 students, 2 educators), CFPP Lecco (11 students, 3 educators), Aspocollege (15 students, 4 educators), LVQ (16 students, 3 educators), and LaorcaLab (6 students, 2 educators). Participants were aged 18–34 and presented mild to moderate cognitive disabilities, including difficulties in attention regulation, working memory, executive functioning, and motor coordination.

2.2 System Description

The VR cycling application was developed in Unity 2021.3 and deployed on Meta Quest 3. The virtual environment included flat paths, uphill segments, and downhill sections to create realistic route variations. Rendering performance was optimized to maintain a stable 90 Hz refresh rate in order to reduce latency and limit cybersickness [9].

The physical setup consisted of a stationary bicycle with resistance modulation linked to virtual terrain conditions. Uphill segments increased pedaling resistance, whereas downhill segments reduced it, reinforcing the perception of slope changes through synchronized visual and physical feedback.

Full-body motion was captured using The Captury Live. Expert cyclist recordings were embedded into the simulation to create a virtual coach able to demonstrate appropriate posture, cadence, and movement patterns. During the sessions, participants' movements were streamed in real time to Unity, enabling avatar mirroring and feedback based on trunk stability, pedaling symmetry, and cadence consistency.

2.3 AI-Driven Virtual Coach

The AI-driven Virtual Coach represented the adaptive core of the system. It continuously monitored cadence, trunk alignment, pedaling symmetry, and movement variability, and delivered simplified visual and verbal cues tailored to the cognitive and motor abilities of the users. Feedback was designed to be clear, supportive, and non-overloading. The coach also adapted terrain intensity and resistance in response to fatigue or instability, promoting both safety and engagement [4].

3 Experimental Procedure

The intervention was conducted over two weeks, with three sessions per week, for a total of six training sessions per participant. Each session lasted approximately 10 min and was supervised by a trained facilitator.

Each session included three phases:

- **Warm-up:** participants established a comfortable cadence and posture in a flat virtual environment.
- **Guided cycling:** the virtual coach provided demonstrations and real-time feedback on posture, cadence, and pedaling symmetry.
- **Independent riding:** participants completed routes including flat, uphill, and downhill segments.

Figure 1 illustrates a representative screenshot of the VR cycling application interface. Task complexity increased progressively through slope variations, route duration, environmental changes, and simple cognitive prompts such as directional cues and memory-based route recall. Before and after selected sessions, participants were shown brief visual summaries of previous performance to support motor awareness and engagement.

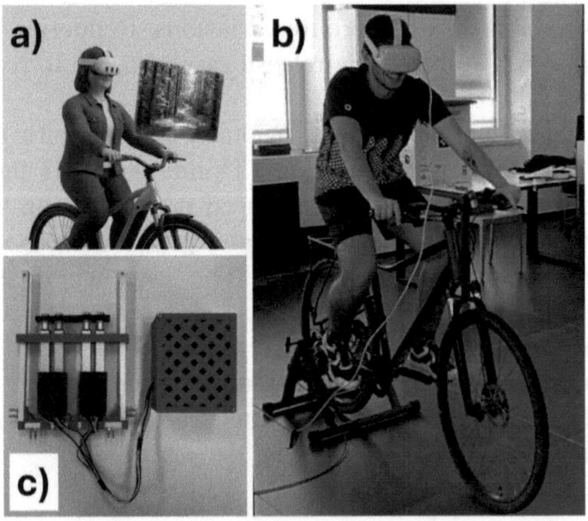

Fig. 1. a) A first-person view of a VR Cycling session. b) The complete setup of the system and c) The linear actuators linked to arduino and unity to simulate different path perceptions (downhill, planar, uphill).

3.1 SUS Protocol

The System Usability Scale (SUS) [2] was used to evaluate participants' perceptions of the VR cycling system and the adaptive physical cycling setup. Although 66 students participated in the intervention, complete SUS responses were obtained from 60 participants. To ensure immediacy of feedback and minimize recall bias, each participant completed the SUS questionnaire at the end of the VR training phase. The SUS was administered using simplified language and icon-supported Likert scales to facilitate accessibility for participants with cognitive disabilities. All responses were collected immediately after the final session, in line with recommended usability testing practices (Fig. 2).

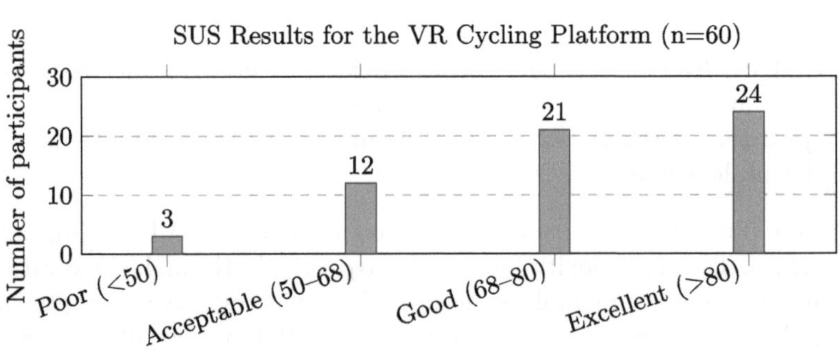

Fig. 2. Distribution of System Usability Scale (SUS) scores for the VR cycling platform across 60 participants.

The System Usability Scale (SUS) results indicated a high level of perceived usability of the VR cycling platform among the 60 participants. The mean SUS score was 79.4 (SD = 8.6), exceeding the commonly accepted usability benchmark of 68. A total of 45 participants (75%) rated the system within the Good to Excellent range, while only 3 participants (5%) reported scores below the acceptable threshold. These findings suggest strong learnability, interaction clarity, and overall user satisfaction, supporting the feasibility of the AI-driven VR cycling system for young adults with cognitive disabilities.

3.2 Cybersickness Symptoms VR Cycling Sessions

To assess the tolerability of the VR cycling intervention, post-session cybersickness symptoms were recorded using an adapted and simplified questionnaire derived from the Simulator Sickness Questionnaire (SSQ). Complete responses were obtained from 60 participants. The instrument focused on core indicators including nausea, visual fatigue, dizziness, disorientation, sweating, and general tiredness.

As summarized in Table 1, symptom intensity remained low across the participant group during VR cycling sessions. The overall mean symptom score was minimal relative to the maximum possible scale value, indicating good tolerability of the immersive experience. Among the reported symptoms, mild fatigue was the most frequently noted, followed by occasional eye strain. Reports of dizziness or disorientation were rare, and no participant experienced severe discomfort requiring session interruption.

A subset of participants reported no symptoms at all, while minor visual fatigue was typically observed during initial exposure to the VR headset or after extended concentration periods. These findings are consistent with previous research demonstrating that immersive applications characterized by stable frame rates, limited abrupt acceleration cues, and gradual environmental transitions are generally well tolerated by individuals with cognitive disabilities.

Overall, the low incidence and mild intensity of cybersickness symptoms confirm that the VR cycling setup was safe, accessible, and suitable for repeated use within the two-week intervention, without negatively affecting participant engagement or motivation.

3.3 International Classification of Functioning, Disability and Health (ICF)

To evaluate functional changes associated with the two-week VR cycling intervention, the International Classification of Functioning, Disability and Health (ICF) framework was employed as a structured assessment tool. The ICF provided a multidimensional perspective, allowing facilitators to monitor variations in cognitive, motor, and participation-related domains throughout the program. This approach supported an individualized and holistic analysis of each participant's development during the immersive and physically integrated cycling sessions.

Table 1. Cybersickness Symptoms After VR Cycling Sessions (n = 60)

Symptom	Mean	SD	Max	% Reporting
Nausea	0.12	0.33	2	8%
Eye Strain	0.48	0.62	3	32%
Dizziness	0.10	0.30	2	7%
Disorientation	0.05	0.22	1	5%
Sweating	0.20	0.45	2	15%
Fatigue	0.95	0.80	3	60%
Total Score	1.90	1.75	6	–

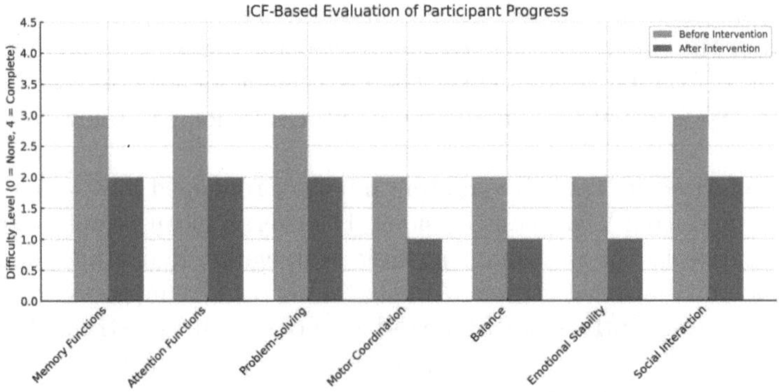

Fig. 3. ICF-based assessment illustrating functional changes across cognitive, motor, and participation domains following the two-week VR cycling intervention. Lower scores correspond to reduced levels of perceived difficulty.

The ICF assessment was administered both before and after the two-week training period to determine short-term functional impact. As shown in Fig. 3, measurable improvements were observed across the evaluated domains, which included attention control, working memory, executive reasoning, motor coordination, balance and trunk stability, emotional regulation, and social interaction.

At baseline, participants generally reported moderate levels of difficulty (mean score 3) in several domains, particularly those related to sustained attention and coordination. Following the intervention, average scores shifted toward mild difficulty levels (mean score 1–2), indicating a positive functional trend. Improvements were especially notable in motor coordination and attention stability, likely reflecting the rhythmic and sustained engagement required during immersive cycling tasks.

These findings suggest that the combined use of VR immersion, adaptive resistance cycling, and AI-guided feedback may contribute not only to motor performance enhancement but also to increased self-confidence, engagement, and perceived autonomy. The standardized ICF structure enabled consistent documentation of individualized progress, reinforcing the value of short-term XR-based interventions within inclusive educational and rehabilitation contexts.

4 Results

The VR cycling platform demonstrated high usability, low cybersickness, and positive short-term functional outcomes.

Usability. The mean SUS score was 79.4 (SD = 8.6), exceeding the benchmark of 68. Most participants (75%) rated the system as Good to Excellent, while only 5% scored it below acceptable levels, indicating strong usability and ease of interaction.

Cybersickness. Symptoms were minimal, with mild fatigue and occasional eye strain being the most common. Reports of nausea, dizziness, and disorientation were rare, and no sessions were interrupted, confirming good tolerability.

Functional Outcomes. ICF-based observations indicated improvements in attention, coordination, and trunk control, along with increased confidence and engagement. These results suggest that immersive cycling with adaptive feedback supports short-term cognitive-motor development.

Qualitative Feedback. Participants reported strong immersion, particularly due to synchronized resistance and visual slopes. The virtual coach was perceived as motivating, and facilitators highlighted an effective balance between challenge and accessibility.

5 Conclusion

This study demonstrates the feasibility and value of combining immersive VR cycling with a physically adaptive stationary bicycle to support cognitive and motor development in young adults with disabilities. Developed in collaboration with local associations, the system addresses key challenges such as attention, memory, and executive control.

A core contribution is the integration of markerless motion capture (The Captury Live) to enable an AI-driven virtual coach providing real-time biomechanical feedback and adaptive guidance. The synchronization between virtual terrain and dynamic resistance enhanced realism and supported sensorimotor engagement in a safe environment.

Over the two-week intervention, participants showed increased confidence, improved cadence stability, better trunk alignment, and enhanced attentional persistence. Observations suggest short-term improvements in coordination and task execution.

The combined use of SUS, SSQ, and ICF provided a comprehensive evaluation of usability, tolerability, and functional outcomes. Overall, the results highlight the potential of AI-enhanced VR cycling as a scalable and inclusive solution for cognitive-motor training in educational and rehabilitation contexts. Future work should include larger samples and long-term validation.

Acknowledgments. The authors would like to express their sincere gratitude to all participating associations and their students for their active involvement, enthusiasm, and invaluable feedback throughout the project. Special thanks are extended to ASPOC, Progetto InAUT, CFPP Lecco, Aspocollege, LVQ, and LaorcaLab, whose collaboration and commitment made the implementation and evaluation of the VR cycling intervention possible. The contribution of their educators and support staff was essential in ensuring accessibility, safety, and meaningful engagement for all participants.

References

1. Aruanno, B., et al.: Enhancing inclusive education for young students with special needs through mixed reality: exploring the potential of cnc milling machine application. Comput.-Aided Des. Appl. **21**(3), 522–535 (2024)
2. Brooke, J.: Sus: a quick and dirty usability scale. Usabil. Eval. Ind. 189–194 (1996)
3. Hartmann, M., Pelz, N., Brehm, M., Seidel, H.P.: Markerless motion capture for rehabilitation and sports science: evaluation of accuracy and usability. Sensors **20**(24), 7035 (2020)
4. Held, R., Gupta, A., Curless, B.: Real-time motion feedback in virtual reality for motor learning. In: Proceedings of IEEE VR, pp. 1–9 (2019)
5. Langer, A., et al.: Vertical locomotion improves horizontal locomotion: effects of climbing on gait and other mobility aspects in Parkinson's disease: a secondary analysis from a randomized controlled trial. J. Neuroeng. Rehabil. **21**(1) (2024)
6. Laver, K.E., Lange, B., George, S., Deutsch, J.E., Saposnik, G., Crotty, M.: Virtual reality for stroke rehabilitation. Cochrane Database Syst. Rev. (11) (2017)
7. de Miranda, A.F., Aires Lins, F.A., Nobrega, O.O., Falcao, T.P.: Evaluation of virtual learning environments for the teaching of students with down syndrome. In: 2017 IEEE International Conference on Systems, Man, and Cybernetics (SMC), pp. 1179–1184 (2017)
8. Mirelman, A., Rochester, L., Maidan, I.: Virtual reality training to improve gait and cognitive function in older adults. Lancet **388**, 1170–1182 (2016)
9. Rebsamen, S., Burkhardt, J.M., Crosetti, M.: A review of virtual reality technologies for sports training and rehabilitation. Front. Virtual Real. **3**, 882892 (2022)
10. Weiss, P.L., Keshner, E.A., Levin, M.F.: Virtual reality for neurorehabilitation: review and future perspectives. J. Neuroeng. Rehabil. **11**(1), 1–12 (2014)

Bridging ICF Functioning and the ISO Classification of Assistive Products Using BERT-Based Semantic Mapping

Sabatina Criscuolo[1](✉), Daniele Spoladore[1], Eleonora Conti[2], and Barbara Volta[2]

[1] Institute of Intelligent Industrial Technologies and Systems for Advanced Manufacturing, National Research Council of Italy, Via Gaetano Previati 1/E, 23900 Lecco, Italy
{sabatina.criscuolo,daniele.spoladore}@cnr.it

[2] Department of Maternal, Child and Adult Medical and Surgical Sciences, University of Modena and Reggio Emilia, Reggio Emilia, Italy
barbara.volta@unimore.it

Abstract. The International Classification of Functioning, Disability and Health (*ICF*) and the *ISO 9999* standard for assistive products are widely adopted in rehabilitation and assistive technology provision. However, the lack of explicit and systematic links between these two classifications limits their interoperability and hampers the development of integrated digital tools for assistive device selection. This paper proposes an automated semantic mapping approach between *ICF* functioning codes and *ISO 9999* categories using BERT-based sentence embeddings. Two sentence-transformer models are compared: a general-purpose model (*all-mpnet-base-v2*) and a domain-specific biomedical model (*BioSimCSE-BioLinkBERT-BASE*). Textual descriptions of 136 *ICF* codes and 123 *ISO 9999* categories are processed through a standardised NLP pipeline; cosine similarity yields a 136×123 matrix from which the top-5 matches per *ICF* code are extracted and independently evaluated by two occupational therapists using a 6-point Likert scale. The biomedical model achieved *Precision@1* = 0.971 and *Precision@3* = 1.0, with an inter-rater agreement of 84.3%. Stratified analysis revealed higher alignment quality for *Activities & Participation* codes than for *Body Functions* codes, indicating a priority area for future semantic enrichment. Results support the integration of the proposed approach into the *Rientr@* decision support platform for return-to-work interventions.

Keywords: ICF · Assistive Technology · ISO9999 · Natural Language Processing · Semantic Alignment

1 Introduction

The Return to Work (RTW) process for individuals with disabilities sustained through occupational injuries requires systematic alignment between functional

K. Miesenberger et al. (Eds.): ICCHP 2026, LNCS 16867, pp. 37–45, 2027.
https://doi.org/10.1007/978-3-032-31308-9_5

limitations and workplace accommodations, including assistive technologies (AT). In this context, the Italian National Institute for Insurance against Accidents at Work (INAIL) promotes the *Rientr@* project, which develops a Decision Support System (DSS) for identifying suitable jobs for people affected by an impairment after a work injury [16]. The system correlates workers' health condition, coded with the International Classification of Functioning, Disability, and Health (*ICF*) [17], and a suitable job with tasks, skills, and abilities, described with the O*NET framework [16], derived from the Standard Occupational Classification (SOC) in the USA. Although the Rientr@ DSS showed significant potential, the adoption of O*NET is not aligned with the use of the European Skills, Competences, Qualifications and Occupations (ESCO), which is a widely adopted classification to describe several characteristics of professions. Therefore, some attempts were made to match the two classifications using Machine Learning (ML) and Natural Language Processing (NLP) techniques [6]. Beyond job matching, the integration of AT into RTW represents a critical challenge often faced by occupational therapists, employers, and social workers. Indeed, inappropriate AT selection often results in abandonment, thus resulting in major barriers to successful work reintegration [7]. Also, across some European regions, AT and their selection cluster around accessibility, affordability, and acceptability: this structural uncertainty makes systematic matching of AT to work needs difficult [12]. Moreover, it is necessary to note that employees' perspectives on assistive technologies often report a lack of knowledge, focus, and training on the use of such technologies [15]. From a clinical perspective, occupational therapists face additional obstacles: insufficient training in AT, time pressure, and the lack of structured evidence-based selection tools hamper consistent practice [11,18].

A candidate resource for structuring AT selection is the *ISO 9999:2022* standard [2], which classifies assistive products hierarchically according to their intended *function*, i.e., what the assistive product is intended to do for the user. Furthermore, to make the ISO aligned with clinical terminology, the classification aligns with *ICF*, particularly, with the *Body function, Activity & participation, Environmental factors* components. This relationship ensures the hierarchy reflects internationally recognized concepts of disability and functioning. This alignment makes ISO 9999 a natural complement to the ICF-based *Rientr@* DSS, provided that a reliable mapping between the two classifications can be established.

Mapping ICF to ISO 9999 has been attempted in a limited number of studies. In 2012, Bassi et al. [3] proposed a mapping between the 1998 version of ISO 9999 and a subset of ICF *Environmental Factors*, with limited practical applicability due to the breadth of that ICF component. Explicit mapping between the two classifications was stated in a 2009 technical report [4], with the aim of indicating what the user of the assistive product can and may expect from it. The report maps all ISO third-level items with all types of ICF third-, fourth, and fifth-level components (including Environmental Factors). Although covering much of the ISO 9999, the report does not describe the mapping methodology adopted.

In 2009, a WHO document [13] constituted the core effort to align ICF "Chapter e1 Products & technology" with ISO 9999 terminology to support interoperable disability data systems. Despite these efforts, no mapping specifically designed to support occupational therapists in RTW interventions currently exists.

To address this gap and support occupational therapists in selecting appropriate assistive technologies, the present work proposes an extension of the *Rientr@* DSS, leveraging an ML-driven approach. Specifically, transformer-based architectures are used to automatically identify and synchronize the ontological representations of ICF and ISO 9999. Finally, a human validation protocol involving occupational therapists is further defined to assess the clinical reliability of the automated matches in real-world rehabilitative settings.

2 Materials and Method

The proposed methodology automates the alignment between *ICF* codes and *ISO 9999* classes to support clinical decision-making in AT selection based on functional limitations. The overall workflow is illustrated in Fig. 1.

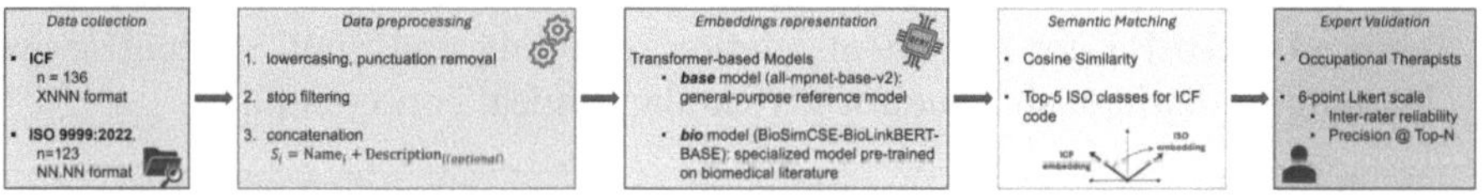

Fig. 1. Schematic representation of the proposed methodology.

2.1 Dataset

The study utilized two datasets. The first comprises 136 *ICF* codes selected from the "Body Functions" and "Activities and Participation" components, restricted to the `XNNN` alphanumeric format (`X` is the component letter and `NNN` is the specific functional level) to ensure granularity and consistency at the functional level most relevant to workplace reintegration. The second consists of a subset of 123 assistive technology codes from *ISO 9999:2022* at the `NN.NN` hierarchical level (corresponding to classes and subclasses) to balance specificity and generalization. For both datasets, each entry includes the official nomenclature and, where available, its technical description.

2.2 NLP Preprocessing and Feature Engineering

Textual descriptors from both taxonomies undergo a standardized preprocessing pipeline to maximize information density. The process consists of *lowercasing and punctuation removal*, and *stopword filtering* to remove non-informative terms (e.g., articles, conjunctions). Each preprocessed entry is then structured as a single concatenated string $S_i = \text{Name}_i + \text{Description}_{i(optional)}$. This representation allows transformer models to exploit the full contextual window, facilitating the identification of semantic links between clinical *ICF* terminology and technical *ISO* specifications, even across entries with varying textual densities.

2.3 Semantic Embedding and Similarity Computation

To capture the semantics of both classifications, *transformer-based models* are employed. These architectures utilize the *self-attention mechanism*, which allows the model to dynamically weight the importance of each word within a description relative to the entire context [19]. Specifically, Bidirectional Encoder Representations from Transformers (BERTs) are leveraged for their bidirectional analysis, considering both preceding and following terms simultaneously [8]. Two models are evaluated to identify the optimal trade-off between general linguistic capability and domain-specific precision:

- *Base* model (`all-mpnet-base-v2`): a general-purpose encoder pre-trained on over one billion sentence pairs [1];
- *Bio* model (`BioSimCSE-BioLinkBERT-BASE`): a biomedical specialist combining LinkBERT for document-relation modeling and SimCSE contrastive learning to distinguish semantically similar clinical concepts [9].

Each preprocessed entry is projected into a dense embedding vector encoding its conceptual meaning. This approach enables the alignment of codes sharing conceptual relevance even in the absence of direct lexical overlap. Following this transformation, pairwise semantic similarity is computed between each *ICF* and *ISO* vector using *cosine similarity*, defined as the cosine of the angle between two vectors [10]. The result is a similarity matrix whose entries range from 0 to 1, where a value approaching 1 signifies a high similarity. For each *ICF* code, the system produces a ranked *top-5* of the most semantically proximate *ISO* classes.

2.4 Expert-Based Validation

The reliability of the automated mappings is evaluated through an independent assessment conducted by two domain experts in two phases. In the first phase, two occupational therapists, a senior expert (Rater 1) and a junior practitioner (Rater 2), independently assessed *ICF-ISO* correspondences using a 6-point Likert scale (1: *Strong Disagreement* to 6: *Strong Agreement*). Inter-rater reliability was quantified via: (i) exact agreement percentage; (ii) weighted Cohen's κ with quadratic weights, which penalises disagreements proportionally to their ordinal distance; and (iii) Spearman's ρ, to assess ranking concordance without assuming score normality. Analyses were performed globally and stratified by rank position (top-1 through top-5) and ICF chapter (`b`: Body Functions; `d`: Activities & Participation). In the second phase, *Precision@k* to measure the percentage of automated suggestions confirmed as correct by the clinicians. A Wilcoxon signed-rank test with Benjamini-Hochberg (BH) correction was applied per rank position to compare cosine similarity distributions between the two models on matched pairs ($n = 136$ per rank).

3 Results and Discussion

3.1 Similarity Matrix and Model Comparison

Each ICF code was mapped to the *ISO 9999:2022* classes, yielding a 136×123 cosine similarity matrix, that quantifies the semantic correlation between clinical descriptors and AT classes. Three metrics are reported: *mean top-1 similarity*, the average of the highest similarity score per ICF code; *top-1 range*, the dispersion of best matches across the dataset; and *mean top-5 similarity*, the average of the five highest-ranked scores per code. The *Bio* model outperformed the *Base* model across all metrics: mean top-1 similarity of 0.426 ($\pm$0.078), with a range of 0.258 - 0.668 versus 0.408 ($\pm$0.105) with a range of 0.184 - 0.617, and mean top-5 similarity of 0.370 ($\pm$0.079) versus 0.333 ($\pm$0.098). The reduced standard deviation of the *Bio* model indicates more consistent matching behaviour across the dataset, suggesting that domain-specific pre-training on biomedical literature provides a more stable semantic space for clinical terminology alignment. Table 1 illustrates the top-5 matches for ICF code `b117` (Intellectual functions) as a representative example.

Table 1. Comparison of Top-5 matches for ICF code `b117` (Intellectual functions).

Bio Model			Base Model		
Rank	ISO Name (Code)	Score	Rank	ISO Name (Code)	Score
1	Cognitive test (04.25)	0.524	1	Cognitive test (04.25)	0.550
2	Enhance cognitive (04.26)	0.412	2	Enhance cognitive (04.26)	0.375
3	Music products (30.12)	0.391	3	Time/Planning (22.28)	0.363
4	Arm/Hand function (24.18)	0.372	4	Home construction (18.24)	0.320
5	Handicraft tools (30.18)	0.338	5	Arm/Hand function (24.18)	0.309

3.2 Expert-Based Validation

Inter-Rater Reliability. A total of 680 *ICF-ISO* correspondences were independently assessed by both raters (136 codes $\times$ 5 ranked matches per code). The *Bio* model yielded an exact agreement of 84.3 %, contrasting with 54.4 % for the *Base* model; at the same time, both models produced near-zero or negative κ values ($\kappa_{\text{Bio}} = 0.049$, $\kappa_{\text{base}} = -0.005$). This pattern is consistent with the prevalence paradox of Cohen's κ [5]: when one rating category dominates, here, score 6 accounted for 88.7 % and 76.2 % of responses for *Bio* and *Base* respectively, κ is systematically suppressed regardless of actual rater concordance, and percentage-based agreement is therefore the more informative metric in this context. A further source of asymmetry was the raters' use of the scale: the junior rater concentrated responses in the range 4–6 (variance: 0.48 for *Bio*, 0.75 for *Base*), whereas the senior rater utilized the full scale (variance: 1.23 and 1.42), consistent with documented leniency bias in novice evaluators [14], motivating the restriction of Phase 2 to Rater 1's scores.

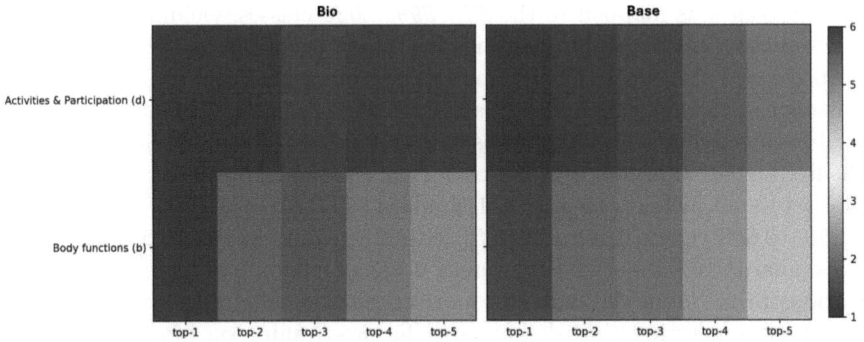

Fig. 2. Expert scores assigned by the senior rater per ICF chapter and rank position, for the *Bio* (left) and *Base* (right) models.

As shown in Fig. 2, stratified analysis by ICF chapter revealed a systematic performance gap: *Activities & Participation* codes (d) consistently received higher expert scores across all ranks and both models, while *Body Functions* (b) codes showed markedly lower scores, particularly at ranks 2–5. This suggests that functional task descriptors are intrinsically better aligned with *ISO 9999* terminology than abstract physiological codes, with direct implications for future ontology design: b-chapter codes may require supplementary semantic enrichment or manual curation.

Predictive Validity of Cosine Similarity. Score distributions (Rater 1) revealed a marked ceiling effect at rank 1 for both models (96.3% and 90.4% of responses scored 6 for *Bio* and *Base* respectively), with variance increasing progressively toward rank 5 (0.47→2.21 for *Bio*; 0.71→3.23 for *Base*). Rather than a methodological limitation, this ceiling effect reflects a positive outcome: the semantic pre-filtering performed by the top-5 selection effectively excludes poor candidates, producing a pool that the expert judges as almost uniformly acceptable at the highest rank. The near-constant score distribution at rank 1, however, renders Spearman's ρ uninformative at that position, and those values are interpreted with caution. At the global level, both models showed a positive and statistically significant correlation between cosine similarity and expert judgment ($\rho_{\mathrm{Bio}} = 0.228$, $\rho_{\mathrm{Base}} = 0.273$), confirming that model confidence is a meaningful proxy for clinical acceptability. The rank-stratified profiles reveal contrasting behaviours: *Base* achieves its highest ρ at rank 1 ($\rho = 0.245$), indicating alignment between model ordering and expert preference, while *Bio* shows a non-significant ρ at rank 1 ($\rho = 0.065$, $p = 0.45$) and reaches its maximum at rank 5 ($\rho = 0.307$). This inversion reflects *Bio*'s compressed similarity range (0.258–0.668 vs. 0.184–0.617), which limits discrimination among top candidates while reliably penalising poor matches at lower ranks.

Clinical Utility. *Precision@k* (threshold ≥ 5) confirmed the clinical utility of both models: *Bio* achieved *Precision@1* $= 0.971$ and *Precision@3* $= 1.0$, versus 0.949 and 1.0 for *Base*. For every ICF code, at least one clinically acceptable match is guaranteed within the first three suggestions regardless of the model used. The Wilcoxon signed-rank test confirmed that *Bio* assigns systematically higher similarity scores across all ranks after BH correction (all $p_{\text{adj}} < 0.05$), with effect sizes increasing from $r = 0.210$ at rank 1 to $r = 0.579$ at rank 5.

Taken together, these results reveal a complementary profile: *Bio* is better suited for shortlist generation, achieving higher *Precision@1* and more consistent top-level scores; *Base* offers better-calibrated rank ordering, making it preferable when the DSS presents a single best-match recommendation.

4 Conclusion

This paper proposed an automated *ICF-ISO 9999* semantic mapping system based on BERT-based sentence embeddings, evaluated through expert validation by occupational therapists. Both models demonstrated high clinical utility, achieving *Precision@3* $= 1.0$, ensuring that at least one acceptable match is always present within the first three suggestions. The *Bio* model proved better suited for shortlist generation, while the *Base* model offered more calibrated rank ordering. Stratified analysis revealed that *Activities & Participation* codes align more naturally with *ISO 9999* terminology than *Body Functions* codes, indicating a priority area for future semantic enrichment. The proposed system constitutes a first step toward integrating automated AT selection support into the *Rientr@* DSS, with broader applicability to rehabilitation and RTW decision-support tools.

Acknowledgments. The authors would like to acknowledge the Italian Institute for Insurance against Accident at Work (INAIL) for funding the project "PR23-SV-P2 âĂŞ Rientr@Returns: Consolidamento tecnologico e ampliamento della destinazione d'uso della piattaforma di simulazione Rientr@" "Technological reinforcement and extension to INAIL users of the Rientr@ simulation platform".

References

1. all-mpnet-base-v2 model (2019). https://huggingface.co/sentence-transformers/all-mpnet-base-v2. Accessed 02 Feb 2026
2. Iso 9999:2022 — assistive products — classification and terminology (2022). https://www.iso.org/standard/72464.html, seventh edition
3. Bassi, G., Simoncello, A., Frattura, L.: Mapping iso 9999 to ICF in health information systems (2012)
4. Bougie, T., Heerkens, Y.: ISO 9999 with ICF-references. WHO, Geneva (2009)
5. Cicchetti, D.V., Feinstein, A.R.: High agreement but low kappa: II. Resolving the paradoxes. J. Clin. Epidemiol. **43**(6), 551–558 (1990)
6. Criscuolo, S., et al.: Towards machine learning-based ontology mapping to bridge o* net and esco skills. In: 2025 IEEE International Conference on Metrology for eXtended Reality, Artificial Intelligence and Neural Engineering (MetroXRAINE), pp. 299–304. IEEE (2025)
7. Gamble, M.J., Dowler, D.L., Orslene, L.E.: Assistive technology: choosing the right tool for the right job. J. Vocat. Rehabil. **24**, 73–80 (2006)
8. Gardazi, N.M., Daud, A., Malik, M.K., Bukhari, A., Alsahfi, T., Alshemaimri, B.: Bert applications in natural language processing: a review. Artif. Intell. Rev. **58**(6), 1–49 (2025)
9. Kanakarajan, K.R., Kundumani, B., Abraham, A., Sankarasubbu, M.: BioSimCSE: BioMedical sentence embeddings using contrastive learning. In: Proceedings of the 13th International Workshop on Health Text Mining and Information Analysis (LOUHI), pp. 81–86. Association for Computational Linguistics, Abu Dhabi (Hybrid) (2022). https://aclanthology.org/2022.louhi-1.10
10. Lahitani, A.R., Permanasari, A.E., Setiawan, N.A.: Cosine similarity to determine similarity measure: study case in online essay assessment. In: 2016 4th International Conference on Cyber and IT Service Management, pp. 1–6. IEEE (2016)
11. Larsen, S.M., Brandt, A., Hounsgaard, L., Kristensen, H.: Occupational therapists' perspectives on an evidence-based, client-centered assistive technology intervention. Br. J. Occup. Ther. **86**, 376–384 (2023). https://doi.org/10.1177/03080226221148409
12. Mishra, S., et al.: Assistive technology needs, access and coverage, and related barriers and facilitators in the who European region: a scoping review. Disabil. Rehabil. Assist. Technol. **19**, 474–485 (2022). https://doi.org/10.1080/17483107.2022.2099021
13. Organization, W.H., et al.: Building bridges between diseases, disabilities and assistive devices: linking the GBD, ICF and ISO 9999: background paper 2, august 2010. World Health Organization, Technical report (2010)
14. Paunov, T., Weck, F., Heinze, P.E., Maaß, U., Kühne, F.: Competence ratings in psychotherapy training-a complex matter. Cogn. Ther. Res. **48**(3), 500–510 (2024)
15. Rasouli, O., Kvam, L., Husby, V.S., Røstad, M., Witsø, A.E.: Understanding the possibilities and limitations of assistive technology in health and welfare services for people with intellectual disabilities, staff perspectives. Disabil. Rehabil. Assist. Technol. **18**, 989–997 (2021). https://doi.org/10.1080/17483107.2021.1963856
16. Spoladore, D., et al.: Towards a knowledge-based decision support system to foster the return to work of wheelchair users. Comput. Struct. Biotechnol. J. **24**, 374–392 (2024)
17. Stucki, G., Cieza, A., Melvin, J.: The international classification of functioning, disability and health: a unifying model for the conceptual description of the rehabilitation strategy. J. Rehabil. Med. **39**(4), 279–285 (2007)

18. Thawisuk, C., Inoue, K., Kaunnil, A., Suyama, N., Kim, M., Ito, Y.: Factors influencing implementation of assistive technology services for older adults from the perspectives of thai occupational therapists: a mixed methods study. Disabil. Rehabil. Assist. Technol. **19**, 859–867 (2022). https://doi.org/10.1080/17483107.2022.2129847
19. Vaswani, A., et al.: Attention is all you need. Adv. Neural Inf. Process. Syst. **30** (2017)

[illegible]

ICT to Support Inclusive Education – Universal Learning Design (ULD)

ICT to Support Inclusive Education-Universal Learning Design (ULD) Introduction to the Special Thematic Session

Marion Hersh[1(✉)] and Barbara Leporini[2]

[1] Biomedical Engineering, University of Glasgow, Glasgow, Scotland, UK
marion.hersh@glasgow.ac.uk
[2] Department of Computer Sc., University of Pisa and ISTI-CNR, Pisa, Italy
barbara.leporini@unipi.it

Abstract. Education plays a fundamental role in individual development and social participation, making it essential to design effective methodologies and tools to support learning. This is particularly critical in the context of inclusive education, where the focus has moved from integration to inclusion, with the aim of enhancing learning opportunities for all. In this context, information and communication technologies (ICT) play a key role, not only for overcoming barriers but also for enriching learning experiences and improving accessibility for a broader range of learners. The emergence of generative artificial intelligence (AI) can provide new opportunities for content adaptation, multimodal interaction, and personalised learning, but also raises very serious challenges related to responsible and ethical use. This Special Thematic Session includes 12 papers, 10 of which are published in this volume, covering a wide range of topics, technologies, and educational contexts. The contributions reflect the diversity and evolution of the field, highlighting how inclusive education is a dynamic and multi-dimensional process.

Keywords: Inclusive Education · Curriculum Accessibility · Barriers · Attitudes · Technology

1 Introduction

Education plays a fundamental role both in individual development and in enabling participation in society and employment. There is therefore a need for methodologies and tools that effectively support learning processes. This is even more critical in inclusive education, as it involves addressing a wide diversity of learners and contexts. Consequently, the perspective has evolved over time from integration-focused on adapting existing solutions to accommodate specific needs-to a broader concept of inclusion [1, 2]. This change has led to the need to move beyond solutions aimed solely at overcoming individual barriers, and instead design approaches that enrich and extend learning opportunities for all [3, 4]. Consequently, inclusive education is not only about supporting students with special educational needs (SEN), but improving the general quality, accessibility and personalisation of educational solutions [5–7].

K. Miesenberger et al. (Eds.): ICCHP 2026, LNCS 16867, pp. 49–56, 2027.
https://doi.org/10.1007/978-3-032-31308-9_6

In this context, information and communication technologies (ICT) play a key role. Digital and assistive technologies are not only tools to overcome barriers otherwise experienced by disabled students, but resources that can enhance learning for everyone. For instance, solutions designed to support blind and low vision students often result in richer, more structured, and more accessible content, which can benefit all learners, following the principles of Universal Design for Learning (UDL) [8]. Similarly, tools that support understanding complex content, such as mathematical expressions or technical materials, can reduce cognitive barriers and facilitate understanding for everyone [9, 10]. This perspective reflects a paradigm in which accessibility and inclusion are not specialised features or add-ons, but key elements of education innovation. Designing for diversity can lead to more effective and engaging learning environments, with benefits to a wider population.

More recently, the rise of generative artificial intelligence (AI) has led to new opportunities in the area of education. AI-based tools can support content adaptation, multimodal representation, and personalised learning experiences, potentially enhancing both accessibility and learning outcomes [11, 12]. However, there are also very serious associated risks and challenges [13–15] and varying views on whether using AI in a thoughtful, ethical and effective way is sufficient to overcome the problems and allow it to be applied without risk to support inclusive education.

The session papers reflect well the current evolution of the field and the diversity of approaches that are being explored. They cover a wide range of topics, technologies, and educational contexts, showing how inclusive education is not a single-direction effort but a multi-dimensional space where different solutions and methodologies are combined.

2 Session Papers

The session contains 12 papers, 10 of which are published in this volume. A brief summary is presented in Table 1 below. They are very varied and have authors from 10 different countries, eight in Europe and two outside. Two papers involve inter-country comparisons. The target learners cover all stages from pre-school to university, as well as teachers and science, technology, engineering and mathematics (STEM) professionals. The most commonly used technologies were artificial intelligence (AI) and video. STEM, particularly mathematics, was the most common subject for interventions.

The session papers can be divided into three main groups: technology design and evaluation, institutional accessibility and barriers, and attitudes to and experiences of existing technologies. The four papers on technology design and evaluation covered an interactive sonification app (Schölch et al.); an audio based role playing game for science, technology, engineering and mathematics (STEM) (Frizzi et al.), a video-based assistive picture book to support reading (Hsieh and Huang); and a system for making Scratch programming accessible (Truillet).

Schölch, Ducci, Garcia Sanchez and Bernareggi present APP-NAME, which uses interactive sonification to explore mathematical functional graphs in 'Audiofunctions + : Interactive Sonification for Inclusive Learning of Function Graphs'. The interface is keyboard-based with attention to screen reader usability and the involvement of experienced screen reader users to ensure this. The app maps function graph properties to

Table 1. Paper overview.

Authors	Type of Paper	Target Learners	Technology	Number	Country
Schölch et al[a]	App development	Screen reader users – secondary and university	Sonification	Not stated	Germany, Italy,Spain
Siqueira et al.[a]	Qualitative study	Visually impaired STEM students & professionals	AI & AT	13	Brazil
Frizzi et al.[a]	Game design	Visually impaired children	AI		Italy
Hsieh & Huang[a]	Design & evaluation	Preschool with developmental delays	Video	3	Taiwan
Hsieh & Chen[a]	Study	5–6 year old disabled preschoolers	Video	47 disabled 67 nondisabled	Taiwan
Theodorou[a]	Theory development	HE with invisible disabilities	AI	N/a	Greece
Nuppenau[b]	Literature review & interviews with disability services	Visually impaired computer science students	N/a	Not stated	Austria
Nuppenau[b]	Design of training programme	Visually impaired pre-university	N/a	N/a	Austria
Coughlan et al.[b]	Comparative study	Disabled university students	Assistive tools	356 Spanish 108UK	Spain&UK
Huang[b]		Primary students with mild cognitive impairments		32 primary students 16 teachers	Taiwan

(continued)

Table 1. *(continued)*

Authors	Type of Paper	Target Learners	Technology	Number	Country
Wu et al.[b]	Study	Special education teachers	Virtual reality	409	Taiwan
Truillet[a]	Technology development	Visually impaired children	Scratch blocks	Not stated	France

[a]Miesenberger, K.; Petrie, H..; Penaz, P. (eds.): ICCHP 2026, Computers Helping People with Special Needs, 20th International Conference; Linz, Austria, Proceedings. Springer (2026).
[b]Petz, A.; Miesenberger, K. (eds.): ICCHP Open Access Compendium „Future Perspectives on Accessibility, AT and eInclusion"; Linz, Austria, Proceedings. Johannes Kepler University Linz (2026).

sound parameters. A preliminary study has been carried out, as well as expert validation by blind experts. Two further studies are planned to test learning outcomes in secondary schools and usability with university students under controlled conditions.

In 'Designing an Accessible Audio-Driven Role-Playing Game for STEM Learning', Frizzi, Forgione, Galesi and Leporini present le Chiavi di Elthar, a multimodal collaborative role playing game. Participants have distinct roles with educational and inclusion aims. The multimodal interface is designed to ensure accessibility with audio descriptions used to provide narration, instructions and challenges. Narrative is central to the game experience and the solution of logical-mathematical and scientific problems is required to progress the story. Narrator and character voices were produced by AI-based text-to-speech systems to improve voice naturalness and express quality. A preliminary evaluation by visually impaired children at a summer camp found that they were able to use it autonomously and liked the audio narration and multimodal interaction. Suggestions were obtained for improvement.

Hsieh and Huang investigated the use of video based assistive picture book to support reading for preschool children with developmental delays in 'Design and Evaluation of a Video Based Assistive Picture Book for Story Comprehension Support in Preschool Children with Developmental Delays'. The book was designed to reduce cognitive load through the use of short video clips, voice-over narration aligned with visual content and guided prompts to direct attention to critical narrative elements. Evaluation using three single case studies with three preschool children with developmental delays found that the approach using cognitive load reduction and multimedia scaffolding was successful. However, the authors recognise the limitations of the small number of participants and the use of a particular design in a controlled context.

Tangible Blocks Go Online (TaBGO) for making Scratch, a frequently used introductory programming platform for young people, accessible to blind learners, is presented by Truillet in 'From Algorithm To Execution: Enabling Everyone To Engage In Programming Activity'. TABGO involves physical blocks for building the algorithm, a webcam, smartphone or other video capture device and tools to convert Scratch files to different formats to allow students to access the results. The blocks are stored in a compartmentalised case to help users locate and assemble them. The author states that the results of preliminary tests have been encouraging, without providing details and proposes further work on improving usability and long term classroom integration.

The four papers on institutional accessibility and barriers discuss an AI-driven cognitive framework (Theodorou); and the development of a peer counselling training programme for visually impaired students (Nuppenau) and present two comparative studies, of the institutional barriers to visually impaired computer science students in Austria, Ireland and Slovenia (Nuppenau); and the experiences of disabled university students in Spain and the UK (Coughlan et al.).

Theodorou introduces an AI-driven cognitive framework based on four interrelated pillars in 'AI-Driven Cognitive Accessibility for People with Non-Visible Disabilities in Higher Education: A Conceptual Framework for Inclusive Digital Systems', They are 1) cognitive accessibility as the desired system outcome; 2) AI seen as a run-time control layer which monitors interaction patterns and regulates interaction complexity and pacing; 3) User control, transparency and self-advocacy, including the ability to understand and override automated decisions; and 4) institutional inclusion, which places cognitive accessibility in the broader higher education (HE) organisational context. The authors suggest that the framework will encourage HE institutions to go beyond compliance-based accessibility to adaptive inclusive digital infrastructures.

The development of a training programme for visually impaired university students is discussed by Nuppenau in 'Peer Counselling to Support Blind and Visually Impaired Pupils in Their Transition to Higher Education'. The development drew on a literature review on mentoring, peer support and inclusive transitions and semi-structured interviews and focus groups with visually impaired school and university students, teachers and parents. The programme covers everything relevant to the school-university transition, including obtaining reasonable adjustments and using AT, with resources in an accessible format. The pilot implementation and evaluation phase involved trained peer counsellors carrying out one-to-one sessions, small group meetings and theme-based workshops with matched students considering HE or in the final years of school. Evaluation involved both metrics, such as participation numbers and session frequency, and pre-and post-intervention student self-reports of confidence and knowledge.

One of the comparative studies considered institutional barriers to visually impaired computer science students in Austria, Ireland and Slovenia in 'Blind and Visually Impaired Students in Computer Science: Institutional Conditions and Paths Towards Proactive University Support in Austria, Ireland and Slovenia' by Nuppenau. This involved a study of relevant legislation and university policies in the three countries, interviews with disability service staff and a literature review of institutional support structures and institutional change. These authors identified five priority areas for improving university support. These are 1) Clear responsibility structures with designated coordinators linking disability services, computer science departments and IT services; 2) quality assurance with regular surveys and course feedback having visual impairment specific indicators; 3) including discipline specific accessibility challenges e.g. non-visual coding in staff training; 4) peer mentoring programmes; and 5) embedding UDL and accessibility in curriculum design from the start. However, further work will be required to develop specific recommendations and investigate their usefulness and how best they can be implemented.

The other comparative study was a bilingual one of the experiences of disabled students in Spanish and UK universities. In 'Context Matters: Comparing What Works for Disabled Students at Spanish and UK Distance Learning Institutions', Coughlan, Iniesto, Castellano-Beltrán and Rodrigo San Juan present a study investigating the subjects studied, how they described their disabilities or support needs, what helped them initially, resources they would suggest, tools or AT used and successful strategies. Administrative differences resulted in differences in disability or support need descriptions with UK universities more open to self-reporting. Spanish responses tended to focus on tutorial or support groups for disabled students, whereas UK institutions focused on one-to-one relationships with tutors. There were also different approaches to examinations and in person and online activities with more in person activities in Spain. The authors suggested the need for a combined analysis of data from disabled students and their study context to fully understand the implications for the appropriate use of tools and strategies.

The four papers on attitudes to and experiences of existing technologies covers ICT and AI support for reading mathematics formulae (Siqueira et al.); the use of short video clips to support mathematics understanding (Hsieh and Chen); the use of picture story books to support literacy and social-emotional learning (Huang); and teacher attitudes to the use of virtual reality (VR) (Wu et al.).

In 'A Qualitative Study on the Use of ICT and AI by STEM Students and Professionals to Support the Reading of Mathematical Formulas', Siqueira, Ribeiro, Andrade and Freire present the results of semi-structured interviews with 13 visually impaired STEM students or professionals aged over 18. All participants reported using various assistive technologies (AT) in their academic and professional work. They all used AI in various ways and started using it at different times, frequently to provide verbal representations of visual mathematical formulae, for instance in the form of descriptions. They also used AI to increase autonomy, but there were some criticisms of AI reliability and a desire for AI integration with screen readers.

Hsieh and Chen investigated the use of short video clips to support mathematics learning by 5–6 year old pre-school children in 'Reducing Interface Message Complexity as Digital Scaffolding: A Study of Mathematical Concept Understanding among Children with Special Educational Needs in Short-Form Video Environments'. The assessment included a concept understanding tool developed by the authors. While this was checked against another tool, further evaluation of the tool before being used in a study would have been desirable. The study found similar mathematics concept understanding by disabled and non-disabled preschoolers when a low complexity interface was used and that the disabled group preferred longer videos as they gave them more time to think and landscape format as they enabled them to 'see more'.

Huang evaluated the CLEPS picture story book programme for socio-emotional learning and literacy instruction with primary school students with mild cognitive impairments in 'Using Chinese Life Education Picture Storybooks as a Supportive Social-Emotional Learning Intervention for Students with Mild Intellectual Disabilities'. The evaluation used a combination of teacher and student reports and teacher assessment of performance. After a two-day workshop, 16 special education teachers implemented the programme in 16 sessions over 12 weeks. The results showed that the approach significantly improved both literacy and social-emotional competencies. The author considered that embedding social-emotional learning into culturally meaningful narratives made the approach accessible, engaging and developmentally appropriate, but notes that the sustainability of the learning gains needs to be investigated.

Wu, Lin, Shen, Chen and Sher used a survey of special education teachers to investigate barriers to implementing virtual reality in the classroom in 'Virtual Reality Adoption Among Special Education Teachers: Explaining the Intention-Behavior Gap'. The survey questions were designed to investigate components of the Technology Acceptance Model 3 (TAM3) and decisions about using virtual reality (VR) in the special education context. Perceived usefulness was found to be the main driver of attitude to using VR, which strongly predicted actual use. Male teachers were found to have significantly greater perceived external control than preschool teachers. The authors consider that the study shows the value of TAM3 in the special education context and the existence of structural constraints to implementing VR. They propose a combination of targeted resource allocation and task-oriented hands-on training to overcome the barriers to using VR.

3 Conclusions

The 12 papers give a good impression of research in the area, the potential of different technologies, the progress that has been made and the considerable work remaining to be done, while recognising that they are only a fraction of the total papers in the field. The use of AI has become significant since the last conference, but there are fewer papers that use co-design and co-production approaches.

References

1. Ainscow, M.: Developing inclusive education systems: what are the levers for change? J. Educ. Change **6**(2), 109–124 (2005)
2. Booth, T., Ainscow, M., Black-Hawkins, K., Vaughan, M., Shaw, L.: Index for inclusion. Developing learning and participation in schools **2** (2002)
3. Evans, K.L.: Universal design for learning. Choral J. **64**(7), 8–21 (2024)
4. Sulaiman, L.H., Tahar, M.M.: Implementation of universal learning design principles by mainstream teacher in inclusive education programs. Spec. Educ. [SE] **2**(1), e0015–e0015 (2024)
5. Gupta, S.S., Henninger IV, W.R., Vinh, M.E.: How do children benefit from inclusion. First steps to preschool inclusion: how to jumpstart your programwide plan. 33–57 (2014)
6. Florian, L.: What counts as evidence of inclusive education? Eur. J. Spec. Needs Educ. **29**(3), 286–294 (2014)
7. Lindner, K.T., Schwab, S., Emara, M., Avramidis, E.: Do teachers favor the inclusion of all students? A systematic review of primary schoolteachers' attitudes towards inclusive education. Eur. J. Spec. Needs Educ. **38**(6), 766–787 (2023)
8. Levey, S.: Universal design for learning. J. Educ. **203**(2), 479–487 (2023)
9. Mayer, R.E.: The future of multimedia learning. J. Appl. Instr. Des. **11**(4), 69–77 (2022)

10. Sweller, J.: Cognitive load theory: what we learn and how we learn. In: Learning, design, and technology: An international compendium of theory, research, practice, and policy, pp. 137–152. Springer International Publishing, Cham (2023)
11. Roll, I., Wylie, R.: Evolution and revolution in artificial intelligence in education. Int. J. Artif. Intell. Educ. **26**(2), 582–599 (2016)
12. Zawacki-Richter, O., Marín, V.I., Bond, M., Gouverneur, F.: Systematic review of research on artificial intelligence applications in higher education–where are the educators? Int. J. Educ. Technol. High. Educ. **16**(1), 39 (2019)
13. Hersh, M.: AI Research: where are the disabled researchers and the voices of disabled people. In International Conference of the Association for the Advancement of Assistive Technology in Europe, (pp. 209–216). Cham, Springer Nature Switzerland (2025)
14. Teo, S.: Artificial intelligence and its 'slow violence' to human rights. AI Ethics **5**, 2265–2280 (2025)
15. Tuset Varela, D.: Artificial intelligence law through the lens of michel foucault: biopower, surveillance, and the reconfiguration of legal normativity. Open J. Soc. Sci. **12**, 189–201 (2024)

Audiofunctions+: Interactive Sonification for Inclusive Learning of Function Graphs

Lukas Schölch[1](✉), Pedro A. Garcia-Sanchez[2], Mattia Ducci[3], and Cristian Bernareggi[3]

[1] Karlsruhe Institute of Technology, Karlsruhe, Germany
lukas.schoelch@kit.edu
[2] University of Granada, Granada, Spain
pedro@ugr.es
[3] University of Turin, Turin, Italy
{mattia.ducci,cristian.bernareggi}@unito.it

Abstract. Audiofunctions+ is a web application for exploring mathematical function graphs through interactive sonification in inclusive learning contexts, with a clear didactic focus: supporting core learning activities around function graphs without adding hints beyond what a standard visual plot would provide.

Audiofunctions+ follows a keyboard-centered interaction paradigm and treats high-quality screen reader usability as a primary requirement. The application combines a visual function plot with sonification at a movable cursor position, offering stepwise and smooth navigation as well as optional batch playback. Sonification maps function values to pitch and adds cues such as panning and earcons while balancing information density and cognitive load.

To support typical graph-reading tasks Audiofunctions+ includes spoken coordinates, points of interest (e.g., discontinuities) exposed during navigation, and user-defined landmarks to enable rapid comparisons across the graph.

Initial validation activities provide indications that the approach works well in practice. The application is already stable, publicly available, and open source on GitHub.

Keywords: Sonification · Math Education · Hci · Universal Learning Design · Function Graph

1 Introduction

Inclusive education for learners with disabilities has been a central objective of educational policy and research over recent decades. Despite significant progress, substantial barriers remain, particularly in science, technology, engineering, and mathematics (STEM) education. In particular, STEM education of students with blindness or low vision presents specific and well-documented difficulties, with

K. Miesenberger et al. (Eds.): ICCHP 2026, LNCS 16867, pp. 57–65, 2027.
https://doi.org/10.1007/978-3-032-31308-9_7

a major obstacle being access to graphical representations, which are ubiquitous in STEM education. Graphs, diagrams, charts, and plots are essential tools for conveying quantitative relationships, trends, and functional dependencies. However, these representations are typically designed for visual inspection and are often inaccessible or only partially accessible to learners with visual impairments. There exist several tools and methods aimed at making function graphs accessible to students with blindness or low vision. One widely used approach is tactile graphics; these preserve the spatial nature of graphs and support the development of mental models, but they are static, often require prior preparation, and can become cluttered for complex functions or data. Another common method involves textual descriptions and value tables of function graphs. These representations are flexible and compatible with screen readers, but they do not provide instantaneous access to global characteristics of a graph or quantitative relationships. The quality and usefulness of text descriptions depend heavily on the author's expertise and awareness of accessibility principles. Overall, none of these methods alone offers a complete and fully satisfactory solution.

Sonification has emerged as a promising non-visual approach for representing function graphs by mapping function properties to sound parameters such as pitch or spatialization. Its dynamic nature can support interactive exploration and help users perceive global trends (e.g., monotonicity, periodicity, and local extrema) through auditory cues. Despite its potential, sonification for function graphs remains difficult to adopt in inclusive educational contexts. Many existing tools are specialized applications that target expert users, require substantial training, and are not properly aligned with everyday classroom needs. This contribution introduces Audiofunctions+, a web application designed to enable students with visual disabilities to explore and understand function graphs in an inclusive classroom setting.

2 Related Work

Sonification is the process of mapping data to sound to improve accessibility, perception, and interpretation of information [3]. Sonification research is grounded in parameter mapping, where data attributes are systematically translated into sound parameters (e.g., pitch, loudness, timbre, and spatialization). This mapping can follow various models. The most used in data visualization and function graph exploration are the following. *(i) Discrete Event-Based Sonification:* provides immediate auditory feedback for specific data points or interactions (e.g., a beep when a cursor intersects a graph line) [2]; *(ii) Continuous Sonification:* uses uninterrupted sound streams to represent evolving data trends, facilitating real-time monitoring [9]; *(iii) Spatial and Narrative Sonification:* enhances comprehension by placing sound in stereo or 3D space or by integrating auditory cues into a storytelling context [4].

Prior to the development of the new version of Audiofunctions+, a literature and software review was performed by the project team[1]. Software tools were

[1] https://sonairgraph.unito.it.

examined according to different categories. Several sonification applications were studied; most of them meant to sonify data and not functions. Sonification of functions is present in *Aural* [6], *MathTrax*[2], *Sonify (R package)*[3], *Audiographs*[4], *SenseMath*[5], and *Desmos*[6].

MathTrax is a discontinued Windows tool that combines function sonification with solver – and classifier – based descriptions. *Audiographs* is a Windows only software to sonify mathematical functions. *SenseMath* is an iOS only application specifically created for didactical purpose with visually impaired people, and allows a non-interactive function exploration by simple playback combined with a metronome. *Desmos graphing calculator* enables to type in the function, plot its graph and explore it using sonification. *Sonify* is a command line tool to sonify univariate data into a continuous sound with time varying pitch, meant to be an alternate to the 'plot' command in R.

The analysis of the mentioned applications resulted in a report [8], which includes further details. While these tools demonstrate the potential of sonification for function graph exploration, none of them fully addresses the requirements of inclusive classroom use. Most are platform-specific, discontinued, or aimed at expert users rather than students in mainstream education. Moreover, existing tools either provide additional interpretive hints that go beyond what a standard visual plot conveys in didactic settings, or they lack interaction features, that would be important for typical graph-reading tasks, such as comparing multiple functions, identifying discontinuities. Furthermore, most tools lack the flexible and intuitive navigation needed to keep learners focused on understanding the graph rather than operating the tool.

These applications and pedagogical studies based on previous versions of Audiofunctions [1], highlight that accessibility in multimodal mathematical tools must be grounded in educational intentionality rather than conceived as a mere technical translation of visual or information. Design choices, such as specific timbral features, can actively shape the construction of mathematical meaning, supporting embodied and perceptually driven understanding. The earlier version of AudioFunctions had several key limitations: it offered limited compatibility with screen readers, lacked tools for managing reference points on function graphs, provided only a small number of earcons and navigation modalities to find out important graph features, and featured a user interface suited to controlled settings for research studies rather than practical use by students in a classroom.

3 Audiofunctions+

Audiofunctions+ is a web application for exploring mathematical function graphs through interactive sonification. Building on the limitations and learnings

[2] https://github.com/TerryHodgson/NASA-MathDescriptionEngine1.0.3.
[3] https://cran.r-project.org/package=sonify.
[4] https://sourceforge.net/projects/audiographs/files/latest/download.
[5] https://enviter.eu/sensemath-making-sense-of-math/.
[6] https://www.desmos.com/calculator.

identified in prior work, Audiofunctions+ aims to be practical for everyday classroom use and to support shared activities by sighted and visually impaired students through a streamlined, screen readerâĂŞfriendly interaction design. It is intended to complement, not replace, established accessible representations such as tactile graphics, and it is designed to not provide additional hints beyond the information available in a standard visual graph.

Audiofunctions+ implements sonification using *JSXGraph*[7] and *Tone.js*[8]. *JSXGraph* renders the graph and provides interaction events, which drive a *Tone.js* audio chain. During the implementation we gathered constant feedback from 3 blind experts and from other sources like the blind association in Spain (ONCE).

3.1 User Interface

To ensure that all users, regardless of the type or degree of visual impairment, can operate the app on equal terms, the entire user interface was designed with a keyboard-centered interaction paradigm. Throughout the design, high-quality screen reader usability was treated as a primary requirement.

The application is built around a single central element: an interactive plot of a mathematical function and a movable cursor on it (Fig. 1a). Sonification is generated only at the current cursor position. To interact with the sonification, users can move the cursor to the left or right along the function in two modes: *(i) stepwise navigation:* pressing the left or right arrow key shifts the cursor by a fixed step size; *(ii) smooth navigation:* holding `[Shift]` while pressing left/right moves the cursor continuously until the keys are released or the plot boundary is reached. As special cases of smooth navigation, users can trigger a "batch sonification" that automatically moves the cursor over the full visible domain once (from left to right), and optionally control the cursor with the mouse. In the latter case, the sonification volume is mapped to the y-distance between the mouse pointer and the function value to provide an additional alignment cue.

Besides the graph, the main view includes only two controls: mute/unmute for sonification and a button that opens a command palette (also via `[Ctrl+K]` or `[Cmd+K]` on macOS). The command palette provides access to all functionality through a compact category list with nested entries, and displays shortcuts (where available) to support incidental learning (Fig. 1b). It can be navigated with arrow keys or the mouse, or queried via typing using fuzzy search with action-specific alternative keywords (e.g., "formula" may suggest "Edit Functions" already after a few characters). The screen reader behaviour, especially in the command palette, was iteratively refined with experienced screen reader users, and more complex features are moved into dialogues to reduce simultaneously presented UI elements and cognitive load. For example, the "Edit Functions" dialogue supports adding, editing, and deleting functions via plain text fields using a lightweight, calculator-like notation without requiring LaTeX or other specialized formats (Fig. 1c).

[7] https://jsxgraph.org.

[8] https://tonejs.github.io/.

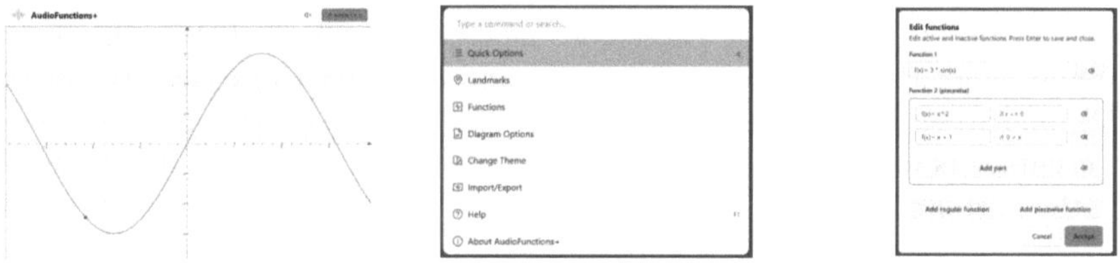

(a) Graph View (b) Command Palette (c) Edit Functions dialog

Fig. 1. Screenshots of Audiofunctions+.

To match the expressive power of sonification to that of a visual function plot, Audiofunctions+ provides additional features, ranging from small utilities (e.g., reading out the current cursor coordinates) to "points of interest" (POIs) and "landmarks". POIs are detected automatically (e.g., discontinuities or "holes"). In visual plots, such locations are usually highlighted with a distinct marker, often shown as a hollow circle, so they can be identified at a glance. In Audiofunctions+, POIs are auditively exposed during smooth navigation via subtle snapping, ensuring that these isolated locations are reliably sonified despite the sampling rate of cursor movement. Landmarks support value-comparisons across larger distances on the graph that are immediate in visual plots but inefficient with sequential sonification. To address this, users can place landmarks at arbitrary positions on the function and then jump directly between these user-defined reference points via keystrokes, enabling rapid back-and-forth comparison without repeatedly traversing and re-sonifying the interval between them.

Audiofunctions+ offers an additional feature for teachers, to prepare exercises and examples that can be shared via links or json files to the students and their colleagues. For didactical purposes, teachers can restrict the functionality of Audiofunctions+ for the shared exercises.

3.2 Sonification

Audiofunctions+ maps function-graph properties of the visible part of the cartesian plane on the screen to sound parameters. Based on the literature, Audiofunctions+ maps the value of the function at the cursor position to the sound pitch (the higher the value of the function, the higher the pitch); panning is mapped to the cursor's x-position within the current view. These mappings leverage the perceptual correspondence between pitch and vertical position, where higher pitches are perceived as higher in space and lower pitches as lower [7], whilst stereo panning exploits humans' ability to perceive the directionality of sound. Sonification is available in two modes: *continuous* (clarinet timbre) and *discrete* (guitar notes). Offering this two sonification modes supports different educational goals.

In addition to these main features, Audiofunctions+ enriches sonification with other sounds and features, always considering a balance between communicated information and cognitive load. These cues include signaling negative values by adding pink noise (because it is not invasive and does not cause high cognitive load [5]); an earcon for crossing the y-axis, and a distinct sound is played whenever the cursor is located where no function value exists or when this value is outside the current view.

4 Validation and First Results

The validation of Audiofunctions+ proceeded in two stages. First, a targeted internal study and an expert validation with blind users were conducted to assess the sonification design and overall accessibility of the application. The insights gained were used to refine Audiofunctions+ before proceeding to the larger studies. Second, two larger studies with the improved version are currently underway to evaluate Audiofunctions+ in realistic educational settings.

4.1 Preliminary Results

To choose a specific technique for spatial sonification, we conducted a small internal study comparing three panning algorithms: Interaural Time Difference (ITD), Interaural Level Difference (ILD), and Head-Related Transfer Function (HRTF). The study compared these algorithms by having 9 participants identify the direction of static and moving sounds mapped to 12 angles (15° each). Results showed that ILD performed best: its root mean square localization error was 3.13, compared to 3.24 (ITD) and 3.98 (HRTF). ILD also scored higher in subjective confidence and response time; for moving audio, ILD produced 25 errors versus 49 (ITD) and 44 (HRTF). Based on these results, ILD was adopted as the panning algorithm in Audiofunctions+.

Following the internal study, we conducted an expert validation with 8 blind users who had not been involved in the development process, in order to assess the accessibility, ease of use, and overall suitability of the application for its intended use. Participants were given a link to the application and a set of structured tasks, but received no dedicated introduction or guided walk-through. Instead, they were asked to read the built-in tutorial independently before proceeding. Tasks covered core interaction scenarios, including stepwise and continuous graph navigation, batch sonification, switching between functions and sonification modes, zooming, coordinate readout, and editing the function set.

All experts rated the application as stable. Seven out of eight considered Audiofunctions+ useful for students, and equally agreed that teachers would benefit from it when introducing mathematical functions in the classroom. However, the qualitative feedback revealed several usability issues and areas for improvement. These were addressed in a subsequent refinement cycle before proceeding to the larger studies. Specific improvements include keyboard shortcut refinements, a redesign of the sonification mode from a per-function setting to a global mode, and an improved in-app tutorial to better guide users through the application's features.

4.2 Ongoing and Planned Studies

Building on these preliminary results, we are currently conducting two larger studies to evaluate Audiofunctions+ in realistic educational settings.

Classroom Study: A didactic classroom study is being carried out in secondary schools to evaluate whether Audiofunctions+ supports students with and without visual impairments in learning about mathematical function graphs. The study uses a methodological sheet with several tasks that was developed by the project team, was validated by both visually impaired experts and methodological experts. Several sessions in different secondary schools across the countries participating in the project took place, with at total of 159 students, of which 17 where visually impaired. Students in the same classroom were arranged in pairs and trios (with all possible combinations). The data is now being categorised and analysed. All tests are aimed to the students. The sharing options for teachers are only used to produce the worksheets for the study.

Usability Study: A controlled online usability study with at least 50 university students is currently underway. Participants are first introduced to the core features in a guided practice environment before independently completing three (randomly ordered) tasks that are designed to require different exploration strategies and feature sets (e.g. function comparison, landmark-based exploration, and view-panning). After each task, participants complete a questionnaire measuring task success as well as perceived usefulness and ease of use of the relevant features. The study concludes with a NASA-TLX assessment and a general questionnaire covering overall interaction concepts and sonification modes. Sessions are recorded, transcribed and anonymised for futher qualitative analysis.

5 Conclusion

Audiofunctions+ presents a rethought approach to exploring function graphs, centered on the didactic value of interactive sonification for inclusive learning scenarios. In contrast to existing sonification tools discussed in Sect. 2, it combines a fully keyboard-centered, screen-reader-friendly interface with features tailored to typical classroom graph-reading tasks, such as flexible navigation, automatic handling of discontinuities, fast switching between functions, landmark-based comparison, and sharing and restriction mechanisms for teachers. Initial feedback from our internal study and expert validation indicates that Audiofunctions+ is stable, accessible, and usable in practice, and supports the intended interaction concept. Building on these results, we are currently conducting a classroom study in secondary schools and an online usability study with university students to obtain more robust quantitative and qualitative evidence on learning outcomes and interaction quality. With its public availability and open-source codebase,[9] Audiofunctions+ is already available as a new modality for introducing mathematical function graphs in inclusive classrooms.

Acknowledgments. The authors are supported by the SONification for Accessible and Inclusive Representation of GRAPHs in Education (SONAIRGRAPH) project, which is an Erasmus+ key action 2 (project no. 2024-1-IT02-KA220-HED-000244481), funded by the European Union. Views and opinions expressed are however those of the author(s) only and do not necessarily reflect those of the European Union or the European Education and Culture Executive Agency (EACEA). Neither the European Union nor EACEA can be held responsible for them.

The authors would like to thank the referees for their detailed reading and the suggestions proposed that certainly helped to improve this manuscript. We would also like to thank the rest of the members of the SONAIRGRAPH project, as well as the many participants of the different validation, methodological and usability tests performed so far.

References

1. Ahmetovic, D., Bernareggi, C., Guerreiro, J., Mascetti, S., Capietto, A.: Audiofunctions.web: multimodal exploration of mathematical function graphs. In: Proceedings of the 16th International Web for All Conference, pp. 1–10. Association for Computing Machinery, New York (2019). https://doi.org/10.1145/3315002.3317560
2. Dobosz, K., Hanak, D.: Audible charts of mathematical functions. In: Miesenberger, K., Peňáz, P., Kobayashi, M. (eds.) Computers Helping People with Special Needs. ICCHP 2024. Lecture Notes in Computer Science, vol. 14750. Springer, Cham (2024). https://doi.org/10.1007/978-3-031-62846-7_25
3. Hermann, T., Hunt, A., Neuhoff, J. (Eds.). The Sonification Handbook. Logos Publishing House, Berlin (2011). https://sonification.de/handbook
4. Hoque, M.N., Ehtesham-Ul-Haque, M., Elmqvist, N., Billah, S.M.: Accessible data representation with natural sound. In: Proceedings of the 2023 CHI Conference on Human Factors in Computing Systems, pp. 1–19. ACM (2023). https://doi.org/10.1145/3544548.3581087
5. Lu, S. Y., Huang, Y. H., Lin, K. Y. Spectral content (colour) of noise exposure affects work efficiency. Noise Health **22**(104), 19–27 (2020). https://doi.org/10.4103/nah.NAH_61_18
6. Roy, T., Boppana, L. Interactive web-based image and graph analysis using Sonification for the Blind. In: Proceedings of the 2022 IEEE Region 10 Symposium (TENSYMP), Mumbai, India (2022). https://doi.org/10.1109/TENSYMP54529.2022.9864411.
7. Rusconi, E., Kwan, B., Giordano, B.L., Umiltà, C., Butterworth, B.: Spatial representation of pitch height: the SMARC effect. Cognition **99**(2), 113–129 (2016). https://doi.org/10.1016/j.cognition.2005.01.004

[9] https://github.com/SONAIRGRAPH/audiofunctions-plus.

8. Spagnuolo, A., Ducci M., Schölch, L., Burgos, M., Tizón-Escamilla, N., Müller, K.: Sonification and Haptic Feedback for Mathematical Graph Accessibility, KIT Scientific Working Papers **265**, Karlsruher Institut für Technologie, Karlsrhuhe (2025)
9. Trayford, J.W., Harrison, C.M.: Introducing strauss: a flexible sonification python package. arXiv preprint arXiv:2311.16847 (2023). https://doi.org/10.21785/icad2023.1978

A Qualitative Study on the Use of ICT and AI by STEM Students and Professionals to Support the Reading of Mathematical Formulas

Monique Scalco Soares Siqueira, Eduardo Augusto Ribeiro, Saimon Gabriel de Andrade, and André Pimenta Freire(✉)

Department of Computer Science, Federal University of Lavras, Lavras, Brazil
apfreire@ufla.br

Abstract. Students with visual impairments face persistent barriers in learning mathematics, particularly regarding access to and interpretation of equations and symbolic expressions. Although technologies have expanded accessibility possibilities, challenges remain in the navigation and autonomous manipulation of complex mathematical content. This qualitative study investigates how visually impaired students and professionals in Science, Technology, Engineering, and Mathematics (STEM) fields use Artificial Intelligence to assist in reading complex mathematical formulas. Semi-structured interviews were conducted with 17 participants, and the data were analyzed using Thematic Analysis. The results indicate that AI is used in conjunction with other assistive technologies, especially screen readers, to translate visual mathematical representations into verbal descriptions. Participants' expectations center on a deeper integration between AI systems and screen readers to enable more fluid and contextualized access to mathematical expressions.

Keywords: Visual Impairments · Mathematical Content · Artificial Intelligence

1 Introduction

Students with visual impairments face recurring obstacles in the process of learning mathematics, particularly concerning the understanding and solving of mathematical equations and expressions. Such difficulties are associated with both the high degree of abstraction of mathematical knowledge and the predominance of visually oriented symbolic representations [3,10].

While the advancement of assistive technologies and Artificial Intelligence-based solutions has expanded access possibilities [11], significant challenges persist regarding the navigation, interpretation, and autonomous manipulation of complex mathematical expressions by students with visual impairments [15,16]. Despite the promises with the advancements of AI (Artificial Intelligence) technology, there is limited knowledge about how people with visual impairments are

K. Miesenberger et al. (Eds.): ICCHP 2026, LNCS 16867, pp. 66–73, 2027.
https://doi.org/10.1007/978-3-032-31308-9_8

actually using these AI systems in real-world academic and professional contexts within Science, Technology, Engineering, and Mathematics (STEM) fields.

In light of this challenge, the present study sought to understand how visually impaired students and professionals in STEM use Artificial Intelligence to support the reading of complex mathematical formulas. To achieve this, the authors conducted a qualitative investigation involving semi-structured interviews with 17 participants.

2 Related Work

People with disabilities face significant educational and career barriers in STEM, leading to underrepresentation, higher unemployment, and lower earnings [8]. This systemic exclusion is compounded by highly visual science and mathematics curricula, making these subjects inherently inaccessible to students with visual impairments [9].

Assistive technologies attempt to mitigate these obstacles but often face limitations. For example, transcribing two-dimensional mathematical formulas into a linear Braille format can cause cognitive overload for the user [13]. Furthermore, producing mathematical Braille is a slow and complex process requiring specialized equipment and trained professionals [5].

Among computer screen readers, NVDA and JAWS are currently the most used [18]. NVDA struggles with mathematical formulas natively, often requiring plugins like Access8Math to enable reliable navigation and interpretation [1]. Conversely, while JAWS offers advanced mathematical navigation [7], its operational complexity demands greater cognitive effort from users [17].

Effective support for these technologies relies heavily on properly structured digital formats. While images with alternative text convey a formula's general idea, they lack the interactive navigation necessary for complex comprehension [14]. In contrast, well-implemented MathML (Mathematical Markup Language) provides screen readers with the possibility of offering structured, internal navigation that facilitates more accurate interpretation.

Given the limitations of traditional tools in providing interactive and autonomous navigation, integrating AI and Assistive Technologies (AT) represents a major advancement in inclusive education [19]. AI-supported screen readers, voice assistants, and NLP (Natural Language Processing) interfaces enhance student autonomy and access to educational content [11]. However, persistent challenges remain, including system accuracy, infrastructure requirements, teacher training gaps, and ethical concerns over data privacy and algorithmic bias.

Ultimately, students with visual impairments consistently struggle with symbol recognition, equations, and graphs [15]. While several technologies have been developed to address these mathematical barriers, their limitations in navigation, manipulation, and semantics highlight the need for continued innovation [2].

3 Method

The study employed semi-structured interviews. They were conducted to facilitate in-depth exploration of participant perceptions while maintaining a guiding structural framework [12]. Participant selection used the snowball sampling technique, a non-probability sampling strategy. According to Flick [6], this approach is particularly suitable for accessing specific groups or hard-to-reach populations where initial participants assist in identifying subsequent informants.

To initiate the sampling process, the researchers selected a key informant with whom they had prior contact, designated as the 'seed.' From this initial informant, subsequent interviewees recommended new participants from their personal networks. This procedure was repeated until the 17th interview, as saturation in data analysis was reached.

Inclusion criteria were defined as follows: voluntary availability to participate; a diagnosed visual impairment; current status as a professional or student in a STEM field; age over 18; and full capacity to provide informed consent. Narratives were transcribed verbatim, without modification or correction, to preserve the fidelity of participant statements. To ensure anonymity, participants' names were replaced with alphanumeric identifiers, ranging from Interviewee 1 to the final participant. The sample included participants from various Brazilian states in all five geographical regions of the country. The states represented were: Ceará (CE), Maranhão (MA), Pernambuco (PE) from the Northeast; Mato Grosso (MT) from the Centre-West; Minas Gerais (MG), from the Southeast; Rio de Janeiro (RJ), and São Paulo (SP) from the Southeast; Pará (PA) from the North and Rio Grande do Sul (RS) from the South.

Of the total number of interviewees, 6 participants have professional experience in the STEM field. Their career paths are concentrated in software development and programming, with proficiency in languages such as Python and Java, as well as in teaching and consultancy roles that integrate communication, technology, and accessibility. Data analysis employed a Thematic analysis [4]. This process led to the construction of three overarching themes that map the relationship between visual impairment and mathematical language: (i) Barriers to accessing mathematical content; (ii) Pre-AI strategies; and (iii) Uses of AI for understanding formulas. Finally, the research was approved by the Research Ethics Committee of the Federal University of Lavras under identifier 88520925.1.0000.5148. Table 1 contains the main demographic information about the participants.

4 Findings

The findings are organized into three themes mapping the trajectory of students and professionals with visual impairments in STEM, from initial hurdles to the adoption of emerging technologies.

Table 1. Participants Profile

ID	Age	Gender	Education	Works in STEM	Disability	State
1	37	M	BSc, MSc and PhD in Physics; Postdoc (ongoing).	No	Blind	MG
2	30	F	BSc in Physics; MSc in Biosciences and Health; PhD (ongoing).	No	Low vision	RJ
3	44	F	BSc and MSc in Social Communication; PhD in Computer Science (ongoing).	Yes	Blind	RJ
4	29	F	BSc in Mathematics; MSc in Computer Science (incomplete).	Yes	Low vision	RJ
5	36	M	BSc in Computer Science; MSc in Educational Technology.	No	Low vision	CE
6	20	M	BSc in Mathematics (ongoing).	No	Blind	MA
7	39	F	BSc in Physics; MSc and PhD in Education.	No	Low vision, monocular	SP
8	35	M	BSc in Computer Science (ongoing).	No	Blind	PE
9	25	M	BSc in Computer Science.	Yes	Blind	RS
10	29	F	BSc in Languages and Spanish (ongoing).	Yes	Blind	PA
11	53	M	BSc, MSc, PhD, Postdoc in Physics.	Yes	Blind	SP
12	52	M	Technical degree in Electrotechnics; Mathematics (incomplete); Pedagogy (ongoing).	No	Blind	MT
13	22	F	BSc in Computer Science (ongoing).	Yes	Blind	MG
14	38	M	BSc in IS; Specialization in InfoSec; MSc in Education Tech; CS Master's (incomplete).	No	Low vision	MG
15	32	M	Technical ed. in Nutrition; BSc in IS (incomplete); Mathematics (ongoing).	No	Blind	MG
16	33	M	BSc in CS and Psychology; CS MSc (incomplete); MSc in Psychology (ongoing).	No	Blind	MG
17	28	M	BSc in Mathematics (ongoing).	No	Blind	RJ

4.1 Barriers to Accessing Mathematical Content

Participants face a continuous chain of obstacles, beginning with physical and attitudinal barriers within educational institutions. Most cited limitations like the absence of tactile paving, audible signaling, and lifts. While some used monitors to navigate campus, the majority depend on classmates or bystanders, occasionally incurring in "minor" accidents that highlight precarious accessibility conditions.

In STEM academic environments, reports highlight a lack of teacher training and accessible teaching materials. Regarding professors, Interviewee 3 points out: "It depends on the professor themselves. There are professors who are more aware of the issue. There are other professors who don't care, and others who don't know but try." This underscores a lack of systematic institutional preparation, shifting the burden of inclusion onto individual teacher initiative.

Teaching materials are rarely provided in accessible formats. Even when adaptation is possible, the time-consuming process compromises the ability to keep pace with coursework. Materials often arrive after the content has been covered, creating learning gaps. Interviewee 6 explains: "Some of these materials we can send to the accessibility office, and the accessibility office converts this material into a digital format that is accessible or converts it into Braille. But because the material is very extensive, it takes a long time, so when it reaches our hands, a good amount of time has already passed."

The intrinsic visual complexity of mathematics imposes additional challenges. As Interviewee 1 states: "I knew I would already have some difficulty because the course is graphic, right? It's visual." Consequently, classmates and monitors remain vital helpers in this learning process.

4.2 Pre-AI Strategies

All interviewees reported using various assistive technologies. Screen readers (including NVDA, VoiceOver, TalkBack, and JAWS) are used by all participants and are considered essential, notably for reading AI-generated responses. Tactile technologies, such as Braille and 3D printing, are used to comprehend spatial concepts like geometry. Participants with low vision also reported using electronic magnifiers and screen magnification software.

4.3 Uses of AI for Understanding Formulas

AI usage emerges at different stages of academic and professional trajectories. For some, AI is incorporated sporadically following a period of distance from dense mathematical content. For others, particularly those in graduate programs or the job market, AI serves as a complementary resource for organizing abstract content.

A central theme is using AI to translate visual mathematical representations into verbal language. Participants use systems like ChatGPT to describe formulas, graphs, and captions. Interviewee 1 explains: "Sometimes there aren't people to help me study, so I go to the Artificial Intelligence and ask it to read to me and describe the graphs. I ask it to say things related to the figure, how it can translate the figure into words. For example, I ask ChatGPT: 'describe this equation in natural language.' It literally explains that 'x' is equal to the summation from one to infinity, transforming everything visual into words. Thus, with the screen reader, I can read the equation."

Similarly, Interviewee 11 stated: "I use ChatGPT to see if it can describe the formula." Interviewee 6 adds: "I send the document and ask it [the AI]: 'Look, describe the graphs, describe the attached images, and transform that content that is missing accents—rewrite it applying the correct accentuation. 'Then I ask it to format it in Markdown. It is a union between assistive technology, which is the screen reader, and what we have today with artificial intelligence."

Beyond formulas, AI broadens autonomy by drafting summaries and organizing complex content. It acts as a learning mediator, assisting in the structuring of reasoning and the optimization of study time. This extends to creating exercises: "I ask it to create exercises and explain the concept of things to me there."

However, some narratives reveal limitations regarding how AI is prompted. A lack of knowledge regarding interaction strategies and precise prompt formulation can compromise results. Dissatisfaction often stems from the mediation of human-machine interaction rather than the tool's potential. Reliability also remains a concern; participants emphasize the need for constant verification, as AI is susceptible to conceptual errors or overly-simplified answers.

Regarding future expectations, participants expect integration between AI and screen readers to make the reading of mathematical expressions automatic and fluid.

> "It would be very cool if there were already something powerful like AI linked to the screen reader, something that could identify, create a formula, or give you a shortcut to say that it is a formula, select the formula and such, I don't know, something like that which was fast and already translated that for me into audio; that would be very good, for sure [Interviewee 5]."

This statement points to the demand for integrated solutions capable of immediate audio translation, which would significantly expand autonomy in accessing mathematical information.

5 Discussion

The relevance of traditional assistive technologies is absolute within the sample, as screen readers are used by all participants, regardless of whether they have low vision or blindness. However, the use of AI for mathematics study is not uniform; while some participants already incorporate it into their routines, others remain unaware of how to use it or are in exploratory and sporadic stages.

Nevertheless, for those who use both technologies, the results demonstrate that the integration between them represents a significant advancement in overcoming barriers in this field. This corroborates findings on how the integration of AI subfields has fostered a rapid evolution of learning and communication tools [19]. This synergy is evidenced by the way AI translates visual mathematical representations into verbal descriptions, allowing screen readers to process information that previously posed persistent obstacles in the interpretation of equations and symbolic expressions.

The data also show that, in practice, this evolution occurs in a hybrid manner: AI does not (yet) replace traditional screen readers but rather enhances them by translating complex visual elements into verbal descriptions. This strategy provides autonomy and speed, enabling access to content that increases academic engagement and student independence [11]. However, this effectiveness is conditioned by the user's competence in formulating precise commands, as flaws in human-machine mediation and AI's susceptibility to conceptual errors still require a judicious approach and constant verification of the results.

6 Conclusions and Future Work

This study makes significant contributions. First, it demonstrates that AI does not operate as an isolated solution, but rather as part of a broader accessibility ecosystem that includes screen readers, tactile resources, and human support. The study highlights how AI usage is mediated by digital literacy, prompt formulation skills, and the critical evaluation of the information presented. The research identifies implications for future development, particularly the need for deeper integration between AI systems and screen readers, as well as improved semantic interpretation of mathematical expressions.

The findings in this study will inform the development of screen reader add-ons to integrate the reading of complex mathematical formulas using artificial intelligence and how this integration should be designed.

Future studies will include the development of proof-of-concept prototypes integrating AI systems and screen readers to read complex mathematical content and the evaluation by people with visual impairments.

Acknowledgments. This study was funded by CAPES, CNPq, FAPEMIG and FINEP. The authors used Gemini as an AI tool solely to revise the text. The authors take full responsibility for the publication's content.

Disclosure of Interests. The authors have no competing interests to declare that are relevant to the content of this article.

References

1. Access8Math Team: Access8math: Math accessibility extension for nvda. NVDA add-on (2025). https://addons.nvda-project.org/addons/access8math.en.html. Accessed 10 Feb 2026
2. Al Shehri, W., Almalki, J., Alshahrani, S.M., Alammari, A., Khan, F., Alangari, S.: Assistive technology acceptance for visually impaired individuals: a case study of students in Saudi Arabia. PeerJ Comput. Sci. **8**, e886 (2022)
3. Ali, A., Khusro, S., Alahmadi, T.J.: Accessible interactive learning of mathematical expressions for school students with visual disabilities. PeerJ Comput. Sci. **10**, e2599 (2024)
4. Braun, V., Clarke, V.: Using thematic analysis in psychology. Qual. Res. Psychol. **3**(2), 77–101 (2006)
5. Dias, A., França, J., Borges, J.A., Silveira, J., Carvalho, M., Borges, M.: Mathematics, computing and braille: Challenges from pedagogy, semiotics and speech synthesis (matemática, computação e braille: Desafios da pedagogia, da semiótica e da síntese da fala). In: Brazilian Symposium on Computers in Education (Simpósio Brasileiro de Informática na Educação-SBIE), vol. 29, p. 1863 (2018)
6. Flick, U.: An Introduction to Qualitative Research. Sage Publications (2022)

7. Freedom Scientific: Jaws: Job access with speech. Commercial Windows software (2025). https://www.freedomscientific.com/products/software/jaws/. Accessed 10 Feb 2026
8. Gordian-Velez, W.: Ensuring the inclusion of people with disabilities in stem education and careers. J. Sci. Policy Gov. **20** (2022)
9. Hayes, C., Proulx, M.J.: Turning a blind eye? removing barriers to science and mathematics education for students with visual impairments. Br. J. Vis. Impair. **42**(2), 544–556 (2024)
10. Juyal, S., Sharma, S., Jadhav, N., Sorge, V., Balakrishnan, M.: Making equations accessible in scientific documents. In: International Conference on Computers Helping People with Special Needs, pp. 22–29. Springer, Cham (2022)
11. Kooli, C., Chakraoui, R.: Ai-driven assistive technologies in inclusive education: benefits, challenges, and policy recommendations. Sustain. Futures **10**, 101042 (2025)
12. Kvale, S., Brinkmann, S.: Interviews: Learning the Craft of Qualitative Research Interviewing. Sage (2009)
13. Maćkowski, M., Kawulok, M., Brzoza, P., Spinczyk, D.: Methods and tools supporting the learning and teaching of mathematics dedicated to students with blindness. Appl. Sci. **13**(12), 7240 (2023)
14. Ribeiro, E., Andrade, S., Freire, A.: Accessibility of mathematical formulas in scientific papers on the web for people with visual impairments in higher education (acessibilidade de fórmulas matemáticas em artigos científicos na web para pessoas com deficiência visual no ensino superior). In: Anais do XXXVI Simpósio Brasileiro de Informática na Educação, pp. 1219–1233. SBC, Porto Alegre, RS, Brasil (2025). https://doi.org/10.5753/sbie.2025.12852
15. Shoaib, M., Fitzpatrick, D., Pitt, I.: Assistive technology-based solutions in learning mathematics for visually-impaired people: exploring issues, challenges and opportunities. Multimedia Tools Appl. **82**(29), 46153–46184 (2023)
16. Shoaib, M., Minghim, R., Fitzpatrick, D., Pitt, I.: Mathematics accessibility in primary education: enhancing mathematics learning skills and overcoming barriers for visually impaired primary students. In: International Conference on Computers Helping People with Special Needs, pp. 192–202. Springer, Cham (2024)
17. da Paixão Silva, L.F., de Faria Oliveira, O., Freire, E.R.C.G., Mendes, R.M., Freire, A.P.: How much effort is necessary for blind users to read web-based mathematical formulae? a comparison using task models with different screen readers. Association for Computing Machinery, New York, NY, USA (2017)
18. WebAIM: Web accessibility in mind – screen reader user survey #10 results (2024). https://webaim.org/projects/screenreadersurvey10/. Accessed 10 Feb 2026
19. Zdravkova, K., Krasniqi, V., Dalipi, F., Ferati, M.: Cutting-edge communication and learning assistive technologies for disabled children: an artificial intelligence perspective. Front. Artif. Intell. **5 - 2022** (2022)

Designing an Accessible Audio-Driven Role-Playing Game for STEM Learning

Maddalena Frizzi[1], Nicola Forgione[1], Giulio Galesi[1], and Barbara Leporini[1,2(✉)]

[1] University of Pisa, Pisa, Italy
barbara.leporini@unipi.it
[2] ISTI-CNR, Pisa, Italy

Abstract. In this work, we present 'Le Chiavi di Elthar', an accessible digital role-playing game designed to support STEM learning for blind and visually impaired children. By combining multimodal interaction, artificial intelligence (AI), and accessibility-by-design principles, the project explores how educational and entertainment games can be developed in a more inclusive and autonomous way.

Keywords: Educational Games · Accessibility · Visual Impairment · Multimodal Interaction · STEM

1 Introduction

Access to STEM disciplines (Science, Technology, Engineering and Mathematics) represents a significant challenge for blind and visually impaired (BVI) children and adolescents, particularly in contexts that are strongly oriented toward the use of visual materials and interfaces [1]. Diagrams, charts, images, and simulations increasingly form the core of educational and playful activities, often making constant support from sighted individuals necessary and consequently limiting the autonomy of students with visual impairments. This issue affects not only knowledge learning, but also motivation and active participation. Game-based learning is widely recognized as an effective strategy for fostering engagement and active learning. However, in the case of BVI users, a significant gap in game accessibility still exists, both in educational and recreational contexts [2, 3]. Many games are inaccessible or require ad hoc adaptations, while solutions specifically designed for people with visual impairments often tend to be simplified, weakly immersive, or highly assisted [4, 5]. Moreover, such solutions rarely support the effective inclusion of BVI players within mixed groups that also include sighted ones. As a result, there is still a limited availability of games capable of combining accessibility, enjoyment, and meaningful integration of STEM content within the gameplay experience [6, 7].

An accessible educational game that effectively includes STEM content could instead support the acquisition of foundational competencies in a motivating way, fostering interest in STEM subjects and potentially encouraging future educational careers in scientific

K. Miesenberger et al. (Eds.): ICCHP 2026, LNCS 16867, pp. 74–81, 2027.
https://doi.org/10.1007/978-3-032-31308-9_9

fields. This work addresses this gap by contributing to the field of Human-Centered and Inclusive Design by proposing 'Le Chiavi di Elthar', an accessible and inclusive digital role-playing game designed for blind and visually impaired children. The game combines STEM knowledge, exercises, and problem-solving activities directly into gameplay through an audio-driven, narrative-based approach, supported by a multimodal interaction system combining audio, voice input, touchscreen gestures, and physical objects equipped with NFC tags. The goal is to demonstrate how a digital game can be designed in an accessible manner and become a rich, motivating, and autonomous environment for learning and exploration in STEM disciplines also for BVI children. The game 'Le Chiavi di Elthar' was developed within a research project aimed at investigating solutions to overcome the barriers encountered by people with visual impairments in accessing STEM content, while simultaneously fostering motivation toward educational pathways in scientific fields. Within this perspective, the game is not conceived as a simple instructional tool, but as a complete ludic experience that restores the value of play as a space for exploration and participation. The project has various objectives: to design an accessible and inclusive play experience that can be effectively used by blind and visually impaired children; to integrate STEM content and problem-solving activities directly into gameplay; to promote player autonomy by reducing the need for external assistance; and to explore the use of artificial intelligence–based technologies as supporting tools for the design and production of accessible narrative and interactive content.

2 Related Work

Game-based learning has proven effective for STEM education, enhancing motivation and learning through interactive and immersive experiences [8]. However, for BVI children, play is often not spontaneous because many games focus on tasks rather than fun [9]. This disconnect stems from a lack of Participatory Design (PD); without involving BVI users in the creative process, developers struggle to move beyond visual-heavy interfaces. Since most educational games rely on visual cues, diagrams, and graphical interfaces, BVI learners face barriers to autonomy and peer interaction [10, 11].

Existing accessible games for BVI children prioritize audio or haptic feedback but are often constrained by simplified mechanics or dependency on sighted assistance [12]; studies show BVI children prefer solitary play and struggle with symbolic pretend play in visual-heavy scenarios [9, 13]. Augmented toys facilitate joint attention but can reduce cooperative play by shifting focus to audio cues [14].

The International Game Developers Association (IGDA) defines game accessibility as playable under limitations like blindness, emphasizing design over assistance to preserve fun [15].

By adopting a participatory approach, developers can ensure mechanics are naturally inclusive. 'Le Chiavi di Elthar' addresses these gaps via audio-narrative gameplay, multimodal inputs (voice, touch, NFC), and AI-STEM challenges for autonomous, inclusive play with sighted peers.

3 Method

The game was developed as an interactive prototype to explore accessibility, multimodal interaction, and narrative-driven STEM learning for blind and visually impaired children. The design process adopted a user-centered, participatory and expert-informed approach, combining requirement analysis grounded in the literature with the direct contributions of the blind author of this work, a blind psychologist, and a typhlologist, and including iterative prototyping and progressive refinement through preliminary user testing. The combination of tactile 3D-printed objects, mobile devices, audio narration, and NFC-based interaction enabled a fully interactive and accessible gameplay experience. During the development process, artificial intelligence–based tools were used in different ways.

4 Game Design

4.1 Structure and Narrative Design

From a ludic perspective, 'Le Chiavi di Elthar' is inspired by the model of collaborative role-playing games. Participants take on distinct roles (knight, druid, rogue, and mage) each associated with specific narrative characteristics and operational functions. This role distribution serves not only a narrative purpose but also explicit educational and inclusive goals, as it promotes active participation by all players and encourages collective discussion and shared decision-making.

Narrative constitutes the backbone of the game experience. The adventure is divided into successive chapters, each set in a different environment and associated with one of the natural elements (forest, river, desert, mountain). This episodic structure allows regulation of the experience's rhythm by alternating moments of narrative exploration with phases of more intense and cognitively demanding interaction. As a result, game progression remains balanced and adaptable to players' abilities, attention span, and cognitive load.

Within the game, solving logical-mathematical and scientific challenges is a necessary condition for overcoming narrative obstacles and advancing the story. Cognitive activity is therefore not presented as an isolated exercise, but as an integral part of the ludic experience. By embedding STEM challenges directly within the narrative flow, the game reinforces motivation and engagement, while supporting learning through play rather than interrupting it.

STEM challenges were designed to cover content primarily aligned with the lower secondary school curriculum, which was identified as the target level for the experience. Questions were reworked to be compatible with a predominantly voice-based mode of interaction and were progressively integrated into the narrative context of the game. Each challenge is introduced through a short narrative description that provides the information necessary to address the problem within the story world. Players can also access a system of progressive hints, which allows the level of support to be adjusted according to the needs of the group. This approach supports gradual and inclusive learning by helping players overcome difficulties without removing the cognitive effort required, thereby avoiding both cognitive overload and frustration. Challenges are distributed throughout the experience according to a controlled progression of difficulty, alternating simpler tasks with more cognitively demanding ones. In later sections of the game, concepts drawn from more advanced disciplines (such as physics or programming) are introduced. In these cases, disciplinary novelty is primarily conveyed through narrative framing and terminology, while the underlying reasoning structure remains grounded in concepts already familiar to the players, thus preserving cognitive accessibility.

Two representative STEM challenges are presented to illustrate different levels of complexity. The first is a spatial reasoning task set in a desert, where players must identify the correct oasis based on temperature distributions and the position of the sun, relying exclusively on non-visual environmental cues in line with an inclusive, audio-based interaction. The second involves multi-step challenges introduced in later stages, requiring players to solve sequential, interconnected problems of increasing cognitive complexity. These tasks include mapping large-scale temporal data onto a 24-h timescale, performing proportional conversions, and applying the results to physics-based and real-world scenarios.

In addition to cognitively oriented challenges, the game also includes physical interaction tasks with the smartphone device, activated through specific NFC tags. These tasks require players to perform actions such as repeated taps, long presses, or dragging gestures on the touchscreen. Such challenges reinforce immersion by associating physical gestures with explicit narrative meanings, strengthening the connection between action, story progression, and player engagement.

4.2 Multimodal Interaction

One of the core contributions of this work lies in the adoption of a multimodal approach, designed to ensure accessibility of the game experience even in the absence of visual information. The auditory channel plays a predominant role: narration, instructions, and challenges are primarily conveyed through spoken descriptions. Environmental sounds and sound effects further support the narrative, both by enhancing immersion and by providing immediate feedback on players' actions [1].

Interaction is enabled through a combination of complementary modalities. Voice interaction is used to answer questions and make narrative choices, allowing players to engage with the game through speech. Touchscreen gestures, such as repeated taps, long presses, and dragging motions, are employed in specific challenges to simulate in-game actions and physical effort. In addition, 3D-printed objects equipped with NFC tags, allow players to activate game functionalities and narrative events through a mobile application developed with MIT App Inventor. Finally, haptic feedback, delivered through device vibration, is used to distribute information across multiple sensory channels, reducing auditory overload while reinforcing interaction cues.

The use of tangible objects and NFC technology replaces traditional visual navigation of digital menus with a concrete and immediate form of interaction. Figure 1 shows the eight tactile objects used for interaction. This design choice supports greater autonomy for BVI players and reduces the need for external assistance. Moreover, the possibility of combining multiple interaction modalities makes the experience flexible and adaptable to individual preferences and abilities, reinforcing inclusivity and user-centered design.

Fig. 1. Set of 3D-printed tangible objects equipped with NFC tags, used for multimodal interaction with the mobile application.

4.3 Use of Artificial Intelligence in the Design Process

During the development process, artificial intelligence–based tools were explored with different roles. AI-based text-to-speech systems were used to generate narrator and character voices, due to their expressive quality and the naturalness of their intonation. The use of these tools enabled rapid iteration of audio content and supported greater variety in character representation, contributing to narrative immersion and clarity. On the other hand, the use of generative models to create STEM challenges did not yield satisfactory results. Therefore, such tools were employed exclusively for formal revision and structural standardization of the questions, while human control over educational design remained essential. Similarly, AI-based generation of sound effects did not yield satisfactory results and was therefore not adopted, leading to the use of externally sourced audio assets. In contrast, image generation tools proved effective in producing visual assets consistent with the narrative, thereby supporting the design process and contributing to a coherent visual representation of the game world. These findings highlight the role of artificial intelligence as a supportive technology for inclusive design, rather than as a replacement for the design process itself.

5 Evaluation

A preliminary evaluation of 'Le Chiavi di Elthar' was conducted with a group of nine blind and visually impaired children during a summer camp dedicated to recreational and educational activities organized by the Regional Association for the Blind in Tuscany (Italy). The evaluation was exploratory and qualitative in nature. Participants interacted with the game using the available multimodal features (See Fig. 2).

Fig. 2. Participants interacting with the game's tactile objects and multimodal features.

Observations and informal feedback were collected during gameplay sessions by one of the authors of this work. Five participants completed a post-test questionnaire evaluating usability, engagement, and perceived accessibility, with responses expressed on a 5-point scale (1 = lowest, 5 = highest). Preliminary results showed positive feedback, with 4 out of 5 participants reporting high engagement and ease of interaction. Participants were able to interact autonomously with the game and showed sustained engagement throughout the narrative experience. The integration of audio-driven narration and multimodal interaction was perceived as intuitive. In addition, the collaborative role-playing structure encouraged discussion and participation among players. Overall, responses were concentrated in the upper range of the scale (4–5), indicating a high level of perceived usability and accessibility, with only minor variability observed in the evaluation of feedback clarity. Table 1 summarizes the main qualitative assessments obtained from the pilot test, which also provided valuable improvement suggestions.

These insights are informing ongoing refinements of the system and will be addressed in future iterations of the game, which will: (1) expand the evaluation using a larger and more diverse sample and quantitative metrics, (2) include comparisons with existing solutions (e.g., haptic-based games) within the discussion, and (3) conduct further data collection and analysis on specific attributes such as accessibility, immersion, and user experience to validate the game's feasibility and educational efficacy.

Table 1. Summary of the main qualitative assessments obtained from the pilot test.

Finding	Implication
All participants were actively involved and reported willingness to repeat the experience	Confirms the effectiveness of the narrative and interactive design in fostering user engagement

(*continued*)

Table 1. (*continued*)

Finding	Implication
More experienced participants found the tasks too simple, and the narrative less engaging than intended	Results should be validated with target users. The system supports future customization of content, difficulty, and narrative
NFC tokens were intuitive and easy to use, improving accessibility compared to traditional interfaces	Supports the adoption of NFC as a core interaction mechanism for accessible gameplay
Participants experienced only part of the game due to time constraints	Future evaluations should ensure full gameplay exposure to obtain more comprehensive results
Tactile activities emerged as the most engaging elements of the experience	Increasing the number and variety of tactile interactions may further enhance engagement

6 Conclusions

In this work, we presented 'Le Chiavi di Elthar', a digital role-playing game that combines educational content with a multimodal interaction system designed to be accessible to blind and visually impaired (BVI) children. The main contribution of this work lies in demonstrating that an accessible, audio-based digital game can effectively integrate STEM content, problem solving, and multimodal interaction for blind and visually impaired children. The project shows that accessibility does not necessarily imply simplification or a reduction of complexity; rather, it can become an opportunity to rethink interaction and learning in a more inclusive and user-centered way. 'Le Chiavi di Elthar' also contributes to the ongoing discussion on the use of artificial intelligence in the design of accessible systems, highlighting both its potential and its limitations. In addition, the proposed game represents a scalable and adaptable model that can be transferred to different educational contexts, disciplines, and age groups, supporting future developments in accessible and inclusive game-based learning.

Acknowledgments. This study is part of the PRIN project 2022HXLH47 "STEMMA- Science, Technology, Engineering, Mathematics, Motivation and Accessibility" (funded by the European Union- Next Generation EU, Mission 4 Component C2 CUP B53D23019500006).

Disclosure of Interests. The authors have no competing interests to declare that are relevant to the content of this article.

References

1. Ghoneim, R., Aljedaani, W., Alghamdi, A.M., Ludi, S.: Educational accessibility in STEM for visually impaired and blind students: a literature review on challenges and support. In: International Conference on Human-Computer Interaction, (pp. 65–86). Cham, Springer Nature Switzerland (2025)

2. Hassan, L.: Accessibility of games and game-based applications: a systematic literature review and mapping of future directions. New Media Soc. **26**(4), 2336–2384 (2024)
3. Neto, L.V., Fontoura Junior, P.H., Bordini, R.A., Otsuka, J.L., Beder, D.M.: Design and implementation of an educational game considering issues for visually impaired people inclusion. Smart Learn. Environ. **7**(1), 4 (2020)
4. Fatima, S., Baalsrud Hauge, J.: Accessibility issues within serious games in engineering education for visual impairment. In: International Conference on Entertainment Computing, (pp. 96–114). Singapore, Springer Nature Singapore (2023)
5. Marichal, S., Rosales, A., González Perilli, F., Pires, A.C., Blat, J.: Auditory and haptic feedback to train basic mathematical skills of children with visual impairments. Behav. Inf. Technol. **42**(8), 1081–1109 (2023)
6. Castaneda, J.A.C., et al.: Designing inclusive tech playful educative solutions for visually impaired learners in STEM education. Smart Learn. Environ. **12**(1), 4 (2025)
7. Pieriboni, G., Buzzi, M., Leporini, B.: Stem education and ICT-enhanced tools for students with disabilities: a five-year review. Univ. Access Inf. Soc. **25**(1), 3 (2026)
8. Li, Y., Chen, D., Deng, X.: The impact of digital educational games on student's motivation for learning: the mediating effect of learning engagement and the moderating effect of the digital environment. PLoS One **XIX** (2024)
9. Skellenger, A.C.: Play as a means for increasing multiple skills of young children with visual impairments. Peabody J. Educ. **67**(2), 36–49 (1990)
10. Agrimi, E., Battaglini, C., Bottari, D., Gnecco, G., Leporini, B.: Game accessibility for visually impaired people: a review. Soft. Comput. **28**(17), 10475–10489 (2024)
11. Bolesnikov, A., Kang, J., Girouard, A.: Understanding tabletop games accessibility: exploring board and card gaming experiences of people who are blind and low vision. TEI '22: Proceedings of the Sixteenth International Conference on Tangible, Embedded, and Embodied Interaction, Association for Computing Machinery, New York (2022)
12. Friberg, J., Gärdenfors, D.: Audio games: new perspectives on game audio. ACE '04: Proceedings of the 2004 ACM SIGCHI International Conference on Advances in computer entertainment technology, Association for Computing Machinery, New York, (2004)
13. Verver, S.H., Vervloed, M.P.J., Steenbergen, B.: Characteristics of peer play in children with visual impairments. Res. Dev. Disabil. **105**, 103714 (2020)
14. Verver, S.H., Vervloed, M.P., Steenbergen, B.: Facilitating play and social interaction between children with visual impairments and sighted peers by means of augmented toys. J. Dev. Phys. Disabil. **32** (2019)
15. IGDA: Game Accessibility White Paper (2004). http://www.igda.org/accessibility/IGDA_Accessibility_WhitePaper.pdf

Design and Evaluation of a Video-Based Assistive Picture Book for Story Comprehension Support in Preschool Children with Developmental Delays

Chia-Yen Hsieh[1] and Jing-Wen Huang[2(✉)]

[1] Department of Early Childhood Education, National Pingtung University, Pingtung City, Taiwan
banduna@nptu.edu.tw

[2] Graduate Institute of Educational Administration, National Pingtung University, Pingtung City, Taiwan
jwhuang@mail.nptu.edu.tw

Abstract. This study examined the design and evaluation of a video-based assistive picture book intended to support story comprehension in preschool children with developmental delays. Grounded in principles of cognitive load reduction and multimedia scaffolding, the intervention was conceptualized as an accessibility-oriented digital tool rather than a passive media resource. A single-case multiple-baseline design across participants was employed to investigate changes in individual narrative comprehension following the introduction of the assistive picture book.

Participants were preschool children enrolled in an early childhood special education setting. Story comprehension was assessed across baseline, intervention, and maintenance phases using a structured, researcher-developed measure capturing key dimensions of narrative understanding. Visual analysis indicated that baseline performance was generally low and unstable. Following the intervention, all participants demonstrated immediate and substantial improvements in comprehension, accompanied by increased performance stability and reduced variability. These gains were largely maintained after the withdrawal of structured intervention sessions.

The findings suggest that the deliberate integration of simplified visual narratives, synchronized narration, and guided prompts can effectively support narrative processing in young children with developmental delays. This study contributes to the literature by demonstrating how theoretically grounded design features can be operationalized into practical assistive tools that enhance inclusive early literacy experiences.

Keywords: Assistive Technology · Story Comprehension · Developmental Delays · Multimedia Learning · SDG 4: Inclusive and Equitable Quality Education

K. Miesenberger et al. (Eds.): ICCHP 2026, LNCS 16867, pp. 82–90, 2027.
https://doi.org/10.1007/978-3-032-31308-9_10

1 Introduction and State of the Art

Preschool children with developmental delays frequently experience difficulties in story comprehension, which can constrain early literacy development and limit meaningful participation in inclusive learning environments (Justice & Kaderavek, 2004). Story comprehension requires the coordination of linguistic processing, attentional control, working memory, and inferential reasoning, capacities that are often compromised in young children with developmental delays (Florit et al., 2011). Given that early narrative understanding serves as a foundation for subsequent academic learning and social participation, ensuring accessible pathways to story comprehension constitutes a critical priority in inclusive early childhood education.

In recent years, digital picture books have become increasingly prevalent in early childhood education. However, evidence suggests that developmental benefits depend more on design quality and intentional scaffolding than on digital exposure alone. Despite this, limited research has examined how digital reading materials can be deliberately designed as assistive supports for children with developmental delays, highlighting a gap between technological availability and accessibility needs.

Against this background, this study examines the design and evaluation of a video-based assistive picture book intended to support story comprehension in preschool children with developmental delays. Conceptualizing digital technology as an assistive solution rather than a passive medium, the study investigates how a targeted design can support narrative comprehension processes within inclusive early childhood settings.

Building on the identified need for intentionally designed digital reading supports, this study pursued three objectives.

1. To design a video-based assistive picture book that operationalizes principles of cognitive load reduction and multimedia scaffolding (Mayer, 2021; Sweller et al., 2019) into concrete design features addressing common barriers to story comprehension among preschool children with developmental delays.
2. To evaluate how the video-based assistive picture book functions in practice as an accessible reading support, with particular attention to its role in supporting narrative comprehension processes and inclusive early literacy engagement.
3. To document changes in individual children's story comprehension processes following the introduction of the assistive picture book design, using a single-case multiple-baseline evaluation approach.

2 Literature Review

2.1 Digital Picture Books and Multimedia in Early Childhood

In recent years, digital picture books and multimedia resources have become increasingly prevalent in early childhood contexts and are often promoted for their potential to enhance engagement and support learning (Takacs et al., 2015). However, growing evidence suggests that digital media exposure alone does not guarantee developmental benefits and may pose risks when it displaces interactive or scaffolded learning experiences. Large scale research has demonstrated that higher levels of unstructured digital media use are associated with reduced parent–child interaction and less favorable developmental outcomes (Madigan et al., 2019), underscoring that the design and context of media use matter more than mere access. Digital tools should therefore be understood not as neutral delivery mechanisms but as elements embedded within broader interactional and accessibility contexts.

2.2 Accessibility Gaps in Digital Reading Materials for Children with Developmental Delays

Despite the routine presence of digital media in young children's lives, relatively little attention has been directed toward the design of digital reading materials that function as assistive supports specifically for children with developmental delays. Many existing digital picture books prioritize visual appeal or entertainment but fail to translate principles of cognitive accessibility into concrete design features that address the cognitive and attentional barriers hindering story comprehension for this population (Bus et al., 2015). Without deliberate design that operationalizes principles of cognitive load reduction and multimedia learning into structured assistive supports (Mayer, 2021; Sweller et al., 2019), digital reading materials risk reproducing rather than reducing existing accessibility barriers.

2.3 Assistive Technology Perspectives and Video Based Approaches

From an assistive technology perspective, effective digital interventions should aim to reduce extraneous cognitive load, direct attention to essential narrative elements, and provide structured scaffolding that supports comprehension processes (Mayer, 2021). Video based formats offer particular promise in this regard, as they enable the integration of simplified visual narratives, synchronized narration, and guided prompts that can be systematically aligned with children's processing capacities. Short form video presentations may further enhance accessibility by constraining information density and supporting sustained attention, considerations that are especially relevant for preschool children with developmental delays.

Taken together, the existing literature highlights a clear need for digital reading materials that move beyond general multimedia enhancement toward deliberately designed assistive supports grounded in cognitive load theory and multimedia learning principles. The present study responds to this need by developing and evaluating a video based assistive picture book specifically designed to address the story comprehension barriers faced by preschool children with developmental delays.

3 Methodology

3.1 Design Overview and Evaluation Approach

This study adopted a design evaluation approach to examine how a deliberately designed video-based assistive picture book functions in practice as an accessible reading support for preschool children with developmental delays. Rather than testing instructional effectiveness through group comparison, the study focused on evaluating whether the proposed design could address identified accessibility barriers to story comprehension and support narrative processing at the individual level.

A single-case multiple-baseline design across participants was employed to evaluate the functioning of the assistive picture book design. This approach is well suited for design evaluation in early childhood and special education contexts, as it allows for systematic examination of changes in individual performance following the introduction of a targeted intervention while maintaining experimental control through staggered implementation. The design enabled the documentation of design-related changes in story comprehension processes across baseline, intervention, and maintenance phases.

3.2 Participants and Context

Participants were preschool children identified with developmental delays and enrolled in an early childhood special education setting. Inclusion criteria included documented developmental delays, basic receptive language ability sufficient to engage with picture book content, and regular attendance during the study period. All participants had prior experience with traditional picture book reading activities but limited exposure to structured digital reading supports designed specifically for accessibility.

The study was conducted in a familiar educational environment to minimize contextual disruption and ensure that observed changes could be attributed to the introduction of the assistive picture book design rather than environmental novelty.

3.3 Design of the Video-Based Assistive Picture Book

The video-based assistive picture book was developed to operationalize principles of cognitive load reduction and multimedia scaffolding into concrete design features supporting story comprehension. The design emphasized accessibility by simplifying narrative structure, highlighting essential story elements, and reducing extraneous visual and auditory information.

Key design features included short-form video presentation, synchronized voice-over narration aligned with visual content, and guided prompts directing attention to critical narrative components such as characters, events, and causal relationships. The short-form format was intentionally selected to constrain information density and support sustained attention, which is particularly relevant for preschool children with developmental delays. The assistive picture book was designed as a structured digital artifact rather than a general multimedia resource, with explicit consideration of how each design feature functioned to support comprehension processes.

3.4 Measures and Evaluation Procedures

Story comprehension was assessed using a researcher-developed Story Comprehension Assessment designed to examine overall changes in narrative understanding following exposure to the video-based assistive picture book. The assessment was informed by commonly identified dimensions of story comprehension in the literature, including information retrieval, sequence organization, causal understanding, and inferential reasoning (Altun, 2018; Hjetland et al., 2017; Rubegni et al., 2021).

Assessment tasks were closely aligned with the narrative content of the video-based picture books and were administered individually after each viewing session. Multiple response formats were employed, including picture-based responses and oral answers, to accommodate the developmental characteristics of the participants. Although scoring procedures accounted for the four dimensions of story comprehension, analyses focused on a composite score to capture overall changes in story comprehension processes consistent with the design evaluation focus of the study.

Content validity was supported through alignment with established theoretical definitions of narrative comprehension and through careful matching of assessment items to the story content of the assistive materials. Reliability was enhanced by standardized administration procedures across all phases and participants, with all assessments conducted by the same trained examiner using predefined scoring criteria. This approach was considered appropriate for documenting individual-level changes in story comprehension within a single-case multiple-baseline design.

3.5 Data Analysis

Data analysis followed standard procedures for single-case design evaluation. Visual analysis was conducted to examine changes in level, trend, and stability of story comprehension performance across phases. Patterns of improvement and maintenance were interpreted in relation to the timing of the introduction of the assistive picture book design, with attention to consistency across participants.

This analytic approach supported the evaluation of how the designed artifact functioned in practice and provided preliminary evidence regarding its potential as an accessible digital reading support for inclusive early childhood education.

4 Results

4.1 Overview of Design Functioning Across Participants

The results document how the video-based assistive picture book functioned in practice as an accessible reading support for preschool children with developmental delays. Using a single-case multiple-baseline evaluation approach, changes in story comprehension performance were examined across baseline, intervention, and maintenance phases for each participant. Visual analysis focused on level, trend, stability, and overlap to evaluate whether the introduction of the assistive design was associated with systematic changes in narrative comprehension processes. Results are reported at the composite level to reflect overall changes in story comprehension processes, consistent with the design evaluation focus of the study.

Across participants, baseline phases were characterized by lower performance levels and variable trends in story comprehension. Following the introduction of the video-based assistive picture book, immediate and substantial changes in performance levels were observed, accompanied by increased stability. Maintenance phases generally demonstrated sustained performance above baseline levels, indicating that the design continued to function as an accessible reading support after the withdrawal of structured intervention sessions.

4.2 Individual-Level Design Functioning

4.2.1 Participant 1

For Participant 1, baseline story comprehension scores ranged from 21 to 33, with a level range of 12 and a mean level of 28.2. Performance during baseline showed limited improvement, with a level change of +4 and a stability index of 60 percent. Trend analysis indicated a stable but low performance pattern.

Following the introduction of the video-based assistive picture book, intervention-phase scores increased markedly, ranging from 75 to 92, with a level range of 17 and a mean level of 83.4. The within-phase level change increased to +13, and stability reached 100 percent, indicating that the assistive design supported consistently high performance. Visual analysis showed no overlap between baseline and intervention data points, suggesting a clear functional relation between the introduction of the design and changes in story comprehension performance.

During the maintenance phase, scores ranged from 67 to 83, with a mean level of 75.8 and a level change of +16. Stability decreased to 60 percent, and overlap with intervention data was observed at 60 percent. Despite this variability, performance remained substantially higher than baseline levels, indicating that the assistive picture book continued to function as a supportive reading tool after the intervention phase.

4.2.2 Participant 2

Participant 2 demonstrated baseline story comprehension scores ranging from 18 to 37, with a level range of 21 and a mean level of 30.2. Baseline performance showed a decreasing trend, with a level change of −8 and stability at 60 percent, indicating limited and unstable narrative comprehension support prior to the introduction of the assistive design.

During the intervention phase, scores increased sharply, ranging from 83 to 100, with a mean level of 92.6. Stability reached 100 percent, and performance remained consistently high throughout the intervention phase. Visual analysis revealed zero overlap between baseline and intervention phases, indicating a strong functional association between the assistive picture book design and improved story comprehension processes.

In the maintenance phase, scores ranged from 79 to 92, with a mean level of 86 and stability remaining at 100 percent. Although a small decrease in level was observed, performance continued to exceed baseline levels substantially, suggesting that the design maintained its supportive function beyond the structured intervention period.

4.2.3 Participant 3

For Participant 3, baseline scores ranged from 17 to 50, with a level range of 33 and a mean level of 27.6. Baseline performance exhibited considerable variability, with a level change of −33 and stability at 60 percent. Trend analysis indicated no clear developmental progression during baseline.

Following the introduction of the video-based assistive picture book, intervention-phase scores increased to a range of 75 to 100, with a mean level of 86.6 and a level change of +21. Stability reached 100 percent, and trend analysis showed a stable pattern at higher performance levels. These findings indicate that the assistive design supported more consistent narrative comprehension processes for this participant.

During the maintenance phase, performance remained at a high level, with stability sustained and no return to baseline patterns. The absence of baseline-level performance during intervention and maintenance phases supports the interpretation that the assistive picture book design functioned effectively as an accessible reading support for this participant.

4.3 Summary of Design Functioning Outcomes

Taken together, the results indicate that the video-based assistive picture book functioned as an effective accessibility-oriented design for supporting story comprehension in preschool children with developmental delays. Across all participants, the introduction of the assistive design was associated with immediate increases in performance levels, reduced variability, and enhanced stability. Maintenance data further suggest that the design continued to support narrative comprehension processes beyond the initial intervention period.

These findings provide converging single-case evidence that the video-based assistive picture book design successfully operationalized principles of cognitive load reduction and multimedia scaffolding into functional design features that addressed common barriers to story comprehension at the individual level.

5 Conclusion and Implications

The present study examined how a video-based assistive picture book functioned as an accessible reading support for preschool children with developmental delays, using a single-case multiple-baseline design. The results indicate that the introduction of the assistive picture book was consistently associated with systematic positive changes in story comprehension processes across participants: performance levels increased, response variability decreased, and gains were maintained beyond the intervention period. The systematic replication of these patterns across staggered baselines strengthens the inference that the observed changes were attributable to the design intervention rather than to maturation or incidental exposure (Kratochwill et al., 2013).

From a design perspective, the findings demonstrate that principles of cognitive load reduction and multimedia scaffolding (Mayer, 2021; Sweller et al., 2019) can be effectively operationalized in accessible digital reading materials for young children with developmental delays. The combination of short-form video format, synchronized narration, and guided prompts appeared to constrain extraneous processing demands while directing attention to essential narrative elements, an approach consistent with evidence that structured multimedia features, rather than rich but unguided content, support comprehension in young learners (Takacs et al., 2015). These results extend prior work on multimedia storybooks (Bus et al., 2015) by illustrating how design features can be tailored specifically as assistive supports for children facing cognitive and attentional barriers to narrative understanding.

Importantly, the findings reframe the role of digital media in early childhood from a passive environmental exposure toward an intentional assistive solution. Concerns that unstructured screen time may displace interactive learning (Madigan et al., 2019) appear to be tied to design quality rather than to the digital medium itself. When reading materials are deliberately designed to scaffold comprehension, digital formats can serve as accessibility-oriented supports within inclusive early literacy contexts.

The study also highlights the value of single-case experimental designs for assistive technology research in early childhood. Such designs offer a rigorous framework for examining how specific design features operate across diverse learners without requiring large homogeneous samples (Horner et al., 2005), complementing group-level research with fine-grained evidence on individual design–user interactions. The video-based format further demonstrates potential as a scalable reading support suitable for one-to-one learning contexts in both educational and home settings.

Several limitations warrant acknowledgment. The study involved a small number of participants and evaluated one specific design artifact within a controlled context; findings are therefore intended to inform design understanding rather than broad generalization. Future research may extend this approach through iterative redesign cycles, complementary qualitative data on user experience, and application across diverse narrative genres and assistive contexts.

Disclosure of Interests. The authors have no competing interests to declare that are relevant to the content of this article.

References

Altun, D.: The efficacy of multimedia stories in preschoolers' explicit and implicit story comprehension. Early Child. Educ. J. **46**(6), 629–642 (2018). https://doi.org/10.1007/s10643-018-0916-8

Bus, A.G., Takacs, Z.K., Kegel, C.A.: Affordances and limitations of electronic storybooks for young children's emergent literacy. Dev. Rev. **35**, 79–97 (2015)

Florit, E., Roch, M., Levorato, M.C.: Listening text comprehension of explicit and implicit information in preschoolers: the role of verbal and inferential skills. Discourse Process. **48**(2), 119–138 (2011)

Hjetland, H.N., Brinchmann, E.I., Scherer, R., Melby-Lervåg, M.: Preschool predictors of later reading comprehension ability: a systematic review. Campbell Syst. Rev. **13**(1), 1–155 (2017). https://doi.org/10.4073/csr.2017.14

Horner, R.H., Carr, E.G., Halle, J., McGee, G., Odom, S., Wolery, M.: The use of single-subject research to identify evidence-based practice in special education. Except. Child. **71**(2), 165–179 (2005)

Justice, L.M., Kaderavek, J.N.: Embedded-explicit emergent literacy intervention I. Lang. Speech Hear. Serv. Sch. **35**(3), 201–211 (2004)

Kratochwill, T.R., et al.: Single-case intervention research design standards. Remedial Spec. Educ. **34**(1), 26–38 (2013). https://doi.org/10.1177/0741932512452794

Madigan, S., Browne, D., Racine, N., Mori, C., Tough, S.: Association between screen time and children's performance on a developmental screening test. JAMA Pediatr. **173**(3), 244–250 (2019). https://doi.org/10.1001/jamapediatrics.2018.5056

Mayer, R.E.: Multimedia learning. 3rd edn. Cambridge University Press (2021)
Rubegni, E., Dore, R., Landoni, M., Kan, L.: The girl who wants to fly: exploring the role of digital technology in enhancing dialogic reading. Int. J. Child-Comput. Interact. **30**, 100239 (2021). https://doi.org/10.1016/j.ijcci.2020.100239
Sweller, J., van Merriënboer, J.J.G., Paas, F.: Cognitive architecture and instructional design: 20 years later. Educ. Psychol. Rev. **31**(2), 261–292 (2019). https://doi.org/10.1007/s10648-019-09465-5
Takacs, Z.K., Swart, E.K., Bus, A.G.: Benefits and pitfalls of multimedia and interactive features in technology-enhanced storybooks: a meta-analysis. Rev. Educ. Res. **85**(4), 698–739 (2015). https://doi.org/10.3102/0034654314566989

Reducing Interface Message Complexity as Digital Scaffolding: A Study of Mathematical Concept Understanding Among Children with Special Educational Needs in Short-Form Video Environments

Chia-Yen Hsieh(✉)

Department of Early Childhood Education, National Pingtung University, Pingtung City, Taiwan
banduna@nptu.edu.tw

Abstract. This study investigates how short-form video interface Message Complexity functions as Digital Scaffolding for preschoolers with Special Educational Needs (SEN) in mathematics learning contexts. Grounded in the Limited Capacity Model of Motivated Mediated Message Processing (LC4MP), a 2 × 2 quasi-experimental design was employed with 114 Taiwanese preschoolers (SEN group, $n = 47$; TD group, $n = 67$) to compare mathematical concept understanding under High-Complexity and Low-Complexity interface conditions. Results revealed that SEN preschoolers performed significantly lower than TD preschoolers under High-Complexity interfaces ($F = 3.502$, $p = .019$), whereas no significant difference emerged under Low-Complexity conditions. Qualitative data corroborated that reduced interface complexity redirected attention toward instructional content. SEN preschoolers also preferred longer videos and landscape interfaces. These findings suggest that interface denoising can transform digital environments into supportive scaffolds, narrowing learning gaps and advancing inclusive digital learning design.

Keywords: Digital Scaffolding · Message Complexity · Special Educational Needs · Limited Capacity Model · SDG 4: Inclusive and Equitable Quality Education

1 Introduction and State of the Art

As artificial intelligence driven algorithms become deeply integrated into contemporary media environments, short-form video has emerged as both a dominant trend and a routine component of preschoolers' everyday experiences. Short-form video is characterized by brief duration, highly condensed content, algorithmic curation, and high frequency updates (Chiencharoenthanakij et al., 2025; Xu et al., 2023). Platforms employ what Xu et al. (2023) conceptualized as "Technological Hooks", in combination with autoplay functions and simple swipe interactions, to repeatedly stimulate users' neural reward systems and trigger dopamine release. Within this mechanism, preschoolers are

K. Miesenberger et al. (Eds.): ICCHP 2026, LNCS 16867, pp. 91–98, 2027.
https://doi.org/10.1007/978-3-032-31308-9_11

able to establish continuous cycles of immediate gratification through simple operations. However, such high intensity sensory stimulation poses a potential risk to preschoolers whose prefrontal cortex is still undergoing critical developmental processes (Chen et al., 2022; Chiencharoenthanakij et al., 2025).

According to Lang's Limited Capacity Model of Motivated Mediated Mes-sage Processing (LC4MP), human cognitive resources are inherently limited. For preschoolers with special educational needs (SEN children), whose capacity to filter irrelevant stimuli is comparatively weaker (Chiencharoenthanakij et al., 2025; Zhu et al., 2025), Tao's (2011) analysis of media structural features provides further insight into the mechanisms underlying attentional disruption. Building on this framework, the present study argues that the distinctive structural characteristics of short-form video, such as rapid shot transitions and salient visual effects, are particularly likely to elicit in-voluntary Orienting Responses. These responses forcibly allocate limited cognitive resources to primary sensory processing, resulting in Cognitive Overload and leaving insufficient resources available for the encoding and comprehension of mathematical concepts.

In response to this challenge, the present study focuses on "Interface Structure". Xu et al. (2023) conceptualized short-form video as a media-rich presentation interface, in which automatic scrolling and full-screen vertical display intensify competition for cognitive resources. Accordingly, this study proposes that reducing Message Complexity can transform sources of distraction into forms of Digital Scaffolding. The purpose of this study is to examine how interface design within algorithmically mediated environments can function as an early-stage preventive support system that facilitates effective learning among preschoolers with special educational needs.

2 Theoretical Framework

2.1 Message Complexity and Cognitive Resource Competition

Short-form videos maintain user engagement through Technological Hooks (Xu et al., 2023). This study operates on their structural features (such as frequent cuts and sudden audiovisual effects) as Message Complexity at the cognitive level. Drawing on Tao (2011), the short-form video browsing environment tends to induce preschoolers to adopt a "Singleton Detection Mode," where attention actively monitors the environment for salient information. In this mode, high-density structural features continuously drive the Automatic Processing mechanism, causing attention to prioritize capturing salient but irrelevant stimuli (such as decorative animations) rather than core educational content. Under the premise of limited resources, secondary tasks commandeer cognitive resources, hindering the encoding of information into long-term memory.

2.2 Specificity of SEN Preschooler and the Need for Digital Scaffolding

The process impacts Preschooler with Special Educational Needs (SEN preschooler) most significantly, as their inhibitory control and ability to filter distractions are weaker (Chiencharoenthanakij et al., 2025; Zhu et al., 2025). This physiological disadvantage makes it difficult for them to disengage from the Automatic Processing mechanism, resulting in a lack of remaining resources for deep construction. Therefore, drawing on the perspectives of Wyeth et al. (2023) and Zhu et al. (2025), this study proposes transforming "Interface Denoising" into "Digital Scaffolding." It is inferred that by removing distracting features that trigger Orienting Responses, the physiological limitations of SEN preschooler can be compensated for, ensuring that resources are reallocated to core learning tasks.

This study aims to explore the impact of short-form video Message Complexity as a form of Digital Scaffolding on the mathematics learning of preschool SEN preschoolers. The specific research questions are as follows:

RQ1: Do SEN preschoolers and typically developing (TD) preschoolers show differences in mathematical concept understanding performance under different interface Message Complexity conditions?
RQ2: Do SEN preschoolers exhibit interface usage preferences (such as video length and presentation orientation) different from TD preschoolers in short-form video learning contexts?
RQ3: How does qualitative data supplement the explanation of differences in preschooler's attention focus and learning experiences during the viewing process under different interface message complexities.

3 Methodology

3.1 Participants and Grouping

This study employed an exploratory mixed-methods design. Using convenience sampling, 114 Taiwanese preschoolers aged 5–6 were recruited. Based on assessments and screening results, participants were divided into a Special Needs Group (SEN Group, n = 47) and a Typically Developing Group (TD Group, n = 67). The SEN Group included preschoolers diagnosed with developmental delays related to attention deficits (i.e., those holding a SEN identification) and preschoolers identified as having potential attention difficulties based on teacher observation checklists (specifically, those scoring below the cutoff on three or more attention items). (In Tai-wan, assessing whether preschooler have special educational needs involves not only referencing comprehensive assessment data from preschooler's hospitals but also simultaneously considering the number of items "falling into the net" [i.e., falling below the standard] on teacher observation checklists. "Falling into the net" indicates that the teacher considers the child has not yet met the standard for that indicator; the more items that fall into the net, the slower the child's development based on teacher observation records. In Taiwan, this is also an important indicator for assessing preschoolers' special educational needs.)

3.2 Experimental Materials and Design

Mathematics short-form videos were selected as experimental materials, given that mathematical concepts possess a high degree of abstraction and require digital media support to make them concrete (Altındağ Kumaş, 2024). This study operationalized the structural features of short-form videos into two types of interfaces to ex-amine their moderating effect on cognitive load: First, the High-Complexity Inter-face (> 5 structural features), which includes frequent shot changes, sudden sound effects, and decorative animations, designed to simulate a high-resource-competition environment and expected to trigger involuntary Orienting Responses (4 videos in total). Second, the Low-Complexity Interface (< 3 structural features), which applies an Interface Denoising strategy by selecting videos with identical instructional content but with reduced irrelevant distractions (Auxiliary Removal), thereby transforming the interface into Digital Scaffolding (4 videos in total).

This study adopted a 2 × 2 (Child Group × Short-form Video Interface Message Complexity) quasi-experimental design. By manipulating interface Message Complexity (High vs. Low), tests were administered to preschoolers in different groups (SEN vs. Typically Developing [TD] preschoolers) to analyze their effectiveness in mathematical concept understanding and subjective preferences (preschoolers in both groups were required to watch all 8 mathematics learning short-form videos). Additionally, before the preschooler watched the videos, parents were asked to fill out a "Child Short-form Video Viewing Habits Questionnaire" (containing 5 items, e.g., "How much time does your child spend using electronic devices to watch short-form videos per day?" and "What electronic devices does your child usually use to watch short-form videos?") to collect background variables on preschooler's short-form video viewing as control variables.

3.3 Measures

The dependent variables in this study were mathematical concept understanding effectiveness and subjective preference. The assessment tools are briefly described as follows:

Mathematical Concept Understanding Effectiveness.
Developed by the researchers, this instrument aimed to measure preschooler's learning effectiveness regarding "number sequence," "number composition," and "number decomposition." There were five questions per category, totaling 15 questions. The test adopted a multiple-choice format; correct answers received 1 point, and incorrect answers received 0 points, with a total score range of 0 to 15. Content validity was used to assess the validity. For reliability, KR-20 (Kuder-Richardson Formula 20) analysis was employed, yielding a KR-20 = .931, indicating high reliability and validity of this assessment tool.

Subjective Preference.
Subjective preference was measured using a 5-point Likert scale. After watching the mathematics learning video, preschoolers were asked to check their level of liking for the video; a higher score indicated a higher preference for the video.

3.4 Data Analysis Strategy

Regarding data analysis, descriptive statistics and Chi-square tests were first used to examine preschooler's short-form video viewing habits. These habits were then included as control variables in subsequent analyses to prevent them from becoming confounding variables affecting the results. Quantitative data were analyzed using Repeated Measures ANOVA to examine the interaction effects between interface and group, analyzing the simple main effects (if the interaction was significant) and their main effects. Additionally, Chi-square tests were used to examine differences in preschooler's subjective preferences. Qualitative data were analyzed using Open Coding. Due to space limitations, the results and discussion are presented together below.

4 Results and Discussion

Based on the research questions (RQ1–RQ3), this study integrates quantitative analysis and qualitative interview data to explain the impact of short-form video inter-face Message Complexity in the context of preschool mathematics learning, discussing it using the Limited Capacity Model (LC4MP) as an explanatory framework.

4.1 Differences in Mathematical Concept Understanding Effectiveness Between Preschooler with Special Needs and Typically Developing Preschooler Under High Message Complexity Interfaces (Corresponding to RQ1)

First, an analysis was conducted to determine whether short-form video interface Message Complexity affects preschooler's mathematical concept understanding effectiveness. The results showed that under the High-Complexity Interface condition, the mathematical concept understanding effectiveness of preschooler with special needs (SEN) was significantly lower than that of typically developing (TD) preschooler ($F = 3.502$, $p = .019$, $\eta^2 = .123$). Qualitative interview data further supplemented this result. When watching High-Complexity Interface videos, the attention of most preschoolers was easily attracted by plot details or decorative elements rather than focusing on the key mathematics teaching points. For example, preschooler only remembered "he was drinking milk" (T3520240923) or "the balloon flew away" (T9520241104); in geometry-related videos, they focused on "drawing a mouse" (T3220240923) rather than the shape itself; some preschooler also only recalled auditory stimuli, such as "I heard 5678..." (T8620241008), but were unable to answer core mathematical concept questions. These results indicate that High-Complexity Interfaces may prompt preschoolers to allocate attention to non-instructional stimuli, thereby hindering the understanding and encoding of mathematical concepts. This phenomenon can be explained by the Limited Capacity Model.

4.2 Changes in Mathematical Concept Understanding Effectiveness of SEN Preschooler Under Low Message Complexity Interfaces (Corresponding to RQ1)

Quantitative results showed that under the Low-Complexity Interface condition, there was no significant difference in mathematical concept understanding effectiveness between the Special Needs Group (SEN) and the Typically Developing Group (TD) ($F = 1.33$, $p = .270$, $\eta^2 = .051$). This result indicates that when interface Message

Complexity is reduced, the learning performance of SEN preschoolers can reach a level similar to that of TD preschoolers. Qualitative data further supported this finding. In the Low-Complexity Interface, preschooler were able to clearly describe the calculation process, for example, "6 balloons… Gave to Qiqi… 4 left" (T4320240923), or explicitly point out the instructional purpose of the video, such as "It teaches me precise measurement" (T6820241014), and even directly grasp the mathematical concept, "Watching this, I knew what 1 plus 1 equals" (T6620241014). Synthesizing the quantitative and qualitative results, the Low-Complexity Interface may effectively reduce distracting stimuli, transforming the interface from a potential source of distraction into Digital Scaffolding that supports learning, thereby compensating for the limitations of SEN preschooler in attention and control processes.

4.3 Interface Usage Preferences of SEN Preschooler in Short-Form Video Contexts (Corresponding to RQ2)

An analysis of the interface usage preferences of preschooler with special needs in short-form video learning contexts revealed that SEN preschooler significantly preferred long videos ($\chi^2(1) = 26.96$, $p < .001$) and landscape interfaces ($\chi^2(1) = 7.43$, $p = .006$). Interview data indicated that preschoolers believed longer videos provided time to "think for a while" (T6920241014), while landscape interfaces were described as "bigger" (T8320240930) and allowing them to "see more" (T11420241104). This preference suggests that when using short-form videos, preschoolers with special needs may tend to choose interface forms with temporal continuity and spatial integrity to maintain visual stability and reduce feelings of uncertainty during the viewing process. These results indicate that interface preference itself can be viewed as a behavioral manifestation of preschooler's needs for the learning environment and serves as an important reference basis for designing inclusive digital learning interfaces in the future.

4.4 Qualitative Data Supplementing Learning Experiences and Social Scaffolding (Corresponding to RQ3)

Beyond attention and learning experiences at the interface level, qualitative data also reveals important social contextual factors influencing preschooler's viewing processes. In the qualitative interview data, multiple preschoolers mentioned "Mom doesn't let me watch," indicating that parental intervention remains largely at the level of control. This phenomenon aligns with the results of Choy et al. (2024), who pointed out that most parents are "Passive Digital Mediators." This finding suggests that the function of Digital Scaffolding exists not only at the interface level but can also extend to the social interaction level. By designing "co-viewing prompts" or guidance nodes within the system, parents can be facilitated to transform from passive regulators into "Active Digital Guides," forming a more supportive interactive relationship among humans, interfaces, and learning content.

5 Conclusion

Adopting the Limited Capacity Model of Motivated Mediated Message Processing (LC4MP) as an explanatory framework, this study explores the impact of short-form video interface Message Complexity in preschool mathematics learning contexts and compares the learning performance and usage preferences of preschooler with Special Educational Needs (SEN) and Typically Developing (TD) preschooler under different interface conditions. The results indicate that under High-Complexity Interface conditions, the mathematical concept understanding effectiveness of SEN preschooler was significantly lower than that of TD preschooler, and qualitative data revealed that their attention was easily diverted to visual or auditory stimuli irrelevant to instructional goals. Conversely, under Low-Complexity Interface conditions, no significant difference in mathematical concept understanding effectiveness was observed between the two groups, and preschoolers were able to more clearly describe calculation processes and instructional key points. These results suggest that through Interface Denoising and the reduction of non-essential stimuli, short-form video interfaces have the potential to transform from sources of distraction into Digital Scaffolding that supports learning, to some extent narrowing the learning gap between SEN and TD preschooler. Furthermore, SEN preschoolers significantly preferred longer videos and landscape interfaces, indicating they may rely more on the visual stability provided by temporal continuity and spatial integrity to support their comprehension processes in short-form video contexts.

Based on these findings, this study recommends that interface Message Complexity be prioritized as a core consideration in the instructional application and design of mathematics short-form videos, prioritizing low-complexity, rhythmically predictable, and visually stable presentation forms to reduce the competition of non-instructional stimuli for attention, which is particularly beneficial for the learning engagement of SEN preschooler. Concurrently, qualitative data also indicate that family digital mediation styles may influence preschooler's viewing experiences, suggesting that the implementation of Digital Scaffolding should not be limited to the interface level but can also extend to parental co-viewing and guidance mechanisms. Limited by conference length constraints and research design, this study represents exploratory findings; future research could validate these findings with larger samples and diverse content types, integrating objective process indicators to deepen the understanding of short-form video interface design and inclusive learning support.

Acknowledgements. The author would like to thank Chen, En Qi for her assistance in data curation.

Disclosure of Interests. The author has no competing interests to declare that are relevant to the content of this article.

References

Altındağ Kumaş, Ö.: The power of digital story in early mathematics education: innovative approaches for preschooler with intellectual disabilities. PLoS ONE **19**(4), e0302128 (2024)

Chen, Y., Li, M., Guo, F., Wang, X.: The effect of short-form video addiction on users' attention. Behav. Inf. Technol. **42**(11), 2893–2910 (2022)
Chiencharoenthanakij, R., et al.: Short-form video media use is associated with greater inattentive symptoms in Thai school-age preschooler: insights from a cross-sectional survey. Brain Behav. **15**(7), e70656 (2025)
Choy, Y.N., Zhang, Z., Luo, Y., Lau, E.Y.H., Wu, D.: Digital parenting in the age of TikTok: Profiles of Chinese preschoolers' short-form video use. Preprint (2024)
Lang, A.: The limited capacity model of motivated mediated message processing. J. Commun. **50**(1), 46–70 (2000)
Tao, C.-C.: How do media stimuli receive attention: salience or relevance? The perspective of cognitive approaches to media. Mass Commun. Res. **107**, 245–290 (2011)
Wyeth, P., Kervin, L., Danby, S., Day, N., Darmansjah, A.: Digital technologies to support preschooler with special needs in early childhood education and care: a literature review. OECD Education Working Papers, No. 294. OECD Publishing (2023)
Xu, Z., Gao, X., Wei, J., Liu, H., Zhang, Y.: Adolescent user behaviors on short video application, cognitive functioning, and academic performance. Comput. Educ. **203**, 104865 (2023)
Zhu, H., Chen, R., Zhao, Y.: FocusView: understanding and customizing informational video watching experiences for viewers with ADHD. In: Proceedings of the 27th International ACM SIGACCESS Conference on Computers and Accessibility (ASSETS'25). ACM (2025)

Context Matters: Comparing What Works for Disabled Students at Spanish & UK Distance Learning Institutions

Tim Coughlan[1](✉), Francisco Iniesto[2], Ana Castellano-Beltrán[3], and Covadonga Rodrigo[2]

[1] The Open University, Milton Keynes, UK
tim.coughlan@open.ac.uk
[2] Universidad Nacional de Educación a Distancia, Madrid, Spain
[3] Universidad de Sevilla, Seville, Spain

Abstract. This research uses survey data collected from disabled students in two large-population distance learning universities in Spain (n = 356) and the UK (n-108) to explore how the use of technologies, strategies and resources varies between contexts. By analysing this in combination with comparison of features of these environments, we identify how the contexts impact on the relevance of particular tools and strategies to disabled students, and the similarities and differences that appear. Themes include differences in how disability is diagnosed and described, as well as how teaching models and institutionally supported tools impact on the guidance that would be relevant. The analysis contributes towards understanding how relevant context-aware guidance could be delivered and provides insights into dimensions of variability across educational contexts.

Keywords: Assistive Technology · eLearning and Education · User Centred Design and User Participation

1 Introduction

Appropriate guidance, strategies and assistive technology choices for disabled people are context dependent, however there is limited research with which to understand these phenomena in education. It is not clear if what works for a person studying in one institution would apply if they were studying elsewhere, or the dimensions through which recommendations could be adjusted. This research therefore aims to understand where and how institutional contexts, across countries, can affect where disability barriers arise, how they are communicated, and overcome. These findings can be applied to develop shared, adaptive systems for guidance and support.

In this study we use a shared survey design to collect and analyse data from disabled students at two universities: Universidad Nacional de Educación a Distancia, Spain (UNED) and The Open University, UK (OU), with open-ended questions to elicit student perspectives on what works for them individually. Both are massive distance learning

K. Miesenberger et al. (Eds.): ICCHP 2026, LNCS 16867, pp. 99–107, 2027.
https://doi.org/10.1007/978-3-032-31308-9_12

institutions with similarities in approach and population, but teaching models, policies, processes, language and culture differ. For example, in Spain, disabilities recognition is a national policy established by law with administrative and legal implications quite different to those in the UK [1]. By analysing comparable data and relating it to differences between the contexts, we explore how these differences impact the assistive tools, strategies and resources that students report as useful.

Our research questions are:

1) How do disabled students across two Spanish and UK institutions describe themselves and the assistive tools and strategies that help them overcome barriers?
2) What can differences between students in these contexts tell us about ways to support recommendations and assistive technology needs across contexts?

2 Background

The relationships between disability and context present theoretical and practical questions debated by disability scholars and represented in internationally-recognised frameworks. For example, the World Health Organisations' International Classification of Functioning, Disability and Health (ICF) represents a biopsychosocial model rationale, emphasising that the same impairment in different environments may or may not lead to a barrier, and appropriate support may remove such a barrier. Hence, while medical models focus on individual conditions, and social models emphasise that society and environment create disability, disability is here located across the individual and environment and shaped by the interactions between these [2].

Prior experiences and variability in impairments affect individual needs, but it is also important to identify how differences between environments impact on disabilities and support to overcome barriers [3]. Ecological Systems Theory [4] provides a structure through which to analyse this, classifying levels of environmental system from the intimate microsystem to the societal macrosystem and change over time (chronosystem).

Deeper understanding of the dimensions through which contextual differences affect the utility of particular technologies, strategies and resources could have significant benefits. For example, [5] AI-based tools could provide personalised guidance to disabled students, drawing on the perspectives of other students [5]. Here we explore how context is important to providing *appropriate* suggestions, as contextual differences may otherwise undermine the relevance of these suggestions.

3 Methodology

Data was collected through a collaborative project to support the participation of disabled students in establishing a knowledge base that links individual descriptions of disabilities with the tools, strategies and resources that students report to be useful in overcoming barriers to their learning. A bilingual survey was devised for students to report this data in Spanish or English to understand how students describe their disabilities and what types of suggestions students share about the support that works for them. The survey questions were collaboratively developed by the research team, and included the following set of core questions asked of participants across both contexts:

1. Subjects you have studied or are studying at the university
2. Describe your disabilities or additional study needs in your own words
3. What helped most when you started your studies
4. Resources you would suggest to a student like yourself, and benefits these had
5. Tools or assistive technologies you use, and benefits these have
6. Strategies that have helped you succeed in your studies.

Participants responded anonymously to reduce concerns about collection of sensitive personally identifiable data. Ethical clearance was given by the OU's Human Research Ethics Committee. The survey was advertised to students with declared disabilities, first at the OU and then at UNED. The English-language survey was advertised to 3,000 OU students. From this, 108 responses were taken forward for analysis. The Spanish-language survey was advertised to 6,968 UNED students with 356 responses analysed.

Categorisations of disability in use vary between the contexts studied, but a shared categorisation is useful to understand populations. Table 1 shows participant disabilities according to a categorisation agreed drawing on previous approaches including [6]. Where more than one category is relevant, multiple categories are included. It was notable in this that UK participants more often described multiple categories of disabilities, hence the overall percentages are higher.

Table 1. Disability categories among participants according to institutions.

	UNED	OU
Sensory disability	81 (22.7%)	28 (25.9%)
Physical disability	133 (37.4%)	63 (61.1%)
Neurodivergence and/or learning difficulties	37 (10.4%)	43 (39.8%)
Psychosocial disability and mental health conditions	101 (28.4%)	77 (56.2%)
Chronic health conditions	82 (23%)	55 (40.1%)

Qualitative responses were analysed through a process of thematic analysis [7]. The data was divided into two parts for this purpose. Firstly, identifying themes in the ways that participants talked about their disabilities, and secondly, the types of suggestions they provided, which indicate the tools, resources and strategies that supported them to overcome barriers to succeeding in their studies. The coding process involved two members of the research team. Each researcher's work was systematically reviewed by the other to ensure rigour and consistency. The same process was followed for the OU and UNED data sets, but this was conducted separately. In this way, different themes and sub-themes could be recognising differences. The OU data was collected in 2022 with an isolated analysis of this reported in [8]. The UNED data was collected in 2024. There is potentially an impact from this related to changing technology, for example some references are made to newer GenAI tools in the UNED data.

4 Findings

Collaborative comparison of the two thematic analyses identified key areas with relative similarities and differences:

4.1 Describing Disabilities

Administrative differences between Spain and the UK can be observed impacting on disability descriptions. For example, Spain is considered to have a strong process of diagnosis and measurement, related in comments such as:

Social phobia, 65% mental disability, operated on for Obstructive Hypertrophic Cardiomyopathy last May/June. Under treatment with oral anticoagulants for mitral valve disease and depression. (UNED).

UK universities are more open to self-reported disabilities but this creates challenges. One distinct topic in descriptions from OU students is lack of diagnosis or late diagnosis and resulting uncertainty:

I have dyslexia but I do not have an official diagnosis due to the cost. (OU).

4.2 Support

Building on the above, participants report a variety of support from both formal services and less formal interactions, that have been important to their success:

The COIE (Student Guidance Centre), UNIDIS (Disability), Student Offices and Secretariats, the entire UNED website, tutorial videos, MOOCs, Forum groups for each course, online or face-to-face tutorials, specific questions at the corresponding associated centre (or any other), etc. (UNED).

I would like to thank the departments that support and assist people with recognized disabilities, in this case UNED - UNIDIS, for their great contribution, efficiency, and daily work. (UNED).

OU data also highlights the contribution of equivalent Disability Support Team services, but presents this more as a starting point to interactions with tutors and peers:

Flexibility and understanding from my tutor initiated by Disability Support Team This has allowed me to have an open and productive dialogue with my tutor about my health struggles, especially about falling behind due to hospital admissions and with assignment deadlines (OU).

Facebook module and interest groups. I found a 'study buddy' on one in my first module and we often study via skype together. The groups can be emotionally supportive and encouraging especially if I have... thought of ending my studies. (OU).

Further sources of support mentioned include the Library and external services for mental health support which have national reach. In this regard, there appear similar categories of support need but these will differ on specifics in each institution and country.

4.3 Teaching and Tuition

Engagement with tutors and tuition is a further theme where similarities and distinct patterns emerge. Responses from UNED tend to focus on the tuition approach and potential for this to directly support groups of disabled students:

A tutorial or support group, led by a professional, is needed to address the needs of individuals with ADD, ADHD, autism spectrum disorder...at the beginning of the course. There is a lot of information out there, and it's difficult to select what's relevant. (UNED).

OU comments are more focused on the one-to-one relationship with an individual tutor. This reflects different ways of working between the institutions:

Don't be afraid to contact your tutor if you don't understand a question or want to run ideas past them to check you understand. This isn't cheating. (OU).

Use of face to face and online activities are distinct in the two institutions and impact on what works. The OU recently moved away from most face-to-face tuition. Respondents highlight how this changes barriers and effective use of technology:

Recorded tutorials and email and remote support from tutors. These have allowed me to receive the required information due to my difficulties in being in a group live (tutorials). Its great having online support at all times. (OU).

I miss having face-to-face tutorials with my Masters, as I found bouncing ideas off of my peers helpful and it gave me the opportunity to spend time with my tutor & get clarity on anything I was struggling with. (OU).

UNED has 64 associated centres in Spain and 15 overseas, which means significant face to face interaction alongside online options and barriers:

Disabled Students who are unable to travel to associate centres for "voluntary" tutorials should have the option of doing them online. If the tutorial, by its nature, can only be done in person, we should be given an alternative option. (UNED).

4.4 Assessment

Exams at UNED are face to face, even with an important number of centres, many students still need to travel, although in particular cases students are allowed to take the exam from home, that decision is made on a case-by-case basis:

Although the courses are online, the exams are always in person, and in cases like mine, with a chronic illness, I can't always attend. Any option to take the exams remotely, for example, would be great. (UNED).

At UNED, they provide, if the student requests it, various forms of support when taking exams, such as a teacher who helps me fill in the boxes on the tests. (UNED).

Adaptations to support disabled students in exams can include increased font size, electronic formats, textual transcriptions, figure descriptions and additional time, while extensions to coursework deadlines are a common adjustment for OU students:

On some occasions I have suggested that examiners establish strategies to extend the exam time, since the ability to concentrate and respond, I insist, in certain cases requires a little more time. (UNED).

Don't be afraid to ask for an extension when you need it - it reduces the panic pressure and gives you some breathing space. Let your tutor and or student support know if you are struggling as they can often give more help and sort things out. (OU).

4.5 Institution-Approved and Sponsored Tools

The data illustrates how the tools an institution chooses to use, or not support, influence students' requirements and the suggestions that are relevant to them. For example:

Adobe Connect (used for online tutorials in OU) has helped even when I didn't know what I was doing. It gives me a good interface to interact with my tutor (OU).

UNED uses Microsoft Teams and has in-house built solutions such that video classes now get AI transcribed subtitles:

At UNED I see the Intecca platform where the recorded classes are located. They have started using AI to create subtitles more quickly and automatically. (UNED).

AI captions and transcripts are now also available in some forms at OU, harnessing in-built features of mainstream tools. Digital tools for communication are clearly important in distance learning, yet the tools and practices around them differ between contexts. Telegram and WhatsApp are not officially permitted at either institution though students report making use of them to form unofficial groups that they value:

What I'm finding most useful are the Telegram and WhatsApp groups for my subjects, thanks to which I've been able to get some books in accessible formats. (UNED).

The choice of mainstream applications adopted by the institution also play an important role which will differ across contexts, offering easy access to assistive tools in conjunction with features of the ways in which learning materials are shared, in this case both UNED and the OU provide students with access to Microsoft Office:

the option of textbooks in "Word version (optimised for screen readers)" is fantastic because I can use the free student Office 365 option "Read it aloud" instead have to pay for apps like "NaturalReader"....I can set the text font to OpenDyslexic ... I can even translate the whole textbook to my mother tongue (OU).

The accessibility options in the Office suite help me to prepare the assignments I have to submit, create summaries, etc. (UNED)".

While there are similarities in reports from OU and UNED students, the importance of these features suggests that institutions using other tools would have significant differences. Alternative choices such as Google Workspace for Education have a significant market share [9]. Providers and institutions also differ within their combinations and configurations of the office suite, learning management system and video conferencing tools that students refer to as essential in the accessibility of their learning.

4.6 Strategies and Tools for Personal Organisation

Strategies and tools for organisation is a shared theme across the contexts. This could be seen as related to the need for distance learners to be self-regulated:

Notion app for organisation, Pomodoro Technique, scheduling, peer communities, past exams, talking to teachers or having someone else talk to them with your questions if you find it difficult. (UNED).

I started using the Pomodoro method while studying...This has helped my motivation and procrastination issues as it's much easier to face tasks if they're broken up into shorter time periods with breaks in between. (OU).

Another consistent topic is how the ability to study can be variable over time due to disabilities, so being ahead and organised is essential. While this is consistent across the contexts it varies in requirements, for example due to how they are assessed:

If you are in a period of difficulty health wise, work backwards from your (assignment). Decipher what is needed... in the guidance then work on those areas first. (OU).

I need to write the same thing several times so I can memorise it and not forget it on exam day. I make my own notes on the computer. (UNED).

5 Discussion and Conclusions

By combining analysis of data from disabled students with analysis of their contexts we unpack how contextual factors impact on the relevance of guidance suggestions. While limited to two institutions, the comparison allows us to identify initial dimensions of variation (see Table 2).

These factors operate unevenly across ecological levels. For example, institutionally supported tools and teaching models have implications for strategies and relevance of assistive features. Face-to-face assessment and provision in UNED introduce mobility-related constraints, while remote provision at the OU shifts the focus towards ongoing communication and time management. At the macrosystem level, culture and process around disability vary between countries. Disability is framed and communicated differently, with more formalised and quantified descriptions in Spain and more self-reported accounts in the UK. Institutional changes over time also impact on relevance. These dimensions shape what is relevant for disabled students and suggest that while there is potential to reuse gathered knowledge on effective strategies, tools and resources, these depend on the interaction between institutional, cultural and temporal factors [3, 6]. This implies that adaptive and AI-based support systems should model these dimensions explicitly if they are to support wide audiences.

Table 2. Summary of contextual differences by theme

Dimension	Contextual differences
Describing Disabilities	Macrosystem: national approaches to diagnosis shape descriptions. Spain reflects formal diagnosis and quantified disability status; the UK data shows more self-reporting, uncertainty and late or missing diagnosis
Disability Support	Microsystem: UNED data emphasises formal institutional services (e.g. UNIDIS), while OU data highlights tutor-based support and peer communities after initial disability support conversations
Teaching and Tuition	Mesosystem: Overall teaching and communication methods shape relevance of strategies and technology Chronosystem: OU has shifted from partly face-to-face to fully online teaching, altering barriers and requirements during students' studies
Assessment	Microsystem/Exosystem: UNED relies on summative assessment through in-person exams and online evaluation through the e-learning platform, while OU uses remote assessment with extensions as a key adjustment providing flexibility for disabled students
Institution-approved and sponsored tools	Macrosystem/Exosystem: institutional communications platforms shape interaction. UNED uses MS Teams for synchronous teaching while OU uses Adobe Connect, alongside informal tools in both contexts
Personal organisation	Microsystem: similar strategies are reported across contexts (e.g. planning, Pomodoro) but demands differ: UNED is shaped by exam preparation, while OU emphasises continuous coursework time management

Acknowledgments. The OU supported this study through its Open Societal Challenges initiative. Francisco and Covadonga´s research is supported by the project: Human-Centered AI: User-Driven Adaptative Interfaces (PID2023-148577OB-C22) funded by MICIU/AEI/https://doi.org/10.13039/501100011033 and by FEDER/UE. Ana Castellano-Beltran's research is supported by the Erasmus+ traineeship grant under the European Union's Erasmus+ Programme.

Disclosure of Interests. The authors have no competing interests to declare that are relevant to the content of this article.

References

1. Agencia Estatal Boletín Oficial del Estado: Royal Decree 888/2022 (2022). https://www.boe.es/buscar/doc.php?id=BOE-A-2022-17105. Last accessed 16 Apr 2026
2. Shakespeare, T.: Disability Rights and Wrongs Revisited. Routledge, pp. 78–80 (2014)
3. Moriña, A.: Inclusive education in higher education: challenges and opportunities. Eur. J. Spec. Needs Educ. **32**(1), 3–17 (2017)
4. Bronfenbrenner, U.: Toward an experimental ecology of human development. Am. Psychol. **32**(7), 513 (1977)
5. Coughlan, T., Iniesto, F.: What should I know? Analysing behaviour and feedback from student use of a virtual assistant to share information about disabilities. Internet High. Educ. **66** (2025)
6. Perera, V.H., Sánchez-Díaz, N., Castellano-Beltrán, A.: Beyond adversity: strategies for academic success from the voices of graduates with disabilities. Disabil. Soc. (2025)
7. Braun, V., Clarke, V.: Reflecting on reflexive thematic analysis. Qual. Res. Sport Exerc. Health **11**(4), 589–597 (2019)
8. Coughlan, T., Iniesto, F., Carr, J.E.: Analysing disability descriptions and student suggestions as a foundation to overcome barriers to learning. J. Interact. Media Educ. **2024**(1) (2024)
9. About Chromebooks: Google for Education Statistics (2026). https://www.aboutchromebooks.com/google-for-education-user-statistics/. Last accessed 16 Apr 2026

From Algorithm to Execution: Enabling Everyone to Engage in Programming Activity

Philippe Truillet(✉)

Univ Toulouse, CNRS, IRIT, Toulouse, France
Philippe.Truillet@utoulouse.fr

Abstract. In France, the visual programming language Scratch is widely used in middle schools due to its ease of use and was officially incorporated into the national curriculum following the 2016 reform. However, this tool relies primarily on visual interaction, which makes it largely inaccessible to blind and visually impaired students.

This article introduces TaBGO (Tangible Blocks Go Online), a tool that allows blind and visually impaired children to design and run Scratch programs independently or in collaboration with sighted peers. TaBGO relies on a set of tangible Scratch blocks, a visual recognition system, and software that automatically translates physical algorithms into Scratch files, along with program transformation tools for non-visual exploration.

Keywords: programming activity · algorithm design · tangible user interfaces · accessibility · autonomy

1 Introduction

Since 2009, numerous surveys have predicted a substantial increase in employment opportunities in the field of computer science. This trend reflects the growing importance of digital technologies in contemporary society. In parallel, computing education has progressively reached younger learners and formal educational contexts. In France, the 2016 educational reform integrated core computing concepts into the middle-school curriculum. To introduce these notions, teachers commonly rely on online visual programming platforms such as Scratch, Blockly, ..., which are designed to be intuitive for beginners.

Although these environments are effective for sighted learners, they are fundamentally based on visual interaction and therefore remain largely inaccessible to blind or low-vision students. This raises an important educational and social challenge: how can we ensure that blind and visually impaired students benefit from the same learning opportunities in computer science as their sighted peers [1].

K. Miesenberger et al. (Eds.): ICCHP 2026, LNCS 16867, pp. 108–114, 2027.
https://doi.org/10.1007/978-3-032-31308-9_13

Beyond the issue of inclusion, programming activities can play a significant role in the sensorimotor and cognitive development of blind adolescents. Middle school represents a critical period for the development of perceptual and motor skills, particularly for students with visual impairments who may face additional developmental challenges. Participating in structured, school-based programming activities can stimulate sensory exploration, motor coordination, and problem-solving skills. Moreover, collaborative programming tasks can foster interaction between sighted and blind students, thereby promoting social inclusion in classroom settings. This paper therefore addresses the following research questions:

1. **RQ1** - Is it possible to provide a non-visual medium that allows visual-impaired (ViP) students to access Scratch programming on an equal footing with sighted students?
2. **RQ2** - Can such a solution be realistically integrated into ordinary educational environments to support inclusive teaching practices?

To answer these questions, we propose a tangible user interface (TUI) composed of physical blocks and a software that translates tangible algorithms into executable Scratch programs.

2 Related Work

Scratch, developed at MIT [2], is one of the most widely used platforms for introducing computing concepts to young learners. Its block-based, visual syntax lowers the barrier to entry for novices. Similar ideas can be found in tangible programming tools such as Bee-Bot, Lighters [4], Torino [5], and other systems that allow children to construct algorithms using physical objects or robots.

Several projects have explored accessibility in block-based environments. Blocks4All [5] and AccessibleBlockly [6] provide auditory and tactile cues to support blind users. Research on Scratch accessibility has also led to prototypes such as Accessi-DV [7] and CodeBox64 [8]. While these systems improve access, they often require assistance from a sighted person or technical expertise for setup and use. While *unplugged programming* is a solution that can be useful for learning computer science, it is limited by the inability to access online digital resources.

TaBGO [9] builds on these approaches with the goal of achieving full autonomy for blind users through a combination of tangible interaction, multimodal feedback, and low-cost open-source technologies.

After creating the first prototypes (see Fig. 1 on the left), we tested our solution using the Wizard of Oz technique. An initial study was conducted [9] on tasks involving the construction of simple algorithms (offered as part of their school curriculum) using physical blocks during four one-hour sessions, focusing on skills acquired in middle school (mathematics, computer science, and music), from 6th to 9th grade by sighted students. The tasks were completed independently or cooperatively by pairs of students. Additional surveys were also conducted to assess the system's perceived usability (SUS), the subjects' cognitive load while performing the tasks (NASA-TLX), and their overall satisfaction. The results were very encouraging: first, the prototypes were easy to use and well received (average SUS score: 58.3), and second, the cognitive load remained low and tasks were completed within the allocated time (the average NASA-TLX score was 13.15). Overall, the tangible blocks were generally preferred over the online Scratch platform.

This initial phase encouraged us to take things further and offer a cross-platform solution that is easy to install and use.

3 TaBGO

TaBGO[1] (Tangible Blocks Go Online) can be divided into three parts, each of which addresses a specific issue:

- some **physical blocks** for building the algorithm
- a video capture device capable of detecting blocks. A fixed, illuminated device equipped with a 4K webcam can be used just like an image captured by a smartphone
- and a **software** for transcribing the blocks into Scratch code.

TaBGO is complemented by a set of tools that allow you to run programs in various non-visual ways. You will find all the necessary stuff at the address listed at the bottom of the page.

3.1 Hardware Design and Overall Architecture

The blocks were designed iteratively to be robust and easy for secondary school pupils to handle. We first worked on the size, shape, colors, and information to be displayed (in Braille or black) for the initial prototypes (see Fig. 1 on the left below). We ultimately chose the blocks designed by graphic designer Alexandre Ilic at INJA (see Fig. 1 on the right).

Although these blocks are less faithful to the visual version of Scratch, they use magnetic, textured blocks. They match the colours of the block types, provide an indented reading path for the program, and display the block in both Braille and black.

The blocks are stored in a compartmentalized case (see Fig. 2) organized by category, which helps users - sighted or blind - to locate and assemble them efficiently. Each block contains a TopCodes[2], which makes it easy to scan using an optical reader, even in low-light conditions.

The software component is coded with Processing.org[3] language and performs two main tasks:

[1] https://github.com/tabgo.

[2] https://github.com/TIDAL-Lab/TopCodes.

[3] https://processing.org.

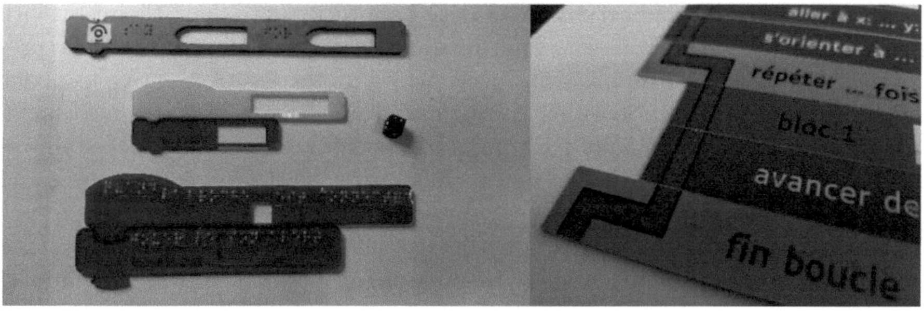

Fig. 1. Some prototypes used during the design phase (on the left), the blocks currently in use designed by A. Ilic (INJA) (on the right).

Fig. 2. The case containing the tangible blocks.

- **visual recognition**. It analyses captured images to detect each block which is associated with a unique TopCodes, its orientation, and any other useful information (cf. Fig. 4) such as *variables*. It is essential to be able to manipulate different values in order to specify the number of repetitions in a loop, an angle, and so on. While we initially favoured the use of Braille dice (cubarithms), which can be handled fairly easily by blind students. We ultimately opted for a 3D modular holder (see prototype in Fig. 3) into which digits can be placed to form a number. This number is then decoded by OCR software during the algorithm's recognition process.
- and **code translation**. These informations are then exported into a structured Scratch sb3 program

Fig. 3. The variable handling prototype.

By generating a standard sb3 file, TaBGO allows users to share their files with sighted users or with Professors and, in some cases, to run and test their programs independently. Emphasis has been placed on the use of iterative feedback loops that can facilitate learning through trial and error. This can also facilitate the gradual acquisition of programming concepts. Real-time processing was deliberately omitted to reduce technical constraints, hardware requirements, and the cognitive load for novice users.

Nevertheless, this solution is not yet complete. Hence, beyond developing a solution that allows blind children to program in Scratch, it was also important to provide stand-alone solutions for testing the programs they create using non-visual methods. Indeed, the exercises typically given to middle school students generally involve creating patterns (triangles, stars, spirals or even house drawings) using the fundamental structures of programming.

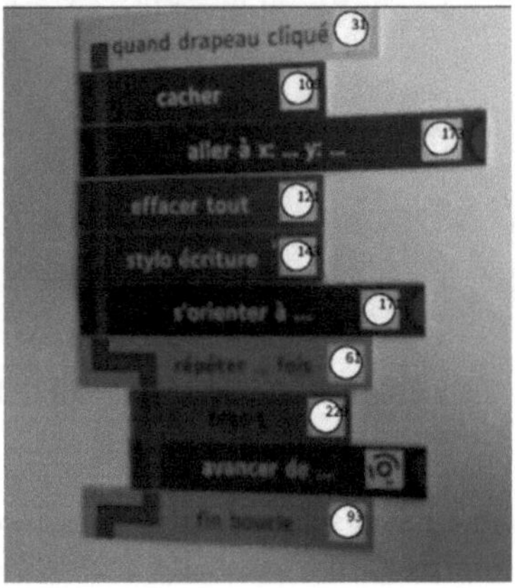

Fig. 4. Detecting blocks by their TopCodes to generate the sb3 file.

Thus, analysing the output is a very important factor in the learning process. Unfortunately, the online platform does not provide non-visual access to this output. That is why we have developed several tools that allow users to explore the results through touch or sound.

3.2 Additional Tools

The first add-on tool (written in Python) automatically converts Scratch programs into SVG (Scalable Vector Graphics files). By using various options, it is possible to generate images that can be printed on thermal relief paper, in 3D, or even allow a small robot like an Ozobot robot to navigate continuously within the image (Fig. 5). This approach allows you to follow the path by placing your finger on the robot. All these solutions provide students with ways to explore autonomously their work.

Fig. 5. An Ozobot robot navigates the figure produced by the sb3 file on the left and Trace generated by the algorithm converted into 3D sound on the right.

Other tools are currently being developed, such as the ability to explore the algorithm's output in 3D. By using stereo sound, it is possible to assign a direction (left-right) and a height (up-down) to audio stimuli in order to recreate a sense of space. For example, when using a pair of headphones, a movement of the Scratch avatar to the right can be associated with a sound on the right so that a visually impaired person can perceive this movement.

These tools are independent of TaBGO and can therefore be used with files generated by the online platform. They are also available for free download on the project's website.

4 Conclusion and Future Work

TaBGO offers a practical, low-cost, multimodal, and non-visual approach to programming with Scratch. It aims to help blind and visually impaired middle school students learn and experiment with algorithms. By combining physical blocks, computer vision recognition with simple techniques, and various forms of feedback, we aim to achieve full autonomy - from algorithm design to execution - while also enabling students to work collaboratively with sighted peers in inclusive classrooms.

Initial informal trials conducted in specially adapted classrooms have yielded encouraging results regarding the manipulation of blocks and the construction of algorithms. The practical use of the tool in the classroom still needs to be evaluated using the programming exercises provided as part of the students' curriculum.

Beyond the questions raised in the introduction to this article—particularly regarding technical feasibility and integration into mainstream schools—research questions remain open regarding its applications:

- How can the proposed approach, which relies on the use of tangible blocks - either individually or in combination - truly help students develop their computer science skills?

- Is the student capable of using the tool as a whole (building algorithms with blocks, recognizing and receiving non-visual feedback on the result) completely independently?
- To what extent is collaboration with other students - and in particular with sighted students - possible?

Acknowledgments. This study was partially funded by UNADEV association (Grant number 2019.49). Thanks to CESDV/IJA Toulouse for their fruitful collaboration on this project.

References

1. Metelja, O., Thieme, A., Brûlé, E., Benett, C., Serrano, M., Jouffrais, C.H.: Toward class-room experiences inclusive of students with disabilities. Interact. **26**(1), 40–45 (2019). https://doi.org/10.1145/3289485
2. Maloney, J., Resnick, M., Rusk, N., Silverman, B., Eastmond, E.: The scratch programming language and environment. ACM Trans. Comput. Educ. (TOCE) **10**(4), 1–15 (2010). https://doi.org/10.1145/1868358.1868363
3. Wang, X., Xing, Q., Jin, Q., Wang, D.: Be a lighting programmer: supporting children collaborative learning through tangible programming system. Int. J. Hum. Comput. Interact. **40**(10), 2622–2640 (2024). https://doi.org/10.1080/10447318.2022.2163783
4. Morrison, C., et al.: Torino: a tangible programming language inclusive of children with visual disabilities. Hum. Comput. Interact. **35**(3), 191–239 (2020). https://doi.org/10.1080/07370024.2018.1512413
5. Milne, L.R., Ladner, R.E.: Blocks4All: overcoming accessibility barriers to blocks programming for children with visual impairments. In: Proceedings of CHI 2018, vol. 2018, pp. 1–10 (2018). https://doi.org/10.1145/3173574.3173643
6. Ludi, S., Simpson, J., Merchant, W.: Exploration of the use of auditory cues in code comprehension and navigation for individuals with visual impairments in a visual program. In: Proceedings of ASSETS, vol. 2016, pp. 279–280 (2016). https://doi.org/10.1145/2982142.2982206
7. Boissel, S., Mallette Accessi, D.V.: Scratch "Scratch débranché en braille et gros caractères", dans la nouvelle revue de l'adaptation et de la scolarisation, n. 77, pp. 183–192. INSHEA (2017). https://doi.org/10.3917/nras.077.0183
8. Wagner, A., Wang, Z.: Evaluating a tactile approach to programming scratch. In: Proceedings of ACMSE, vol. 2019, pp. 226–229 (2019). https://doi.org/10.1145/3299815.3314464
9. Andriamahery-Ranjalahy, K.H., Berquez, L., Jessel, N., Truillet, P.: TabGO: towards accessible computer science in secondary school. In: Antona, M., Stephanidis, C. (eds.) HCII 2021. LNCS, vol. 12769, pp. 12–24. Springer, Cham (2021). https://doi.org/10.1007/978-3-030-78095-1_2

Virtual Reality Adoption Among Special Education Teachers: Explaining the Intention-Behavior Gap

Ching-Hsuan Wu[1](✉), Mu-En Lin[1], Tzu-Yu Shen[1], Chih-Hsuan Chen[1], and Yung-Ji Sher[2]

[1] Department of Special Education, National Taitung University, 369, Sec. 2, University Rd., Taitung, Taiwan (R.O.C.)
may881027@gmail.com, paul890401957@gmail.com, ta895105@gmail.com

[2] Department of Special Education and Graduate Institute of Rehabilitation Counseling and Gerontological Wellbeing, National Taiwan Normal University, 162, Sec. 1 Heping East Road, Taipei, Taiwan (R.O.C.)
siaa@ntnu.edu.tw

Abstract. Virtual Reality (VR) offers transformative potential for special education, yet a persistent "high intention, low adoption" paradox limits its integration. To diagnose this implementation gap, this study utilizes the Technology Acceptance Model 3 (TAM3), specifically examining the role of environmental resources as a critical adoption threshold. Based on a survey of 409 special education teachers in Taiwan, we applied Partial Least Squares Structural Equation Modeling (PLS-SEM) to analyze the determinants of Usage Behavior. The results indicate that Perceived Usefulness (PU, β =.75) and Perceived Ease of Use (PEOU, β =.61) drive Attitudes Toward Using (ATU). Crucially, while Behavior Intention (BI) strongly predicts Actual System Use (ASU, β =0.81), it is heavily contingent upon perception of External Control (EC). The significant variability in EC highlights a structural digital divide, particularly disadvantaging preschool and elementary sectors. We conclude that to bridge this gap, policy interventions must prioritize precise resource allocation and task-oriented technical support, ensuring that teacher enthusiasm translates into sustainable classroom practice.

Keywords: Computer Self-efficacy · Extended Technology Acceptance Model (TAM3) · Special Education Teachers · Structural Equation Modeling (SEM) Virtual Reality Technology

1 Introduction

Virtual Reality (VR) has emerged as a promising assistive technology in special education, characterized by its capacity to create immersive, controllable, and repeatable learning environments [1]. These features are particularly beneficial for students with Autism Spectrum Disorder (ASD) and Attention Deficit Hyperactivity Disorder (ADHD), facilitating the acquisition of social skills and cognitive scaffolding in a safe setting [7,

K. Miesenberger et al. (Eds.): ICCHP 2026, LNCS 16867, pp. 115–121, 2027.
https://doi.org/10.1007/978-3-032-31308-9_14

8]. However, a significant gap remains between the pedagogical potential of VR and its routine implementation in classrooms [5]. This phenomenon, described as the "high intention, low adoption" paradox, suggests that positive teacher attitudes do not automatically translate into consistent usage behavior [10], identifying the determinants behind this discrepancy is critical. While previous studies often cite hardware costs as the primary barrier [10], this explanation may be insufficient to fully capture the complexity of the adoption process in special education. Teachers in this field typically exhibit strong "task-oriented" traits, theoretically predisposing them to adopt effective tools [5, 9]. We posit that the bottleneck lies less in individual motivation and more in the perception of External Control (EC)—specifically, the availability of organizational resources and technical support [5]. Without these external enablers, even highly motivated teachers may face structural difficulties in crossing the threshold from intention to action [3, 14].

To empirically investigate this structural barrier, this study integrates the Technology Acceptance Model 3 (TAM3), which specifically accounts for environmental facilitators [12]. We conducted a survey of 409 special education teachers in Taiwan, analyzing the data via Partial Least Squares Structural Equation Modeling (PLS-SEM). This approach allows for a rigorous assessment of how environmental support moderates the transition to usage. The findings aim to offer evidence-based recommendations for policymakers to optimize resource allocation, helping bridge the digital divide and ensuring that digital inclusion efforts result in tangible classroom practices.

2 State of the Art

2.1 Theoretical Framework: Why TAM3?

While the classical Technology Acceptance Model (TAM) identifies Perceived Usefulness and Ease of Use as core predictors, it often falls short in explaining adoption behaviors within resource-constrained educational environments. Although the Unified Theory of Acceptance and Use of Technology (UTAUT) offers macro-level explanatory power, it lacks the granularity required to diagnose specific practical bottlenecks in special education [3]. In contrast, TAM3 [12] provides a more nuanced framework by introducing "External Control" (EC) and "Computer Self-Efficacy (CSE)" as distinct antecedents. EC is particularly critical in this context, as it directly quantifies the degree of administrative and infrastructural support. This theoretical lens allows for a precise diagnosis of the "high intention, low usage" paradox, shifting the analytical focus from individual psychological willingness to structural and environmental enablers.

2.2 Alignment Between VR Technology and Special Education Needs

The pedagogical affordances of Virtual Reality (VR)—specifically immersion, controllability, and safety—demonstrate a precise fit with special education requirements. Literature indicates that VR provides error-tolerant environments for repetitive practice, significantly enhancing attention regulation in students with ADHD [7]. Furthermore, it scaffolds social interaction skills for students with ASD [9, 13], and facilitates the acquisition of vocational skills [2]. These functional benefits directly address practical teaching dilemmas, resonating with the strongly "task-oriented" nature of special education teachers and serving as a primary driver for their adoption intention.

2.3 The Implementation Gap: From Efficacy to Structural Constraints

Despite the clear pedagogical fit, a significant implementation gap persists. The transition from "laboratory efficacy" to "classroom reality" is stifled by structural constraints: high maintenance costs, limited hardware accessibility, and a scarcity of longitudinal adoption studies [10, 11]. Within the TAM3 framework, these systemic barriers represent a critical deficit in "External Control" (EC). While prior research has predominantly focused on efficacy verification (does it work?), this study shifts the analytical lens to adoption mechanics (why is it not used?) [10, 11], positing EC as the decisive structural factor that blocks the translation of high intention into actual teaching behavior.

3 Methodology

3.1 Research Framework and Participants

This study utilizes TAM3 [12], integrating Computer Self-Efficacy (CSE) and External Control (EC) as key antecedents. An online survey using purposive sampling targeted special education teachers in Taiwan (April–May 2025). Mandatory response settings ensured zero missing data. Of 410 submissions, 409 valid responses were retained (99.8% effective rate). The sample comprises primarily female elementary school teachers aged 31–40, reflecting the current demographic structure of the local special education workforce.

3.2 Instruments

Measurement items were adapted from Venkatesh & Bala [12] and Davis [4], then translated and modified to align with specific special education scenarios (e.g., reframing "system use" as "instructional integration"). A 5-point Likert scale measured constructs including PU, PEOU, ATU, CSE, BI, EC, and ASU. A pilot test confirmed linguistic clarity and content validity prior to distribution. (Cronbach's $\alpha = .74 \sim .96$).

3.3 Data Analysis Strategy

PLS-SEM (via SmartPLS 3.0) was selected for its robust handling of prediction-oriented models and non-normal data. The analysis followed a standard two-stage procedure: (1) Measurement Model: Assessed reliability (CR, Cronbach's α) and validity (AVE > .50; HTMT < .90) to ensure psychometric soundness; (2) Structural Model: Employed bootstrapping (5,000 subsamples) to test path coefficients (β) and hypotheses, utilizing R^2 and SRMR to evaluate overall model fit.

4 Results

4.1 Measurement Model and Descriptive Statistics

Descriptive analysis reveals a critical dichotomy: while teachers exhibited high Behavioral Intention ($M = 4.01 \sim 4.22$), reflecting strong adoption motivation, External Control (EC) showed the highest variability ($SD = .91 \sim 1.25$). This high standard deviation in EC quantitatively corroborates the "uneven resource distribution" across schools. Regarding psychometric properties, the measurement model demonstrated robust reliability and validity. All constructs exceeded the recommended thresholds: Composite Reliability (CR) ranged from .77 to .90, and Average Variance Extracted (AVE) surpassed .50. Furthermore, discriminant validity was established as all Heterotrait-Monotrait (HTMT) ratios remained below the conservative threshold of .90 [6].

4.2 Structural Model Assessment

The structural model assessment, conducted via bootstrapping (5,000 subsamples), supported all proposed hypotheses (H1–H6). The model demonstrates substantial explanatory power, accounting for 65% of the variance in behavior. Key path coefficients indicate that Perceived Usefulness ($\beta = .75$, $p < .001$) is the dominant driver of Attitude Toward Using, surpassing Perceived Ease of Use ($\beta = .61$, $p < .001$) serve as the core drivers of Attitude. Attitude, in turn, strongly predicts Behavioral Intention ($\beta = .76$, $p < .001$), which is subsequently strongly associated with Actual System Use ($\beta = .81$, $p < .001$). Crucially, the antecedents specific to TAM3—Computer Self-Efficacy ($\beta = .76$) and External Control ($\beta = .44$)—both exerted significant positive effects on Behavior Intention. This confirms that adoption is jointly driven by individual capability and environmental support (Table 1).

Table 1. Results of Hypothesis Testing for the Structural Model

Hypo	Path Relationship	Expected Direction	Path Coeff	t	p	Result
H1	PU → ATU	Positive	0.75**	12.64	0.00	Supported
H2	PEOU → ATU	Positive	0.61**	4.58	0.00	Supported
H3	ATU → BI	Positive	0.76**	9.82	0.00	Supported
H4	EC → BI	Positive	0.44*	2.46	0.01	Supported
H5	CSE → BI	Positive	0.70**	6.51	0.00	Supported
H6	BI → ASU	Positive	0.81**	33.62	0.00	Supported

$p < .05$*, $p < .01$**

4.3 Group Differences and Structural Constraints

Difference analysis (t-test/ANOVA) highlighted significant demographic disparities. At the individual level, male teachers reported significantly higher Computer Self-Efficacy (CSE) and Ease of Use (PEOU) compared to female teachers ($p < .05$). More critically, at the structural level, junior high school teachers perceived significantly higher External Control (EC) than those in preschool settings ($p < .001$). This finding provides empirical evidence of a "digital divide" rooted in resource allocation rather than teacher motivation. Notably, operational experience did not significantly moderate Behavioral

Intention, suggesting that high motivation is ubiquitous across the workforce. However, the translation of this intention into practice remains strictly gated by the availability of environmental resources (Fig. 1).

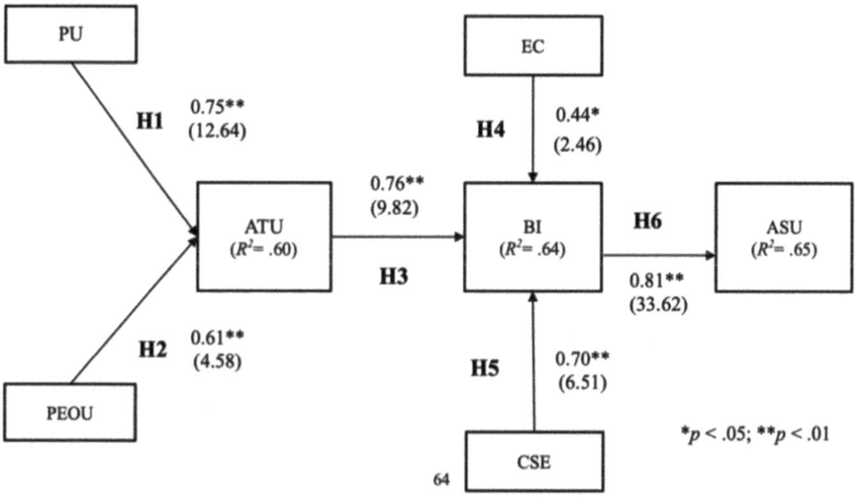

Fig. 1. Path verification diagram of the research model (path coefficients and *t*-values)

4.4 Discussion and Implications

This study empirically validates the applicability of TAM3 in special education, elucidating the decision-making process from intention to behavior. The results confirm the "task-oriented" nature of special education teachers: their adoption decisions are primarily driven by Perceived Usefulness ($\beta = .75$), indicating that VR is evaluated strictly on its ability to align with Individualized Education Program (IEP) goals and scaffold learning. However, a critical "intention-behavior gap" was identified, significantly influenced by the perception of External Control (EC). While motivation is high across the board, actual implementation is gated by structural constraints rather than individual unwillingness. The significant variance in EC ($SD = 1.25$) highlights an uneven distribution of resources, particularly disadvantaging preschool and elementary sectors.

To bridge this digital divide, we propose a two-tiered strategy: (1) Targeted Resource Allocation: Administrative authorities should prioritize specific infrastructure investments—such as dedicated maintenance budgets, flexible procurement models, and on-site technical support staff—in preschool and elementary special education, addressing the structural deficits identified in the difference analysis; (2) Capacity Building: Professional development should shift from general awareness to "task-oriented" hands-on training, specifically designed to enhance Computer Self-Efficacy (CSE).

In conclusion, substantive VR integration requires more than just teacher enthusiasm; it demands a robust support ecosystem. Only by ensuring resource availability and reducing technical thresholds can the field overcome environmental constraints and realize the full pedagogical potential of VR. However, several limitations should be noted. Actual

System Use (ASU) was measured via self-reported frequency, which may introduce common-method bias inherent in cross-sectional surveys. Future studies should incorporate objective usage logs to further validate these findings, and involve diverse stakeholders—including students with disabilities, parents, and therapists—through participatory design. Additionally, investigating whether these structural adoption barriers persist across other fields of Assistive Technology (AT) would provide a more comprehensive perspective on the inclusive digital ecosystem.

Disclosure of Interests. The authors have no competing interests to declare that are relevant to the content of this article.

References

1. Angra, S., Jangra, S., Gulzar, Y., Sharma, B., Singh, G., Onn, C.W.: Twenty-two years of advancements in augmented and virtual reality: a bibliometric and systematic review. Front. Comput. Sci. **7**, 1470038 (2025). https://doi.org/10.3389/fcomp.2025.1470038
2. Chang, I.H., Sher, Y.J., Hung, R.C., Tai, K.H.: A study on the usability of virtual reality vocational skills training for students with autism in vocational high schools. J. Spec. Educ. **55**, 39–80 (2022). https://doi.org/10.53106/207455832022060055002
3. Chiu, Y.L., Wang, J.C.: Exploring the behavioral intention of elementary school teachers in Kaohsiung City towards using iPads for teaching under the "Tablets for Every Student" program through the Unified Theory of Acceptance and Use of Technology. J. Ind. Technol. Educ. **6**, 110–128 (2023). https://doi.org/10.6306/JITE.202307_(16).0007
4. Davis, F.D.: Perceived usefulness, perceived ease of use, and user acceptance of information technology. MIS Q. **13**(3), 319–340 (1989). https://doi.org/10.2307/249008
5. Dechsling, A., Vister, O.M., Johansen, T.E., Børtveit, L., Herikstad, Y., Nordahl-Hansen, A.: Implementing virtual reality in special education: teachers' perspectives. Int. J. Disabil. Dev. Educ. 1–16 (2024). https://doi.org/10.1080/1034912X.2024.2427603
6. Henseler, J., Ringle, C.M., Sarstedt, M.: A new criterion for assessing discriminant validity in variance-based structural equation modeling. J. Acad. Mark. Sci. **43**(1), 115–135 (2015). https://doi.org/10.1007/s11747-014-0403-8
7. Hung, S.H.: The effectiveness of using immersive virtual reality jazz drumming games to reduce interfering behaviors in students with Attention Deficit Hyperactivity Disorder. Master's thesis, National Taiwan Normal University (2025). (Unpublished)
8. Lin, P.R., Lin, C.T.: Small fish can also drive submarines: an action research on electric wheelchair intervention for students with profound and multiple disabilities. Bull. Spec. Educ. **38**(2), 99–125 (2013). https://doi.org/10.6172/BSE.201307.3802005
9. Meng, Y.R., Yeh, C.C.: A study of the effectiveness of social skills learning for students with autism in primary and junior high schools through virtual reality instruction system. J. Educ. Commun. Technol. **23**, 39–58 (2020). https://doi.org/10.6137/RECT.202008_(123).0003
10. Samala, A.D., Rawas, S., Rahmadika, S., Criollo-C, S., Fikri, R., Sandra, R.P.: Virtual reality in education: global trends, challenges, and impacts—game changer or passing trend? Discov. Educ. **4**(1), 1–45 (2025). https://doi.org/10.1007/s44217-025-00650-z
11. Stracke, C.M., et al.: Immersive virtual reality in higher education: a systematic review of the scientific literature. Virtual Real. **29**(2), 1–21 (2025). https://doi.org/10.1007/s10055-025-01136-x

12. Venkatesh, V., Bala, H.: Technology acceptance model 3 and a research agenda on interventions. Decis. Sci. **39**(2), 273–315 (2008). https://doi.org/10.1111/j.1540-5915.2008.00192.x
13. Yeh, C.C., Meng, Y.R.: Effectiveness of Virtual Reality Social Skills Training for Students with Autism and Social Difficulties Observed Through Behavior and Brain Waves. Appl. Sci. **15**(9), 4600 (2025). https://doi.org/10.3390/app15094600
14. Yeh, C.F., Yang, H.S.: Applying virtual reality and digital game-based learning to local culture teaching for elementary school students: An empirical study on learning effectiveness and local identity. J. Educ. Commun. Technol. **126**, 1–19 (2021). https://doi.org/10.6137/RECT.202108_(126).0001

New Methods for Creating Accessible Material in Higher Education

New Methods for Creating Accessible Material in Higher Education
Introduction to the Special Thematic Session

Michaela Hanousková[1], Lukáš Másilko[1], Karin Müller[2], Svatoslav Ondra[1](✉), Andrea Petz[3], and Thorsten Schwarz[2]

[1] Masaryk University, Brno, Czech Republic
{hanouskova,masilko,ondra}@teiresias.muni.cz
[2] Karlsruhe Institute of Technology (KIT), Karlsruhe, Germany
{karin.e.mueller,thorsten.schwarz}@kit.edu
[3] Integriert Studieren, Johannes Kepler University, Linz, Austria
andrea.petz@jku.at
https://www.teiresias.muni.cz/ , https://www.access.kit.edu/english/ ,
https://www.jku.at/institut-integriert-studieren/

Abstract. This paper introduces the Special Thematic Session (STS) on *New Methods for Creating Accessible Material in Higher Education* [1]. Inclusive education, as mandated by the UN Convention on the Rights of Persons with Disabilities, demands universities to provide accessible study conditions. However, many study materials lack accessibility especially for visual content such as graphics and there are only few universities that offer a regular literature transfer service. Therefore, most students have to create solutions themselves. It is therefore necessary to develop new standardized methods and tools that make it easier for students with visual impairments and print disabilities to access visual and STEM content of teaching material and exams e.g. by generating captions of charts, providing standardized descriptions and making graphics available tactilely.

Keywords: Accessibility · Higher Education · Inclusive Education · Disability · STEM Accessibility

1 Introduction

Access to education is crucial for all people, regardless of their individual circumstances or limitations. This principle is not only a matter of equality, but also a cornerstone of an inclusive society that values and promotes the diversity and uniqueness of each individual. In the pursuit of inclusive education, as mandated by Article 24 of the UN Convention on the Rights of Persons with Disabilities, access to higher education is recognized as a fundamental right. This applies not only to physical accessibility, but also to the area of teaching materials; universities and other institutions are obliged to provide barrier-free study conditions. Thus, it is crucial that institutions in higher education make their teaching and

K. Miesenberger et al. (Eds.): ICCHP 2026, LNCS 16867, pp. 125–130, 2027.
https://doi.org/10.1007/978-3-032-31308-9_15

learning materials accessible to ensure that all students can benefit equally from educational opportunities.

A UNESCO report [2] emphasizes the importance of accessible educational materials and highlights that they can help make education systems more inclusive and promote participation for all students. Furthermore, UNESCO stresses that the provision of accessible materials is not only an ethical imperative, but also an important prerequisite for achieving the Sustainable Development Goals.

The benefits of providing accessible materials are manifold. It's not just about meeting legal requirements, but also about creating an inclusive learning environment where all students can reach their full potential. Accessible materials not only help people with disabilities, but also mainstream students who may benefit from alternative ways of presenting or accessing learning.

However, many educational institutions do not provide fully accessible teaching and learning materials or are even not aware of their obligation to provide all students with access to teaching materials. It is mostly up to the students to decide how they obtain the teaching materials and how they are made accessible, for example by hiring assistants to convert literature, teaching them how to make documents accessible or asking lecturers to make their material available digitally so that they at least have access to the content.

This has far-reaching implications for how people with disabilities access education. A lack of accessible materials can lead to students with disabilities or other special needs being excluded from full participation in academic life.

A possible solution involves new methods like artificial intelligence or LLMs (Large Language Models) that show potential in e.g. automatically describing complex structures like tables or mixed/non-text elements like pictures, graphs, charts etc.

However, first examples show that this process only works semi-automated in the moment - a human supervision is needed to check e.g. the descriptions on completeness but also on a logically appropriate cue, a red thread through the picture or even chart described.

Often, pictures and other mixed/non-text alternatives are used additionally to text - and a verbose description of an element that is fully explained in one of the paragraphs above does keep the readers from efficiently grabbing the idea, use the provided content and results in using up the readers' time and attention.

In the moment, the powerful algorithms of an LLM or AI are not able to link mixed/non-text elements to information/positions in a text or understand the text around non-textual content and are also not able to decide whether the information in it must be explained and represented or can easily be discarded.

So a certain amount of research, definition and standardisation work needs to be done before these technologies can reach their full potential and find their way into making up complex structures and mixed/non-textual content accessibly and usable instead building up new barriers.

This Special Thematic Session (STS)[1] seeks to explore the multifaceted challenges associated with creating accessible teaching and learning materials in

[1] The current paper is a slightly modified version of [8].

higher education for students with visual impairments and print disabilities. By examining tools, methodologies, and best practices, this session endeavors to equip educators and institutions with the knowledge and resources necessary to foster truly inclusive learning environments.

2 Current Solutions to Improve Access to Teaching Material

Teaching material includes a wide range of document types, from handwritten and digital notes to scientific papers, lecture slides, video lectures, books, and assignments. In addition, they frequently comprise graphical content in two and three dimensions, which are essential for class participation, lab activities, and examinations. However, despite these mandates, a significant portion of educational materials remains inaccessible to students with visual impairments.

Addressing this accessibility gap necessitates a comprehensive approach, tailored to the unique needs and working methods of individual students.

In the following paragraphs, we present four approaches that developed new solutions on how to improve the accessibility of teaching materials, addressing the barriers in access to math formulae, function graphs, IPA symbols, as well as to video lectures and lecture slides in general.

2.1 Accessibility of Graphics

While information is often presented visually by pictures, schemes, charts, or graphs to summarize complex content, it is not accessible to blind individuals. There are currently three main possibilities to make them accessible: (i) creating a description, (ii) substituting the graphical content with another form (e.g., replacing charts with tables), and/or (iii) providing a tactile graphic that allows blind users to explore graphical content via touch. Toyoda et al. [7] proposed to combine (i) and (iii) to access mathematical function graphs. Their system simultaneously generates rule-based audio descriptions and tactile graphics from mathematical expressions. By adopting a rule-based approach using numerical analysis, the system ensures high consistency and reproducibility in the generated text, preventing variations that might occur with different human test creators. This is vital for university entrance examinations where fair conditions are important. Evaluation with sighted students confirmed that these descriptions allowed participants to accurately reconstruct the graphs, demonstrating the system's ability to help users form precise mental images of mathematical structures. Furthermore, based on feedback from a blind faculty member, the system was enhanced to describe complex relationships between multiple graphs, such as parallelism and intersections, which are difficult to perceive through touch alone. Automatically generated description of a graph that is provided together with its tactile form aims to support comprehension and efficiency of a reader when exploring the tactile graph.

Until recently, descriptions were mainly created manually by experts who decided which content of a graphic was most essential and then described it in words. It is usually up to the experts how they describe and structure a description. Now, gradually, it is possible to involve automated tools (either based on AI, or not) in the process of describing visual information. Toyoda et al. [7] based on Sobota et al. [6] have recognized the lack of standardized descriptions for mathematical function graphs, particularly for blind individuals, and they propose to develop a comprehensive description standard in a user-centered design process. Thus, it is better ensured that the descriptions are more standardized, structured and reproducible.

2.2 Accessibility of Documents

Since people who rely on modern assistive technologies are largely dependent on the existence of digital versions of learning materials, one would expect that in today's digital age, document accessibility would be a simple and solved issue. While the easy availability of digital tools for the creation and editing of documents has brought with it the existence of a massive number of digital documents, paradoxically, it has not yet ensured their greater accessibility. The emphasis on the visual aspect, but the omission of technical correctness of the typesetting, often brings difficulties not only to users of assistive technologies. Moreover, complexity and difficulties in accessibility of learning materials arise from the fact that they include not only text documents, but e.g. lecture slides, video recordings, 2D complex spreadsheets, etc.

Kobayashi et al. [4] have focused on obstacles in the accessibility of text documents that are caused by a symbolic alphabet used in a document, namely the International Phonetic Alphabet. Compared to other typical accessibility issues, such as math formulae and other STEM symbolic expressions, this is quite unheeded area of document accessibility. Their proposed solution is a low-cost, intuitive system that utilizes a standard laptop, a webcam, and swell-paper tactile sheets to teach IPA phonetic symbols. Using augmented reality (AR) markers and the Google MediaPipe library, the system tracks finger positions to provide immediate audio feedback when specific tactile symbols are touched. This approach allows students to explore spatial organization within an IPA chart tactually while receiving auditory pronunciation feedback without needing expensive dedicated devices. Preliminary evaluations showed high engagement, with participants comparing the interactive learning process to a "game-like" experience.

Komada et al. [5] address the main barriers in accessibility of PowerPoint slides. They integrate generative AI and iterative human-in-the-loop personalization in order to generate alternative text of graphics, detecting reading order and also recognizing mathematical formulae. Their system employs a two-stage architecture. Stage 1 performs automated format conversion (alt-text, reading order, math OCR), while Stage 2 applies user-guided personalization. A key contribution is the use of a structured user profile schema that captures individual needs, including assistive technology context, preferred description styles (e.g., concise vs. narrative), and cognitive style parameters. By positioning educators and disabled users as active authors through natural-language interaction, the system ensures that accessible content is semi-automatically tailored to the specific disability context and curricular needs of the student.

Anderer et al. [3] have proposed a prototype of the AI-driven system that guides user to make a video lecture and related PDF lecture slides more accessible. The system allows users to ask a chatbot about visual content in video frames and facilitates semantic navigation through lecture transcripts. Additional features include notification sounds for slide transitions and customizable prompts to tailor how image descriptions are generated. Authors have focused on a long-term study of usability (semester-long evaluation) in order to get much more valuable feedback. The longitudinal study revealed that factors like technical friction and high cognitive load are significant barriers to technology adoption, findings that were not evident in short-term tests. They advocate for frequent communication with participants and transparency regarding technical challenges to prevent user frustration.

3 Conclusion

In summary, the contributions of this Special Thematic Session stress the importance of enhancing accessibility and inclusivity in higher education. The presented approaches apply innovative tools, methods, and develop standards that enable educators and institutions to improve equitable access to learning materials for all students, regardless of their abilities. There are still many research questions which have not yet been answered. The new approaches are promising that materials can be made accessible more quickly in the future by overcoming barriers (semi-)automatically and access to information is facilitated for all.

References

1. Müller, K., Stiefelhagen, R., Hanousková, M., Ondra, S., Másilko, L., Petz, A.: STS new methods for creating accessible material in higher education. In: Miesenberger, K., Petrie, H., Peňáz, P. (eds.), ICCHP 2026, Computers Helping People with Special Needs, 20th International Conference; Linz, Austria, Proceedings. Springer (2026)
2. UNESCO. Every learner matters and matters equally: making education inclusive; background document, UNESCO, Paris. https://unesdoc.unesco.org/ark:/48223/pf0000388991.locale=en
3. Anderer, K., Müller, K., Wölfel, M.: Lessons learned for long-term accessibility studies: a case study with blind and low vision students on a prototype for accessing video lectures. In: Miesenberger, K., Petrie, H., Penaz, P. (eds.), ICCHP 2026, Computers Helping People with Special Needs, 20th International Conference; Linz, Austria, Proceedings. Springer (2026)
4. Kobayashi, M., Kobayashi, Y. Tactile IPA chart with audio feedback for visually impaired students. In: Petz, A., Miesenberger, K. (eds.): ICCHP Open Access Compendium "Future Perspectives on Accessibility, AT and eInclusion"; Linz, Austria, Proceedings. Johannes Kepler University Linz (2026)

5. Komada, T., Yamaguchi, K.: AIDE: Integrating generative AI and user-guided personalization for accessible STEM education. In: Miesenberger, K., Petrie, H., Penaz, P. (eds.), ICCHP 2026, Computers Helping People with Special Needs, 20th International Conference; Linz, Austria, Proceedings. Springer (2026)
6. Sobota, Z.E., Freese, A.-C., Schwarz, T., Müller, K.: Towards establishing a description standard of mathematical function graphs for people with blindness. In: Miesenberger, K., Kobayashi, M., Penaz, P. (eds.) ICCHP 2024, Computers Helping People with Special Needs, 19th International Conference, Springer, Linz, Austria, Proceedings (2024)
7. Toyoda, R., Ashida, C., Fujiyoshi, A.: Automatic generation of audio descriptions and tactile graphics for function graphs to support visually impaired students in university entrance examinations. In: Miesenberger, K., Petrie, H., Penaz, P. (eds.), ICCHP 2026, Computers Helping People with Special Needs, 20th International Conference; Linz, Austria, Proceedings. Springer (2026)
8. Hanousková, M., et al.: STS new methods for creating accessible material in higher education. In: Miesenberger, K., Peňáz, P., Kobayashi, M. (eds.) Computers Helping People with Special Needs. ICCHP 2024. LNCS, vol. 14750. Springer, Cham (2024). https://doi.org/10.1007/978-3-031-62846-7_34

AIDE: Integrating Generative AI and User-Guided Personalization for Accessible STEM Education

Toshihiko Komada[1,2](✉) and Katsuhito Yamaguchi[1,2]

[1] Nihon University, Funabashi, Chiba 274-8501, Japan
eugene@sciaccess.net
[2] NPO: Science Accessibility Net, Fukuoka, Fukuoka 814-0001, Japan
komada.toshihiko@nihon-u.ac.jp

Abstract. PowerPoint slides remain the dominant medium for university STEM instruction, yet present significant accessibility barriers, particularly for visual impairment and dyslexia. While generative AI has progressed on format-level challenges such as alt-text and reading-order detection, personalization to individual needs remains beyond generic AI. We present AIDE (Automated Inclusive Document Engine), integrating generative AI with co-design and iterative human-in-the-loop (HITL) personalization to transform inaccessible STEM slides into individually customized accessible materials. Unlike prior systems where HITL serves quality assurance, AIDE positions educators, support staff, and disabled users themselves as active authors of their accessible content through natural-language interaction. Preliminary consultations with nine stakeholders—four educators with disability support expertise, four disabled individuals, and one expert participant proficient in screen reader operation—suggest that personalization needs exceed what generic approaches can accommodate. We outline integration with deployed accessibility infrastructure and a roadmap toward scalable personalized accessibility.

Keywords: Accessibility · STEM Education · Personalization · Human-in-the-Loop · Generative AI · Co-Design

1 Introduction

PowerPoint slides dominate university STEM instruction but present accessibility barriers: missing alternative descriptions, inaccessible mathematical notation, and undetected reading order [8,21]. The European Accessibility Act [6] makes addressing these barriers a legal as well as pedagogical imperative.

Generative AI has progressed on format-level challenges such as alt-text generation and reading-order detection [15], but personalization to individual needs—disability context, curricular specifics, cognitive style—remains beyond generic solutions [14].

K. Miesenberger et al. (Eds.): ICCHP 2026, LNCS 16867, pp. 131–139, 2027.
https://doi.org/10.1007/978-3-032-31308-9_16

We present AIDE (Automated Inclusive Document Engine). Our contributions are threefold. *First*, we articulate a conceptual separation between format-level and personalization-level challenges, realized as a two-stage architecture: an abstraction layer decouples the pipeline from the vision-language model, while the Model Context Protocol [2] supplies external knowledge sources—profiles, curriculum context—to the generation process. *Second*, we propose an accessibility-specific user profile coupled with human-in-the-loop refinement, repositioning HITL from quality assurance to authoring by non-experts. *Third*, we situate AIDE as a continuation of deployed Japanese accessibility infrastructure—InftyReader Online [21] and Chatty Library [20]—rather than an isolated prototype.

2 State of the Art

Efforts to automate STEM document accessibility progress along a three-stage trajectory. At *recognition*, the InftyReader family pioneered integrated OCR for mathematical documents [18]. At *structuring*, InftyReader Online extends this to end-to-end conversion of PDF and PowerPoint into accessible forms such as Fixed-layout DAISY, targeting dyslexic learners [21]. These systems establish the conversion substrate on which a *personalization* stage such as AIDE operates. Generative AI has begun to complement this trajectory: vision-language models support alt-text generation [15] and image interpretation addressing dyslexia and dyscalculia [14], while retrieval-based alternative-text generation mitigates fully automated captions [12]. Persistent hallucination and semantic inaccuracy remain [10], motivating a design in which human oversight is a structural component of the pipeline.

While generative AI scales alt-text production, human oversight remains essential for semantic accuracy [15], and large vision-language models are prone to factual hallucinations [10]. Taxonomies of human-in-the-loop machine learning distinguish human-as-annotator from human-as-co-learner configurations [11], and human-AI interaction guidelines emphasize preserving user control across iterative refinement [1]. Existing HITL systems for accessibility—retrieval-based alt-text [12] and natural-language diagram access [13]—treat human involvement as quality assurance rather than personalization authoring.

Deployed Japanese accessibility infrastructure such as Chatty Library [20] and InftyReader Online [21] offers a pragmatic deployment foundation. *Participatory design* originates in Scandinavian information-systems research [17]; contemporary *co-design* foregrounds sustained designer–user collaboration [4,16]. Neither tradition, to our knowledge, has previously been combined with generative AI pipelines for personalized STEM accessibility.

None of these strands combines the three axes that AIDE proposes: (i) a structured user profile schema coupling disability context, content preferences, cognitive style, and course context as first-class personalization inputs; (ii) a two-stage architectural separation with a standardized interface for injecting external knowledge sources into the generation pipeline; and (iii) positioning as a continuation of deployed accessibility infrastructure [20,21]. AIDE addresses all three jointly.

3 AIDE System Design

3.1 System Architecture

AIDE is a two-stage pipeline. Stage 1 (format conversion) ingests native slide artifacts and emits a structured, accessibility-aware intermediate representation. Stage 2 (personalization) applies user-profile-driven transformations with human-in-the-loop refinement. Figure 1 shows the data flow from raw slides to personalized accessible output.

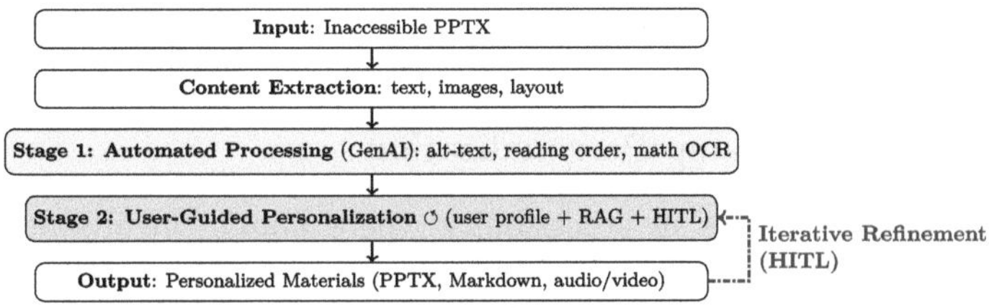

Fig. 1. AIDE system architecture. A two-stage pipeline converts inaccessible PPTX into personalized accessible materials. Stage 1 performs automated format conversion (alt-text, reading order, math OCR); Stage 2 applies user-guided personalization with iterative HITL refinement.

Stage 1 targets Microsoft PowerPoint (.pptx). Office Open XML parsing is performed with `python-pptx`; agent orchestration via Claude Code [3] assists content extraction (text runs, shape geometry, embedded images, reading order). Mathematical notation present as imagery is routed to symbolic OCR pathways that preserve LaTeX-level structural fidelity.

The stage emits a JSON intermediate representation (IR) accessibility-aware by construction. Each node records a WCAG 2.2 role [19], preliminary alternative text from the vision-language model, a confidence signal used by Stage 2 to prioritize review, and course-context fields supporting retrieval-augmented grounding [9] via curriculum-local context (runtime retrieval from external knowledge bases is planned as future work).

AIDE employs an abstraction layer that separates core pipeline logic from the underlying vision-language model, enabling future substitution as the model landscape evolves. The current implementation uses Gemini as the generative backbone. Complementarily, the Model Context Protocol [2] provides a standardized interface for injecting external knowledge sources—including user profiles, curriculum context for RAG-based grounding, and auxiliary processing tools—into the generation process, decoupling knowledge provision from model choice.

3.2 Co-Design Process Informed by Participatory Design Principles

AIDE's design process is informed by the participatory design tradition [17], the principle of direct participation by disabled people [5], and by contemporary *co-design* practice foregrounding sustained designer–user collaboration [4,16]. We characterize the current stage as *formative co-design* [16]: nine stakeholders—four educators with disability support expertise, four disabled individuals, and one expert participant proficient in screen reader operation—informed design commitments through semi-structured consultations and one think-aloud session. Summative co-design [4]—iterative cycles with a stable cohort—is deferred to the planned field study (Sect. 5.5).

Participatory design principles here are methodological rather than procedural: consultations surfaced the diversity of description-style preferences that motivated the `description_style` and `image_detail_level` fields (Sect. 3.4), while the usability session validated non-expert natural-language refinement.

3.3 Human-In-The-Loop Personalization

Unlike prior HITL systems in accessibility where human involvement primarily serves quality assurance [12,13], AIDE repositions HITL as the mechanism through which personalization is *authored*. The user profile (Sect. 3.4) supplies initial constraints; iterative natural-language feedback refines them in context. We do not assume the authoring party is an accessibility expert: educators, support staff, and disabled users themselves can act as authors of their accessible content without first becoming familiar with accessibility metadata languages.

Table 1 contrasts prior HITL accessibility tools with AIDE along four dimensions—purpose, users, iteration, and *authorship*, the fourth being new: prior systems treat human-generated input as correction signal, whereas AIDE treats it as authoring intent.

Table 1. Comparison of human-in-the-loop approaches in accessibility research.

Dimension	Prior Work	AIDE
Purpose	Quality assurance	Personalization
Users	Domain experts	Including non-experts
Iteration	Single verification	Iterative refinement
Authorship	Correction signal	Authoring intent

Three commitments further distinguish AIDE's loop: *curriculum-aware* grounding via RAG [9], *instructional alignment* between profile and output, and a lightweight *profile-selection heuristic* that interprets early user turns as evidence for refining profile fields. Formal evaluation is planned as future work.

3.4 User Profile Schema

A core contribution of AIDE is a structured user profile coupling disability context, content preferences, cognitive style, and course context as first-class inputs to personalization. Table 2 presents ten fields across four dimensions: D1 captures assistive-technology context; D2 encodes description style, mathematical representation, and image detail preferences; D3 represents cognitive style parameters; and D4 binds the profile to a course through a retrieval key for RAG [9]. Fields are annotated by provenance: *impl* marks those currently instantiated; *obs* marks requirements surfaced during consultations and scheduled for subsequent integration.

Table 2. AIDE User Profile schema: four dimensions, ten fields.

Dimension	Field	Example Values
D1: AT Context	`disability_type`[a]	visual_impairment, dyslexia, low_vision
	`assistive_technology`	NVDA, JAWS, VoiceOver, TalkBack
D2: Content Preferences	`description_style`	concise_factual, narrative_trend, structured_bullet
	`math_representation`	mathml, natural_language, latex_verbal
	`image_detail_level`	brief, detailed, trend_based
D3: Cognitive Style	`reading_pace`	slow, normal, fast
	`cognitive_load_preference`	minimal, moderate, dense
	`technical_vocabulary_familiarity`	novice, intermediate, expert
D4: Course Context	`course_id`	string (RAG retrieval key)
	`language`	en, ja, de, ...

[a] Indicative examples; the schema accepts any disability category aligned with WCAG 2.2 perspectives, including auditory, motor, cognitive, and co-occurring conditions.

4 First Results from Stakeholder Consultation

We conducted preliminary consultations with nine stakeholders: four educators with disability support expertise, four disabled individuals, and one expert participant proficient in screen reader operation who engaged in a think-aloud session on an early prototype. The central observation is that personalization needs were substantially more diverse than a single accessibility template can accommodate: participants requested different description-detail levels, different trade-offs between narrative and bulleted framing, and distinct preferences over how mathematical notation should be rendered aloud—from MathML verbalization to informal paraphrase. These observations directly motivated the user-profile schema (Sect. 3.4).

Our sample spanned visual impairment and low vision but did not include dyslexic participants; dyslexia-oriented design remains informed by prior work [14,21] and will be broadened in the planned field study. For mathematical content—several participants' most error-prone area—AIDE is designed to bridge to symbolic recognition via InftyReader Online [21]. Consultations were deliberately structured as formative co-design with alternating educator and disabled-user groups [16]; an IRB-approved summative field study is outlined in Sect. 5.5.

5 Discussion

5.1 Conceptual Framing

At the heart of AIDE is a conceptual separation between *format-level* accessibility challenges—increasingly tractable by automated pipelines—and *personalization-level* challenges, which are not. This separation frames the Discussion on generative-AI risks, scalability, and distinctive contributions.

5.2 Mitigating Hallucinations in Accessible Content Generation

Hallucination risk is a well-documented limitation of generative AI in educational contexts [10,15]. AIDE addresses this through a defense-in-depth strategy that leverages its architectural choices as structural safeguards.

First, the human-in-the-loop personalization loop (Sect. 3.3) is itself a verification mechanism: users review AI output, identify inaccuracies, and provide corrective natural-language feedback. Designed primarily for personalization, this loop concurrently serves as hallucination verification.

Second, the system grounds generation in course-specific context via retrieval-augmented generation [9], reducing reliance on parametric memory for domain-specific content.

Third, the user-profile schema (Table 2) constrains output along stylistic and cognitive dimensions, narrowing the latitude for creative embellishment that manifests as hallucinated detail.

Fourth, the abstraction layer admits future cross-validation between independent vision-language models as a future extension.

Finally, for mathematical content—where hallucination risk is highest—the modular pipeline admits integration with symbolic OCR systems such as InftyReader Online [21], offering a verification pathway grounded in deterministic recognition.

Formal measurement of these layers' effectiveness remains future work. Positioning hallucination mitigation as a structural property rather than a post-hoc filter reflects AIDE's principle that accessibility requires user agency throughout generation.

5.3 Scalability Through Amortized Personalization

A legitimate concern about human-in-the-loop systems is whether iterative feedback scales beyond individual use cases. AIDE addresses this through an *amortized feedback cost* model rather than per-document human effort.

User profiles (Table 2) are constructed once per user and reused across subsequent documents. In a course with many lecture slides, profile construction cost is incurred only once, while per-document refinement *tends to decrease* as profile coverage improves—though not monotonically, since individual documents may surface new preferences. Based on design intent, we target two to three refinement iterations per document—sufficient for meaningful adjustment while bounded to avoid cognitive fatigue; formal measurement is planned.

The three usage scenarios in Sect. 3.2 further distribute cost across organizational roles: in educator-driven deployment, a single instructor profile serves an entire class; in support-staff-driven deployment, accessibility specialists configure profiles for multiple students; and user-driven deployment supports individual self-service. These scenarios reflect realistic accessibility workflows in higher education.

The feedback required in Stage 2 is inversely related to the accuracy of Stage 1 format conversion. As generative AI models improve, human effort converges toward bounded preference-specification rather than unbounded error correction.

Future work includes iterative profile learning, community-shared profile templates, and integration with Chatty Library [20] and InftyReader Online [21], whose symbolic recognition pathway for mathematical content provides a deployment foundation for community-scale amortization. These mechanisms position HITL not as a bottleneck but as a bounded, one-time investment whose returns grow with continued use.

5.4 Distinctive Contributions

Placed against the state-of-the-art reviewed in Sect. 2, AIDE occupies a distinctive position along three complementary axes: (i) conceptual separation of format-level from personalization-level challenges, extended to the specific demands of STEM content and realized as an architecture-level decoupling between pipeline logic and generative backbone; (ii) a repositioning of human-in-the-loop interaction from expert quality assurance to authoring by non-experts; and (iii) explicit design for deployment on top of existing accessibility infrastructure. To our knowledge, the combined framing of these three axes as a unified design agenda has not been articulated in prior work, even where individual components have precedents.

5.5 Integration, Limitations, and Future Work

Integration is planned through Chatty Library [20] and InftyReader Online [21]. The current work reports formative co-design [7, 16]; an IRB-approved field study with a stable cohort is planned for summative evaluation of iteration counts, hallucination mitigation, and scalability. Limitations include the absence of dyslexic participants—a gap given the literature on dyslexia and dyscalculia [14]—and the single-model implementation, whose abstraction layer admits model substitution and future cross-validation as separate concerns from the Model Context Protocol's knowledge-injection role.

Acknowledgments. This work was supported by JSPS KAKENHI Grant Numbers JP24K06248 and JP25H00559. The authors thank A. Fujiyoshi and M. Suzuki for their valuable contributions to the InftyProject and related discussions that informed AIDE's design. We also thank the nine stakeholder participants whose consultations shaped AIDE's design commitments. The authors used large language models (Anthropic Claude, Google Gemini, and OpenAI Codex) to assist with text condensation and stylistic refinement under author supervision; all suggestions were reviewed and approved by the authors, who take full responsibility for the content of the manuscript.

Disclosure of Interests. The authors have no competing interests to declare.

References

1. Amershi, S., et al.: Guidelines for human-AI interaction. In: Proceedings of the 2019 CHI Conference on Human Factors in Computing Systems (CHI '19), pp. 1–13. ACM, Glasgow, Scotland UK (2019)
2. Anthropic: Model context protocol specification (2024)
3. Anthropic: Claude code: Agent skills for document processing (2025), source-available; governed by Anthropic Terms of Service
4. Bratteteig, T., Wagner, I.: Unpacking the notion of participation in participatory design. Comput. Support. Coop. Work (CSCW) **25**(6), 425–475 (2016)
5. Charlton, J.I.: Nothing About Us Without Us: Disability Oppression and Empowerment. University of California Press, Berkeley, CA (1998)
6. European Parliament and Council of the European Union: Directive (EU) 2019/882 of the European Parliament and of the Council of 17 April 2019 on the accessibility requirements for products and services (European Accessibility Act). Official Journal of the European Union, L 151, 7 June 2019 (2019)
7. Faulkner, L.: Beyond the five-user assumption: benefits of increased sample sizes in usability testing. Behav. Res. Methods Instrum. Comput. **35**(3), 379–383 (2003)
8. Komada, T., Yamaguchi, K., Suzuki, M.: Multilingual support for accessibility in PowerPoint STEM contents. In: Proceedings of the AAATE 2023. Studies in Health Technology and Informatics, vol. 306, pp. 144–150. IOS Press (2023)
9. Lewis, P., et al.: Retrieval-augmented generation for knowledge-intensive NLP tasks. Adv. Neural Inf. Process. Syst. **33**, 9459–9474 (2020)
10. Liu, H., et al.: A survey on hallucination in large vision-language models. arXiv preprint arXiv:2402.00253 (2024). v2, May 2024
11. Mosqueira-Rey, E., Hernández-Pereira, E., Alonso-Ríos, D., Bobes-Bascarán, J., Fernández-Leal, Á.: Human-in-the-loop machine learning: a state of the art. Artif. Intell. Rev. **56**(4), 3005–3054 (2023)
12. Moured, O., et al.: Alt4Blind: a user interface to simplify charts alt-text creation. In: Miesenberger, K., Peňáz, P., Kobayashi, M. (eds.) Computers Helping People with Special Needs. ICCHP 2024. LNCS, vol. 14750, pp. 420–428. Springer, Cham (2024). https://doi.org/10.1007/978-3-031-62846-7_35

13. Murillo-Morales, T., Miesenberger, K.: Effective non-visual access to diagrams via an augmented natural language interface. In: Miesenberger, K., Kouroupetroglou, G., Mavrou, K., Manduchi, R., Covarrubias Rodriguez, M., Penáz, P. (eds.) Computers Helping People with Special Needs. ICCHP-AAATE 2022. LNCS, vol. 13341, pp. 63–72. Springer, Cham (2022). https://doi.org/10.1007/978-3-031-08648-9_9
14. Nieddu, G., Gerazov, B., Pagliara, S.M., Zurru, L.A., Carrisi, M.C.: Evaluating large multimodal models for inclusive mathematics education: addressing dyslexia and dyscalculia in higher education. In: Mavrou, K., Encarnação, P. (eds.) Technology for Inclusion and Participation for All: Recent Achievements and Future Directions. AAATE 2025, pp. 224–231. Springer, Cham (2025). https://doi.org/10.1007/978-3-032-01628-7_28
15. Risi, M.: Comparative study on Gen-AI models to write alt text. In: Mavrou, K., Encarnação, P. (eds.) Technology for Inclusion and Participation for All: Recent Achievements and Future Directions. AAATE 2025, pp. 217–223. Springer, Cham (2025). https://doi.org/10.1007/978-3-032-01628-7_27
16. Sanders, E.B.N., Stappers, P.J.: Co-creation and the new landscapes of design. CoDesign **4**(1), 5–18 (2008)
17. Spinuzzi, C.: The methodology of participatory design. Tech. Commun. **52**(2), 163–174 (2005)
18. Suzuki, M., Tamari, F., Fukuda, R., Uchida, S., Kanahori, T.: INFTY: an integrated OCR system for mathematical documents. In: Proceedings of the 2003 ACM Symposium on Document Engineering (DocEng '03), pp. 95–104. ACM, Grenoble, France (2003)
19. W3C: Web content accessibility guidelines (WCAG) 2.2. W3C Recommendation, 5 October 2023 (2023)
20. Yamaguchi, K., Komada, T., Suzuki, M.: ChattyBox: Online accessibility service using Fixed-Layout DAISY. In: Miesenberger, K., Peňáz, P., Kobayashi, M. (eds.) Computers Helping People with Special Needs. ICCHP 2024. LNCS, vol. 14750, pp. 167–174. Springer, Cham (2024). https://doi.org/10.1007/978-3-031-62846-7_20
21. Yamaguchi, K., Komada, T., Suzuki, M.: Online conversion service of PDF/PowerPoint into accessible forms for dyslexic students. In: Mavrou, K., Encarnação, P. (eds.) Technology for Inclusion and Participation for All: Recent Achievements and Future Directions. AAATE 2025, pp. 33–40. Springer, Cham (2025). https://doi.org/10.1007/978-3-032-01628-7_5

Automatic Generation of Audio Descriptions and Tactile Graphics for Function Graphs to Support Visually Impaired Students in University Entrance Examinations

Riko Toyoda, Chiyori Ashida, and Akio Fujiyoshi(✉)

Graduate School of Science and Engineering, Ibaraki University, Hitachi, Japan
{25nm756x,25nm703n,akio.fujiyoshi.cs}@vc.ibaraki.ac.jp

Abstract. Function graphs play an important role in mathematics examinations for university entrance in Japan. However, for visually impaired students who use braille, only tactile graphics are provided, and sufficient information accessibility is not ensured. This paper proposes guidelines for standardized audio descriptions for function graphs used in mathematics examinations, and a system that simultaneously generates audio descriptions and tactile graphics from mathematical expressions. The standardized audio descriptions systematically explain the overall shape and mathematical characteristics of function graphs. By using the proposed system on a regular basis, visually impaired students can understand function graphs and solve related problems within the limited time available in examinations. To evaluate the effectiveness of the audio descriptions, an experiment was conducted with sighted university students, and the results confirmed that all participants were able to accurately draw the graphs using only the audio descriptions. Furthermore, based on feedback from a totally blind university faculty member, an additional function was implemented to describe the relationships between multiple graphs.

Keywords: Visually Impaired · Tactile Graphs · Accessibility

1 Introduction

In Japan, visually impaired students who study science and engineering subjects using braille must understand the shapes and mathematical properties of function graphs through tactile graphics. Tactile graphics are widely used in examinations, including university entrance examinations, and often serve as the only form of reasonable accommodation for braille users.

However, tactile graphics present several challenges. Understanding the overall shape of a graph requires a considerable amount of time, and in regions where the density of dots is high, it becomes difficult to accurately perceive

K. Miesenberger et al. (Eds.): ICCHP 2026, LNCS 16867, pp. 140–147, 2027.
https://doi.org/10.1007/978-3-032-31308-9_17

coordinates and shapes. In addition, in recent years, as the importance of data literacy has been increasingly emphasized, changes in the formats of university entrance examination questions have become a serious issue. Figure 1 shows function graphs presented in the 2024 Japanese Common Test for University Admissions. In the same subject in the 2023 examination, two function graphs were included, but both served only as reference figures to explain the problem setting. In contrast, in the 2024 examination, all twenty-four function graphs were presented as answer choices, requiring examinees to read and compare their contents. Such changes in question formats place visually impaired examinees at a disadvantage under the constraint of limited examination time.

This study proposes guidelines for standardized audio descriptions for function graphs in mathematics examination and presents a system that generates audio descriptions and tactile graphs from mathematical expressions, aiming to foster educational equity and support for visually impaired students. The standardized audio descriptions systematically explain the overall shape and mathematical characteristics of function graphs. The proposed system emphasizes consistency and reproducibility in the generated audio descriptions and employs a rule-based approach based on numerical analysis to generate explanatory text. By providing descriptions according to predefined rules, the system prevents variations in descriptive content and expression across different test creators, thereby enabling examinees to work under consistent conditions.

The effectiveness of the proposed audio descriptions was evaluated through an experiment involving sighted university students, which confirmed that all participants could accurately reconstruct the graphs using only the audio descriptions. Furthermore, based on feedback from a visually impaired faculty member, the system was enhanced with an additional function to describe the relationships between multiple graphs.

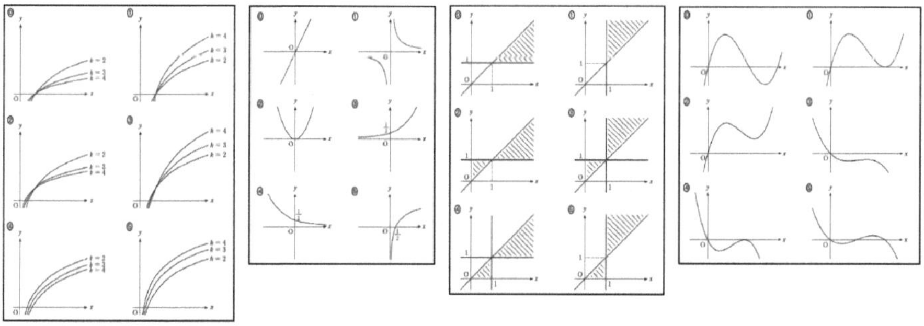

Fig. 1. Function graphs presented in the Mathematics II and Mathematics B section of the 2024 Japanese Common Test for University Admissions.

2 Standardized Audio Descriptions for Function Graphs

2.1 Overview

The audio descriptions proposed in this study are designed to enable examinees to efficiently grasp the overall shape and key mathematical characteristics of graphs within the limited time available in examinations. By presenting information about graphs through audio descriptions prior to tactile exploration, the system helps form a mental image of the graph and enhances understanding of tactile information. For example, in multiple-choice problems involving several graphs, as shown in Fig. 1, audio descriptions allow examinees to eliminate inappropriate options at an early stage. This provides a form of reasonable accommodation that enables visually impaired examinees to narrow down answer choices in a manner analogous to the visual process used by sighted examinees.

This study adopts a rule-based approach based on numerical analysis to generate explanatory text. In examination settings, inconsistencies in descriptive content or expression may confuse examinees and undermine fairness. By following predefined rules, the proposed method suppresses variation in expression and achieves consistent and standardized audio descriptions.

2.2 Related Work

Describing function graphs through text or audio is one of the primary approaches, alongside tactile graphics, for conveying mathematical content to individuals with visual impairments. For instance, [1] provides comprehensive guidelines for explaining various types of diagrams, including function graphs. In Japan, [2] serves as a manual for producing audio materials designed to be used in conjunction with tactile graphics and large-print textbooks for visually impaired students. Sobota et al. [3] proposed an approach to standardizing descriptions of function graphs for people with visual impairments. The aim of their study is to establish standardized descriptions that enable visually impaired individuals to understand university-level function graphs more efficiently. They analyzed how the order and structure of descriptions affect the comprehension of function graphs and identified the components that constitute a standardized description.

In their work, a standardized description consists of the following components. First, metadata such as the graph type, title, and caption are presented. Next, information about the coordinate system is described, including axis ranges, tick spacing, and displayed quadrants. Background information, referred to as the environment, is provided only when numerical scales are unavailable. This is followed by the function name and a left-to-right description of the function. In addition to continuous sentences describing the graph's behavior, a separate list of key coordinates such as extrema and intercepts is included to improve information retrieval. Finally, other characteristics such as symmetry or special points are added.

We also refer to the four-level model by Lundgard et al. [4] to determine the level of information to include.

2.3 Design of Standardized Audio Descriptions

In this study, audio descriptions were designed with reference to the prior work described in Sect. 2.2, with a focus on use in examinations such as university entrance examinations. The primary targets of this study are polynomial functions and conic sections, specifically ellipses and hyperbolas, which frequently appear in Japanese high school mathematics and university entrance examinations. Audio descriptions were constructed based on the characteristics of each type of function. While the prior work explains each component in separate sections, this study emphasizes enabling examinees to grasp the overall shape of graphs within a limited time and therefore adopts continuous descriptions whenever possible. In addition, the descriptions were designed to be concise and composed of short sentences to facilitate repeated listening.

Detailed information related to the coordinate system was omitted because the proposed system automatically determines an optimal plotting range that includes all quadrants based on numerical analysis. In addition, the function name and the environment component, which provides background information, were excluded due to the system design that generates descriptions immediately from mathematical expressions alone. Furthermore, to prevent time loss caused by redundant information, the list of coordinates was not presented separately.

Description for Polynomial Functions. The description for polynomial functions is as follows. First, the degree of the function is stated, followed by the quadrant in which the graph begins. Next, the behavior and characteristics of the graph are described in order from smaller to larger values of x. This includes changes in y as x increases, transitions between quadrants, and key coordinates such as intercepts, extrema, and inflection points. In the case of a linear function, the slope of the graph is also described. Accordingly, the description for $y = x^3 - 3x^2 + 4$ is given as follows.

> It is the graph of a cubic function. The function starts in the third quadrant. As x increases, y rises. It intersects at $(-1, 0)$, enters the second quadrant, and continues to rise. It reaches a local maximum at $(0, 4)$, then enters the first quadrant and falls. It reaches a local minimum at $(2, 0)$ and then rises. There is an inflection point at $(1, 2)$.

Descriptions for Conic Sections Other Than Parabolas. Conic sections, including ellipses and hyperbolas, have shapes that are defined by geometric parameters. Therefore, in the audio descriptions of conic sections, descriptions that emphasize the continuous behavior of the graph were avoided, and the explanatory text was structured in a list-based format that enumerates mathematical features. Accordingly, the description for $\frac{x^2}{4} + \frac{y^2}{9} = 1$ is given as follows.

It is an ellipse. The center is at $(0, 0)$. The x-intercepts are $(-2, 0)$ and $(2, 0)$. The y-intercepts are $(0, -3)$ and $(0, 3)$. The semi-minor axis is 2 and the semi-major axis is 3. The foci are at $(0, \sqrt{5})$ and $(0, -\sqrt{5})$.

Descriptions of Relationships Between Two Functions. When two mathematical expressions are provided, the description begins by stating the types of graphs. Then, each function is described individually. Finally, the relationship between the two functions is explained, including whether they intersect and whether they are parallel.

3 Implementation of the System

The proposed system is implemented in Python using external libraries SymPy, Matplotlib, and pyttsx3. Figure 2 shows the system's interface, and Fig. 3 shows the schematic overview of the generation pipeline. The system's processing consists of three main stages: computer algebra system, rule-based generator, and multimodal output. First, the input mathematical expressions are symbolically analyzed using the SymPy library. In this stage, the system identifies key coordinates such as local extrema, x/y intercepts, and inflection points by calculating derivatives and solving equations. These extracted mathematical features are stored as structured data.

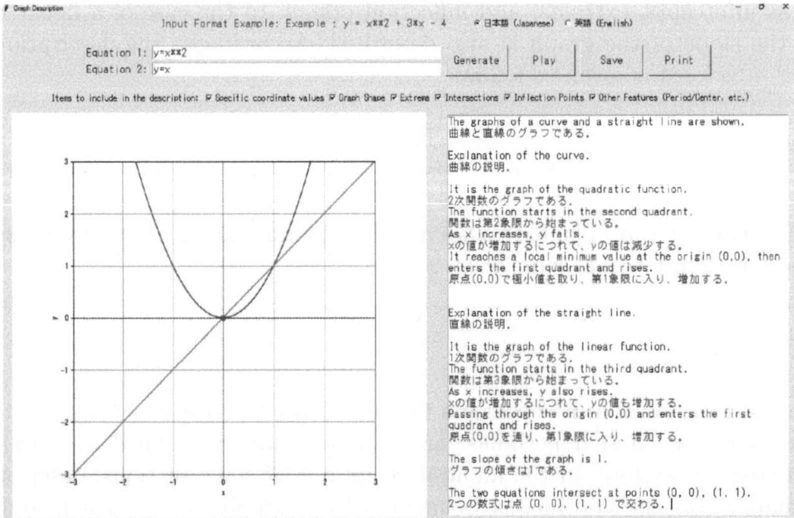

Fig. 2. System's interface. In the screen, a description is presented in both Japanese and English for ease of understanding.

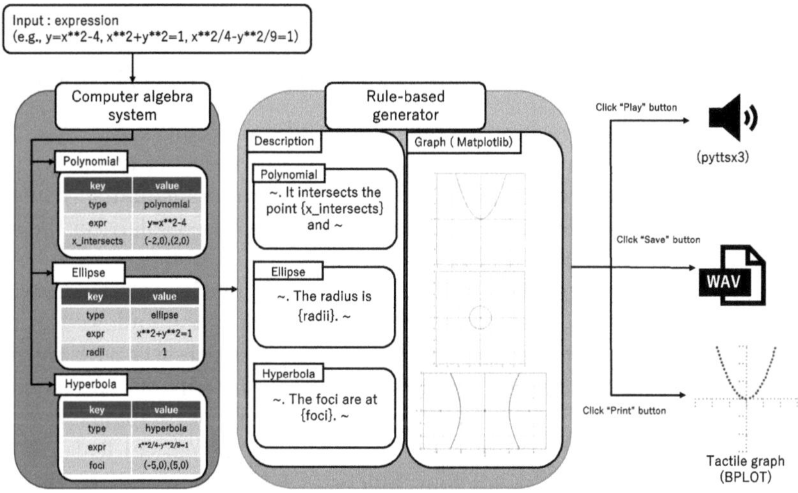

Fig. 3. Schematic overview of the generation pipeline.

The function for automatically generating explanatory text for audio descriptions generates descriptions in a rule-based manner based on the design principles described in Sect. 2 and on features extracted through numerical analysis of function graphs. The generated descriptions support both Japanese and English, and users can select their preferred language. According to the selected language, the explanatory text is generated and corresponding audio descriptions are produced. In addition, the generated text can be converted into speech using text-to-speech technology and played back or saved as audio data in WAV format. The generated description is displayed in an editable text box within the UI. Users can manually modify the text to suit their specific needs, and the updated content is immediately reflected in the audio output when the "Play" button is pressed. This feature allows for real-time adjustment of the information provided to the examinee.

To accommodate various examination scenarios, the system allows users to customize the descriptive content through checkboxes in the UI, as seen in Fig. 2. These checkboxes include options such as "Specific coordinate values", "Graph shape", "Extrema", "Intersection points", and "Other features (inflection points, etc.)". The description generation engine dynamically filters the analyzed data based on these selections. Only the selected elements are integrated into the final textual and audio descriptions, while unselected elements are automatically excluded.

The function for generating data for tactile graphics produces tactile graphic data from the input mathematical expressions and saves it as files compatible with the tactile graphics creation system BPLOT [5]. This function enables output using BPLOT on braille printers installed in many special needs schools, such as the ESA721 (JTR) and the Everest-D V5 (Index Braille).

4 Evaluation

4.1 Study 1: Redrawing Graphs Based on Audio Descriptions

As the first stage of evaluating the generated audio descriptions in this study, an experiment was conducted with four sighted university students to verify whether the geometric characteristics of the graphs were adequately conveyed. Participants were instructed to reconstruct the graphs based solely on the audio descriptions provided by the system.

The experiment utilized four different types of functions and curves: two cubic functions, an ellipse, and a hyperbola. Participants were allowed to listen to each description three times, drawing the graphs concurrently with the audio playback. Figure 4 shows the graphs drawn by four participants corresponding to each tested function. The results confirmed that all participants were able to accurately reproduce the overall shape and key mathematical features, such as extrema and intercepts, for all four functions when compared to the original graphs. This suggests that the generated descriptions successfully cover the essential mathematical structure of the functions.

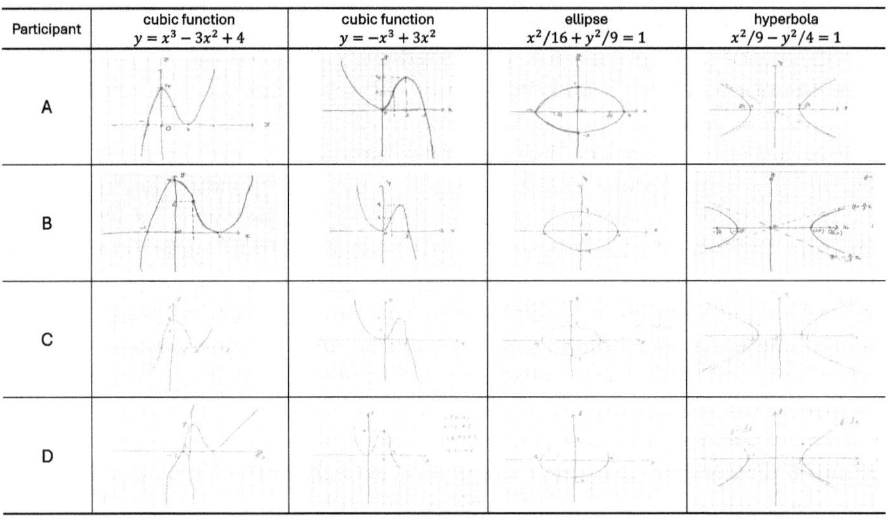

Fig. 4. Redrawn Graphs Based on Audio Descriptions.

4.2 Study 2: Feedback from a University Faculty Member

Second, we obtained feedback through informal discussions with a totally blind university faculty member. The feedback revealed that perceiving relationships between multiple graphs such as parallel relationships is particularly difficult when relying on tactile graphics alone. Based on this finding, we extended the system to describe the relationships between two functions, such as intersections or parallelism, providing multimodal support that compensates for the limitations of tactile perception.

5 Conclusion

This study developed a system to improve information accessibility in mathematics learning and university entrance examinations for visually impaired students by automatically generating audio descriptions and tactile graphics for function graphs. By adopting a rule-based approach, the generated descriptions maintain consistency for use in examinations. Evaluation experiments with sighted participants confirmed that our rule-based descriptions provide sufficient information for accurate graph reconstruction. This demonstrates the system's effectiveness in providing comprehensive information accessibility, ensuring that essential mathematical characteristics are conveyed regardless of the curve type. Furthermore, feedback from a blind faculty member revealed the difficulty of perceiving parallel relationships tactilely, leading to the implementation of graph-relationship descriptions.

Future research will focus on verifying the system with visually impaired high school students. This includes evaluating its effectiveness through mathematics tests and its utility as a tactile graphics aid. Additionally, we aim to expand the system's coverage to include trigonometric functions, exponential functions, and inequalities, covering all graph types in the Japanese Common Test. Finally, we plan to develop a web-based application for daily educational use to foster a fairer examination environment.

References

1. NCAM, DIAGRAM Center. http://diagramcenter.org/table-of-contents-2.html. Accessed 15 Apr 2026
2. Japan Lighthouse: Manual for Producing Audio-Translated Teaching Materials for Visually Impaired Students. https://www.lighthouse.or.jp/iccb/wp-content/uploads/features/6f10fe9bfc8b0d57442dee41856619471.pdf. Accessed 15 Apr 2026. In Japanese
3. Sobota, Z.E., Freese, A.C., Schwarz, T., Müller, K.: Towards establishing a description standard of mathematical function graphs for people with blindness. In: Miesenberger, K., Peňáz, P., Kobayashi, M. (eds.) Computers Helping People with Special Needs. ICCHP 2024. LNCS, vol. 14750, pp. 313–321. Springer, Cham (2024). https://doi.org/10.1007/978-3-031-62846-7_38
4. Lundgard, A., Satyanarayan, A.: Accessible visualization via natural language descriptions: a four-level model of semantic content. IEEE Trans. Vis. Comput. Graph. **28**(1), 93–103 (2021). https://doi.org/10.1109/TVCG.2021.3114770
5. Fujiyoshi, M., Fujiyoshi, A., Tanaka, H., Ishida, T.: Universal design tactile graphics production system bplot4 for blind teachers and blind staffs to produce tactile graphics and ink print graphics of high quality. In: Miesenberger, K., et al. (eds.) ICCHP 2018. LNCS, vol. 10897, pp. 167–176. Springer, Cham (2018). https://doi.org/10.1007/978-3-319-94274-2_23

Lessons Learned for Long-Term Accessibility Studies: A Case Study with Blind and Low Vision Students on a Prototype for Accessing Video Lectures

Katharina Anderer[1,2(✉)], Karin Müller[2], and Matthias Wölfel[1]

[1] Karlsruhe University of Applied Sciences, Karlsruhe, Germany
[2] Karlsruhe Institute of Technology, Karlsruhe, Germany
katharina.anderer@kit.edu

Abstract. Long-term studies in the field of human-computer interaction are an important intermediate step in verifying whether technologies are also suitable in the long run. In this study, we wanted to investigate the long-term benefits of a prototype that helps blind and low vision students gain better access to their lecture material. We conducted feedback interviews over the course of a semester. There was positive feedback on the adaptive responses of the prototype, the increased autonomy to work through lecture material, as well as the possibility to discuss questions with AI. The interviews revealed new ideas to improve the prototype. However, a high cognitive load, among other factors, was still preventing adoption. These findings were not evident from the short-time testing. In addition, the findings suggest that future research might benefit from more frequent communication, a smaller, highly motivated cohort, and transparency about technical frictions as a mechanism to prevent frustration and increase interaction with the prototype.

Keywords: HCI · Accessibility · Blind and Low Vision Students · Prototype for Accessing Lectures · Longitudinal Studies

1 Introduction

In the field of education, the lack of accessibility of study materials for students with visual impairments remains a major problem. Blind students and students with low vision (BLV) often report that they need a lot of time and effort to work through the study material [1]. In the context of live lectures or lecture videos, keeping track of the current slide or making sense of the visuals are some of the main barriers for BLV students [1]. One major reason for this is that visuals are often not explicitly described by lecturers or only at certain semantic levels [2, 11]. To address barriers, students often develop strategies such as focusing on the audio content, asking peers, or revealing their disability [20].

K. Miesenberger et al. (Eds.): ICCHP 2026, LNCS 16867, pp. 148–156, 2027.
https://doi.org/10.1007/978-3-032-31308-9_18

To address these challenges, in a previous work, we developed a prototype of a web application, called 'LectureAssistant', to make lecture videos more accessible to BLV students [1]. The prototype allows users to ask a chatbot about the visual content of the current video frame, or helps navigate to a different video position based on semantic similarity between the user's query and the lecture transcript [1]. A first evaluation of the prototype revealed that although the students were optimistic that the prototype would be helpful to them, some stated that only long-term use could give them a clear opinion of whether the prototype is actually beneficial. Furthermore, the prototype evaluation was conducted within a standardized setting, which carries the risk of creating a working scenario that does not mirror the natural working processes of the students [16].

Although short-term usability tests are common in human-computer interaction research, they fail to capture the dynamic interplay between technology and user behavior over time. Errors, frustration, and satisfaction can change greatly over time [9,10,13]. Therefore, short-time testing cannot anticipate whether the technology has the potential to be adopted. In contrast, long-term studies allow users to familiarize themselves with a new technology [9,16].

In this work, we conducted a semester-long evaluation of 'LectureAssistant' prototype to allow users to use it in a more realistic scenario with their own material. In particular, we considered the following research question.

RQ1: Do blind people and people with low vision perceive a benefit of the prototype application with respect to their daily study?

For the case that students would not adopt the new technology, we also wanted to investigate the factors preventing the adoption of the prototype.

RQ2: What are the factors that prevent the adoption of the prototype?

Our research contributes to the improvement of an accessible video lecture application and details challenges of longitudinal accessibility studies.

2 Related Work

Although longitudinal studies in general HCI are well-established [3–5,8,12], accessibility research faces unique challenges, such as a high need for customization [6]. BLV often 'hack' the behavior of assistive technology to better meet their needs, as observed by [6].

In a study, Rodrigues et al. [15] tested the adoption of blind users when using accessibility services on smartphones for 8 weeks. The initial contact with the new functions of the accessibility services was, in general, overwhelming and frustrating, as there were many new functions to memorize and the tutorial was sometimes misleading [15]. Therefore, keeping participants motivated to continue to use new devices, even after a frustrating first contact, is a major challenge.

Opinions about the usefulness or usability of technology can change over time, either towards being more optimistic, as observed in the study by [15], or towards abandoning it. The reasons for the latter were analyzed, especially for assistive technology, by [14] and grouped into four categories: lack of consideration of user opinion, lack of affordability, poor device performance, and change in user needs or priorities. This underlines the importance of including end-user opinions from the beginning and providing efficient solutions that are affordable for everyone. There are several other possible reasons for abandonment or dissatisfaction, such as assistive technology that is inefficient or difficult to operate, or psychosocial factors such as fear of being stigmatized, which are summarized by [7]. A study by [18] proposed a training framework to improve the acceptance and use rates of a mobile navigation app for blind people, arguing that appropriate training plays an important role in adoption. The framework makes suggestions to present a new application in a way that motivates end-users to use it, pointing to benefits such as increased autonomy and training in a familiar environment with tasks that are feasible and understandable [18].

3 Method

In the following, we will first briefly describe the prototype's functions and interface, the study design, and then describe participants and their on-boarding. Finally, we detail the analysis of the feedback interviews.

Short Description of the Prototype. The prototype is a web application that allows the user to upload lecture videos and PDF lecture slides as a lecture session which is detailed by [1]. Each session then allows the user to watch and listen to the video. In addition, the transcript of the lecture is processed and is displayed next to the video within a session. The user can navigate to it also via screen reader and navigate through the transcript via chapters and summaries, or the original transcript text. A chatbot window further allows the user to ask visual questions about the current video frame or lecture slide, or to navigate the video to a video position related to the user's query. In addition to the work of [1], the user can also enable a notification sound for slide transitions and write a default prompt to give the chatbot instructions on how image descriptions should be designed. Like this, the user can customize the descriptions for images, a need identified by [1,11]. In addition, there is a slide description window where an alternative text description of the current video frame or PDF slide is provided to the user as an overview.

Study Design. We chose the course of a whole semester as an adequate period of time to conduct a long-term study for a lecture assistant tool, as this should include phases of high and low study load. During this period, the goal was to conduct 2–3 feedback interviews with the participants, including questions about satisfaction with the prototype, how they might have changed their study workflow, what functions worked well, and which did not. However, as we describe in the results section, we could not realize the intended number of feedback interviews with all participants, as many participants did not use it frequently or not at all. The study has been approved by the ethics committee and the data protection office of our university.

Participants. We recruited eight participants by contacting accessibility representatives from universities in Germany, who further emailed the invitation. We required that they are currently enrolled in a university and attend at least one course, as well as having a vision impairment. One participant was a guest listener, attending two university lectures as a retiree. All participants had a vision of less than 10%. The study backgrounds were diverse, including psychology, sports sciences, biology, leisure studies, computer sciences, and physics. While two participants worked visually, five worked with a screen reader, and one worked visually and with a screen reader. Table 1 provides an overview of the characteristics of the participants.

Table 1. Background and Demographic Data of Participants

ID	Gender	Age	Vision	Working Style	AI experience	AI-Tools
P1	m	60–65	blind	screen reader and braille display	little	Microsoft Copilot
P2	m	25–30	blind	screen reader	a lot	Seeing AI, Envision Glasses
P3	m	20–25	2–5%	screen reader	a lot	self-hosting AI for making material accessible
P4	w	20–25	5–10%	visually working with iPad	a bit	ChatGPT
P5	m	25–30	4%	visually working with iPad	a lot	Ray-ban Meta glasses
P6	w	20–25	2%	visually and screen reader	little	
P7	w	20–25	blind	screen reader	a lot	SeeingAI, EnvisionAI, ChatGPT etc.
P8	w	25–30	blind	screen reader	little	

On-Boarding. In an initial interview, we asked about demographic data and their interest in and use of AI technology and technology in general. We were also interested in how students already worked with lecture videos, and which barriers they might encounter when using them. In the same session, we introduced participants to the functionalities of the prototype. The entire on-boarding session took between 1 and 1.5 h.

Feedback Sessions. The feedback sessions were conducted remotely and were scheduled for one hour. We used semi-structured interviews, asking, for example, about barriers, suggestions, and the participants' workflow. In addition, we analyzed the feedback emails from the participants and incorporated their written feedback into the analysis. Data were analyzed with a reflexive thematic analysis by combining deductive coding, based on our structured interview guide, with inductive coding to capture emergent themes from the responses of participants. Feedback interviews were conducted in a remote video chat session with P1–P3, P5, and P8. From the others, we could get written feedback via email on the reasons why they did not use the prototype or stopped using it.

4 Results

Here, we report findings from the participants' feedback. Feedback was grouped into the following themes: adaptive responses and autonomy, optimizing user flow and compatibility issues, multi-modal interaction & sensory integration, and factors preventing adoption.

Adaptive Responses and Autonomy

Feedback about the benefits of the prototype included that it *"is a fundamental enrichment, as [it] allows me to work through specific content on my own for the first time"* (P1). P1 reported listening only to the audio of a lecture video to understand its content before being introduced to the prototype. In addition, P1 reported that automatism, such as providing the text of a lecture slide, has improved the intuitivism of the prototype. P1 also considered it useful to ask the chatbot for flexible formulas in Unicode or LaTeX. P5 stated to *"definitely see a benefit, especially at events that can be very confusing [...] where you can then revisit the content of the lecture afterwards"*. Furthermore, *"the possibility of discussing content with AI is very useful"* (P5).

Optimizing User Flow and Compatibility Issues

Most of the participants wished for a more ergonomic and efficient user flow, with the aim of reducing cognitive load and friction points. P1 considered that the prototype was not yet efficient: *"If I had to keep up with the sequence of exercises in the lecture and understand the lecture content within a week to solve the problems, I would fail. [...] I am typing a lot for very little content."* Similarly, P5 explained that he was not motivated to use the prototype due to a lack of satisfactory usability. P1 suggested having a more granular video rewind function, which we directly implemented similarly to YouTube, with keys 1–9 to navigate to 10% to 90% of the video. P2 suggested reducing the number of steps the user takes by navigating directly to the session after uploading the video, instead of staying on the overview page, improving the sorting of uploaded sessions, and implementing a drag-and-drop functionality for uploading videos, instead of having to navigate through the file system.

Multi-modal Interaction & Sensory Integration

Other suggestions were for a more holistic experience, including the possibility for the AI to navigate the page, relieving the user of this task, or to provide voice input and output for the chatbot, making it possible to use the app without keyboard, screen reader, or braille, even *"from the couch"* (P2). P1 also commented on difficulties in integrating all the different information streams that come in simultaneously: The slide description of the current video frame, the transcript, and the audio, stating that *"the app lacks a concept that suggests to blind users how the simultaneous streams of information can be captured sequentially"*. To solve this issue, P1 suggested automatically stopping the video whenever the slide was changing, and the slide description information has been updated. These suggestions indicate that participants envisioned hands-free or eyes-free interaction with the prototype through voice input or AI navigation.

Factors Preventing Adoption

Only one participant used the prototype weekly (P1), while the other participants tested it a few times and then stopped. Therefore, we only conducted the intended feedback sessions with P1, P2, P3, and P5. However, the other participants gave their feedback via e-mail about why they stopped using it.

P2 and P3 reported compatibility issues with the browser and screen reader as the main reason. P3 reported that the web app did not work well for the Orca screen reader and with Firefox, but worked well with the talk-back screen reader and Android. Finding out what combination of browser, OS and screen reader worked well, required effort for the participants. Screen readers such as Jaws already excessively occupy shortcuts that were also defined for the web app. Users had to deactivate the screen reader shortcuts to be able to use the shortcuts, leading to additional steps.

P6 and P7 the lecture material provided by the university was accessible enough. P8 explained that the prototype seemed more complex than the AI app she already used, and the effort to learn a new interface was daunting.

A crucial factor was that uploading large videos took a long time and sometimes failed. When P5 used the prototype for the first time, the video upload failed, leading *"to a kind of frustration reaction, so to speak, that [he] simply did not think about using the tool again when [he] needed it."*

For P8, we tried to request the video material from the lecturers, but they did not want to record and share their online lectures, so in this case, potentially useful material remained unavailable.

For P5, an aspect was the appearance, explaining that for him, *"a product really has to look good [...] and the user interface must be logical and structured so that [he] enjoy[s] using it."*

5 Discussion and Conclusions

In this study, we gathered feedback from BLV students over the course of a semester on the usability and usefulness of a lecture video platform. The prototype-specific findings of the study include that although functions such as providing adaptive responses or automatic slide-to-text extraction met a clear need, extraneous cognitive load [17] was introduced by technical friction. The participant's feedback made clear that it is further important to work on a smoother user flow and well-integrated information streams. RQ1 could only be answered to a limited extent as a lack of adoption prevented changes in the student's workflows.

In academia, it is usually out of scope to develop a production-ready state compared to a proof-of-concept prototype. Regarding the lessons learned from the study, the lack of technical stability and interoperability caused many users to abandon the prototype after their first attempt. We defined prototype-specific shortcuts compatible with Safari, Chrome, and VoiceOver that were often not compatible with other browsers, such as Firefox, or screen readers such as Orca. Future long-term studies need to make sure that the prototype for testing is compatible with a wide variety of tools, and if not, potentially specify the browsers and screen readers that should be used. However, this could limit the potential pool of participants or increase development resources. To prevent abandonment in future longitudinal accessibility studies, researchers should maintain frequent, close communication with a smaller, highly motivated cohort. This could be achieved by regular meetings, where different tasks cover the most important functions. In retrospect, we should have set clear expectations for using the prototype regularly until the participants had become familiar with it. Furthermore, future studies might benefit from transparency by explicitly framing technical friction as a collaborative "problem-solving".

Participants' suggestions for an AI with which they could interact on the couch, or which they could ask to navigate the app, underline the wish for a more intuitive user interface. This might increase the relative advantage perceived by the user [19] by reducing the interaction cost and providing a clear benefit over established AI workflows.

Technical friction often prevented a deeper interaction with features such as slide descriptions or visual question-answering of the chatbot. However, these challenges provide a key "lesson learned": future longitudinal accessibility research should focus more on a transparent, communicative research strategy that manages user expectations through a more participatory, active partnership when interoperability cannot be assured.

References

1. Anderer, K., Müller, K., Strobel, L., Wölfel, M., Niehues, J., Gerling, K.: Making lecture videos accessible for students who are blind or have low vision through ai-assisted navigation and visual question answering. In: Proceedings of the 27th International ACM SIGACCESS Conference on Computers and Accessibility, pp. 1–15 (2025)
2. Anderer, K., Wölfel, M., Niehues, J.: Identifying the information gap for visually impaired students during lecture talks. In: 2024 IEEE Symposium on Visual Languages and Human-Centric Computing (VL/HCC), pp. 168–173. IEEE (2024)
3. Chattopadhyay, D., O'Hara, K., Rintel, S., Rädle, R.: Office social: presentation interactivity for nearby devices. In: Proceedings of the 2016 CHI Conference on Human Factors in Computing Systems, pp. 2487–2491 (2016)
4. Fan, X., Luo, W., Wang, J.: Mastery learning of second language through asynchronous modeling of native speakers in a collaborative mobile game. In: Proceedings of the 2017 CHI Conference on Human Factors in Computing Systems, pp. 4887–4898 (2017)
5. Harbich, S., Hassenzahl, M.: User experience in the work domain: a longitudinal field study. Interact. Comput. **29**(3), 306–324 (2017)
6. Herskovitz, J., Xu, A., Alharbi, R., Guo, A.: Hacking, switching, combining: understanding and supporting diy assistive technology design by blind people. In: Proceedings of the 2023 CHI Conference on Human Factors in Computing Systems, pp. 1–17 (2023)
7. Hocking, C.: Function or feelings: factors in abandonment of assistive devices. Technol. Disabil. **11**(1–2), 3–11 (1999)
8. Jungselius, B., Weilenmann, A.: Tracing change in social media use: a qualitative longitudinal study. In: Proceedings of the 2025 CHI Conference on Human Factors in Computing Systems, pp. 1–14 (2025)
9. Karapanos, E., Gerken, J., Kjeldskov, J., Skov, M.B.: Introduction to "advances in longitudinal HCI research". In: Karapanos, E., Gerken, J., Kjeldskov, J., Skov, M.B. (eds.) Advances in Longitudinal HCI Research. Human–Computer Interaction Series, pp. 1–7. Springer, Cham (2021). https://doi.org/10.1007/978-3-030-67322-2_1
10. Kjærup, M., Skov, M.B., Nielsen, P.A., Kjeldskov, J., Gerken, J., Reiterer, H.: Longitudinal studies in HCI research: a review of CHI publications from 1982–2019. In: Karapanos, E., Gerken, J., Kjeldskov, J., Skov, M.B. (eds.) Advances in Longitudinal HCI Research. Human–Computer Interaction Series, pp. 11–39. Springer, Cham (2021). https://doi.org/10.1007/978-3-030-67322-2_2
11. Lundgard, A., Satyanarayan, A.: Accessible visualization via natural language descriptions: a four-level model of semantic content. IEEE Trans. Vis. Comput. Graph. **28**(1), 1073–1083 (2021)
12. Melo, B., Andrade, R., Darin, T.: Longitudinal user experience studies in the iot domain: a brief panorama and challenges to overcome. In: Proceedings of the 21st Brazilian Symposium on Human Factors in Computing Systems, pp. 1–13 (2022)
13. Mendoza, V., Novick, D.G.: Usability over time. In: Proceedings of the 23rd Annual International Conference on Design of Communication: Documenting & Designing for Pervasive Information, pp. 151–158 (2005)
14. Phillips, B., Zhao, H.: Predictors of assistive technology abandonment. Assist. Technol. **5**(1), 36–45 (1993)

15. Rodrigues, A., Montague, K., Nicolau, H., Guerreiro, T.: Getting smartphones to talkback: understanding the smartphone adoption process of blind users. In: Proceedings of the 17th International ACM Sigaccess Conference on Computers & Accessibility, pp. 23–32 (2015)
16. Rogers, Y., Marshall, P.: Research in the Wild. Morgan & Claypool Publishers, San Rafael (2017)
17. Sweller, J., Chandler, P.: Why some material is difficult to learn. Cogn. Instr. **12**(3), 185–233 (1994)
18. Theodorou, P., Meliones, A.: Towards a training framework for improved assistive mobile app acceptance and use rates by blind and visually impaired people. Educ. Sci. **10**(3) (2020). https://www.mdpi.com/2227-7102/10/3/58
19. Wang, Y., Meister, D., Wang, Y.: Reexamining relative advantage and perceived usefulness: an empirical study. Int. J. Inf. Commun. Technol. Educ. (IJICTE) **7**(1), 46–59 (2011)
20. Wilkens, L.: Using videos in higher education: experiences of students with visual impairment. Br. J. Vis. Impair.

Inclusive and Intelligent Digital Healthcare

Intelligent, Inclusive, and Integrated Digital Healthcare: Foundations for Equitable and Trustworthy Care Innovation

Yehya Mohamad[1,2(✉)] and Carlos A. Velasco[1]

[1] Fraunhofer Institute for Applied Information Technology (FIT), Sankt Augustin, Germany
{yehya.mohamad,carlos.velasco.nunez}@fit.fraunhofer.de

[2] Computer Science Department, German University of Technology in Oman, Muscat, Sultanate of Oman

Abstract. Intelligent and inclusive digital healthcare responds to demographic ageing, rising multimorbidity, workforce shortages, and the need to provide equitable care for elderly people and persons with disabilities. This introductory paper outlines foundations and challenges of the domain, human-centered design, integrated care pathways, interoperability, privacy and security, ethics, and workforce capacity. Finally, it positions the ten accepted contributions of this Special Thematic Session (STS) and summarizes the role and contribution of each paper.

Keywords: Digital health · accessibility · inclusive design · integrated care · interoperability · privacy and security · explainable AI · digital health literacy

1 Introduction

Healthcare and care systems are being reshaped by demographic change and increasing care complexity. Aging populations, rising chronic disease prevalence, workforce shortages, and escalating costs are creating an environment that demands innovative technological solutions. Many people now live longer with chronic conditions [1]. A growing share of care is delivered outside hospitals, at home, in community settings, or in long-term care facilities. Digital health technologies are therefore increasingly expected to support continuity of care, patient empowerment, resource-efficient service delivery and pandemic situations.

However, digital transformation is not automatically inclusive or effective. Older adults, people with disabilities, and informal caregivers often face barriers related to accessibility, usability, literacy, affordability, and trust [4]. Simultaneously, healthcare organisations must contend with fragmented data landscapes where valuable clinical information remains siloed across incompatible systems, limiting the potential for comprehensive patient understanding and evidence-based decision-making [5]. Intelligent and inclusive digital healthcare addresses these gaps by treating accessibility, participation, and interoperability as core design goals rather than afterthoughts.

The research domain can be understood through three intertwined lenses:

K. Miesenberger et al. (Eds.): ICCHP 2026, LNCS 16867, pp. 159–166, 2027.
https://doi.org/10.1007/978-3-032-31308-9_19

- Intelligence, data-driven support, adaptation, and prediction, including agentic AI capable of goal-directed reasoning and autonomous workflow execution.
- Inclusion, accessibility, usability, equity, and affordability across diverse user groups and care settings.
- Integration, coordination across actors, settings, and data systems, supported by interoperable architecture and trustworthy governance.

2 Domain Foundations: Intelligent, Inclusive, and Integrated

2.1 Intelligent Digital Healthcare

"Intelligent" digital healthcare refers to computational capabilities that support decision-making, monitoring, prediction, and personalization. Current AI applications have demonstrated meaningful impact, particularly in radiology, digital pathology, and specialized diagnostic tasks. The field is rapidly evolving beyond isolated, reactive tools toward proactive, agentic systems.

This shift involves moving from conventional AI that responds to prompts in isolation toward agentic architectures in which specialized AI agents can reason, plan, and execute complex clinical workflows [7]. Such agentic AI systems are capable of autonomous operation and goal-driven behavior with minimal human intervention, decomposing complex objectives and coordinating specialized agents across disparate systems [7].

Realizing this potential requires addressing known limitations: AI "hallucinations" remain a concern, with studies showing significant diagnostic error rates in some generative AI applications; only around half of consumers currently believe AI can meaningfully improve healthcare; and data fragmentation is identified as a critical barrier by most healthcare professionals and AI developers. Trustworthy intelligence therefore depends not only on model performance, but on explainability, uncertainty quantification, bias monitoring, and continuous clinical validation [8].

2.2 Inclusive Digital Healthcare

"Inclusive" digital healthcare goes beyond compliance checklists. It encompasses accessible interaction modalities, low-threshold onboarding, support for diverse cognitive and sensory needs, and designs that acknowledge digital exclusion and differences in technology affinity. Inclusiveness also concerns affordability and frugality, because high-cost or heavy infrastructure solutions can exclude both users and care organizations.

In practice, inclusive design is operationalized through multimodal interfaces, combining text, voice, and visual inputs, that accommodate diverse user abilities and preferences. Patient-facing tools, such as virtual assistants that support symptom reporting via validated questionnaires, personalized care plan views, and tailored educational materials, exemplify how intelligent systems can simultaneously advance both accessibility and clinical utility. Multilingual capabilities further extend inclusion across linguistically diverse populations and healthcare systems.

2.3 Integrated Digital Healthcare

"Integrated" digital healthcare recognizes that care is inherently distributed. Families, professionals, and organizations work across administrative and institutional boundaries, and information discontinuities routinely shift coordination burdens onto patients and caregivers. Digital systems must therefore support coordination, information sharing, and continuity without increasing administrative load or undermining autonomy.

Federated architecture extends this further by enabling cross-institutional and cross-border collaboration without requiring direct data sharing, preserving data sovereignty while supporting population-level insights [5].

Together, these foundations suggest that inclusive healthcare innovation must connect human-centered design with interoperable infrastructures, regulatory compliance, and trustworthy governance. The adherence to frameworks such as General Data Protection Regulation (GDPR), the EU AI Act [11], and the European Health Data Space (EHDS) is increasingly shaping what responsible deployment looks like in practice.

3 Design and Implementation Principles

Work on accessible, smart, and integrated healthcare systems highlights a practical, iterative development approach grounded in human-centered design. An ISO 9241-inspired cycle, analyzing context of use, elicitation of user requirements, implementation of prototypes, and evaluating prototypes, keeps end users in focus while enabling refinement across iterations [12].

User involvement is operationalized through interviews with end users, ideation workshops with health professionals, and the explicit identification of key use scenarios and use cases. A recurring lesson is that requirements must be testable. User requirements are best documented with a clear summary of what the system should do, a rationale explaining why the requirement matters and for whom, and a fit criterion expressing quantified goals or acceptance criteria against which implementation can be verified.

Illustrative integrated care platforms combine patient empowerment applications, clinician dashboards, home and health monitoring, and communication services. Typical characteristics include health data interoperability, security and privacy controls, scheduling support, interface customization and accessibility, integrated communication (chat, audio, video), and alignment to interoperability and data protection requirements. Compliance-by-design approaches, in which regulatory requirements are embedded into system architecture and training pipelines from the outset, rather than retrofitted post-development, represent an emerging best practice that reduces regulatory risk and accelerates the path to clinical deployment.

4 Review of the Special Thematic Session Contributions

The review is organized to reflect the layered nature of intelligent and inclusive digital healthcare.

First, contributions on assistive and therapeutic technologies demonstrate how inclusive interaction can be designed and evaluated in concrete intervention settings (robot/VR storytelling; theory-guided conversational support).

Second, papers on intelligent monitoring and navigation illustrate frugal and explainable AI for longitudinal prediction and accessibility-oriented wayfinding systems that consider both user needs and organizational workflows.

Third, methodological and capacity-building contributions address the enabling conditions for integrated care. Methods to elicit design knowledge across stakeholders, evidence on workforce digital skills and emerging skill needs, and frameworks for digital health literacy and ethical reflection.

Finally, the STS includes contributions that broaden the integrated-care lens to caregiver wellbeing and psychosocial support, highlighting that inclusive digital healthcare must account for family systems, and burden. The accepted papers contribute complementary building blocks for intelligent and inclusive digital healthcare.

The following subsections provide a short description of each contribution's focus, role in the domain, and specific contribution.

- **Storytelling Integrated into a Socially Assistive Robot and Virtual Reality for Speech and Language Therapy:** This paper [13] examines technology-mediated storytelling as a tool for speech and language therapy, comparing two intervention modalities: storytelling supported by a physical NAO robot and storytelling delivered in a virtual reality environment with a virtual NAO avatar. Children's narrative utterances are recorded and analyzed across morphological and syntactic parameters, enabling a structured comparison of which grammatical competences are elicited in each modality. The contribution advances inclusive therapy technology by providing evidence that both embodied and virtual systems can support narrative production, while also highlighting individual differences that matter for tailoring interventions.
- **Frugal and Explainable AI for Accessible Longitudinal Monitoring of Parkinson's Disease:** This work [18] proposes a frugal longitudinal framework to predict short-term motor severity in Parkinson's disease using baseline clinical assessments, explicitly aiming to reduce dependence on costly neuroimaging. Methodological rigor is emphasized through leakage prevention with patient-level partitioning and transparent evaluation, and model behavior is made interpretable via SHAP-based feature attribution. The paper contributes an inclusion-oriented pattern for clinical AI: resource-aware feature sets combined with explainability to support trust and potential use in low-resource or remote care settings.
- **A Study of Acceptance and Commitment Therapy (ACT) Combined with an AI System for Spinal Cord Injuries:** This paper [14] develops an ACT-guided conversational AI framework that formalizes ACT's six core processes as dialogue governance principles for large language model interaction. An implemented ACT-AI chat agent routes users through structured modules and evaluates feasibility using interaction logs and pre/post measures, framing the system as self-help support. The contribution's key role is demonstrating how "intelligence" can be constrained and made reproducible by grounding conversational behavior in a validated therapeutic model rather than ad hoc prompting.
- **Evaluating Healthcare Staff Perceptions of AI-Enabled Indoor Wayfinding Technologies:** This study [20] addresses accessibility challenges in complex healthcare facilities by investigating staff perspectives on AI-enabled indoor wayfinding and

the operational consequences of current navigation barriers. The work links universal design goals (personalized routing for diverse needs) with organizational impacts such as staff time spent assisting lost visitors and potential inefficiencies. Its contribution is to foreground stakeholder and workflow considerations for deploying accessibility-aware navigation systems in real healthcare environments.

- **Eliciting Design Knowledge for Care Coordination Through Multi-Actor Eco-Map Comparison:** This methodological contribution [21] introduces a multi-actor eco-map comparison method to elicit design knowledge in care coordination contexts that span multiple organizations and administrative boundaries. By analyzing convergences and divergences across actors' eco-maps, the method surfaces structural issues such as "family-as-hub" coordination burdens and translates them into traceable design principles and requirements. The paper strengthens integrated-care design practice by providing a structured pathway from stakeholder perspectives and scenarios to actionable requirements and prototype probes.
- **Evidence-based Monitoring of Digital Skills in Long-term Care and Implications for Future Training:** This paper [15] reports on a longitudinal survey across ten European countries examining digital skills relevance, gaps, and technology usage in long-term care among care workers and managers. Findings highlight persistent gaps in areas such as digital communication/collaboration, content creation, safety, and problem solving, with role-specific differences between managers and frontline workers. The contribution anchors the workforce dimension of inclusive digital healthcare by providing evidence for targeted, low-threshold training and organizational strategies that support adoption.
- **Care4Skills: Using Unusual Methods to Anticipate Emerging Skill Needs in the Long Time Care Sector:** This contribution [17] proposes a data mining and machine-learning pipeline that crawls job listings and uses large language models to extract and cluster skills relevant to long-term care work. By relying on real-world job market requirements rather than surveys alone, the approach aims to identify emerging digital skills and tool knowledge, including regional patterns. The paper complements survey-based monitoring by offering an automated, continuously updatable method to inform curricula and reskilling materials aligned with evolving digitalization in care.
- **Health for All: Digital Health Literacy and Ethics as Foundations for Sustainable Digital Health Solutions:** This paper [22] presents an integrated approach combining a Digital Health Lab for experiential learning, a modular literacy training concept, and an "Ethics as an Opportunity" reflection card set. The framework addresses adoption barriers by linking hands-on exposure to technologies with structured reflection on privacy, data protection, autonomy, and inclusiveness. Its contribution is to position literacy and ethics as enabling infrastructure for sustainable and responsible digital health, supporting trust and long-term integration into practice.
- **Bridging the Support Gap: A Digital Mindfulness and Peer-Support Ecosystem for Parents of Children with Autism in Poland:** This conceptual paper [16] addresses caregiver burden by proposing a mobile-based ecosystem that combines asynchronous mindfulness micro-interventions with peer-validated community support. Design requirements include short, low-effort exercises, explicit self-compassion mechanisms, and moderated community features to reduce isolation and

stigma. The contribution broadens inclusive digital healthcare beyond patient-facing tools by highlighting caregiver wellbeing as a prerequisite for sustainable care.

- **Inclusive and Intelligent Digital Healthcare:** This contribution [22] frames the domain by highlighting demographic change, the need for accessible and integrated systems across care environments, and the enabling role of digital health technologies such as analytics, IoT ecosystems, and machine learning. It also foregrounds interoperability standards, regulatory and governance considerations, and privacy, security, and ethical issues as essential for deployment. As a unifying anchor, it connects the accepted papers to a shared agenda: designing and evaluating digital health solutions that are simultaneously intelligent, accessible, and integrated into real care ecosystems.

5 Cross-Cutting Synthesis: Toward Accessible, Smart, and Integrated Care

Across the STS, several cross-cutting themes map directly to the design and implementation principles established in accessible, smart, and integrated healthcare systems work.

First, multiple papers emphasize grounding design in context-of-use: staff experiences in wayfinding, caregiver experiences in autism support, and multi-actor eco-map perspectives in care coordination all function as scenario-level evidence that shapes requirements. Second, the volume illustrates "responsible intelligence". Predictive modelling is paired with explainability and leakage-aware evaluation; conversational AI is paired with theory-based governance; and adoption is paired with literacy and ethics frameworks. These patterns make intelligence more transparent and controllable in real care contexts. Third, inclusion is addressed at different layers: accessible therapeutic interaction (robot/VR), accessible navigation, frugal monitoring for low-resource settings, and skill and literacy development to reduce digital exclusion. Together, these layers reflect the need for integrated platforms that combine patient empowerment, professional dashboards, monitoring, and communication while meeting security, privacy, and interoperability requirements.

Finally, several contributions highlight the socio-technical nature of integration. The most effective digital health solutions are those that reduce coordination burdens, support shared understanding, and align with organizational workflows, reinforcing the importance of iterative, user-involved development and testable requirements.

6 Conclusion and Outlook

The ten contributions in this session demonstrate that intelligent and inclusive digital healthcare requires more than novel technologies:

It requires human-centered design, explicit and testable requirements, trustworthy and explainable intelligence, and integrated infrastructures that enable secure and interoperable care. Future work should strengthen evidence on long-term adoption and outcomes, develop scalable co-creation and evaluation methods, and advance architectures that enable cross-organizational coordination while respecting privacy and user control. The papers collected here provide practical building blocks toward accessible, smart, and integrated healthcare systems for elderly people and people with disabilities.

References

1. James, N.D., et al.: The Lancet Commission on prostate cancer: planning for the surge in cases. The Lancet **403**(10437), 1683–1722 (2024). https://doi.org/10.1016/S0140-6736(24)00651-2
2. Global strategy on digital health 2020-2025. World Health Organization, Geneva (2021)
3. Whitelaw, S., et al.: Applications of digital technology in COVID-19 pandemic planning and response. The Lancet Digital Health **2**(8), e435–e440 (2020)
4. Cajander, Å., et al.: Barriers to and Facilitators of Digital Health Technology Adoption Among Older Adults With Chronic Diseases: Updated Systematic Review. JMIR Aging **8**(1), e80000 (2025)
5. Hamiti, F., et al.: A Data Space infrastructure supporting the integration of clinical data nodes and cancer registries. In: DSAI 2024, ACM (2024). https://doi.org/10.1145/3696593.3696627
6. Srinivasu, P.N., Aruna Kumari, G.L., Ahmed, S., Alhumam, A.: Exploring Agentic AI in Healthcare: A Study on Its Working Mechanism. Front. Med. **12**, 1753443 (2026). https://doi.org/10.3389/fmed.2025.1753443
7. Sadeghi, Z., et al.: A Review of Explainable Artificial Intelligence in Healthcare. Comput. Electr. Eng. **118**, 109370 (2024)
8. Pongrac, E., et al.: Toward Inclusive Design Heuristics for Digital Health Interventions for the Aging Population: Scoping Review. JMIR **27**(1), e79449 (2025)
9. Tabari, P., et al.: State-of-the-Art FHIR-Based Data Model and Structure Implementations: Systematic Scoping Review. JMIR Med. Inform. **12**, e58445 (2024)
10. European Parliament and Council: Regulation (EU) 2024/1689 laying down harmonised rules on artificial intelligence (Artificial Intelligence Act). Official Journal of the European Union, L, 2024/1689 (2024)
11. ISO 9241-210:2019. Ergonomics of human-system interaction — Part 210: Human-centred design for interactive systems. International Organization for Standardization
12. Andreeva, A., Padareva-Ilieva, G., Lekova, A., Stefanov, T.: Storytelling Integrated into a Socially Assistive Robot and Virtual Reality for Speech and Language Therapy. In: Miesenberger, K., Petrie, H., Penaz, P. (eds.) ICCHP 2026, Computers Helping People with Special Needs, 20th International Conference; Linz, Austria, Proceedings. Springer (2026)
13. Chien-Wen, S., Valdez Sanchez, M., Chen, C.: A Study of Acceptance and Commitment Therapy (ACT) Combined with an AI System for Spinal Cord Injuries: In: Miesenberger, K., Petrie, H., Penaz, P. (eds.): ICCHP 2026, Computers Helping People with Special Needs, 20th International Conference; Linz, Austria, Proceedings. Springer (2026)
14. Matausch-Mahr, K.: Evidence-based Monitoring of Digital Skills in Long-term Care and Implications for Future Training. In: Miesenberger, K., Petrie, H., Penaz, P. (eds.) ICCHP 2026, Computers Helping People with Special Needs, 20th International Conference; Linz, Austria, Proceedings. Springer (2026)
15. Trela, L., Krzeminska: Nina Bridging the Support Gap: A Digital Mindfulness and Peer-Support Ecosystem for Parents of Children with Autism in Poland. In: Petz, A., Miesenberger, K. (eds.) ICCHP Open Access Compendium, Future Perspectives on Accessibility, AT and eInclusion; Linz, Austria, Proceedings. Johannes Kepler University Linz (2026)
16. Punz, M.: Care4Skills: Using Unusual Methods to Anticipate Emerging Skill Needs in the Long Time Care Sector. In: Petz, A., Miesenberger, K. (eds.) ICCHP Open Access Compendium "Future Perspectives on Accessibility, AT and eInclusion"; Linz, Austria, Proceedings. Johannes Kepler University Linz (2026)
17. Bouraoui, A., Haouari, N., Belazreg, N.: Frugal and Explainable AI for Accessible Longitudinal Monitoring of Parkinson's Disease. In: Miesenberger, K., Petrie, H., Penaz, P. (eds.) ICCHP 2026, Computers Helping People with Special Needs, 20th International Conference; Linz, Austria, Proceedings. Springer (2026)

18. Schaur: Melanie From Care Crisis to Digital Transformation? Digitalization and Assistive Technologies in European Long-Term Care. In: Miesenberger, K., Petrie, H., Penaz, P. (eds.) ICCHP 2026, Computers Helping People with Special Needs, 20th International Conference; Linz, Austria, Proceedings. Springer (2026)
19. Joseph, S., Darby, D., Namboodiri, V., Tucker, R.: Evaluating Healthcare Staff Perceptions of AI-Enabled Indoor Wayfinding Technologies. In: Petz, A., Miesenberger, K. (eds.) ICCHP Open Access Compendium „Future Perspectives on Accessibility, AT and eInclusion"; Linz, Austria, Proceedings. Johannes Kepler University Linz (2026)
20. Schaur Moro, S., Osaki, Y., Ohashi, T.: Eliciting Design Knowledge for Care Coordination Through Multi-Actor Eco-Map Comparison : A Single-Case Methodological Study. In: Miesenberger, K., Petrie, H., Penaz, P. (eds.) ICCHP 2026, Computers Helping People with Special Needs, 20th International Conference; Linz, Austria, Proceedings. Springer (2026)
21. Wohofsky, L., Krainer, D.: Health for All - Digital Health Literacy and Ethics as Foundations for Sustainable Digital Health Solutions. In: Petz, A., Miesenberger, K. (eds.) ICCHP Open Access Compendium "Future Perspectives on Accessibility, AT and eInclusion"; Linz, Austria, Proceedings. Johannes Kepler Universi-ty Linz (2026)

Storytelling Integrated into a Socially Assistive Robot and Virtual Reality for Speech and Language Therapy

Anna Andreeva[1,2](✉), Gergana Padareva-Ilieva[1], Anna Lekova[2], and Tsvetelin Stefanov[2,3]

[1] South-West University "Neofit Rilski", 66 Ivan Mihailov Str., 2700 Blagoevgrad, Bulgaria
anna_andreeva@swu.bg
[2] Institute of Robotics, Bulgarian Academy of Sciences, 1113 Sofia, Bulgaria
[3] University of Library Studies and Information Technologies, 69A Shipchenski Prohod Blvd., 1574 Sofia, Bulgaria

Abstract. This study explores the effectiveness of technology-enhanced storytelling interventions in supporting narrative development in children with language disorders. Narrative skills are crucial for communication, academic achievement, and social interaction, yet children with language disorders often experience persistent difficulties in storytelling. The research compares three speech and language therapy conditions: human–robot interaction using the socially assistive robot NAO, virtual reality interaction with a robot avatar, and traditional human–human therapy. Eight children aged 4 to 13 participated in structured storytelling sessions across all three conditions. Their narratives were audio-recorded, transcribed, and analyzed in terms of key morphological and syntactic parameters. Results show that four children demonstrated similar performance across all conditions, while others exhibited individual variability. Some performed better in robot-assisted and traditional settings, whereas others showed improvement in virtual reality. Overall, the findings suggest that both physical and virtual technological environments can enhance engagement and support linguistic development. Although differences between conditions were not substantial, each modality demonstrated potential benefits. These results support the integration of socially assistive robots and virtual reality as complementary tools in speech and language therapy, while further research is needed to examine their long-term effects.

Keywords: Socially Assistive Robots · Virtual Reality · Speech and Language Therapy · Children with Language Disorders · Storytelling

1 Introduction

Technology is increasingly integrated into speech and language therapy, offering flexible, accessible, and effective tools that can enhance engagement, support independent practice, and improve therapeutic outcomes. When used alongside traditional methods, different types of technologies such as computers, robots, mixed reality, conversation

K. Miesenberger et al. (Eds.): ICCHP 2026, LNCS 16867, pp. 167–174, 2027.
https://doi.org/10.1007/978-3-032-31308-9_20

artificial intelligence and others enable therapists to target both clinical goals and digital participation, expanding the reach and impact of therapy [1]. Technology offers a promising opportunity for supporting the standard speech and language therapy (SLT) interventions in the development of storytelling skills [2, 3].

Narrative skills involve the abilities to understand and to express needs, feelings, thoughts and ideas. Children with language disorders often experience persistent difficulties with narration, literacy, academic achievement and social interaction. Additionally, the challenges, even the inabilities, in expressing thoughts and needs through narration can lead these children to feel frustrated and helpless, which may in turn contribute to behavioral problems, reduced engagement in school and negative impact on their life [4]. Evidence suggests that storytelling-based language intervention can lead to improvements in oral language, reading, and verbal working memory for children with language disorders [5].

2 State of the Art

According to the fifth edition of the Diagnostic and Statistical Manual of Mental Disorders (DSM-5) language disorders is characterized by persistent difficulties in understanding and producing language across the different modalities such as spoken, written, or sign language. The language skills are significantly below the norms for the age. Research has shown that children with language disorders experience significant challenges in narration skills. They often produce narratives with impaired components, for example difficulties to establish the characters, initiating events, internal responses and plans, consequences and reactions [6]. These difficulties highlight the importance of implementing narrative-based interventions that support the development of good storytelling skills.

Narrative intervention is an effective and adaptable approach in SLT, supporting language development in children with language disorders. Children are engaged in listening to and telling or retelling stories through structured supportive techniques such as pictures, sequencing tasks etc. [4, 7]. The advances in interventions supported by technology, including storytelling approaches integrated in Socially Assistive Robot (SAR) and Virtual Reality (VR), offer promising opportunities to develop narrative skills by providing structured, engaging, and multimodal environments for the individual needs of children with language disorders.

The technology-implemented storytelling can suggest an alternative by engaging children in language-learning activities, not as a replacement for adults (parents, caregivers or speech and language therapist) but as a tool that models supportive behaviors. Research of [8] shows that children can learn new words just as effectively from a robot as from a human interaction partner. The study by [9] compared storytelling experiences for individuals with neurodevelopmental disorders in two settings: human–human interaction and robot–human interaction, finding that the robot created a more engaging experience. The review of [10] established that social robots can help children develop storytelling skills and participate more actively in conversations, with robot-delivered stories often perceived as more entertaining.

Through immersive settings, VR technologies in therapy provide children with communication disorders with new interactive ways to improve their speech and language abilities. A review of VR scenarios for SLT concluded that most research focuses on a limited range of conditions such as ASD, Specific Language Impairment, Intellectual Disabilities, Dyslexia and Hearing Disorders. Studies mainly target skills like communication, conversation, and vocabulary [11]. However, ethical considerations in VR applications remain underexplored beyond basic research protocols, such as interaction time, evaluation process, assessment for cybersickness etc.

The aim of the study is to exam the children's provoked narrative in three conditions: human – robot, virtual avatar robot – human (VR) and human-human interactions during storytelling SLT sessions.

3 Methodology

The participants in the interventions consist of eight children with language disorders. The ages of the children (3 females and 5 males) range from 4 to 13 years ($M = 7.88$; $SD = 2.9$;). The study was conducted at Center of Logopedics at South-West University "Neofit Rilski" in Blagoevgrad, Bulgaria. The study was reviewed and approved by the Ethics Committee (South-West University "Neofit Rilski", protocol N 2410–1/29.10.2024).). Written informed consent was obtained from the parents of all participating children. The participants' personal information was anonymized to maintain confidentiality.

This study investigates participation in three intervention conditions of storytelling. Each child participated in three storytelling sessions, one per condition. During each session, children were prompted to produce a narrative in interaction with either the NAO robot, the NAO avatar in VR or the speech and language therapist. Sessions lasted approximately 5 min and were conducted individually in a quiet room. Each story is illustrated by three cards presenting the sequence of actions in time. There is a fourth card, which is intentionally placed as false card.

The narrative utterance of each child was audio-recorded with PRAAT software (https://www.fon.hum.uva.nl/praat/). Narrative data were manually transcribed and analyzed by a speech and language therapist and a linguist. Analyses focused on narrative macrostructure elements and overall narrative quality as part of the assessment methodology described in [12]. After the sessions each child filled in a questionnaire about the interaction. The rating scale was with three options: frowning emoji face for "Disagree", neutral emoji face for "Neutral" and smiling emoji face for "Agree". For the VR interaction questionnaire there was a specific item asking the children about sickness or general discomfort during or after the session. The parents were asked to monitor their children for symptoms related to cybersickness such as headache, fatigue, dizziness, difficulties in focusing, sweating, increased salivation etc. considering the studies of [13].

The first condition employed socially assistive robot Nao. The participants are a child with language disorder, the robot and the speech and language therapist. Within the framework of the ATLog project (https://atlog.ir.bas.bg/en), we developed the interactive scenario "Tell Me a Story" in Choregraphe (software for programing interactive scenarios) and integrated it in the ATLog platform. Nao is situated opposite the child, on a table. The child chooses the story. The therapist puts the three consecutive pictures in front of the child and starts the session. The robot is telling the short story. The Nao utterance is prerecorded audio uploaded into it. The robot is programed to make gestures and move the body to look more natural and to have human-like behavior. At the end of the story the speech and language therapist mixed the pictures. Nao asks the child to put the pictures in the correct order and to retell the story.

The second condition was conducted in VR, employing a virtual avatar if the robot Nao. The participants are a child with language disorder, the speech and language therapist and the virtual robot Nao. A web-based VR version of the interactive scenario "Tell Me a Story" (see Fig. 1) has been developed, using the Node.js, Express.js, Three.js, HTML, CSS and JavaScript technology stack.

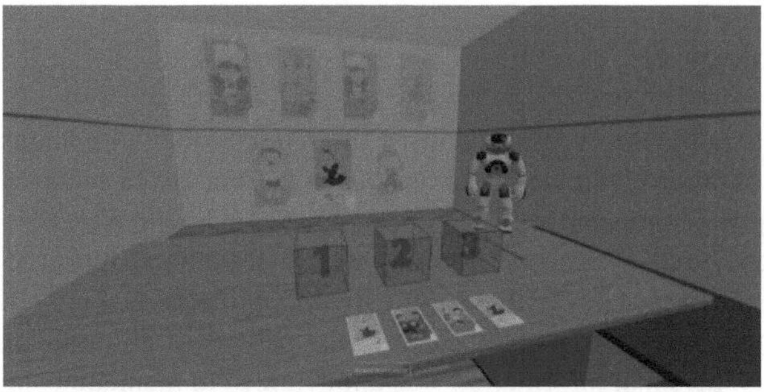

Fig. 1. Scene from the VR session for storytelling

In the VR serious game, the player stands in front of a desk on which 4 cards are positioned below eye level, while 3 boxes are arranged at eye level. The cards on the desk are presented in a randomized order. At the beginning of the game, the player listens to the complete story. Afterwards, each individual story event is narrated only once. The player must then identify the appropriate card and place it in the appropriate box. The boxes represent the chronological sequence of the story events. Once all relevant story moments have been correctly selected and arranged, the player must retell the entire story they initially chose. During the session the VR room is projected in the Meta Quest Pro for the child and on a computer screen (streaming) for the speech and language therapist.

The third condition represented a classical therapy session. The speech and language therapist is using a storytelling method with one child with langue disorders. The story is illustrated into three sequenced pictures. First the speech and language therapist presented the story supported by three pictures. After that, the pictures are mixed. The child must put the pictures in the correct order and to retell the story.

4 Results

After the VR sessions, none of the participating children and their parents reported symptoms related to cybersickness, such as headaches, fatigue, dizziness, difficulty focusing, sweating, or increased salivation.

All questionnaires about the interactions filled in by each child were positive with predominant smiling emoji faces. The questionnaire evaluated children's experience with the technology storytelling game, focusing on clarity of instructions, ease of interaction (selecting, pointing, and moving objects), and control methods (hands and joystick). It also assessed visual and auditory perception, comfort while using the VR equipment/ interacting with the robot Nao, and overall enjoyment of the activity. The only difference was found in the control methods in the VR. Younger children preferred to use joysticks, whereas older children preferred to use their hands.

Audio files of each child include child's speech during the storytelling session. PRAAT has been used to manually label speech segments. Then, for quantitative measuring, the intervals with child's storytelling have been analyzed for particular grammatical parameters both the morphological and syntactic levels. At the morphological level, we evaluated the children's ability to maintain gender and number agreement, subject–predicate agreement. At the syntactic level, we analyzed the structure and complexity of the children's sentence production which included the use of single-component sentences, two-component sentences, and expanded sentences that included modifiers, objects, definitions, complements or other elaborative elements. The ability to form complex sentences that involve subordinate clauses reflecting causal, temporal or other logical relationships is also assessed. Grammatical and logical arrangement of words within a sentence in a grammatically correct word order is evaluated too (see Table 1).

Table 1. Assessment of linguistic competences and parameters.

Linguistic competences	Parameters
Grammatical competences (Morphology)	1. agreement by gender and number within N + Adj/Pron Phrase 2. agreement within predicate – subject relation N + V Phrase
Grammatical competences (Syntaxes)	3. Single-component sentences
	4. Sentences containing subject + predicate – Subject + Verb)
	5. Extended sentences (in which, in addition to the subject and predicate, other words are present that clarify them – definitions, complements, etc.)
	6. Compound sentences
	7. Correct word order

The recordings of each child were carefully and independently evaluated based on the presence/absence of the seven parameters by two specialists - a phonetician / linguist, and a speech-language therapist.

The results are shown in Table 2. For two of the subjects (4 and 5), five of the monitored components of grammatical competence are present in the three types of storytelling: they maintain agreement by gender and number, subject-predicate agreement, produce sentences containing both subject and predicate, demonstrate correct word order, and even produce compound sentences. Two of the subjects (1 and 7) show better performance in terms of grammatical competence during storytelling with the robot and the therapist than during VR storytelling. This is particularly evident in Subject 1, who, while narrating a story to the robot or the human professional, maintains agreement by gender and number, subject-predicate agreement, produces sentences containing both subject and predicate, and demonstrates correct word order. In contrast, during VR storytelling, Subject 1 maintains sporadically and with the help of the therapist one of these competences on morphological level – subject-predicate agreement - and, at the syntactic level, produces predominantly single-component sentences.

Table 2. Comparison of children's utterance between the three storytelling sessions (Qualitative analyses/Grammar competences).

Subjects	Storytelling with robots (№ of parameter from Table 1)	Storytelling VR (№ of parameter from Table 1)	Storytelling with speech and language therapist (№ of parameter from Table 1)
1	1, 2, 4, 7	2, 3	1, 2, 4, 7
2	1, 2, 3, 4, 7	1, 2, 4, 6, 7	1, 2, 4, 7
3	3, 4	1, 2, 3, 4	1, 3, 4
4	1, 2, 4, 6,7	1, 2, 4, 6, 7	1, 2, 4, 6,7
5	1, 2, 4, 6, 7	1, 2, 4, 6, 7	1, 2, 4, 6, 7
6	2, 4	2, 3	2, 3, 4
7	1, 2, 4, 6, 7	2, 4, 6, 7	1, 2, 4, 6, 7
8	2, 3, 4	2, 3, 4	2, 3, 4, 7

In Subject 7, storytelling with the robot/ human reveals the presence of only one additional parameter – maintaining agreement by gender and number – which is not observed when the child tells a story in VR. Regarding the remaining components (2, 4, 6, and 7), these are maintained by the speaker in all types of storytelling.

A clear difference between the competences manifested in the three sessions of storytelling is also observed in Subject 3, though in this case in favor of VR storytelling. While narrating the VR story, Subject 3 maintains agreement by gender and number and subject – predicate agreement, in addition to producing single-component sentences and sentences containing both subject and predicate.

It can also be stated that Subject 2 demonstrates an increase in grammatical competence during VR storytelling, expressed in the production of compound sentences, which are absent from the subject's speech when narrating to the robot or with the speech and language therapist.

Observations show a slightly higher use of compound sentences in VR storytelling compared to robot-assisted or human interaction, although the difference is not significant. This may be influenced by task order, but it also suggests that VR can help elicit existing grammatical competences. It is important to note, however, that when referring to compound sentences in the clients' speech, this involves two or three simple sentences linked by conjunction. There is a lack of ability to form complex sentences that involve subordinate clauses reflecting causal, temporal, or other logical relationships.

Agreement by gender and number occurs less frequently in VR storytelling than in stories told to the robot or the therapist, although again the difference is minimal. Overall, such agreement is not frequently observed in the children's speech, which is likely the reason for the absence of extended sentences (i.e., sentences in which, other elements are present, such as modifiers, complements, etc.) too.

Sentences without connectors, as well as constructions lacking prepositions, are also observed, which is indicative of a deficit at the linguistic level normal for some of clients involved.

5 Conclusion

This study examined the impact of technology-enhanced storytelling on the narrative and grammatical abilities of children with language disorders by comparing three intervention conditions: SAR interaction, VR storytelling, and traditional human–human therapy. The findings demonstrate that all three approaches are capable of eliciting narrative production and supporting the development of core grammatical competences at both morphological and syntactic levels. Although individual differences were observed with some children demonstrating stronger performance in robot-assisted storytelling and others in VR storytelling. The findings indicate that both physical embodiment and virtual embodiment can stimulate children's linguistic capacities and encourage the use of grammatically relevant structures, even in the presence of persistent language difficulties. These results support the use of both technologies in storytelling as facilitating tools in SLT. Future studies with larger participant samples and controlled task sequencing are needed to further investigate their relative effectiveness and long-term impact on grammatical development and narrative skills.

Acknowledgments. This study was funded by the Bulgarian National Scientific Research Fund (project number No KP-06-H67/1).

Disclosure of Interests. The authors have no competing interests to declare that are relevant to the content of this article.

References

1. Leinweber, J., et al.: Technology use in speech and language therapy: digital participation succeeds through acceptance and use of technology. Front. Comm. **8**, 1176827 (2023)
2. Lin, C., Šabanović, S., Dombrowski, L., Miller, A.D., Brady, E., MacDorman, K.F.: Parental acceptance of children's storytelling robots: A projection of the uncanny valley of AI. Front. Robo. AI **8**, 579993 (2021)
3. Chubb, J., Missaoui, S., Concannon, S., Maloney, L., Walker, J.A.: Interactive storytelling for children: A case-study of design and development considerations for ethical conversational AI. Int. J. Child-Comp. Interact. **32**, 100403 (2022)

4. Bar-On, A., Ravid, D., Dattner, E. (eds.): Handbook of communication disorders: Theoretical, empirical, and applied linguistic perspectives, Vol. 15. Walter de Gruyter GmbH & Co KG (2018)
5. Pauls, L.J., Archibald, L.M.: Cognitive and linguistic effects of narrative-based language intervention in children with Developmental Language Disorder. Autism & Developmental Language Impairments 6 (2021)
6. Favot, K., Carter, M., Stephenson, J.: The effects of oral narrative intervention on the narratives of children with language disorder: A systematic literature review. J. Dev. Phys. Disabil. **33**(4), 489–536 (2021)
7. Spencer, T.D., Petersen, D.B.: Narrative Intervention: Principles to Practice. Lang. Speech Hear. Serv. Sch. **51**(4), 1081–1096 (2020)
8. Kory, J., Breazeal, C.: Storytelling with robots: Learning companions for preschool children's language development. The 23rd IEEE International Symposium on Robot and Human Interactive Communication, pp. 643–648 (2014)
9. Fisicaro, D., Pozzi, F., Gelsomini, M., Garzotto, F.: Engaging persons with neurodevelopmental disorder with a plush social robot. In: Proceedings of the 14th ACM/IEEE International Conference on Human-Robot Interaction (HRI '19), pp. 610–611. IEEE Press (2020)
10. Georgieva-Tsaneva, G., et al.: Exploring the Potential of Social Robots for Speech and Language Therapy: A Review and Analysis of Interactive Scenarios. Machines **11**(7), 693 (2023)
11. Rasheva-Yordanova, K., Kostadinova, I., Georgieva-Tsaneva, G., Andreeva, A., Tsvetkova, P., Lekova, A.: A comprehensive review and analysis of virtual reality scenarios in speech and language therapy. TEM Journal **14**(2), 1895–1907 (2025)
12. Padareva-Ilieva, G., Andreeva, A., Lekova, A., Simonska, M.: Assessment of speech and language therapy assisted with social robots and virtual reality: phonetic and linguistic analysis of speech. In: Mavrou, K., Encarnação, P. (eds.) Technology for Inclusion and Participation for All: Recent Achievements and Future Directions. AAATE 2025, pp. 359–366. Springer, Cham (2025)
13. Eudave, L., Martínez, M.: To VR or not to VR: assessing cybersickness in navigational tasks at different levels of immersion. Frontiers in Virtual Reality **6**, 1518735 (2025)

A Study of Acceptance and Commitment Therapy Combined with an AI System for Spinal Cord Injury

Chien-Wen Shen[1,2], Marycielo Valdez Sanchez[1(✉)], and Chen Chen[1]

[1] Department of Business Administration, National Central University, Taoyuan 32001, Taiwan
marycielovs@g.ncu.edu.tw

[2] Asian Institute of Impact Measurement and Management, Taoyuan 32001, Taiwan

Abstract. Large language models enable conversational systems that support naturalistic and adaptive interaction at scale. In digital mental health, such systems may function as accessible self-help complements in settings with limited service capacity, including support for people living with spinal cord injury. This study develops an ACT-guided AI system framework that formalises ACT's six core processes as governance principles for large language model-based conversational systems. The framework is operationalised through the ACT-AI Chat Agent, a self-guided support protocol delivered through six ACT practice modules across a 10-day intervention. An exploratory feasibility study was conducted in a spinal cord injury rehabilitation context in Taiwan using interaction logs, engagement indicators, and pre-post measures of anxiety, depression, and psychological flexibility analysed with Wilcoxon signed-rank tests. Findings indicate feasible protocol completion, sustained engagement, and modest directional improvement in emotional symptoms, while changes in psychological flexibility remained limited and non-significant. The protocol is intended to complement, not replace, professional care, and findings should be interpreted as feasibility signals rather than evidence of clinical effectiveness.

Keywords: AI System · Conversational Systems · AI Chat Agent · Acceptance and Commitment Therapy (ACT) · Spinal Cord Injury

1 Introduction

Recent advances in large language models enable a new class of conversational systems that support naturalistic, adaptive interaction at scale [1]. In digital mental health, such systems are framed as accessible self-help complements in settings with limited service capacity, particularly for people living with physical disabilities and chronic conditions [2], including spinal cord injury. More than 14.5 million people worldwide lived with spinal cord injury in 2021 [3]. Beyond

K. Miesenberger et al. (Eds.): ICCHP 2026, LNCS 16867, pp. 175–182, 2027.
https://doi.org/10.1007/978-3-032-31308-9_21

functional impairment, spinal cord injury is often accompanied by psychological distress and psychosocial challenges [4].

Conversational agents in mental health have evolved from rule-based systems to machine learning and natural language processing approaches with improved responsiveness and engagement [2]. However, many systems remain weakly grounded in validated therapeutic models and often emphasize linguistic performance over process-consistent guidance. Acceptance and Commitment Therapy (ACT), a third-wave cognitive behavioural approach centred on psychological flexibility, offers a process-based framework for structuring supportive interactions through six core processes that help individuals relate more adaptively to distress and act in accordance with personally held values [5]. Among people with spinal cord injury, psychosocial interventions have largely relied on cognitive behaviour therapy (CBT), a structured psychotherapeutic approach that seeks to reduce psychological distress by helping individuals identify and modify maladaptive thoughts and behaviours [6]. Guided online CBT formats have also shown feasibility in a population with spinal cord injury [7]. By contrast, ACT-grounded self-help conversational systems remain underexplored [2]. In settings with limited service capacity, self-help approaches may expand access [2]. However, adherence challenges in unguided formats highlight the value of more structured and engaging interventions [8].

In response to this gap, this study develops an ACT-guided AI system framework. The framework formalises ACT's six core processes as governance principles for large language model-based conversational systems. To demonstrate applicability, the framework is operationalised through the ACT-AI Chat Agent, using a self-guided support protocol for individuals with spinal cord injury. An exploratory feasibility study then evaluates feasibility and initial outcome signals in a spinal cord injury rehabilitation context in Taiwan using interaction logs, engagement indicators, and pre-post measures of anxiety, depression, and psychological flexibility assessed with the Hospital Anxiety and Depression Scale (HADS) and the Comprehensive Assessment of Acceptance and Commitment Therapy Processes (CompACT), with pre-post differences analysed using Wilcoxon signed-rank tests. By positioning ACT as a governance framework for conversational AI and empirically examining a concrete instantiation, this work contributes a structured design approach for theory-informed large language model (LLM) interaction and provides early feasibility evidence for subsequent controlled and comparative evaluations.

2 State of the Art

Conversational agents have long been investigated in human computer interaction and digital mental health [2]. Early systems relied on rule-based or decision-tree architectures that limited adaptability, whereas later machine learning and natural language processing improved responsiveness and scalability. Large language models (LLMs) further extend conversational flexibility but introduce risks related to controllability, consistency, and domain alignment [9]. In digital mental health, Woebot used scripted dialogue based on cognitive behaviour therapy with engagement and short-term symptom improvement [10], while systems such as SELMA added free-text interaction to increase naturalness and perceived relational closeness [11]. Yet most remain content-delivery tools with opaque, non-reproducible dialogue governance, and LLM-based mental health apps often rely on ad hoc prompting with limited process assurance across sessions and users. ACT provides a process model centred on psychological flexibility through six core processes: Acceptance, Cognitive Defusion, Present Moment, Self-as-Context, Values, and Committed Action [5]. Pilot ACT chatbots appear feasible while also highlighting the need for explicit therapeutic specification in automated dialogue [12]. Evidence also supports ACT, including technology-mediated interventions, in chronic disease and physical disability populations, including spinal cord injury [13]. Under mobility constraints, cognitive behaviour therapy programmes have shown feasibility, although adherence and personalisation remain persistent challenges [7]. However, prompt designs that encode ACT processes as explicit dialogue governance for LLM interaction remain limited; the present study operationalises that layer in a large language model-based self-help system for spinal cord injury.

3 Methodology

The study proposes an ACT-guided AI system framework that formalises ACT's six core processes as dialogue governance principles for LLM interaction. The framework is operationalised through an implemented ACT-AI Chat Agent, which constitutes the artefact evaluated in the feasibility study (Fig. 1). The LLM was accessed through the ChatGPT interface (OpenAI) using GPT-4. The ACT-AI Chat Agent is not trained or fine-tuned, and no external datasets are used for model adaptation. The ACT-AI Chat Agent operates as a dialogue layer guided sequentially by rules and a standardised prompt structure, mediating bidirectional communication between the user and an LLM aligned with the six ACT core processes.

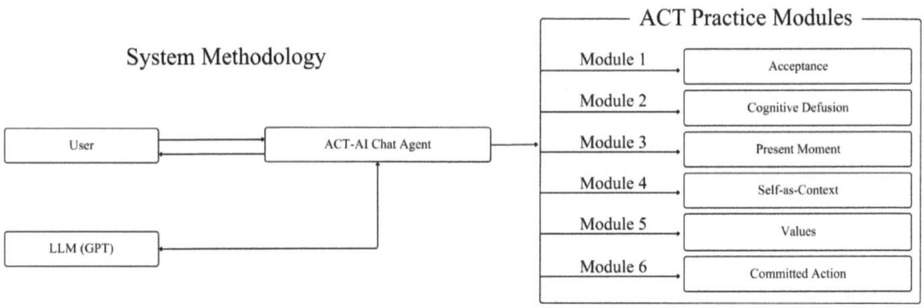

Fig. 1. ACT-AI Chat Agent framework and ACT practice modules for self-help interaction.

Participants received a ChatGPT manual specifying initial requirements to ensure protocol consistency, including the creation of a personal ChatGPT account and the use of separate chat sessions. Participants also received the ACT-AI Chat Agent Practice Manual, which provided an introduction, a guided conversational interaction, and a reflective closure for each module. The study used SurveyCake to deliver the manuals as the platform provides daily completion records. The practice manual was developed based on ACT practice materials and self-help manuals [14–16]. The six practice modules are summarised in Table 1, and the complete manual is available in the project repository. Following a pre-deployment walkthrough with rehabilitation-centre staff, the manual was iteratively revised to fit real-world spinal cord injury rehabilitation contexts and support self-help use. Participant feedback was captured through post-module ratings and brief written reflections for support feasibility assessment and protocol refinement. During the first 6 days, the six ACT practice modules were delivered, and participants copied and pasted the standardised prompts into ChatGPT, followed by four consolidation days (Days 7 to 10) to reinforce practice and reflection before post-assessment. Engagement time per session was estimated at 30–60 min, depending on individual pace and depth of reflection.

Table 1. ACT module operationalisation.

ACT module and purpose	Prompt logic and governance
Acceptance. Encourages acceptance of internal experiences and reduces struggle with distress	Metaphor-based explanation and brief self-check questions with bounded responses
Cognitive Defusion. Promotes distance from evaluative thoughts	Short defusion explanation and description-versus-evaluation exercises with structured prompting
Present Moment. Trains present-focused awareness	Brief attention-guiding exercises that redirect focus to current experience
Self-as-Context. Cultivates an observer perspective toward self-labels	Chessboard metaphor and guided observer-perspective questions
Values. Clarifies personally held values	Values-oriented metaphors and brief clarification questions with standardised elicitation
Committed Action. Translates values into goals and anticipated action	Structured goal-setting and obstacle-anticipation prompts with bounded forward planning

Note. The practice manual, including the full set of standardised copy-and-paste prompts, is available in the project repository: https://github.com/Marycielovs/ACT-AI_SCI.git

Responses were generated from the user's current input and within-session conversational context. Persistent cross-session memory was unnecessary; when cross-day continuity was needed, participants provided a brief recap or a neutral summary was generated from the prior session transcript under the practice manual. The system design supports reproducibility of interaction policies while allowing context-sensitive reflection within defined governance constraints.

Participants were recruited through a spinal cord injury rehabilitation foundation in Taiwan that provides long-term rehabilitation, counselling, and social support. The foundation distributed the study invitation through internal channels. Eligibility required a confirmed spinal cord injury diagnosis, ability to use an online text-based platform, and willingness to follow a 10-day self-guided support protocol. To reflect spinal cord injury heterogeneity and test feasibility across diverse profiles, no restrictions were imposed by injury level, completeness, or time since injury. Participation was voluntary and uncompensated; written informed consent was obtained and no financial or material incentives were offered. Participants could withdraw at any time. The intervention was framed as self-help support rather than clinical treatment, and participants were instructed to discontinue use and seek professional care at the centre if distress arose. Interaction data were stored with restricted access and anonymised for research use; the protocol underwent the foundation's internal ethics review.

A single-group pre-test-post-test feasibility design was employed. Participants completed baseline measures prior to initiating the protocol and post-test measures after completing the 10-day intervention window. Anxiety and depression were assessed using the HADS, and psychological flexibility processes were assessed using the CompACT measure at baseline and post-intervention. Dialogue logs were collected to assess feasibility, engagement, and adherence to the prescribed module sequence, and to support subsequent textual analysis. Records were excluded if questionnaire completion time was under 5 min on more than three occasions or if dialogue logs were missing, consistent with predefined data quality criteria. Pre-post differences were evaluated using Wilcoxon signed-rank tests, selected to match the paired design and small sample feasibility context; the feasibility design was not intended to establish causal effects or comparative effectiveness. The methodological focus was on implementability and acceptability, with outcome measures included to support exploratory assessment and inform subsequent controlled evaluations.

4 Results

The recruitment and screening process resulted in a progressive refinement of the study sample. Approximately twenty individuals with spinal cord injury attended the initial introductory session conducted at the collaborating rehabilitation centre. Seventeen individuals subsequently consented to participate and initiated the 10-day self-guided support protocol. After data quality checks (70.6% retained), 12 participants with paired pre/post questionnaires and valid interaction logs comprised the final analytic sample for outcome analysis. The final analytic sample was predominantly male (11 of 12). Participants represented heterogeneous spinal cord injury profiles, including variation in injury level (50% cervical; 42% thoracic; 8% lumbar).

Interaction logs and platform records indicated that participants were able to engage with the ACT-AI Chat Agent throughout the protocol, with an average observed engagement duration per session ranging from 23 to 60 min depending on the ACT core process addressed. All retained participants completed the prescribed sequence of ACT practice modules over the 10-day period, and no technical failures or system interruptions were observed. Completion timestamps further suggested sustained engagement across modules, with session duration varying by module. For example, exercises related to contact with the present moment and self-as-context were associated with longer interaction durations, whereas values clarification activities showed shorter yet consistent engagement, while remaining within the expected range defined by the protocol.

As shown in Table 2, pre-post comparisons of emotional symptoms assessed using the HADS indicated a consistent directional decrease in anxiety, depression, and overall emotional distress following completion of the self-help protocol. HADS total decreased from 13.83 to 11.91 ($p = 0.081$), indicating a modest directional improvement. Wilcoxon tests were non-significant and changes were modest, so findings are best interpreted as feasibility signals rather than evidence of clinical effectiveness.

Table 2. Pre-post outcomes for emotional symptoms and ACT-related processes.

Measure	Pre-test mean	Post-test mean	Wilcoxon p-value
HADS			
Anxiety	6.75	5.75	0.079
Depression	7.08	6.16	0.103
Total emotional distress	13.83	11.91	0.081
CompACT			
Experiential openness	25.67	27.58	0.286
Behavioural awareness	13.33	13.67	0.632
Valued action	18.58	18.50	0.831
CompACT total	57.58	59.75	0.283

Pre-post comparisons related to ACT psychological flexibility processes assessed using the CompACT measure showed small directional changes across subscales and in the total score following the intervention period. Increases were observed primarily in domains related to experiential openness, which increased from 25.67 to 27.58 ($p = 0.286$), while behavioural awareness and valued action remained relatively stable. None of the observed differences reached statistical significance according to Wilcoxon signed-rank tests. These results suggest limited detectable change in self-reported ACT processes over the short intervention window and are consistent with the exploratory scope of the study.

5 Discussion

Findings support the feasibility of an ACT-guided AI system framework, operationalised through the ACT-AI Chat Agent based on a self-guided support protocol for people with spinal cord injury in a rehabilitation context. Interaction logs, completion records, and engagement indicators suggest that participants were able to follow the prescribed ACT practice modules and engage with the ACT-AI Chat Agent without technical interruption, supporting the practical feasibility of the structured protocol. Directional reductions in anxiety, depression, and overall emotional distress are consistent with the potential of the protocol as a low-intensity supportive resource, whereas limited and non-significant change in CompACT scores indicates that a 10-day protocol may be insufficient to produce measurable change in ACT-related processes. Several constraints limit interpretation, including the small sample, single-group design, short intervention window, and absence of a control condition. The protocol is intended to complement, not replace, professional care, and current findings should be interpreted as feasibility and protocol signals rather than evidence of clinical effectiveness. Because delivery relied on the standard ChatGPT interface, exact output reproducibility over time may be limited as the platform evolves. Future research should strengthen safety procedures, clarify dialogue governance more explicitly, and evaluate ACT process fidelity with greater methodological precision, including study-specific implementations grounded in ACT materials, comparative testing across LLM backends, and more gender-balanced recruitment.

6 Conclusions

The study develops and operationalises an ACT-guided AI system framework for large language model-based conversational support in spinal cord injury rehabilitation. The ACT-AI Chat Agent demonstrates that a structured, process-based self-guided support protocol can be delivered in a feasible manner within a rehabilitation setting. Although findings do not establish clinical effectiveness, results support the potential of theory-informed conversational systems as accessible complements in settings with limited service capacity. A key contribution lies in operationalising ACT's core processes into a structured self-help protocol for LLM-based support. Further research should evaluate the framework in larger controlled studies with longer intervention periods.

References

1. Bharathi Mohan, G., Prasanna Kumar, R., Vishal Krishh, P., et al.: An analysis of large language models: their impact and potential applications. Knowl. Inf. Syst. **66**(9), 5047–5070 (2024). https://doi.org/10.1007/s10115-024-02120-8

2. Vaidyam, A.N., Wisniewski, H., Halamka, J.D., Kashavan, M.S., Torous, J.B.: Chatbots and conversational agents in mental health: a review of the psychiatric landscape. Can. J. Psychiatry **64**(7), 456–464 (2019). https://doi.org/10.1177/0706743719828977
3. Kim, M., Jeong, W., Jang, S., Park, J.H., Bae, Y., Lee, S.W.: Spinal cord injury epidemiology and causes: a worldwide analysis with 2050 projections. Healthcare **13**(20), 2552 (2025). https://doi.org/10.3390/healthcare13202552
4. Post, M., van Leeuwen, C.M.: Psychosocial issues in spinal cord injury: a review. Spinal Cord **50**(5), 382–389 (2012). https://doi.org/10.1038/sc.2011.182
5. Hayes, S.C., Pistorello, J., Levin, M.E.: Acceptance and commitment therapy as a unified model of behaviour change. Couns. Psychol. **40**(7), 976–1002 (2012). https://doi.org/10.1177/0011000012460836
6. Mehta, S., Orenczuk, S., Hansen, K.T., et al.: An evidence-based review of the effectiveness of cognitive behavioural therapy for psychosocial issues post spinal cord injury. Rehabil. Psychol. **56**(1), 15–25 (2011). https://doi.org/10.1037/a0022743
7. Mehta, S., Hadjistavropoulos, H., Nugent, M., et al.: Guided internet-delivered cognitive behavioural therapy for persons with spinal cord injury: a feasibility trial. Spinal Cord **58**(5), 544–552 (2020). https://doi.org/10.1038/s41393-019-0398-6
8. Cuijpers, P., Schuurmans, J.: Self-help interventions for anxiety disorders: an overview. Curr. Psychiatry Rep. **9**(4), 284–290 (2007). https://doi.org/10.1007/s11920-007-0034-6
9. Huang, L., Yu, W., Ma, W., et al.: A survey on hallucination in large language models: principles, taxonomy, challenges, and open questions. ACM Trans. Inf. Syst. **43**(2), Article 42 (2025). https://doi.org/10.1145/3703155
10. Fitzpatrick, K.K., Darcy, A., Vierhile, M.: Delivering cognitive behaviour therapy to young adults with symptoms of depression and anxiety using a fully automated conversational agent (Woebot): a randomized controlled trial. JMIR Ment. Health **4**(2), e19 (2017). https://doi.org/10.2196/mental.7785
11. Hauser-Ulrich, S., Künzli, H., Meier-Peterhans, D., Kowatsch, T.: A smartphone-based health care chatbot to promote self-management of chronic pain (SELMA): pilot randomized controlled trial. JMIR Mhealth Uhealth **8**(4), e15806 (2020). https://doi.org/10.2196/15806
12. Stapleton, A., Lavelle, J.M., McHugh, L.: Chatbot-delivered acceptance and commitment therapy with adolescents: a pilot randomized controlled trial. PsyArXiv preprint (2022). https://doi.org/10.31234/osf.io/j2kpt
13. Khanjani, M.S., Kazemi, J., Younesi, J., et al.: The effect of acceptance and commitment therapy on psychological flexibility and emotional regulation in patients with spinal cord injuries: a randomized controlled trial. Iran. J. Psychiatry Behav. Sci. **15**(2), e105378 (2021). https://doi.org/10.5812/ijpbs.105378
14. Hayes, S.C., Strosahl, K.D. (eds.) A Practical Guide to Acceptance and Commitment Therapy. Springer, US (2004). https://doi.org/10.1007/978-0-387-23369-7
15. Ciarrochi, J.V., Bailey, A.: ACT practical handbook: integrating cognitive behavioural therapy and acceptance and commitment therapy. Traditional Chinese translation by Zhang, B.-S. Chang Laoshi, Taipei (2016). https://reading.udn.com/onlineViewer/pdfTrialViewer/107668
16. Hayes, S.C., Smith, S.: Get Out of Your Mind and Into Your Life: The New Acceptance and Commitment Therapy. Traditional Chinese translation by Zhang, B.-S., Ding, Y.-F., Su, Y.-X. Chang Laoshi Wenhua, Taipei (2017). https://www.airitibooks.com/Detail/Detail?PublicationID=P20180104002

Evidence-Based Monitoring of Digital Skills in Long-Term Care and Implications for Future Training

Kerstin Matausch-Mahr(✉)

Johannes Kepler University Linz, Linz, Austria
kerstin.matausch-mahr@jku.at

Abstract. Long-term care systems throughout Europe are undergoing a period of significant transition. Growing demand for long-term care, influenced by demographic changes, is facing a fluctuating workforce, staff shortages, low pay, financial cuts, unbalanced levels of digitalization, technological development, and a workforce that needs training. A four-year longitudinal study aims to contribute to the Europe-wide discussion and digital transformation in the sector by providing findings. Thus far, this study has examined the state of knowledge regarding digital and person-centered skills, skills gaps, training needs and technological usage in ten European countries. The study sheds light on a complex system. It indicates a continuing predominance of person-centered care, as well as a growing demand for and interest in digital skills. It also highlights national differences and differences among staff categories, emphasizing the need for digital upskilling across countries and categories.

Keywords: Long-Term Care · Skills · Training · Assistive Technologies · Digitalization

1 Introduction

Demographic trends indicate an increasing proportion of older people, leading to a growing share of people having a need for support. Moreover, about 135 million people are living with a disability within the Member States of the WHO European Region [1]. Some of them are asking for long-term care which "consists of a range of services and assistance for people who, as a result of mental and/or physical frailty and/or disability over an extended period of time, depend on help with daily living activities and/or are in need of some permanent nursing care" [2]. While in 2020, 11.6% asked for care services, the share will grow up to 14.1% in 2070, demonstrating an increase in care of 21% among people aged 50 + [3].

Digitalization and digital transformation are fundamentally changing long-term care in Europe. This highlights the importance of digital skills for caregivers and social service managers. Simultaneously, the "healthcare sector is more digitalized than the EU sectors on average, … about a fifth of workers in social care sectors do not use

K. Miesenberger et al. (Eds.): ICCHP 2026, LNCS 16867, pp. 183–190, 2027.
https://doi.org/10.1007/978-3-032-31308-9_22

digital devices – including computers, laptops, tablets and smartphones - at all … These workers – both those who deal directly with clients and those in auxiliary jobs – may be missing out on the benefits of digitalization, automation and robotics" [4]. This demonstrates a gap between societal trends, technological conditions, and real care. These challenges are addressed by political initiatives such as the European Care Strategy introduced by the European Commission [5] which is referring to higher quality and improved access to care. The Council Recommendation on access to affordable, high-quality long-term care emphasizes the importance of improved training to prepare the care workforce with the necessary skills, including digital skills. The Digital Health Action 2023–2030 highlights working infrastructures, safe data, digital training and simultaneously provide user-focused [6]. The Blueprint on Digital Transformation of Health Care for the Ageing Society demands for digital upskilling as well as shared vision, while the Pact for Skills und large-scale skills partnership targets upskilling of 60% of the long-term care workforce annually till 2030 [7, 8]. DigComp [9] as well as the EU Skills Agenda [10] are essential frameworks for defining relevant digital skills at a general level and are also relevant for the long-term care sector.

The paper is structured as follows: Sect. 2 provides a review of the current research situation regarding digitalization in long-term care by analyzing the state of the art. Section 3 outlines the methodology, using a systematic quantitative design, data sources, and the synthesis approach. Section 4 presents the results, highlighting cross-national findings and comparing relevant details. Section 5 discusses the findings in relation to existing literature, reflects on policy and practice implications, limitations and directions for future research.

2 State of the Art

Various studies focus digitization in care, but the number of studies related to digital skills for caregivers in long-term care is limited. A systematic literature review (SLR) on the acceptance of digital technology among nursing staff in geriatric long-term care indicates that the acceptance of digital technologies heavily depends on individual factors such as personal digital skills and the perceived relevance of technology, as well as organizational factors such as access to training or the involvement of employees in implementation processes [11]. Another study highlights the close connection between digital skills and person-centered skills in care, particularly the ability to use digital tools with empathy and a focus on usability for service users. Key digital skills include assessing online information and judging the usefulness of technologies in specific care situations. It highlights strengthening the digital knowledge, skills, and attitudes of care workers to optimize digital transformation in the aged care sector [12]. This asks for an evidence-based monitoring on digital skills, suggestions for adjusted training as well as an attitude monitoring of people working in long-term care as described in the following section. These findings indicate that digital and person-centered competencies are interconnected and that digital tools should be user-centered. Other studies associate higher digital competence levels with age, higher education, inpatient care as well as stronger perceived support from management, organizational structures and colleagues [11, 13]. In general, findings highlight the close socio-technical relationship of digitization in care, as well as the association between acceptance of digital technologies and individual factors and access to training.

3 Methodology

The underlying methodological approach aims to identify and describe the stakeholders involved, long-term care organization in the countries as well as aspects impacting the long-term care sector in the surveyed countries. It also focuses on emerging skill qualifications, particularly digital and person-centered skills, such as empathy, teamwork, advocacy, and strength-based practice. This approach also aims to recognize skill trends in the sector and to define adequate training programs to overcome skill gaps resulting from the COVID-19 pandemic and digital transition in long-term care.

The following staff categories, basing on ESCO guidelines [9], were pre-defined as target groups: 1. Social Work Assistant, 2. Social Care Workers, 3. Nursing Professionals, 4. Social Service Managers.

A longitudinal study design was selected, based on a mixed methods design combining document analysis, qualitative expert interviews (n = 182 including 115 interviews with care workers, 67 with managers), focus groups, an analysis of formal and informal initial and continuing training programs in ten European countries and an annual cross-national quantitative online survey targeting the above-mentioned target groups. Each method was selected to identify complementary perspectives. The methodological approach was conducted in ten European countries: Belgium, Bulgaria, Czech Republic, Finland, France, Greece, Hungary, Italy, Netherlands, Spain.

This paper presents the quantitative considerations and findings of the first two surveys in 2024 and 2025, which are part of a longitudinal panel study using refreshment samples [14, 15]. The study is to be continued until 2027. Refreshment samples are essential due to significant panel attrition. The reasons for this are unclear and may be related to budget cuts and staff reductions, as well as various LTC structures. The quantitative methodology used standardized online questionnaires to collect systematic comparable data. An online survey platform with accessibility features was used to implement the surveys [16]. All participants were informed about the voluntary nature of their participation, their data privacy rights, and the purpose of the questionnaire. At the end, there was a section where interested individuals could sign up to become panel participants.

The entire care staff in the ten chosen countries constituted the population from which the sample for the longitudinal study was drawn, taking into account data from Eurostat and Eurofound [4, 17]. Data was collected through various channels, such as networks, direct face-to-face interaction during meetings, and social media. Due to national differences in recruitment strategies, response rates vary between countries, which is why a descriptive analytical approach was adopted. The first survey was answered by 567 respondents (322 care workers; 245 managers), indicating relevant outcomes for the long-term care systems. The second survey had a significant panel attrition with 182 respondents (141 care workers, 41 managers). For an analysis of panel effects, the sample had to be reduced to those who stated that they also answered the first questionnaire, limiting the informative value of findings and particularly those of single countries (95 respondents: 68 care workers, 27 managers). The first quantitative survey identified conditions of work, person-centered and digital skills of the care workforce, their usage of technology, training used, skill needs as well as relevant statistical data. Skill categorization was based on the ESCO and 21st century skills frameworks [18, 19]. The second one examined skills evolution by using the prior categorization of skills as well as a subjective recognition of emerging trends in long-term care. They focused on the following research questions:

- How relevant are digital skills for care workers and managers in the ten countries?
- What digital skills do care workers and social care managers possess?
- What technology do they use?
- Which aspects impact the long-term care sector?

4 Results

The following results present the findings from the first two surveys of a longitudinal study which will continue until 2027. Trends relating to skills among the panel of care workers and managers are already visible and are discussed in the relevant sections.

4.1 Relevance of Digital Skills for the Care Workforce

Both care workers and social service managers considered basic digital information literacy and basic digital communication as relevant, including emailing, data storage and data movement. This contradicts the view held by managers who considered digital skills to be more relevant for their workforce than care workers perceived themselves. For instance, they recognized digital content creation and digital safety skills related to software installation, password management and changing settings as important for caregivers, indicating the relevance of digitalization for the long-term care sector.

Managers usually considered the aforementioned information and communication literacy as well as a wider range of digital skills as relevant for their daily work. This demonstrates the diversity of their field, even though many of these skills were only occasionally relevant for work.

Additionally, the importance attributed to digital skills varied by country. For instance, digital collaboration tools were considered more relevant in the Czech Republic, Finland, Spain, and the Netherlands. Digital accessibility, on the other hand, was considered more relevant in Spain, France, the Netherlands, and Bulgaria, with moderate levels of importance. Digital safety was widely considered to be less relevant than other digital areas. Despite this result, Czech, Finish, and Dutch care workers were more aware of this issue.

4.2 Digital Skills of the Care Workforce

As the relevance ranking suggested, the competency levels for digital skills were lower than those for people-centered skills. Care workers mostly possessed basic digital skills for information and data literacy, communication and collaboration. They had low to moderate skill levels related to 1) digital content creation, including using mobile devices to create and share multimedia; 2) digital safety, including password renewal; and 3) digital problem-solving, including setting adjustments of software and data movement between devices.

Compared to care workers, social care managers demonstrated more and better-developed skill levels, which tended to be in the upper range. They possessed advanced skills related to digital information and data literacy as well as digital communication. In terms of content creation, digital security, and problem-solving skills, managers demonstrated intermediate to advanced proficiency. There were regional differences in terms of safety and problem-solving skills, with Spain, Finland, France, and the Netherlands showing more developed competencies. This points to differences in long-term care systems and possibly more advanced IT infrastructures.

The findings demonstrated that care workers may benefit less from digital skills, as their training completion rates varied across countries. Some countries had high participation rates for continuing training and certificates among care workers and managers, partially driven by legal requirements, while others demonstrated a training rate of 60 to 70 per cent within the last five years. Most training focused on person-centered skills, but digital skills were becoming increasingly important, suggesting that care workers' digital skills are developing, albeit slowly and remain limited. These results indicate limited readiness for digital tasks. Fortunately, significant and often highly significant correlations between digital skills were identified: Digital training enhances other digital skills. This requires the use of technology, the results of which are described below.

4.3 Usage of Technologies

While internet and computer usage were common among care workers and managers across the surveyed countries, smartphones were already rare in use. Belgian, Finnish, French, and Dutch care workers as well as most of the managers used them, except in Hungary. This indicates different care systems, as well as potentially varied organizational readiness and mindsets. Furthermore, technologies such as safety devices; tools for medication management, health recording, chronic disease management; and smart pill bottles were hardly in use. Generally, Finnish and Dutch managers and care workers demonstrated a more diverse usage of technologies, which again indicates greater digital readiness and skills. Overall, technology usage was limited to a few devices.

4.4 Aspects Impacting the Long-Term Care Sector

Respondents across countries agreed that staff and budget cuts are having a significant impact on the sector. Digitalization was also considered impactful, though the degree of impact varied by staff category and country. Managers in most of the countries considered it to have a moderate to high impact on the sector, with the exception of Bulgarian and Hungarian ones who recognized digitalization as moderately relevant. Attitudes among care workers were more varied. While Belgian, Czech, Dutch, and Finnish care workers assessed it as more impactful, Hungarian and Bulgarian caregivers had a contrasting attitude.

5 Discussion and Conclusion

This study examined how digital skills, skill gaps, training needs and technological usage are structured in ten European countries. It aimed to contribute implications for future training and a better readiness of the sector for its digital transformation. Although the target groups need to have a wide range of skills including digital competences [9, 18–20], the surveys revealed critical aspects related to digital skills that impact work, policy, and training. The studies conducted to date indicate a dominance of person-centered skills such as empathy, teamwork, and direct face-to-face communication, highlighting their relevance for daily work. Digital skills were considered relevant. There is also a growing interest in digital skills, yet the assessment of their relevance and the associated competence levels remained inadequate. One takeaway is that direct care—and thus person-centered skills—remain essential. This suggests that technology complements personal care.

The analysis showed that the implementation of technology varied across countries, indicating different care systems, organizational readiness, technical infrastructure and competence levels among care workers and managers, as well as potentially different mindsets among the workforce. There is a widespread need for digital training and even workers in countries with higher levels of technology use have gaps in their digital knowledge when it came to problem-solving, multimedia, and digital safety – areas that are critical for reporting, monitoring, and telecare. Another takeaway is a cross-border need for digital training as only basic skills were widespread among the countries.

Moreover, the results shed light on the need for more targeted communication of the aforementioned needs. Managers considered digital skills to be more relevant for their workforce than they themselves recognized, highlighting the importance of communicating this perception to the workforce as well as balancing training in a sector impacted by staff shortages, budget cuts, high emotional demands, and varying staff-user rates [4, 21].

One key takeaway is that digital transformation in long-term care remains complex. There is a complexity of the requirements and the sector. Digital transformation asks for an appropriate mindset, including organizational readiness and top-down support for the care workforce, appropriate communication, continuing training as well as constant political will and support. The findings indicate that initiatives such as the EU Skills Agenda [10] and DigComp [9] remain relevant for a digital transition in long-term care and need to find their ways directly to the workforce. The results suggest the need for close socio-technical systems in which people and technology collaborate to deliver long-term care effectively.

Last but not least, limitations exist related to varying and partially small sample sizes across the surveyed countries. Moreover, the study mostly reached non-migrating care workers and those working full time, whereas caregivers predominantly work part time [4]. Yet, the study had a sufficiently comprehensive sample to draw conclusions for a cross-country analysis within the long-term care systems in Europe. Finally, there are still discrepancies between the current situation and the ideal implementation at a national level, as the data indicate existing national differences. To ensure a sustainable digital transformation in long-term care, future research should also focus participatory approaches that give a voice to both professionals and those affected, utilizing longitudinal or multi-stage study designs, potentially making them co-designers of training programs.

Acknowledgements. We thank the European Commission, EASPD, and all the members of the Care4Skills consortium for their continued efforts to create a sustainable European blueprint model for long-term care and its digitalization.

References

1. WHO: Disability: https://www.who.int/europe/news-room/fact-sheets/item/disability. Last accessed 13 April 2026
2. European Union: Long-term care - Employment, Social Affairs and Inclusion, https://employment-social-affairs.ec.europa.eu/policies-and-activities/social-protection-social-inclusion/social-protection/long-term-care_en. Last accessed 13 April 2026
3. Joint Research Centre Europe: Long-term care needs in the EU on the rise, due to demographic change - Joint Research Centre, https://joint-research-centre.ec.europa.eu/jrc-news-and-updates/long-term-care-needs-eu-rise-due-demographic-change-2024-02-02_en. Last accessed 13 April 2026
4. Eurofound, Dubois, H., Leončikas, T., Molinuevo, D., Wilkens, M.: Long-term care workforce: employment and working conditions. Publications Office of the European Union (2020)
5. European Commission: European Care Strategy for caregivers and care receivers, https://ec.europa.eu/commission/presscorner/detail/en/ip_22_5169. Last accessed 15 January 2025
6. World Health Organization: Regional digital health action plan for the WHO European Region 2023–2030, https://iris.who.int/server/api/core/bitstreams/05678ea1-4e26-4f88-9802-f32cdcd9415a/content (2022)
7. European Union: Pact for Skills: launch of large-scale skills partnership for long-term care - Employment, Social Affairs and Inclusion, https://employment-social-affairs.ec.europa.eu/news/pact-skills-launch-large-scale-skills-partnership-long-term-care-2023-04-20_en. Last accessed 13 April 2026
8. European Union: Blueprint on Digital Transformation of Health and Care for the Ageing Society | Shaping Europe's digital future, https://digital-strategy.ec.europa.eu/en/library/blueprint-digital-transformation-health-and-care-ageing-society. Last accessed 16 April 2026
9. Centre, E.C.J.R.: DigComp 3.0 Explorer, https://digcomp-eu.com/. Last accessed 17 April 2026
10. European Union: Policies | Shaping Europe's digital future, https://digital-strategy.ec.europa.eu/en/policies. Last accessed 17 April 2026
11. Iseni, J., Swoboda, W., Houben, D., Hilla, R.: Acceptance of digital technology among nursing staff in geriatric long-term care: systematic review. JMIR Nursing **9**, e82223 (2026). https://nursing.jmir.org/2026/1/e82223. https://doi.org/10.2196/82223
12. GRay, K., Butler-Henderson, K., Day, K.: A digitally capable aged care workforce: demands and directions for workforce education and development. JMIR Aging. 8 (2025). https://doi.org/10.2196/54143
13. Mikkonen, K., et al.: Digital health competence among healthcare professionals: a cross-sectional cluster analysis across 19 countries and regions. Int. J. Nurs. Stud. **176**, 105348 (2026). https://doi.org/10.1016/j.ijnurstu.2026.105348

14. Sand, M., et al.: Creating design weights for a panel survey with multiple refreshment samples: a general discussion with an application to a probability-based mixed-mode panel. Methods, Data, Analyses **19**, 4–22 (2025). https://doi.org/10.12758/mda.2025.01
15. Schnell, R.: Survey-Interviews. SpringerVS, Wiesbaden (2019)
16. SoSci: SoSci Survey ▶ Onlinebefragung, DSGVO-konform, deutsches Unternehmen, https://www.soscisurvey.de/de/index. Last accessed 17 April 2026
17. Eurostat: Population change - Demographic balance and crude rates at national level, https://ec.europa.eu/eurostat/databrowser/product/page/DEMO_GIND (2022). https://doi.org/10.2908/DEMO_GIND
18. ESCO: European Skills, Competences, Qualifications and Occupations: Occupations, https://esco.ec.europa.eu/en/classification/occupation-main. Last accessed 17 April 2026
19. Chen, D.: Toward an understanding of 21st-century skills: From a systematic review. Int. J. Educ. Vocat. Guidance **23**, 275–294 (2023). https://doi.org/10.1007/s10775-021-09511-1
20. Buitrago, M., et al.: Social services in Europe: adapting to a new reality. Eurofound, Luxembourg (2023). https://doi.org/10.2806/347055
21. Spasova, S., et al.: Challenges in long-term care in Europe: A study of national policies. Brussels (2018). https://doi.org/10.2767/84573

Frugal and Explainable AI for Accessible Longitudinal Monitoring of Parkinson's Disease

Amina Bouraoui[1,2(✉)], Nour Haouari[1], and Nourhene Belazreg[1]

[1] Institut Supérieur des Technologies Médicales, University of Tunis El Manar, Tunis, Tunisia
amina.bouraoui@istmt.utm.tn

[2] RIADI Laboratory, ENSI, University of Manouba, Manouba, Tunisia

Abstract. Parkinson's disease is a progressive neurodegenerative disorder that affects motor function, daily living activities, and long-term independence, making continuous monitoring essential for effective care. However, disease progression is highly heterogeneous, with patients experiencing motor disability and functional decline at different rates. Predicting short-term deterioration over a 12-month horizon is therefore critical for patient-centered care, enabling clinicians, patients, and caregivers to anticipate changes and organize home-based monitoring or mobility interventions before critical events occur.

In many clinical settings, monitoring remains dependent on expensive diagnostic tools such as neuroimaging, which are often unavailable in low-resource environments, limiting equitable access to care. This disparity is particularly evident in contexts where advanced infrastructure is concentrated in urban centers, restricting access for underserved populations. Addressing this gap is essential for promoting accessible healthcare and digital inclusion.

In this study, we leverage longitudinal data from the Parkinson's Progression Markers Initiative (PPMI) to model 12-month motor progression using baseline clinical assessments. We propose a frugal and explainable machine learning framework that relies solely on routinely collected clinical variables, avoiding dependence on cost-prohibitive imaging modalities. A rigorous evaluation protocol based on patient-level grouped cross-validation is employed to prevent data leakage and ensure reliable performance estimation. Model interpretability is achieved through SHAP-based feature attribution, providing clinically meaningful insights into the factors driving motor progression.

Keywords: accessible healthcare · Parkinson's disease · frugal AI · remote monitoring · digital inclusion

1 Introduction

Parkinson's disease has emerged as one of the most pressing global health crises of our time, sparking a worldwide call for more integrated research and smarter

K. Miesenberger et al. (Eds.): ICCHP 2026, LNCS 16867, pp. 191–198, 2027.
https://doi.org/10.1007/978-3-032-31308-9_23

clinical strategies [1]. The difficulty in managing Parkinson's disease (PD) lies in its unpredictability. Because the disease is so heterogeneous, patients experience motor decline at vastly different rates and in different ways. Being able to predict short-term deterioration is vital for practical care, as it allows families and clinicians to plan for home-based interventions or mobility aids before a crisis occurs. However, in many clinical settings, monitoring is tethered to expensive diagnostic tools like DaTScan imaging. While these scans offer deep biological insights, they are often unavailable in remote or low-resource areas, creating a substantial gap in healthcare access [1,2]. This is a reality in many regions, including Tunisia, where advanced neuroimaging is often concentrated in major urban centers, leaving many patients without the benefits of high-tech diagnostics. To address these gaps, this study utilizes data from the Parkinson's Progression Markers Initiative (PPMI), a landmark longitudinal study dedicated to identifying the biomarkers that track PD over time. By leveraging the PPMI's clinical datasets, we explore the evolution of motor and non-motor symptoms, staying aligned with the initiative's original goal of understanding disease progression [3]. Positioned at the intersection of eHealth and disability-related monitoring, this work leverages frugal prediction to enhance accessible care and digital inclusion, particularly in resource-constrained environments. It offers a threefold contribution: (i) a frugal longitudinal framework for predicting motor severity using only commonly collected clinical variables, eschewing costly neuroimaging; (ii) a rigorous evaluation protocol that tackles core challenges in longitudinal modeling, such as temporal and patient-identity leakage via strict patient-level partitioning; (iii) enhanced transparency via SHAP-based feature attribution, pinpointing clinical factors linked to short-term motor decline and enabling interpretable, clinically actionable predictions.

2 State of the Art

To move toward more objective assessments, researchers have spent significant time exploring how wearable sensors can track motor symptoms in Parkinson's disease. A broad review of existing literature highlights how these technologies allow for continuous, home-based monitoring of tremors, gait, and motor fluctuations, providing a much more detailed picture than traditional, "snapshot" clinical visits [4]. Recent breakthroughs have shown that by pairing wearable inertial sensors with machine learning, we can pick up on subtle motor abnormalities that might otherwise go unnoticed. These sensor-based methods are not only effective at distinguishing Parkinson's patients from healthy individuals but also show promise in identifying the very first "prodromal" motor signs in the earliest stages of the disease [5]. Specific applications have also proven quite accurate; for instance, using a convolutional neural network to analyze gait data has allowed researchers to estimate MDS-UPDRS-III motor severity scores. Because these predicted scores align so closely with actual clinical evaluations, they provide strong evidence that wearables can reliably monitor how the disease is progressing [6]. At the same time, the field has seen a shift toward more sophisticated longitudinal modeling. Using data from the PPMI, researchers have demonstrated that it is possible to forecast motor decline over time. One successful approach involved a Bayesian multivariate framework that predicted annual changes in motor scores, results that were later validated in an independent cohort of patients [3]. In current diagnostic practice, dopamine transporter imaging (DaT-SPECT) is widely regarded as a reference technique for quantifying nigrostriatal dopaminergic loss in Parkinson's disease. Analyses based on PPMI data have shown that reduced striatal DaT binding, particularly at early stages, is associated with poorer motor outcomes and can act as a marker of disease evolution [7]. Despite their biological importance, DaTScans are expensive, require specialized equipment, and are often performed infrequently. For many healthcare systems and patients in underserved regions, these scans are simply too costly or inaccessible to be used for routine monitoring.

3 Methodology

3.1 Data Source

For this study, we drew our data from the Parkinson's Progression Markers Initiative (PPMI). The PPMI is a landmark, long-term observational study designed specifically to identify and validate the biomarkers needed to track how Parkinson's evolves. By utilizing this clinical dataset, we aim to map out the patterns of both motor and non-motor symptom progression, staying true to the study's original mission [3].

3.2 Prediction Task and Features

Our primary goal was to predict short-term motor progression. Specifically, we set out to forecast a patient's MDS-UPDRS Part III motor severity score at a 12-month horizon using only their baseline information. The features we used included basic clinical markers: initial motor severity, functional autonomy, age, and sex. We also included an interaction term between age and baseline motor severity to capture more nuanced trends. For the sake of comparison, we also tested an extended version of the model that included striatal binding ratios from DaTScans. This focus on clinical features is supported by recent research showing that even subtle motor abnormalities can be captured and used effectively in longitudinal modeling [5].

3.3 Handling Missing Data

The task involves predicting 12-month motor progression from baseline clinical data. We included only patients with complete baseline variables and corresponding 12-month follow-up measurements. All evaluations used patient-level partitioning via unique identifiers (PATNO), supporting grouped cross-validation and preventing data leakage across training and test sets. For missing values, we adopted a conservative, clinically aligned strategy: forward filling within patient trajectories to maintain temporal coherence (assuming stability in certain variables between visits), followed by median imputation for residuals selected for its outlier robustness and alignment with a frugal, transparent pipeline. Advanced imputation methods warrant future investigation to better model variable interdependencies.

3.4 Methodological Rigor and Leakage Prevention

To ensure our findings were scientifically sound, we followed current best practices for machine learning in clinical research [8]. One of the most critical steps was preventing "data leakage," a common pitfall where a model accidentally "sees" a patient's future or identity during training. We implemented a strict patient-level split, ensuring that no data from a single patient's history could ever appear in both the training and testing phases [9]. To further account for any variability in how the data was partitioned, we evaluated the models using patient-level GroupKFold cross-validation. All performance results are reported as the mean and standard deviation across these different folds to provide a transparent view of the model's reliability.

3.5 Modeling and Explainability

We compared three different modeling approaches: a "persistence" baseline (which simply assumes the last known score remains the same), a standard linear regression, and a more sophisticated non-linear XGBoost regressor. Because we believe clinical models should never be a "black box," we used SHAP (SHapley Additive exPlanations) to provide clarity. This is a widely respected method that allows us to see exactly which features are driving the model's predictions, making the results much more interpretable for clinicians [10].

4 Results

Whether we utilized clinical data in isolation or integrated multimodal inputs, the "frugal" XGBoost model consistently edged out the simple persistence baseline. It remained competitive with standard linear regression and frequently achieved superior performance. Specifically, within the clinical-only framework, the non-linear model achieved the most precise results, yielding both the lowest error and the highest explained variance. These results indicate that motor progression over a 12-month horizon is far more nuanced than a tidy, straight line. It isn't simply a matter of symptoms plateauing or declining at a fixed, predictable speed.

An important observation is that incorporating DaTScan features did not yield measurable performance gains. Instead of improving predictive accuracy, these features often introduced noise, leading to greater variability across different data folds. For the specific task of tracking short-term changes, this suggests that the high cost and logistical hurdles of neuroimaging may not be justified for this prediction task, as no additional predictive benefit was observed. Routine, accessible clinical assessments appear to provide the most reliable predictive value.

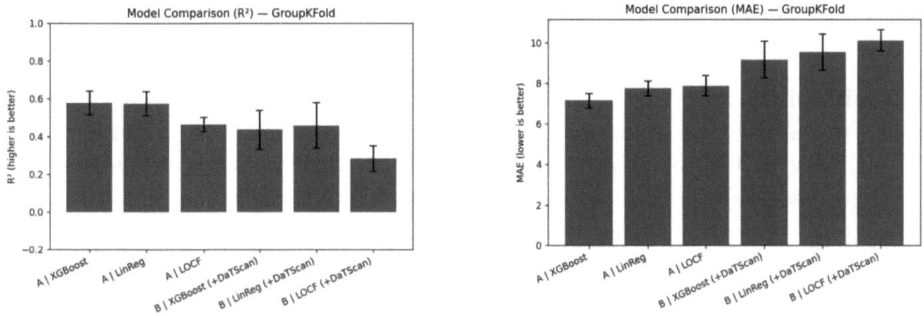

Fig. 1. Performance comparison (Frugal vs Full, MAE and R^2).

As shown in Fig. 1, the frugal XGBoost model consistently outperformed both the naive persistence (LOCF) baseline and linear regression across patient-level cross-validation folds, underscoring the limited capacity of persistence-based and linear models to capture short-term variations in motor severity.

Across all configurations, the frugal model achieved the lowest prediction error and highest explained variance. The inclusion of DaTScan features did not result in consistent performance improvements and was associated with increased variability across folds. Collectively, these findings suggest that, for short-term prediction tasks, standard clinical measures offer sufficient and more stable predictive value compared to resource-intensive neuroimaging modalities.

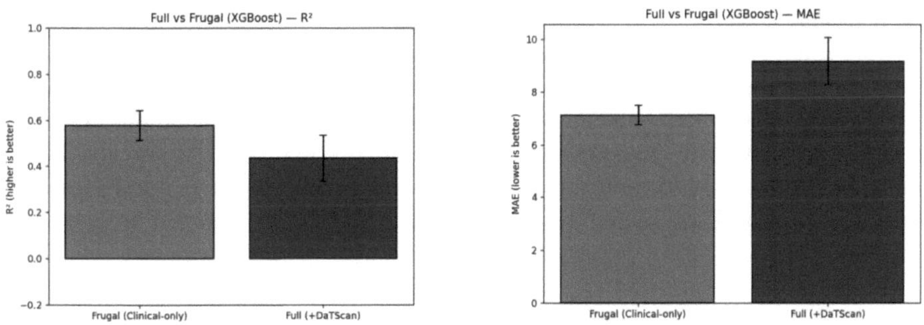

Fig. 2. Full vs Frugal XGBoost (effect of DaTScan).

As illustrated in Fig. 2, the inclusion of DaTScan-derived features did not yield systematic performance gains compared to the frugal configuration, suggesting that high-cost neuroimaging contributes marginally to short-term motor severity prediction in this setting.

4.1 Frugality, Explainability, and Inclusion

Frugality. The frugality of the proposed framework is reflected in the observation that baseline clinical features alone were sufficient to achieve strong predictive performance. Excluding neuroimaging did not compromise accuracy, supporting a modeling strategy compatible with low-resource healthcare settings.

Explainability. SHAP-based feature attribution analysis of the frugal XGBoost model revealed that baseline motor severity, functional autonomy, and age were the primary drivers of predicted motor severity at 12 months, while sex contributed marginally. The direction and magnitude of these effects were clinically consistent, supporting transparent interpretation of model behavior.

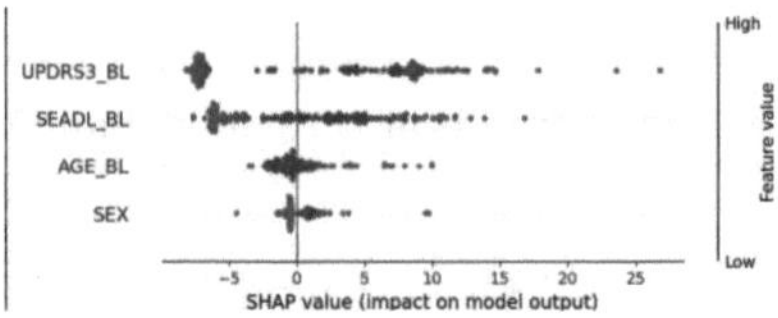

Fig. 3. SHAP summary plot.

As shown in Fig. 3, SHAP-based explainability analysis indicated that baseline motor severity, daily living function, cognitive status, and age were the primary drivers of predicted motor decline. In contrast, neuroimaging and additional sensor-derived variables contributed marginally to model performance.

Inclusion. Although telemedicine has the potential to improve access to Parkinson's disease care, its real-world adoption remains uneven. Practical obstacles persist, including the limits of remote neurological assessment, differences in patients' familiarity with digital tools, and unreliable internet access in some settings [4]. To better ground these issues, we conducted a small, informal exploratory survey in Tunisia ($n = 10$), focusing on how patients perceive barriers to hospital-centered monitoring. These insights are provided purely for contextualization and are meant to inform future work, not to serve as empirical evidence.

5 Discussion

This study shows that near-term motor evolution in Parkinson's disease can be predicted using a frugal and explainable machine learning framework based on routinely collected clinical data. By avoiding reliance on costly neuroimaging, the approach supports accessible and resource-efficient monitoring, particularly in low-resource settings.

From a clinical perspective, predicting 12-month motor decline may enable earlier intervention, improved follow-up, and more personalized care. It also supports monitoring beyond hospital settings, including home-based and everyday care environments.

This work is primarily based on secondary clinical data and should be viewed as a methodological step toward accessible digital health solutions. User involvement remains limited and will be expanded in future work through patient and caregiver integration. Several limitations must be acknowledged. The study relies on a specific cohort, which may limit generalizability. In addition, median imputation, while simple and robust, may not capture complex data dependencies and should be refined in future studies.

Finally, the inclusion of imaging features derived from DaTScan, including putamen binding ratios, did not consistently improve performance. This suggests that routine clinical data may be sufficient for short-term prediction.

6 Conclusion

Using data from the PPMI cohort, this study shows that short-term motor progression over a 12-month horizon in Parkinson's disease can be anticipated using frugal modeling approaches based on standard clinical measures. By deliberately avoiding dependence on costly neuroimaging and by enforcing a careful evaluation strategy that prevents information leakage, we illustrate that transparent and interpretable models can still provide useful short-term predictions under realistic constraints. While the results presented here rely on baseline clinical data, we developed the proposed framework with future extensions in mind, particularly the integration of wearable-derived motor features as such data become more accessible. In settings where advanced imaging is difficult to obtain due to cost or infrastructure limitations, this short-term and resource-aware approach offers a practical direction for more accessible digital monitoring of Parkinson's disease.

References

1. Dorsey, E.R., Bloem, B.R.: The Parkinson pandemic-a call to action. JAMA Neurol. **75**(1), 9–10 (2018)
2. Marek, K.: The Parkinson's progression markers initiative (PPMI). Prog. Neurobiol. (2011)
3. Latourelle, J.C.: Bayesian multivariate modeling of Parkinson's disease progression using PPMI longitudinal data. PLoS ONE (2017)
4. Pham, T., Bonnet, C., Prigent, G.: Estimating MDS-UPDRS-III motor severity from gait data using deep learning. NPJ Digit. Med. **4**, 176 (2021)
5. Paganoni, S., Simmons, Z., Cohen, B.H.: Telemedicine in the management of Parkinson's disease: achievements, challenges, and future perspectives. J. Parkinson's Dis. **12**(4), 1291–1303 (2022)
6. Rovini, E., Maremmani, C., Cavallo, F.: How wearable sensors can support Parkinson's disease diagnosis and treatment: a systematic review. Front. Neurosci. **13**, 555 (2019)

7. Trinh, J., Gasser, T., Berg, D.: Dopamine transporter imaging as a predictor of motor progression in Parkinson's disease. Neurology **100**(12), e1254–e1263 (2023)
8. Bernett, C., Kather, J.N., McKinney, S.M.: Guiding questions to avoid data leakage in clinical machine learning. Nat. Mach. Intell. **6**, 139–145 (2024)
9. Koçak, B., Jethanandani, A., Rieke, N.: Must-have qualities of clinical research on artificial intelligence. Nat. Med. **29**, 1346–1355 (2023)
10. Ponce-Bobadilla, A., et al.: A practical guide to SHAP analysis for explainable machine learning in biomedical research. Briefings Bioinf. **25**(1), bbad518 (2024)

From Care Crisis to Digital Transformation? Digitalization and Assistive Technologies in European Long-Term Care

Melanie Schaur(✉)

Johannes Kepler University Linz, Linz, Austria
melanie.schaur@jku.at

Abstract. Digitalization and the increasing use of assistive technologies are reshaping long-term care (LTC) systems across Europe in response to demographic ageing, workforce shortages, and growing care complexity. While technological innovation is often presented as a solution to structural challenges in care provision, empirical comparative evidence on how these technologies are implemented in practice remains limited. This study analyses national long-term care sector reports from multiple European countries to examine the current role of digitalization and assistive technologies in care delivery, organizational practices, and workforce adaptation. Using a qualitative comparative synthesis of national reports based on stakeholder interviews and sectoral analyses, the study identifies key patterns in technological adoption, including the widespread use of digital documentation systems, communication technologies, monitoring devices, and rehabilitation-support tools. The findings indicate that digital technologies generally complement rather than replace human caregiving, contributing to hybrid care models that combine technological support with relational care practices. Implementation remains uneven across countries and organizations, shaped by policy frameworks, infrastructure, workforce competencies, and ethical considerations such as privacy and trust. The study highlights the importance of organizational readiness, continuous workforce training, and ethical governance in ensuring that digital transformation supports sustainable and person-centered long-term care systems. These findings contribute comparative empirical insights into the evolving role of digitalization and assistive technologies in European LTC contexts.

Keywords: Long-Term Care · Assistive Technologies · Digitalization

1 Introduction

Long-term care (LTC) systems across Europe are undergoing significant transformations in response to demographic ageing, increasing prevalence of chronic conditions, and persistent workforce shortages [1]. Forecasts suggest that the proportion of individuals requiring long-term care will grow from 11.6% in 2020 to 14.1% by 2070, implying a projected 21% increase in the number of people aged 50 and older requiring LTC

K. Miesenberger et al. (Eds.): ICCHP 2026, LNCS 16867, pp. 199–207, 2027.
https://doi.org/10.1007/978-3-032-31308-9_24

compared with 2020 [2, 3]. These demographic developments are part of broader global ageing trends that are expected to affect labor markets, health systems, and demand for social services, including long-term care provision [4].

Within this context, digitalization and the growing use of assistive technologies have emerged as key areas of policy attention and sectoral innovation. Technologies such as digital documentation systems, telecare platforms, monitoring devices, communication tools, and emerging artificial intelligence (AI) applications are increasingly integrated into care provision with the aim of improving efficiency, supporting autonomy, and addressing structural pressures on care systems. At the policy level, digital technologies are frequently framed as potential solutions to workforce shortages and rising care demands, although their implementation remains uneven and socially embedded rather than purely technological [5].

Assistive technologies, broadly understood as devices, systems, and services that support functional abilities and independence among persons with disabilities or age-related limitations, play a particularly important role in this transformation. Research indicates that these technologies can enhance quality of life, support independent living, and reduce physical and administrative burdens on care professionals while improving coordination between caregivers and care users [6–8]. However, evidence consistently suggests that assistive technologies complement rather than replace human caregiving, contributing to hybrid care arrangements that combine technological support with relational care practices [9].

Despite increasing technological adoption, the integration of digital tools, especially digital tools using AI, into long-term care raises important organizational, professional, and ethical questions. Studies highlight concerns related to privacy, autonomy, data security, and trust, particularly when monitoring technologies or data-intensive systems are introduced into care environments [10]. Acceptance of assistive technologies among care users and professionals depends not only on technological functionality but also on perceived reliability, ethical governance, and the extent to which technologies align with person-centered care values [11]. At the same time, digitalization has implications for care workforce competencies and organizational practices. Care professionals are increasingly required to develop digital skills, integrate technological tools into everyday care routines, and navigate new forms of technologically mediated interaction with care users and families. Existing research suggests that technologies are generally perceived as supportive tools rather than substitutes for professional care, emphasizing the continued importance of relational and emotional dimensions of caregiving even within technologically enhanced environments [12].

Despite growing interest in digital health technologies and assistive devices, comparative empirical evidence on how digitalization is implemented in long-term care systems across national contexts remains limited. This study addresses this gap by analyzing national long-term care reports from multiple European countries. It is guided by the following research question: How are digitalization and assistive technologies being implemented in European long-term care systems, and what implications do national reports identify for care practices, workforce roles, and organizational transformation? By examining cross-national sector reports, the study aims to provide empirically grounded insights into how digitalization is shaping contemporary long-term care.

The paper is structured as follows: Sect. 2 provides a review of the current situation regarding digitalization and assistive technologies in LTC by analyzing the state of the art. This section highlights the potential of these technologies at a systems level, as well as the challenges of their implementation. It also addresses issues related to inclusion and the digital divide, workforce and organizational dynamics, ethical considerations, and trust. Section 3 details the methodology, including the comparative qualitative design, data sources, composition of interviews across countries, and the thematic synthesis approach. Section 4 presents the results, synthesizing cross-national patterns in technology adoption, administrative digitalization, workforce implications and ethical-relational dynamics. Section 5 discusses the findings in relation to existing literature, outlines policy and practice implications, reflects on limitations and concludes with directions for future research.

2 State of the Art

Digitalization and the increasing use of AT are reshaping long-term care systems, driven by demographic ageing, rising chronicity, and persistent workforce shortages, while also reflecting broader policy ambitions to modernize care delivery through information and communication technologies, AI, robotics, and remote care infrastructures. Within healthcare policy and implementation discourses, these technologies are frequently positioned as system-level solutions to fragmented care and strained resources, promising improved coordination, proactive management of chronic needs, and expanded reach via telemedicine and remote care technologies, even though operationalization and implementation details often remain underspecified in practice [9].

Empirical work on the relationship between AT and personal care suggests that technologies may, under certain conditions, reduce reliance on informal care while simultaneously complementing formal care, indicating that substitution is neither uniform nor straightforward and depends on user characteristics such as cognitive ability and social resources [13]. At the same time, inclusive digitalization remains contested because persistent digital divides shape who can benefit from technological change: Older adults and LTC residents may face exclusion due to limited access to devices or connectivity, insufficient skills, lack of institutional support, and functional limitations that require assistance for ICT use. The COVID-19 pandemic made these inequalities particularly visible: While ICT-mediated contact (e.g., video calls) was widely promoted as a remedy for isolation in residential care, many residents could not fully participate due to barriers in infrastructure, support, and skills, illustrating how "digital push" dynamics can reproduce or intensify social exclusion if accessibility is not addressed [9]. Workforce and organizational dimensions are equally central in the literature: Implementing AT, robotics, and digital tools may alter workplace culture and care practices and can evoke ambivalent responses among staff, making leadership, training, and organizational readiness critical determinants of uptake. In LTC facilities, ethical acceptability is repeatedly identified as a core condition of successful deployment, with stakeholder concerns clustering around privacy, autonomy, safety, cost, surveillance, and the dignity of residents, especially where pervasive monitoring technologies (e.g., video/audio, wearables, environmental sensors) are introduced [10]. These concerns connect directly to trust in care relationships: Recent evidence synthesized across studies indicates that AT can influence trust dynamics between caregivers and care receivers by shaping perceptions of reliability, competence, intrusiveness, and control, with trust operating as a key mediating factor in whether technologies are accepted and meaningfully integrated into care practices [9]. A growing socio-technical and science-and-technology-studies-oriented strand further highlights that policy narratives often frame healthcare and care work as "in crisis," while promoting digitalization, AI, and robotics as pathways toward "good care" and "good work," thereby shaping expectations and governance strategies for technological futures in care [5].

These considerations underline the importance of empirical research examining how digitalization and AT are actually implemented in long-term care settings, as comparative evidence on their real-world implications for care practices, workforce dynamics, and organizational change remains scarce.

3 Methodology

The study adopted a qualitative comparative research design based on secondary analysis of national reports examining digitalization and assistive technologies in the European long-term care sector. The reports followed a shared template and a semi-structured interview guide was provided to ensure cross-country comparability while allowing contextual specificity. The sections included addressed workforce characteristics, digitalization practices, skills development, assistive technology use, and organizational challenges. The included countries were Belgium, Bulgaria, Czech Republic, Finland, France, Greece, Hungary, Italy, Netherlands and Spain. The countries represented multiple European contexts, covering diverse long-term care systems and organizational settings such as residential care, home care services, disability support services, and community-based care organizations.

The reports are based on qualitative, semi-structured interviews with experts on skills in long-term care, which were conducted as part of the European sectoral cooperation initiative Care4Skills. The interviews were held with: Social service managers [14], care workers [15], nursing professionals [16], and social work assistants [17]. For the sake of methodological simplicity, the latter three staff categories have been grouped together under the heading 'care workers' (Table 1).

Overall, 182 interviews were analyzed, including 115 interviews with care workers and 67 with social service managers. In most countries, care workers constitute the larger share of interviewees, reflecting their central role in everyday long-term care provision, while managers provide organizational and strategic perspectives. The number of interviews varies by country, with the highest representation of care workers in Hungary, Greece, and the Czech Republic, and a more balanced distribution between professional groups in countries such as Finland and Bulgaria.

The analysis focused specifically on the adoption and use of assistive technologies and their impact on care delivery, workforce competencies, and user autonomy. A thematic qualitative synthesis was conducted in three stages. First, national reports were reviewed to identify references to digital technologies in care, assistive technologies supporting autonomy, workforce digital skills, barriers to inclusion, and impacts on care

Table 1. Qualitative Expert Interviews (Source: Own Representation)

Country	Interviews with Care Workers	Interviews with Social Service Managers
Belgium	6	5
Bulgaria	5	5
Czech Republic	15	5
Finland	10	10
France	9	11
Greece	15	5
Hungary	16	9
Italy	14	5
Netherlands	11	4
Spain	14	8
Total	**115**	**67**

delivery and user experience. Second, an inductive thematic coding process identified recurring themes such as types and contexts of assistive technology use, challenges, digital literacy and training needs, and the ethical and relational implications of technological care, while documenting cross-country similarities and differences.

The comparative synthesis examined broader structural patterns across the European long-term care sector, including variations in technology adoption, workforce skill gaps, and organizational readiness for digital transformation.

4 Results

The comparative analysis of national long-term care reports reveals a growing but uneven integration of digitalization and assistive technologies across the examined European care systems. While all analyzed countries report some degree of technological adoption, the extent, strategic orientation, and organizational embedding of digital tools vary substantially depending on national policy priorities, funding structures, and institutional readiness. In most contexts, digitalization appears to be evolving incrementally rather than through comprehensive transformation strategies, with technological adoption often occurring in response to specific organizational needs rather than as part of coordinated sector-wide reforms.

Assistive technologies are most frequently reported in relation to safety monitoring, communication support, and rehabilitation practices. Sensor-based monitoring systems, alarm technologies, and remote observation tools are commonly used to enhance safety and support independent living, particularly in home-care settings. Communication technologies, including digital platforms facilitating interaction between care professionals, care users, and families, are widely adopted across countries and are often perceived as improving coordination and reducing social isolation. Rehabilitation-related technologies, such as digitally supported physiotherapy or cognitive support tools, are present in several national contexts, although their adoption remains uneven and closely linked to resource availability and organizational innovation capacity.

Administrative digitalization represents another prominent dimension of technological integration. Electronic care records, digital reporting systems, and communication platforms are widely implemented to improve documentation efficiency and coordination across care teams. However, the reports highlight considerable variability in infrastructure quality, interoperability of systems, and staff digital competencies. In some cases, partial digitalization has introduced new complexities, including parallel documentation systems or additional administrative workload during implementation phases, suggesting that technological adoption does not automatically translate into efficiency gains.

Workforce implications emerge consistently across the national reports. Digitalization requires new professional competencies, including technical skills, data interpretation abilities, and capacity to integrate technological tools into relational care practices. Many care professionals report ongoing adaptation challenges and emphasize the need for continuous training and organizational support. Importantly, technologies are generally perceived as augmenting rather than replacing care work, particularly when they reduce physically demanding tasks or administrative burdens while preserving opportunities for interpersonal interaction. This perception underscores the continuing centrality of relational care even within increasingly technologized care environments.

Ethical considerations and relational dynamics also shape technology adoption. Concerns regarding privacy, surveillance, data security, and autonomy frequently accompany the introduction of monitoring technologies. Trust between care users, professionals, and families emerges as a key condition for successful implementation. Technologies are most positively evaluated when they are perceived as supporting autonomy and safety without undermining interpersonal relationships. Overall, the results suggest that digitalization in long-term care is characterized by pragmatic integration into existing care practices rather than radical transformation, with organizational readiness, workforce competencies, and ethical considerations playing decisive roles.

5 Discussion and Conclusion

This study examined how digitalization and assistive technologies are being implemented in European long-term care systems and what implications national reports identify for care practices, workforce roles, and organizational transformation. The analysis demonstrates that technological adoption is widespread but uneven, reflecting differences in national policy frameworks, organizational readiness, infrastructure investment, and workforce competencies.

Assistive technologies are primarily used to support safety, communication, coordination, and autonomy among care users, while digital documentation systems and communication platforms contribute to organizational efficiency. However, technologies generally complement rather than replace human caregiving, reinforcing hybrid care models that combine technological support with relational care practices. Workforce adaptation remains a key challenge, with increasing demand for digital competencies alongside continued emphasis on interpersonal caregiving skills.

The findings highlight that successful digital transformation in long-term care requires more than technological innovation alone. Organizational readiness, workforce training, ethical governance, and sustained policy support are critical for ensuring that digitalization enhances rather than disrupts care provision. Future research should further investigate long-term impacts of technological integration, cross-national differences in implementation strategies, and mechanisms for supporting inclusive and sustainable digital transformation in long-term care systems.

Furthermore, the findings provide empirical support for the growing recognition that digitalization in long-term care represents a socio-technical transformation rather than a purely technological process. Consistent with existing literature, assistive technologies tend to complement rather than substitute human caregiving, contributing to hybrid care models that combine digital support with relational, person-centered care practices. This challenges narratives that present technology primarily as a solution to workforce shortages and highlights the importance of organizational, professional, and relational dimensions in shaping technological outcomes.

Workforce adaptation emerges as a particularly significant factor. The introduction of digital technologies reshapes professional roles by requiring new competencies while simultaneously reinforcing the importance of interpersonal caregiving skills. Training provision, organizational learning, and leadership support appear central to facilitating this transition. Without adequate investment in workforce development, digitalization risks creating additional stress for care professionals rather than alleviating workload pressures.

Ethical considerations remain central to technological adoption in care settings. Privacy, autonomy, and trust concerns are not peripheral issues but fundamental determinants of acceptance among care users, families, and professionals. Technologies perceived as intrusive or poorly governed may undermine trust relationships, whereas those integrated transparently into person-centered care practices can enhance safety and confidence. These findings highlight the need for robust ethical governance frameworks accompanying technological innovation.

Importantly, the findings also suggest that digitalization does not automatically produce efficiency gains or improved care outcomes. Implementation challenges, interoperability issues, and uneven digital literacy can limit potential benefits. This reinforces the importance of viewing digital transformation as an ongoing organizational and social process rather than a technical solution.

Limitations of the study: The study is based on secondary data analysis, drawing on national reports rather than primary interview material, which limits control over data collection procedures and consistency. Although a common reporting template was applied, the depth and level of detail vary across countries, affecting comparability to some extent. In addition, the rapid evolution of assistive technologies means the findings reflect a particular moment in time rather than a definitive or long-term overview. Despite these constraints, the comparative synthesis still offers valuable insights into emerging patterns of digitalization and accessibility within European long-term care systems. The study indicates that the future of long-term care will likely involve increasingly hybrid care arrangements combining technological tools with human caregiving. Achieving sustainable and equitable outcomes will require coordinated policy action, workforce development strategies, ethical governance, and continued empirical research into the real-world impacts of assistive technologies across diverse care systems. The study adopts a socio-technical perspective, recognizing that technological adoption in long-term care involves not only technical innovation but also organizational practices, professional identities, accessibility considerations, and relational aspects of care.

References

1. European Commission: Communication from the Commission to the European Parliament, the European Economic and Social Committee and the Committee of the Regions on the European Care Strategy, https://eur-lex.europa.eu/legal-content/EN/TXT/PDF/?uri=CELEX:52022DC0440 (2022)
2. Belmonte, M..: Demographic microsimulation of long-term care needs in the European Union: prototype for a microsimulation model projecting the demand for long term care up to 2070. Publications Office of the European Union, Luxembourg (2023)
3. Joint Research Centre: Long-term care needs in the EU on the rise, due to demographic change - European Commission, https://joint-research-centre.ec.europa.eu/jrc-news-and-updates/long-term-care-needs-eu-rise-due-demographic-change-2024-02-02_en. Last accessed 15 January 2025
4. World Health Organization: UN Decade of Healthy Ageing: Plan of Action 2021–2030 (2020)
5. Breuer, S., Müller, R.: Digitalization, AI, and robotics for good care and work? German policy imaginaries of healthcare technologies. Sci. Pub. Policy **51**, 951–962 (2024). https://doi.org/10.1093/scipol/scae036
6. Anderson, W.L., Wiener, J.M.: The Impact of Assistive Technologies on Formal and Informal Home Care. Gerontologist **55**, 422–433 (2015). https://doi.org/10.1093/geront/gnt165
7. Periša, M., Teskera, P., Cvitić, I., Grgurević, I.: Empowering people with disabilities in smart homes using predictive informing. Sensors **25**, 284 (2025). https://doi.org/10.3390/s25010284
8. World Health Organization: Assistive technology, https://www.who.int/news-room/fact-sheets/detail/assistive-technology. Last accessed 08 May 2024
9. Zheng, K., Han, F., Yang, S., Li, N.: Building trust in long-term care settings using assistive technology: a systematic review. Front. Rehabil. Sci. **5**, 1492104 (2024). https://doi.org/10.3389/fresc.2024.1492104
10. Schaur, M., Matausch-Mahr, K.: Assistive technology using artificial intelligence in the long-term care sector for persons with disabilities: A systematic literature review. Technol. Disabil. **37**, 259–269 (2025). https://doi.org/10.1177/10554181251355420
11. Dorsten, A.-M., Sifford, K.S., Bharucha, A., Mecca, L.P., Wactlar, H.: Ethical Perspectives on Emerging Assistive Technologies: Insights from Focus Groups with Stakeholders in Long-Term Care Facilities. J. Empir. Res. Hum. Res. Ethics **4**, 25–36 (2009). https://doi.org/10.1525/jer.2009.4.1.25
12. Hasseler, M.: Digitalization and new technologies in care – concepts and potentials for nursing care provision. In: Rubeis, G., Hartmann, K.V., Primc, N. (eds.) Digitalisierung der Pflege, pp. 103–116. V&R Unipress, Göttingen (2022). https://doi.org/10.14220/9783737014793.103
13. Agree, E.M., Freedman, V.A., Cornman, J.C., Wolf, D.A., Marcotte, J.E.: Reconsidering substitution in long-term care: when does assistive technology take the place of personal care? The J. Gerontol. Series B. **60**, S272–S280 (2005). https://doi.org/10.1093/geronb/60.5.S272
14. European Commission; Directorate General for Employment, Social Affairs & Inclusion: Social Services Manager (2024).
15. European Commission; Directorate General for Employment, Social Affairs & Inclusion: Social Care Worker (2024).

16. European Commission; Directorate General for Employment, Social Affairs & Inclusion: Nursing Professional, http://data.europa.eu/esco/isco/C2221. (2024)
17. European Commission; Directorate General for Employment, Social Affairs & Inclusion: Social Work Assistant (2024).

Eliciting Design Knowledge for Care Coordination Through Multi-Actor Eco-Map Comparison: A Single-Case Methodological Study

Seiya Moro[1,2](✉), Yutaka Osaki[1], Sota Takagi[1], and Takumi Ohashi[1]

[1] Institute of Science Tokyo, Meguro City, Japan
moro.s.aa@m.titech.ac.jp

[2] Research Fellowships for Young Scientists, Japan Society for the Promotion of Science, Chiyoda-ku, Japan

Abstract. Care coordination in disability and family support often spans multiple organizations and institutional boundaries, leaving families to manage fragmented communication, repeated explanations, and unclear pathways to support. Although eco-maps are widely used to visualize relationships between families and surrounding systems. This paper proposes a multi-actor eco-map comparison method for eliciting design knowledge in complex care coordination settings. Using a single-case methodological study, we conducted two focus group interviews around the same case involving a child with severe intellectual disability: one with institutional actors (local government and welfare professionals) and one with parent mentors. By comparing convergences and divergences across the resulting eco-maps, we identified structural conditions such as weak lateral ties among support actors, the family's role as an information hub, and differences between formal access perspectives and lived continuity experiences. These insights were translated into intermediate-level design knowledge, design principles, and concrete requirements for socio-technical intervention. A high-fidelity prototype was then developed as a design probe to explore the plausibility of these requirements. The contribution of this study is methodological: it demonstrates how multi-actor eco-map comparison can make coordination structures analytically visible and support traceable translation from stakeholder perspectives to design principles and requirements.

Keywords: eCare Coordination · Eco-Map · Design Knowledge Elicitation · Design Principles and Requirements · Disability Family Support

1 Introduction

Care coordination in disability and family support spans multiple organizations, professions, and administrative boundaries. Families often need to interact simultaneously with healthcare, welfare, education, and peer support systems. Although care coordination is intended to organize these activities so that appropriate support can be delivered,

K. Miesenberger et al. (Eds.): ICCHP 2026, LNCS 16867, pp. 208–215, 2027.
https://doi.org/10.1007/978-3-032-31308-9_25

fragmentation, role ambiguity, and discontinuities in information exchange often persist in practice [1]. As a result, families may face repeated explanations, unclear pathways, and the burden of mediating communication across stakeholders.

These challenges are particularly pronounced in support contexts involving children and adults with severe intellectual disabilities, where needs are often long-term, evolving, and distributed across multiple domains of everyday life. In such contexts, support cannot easily be reduced to a single service encounter or a single user need. The issues faced by families and support actors are shaped by interdependent conditions across multiple levels, including institutional arrangements, relationships among support organizations, and everyday caregiving experiences. This makes the design of support tools difficult: a conventional human-centered design approach focusing only on immediate user needs at the micro level may overlook structural conditions at the macro and meso levels that also shape coordination practice.

Design research has emphasized the importance of intermediate-level design knowledge, such as strong concepts, that can connect empirical findings and concrete design decisions [2]. For complex care coordination settings, what is needed is not only an understanding of individual user experiences, but also an approach that can reveal how different actors perceive the support structure and where intervention may be needed across levels. Eco-maps offer one way to visualize a family's relationships with surrounding systems and have long been used for assessment and planning in social work and care contexts [3]. However, eco-maps are typically treated as descriptive tools or as single co-constructed representations. Their potential as a design approach for eliciting design-relevant knowledge across multiple actor perspectives has remained underexplored. Participatory design and probe-based approaches have likewise shown that artifacts can help elicit tacit knowledge and situated practices [4, 5]. Building on this perspective, we use eco-maps not simply to describe care situations, but to support the design of a care coordination tool by making visible the structural tensions and differing viewpoints that shape support practice.

This paper presents a methodological approach for eliciting design knowledge in complex care coordination through multi-actor eco-map comparison. Using a single family support case involving a child with severe intellectual disability, we compare eco-maps created by institutional actors and parent mentors, interpret the resulting differences across macro, meso, and micro levels, and translate these insights into design principles, requirements, and a prototype as a design probe.

2 Related Work

Eco-maps have been widely used to visualize a family's relationships with surrounding formal and informal systems, particularly in social work and care contexts, to support assessment and planning [3]. They provide a structured way to represent stakeholders, relationship strength, and flows of interaction around a focal family. However, eco-maps are typically constructed as a single, co-created representation that integrates multiple perspectives into one map.

While this is useful for shared understanding, it also tends to smooth over differences between stakeholders. As a result, eco-maps are rarely used to explicitly capture or analyze divergences in how different actors perceive the same coordination structure. From a design perspective, this raises an open question: how can eco-maps be used not only as descriptive tools, but also as analytical artifacts to reveal structurally different viewpoints and inform design decisions?

3 Methodology

3.1 Study Design and Overview

This study is methodology-oriented design research using a single case to define and demonstrate a method, not to generalize outcomes about care coordination effectiveness. The unit of analysis is the design knowledge elicited through multi-actor comparison and its translation into design principles and requirements.

We applied the method to one family support case involving a child with severe intellectual disability and multiple support stakeholders. Two separate focus group interviews (FGI) sessions were conducted to co-construct eco-maps from different actor perspectives:

- Operational/institutional side: local government and welfare professionals ($n = 12$).
- Peer support side: parent mentors ($n = 4$).

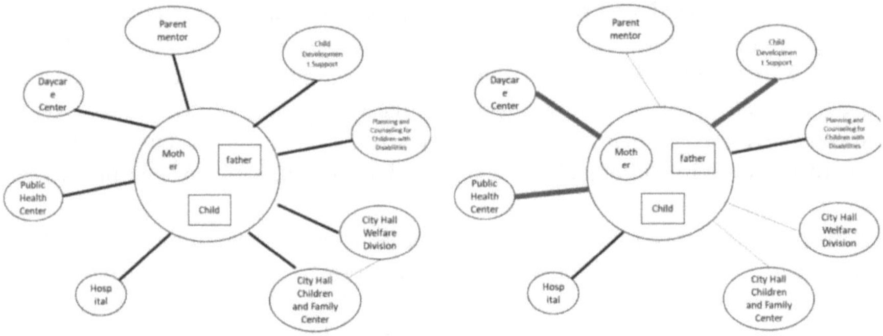

Fig. 1. Eco-maps co-constructed by the institutional group and the parent-mentor group for the samecase (Left: Institutional group, Right: Parent-mentor group)

A UI prototype was then created as a design probe. We then conducted exploration interviews with three parents, and one welfare support professional to collect formative feedback on the proposed requirements and interaction concepts. In this study, we use the term intermediate design knowledge to refer to structured design-relevant insights that bridge observed coordination patterns and concrete design decisions, such as design principles and requirements.

3.2 Defining the Multi-Actor Eco-Map Comparison Method

Eco-map construction. Each FGI co-created an eco-map by placing the focal family at the center and arranging surrounding stakeholders around it. Figure 1 shows the two eco-maps co-constructed by the institutional group and the parent-mentor group for the same case, which served as the basis for the comparison reported in Sect. 4.

3.3 Multi-Actor Comparison and Translation Procedure

We define the proposed method as a four-step process that translates differences across eco-maps into design knowledge and requirements.

Step A: Difference extraction: Convergences and divergences across the eco-maps were identified by comparing the actors represented, the relationships shown, and the overall coordination patterns.

Step B: Structural interpretation: interpret differences as structural conditions (e.g., "weak lateral ties," "family-as-information-hub," "different framings of entry and continuity").

Step C: Design knowledge articulation: express intermediate knowledge as intervention points, design foci, and candidate mechanisms, organized across macro/meso/micro layers.

Step D: Translation and traceability: translate design knowledge into design principles (DP) and requirements (R) and explicitly link each DP/R back to the corresponding extracted differences and structural interpretations.

4 Findings: Design Knowledge Elicited by the Method

This section reports design knowledge made visible through multi-actor eco-map comparison, rather than claiming improved coordination outcomes.

4.1 Convergent Insight: "Family-As-Hub" Under Weak Lateral Ties

Both eco-maps placed the family at the center of dense relationships, while lateral links among support organizations were sparse. This suggests that information often travels through the family, reframing caregiver burden as a structural network issue rather than only an individual one.

4.2 Divergent Framing: Formal Access vs Entry/Continuity Experience

The institutional view emphasized formal access points (windows, procedures, resources), whereas the parent-mentor view emphasized entry/continuity experiences (hesitation, psychological load, and peer support). The implication is that design should bridge these frames-otherwise it risks overlooking either experiential barriers or procedural constraints.

4.3 Multi-Layer Articulation (Macro/Meso/Micro) of Bottlenecks

Figure 2 shows bottlenecks across three layers elicited by the comparison: macro (low portability/standardization of child information and limited proactive involvement mechanisms), meso (weak cross-stakeholder ties and episodic coordination), and micro (repeated explanations, reduced agency, and delayed sensemaking/acceptance).

4.4 A Reinforcing Negative Loop as Design Knowledge

These layers can reinforce one another: weak lateral ties → family-as-hub → repeated burden → reduced agency → delayed connection → more ad hoc coordination → persistently weak lateral ties. This shifts the design focus from adding features to interrupting the reinforcing conditions.

5 Translating Design Knowledge into Design Principles and Requirements

Based on the design knowledge elicited through multi-actor eco-map comparison, we derived a set of design principles (DP) and corresponding requirements (R). The principles function as decision criteria that guide design directions, while the requirements specify implementable conditions. Each principle and requirement is grounded in the structural findings reported in Sect. 4, ensuring traceability from observed differences to design decisions.

5.1 Design Principles (DP)

DP1: De-brokering the family (reducing hub burden).

To address the "family-as-hub" structure identified in Sect. 4.1, the design should reduce the need for families to repeatedly mediate information across stakeholders. This includes enabling reuse and controlled sharing of core information to avoid redundant explanations.

DP2: Standardize and make information portable.

In response to macro-level fragmentation (Sect. 4.3), information should be structured in a way that supports portability across contexts. A "common core + purpose-specific views" model allows different stakeholders to access relevant information without requiring families to reformat or reinterpret it for each interaction.

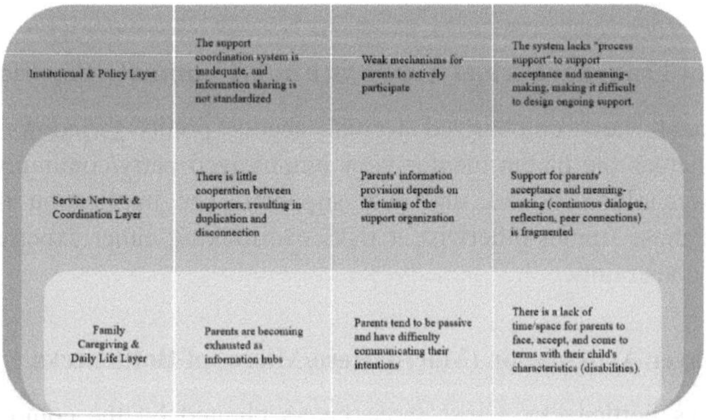

Fig. 2. Structural bottlenecks via multi-actor eco-map comparisons

DP3: Support caregiver agency (from reactive to proactive).

Given the micro-level findings of reduced agency (Sect. 4.3), the design should enable caregivers to prepare, articulate priorities, and act proactively rather than only responding to institutional interactions or events.

DP4: Support sensemaking and continuity.

Addressing both the experiential gap identified in Sect. 4.2 and the delays in sensemaking (Sect. 4.3), the design should support reflection, interpretation, and continuity of experience. This includes connecting everyday experiences with decision-making processes and future actions.

5.2 Requirements (R)

Based on the above principles, we specify the following requirements as concrete design conditions:

R1: Whole-network overview.

The system should visualize key stakeholders and their relationships in a single view, enabling users to understand the overall coordination structure. This requirement primarily supports DP1 and DP2 by making coordination structures visible beyond isolated encounters.

R2: Perspective bridging.

The system should support switching or comparing different viewpoints (e.g., institutional vs caregiver perspectives) to reduce blind spots and align understanding. This requirement primarily supports DP3 and DP4, while also contributing to DP1 by reducing misalignment across actors.

R3: Gap detection.

The system should highlight weak or missing connections, as well as unclear pathways, to make structural issues visible. This requirement primarily supports DP1 and DP2 by revealing where coordination burden and fragmentation arise.

R4: Next-action guidance.

The system should provide actionable guidance, such as who to contact, what to prepare, and suggested questions, to support navigation of the coordination process. This requirement primarily supports DP3 and DP4 by helping caregivers act proactively and sustain continuity across interactions.

R5: Integration of informal and peer support.

The system should represent informal and peer-based resources alongside formal services, reflecting the role of peer support identified in Sect. 4.2. This requirement primarily supports DP3 and DP4 by connecting everyday experience, emotional support, and decision-making.

6 Prototype as Design Probe

To make the derived design requirements concrete and discussable, we developed a high-fidelity UI prototype in Figma. The prototype was informed by the design principles and implemented the requirements derived from them. Figure 3 shows the prototype screens created to address the structural bottlenecks identified across macro, meso, and micro levels. The interface labels are in Japanese. Key labels include 「子育て記録」(Care log), 「つぶやく」(Micro-posts), 「みんなの呟き」(Peer posts feed), and 「基本情報」(Basic info/Life Support File). These functions were designed not as isolated features, but as concrete manifestations of the previously derived design principles and requirements.

6.1 Core Functions Instantiated in the Probe

The probe instantiated selected functions derived from the requirements presented in Sect. 5.2:

- Care log (DX records): captures events and issues for later reuse in consultation and sharing.
- Micro-posts ("murmurs"): support the externalization of concerns and everyday reflections.
- Peer posts feed: enables users to explore experiences and practices shared by other caregivers.
- Life Support File: provides a portable child profile for controlled sharing across settings.

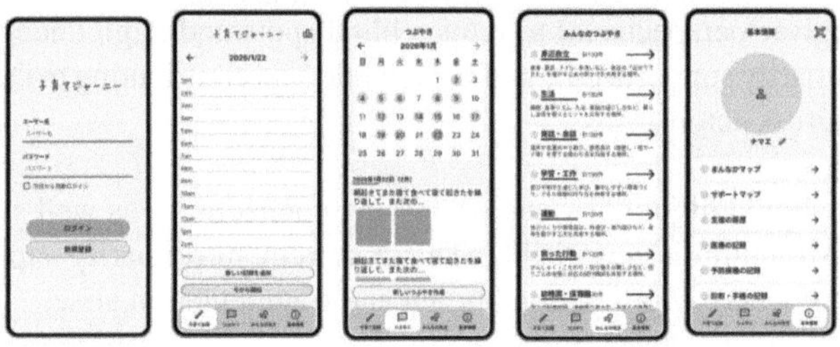

Fig. 3. Prototype screens addressing the three-level bottlenecks. *UI labels are in Japanese. Key labels:* 「子育て記録」 *= Care log,* 「つぶやく」 *= Micro-posts ("Tweet"),* 「みんなの呟き」 *= Peer posts feed,* 「基本情報」 *= Basic info (Life Support File).*

6.2 Exploratory Probe Interviews (3 Parents, 1 Welfare Support Professional)

Exploratory interviews with one welfare support professional and three parents were conducted to discuss the prototype functions as formative interaction concepts rather than as a formal evaluation. Participants valued the integration and reuse of fragmented child-related information across settings, particularly for reducing repeated explanations. They also regarded peer-sharing as potentially useful only when supported by similarity-sensitive matching across families' situations. At the same time, concerns were raised regarding open-sharing environments, especially in relation to privacy, sensitive information, and moderation. Overall, the interviews clarified three practical conditions for future refinement: information centralization, peer matching, and sharing governance.

7 Discussion and Conclusion

This paper has presented a methodological approach for eliciting design knowledge in complex care coordination through multi-actor eco-map comparison. By treating differences across actors as analytically valuable rather than as noise, the approach made it possible to surface structural tensions that would be difficult to capture in a single co-constructed representation, including weak lateral ties, family-as-hub conditions, and divergences between formal access and lived continuity perspectives. In this way, the method supported the translation of cross-actor differences into multi-level design knowledge and traceable design principles and requirements.

The prototype phase served not as a validation of effectiveness, but as a design probe that helped concretize the derived requirements and examine their practical relevance. The exploratory interviews further clarified conditions for future refinement, particularly around information centralization, similarity-sensitive peer matching, and sharing governance. At the same time, this study has several limitations: it is based on a single case, depends partly on facilitation and interpretation, and does not establish generalizable claims about coordination outcomes or system effectiveness.

In conclusion, the contribution of this paper is methodological. It demonstrates how multi-actor eco-map comparison can function as a structured way to elicit design knowledge from complex coordination settings and to connect stakeholder differences to traceable design decisions.

Acknowledgement. Use of AI in writing. Generative AI was used to assist language editing and drafting during manuscript preparation. The authors reviewed and revised all generated text and took full responsibility for the final content.

References

1. McDonald, K.M., et al.: Closing the Quality Gap: A Critical Analysis of Quality Improvement Strategies, Vol. 7: Care Coordination. Agency for Healthcare Research and Quality (AHRQ) (2007)
2. Höök, K., Löwgren, J.: Strong concepts: Intermediate-level knowledge in interaction design research. ACM Transactions on Computer-Human Interaction (TOCHI) **19**(3), Article 23 (2012)
3. Hartman, A.: Diagrammatic assessment of family relationships. Social Casework **59**(8), 465–476 (1978)
4. Gaver, W., Dunne, T., Pacenti, E.: Design: Cultural probes. Interactions **6**(1), 21–29 (1999)
5. Sanders, E.B.-N., Stappers, P.J.: Co-creation and the new landscapes of design. CoDesign **4**(1), 5–18 (2008)

Indoor and Outdoor Navigation for Disabled People: Challenges and Opportunities

Indoor and Outdoor Navigation for Disabled People: Challenges and Opportunities

Navigation for People with Disabilities and Older People: Current Challenges and Opportunities Introduction to the Special Thematic Session

Helen Petrie[1(✉)], Gerhard Weber[2], and Anna Bramwell-Dicks[2]

[1] University of York, York, UK
helen.petrie@york.ac.uk
[2] University of Technology, Dresden, Germany
gerhard.weber@tu-dresden.de, anna.bramwell-dicks@york.ac.uk

Abstract. Navigation presents many challenges for everyone, but particularly for people with disabilities or older people. This Special Thematic Session (STS) brought together researchers and practitioners interested in the use of technology to support people with disabilities and older people in navigation, including both indoor and outdoor navigation in the real world, as well as navigation in virtual worlds. Technologies such as GPS, robotics and AI have provided many advances in independent, safe navigation for these groups, but there are always new technologies emerging and many challenges to be addressed. Papers at the STS presented an interesting range of challenges and opportunities, including investigating users' needs, the use of new technologies such as LiDAR and other sensing systems, better solutions to issues which have been addressed previously such as indoor navigation, understanding traffic lights, and issues around micro or near-field navigation for people with visual disabilities.

Keywords: Navigation · Wayfinding · Obstacle Detection · People with Disabilities · Older People

1 Introduction and Background

Navigation can be a problem for everyone from time to time. Whether it is trying to find one's way in an unfamiliar town or in the country, in a complex office building, or a hospital, airport or museum. Increasingly, we need to navigate through virtual environments as well as physical ones. For people with disabilities and older people, these situations can be particularly challenging. This in turn means that disabled and older people may miss opportunities for work and leisure, are less independent, and have poorer quality of life overall.

Recently developed technologies have provided exceptional advances in relation to navigation for everyone, from GPS guidance and digital maps to beacon-based audio guides in museums. These developments have also been very important to disabled and older people, for example providing pedestrian navigation systems for visually disabled people using GPS and digital maps. Other technologies have supported people with

K. Miesenberger et al. (Eds.): ICCHP 2026, LNCS 16867, pp. 219–224, 2027.
https://doi.org/10.1007/978-3-032-31308-9_26

physical disabilities, for example development of power wheelchairs with autonomous navigation and exoskeletons for mobility. However, many gaps remain and new technologies are constantly emerging which might be beneficial for older and disabled people. This Special Thematic Session (STS) was an opportunity for researchers and practitioners to present recent research on technologies for navigation for disabled and older people, and on the gaps in research which need to be addressed.

Research on human navigation covers a wide range of topics and issues, traditionally about navigation in the physical world, but increasingly navigation in the digital world. Considering navigation in the physical world, at the broadest level we can think of navigation in outdoor spaces having a particular set of challenges for disabled and older people, while navigation in indoor spaces has its own set of challenges, although there are some challenges which apply to navigation in all environments. Outdoor spaces can range from very crowded urban environments with many vehicles, pedestrians and obstacles, to rural environments with complex terrain, animals and different obstacles. Indoor spaces also include many different types of environments to navigate, from large office buildings with complex corridor and room layouts to buildings with large open spaces such as train stations or airports.

Another aspect of navigation, particularly important for disabled and older people, is the dimension of micro-navigation versus macro-navigation, also referred to locomotion versus wayfinding or near- versus far-field navigation (see more detailed discussion of these terms in [9, 15, 18, 20, 24, 26]). The first term in the pairs refers to finding one's way through the immediate environment whereas the second term refers to finding and following a route usually with a destination in mind.

For people with visual disabilities micro-navigation is a particular challenge as there may be obstacles at both foot level (in urban environments swinging signs on pavements, street furniture such as benches and fire hydrants to name a few) and head height (e.g. overhanging branches) that they will not detect. There is also the challenge that without visual feedback humans tend to veer off a straight path, which can be problematic for visually disabled pedestrians. Use of a long cane or guide dog helps address both these challenges, but neither are perfect solutions and many technological solutions have been offered in this area. These solutions range from early systems to detect obstacles and provide tactile or auditory warnings (for example the Mowat Sensor [21, 22] and Sonic Guide [13, 14]) to numerous additions to the long cane (for example the LaserCane, [6], UltraCane [10]). However, none of these solutions have been widely adopted by users, for a variety of reasons [8], so this is still an area which could be addressed with technology.

For people with mobility disabilities, such as wheelchair users, changes in levels of surfaces (potholes, curb drops, steps) are challenges in micro-navigation (although flights of stairs might be better categorized as part of macro-navigation) as they can create insurmountable barriers. Interestingly, solutions to this challenge to support wheelchair users can also benefit other users, particularly visually disabled users, who find information about changes in surface in general positively useful in navigation and information about potentially dangerous changes in surfaces, such as potholes important to be able to avoid them (although a guide dog is likely to avoid that particular potential danger). Older people also may feel unsteady on their feet and benefit from information about surfaces [25]. However, this area also highlights the problem of conflicts between support for different user groups, so a holistic approach is always needed. Tactile paving to indicate street crossings and appropriate routes through large spaces can be beneficial for visually disabled people but create new challenges for wheelchair users and older people. Dropped kerbs assist wheelchair users in crossing roads but remove a source of information about the edge of the pavement for visually disabled people. These conflicts are not common, but they do occur.

For people with visual disabilities, macro-navigation in unknown locations was until recently a major barrier. People with visual disabilities would be trained to navigate particular routes, for example between their home and school or place of work, however being able to go somewhere new with only a long cane or guide dog was a very daunting task which many people would not undertake. The advent of digital maps linked with GPS tracking has largely overcome this barrier and allowed people with visual disabilities to become much more independently mobile with personal navigation systems [19, 24]. Originally these systems required expensive, specialist devices, but are now available on smartphones, providing much more convenient access (for example Ariadne GPS [2], Blindsquare [5] Lazarillo [17]). Of course, smartphones are still expensive devices, so affordability is still a potential barrier.

Finding accessible and safe routes is also potentially a challenge for people with mobility disabilities and older people. As mentioned above, for people with mobility disabilities, including users of wheelchairs and other mobility aids, flights of stairs are obviously insurmountable barriers, as are steep slopes, and surfaces not suitable for their mobility aid. Routes need to be planned to avoid such barriers. In addition, for older people barriers include very busy roads which may be difficult to cross, environments which may be poorly lit at night and routes which have steep slopes [25]. Other people can benefit in a more positive way from route planning systems based on digital maps. For example, for neurodivergent people and those with anxiety or learning difficulties, being able to plan a route and do a virtual walk along the route on a digital map with a street view, can boost confidence in then navigating the route in reality.

2 Contributions

The papers presented in the session covered an interesting range of topics in navigation for disabled and older people. Six of the eight papers addressed challenges for people with visual disabilities and two addressed challenges for people with mobility disabilities, one specifically for wheelchair users and the other for people who use a range of different mobility aids. There were three papers each focusing either on indoor or outdoor navigation issues, as well as one paper which addressed all aspects of navigation.

In relation to research for people with visual disabilities, the papers covered an interesting range of challenges relevant to both indoor and outdoor navigation. Isaksson-Daun [11] addressed the fact that great advances in outdoor far-field or macro-navigation have been made using technologies such as GPS and digital maps, as discussed above, there has been less progress in near-field or micro-navigational support despite some early successful results [27], with most visually disabled people relying on a long cane or guide dog. Therefore, he has created a system for conducting user tests on depth-based near-field navigation for people with visual disabilities to detect obstacles such as stairs.

Král & Tibor [16] explored the potential of extending LiDAR (Light Detection and Ranging) technology for 3D scanning to assist in navigation by improving the accuracy of sensing and mapping the environment. Vertical structures can be dangerous if they appear at the head level and the reason for many types of obstacles for people who are blind have to protect themselves. At the same time (downward) stairs are hard to detect without good 3D models of the environment. On the other hand, van der Bie et al. [4] addressed the challenge of understanding visual traffic lights, a well-known challenge for pedestrians with visual disabilities in navigating the outdoor urban environment, but one still without totally satisfactory solutions. Auditory and tactile signals can be added to the panels where pedestrians request a light change, but these have not been very successful. As van der Bie et al. [4] noted, these can be turned off in the evening (particularly if the auditory signal disturbs nearby residents), are often broken, or only installed at some crossings. Van der Bie et al. propose a solution in which the visually disabled pedestrian carries their own device which detects the status of the traffic light (it would be even better if this could be an app on a smartphone so that people did not need to carry an extra device and remember to take it with them). It is also interesting that this solution highlights a long-standing debate in accessibility, where we question if it is better to equip the environment (i.e. put the appropriate equipment on every traffic light which then becomes the responsibility of the relevant authorities to maintain) or to equip disabled individuals, which then places more responsibility on those individuals.

Comai et al. [7] addressed the challenge of information about surfaces from the point of view of smart wheelchair users, although as discussed above surface information can potentially help other groups such as people with visual disabilities and older people if such data are made available through digital maps. Their work proposes a low-cost sensing and analysis framework for automatic surface condition monitoring. It is geared to wheelchair users as it uses a wheelchair as a mobility proxy to capture the physical interaction between user and environment, but one can imagine the approach being extended to information for other groups.

Turning to indoor navigation issues for people with visual disabilities, Abraham & Namboodiri [1] carefully built on the knowledge that visually disabled people who use a long cane often navigate in indoor spaces by following wall lines with their cane. They incorporated "wall-trailing", as it is sometimes known, as part of the guidance offered by an indoor navigation system. This is an excellent example of how important it is to have a deep understanding of potential users when developing assistive technology solutions. Yu et al. [26] addressed an interesting challenge that is a new consequence of using advanced technologies for people with disabilities, the fact that vision-based indoor navigation systems may detect the faces of people in the vicinity of the user. Their research investigated the challenge of whether blurring the faces of such people compromises the accuracy of the navigation system, fortunately they find it does not.

It was particularly encouraging to see that two of the papers [3, 12] investigated user needs. Too often researchers develop solutions without enough consideration of what issues are most important to potential users of a system. Joseph and Hakansson [12] point out "uncertainty is a stronger barrier than the act of wayfinding itself" as the main result of their large survey among people in need of a better navigation system. Temporal changes remain as the biggest reason for increasing uncertainty and will limit mobility if not addressed in future work.

Interestingly, all the papers in the STS focus on using technologies to support navigation in real, physical world environments. Increasingly, however we are having to navigate complex 3D virtual worlds both for entertainment purposes (e.g. in video games) or to support access to the real world (e.g. route planning via Street Views). This presents a significant opportunity for researchers to explore how these emerging and improving approaches to provide better access for navigating indoor and outdoor physical spaces, can be adapted to enhance accessibility within virtual environments. Future work should consider the transferability of physical navigation frameworks and approaches to virtual contexts, to address accessibility challenges within virtual spaces as well.

Disclosure of Interests. The authors have no competing interests to declare that are relevant to the content of this article.

References

1. Abraham, A., Namboodiri, V.: Beyond Turn-by-Turn: Wall-Trailing Indoor Navigation for Blind Users. In: Miesenberger, K., Petrie, H.., Penaz, P. (eds.) ICCHP 2026, Computers Helping People with Special Needs, 20th International Conference; Linz, Austria, Proceedings. Springer (2026)
2. Ariadne GPS: https://www.iaccessibility.com/apps/low-vision/index.cgi/product?ID=9
3. Bamdad, B.M., Günther, M., Darvishy, A.: Navigating Independence: A Survey of Visually Impaired People's Experiences and Needs. In: Petz, A., Miesenberger, K. (eds.) ICCHP Open Access Compendium "Future Perspectives on Accessibility, AT and eInclusion"; Linz, Austria, Proceedings. Johannes Kepler University Linz (2026)
4. van der Bie, J., et al.: Supporting Accessible Street Crossing for Persons with a Visual Impairment using a Handheld Traffic Light Detector. In: Miesenberger, K., Petrie, H., Penaz, P. (eds.) ICCHP 2026, Computers Helping People with Special Needs, 20th International Conference; Linz, Austria, Proceedings. Springer (2026)
5. Blindsquare app. https://www.blindsquare.com/
6. Bolgiano, D., Meeks, E.: A laser cane for the blind. IEEE J. Quantum Electron. **3**(6), 268 (1967). https://doi.org/10.1109/jqe.1967.1074528
7. Comai, S., et al.: Smart Wheelchair System for Surface Type Classification and Obstacle Detection. In: Miesenberger, K., Petrie, H.., Penaz, P. (eds.) ICCHP 2026, Computers Helping People with Special Needs, 20th International Conference; Linz, Austria, Proceedings. Springer (2026)
8. Dos Santos, A.D.P., Medola, F.O., Cinelli, M.J., Garcia Ramirez, A.R., Sandnes, F.E.: Are electronic white canes better than traditional canes? A comparative study with blind and blindfolded participants. Univ. Access Inf. Soc. **20**(1), 93–103 (2021)
9. Goldschmidt, M.: Orientation and mobility training for people with visual impairments. In: Mobility of Visually Impaired People: Fundamentals and ICT Assistive Technologies. Springer (2018)
10. Hoyle, B., Waters, D.: Mobility AT: The batcane. In: Hersh, M., Johnson, M. (eds.) Assistive Technology for Visually Impaired and Blind People. Springer, London (2008). https://doi.org/10.1007/978-1-84628-867-8_6

11. Isaksson-Daun, J.: A Depth-Based Mobility Aid Development Platform for Users with Blindness and Low Vision. In: Petz, A., Miesenberger, K. (eds.) ICCHP Open Access Compendium "Future Perspectives on Accessibility, AT and eInclusion"; Linz, Austria, Proceedings. Johannes Kepler University Linz (2026)
12. Joseph, S., Hakansson, N.: Design Requirements for Accessible Indoor Wayfinding Technologies Supporting People with Mobility Disabilities. In: Miesenberger, K., Petrie, H., Penaz, P. (eds.) ICCHP 2026, Computers Helping People with Special Needs, 20th International Conference; Linz, Austria, Proceedings. Springer (2026)
13. Kay, L.: Ultrasonic spectacles for the blind. Proceeding of the Conference on Sensory Devices for the Blind, p 275–290. St. Dunstan's (1966)
14. Kay, L.: A sonar aid to enhance spatial perception of the blind: Engineering design and evaluation. Radio and Electronic Engineer **44**(11), 605–627 (1974). https://doi.org/10.1049/ree.1974.0148
15. Kilian, J., Neugebauer, A., Scherffig, L., Wahl, S.: The unfolding space glove: a wearable spatio-visual to haptic sensory substitution device for blind people. Sensors **22**, 1859 (2022)
16. Král, R., Vince, T., Molnár, J.: Design and Calibration of a Wearable 3D LiDAR for Assistive Navigation of People with Visual Impairment. In: Miesenberger, K., Petrie, H., Penaz, P. (eds.) ICCHP 2026, Computers Helping People with Special Needs, 20th International Conference; Linz, Austria, Proceedings. Springer (2026)
17. Lazarillo app. https://lazarillo.app/theapp/
18. Loomis, J.M., Da Silva, J.A., Fujita, N., Fukusima, S.S.: Visual space perception and visually directed action. J. Exp. Psychol. Hum. Percept. Perform. **18**(4), 906 (1992)
19. Loomis, J.M., Golledge, R.G., Klatzky, R.L., Speigle, J.M., Tietz, J.: Personal guidance system for the visually impaired Proceedings of the first annual ACM conference on Assistive technologies, Marina Del Rey, California, USA (1994). https://doi.org/10.1145/191028.191051
20. Montello, D.R., Sas, C.: Human factors of wayfinding in navigation. CRC Press/Taylor & Francis, International Encyclopedia of Ergonomics and Human Factors (2006)
21. Morrissette, D.L., Goodrich, G.L., Hennessey, J.J.: A follow-up study of the Mowat Sensor's applications, frequency of use, and maintenance reliability. J. Visual Impair. Blindn. **75**(6), 244–247 (1981). https://doi.org/10.1177/0145482X8107500603
22. Pressey, N.: Mowat sensor. Focus **11**(3), 35–39 (1977)
23. Sánchez, J., de la Torre, N.: Autonomous navigation through the city for the blind Proceedings of the 12th international ACM SIGACCESS conference on Computers and accessibility. Orlando, Florida, USA (2010). https://doi.org/10.1145/1878803.1878838
24. Strothotte, T., et al.: Development of dialogue systems for a mobility aid for blind people: initial design and usability testing. Proceedings of ASSETS '96: The Second Annual Conference on Assistive Technology. ACM Press, New York (1996). ISBN 0-89791-776-6
25. Swallow, D., Petrie, H., Power, C., Edwards, A.D.N.: Using photo diaries to elicit user requirements from older adults: a case study on mobility barriers. In: Proceedings of the 15th IFIP International Conference on Human-Computer Interaction (INTERACT 2015). Springer (2015)
26. Yu, J., Bhadane, D., Yang, Y., Namboodiri, V.: Integrating Face Blurring into Vision-Based Indoor Navigation: Privacy-By-Design. In: Miesenberger, K., Petrie, H., Penaz, P. (eds.) ICCHP 2026, Computers Helping People with Special Needs, 20th International Conference; Linz, Austria, Proceedings. Springer (2026)
27. Zeng, L., Simros, M., Weber, G.: Camera-based mobile electronic travel aids support for cognitive mapping of unknown spaces. In: Proceedings of the 19th international conference on human-computer interaction with mobile devices and services, pp. 1–10 (2017)

Supporting Accessible Street Crossing for Persons with a Visual Impairment Using a Handheld Traffic Light Detector

Joey van der Bie[1,2(✉)], Anouar Douiyeb[1], Olivia van Eijk[1], Sara ter Haar[1], Alieke Ossevoort[1], Inge van 't Wout[1], Marc te Riele[3], Johan Camps[3], Margriet Pol[1], Krista Overvliet[2], and Albert Postma[2]

[1] Occupational Therapy: Technology and Participation, Centre of Expertise Urban Vitality, Amsterdam University of Applied Sciences, Amsterdam, The Netherlands
j.h.f.van.der.bie@hva.nl

[2] Experimental Psychology and Helmholtz Institute, Utrecht University, Utrecht, The Netherlands

[3] Step Hear Nederland, Son en Breugel, The Netherlands

Abstract. Safe street crossing at busy urban intersections is a challenge for persons with visual impairment (PVI). Many intersections in the Netherlands are equipped with traffic light for cars, cyclist and pedestrians, but lack accessible pedestrian signals for PVI. This results in unsafe situations where PVI cannot adhere to the traffic signals, because they do not have reliable access to the visual information required to determine when it is safe to proceed. We investigated whether accessible street crossing could be facilitated by a handheld traffic light detector that can be placed by the pedestrian directly on a traffic light. Through tactile and auditory indicators, the PVI is notified when the light turns green. We field tested our detector with four PVI at a busy intersection in Amsterdam. Insights were gathered through observations, the System Usability Scale (SUS) and an interview. The results show the detector increased accessibility and users highly value the system (SUS score: 94.4), but crossing at a pedestrian island could still causes problems. Therefore, we would recommend training with the device in advance, especially at complex crossings.

Keywords: Assistive Technology (AT) · (e) Accessibility · blind · visually impaired · crossing · intersection · navigation · Sensor Technology · traffic light

1 Introduction

Independent mobility is a significant challenge for persons with visual impairments (PVI). Particularly in urban environments where navigating intersections safely is difficult due to: the environmental noise that disrupt the hearing; complex crossings with multiple lanes that are to be crossed; and the busy traffic that requires attention [3, 12]. Due to their impairment, PVI cannot rely on the visual traffic signals and mostly have to rely on auditory cues. Relying on auditory cues is difficult and can be dangerous.

K. Miesenberger et al. (Eds.): ICCHP 2026, LNCS 16867, pp. 225–231, 2027.
https://doi.org/10.1007/978-3-032-31308-9_27

The sounds of approaching vehicles are frequently obscured by ambient environmental noises, while acoustic signals are distorted by surrounding features such as bends and objects [3]. Electric vehicles are even more difficult to detect [2]. Furthermore PVI often overestimate the vehicle distance, which can lead to dangerous crossing behaviour [5].

To make the crossing safer, traffic signals can be equipped with accessible pedestrian signals (APS), although different in each country, APS's produce a ticking sound to indicate when it is safe to cross and where to walk towards [4]. However, in practice many intersections lack APS, they are turned off in the evenings, or are broken, leaving many street crossings inaccessible [1].

We investigated whether accessibility at street crossings without APS could be facilitated by using a handheld light detector that translates pedestrian and cycling green light indicators into haptic vibration patterns and audio tones. We designed a prototype and performed a pilot field test with PVI in Amsterdam. In this paper, we introduce the device and present the test results.

2 Related Research in Accessible Street Crossing Aids

Previous research in assistive technology for accessible street crossing has explored the use of computer vision (CV) and wireless communication in various form factors. When considering wearable navigation technology, PVI prefer a small, lightweight, easy to use, reliable device that provides real-time response [6].

Integrating wireless communication in the traffic light to communicate with the navigation app of the smartphone, allows the traffic signal to provide detailed information on: street crossing safety; approaching vehicles; and position on the street crossing [13]. Still, this asks for more technological integration in traffic lights than an APS, has limitations on the maximum number of users and does not create a safer environment than an APS would.

The advancements in both CV and smartphone processing power have enabled sophisticated image processing capabilities in a wearable formfactor that can identify traffic signals and detect oncoming vehicles in real time [10]. However, even after user training, it remains difficult to point the camera towards the correct target, to avoid motion blur and hold the phone at the correct angle [7, 8, 10]. Indeed, reports about commercially available detection apps are mixed on detection accuracy and ease of use [15]. This shows that while technically feasible, in practice using a smartphone for identifying traffic signals is still difficult and not ready for daily usage.

More advanced CV systems have been explored in formfactors such as wearables [11], smart white canes [9] and autonomous guiding systems [14]. However, they are still in early research phase, being currently unpractical for daily usage and have limited reliability, with detection rates of green lights between 60 and 94%.

3 Introducing Zebrapod

To increase accessibility at traffic lights without APS, we co-created with an experience expert PVI a handheld device that can reliably detect and communicate when a traffic light is green. Through our talks we concluded the device should be small, light, fit in a pocket or purse, and work directly when activated, independent of other (smart) devices. Further reliability was important for safe street crossing, the person using the device should not be in doubt if the device was working or was providing a false positive signal. This resulted in the Zebrapod: A handheld device that is placed directly at a body height mounted pedestrian or cycling signal light source to receive confirmation of the green light (Fig. 1A). The Zebrapod uses a light detector to provide real-time tactile and auditory indicators when the light is green. A foam ring (Fig. 1B) allows the device to fit the traffic light housing to block ambient light and ensure accurate readings. When in doubt about working conditions, the left button can be activated to test the actuators. The right button activates the detection mode.

We used a low-tech hardware solution with widely available components keeping material costs below six euros and power demands low (Fig. 1C). The whole system is powered by a 3V coin cell battery and only active when a button is pressed. A vibration motor and piezo buzzer provide the tactile and auditory indicators. They are activated through a transistor, when enough light is shined on the Light Dependent Resistor. A resistor is used to balance the light threshold.

A B C

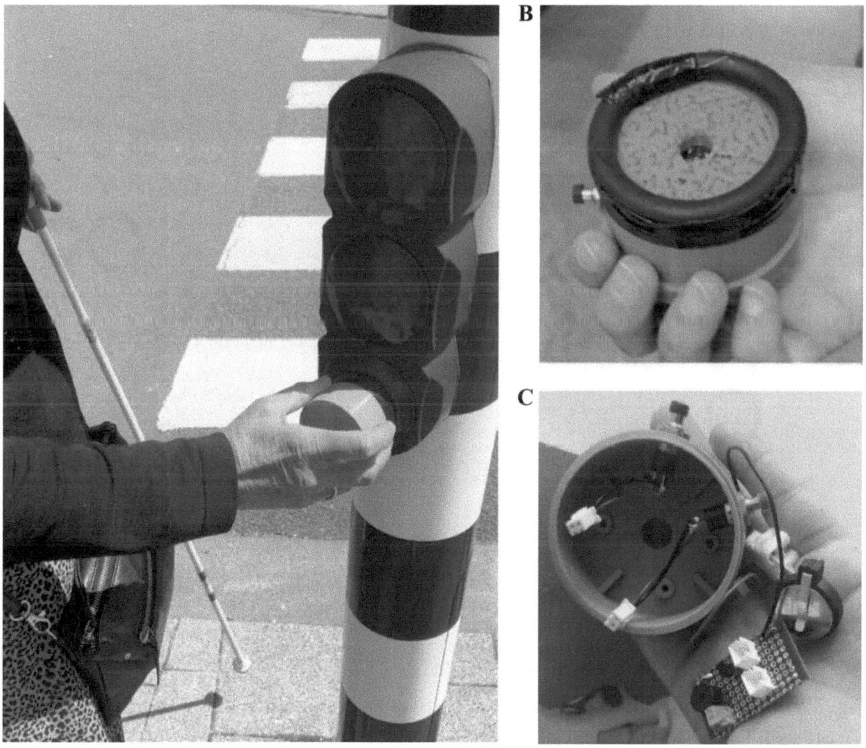

Fig. 1. A Participant detecting the green light with the Zebrapod; **B** The Zebrapod with the 3D printed casing and foam ring matching the size of a small traffic light; **C** Inside the Zebrapod showing the hardware components.

4 Methodology

The effectiveness of our approach was evaluated through a field test by PVI in Amsterdam. Insights were gathered through observations, the System Usability Scale (SUS) and an interview. Participants were selected based on the inclusion criteria: presence of a visual impairment; ability to ambulate independently on foot; and absence of comorbidities. Informed consent was obtained from all participants.

The evaluation was conducted along a predefined route at an intersection with multiple combined cyclist- and pedestrian-crossings with small body height placed light indicators (Fig. 2). Participants first walked on a double lane crossing with a pedestrian island between, followed by a single lane crossing. The route was traversed under guidance, during which the cyclist traffic buttons and lights were identified, and participants were given an opportunity to familiarize themselves with the device by placing it on the green light. Subsequently, participants continued the route while accompanied by a researcher.

Video recordings were used for observational analysis of user-device interactions. Following the route completion, the SUS was administered to determine perceived usability, supplemented by a semi-structured interview for additional insights in safety, accessibility and user experience.

Fig. 2. Test situation with indication of light activation button and indicator light of a double lane crossing with a pedestrian island and a single lane crossing. Participants walked from A to B and back to A.

5 Results

Four adults (three male, one female) participated in the study. Three participants used a white cane for daily navigation. Participant 1 could only distinguish between light and dark. Participant 2 experiences very blurred vision but could perceive colors. Participant 3 possessed a visual field of only 5%, with near vision limited to very close distances. Participant 4 had vision less than 5% in one eye and 20% in the other.

All participants gave the system a high usability score, with an average SUS score of 94.4 (SD 2.6) of 100. Indicating the device is highly acceptable for usage without requiring significant training or modification. Almost all questions were scored maximum or near maximum by all participants. Frequency of use and confidence while using were scored lower by two participants.

In the interview, participants were very positive about the device. They could easily identify the sound and vibrations and would be interested in using the device when available. All participants found the device reliable, would feel safe in using this device independently, were not afraid with collisions with cyclists and would recommend it to other PVI. Recommendations were made to make the device thinner, have smaller and marked buttons, and to be fitted with a cord to make it easier to carry or to be able to connect it to the white cane.

We observed that after the learning phase all participants successfully applied the device on the route. The light could be easily identified, and the device effectively applied to the light. There were no issues with false positives. One participant placed the device on the red-light indicator, having the device vibrating when to wait and stopping vibration when the red light was off. Demonstrating a new effective usage method.

Only at the start of the test, two participants were hesitant on relying fully on the device. When the device vibrated, they first asked the experimenter for confirmation to safely cross the street.

While crossing the street, the participants had no indication if the light was still green. At the pedestrian island between the car lanes, uncertainties arose whether continuing was safe. Since cyclists travel at higher speeds than pedestrians, it was reasonable to assume the light might have turned red. Two of the participants chose to stop at the island and asked the experimenter for help.

Despite the participants walking near the cycling lane, no physical interaction or problems with cyclists occurred during the test.

6 Discussion

We investigated whether a handheld traffic light detection device could facilitate accessible street crossing for PVI. The results show that users were able to reserve their attention on monitoring environmental hazards while receiving confirmation of safe street crossing. Both the open questions as the SUS average score of 94.4, indicate a high level of perceived usability among participants with minor improvement recommendations. Participants expressed strong interest in the future availability of the device.

However, limitations regarding the effectiveness at intersections with pedestrian islands show safety issues might still occur for some PVI's. To limit this risk, users could first get training to get familiar with the specific street crossing, and the time it takes for a safe street crossing.

Although the application of the device on a body height mounted traffic light fits a specific use case, it does provide a clear accessibility advantage over non-use. Without the device, PVI lack any indication of a green traffic light, substantially increasing the risk of collisions with vehicles or cyclists. Especially at busy urban street crossings, all extra safety information can help. And typically, at these street crossings the body height lights are places in countries as The Netherlands, Belgium, Denmark and in some parts of London, United Kingdom.

The speed, ease of use and low battery requirements give the device an advantage over smartphone applications using computer vision (CV). Although a similar application can be developed to embed the functionality of detecting a green traffic light in a smartphone app, it is likely that it would experience the same interaction issues as the current CV solutions we found in the literature, as discussed in the introduction [7, 8, 10]: a smartphone app may not provide the same reliability with more false positives, due to faults in the CV algorithm or interference of sun light. Further, the extra steps a user needs to take, reduce ease of use and overall speed over a dedicated device. Launching a camera functionality in a smartphone requires several seconds on a mid-tier smartphone, even when activated through a shortcut. After activation and detection, the app needs to be closed to prevent battery drain, this all while or before starting to cross. Every extra action that needs to be taken, distracts from paying attention to the environment, and can potentially lead to new safety issues. Last, for effective light/dark difference detection sunlight needs to be blocked as we did with our soft ring, applying this ring on a smartphone requires a custom thick smartphone cover. This makes the smartphone difficult to hold or store in a pocket. Still, we have not tested this implementation and encourage future research in comparing a smartphone implementation to a dedicated solution, to see differences in effectiveness and experience.

Taking the feedback of the participants in consideration, for future research we would recommend improving the device to an even smaller more polished form factor with a wearable cord. Further, given the hesitation at the start of the test of two participants, we are interested in performing a long duration usability test with more participants, to determine the effectiveness for everyday independent usage at different settings.

Disclosure of Interests. A Large Language Model was used for translating and paraphrasing sections to formal English. This research was supported by the Dutch Research Council NWO grand 023.023.065 "Blind Navigeren op Navigatieberichten".

References

1. van Dijck, G., van Wieren, D., Zondag, P.: Akoestische signalering bij verkeerslichten voor mensen met visuele beperking. CROW-KpVV, Ede, the Netherlands (2023)
2. Emerson, R.W., Naghshineh, K., Hapeman, J., Wiener, W.: A Pilot Study of Pedestrians with Visual Impairments Detecting Traffic Gaps and Surges Containing Hybrid Vehicles. Transp Res Part F Traffic Psychol Behav **14**, 117–127 (2011). https://doi.org/10.1016/j.trf.2010.11.007

3. Emerson, R.W., Sauerburger, D.: Detecting Approaching Vehicles at Streets with No Traffic Control. J Vis Impair Blind **102**, 747 (2008)
4. Harkey, D.L., Carter, D.L., Barlow, J.M., Bentzen, B.L.: Accessible pedestrian signals: A guide to best practices. Natl Coop Highw Res Program Contract Guide NCHRP Proj (2007)
5. Hassan, S.E.: Are normally sighted, visually impaired, and blind pedestrians accurate and reliable at making street crossing decisions? Invest. Ophthalmol. Vis. Sci. **53**, 2593–2600 (2012). https://doi.org/10.1167/iovs.11-9340
6. Hersh, M.: Wearable Travel Aids for Blind and Partially Sighted People: A Review with a Focus on Design Issues. SENSORS 22 (2022). https://doi.org/10.3390/s22145454
7. Hong, J., Coughlan, J.M.: Enhancing walk-light detector usage for the visually impaired: a comparison of VR exploration and verbal instructions. Int. Web. Conf. **2024**, 139–149 (2024). https://doi.org/10.1145/3677846.3677849
8. Ivanchenko, V., Coughlan, J., Shen, H.: Real-Time Walk Light Detection with a Mobile Phone. In: Miesenberger, K., Klaus, J., Zagler, W., Karshmer, A. (eds.) Computers Helping People with Special Needs, pp. 229–234. Springer, Berlin, Heidelberg (2010)
9. Mai, C., et al.: A Smart Cane Based on 2D LiDAR and RGB-D Camera Sensor-Realizing Navigation and Obstacle Recognition. Sensors 24 (2024). https://doi.org/10.3390/s24030870
10. Mascetti, S., Ahmetovic, D., Gerino, A., Bernareggi, C., Busso, M., Rizzi, A.: Supporting Pedestrians with Visual Impairment During Road Crossing: A Mobile Application for Traffic Lights Detection. In: Miesenberger, K., Bühler, C., Penaz, P. (eds.) Computers Helping People with Special Needs, pp. 198–201. Springer International Publishing, Cham (2016)
11. Son, H., Weiland, J.: Wearable System to Guide Crosswalk Navigation for People With Visual Impairment. Front Electron 2 (2022). https://doi.org/10.3389/felec.2021.790081
12. Szpiro, S., Zhao, Y., Azenkot, S.: Finding a store, searching for a product: a study of daily challenges of low vision people. In: Proceedings of the 2016 ACM International Joint Conference on Pervasive and Ubiquitous Computing, pp. 61–72. Association for Computing Machinery, New York, NY, USA (2016)
13. Theodorou, P., Tsiligkos, K., Meliones, A., Filios, C.: An Extended Usability and UX Evaluation of a Mobile Application for the Navigation of Individuals with Blindness and Visual Impairments Outdoors—An Evaluation Framework Based on Training. Sensors 22 (2022). https://doi.org/10.3390/s22124538
14. Zheng, Z., Cheng, J., Jin, F.: TFP-YOLO: Obstacle and Traffic Sign Detection for Assisting Visually Impaired Pedestrians. Sensors 25 (2025). https://doi.org/10.3390/s25185879
15. Oko - Cross streets and Maps App. In: App Store (2025). https://apps.apple.com/us/app/oko-cross-streets-and-maps/id1583614988. Accessed 2 Feb 2026

Smart Wheelchair System for Surface Type Classification and Obstacle Detection

Sara Comai[1(✉)], Isabel Pfannkuche[2], Giovanni Locatelli[2], Vittorio Scotti[2], Sebastian Andrei Patcas[2], Alessandro Campi[1], and Fabio Salice[1]

[1] Department of Electronics, Information and Bioengineering (DEIB), Politecnico di Milano, 20133 Milan, Italy
sara.comai@polimi.it

[2] Department of Physics, Politecnico di Milano, 20133 Milan, Italy

Abstract. The independent mobility of wheelchair users is significantly constrained by the quality of urban road surfaces, yet current navigation tools typically lack granular data on terrain texture and vibration comfort. This paper presents a low-cost, embedded sensor system designed to automatically classify road surface types (e.g., asphalt, cobblestones, granite) and detect hazardous irregularities using a standard motorised wheelchair equipped with four accelerometers and a GPS module.

A critical challenge in inertial terrain classification is the dependency of vibration magnitude on transit velocity, where high-speed travel on smooth surfaces often mimics the signal energy of rough terrains. To address this, we propose a physics-informed normalisation protocol that scales acceleration amplitudes based on kinetic energy models and applies a geometric Doppler correction to spectral frequency bands. Features extracted from this normalised domain are processed by a Random Forest classifier to identify five distinct urban terrains, followed by a context-aware post-processing stage that utilises Kurtosis and sensor fusion to decouple structural roughness from distinct hazards like potholes.

Experimental validation conducted in an urban environment demonstrated a global classification accuracy of 70.32%, with a high robustness in distinguishing smooth asphalt from complex textures like cobblestone. These results confirm the feasibility of using consumer-grade inertial sensors to generate objective, dynamic accessibility maps for smart city applications.

Keywords: Urban accessibility · Terrain classification · Assistive technology · Smart mobility · Accelerometer data

1 Introduction

Ensuring full accessibility of public spaces is a prerequisite for autonomy, safety, and equal participation in urban life, particularly for people using wheelchairs and individuals with mobility impairments [1]. While accessibility is often discussed in terms of architectural barriers [2], the quality of ground surfaces

K. Miesenberger et al. (Eds.): ICCHP 2026, LNCS 16867, pp. 232–239, 2027.
https://doi.org/10.1007/978-3-032-31308-9_28

remains an under-addressed factor affecting everyday mobility. In urban environments, surface defects such as potholes, uneven sidewalks, deteriorated pavements, cobblestones, and abrupt slopes can significantly increase physical effort, induce discomfort and fatigue, and raise the risk of falls or loss of control. These issues affect not only wheelchair users, but also pedestrians with reduced balance and people with visual impairments. Despite their pervasive impact, surface-related accessibility barriers are rarely monitored systematically, creating a gap between urban accessibility planning and the real, lived experience of navigating public space.

A key limitation of current approaches is the lack of objective, quantitative measures of surface-induced discomfort and safety. Existing navigation and mapping tools typically optimise for distance or travel time, but do not account for the physical effort, vibration exposure, and stability experienced by users during movement. As a consequence, accessibility is still largely treated as a binary concept (accessible/inaccessible), and not as a continuous property reflecting the actual quality of traversal.

As a result, people using wheelchairs often have to rely on trial-and-error navigation, without reliable tools to anticipate comfort, safety, or physical strain along a route. Collaborative mapping platforms (e.g., Wheelmap, OpenSidewalks, AccessMap) provide valuable community-driven annotations on accessibility elements such as ramps, crossings, and architectural barriers [3,4]. However, these contributions are largely qualitative and often overlook the measurable effects of pavement conditions on wheelchair comfort and safety.

Non-intrusive sensing technologies have been widely explored in assistive and ambient intelligence contexts to monitor human activity and environmental interactions for wheelchair users, often relying on low-cost sensor configurations including accelerometers [5].

This work proposes a low-cost sensing and analysis framework for *automatic road-condition monitoring*, using a wheelchair as a mobility proxy to capture the physical interaction between user and environment. Multiple inertial sensors distributed on the wheelchair frame, together with GPS localization, are used to (i) classify the traversed surface type and (ii) detect localized hazards such as potholes, steps, cracks, and steep slopes.

The main contributions of this work can be summarised as follows:

- A physics-based normalisation strategy that reduces the dependency of vibration features on traversal speed;
- A distributed sensing configuration based on multiple inertial sensors mounted on the wheelchair frame, allowing the capture of both global and localised vibration patterns;
- A lightweight machine learning pipeline combined with context-aware post-processing to distinguish between inherent surface roughness and hazardous local anomalies;
- An application perspective toward dynamic, data-driven accessibility mapping, where routes can be evaluated not only in terms of distance but also in terms of comfort and safety.

In the remainder of the paper, in Sect. 2, we report related work; Sect. 3 details the proposed method; Sect. 4 presents the obtained results; finally, Sect. 5 concludes.

2 Related Work

Most road-condition sensing solutions for wheelchairs rely on inertial measurement units (IMUs) to capture vibrations and infer slope/roughness [6]. To avoid the usage of dedicated hardware such as Arduino boards, several researchers have opted for smartphones/iPods, which integrate similar sensors and allow faster data acquisition and processing [7], sometimes combining inertial data with images captured by the built-in camera for the estimation of road clearance and obstacle height [8]. In nearly all cases, a GPS receiver was also employed to record the travelled path and produce color-coded accessibility maps.

These approaches demonstrate the feasibility of vibration-based surface analysis. However, the effect of traversal speed on vibration signals is typically not explicitly addressed, leading to ambiguities between smooth surfaces at high speed and rough surfaces at low speed.

The physical configuration of the sensors plays a crucial role in ensuring both sensitivity and stability when capturing vibrations transmitted from the ground to the wheelchair frame. Several authors have compared different mounting strategies, assessing their influence on signal quality and the capability to detect small surface irregularities. Single-point mounting on the front wheel of a bicycle can recognize potholes and unevenness on sidewalks, although tailored to bikes [4]. Fixed at the center of the frame of a wheelchair can average vibrations and reduce user-motion artifacts [9], while on the lower central section of the frame can improve vertical sensitivity and reduce lateral noise [6].

Alternative sensing (e.g., laser-based) enables 3D obstacle detection but increases mechanical complexity and calibration requirements [10].

More recently, distributed sensor architectures have been investigated, placing multiple units at various points on the chassis [7]. This configuration aims to capture localised vibrations and reconstruct a dynamic three-dimensional profile of the terrain, enabling a more accurate distinction between vertical and lateral oscillations.

However, most existing systems still rely on either single-point measurements or do not explicitly exploit spatial correlations between multiple sensors, limiting their ability to distinguish between global surface roughness and localised events such as potholes or steps.

On the analytics side, classical pipelines segment signals into short windows, extract time-domain features, and apply lightweight classifiers [6,11]; other works employ neural networks to improve robustness across conditions [10].

Building on these directions, we adopt a *distributed-IMU configuration* (four corners of the frame) and a *physics-informed normalization* to reduce speed dependence. The proposed configuration allows the detection not only of general road surface conditions but also of localised irregularities such as steps and elevation changes, thus overcoming the limitations of previous single-point models.

3 Methodology

The proposed system uses a wheelchair as a sensing platform for road-condition monitoring, enabling direct measurement of vibration and motion in real-world mobility scenarios. The system is designed as a proof-of-concept under controlled acquisition conditions, allowing repeatable measurements while preserving realistic interaction between user and terrain. Four inertial measurement units (IMUs) are mounted at the corners of the wheelchair frame (front-left, front-right, rear-left, rear-right) to capture spatially distributed accelerations and rotations. This configuration allows both global vibration intensity and local asymmetries to be observed. A GPS module provides geolocation and timestamping for all measurements. Sensor data are sampled at 50 Hz and processed in sliding windows of 2 s duration. Before analysis, a 25 Hz low-pass filter is applied to attenuate high-frequency noise unrelated to terrain interaction.

The processing pipeline consists of four main stages: data acquisition, signal preprocessing and normalization, feature extraction, and classification with context-aware anomaly detection.

For each window, a compact set of features is extracted to characterise both continuous surface roughness and impulsive hazards. These include acceleration Root Mean Square (RMS) and standard deviation, spike count above a predefined threshold, kurtosis to capture impulsive shocks, gyroscope RMS and kurtosis to quantify pitch and roll instability, band-limited power spectral density (PSD) energy, and differential vibration between left/right and front/back sensors to detect slopes or uneven loading. GPS latitude, longitude, and altitude are retained to provide spatial context.

A major challenge in vibration-based terrain analysis is the dependency of signal amplitude and frequency on traversal speed. To mitigate this effect, each window is normalised to a reference speed v_{ref} (corresponding to the average training speed) using the instantaneous GPS-derived speed v_{real}:

$$K = \frac{v_{real}}{v_{ref}}. \tag{1}$$

Assuming that vibration energy scales approximately with the square of speed, the acceleration signal is normalised as:

$$a_{norm}(t) = \frac{a(t)}{K^2}. \tag{2}$$

In addition, to compensate for the speed-induced shift of temporal frequencies, the PSD integration bands are adapted according to:

$$\text{Band}_{adaptive} = [f_{start} \cdot K,\ f_{end} \cdot K]. \tag{3}$$

This normalization reduces the influence of speed on the signals, enabling the model to better capture the actual properties of the surface. It also preserves the same spatial wavelengths of pavement texture across different speeds, improving the consistency of spectral features.

Terrain classification uses a Random Forest classifier trained on normalised feature vectors, yielding robust surface-type classification with limited computational requirements. Hazard detection is then implemented through context-aware post-processing rather than a standalone anomaly detector. Isolated predictions of rough terrain occurring within longer smooth segments are re-evaluated as potential local hazards. Candidate events are confirmed using sensor-fusion indicators, such as extreme kurtosis for vertical impacts and high gyroscope kurtosis for tilt-related disturbances, and are subsequently geolocated via GPS. This strategy enables discrimination between inherently rough surfaces and localized defects associated with a higher safety risk.

4 Experimental Results and Conclusions

The proposed system is a proof-of-concept and was validated with a wheelchair user through a series of experiments conducted on multiple urban routes around Politecnico di Milano. The evaluation focuses on validating the feasibility and robustness of the sensing and analysis pipeline under controlled but realistic mobility conditions. Data were collected using a motorized wheelchair driven at controlled, constant speeds, on representative pavement types commonly found in the city, including smooth asphalt, worn asphalt, granite slabs and blocks, rectangular pavement tiles, and cobblestones. The test routes also intentionally included localized hazards such as potholes, curbs, steps, and cracks. Each experimental run lasted between 4 and 6 min, while an extended 12-min run traversed all surface types to evaluate performance over longer and more heterogeneous paths.

Using the speed-normalized feature set, the Random Forest classifier achieved a global terrain classification accuracy of 70.32% on the extended validation run. This is compatible with the inherent challenges of real-world data, which present noise and overlapping patterns for similar pavement types and are influenced by speed and micro-events due to user-induced dynamics. In fact, the system performed particularly well on smooth asphalt, with a Recall of 0.93 and an F1-score of 0.84, reflecting the stability and low-vibration characteristics of this surface. Instead, misclassifications mainly occur among highly irregular surfaces with overlapping vibration signatures (e.g., cobblestones and worn asphalt), which have comparable effects on user comfort.

Figures 1 and 2 provide an insight into the discriminative power of the extracted features. While RMS captures the overall vibration energy, it is not always sufficient to distinguish between surfaces with similar roughness levels. For example, worn asphalt and granite may exhibit comparable RMS values. However, their spectral signatures differ significantly, as shown in the PSD representation, where distinct frequency peaks emerge. This confirms that combining energy-based and frequency-based features enables robust terrain classification under real-world conditions.

As shown in Fig. 3, the system distinguishes smooth, low-effort surfaces from potentially unsafe conditions, supporting user-relevant assistive feedback during

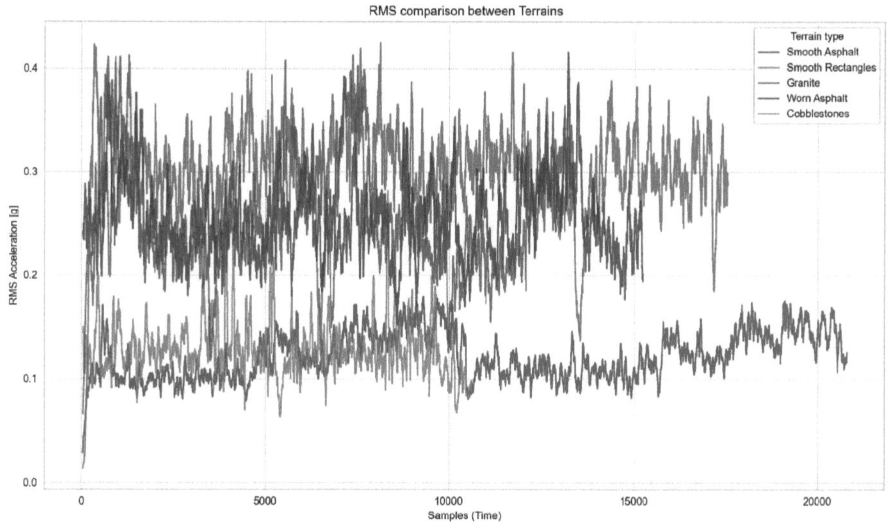

Fig. 1. RMS of acceleration signals across different terrain types, reflecting the overall vibration energy. Several surfaces exhibit overlapping values, highlighting their limited discriminative power when used alone.

wheelchair mobility. The temporal consistency of the classification, combined with context-aware filtering, results in coherent surface segments.

Hazard detection further benefited from the context-aware post-processing logic. High-variance and rhythmic vibrations on inherently rough surfaces (e.g., cobblestones) were not systematically classified as hazardous, resulting in a reduced number of false positives. In contrast, isolated shocks occurring on smoother pavements were consistently detected when confirmed by impulsive features (high kurtosis) and/or rotational instability (high gyroscope kurtosis). This behavior demonstrates the feasibility of separating “rough road type” from “dangerous local defect,” a critical requirement for assistive navigation systems.

Overall, these results indicate that the proposed approach can provide objective, continuous, and geolocated assessments of pavement comfort and hazards from the perspective of wheelchair mobility. Although evaluated on a limited number of users, the results demonstrate that meaningful and consistent patterns can be extracted from low-cost inertial sensing in real-world conditions.

Future work will focus on expanding the experimental validation across multiple users and wheelchair configurations, as well as exploring broader deployment scenarios such as crowd-sourced accessibility mapping and integration with navigation systems.

Finally, while this work focuses on a distributed sensing configuration to maximize fidelity to the user’s physical experience, such systems could also serve as reference platforms for learning and calibrating more scalable smartphone-based solutions through parallel data collection.

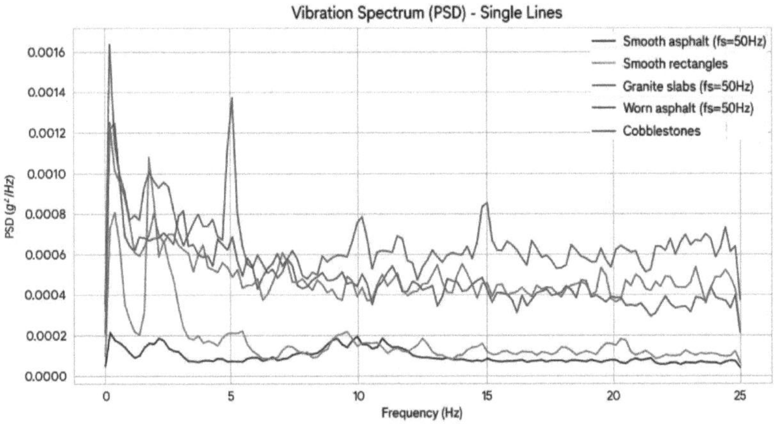

Fig. 2. Power Spectral Density (PSD) of vibration signals for different terrain types. Distinct frequency patterns enable better discrimination between terrains with similar RMS values.

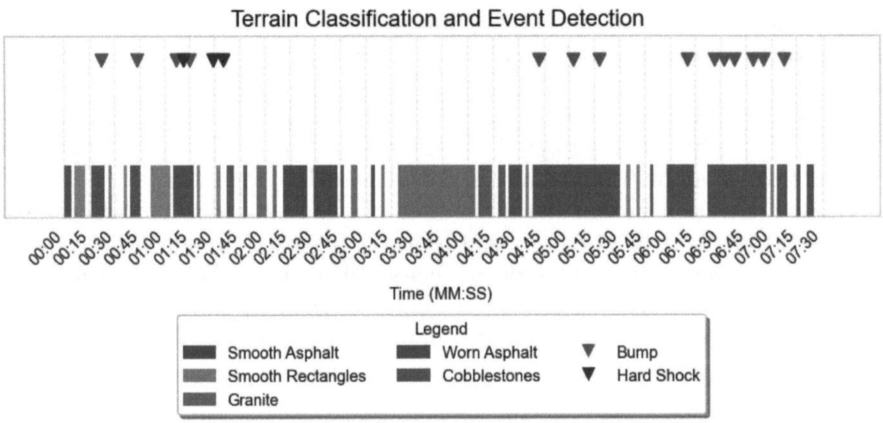

Fig. 3. Example of context-aware surface classification and hazard detection during real-world wheelchair mobility.

References

1. Comai, S., De Bernardi, E., Matteucci, M., Salice, F.: Maps for easy paths (MEP): enriching maps with accessible paths using MEP Traces, pp. 254–263. Springer International Publishing (2017). https://doi.org/10.1007/978-3-319-61949-1_27
2. Comai, S., Kayange, D., Mangiarotti, R., Matteucci, M., Yavuz, S.U., Valentini, F.: Mapping city accessibility: review and analysis. In: Studies in Health Technology and Informatics, vol. 217, pp. 325–331. IOS Press (2015). pMID: 26294492
3. Mobasheri, A., Deister, J., Dieterich, H.: Wheelmap: the wheelchair accessibility crowdsourcing platform. Open Geospatial Data, Softw. Stand. **2**(27) (2017). https://doi.org/10.1186/s40965-017-0040-5

4. Luo, J.: Leveraging raspberry pi and sensor technology to assess sidewalk accessibility: enhancing travel experiences for handicapped individuals. In: 2024 7th International Conference on Universal Village (UV), pp. 1–5 (2024)
5. Salice, F., de Vellis, M., Gwyn Barbieri, A., Masciadri, A., Comai, S.: Nonintrusive monitoring and detection of sitting and lying persons: a technological review. IEEE Access **12**, 178875–178897 (2024)
6. Santic, M., Pomante, L., Fazio, U., Fucci, L.: Wheelchair embedded device for road surface classification and obstacle detection. In: 2024 13th Mediterranean Conference on Embedded Computing (MECO), pp. 1–5 (2024)
7. Watanabe, T., Takahashi, H., Iwasawa, Y., Matsuo, Y., Eguchi Yairi, I.: Weakly supervised learning for evaluating road surface condition from wheelchair driving data. Information **11**(1) (2020). https://www.mdpi.com/2078-2489/11/1/2
8. Damaceno, R.J.P., Ferreira, L., Miranda, F., Hosseini, M., Cesar, Jr., R.M.: Sideseeing: a multimodal dataset and collection of tools for sidewalk assessment (2024). https://arxiv.org/abs/2407.06464
9. Kojima, K., Taniue, H., Kaneko, J.: Mahalanobis distance-based road condition estimation method using network-connected manual wheelchair. In: 2016 IEEE International Conference on Consumer Electronics-Taiwan (ICCE-TW), pp. 1–2. IEEE (2016)
10. Mamun, S.A., Suzuki, R., Lam, A., Kobayashi, Y., Kuno, Y.: Terrain recognition for smart wheelchair. In: Huang, D.-S., Han, K., Abraham, A. (eds.) Intelligent Computing Methodologies, ser. Lecture Notes in Computer Science, vol. 9772, pp. 461–470. Springer International Publishing, Cham (2016). https://doi.org/10.1007/978-3-319-42297-8_43
11. Sarcevic, P., et al.: Online outdoor terrain classification algorithm for wheeled mobile robots equipped with inertial and magnetic sensors. Electronics **12**(15) (2023). https://www.mdpi.com/2079-9292/12/15/3238

Design and Calibration of a Wearable 3D LiDAR for Assistive Navigation of People with Visual Impairment

Richard Král(✉), Tibor Vince, and Ján Molnár

Technical University of Košice, Letná 1/9, 040 01 Košice, Slovakia
richard.kral@tuke.sk

Abstract. This paper presents the design and calibration of a wearable 3D LiDAR system intended for assistive navigation of people with visual impairment. The proposed approach addresses limitations of existing solutions, such as high cost, limited spatial resolution, and computational complexity. The system integrates a single-point time-of-flight (ToF) LiDAR sensor with a two-axis mechanical scanning mechanism, enabling dense spatial sensing and real-time environment perception.

A novel calibration method is introduced to convert Hall sensor signals into accurate angular deflection, addressing hysteresis and non-monotonic behavior through branch-specific modeling and signal segmentation. The resulting system enables the reconstruction of 3D point clouds from synchronized range and angular measurements. A proof-of-concept implementation demonstrates the feasibility of the proposed approach, highlighting its potential for low-cost and energy-efficient wearable deployment.

Future work focuses on full system integration, user feedback design, and experimental validation in real-world navigation scenarios involving visually impaired users.

Keywords: Wearable LiDAR · Assistive Navigation · Visual Impairment · 3D Sensing · Point Cloud Reconstruction

1 Introduction

Independent mobility and safe navigation remain central prerequisites for social participation and quality of life for people with visual impairment (PVI). Although a wide range of electronic travel aids and "smart" canes has been proposed, many solutions still face practical barriers, most commonly high cost, the need for computationally demanding processing, or limited sensing performance. Ultrasound-based approaches often suffer from lower spatial resolution and reduced accuracy in complex environments. To address these limitations, an affordable and energy-efficient assistive concept is proposed based on wearable 3D LiDAR scanning, enabling dense spatial sensing and environment reconstruction from point-cloud data. The current stage of the system design is presented and key directions for further development and validation are outlined.

K. Miesenberger et al. (Eds.): ICCHP 2026, LNCS 16867, pp. 240–247, 2027.
https://doi.org/10.1007/978-3-032-31308-9_29

2 State of the Art

2.1 Navigation and Spatial Orientation Aids

User needs in assistive navigation have been investigated in prior work, including a user study conducted with visually impaired participants, which identified independent navigation and spatial orientation as the most critical unmet need in daily life. The study further highlighted that existing solutions are often insufficient in terms of usability, integration, and real-world applicability, motivating the development of more effective navigation aids [1].

Wearable navigation and orientation aids for visually impaired users have been widely investigated, with research focusing on improving independent mobility through sensing and feedback. Traditional approaches are primarily based on smart cane extensions, where embedded sensors provide obstacle detection and navigation assistance [2, 3]. These systems preserve familiarity but are typically limited in sensing range and spatial resolution.

To overcome these limitations, wearable solutions have been proposed, integrating sensing directly into clothing or head-mounted devices. Examples include smart garments and wearable systems that enhance mobility through embedded sensing and feedback mechanisms [4], as well as smart-glasses-based solutions providing hands-free interaction [5]. While these approaches improve usability, they often remain constrained by sensing capability or system complexity.

Beyond wearable systems, more advanced concepts include robotic and autonomous navigation aids. The CaBot system represents a mobile robotic guide that assists visually impaired users through autonomous navigation and environment perception, demonstrating improved guidance capabilities in structured environments [6].

Another important research direction focuses on SLAM-based navigation systems, where spatial understanding is achieved through real-time localization and mapping. Visual SLAM approaches have been implemented to support navigation services for visually impaired users, enabling environment reconstruction and positioning [7]. More recently, survey studies have summarized the role of SLAM techniques in assistive navigation, highlighting both their potential and limitations in real-world deployment [8]. Despite these advances, existing approaches remain limited by trade-offs between sensing capability, system complexity, and practical usability.

Beyond research prototypes, commercially available solutions demonstrate current deployment possibilities. These systems typically rely on camera-based sensing combined with audio or haptic feedback. Examples include Lumen, which uses AI-based scene analysis with multimodal feedback, Sixth Sense, which integrates external sensors with audio and haptic output, and head-mounted systems such as SuperBrain and Niira that translate visual information into tactile or auditory cues [9–12]. Despite these advances, existing solutions remain limited in functionality, integration, and practical usability.

2.2 Open Limitations and Motivation for LiDAR

Despite intensive development, several limitations persist. A key barrier remains the high cost of commercially available solutions, which can make them inaccessible to a substantial portion of the target population. Complexity of use is a further obstacle, as many systems require training and may be difficult to operate reliably in everyday contexts.

Spatial perception in orientation and navigation aids is typically constrained by the properties of the underlying distance-sensing modality. In this context, LiDAR-based ranging offers relevant advantages over ultrasonic sensors and stereo-camera approaches. Ultrasonic sensing is generally poorly suited for precise ranging and fine spatial discrimination, especially in complex scenes and for small or angled obstacles. Stereo vision can provide dense depth cues, but robust depth estimation typically requires substantial computational resources and can be sensitive to lighting conditions and texture-poor surfaces. By contrast, single-point LiDAR sensors can provide direct distance measurements with high repeatability and can operate with relatively modest processing requirements, which reduces CPU load compared to stereo reconstruction. In addition, modern compact LiDAR modules can reach ranges on the order of up to 9 m while maintaining useful accuracy for obstacle-relevant distances, which is difficult to achieve consistently with low-cost ultrasound and computationally lightweight stereo pipelines. At the same time, modern single-point LiDAR sensors are increasingly affordable, lightweight, compact, and wearable; however, they differ in maximum measurement frequency (critical for building 2D/3D representations), robustness to ambient light, and maximum range. In contrast, 2D and 3D LiDAR systems remain substantially more expensive, bulkier, and more power-demanding [13–17]. Therefore, the development of an affordable wearable 3D LiDAR system remains a relevant and timely research direction.

3 Methodology

The proposed system is a wearable 3D LiDAR sensing unit for real-time spatial perception and assistive navigation. The system integrates a single-point ToF LiDAR sensor (Benewake TFS20-L), a two-axis mechanical scanning unit, and a microcontroller (MCU) for control and data processing. The overall dimensions of the 3D LiDAR are approximately 63 × 78 × 78 mm, enabling compact wearable deployment.

The LiDAR sensor operates at 905 nm with a measurement range up to 20 m under optimal conditions and typically 9–15 m in practical environments. It provides ±6 cm accuracy (0.2–6 m), ~1% beyond this range, precision of ~2 cm, and frame rates up to 250 Hz, while maintaining low power consumption (≤0.43 W) and ambient light resistance up to 100 klux, allowing outdoor operation [14].

To achieve spatial coverage, the sensor is integrated with a two-axis oscillatory scanning mechanism driven by electromagnetic actuation. The system operates near resonance using torsion springs, permanent magnets, and excitation coils (Figs. 1 and 2). The horizontal and vertical oscillations are driven at approximately 3 Hz and 14 Hz, forming a Lissajous pattern that maximizes spatial coverage while maintaining energy efficiency. The oscillation amplitudes are approximately ±19° and ±33°, resulting in a field of view of about 38° and 66°.

The MCU synchronizes LiDAR measurements with angular motion and transmits processed data via UART for real-time visualization, while user feedback is provided via a wireless interface. The total power consumption of the sensing unit is approximately 2 W, making it suitable for battery-powered wearable applications.

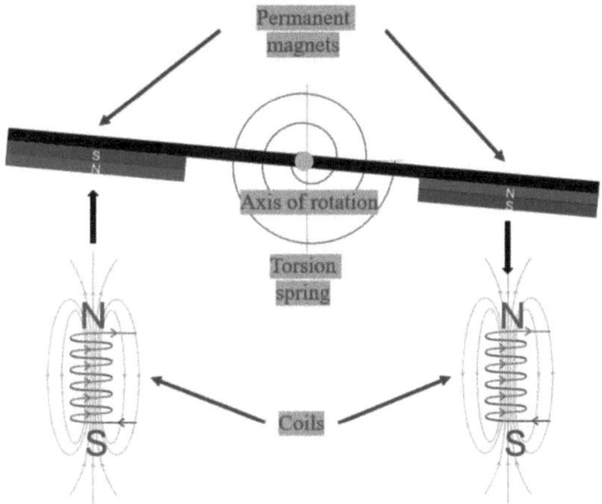

Fig. 1. Principle of the two-axis mechanical scanning unit illustrating electromagnetic actuation using coils and permanent magnets, with torsion springs providing restoring torque and defining the oscillatory behavior.

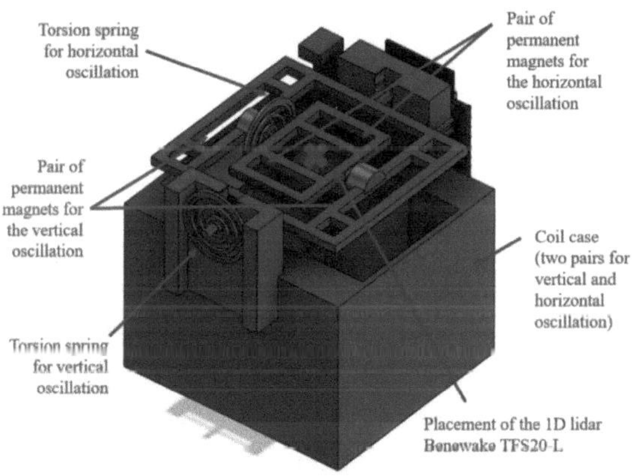

Fig. 2. 3D model of the proposed two-axis scanning unit showing the arrangement of magnets, coils, and torsion springs enabling independent oscillation in horizontal and vertical axes.

Calibration of the Hall-sensor ADC output to instantaneous angular deflection is performed by referencing the Hall signal to a geometry-derived angle computed from LiDAR ranging to a planar target. Because the beam is oblique to the target, the measured slant range $r(t)$ is converted to a reference deflection $\theta_{\mathrm{ref}}(t)$ using trigonometric relations with the known perpendicular distance d and zero-deflection offset α (Fig. 3, left). A nearly constant time lag between the Hall waveform and $\theta_{\mathrm{ref}}(t)$ is estimated by correlation and compensated using sub-sample shifting with interpolation.

To address hysteresis and non-monotonic behavior in the magnet–Hall sensing chain, a single global mapping is avoided. Instead, the oscillation is segmented directly from the Hall waveform by detecting maxima/minima using a plateau-center criterion on a lightly smoothed ADC signal. Each sample is assigned to an increasing or decreasing branch (ADC rising/falling), corresponding to the upper and lower hysteresis branches in Fig. 3, respectively, and parameterized by a normalized half-cycle coordinate $u \in [0,1]$ between successive turning points, resolving the two-valued ADC–angle ambiguity. For each branch and u-bin, robust median aggregation in narrow ADC bins yields knot points, and the final conversion uses interpolation between knots.

A stable and repeatable conversion from Hall-sensor ADC readings to angular deflection was achieved during dynamic oscillation for a single deflection axis (the vertical scan axis of the envisioned 3D LiDAR) (Fig. 3). Direction-dependent discrepancies caused by hysteresis were mitigated by separate calibration of the increasing/decreasing branches combined with half-cycle indexing via u, which removed the two-valued mapping in the problematic region and improved continuity of the reconstructed angle over full cycles. Robust median binning attenuated noise and sporadic outliers, producing cleaner angle trajectories and more stable proof-of-concept 3D point-cloud reconstruction.

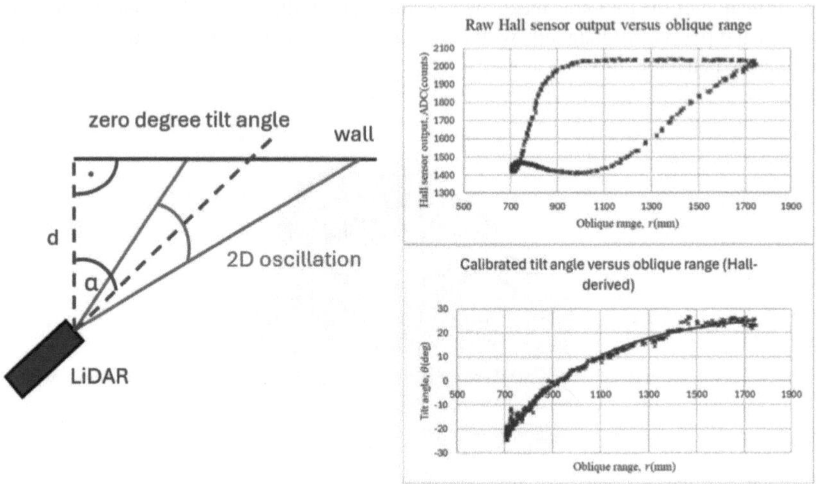

Fig. 3. Raw and calibrated sensor relationships for oblique-range acquisition for a single oscillation axis (up: Hall ADC code vs. range; down: Hall-derived tilt angle vs. range). The plots illustrate the nonlinear and hysteretic behavior of the sensing chain and the improvement achieved through calibration.

4 Results

A proof-of-concept 3D reconstruction pipeline was implemented by combining LiDAR range samples with time-resolved beam direction obtained from the oscillator deflection signals. For each measurement instant, a 3D point coordinates was computed from the measured range together with the corresponding steering angles, enabling conversion from polar measurements to Cartesian coordinates and accumulation into a point cloud using custom Python-based application. As expected for a proof-of-concept implementation, standard preprocessing steps were applied to the raw measurements, including outlier rejection and temporal aggregation. The resulting point clouds demonstrate that the system is capable of capturing structured spatial data suitable for further processing and navigation-relevant analysis. These results confirm the feasibility of the proposed scanning and calibration concept and provide a solid foundation for systematic optimization in subsequent development stages.

During simultaneous dual-axis operation, calibration stability is not uniformly preserved over the entire acquisition; therefore, representative stable intervals are used for proof-of-concept visualization. An example point-cloud reconstruction is shown in Fig. 4, illustrating that the scanning concept can provide structured spatial returns suitable for further refinement, including improved dual-axis calibration consistency, more systematic denoising, and quantitative evaluation in realistic navigation scenarios.

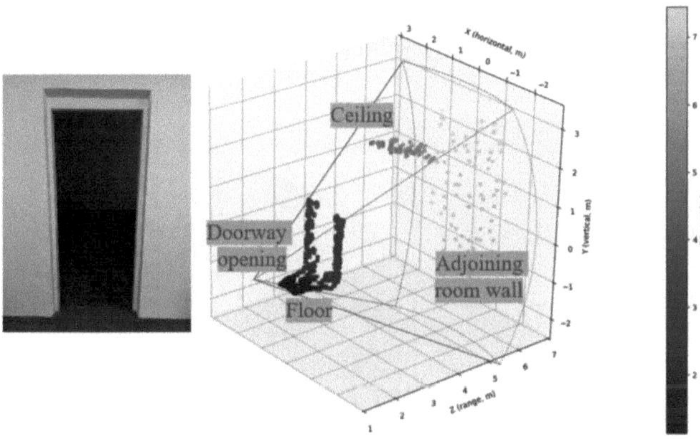

Fig. 4. Reconstructed 3D point cloud of an indoor scene containing a doorway and adjacent space. The point distribution reveals depth discontinuities corresponding to the opening, demonstrating the system's ability to identify traversable areas.

5 Future Directions

Before full wearable integration, further experimental validation is required for simultaneous two-axis operation, as horizontal and vertical oscillation will be driven concurrently in the final system. The key next step is the practical integration of the 3D LiDAR system into a truly wearable form factor. Given the current dimensions of the scanning module, initial housing is planned in a chest-mounted waist bag (Fig. 5) to provide sufficient internal volume while remaining visually unobtrusive. Placement close to the body's centerline is expected to be functionally beneficial, as the sensed region of interest is naturally aligned with torso orientation and the viewing direction is steered by turning the chest toward the intended exploration area. In parallel, miniaturization and mechanical refinement are planned, with the goal of reducing volume, mass, and power consumption to enable integration into clothing in later development stages.

Future work is also directed toward the design of an effective user-feedback channel that translates sensed spatial information into actionable mobility cues. The selection of the feedback modality (haptic and/or audio), its placement on the body, and the encoding of spatial information were not only considered conceptually but also discussed with experts from the Teiresias Center at Masaryk University during a research stay. These findings, together with the proposed feedback design, are further elaborated in [18]. Based on these insights, the feedback system will be iteratively refined to minimize cognitive load while preserving usability in everyday navigation scenarios.

Finally, a structured user study with participants with visual impairment is planned to validate safety and practical utility in realistic conditions. The evaluation will include both indoor and outdoor navigation tasks, where participants will be required to independently navigate through environments containing typical obstacles such as walls, doorways, and open spaces. Performance metrics will include obstacle avoidance success rate, navigation efficiency (e.g., task completion time and walking speed), and the frequency of collisions or near-miss events. In addition, subjective measures such as perceived cognitive load, comfort, and user acceptance will be collected through standardized questionnaires and interviews. Based on these results, the system will be iteratively improved and subsequently validated in extended real-world trials.

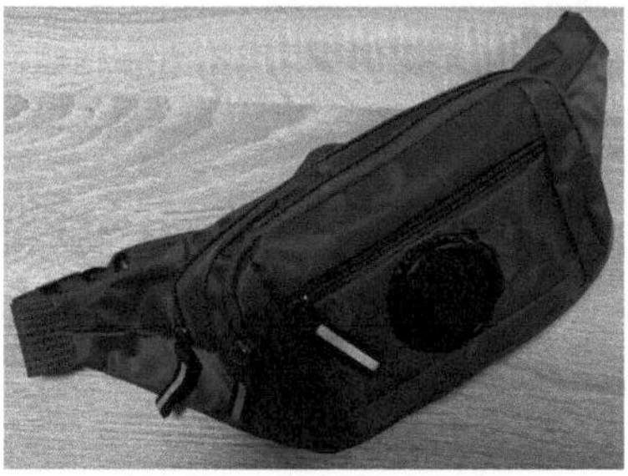

Fig. 5. Proposed chest-mounted waist-bag enclosure for the wearable 3D LiDAR prototype.

Acknowledgments. The paper has been prepared under support of Slovak grant project KEGA 038TUKE-4/2025.

References

1. Král, R., Jacko, P., Vince, T.: Low-Cost multifunctional assistive device for visually impaired individuals. IEEE Access **13**, 56326–56337 (2025). https://doi.org/10.1109/ACCESS.2025.3554366
2. Apu, A.I., Nayan, A.-A., Ferdaous, J., Kibria, M.G.: IoT-Based smart blind stick. Lecture Notes on Data Engineering and Communications Technologies. Springer Singapore, pp. 447–460 (2021). https://doi.org/10.1007/978-981-16-6636-0_34
3. Minatani, K.: Proposal for a versatile smart white cane infrastructure using a 3D printer: as a R&D platform and a practical product design. Proceedings of the 17th International Conference on Pervasive Technologies Related to Assistive Environments. ACM, pp. 21–26 (2024). https://doi.org/10.1145/3652037.3652064
4. Bhatlawande, S., Borse, R., Solanke, A., Shilaskar, S.: A smart clothing approach for augmenting mobility of visually impaired people. IEEE Access **12**, 24659–24671 (2024). https://doi.org/10.1109/ACCESS.2024.3364915
5. Poy, Y.-L., Darmaraju, S., Goh, C.-H., Kwan, B.-H.: Standalone smart glass system for the blind and visually impaired. 2024 IEEE 14th Symposium on Computer Applications; Industrial Electronics (ISCAIE). IEEE, pp. 239–244 (2024). https://doi.org/10.1109/iscaie61308.2024.10576410

6. Guerreiro, J., et al.: CaBot: designing and evaluating an autonomous navigation robot for blind people. In: Proceedings of the 21st International ACM SIGACCESS Conference on Computers and Accessibility (ASSETS '19). Association for Computing Machinery, New York, NY, USA, pp. 68–82 (2019). https://doi.org/10.1145/3308561.3353771
7. Nguyen, Q.-H., et al.: A visual SLAM system on mobile robot supporting localization services to visually impaired people. In: Computer Vision—ECCV (Lecture Notes in Computer Science). Berlin, Germany: Springer, pp. 716–729 (2015). https://doi.org/10.1007/978-3-319-16199-0_50
8. Bamdad, M., Scaramuzza, D., Darvishy, A.: SLAM for visually impaired people: a survey. (2022). arXiv:2212.04745
9. Lumen: Lumen. [quoted 8 Jan 2026], available on the internet: https://www.dotlumen.com/
10. HopeTech: Sixth sense. [quoted 9 Jan 2026]. available on the internet: https://www.hopetech.vision/
11. 7sense: SuperBrain. [quoted 9 Jan 2026]. available on the internet: https://7sense.ee/toode/superbrain-i/
12. Sensotec and Eyesynth: Niira [quoted 10 Jan 2026]. available on the internet: https://www.pro.sensotec.com/post/niira-glasses-launch
13. Benewake TFmini Plus (1D LiDAR). [quoted 10 Jan 2026]. available on the internet: https://en.benewake.com/TFminiPlus/index.html
14. Benewake TFS20-L (1D LiDAR, dToF). [quoted 10 Jan 2026]. available on the internet: https://en.benewake.com/TFS20L/index.html
15. ST VL53L8CX (8×8 ToF array): [quoted 11 Jan 2026]. available on the internet: https://www.st.com/en/imaging-and-photonics-solutions/vl53l8cx.html
16. DFROBOT LD19 (2D LiDAR): [quoted 12 Jan 2026]. available on the internet: https://www.dfrobot.com/product-2610.html?srsltid=AfmBOoqpT4viWRq0Gg-lE3rmNZIq3QbK1kX1-h1u5946pcBKi6A1ufry
17. Velodyne VLP-16 (3D LiDAR): [quoted 12 Jan 2026]. available on the internet: https://www.mapix.com/lidar-scanner-sensors/velodyne/velodyne-puck-vlp16/
18. Král, R., Vince, T.: Optimal haptic feedback for spatial navigation and orientation of visually impaired individuals. Electr. Eng. Inform. **16s**, 207–212 [online]. ISBN 978-80-553-4854-4

Integrating Face Blurring Into Vision-Based Indoor Navigation: Privacy-By-Design

Jun Yu[1], Deven Bhadane[1], Yitian Yang[1(✉)], and Vinod Namboodiri[1,2]

[1] Department of Computer Science and Engineering, Lehigh University, Bethlehem, PA 18015, USA
{juy220,dyb323,yiy523,vin423}@lehigh.edu
[2] Department of Biostatistics and Health Data Science, Lehigh University, Bethlehem, PA 18015, USA

Abstract. Vision-based indoor navigation offers scalable guidance for complex environments but raises significant ethical concerns regarding the incidental capture of bystander faces. This work investigates the intersection of privacy and utility in smartphone-based navigation agents. We specifically examine whether face anonymization compromises the accuracy of Absolute Pose Regression (APR) models. Contrary to the intuition that removing visual information hinders localization, our empirical results on a multi-floor dataset suggest that face blurring acts as a regularizer. By suppressing high-frequency transient features (faces), the privacy-preserving process directs the model to attend to stable visual cues, thereby improving localization accuracy in the test cases. These findings argue for a "privacy-by-design" approach, demonstrating that ethical constraints can align with, rather than oppose, technical robustness.

Keywords: Indoor Navigation · Privacy-Preserving Vision · Face Anonymization · Camera Pose Regression · Assistive Technology

1 Introduction

Vision-based indoor navigation has emerged as a scalable solution for complex environments, leveraging smartphone cameras to align visual features with building maps [5,17]. Existing systems such as ViNav [5], UNav [23], Clew Maps [14], and NaVIP [24,25] demonstrate the growing practicality of camera-based guidance, but the deployment of such "always-on" cameras in public spaces creates inherent tension between assistive utility and bystander privacy (Fig. 1). Unlike passive sensor-based methods, vision pipelines capture rich environmental data, raising significant ethical issues and potential regulatory violations regarding bystander anonymity [1,2]. In public spaces such as university buildings, libraries, or transit hubs, incidental face capture may lead to bystander discomfort, reduced social acceptability, and potential regulatory concerns under privacy frameworks such as the GDPR and CCPA [6].

K. Miesenberger et al. (Eds.): ICCHP 2026, LNCS 16867, pp. 248–255, 2027.
https://doi.org/10.1007/978-3-032-31308-9_30

Fig. 1. A visually impaired user navigating the Health, Science, and Technology Building with a smartphone-based indoor navigation setup. The system captures the surrounding environment to estimate pose.

Prior work has predominantly focused on maximizing navigation accuracy (e.g., ViNav [5], UNav [23]) or analyzing general privacy in smart cameras [3], leaving the intersection of bystander privacy and assistive navigation underexplored. Despite the increasing adoption of vision-based localization in academia and industry [5,14,23], current literature offers limited attention to these privacy implications in assistive-navigation settings [3,10,13,16]. In this work, we adopt a privacy-by-design approach to address a key technical challenge in deep learning-based navigation: the tendency of Absolute Pose Regression (APR) models to "memorize" training data, including transient objects like people. To address this, we implement a strict privacy-by-design training protocol. We hypothesize that training exclusively on anonymized data serves a dual purpose: it satisfies ethical compliance by design and acts as a regularizer, preventing the model from utilizing facial features as landmarks. We therefore examine whether automatic face blurring can be integrated into a visual localization pipeline without sacrificing accuracy, and we complement the performance study with attention analysis to test whether APR models rely on transient human cues or stable architectural structure. This paper presents an empirical evaluation of this hypothesis, demonstrating how this constraint can enhance privacy without compromising navigation reliability.

2 Related Work

Indoor Navigation. Indoor navigation has traditionally relied on infrastructure-supported or sensor-based solutions, including BLE- and WiFi-based systems [4,18,19], but recent camera-based approaches offer a more scalable alternative. Representative vision-driven systems include ViNav [5], UNav [23], Clew Maps [14], and NaVIP [24,25], which reduce infrastructure dependence but vary in how they handle localization drift, energy use, and robustness in dynamic spaces.

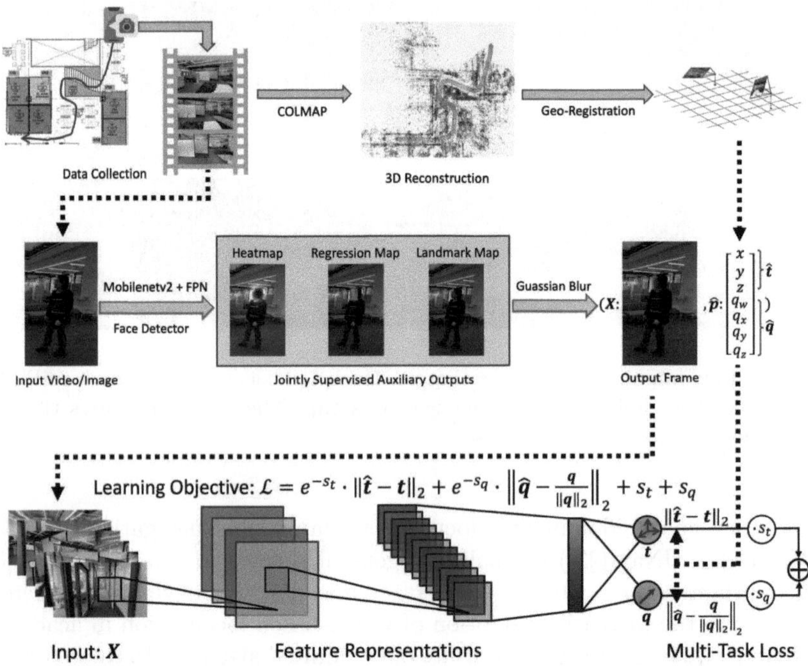

Fig. 2. Workflow for generating face-blurred frames and integrating them into camera-pose estimation. Collected video frames are processed with COLMAP for 3D reconstruction and geo-registration to obtain pseudo-ground-truth poses. In parallel, face detection and Gaussian blur produce anonymized frames. The anonymized frames and pose labels are used to train the camera pose estimation model with a multi-task loss.

Privacy-Preserving Systems. Privacy-preserving vision research has examined broader smart-camera concerns, including user control over captured data and privacy-aware visual processing pipelines [3,7,15]. However, prior work has rarely focused on bystander privacy in assistive indoor navigation, where the ethical challenge is not only scene understanding but also the incidental capture of identifiable people in shared indoor environments.

3 Methodology

We implement a modular pipeline that decouples the privacy mechanism from the localization engine. This allows us to evaluate the impact of anonymization independently of the specific navigation architecture (Fig. 2). Raw videos are decomposed into frames, and pseudo-ground-truth poses are obtained through COLMAP before geo-registration to floor plans, allowing the privacy-preserving preprocessing to remain decoupled from pose learning [20].

3.1 Privacy-Preserving Preprocessing

We utilize CenterFace [22], a lightweight anchor-free detector optimized for mobile edge devices, to identify bystander faces. Detected regions are subjected to a Gaussian blur ($\mathbf{I}_{\text{blurred}} = \text{Blur}(\mathbf{I}, k)$), where the kernel size k adapts to the bounding box dimensions. This isotropic smoothing eliminates identifiable biometric features (eyes, nose) while preserving the coarse spatial occupancy of the person, ensuring the navigation model still recognizes the presence of an obstacle without retaining identity. The blur kernel scales with the detected face size so that identity-bearing facial detail is suppressed while the coarse scene layout remains intact.

3.2 Camera Pose Estimation

We adopt an Absolute Pose Regression (APR) framework to regress the 6-DoF camera pose $[\boldsymbol{t}, \boldsymbol{q}]$ from anonymized images. Our architecture attaches a PoseNet-style dense regression head [12] to a convolutional feature extractor. To evaluate the trade-off between accuracy and mobile efficiency, we implement this framework with two distinct backbones: ResNet-34 [8] (standard) and MobileNet-V3 [9] (lightweight).

The model minimizes a homoscedastic uncertainty-based multi-task loss [11]:

$$\boldsymbol{L}(I) = e^{-s_x} \|\hat{\boldsymbol{t}} - \boldsymbol{t}\| + e^{-s_q} \left\| \hat{\boldsymbol{q}} - \frac{\boldsymbol{q}}{\|\boldsymbol{q}\|} \right\| + s_x + s_q \tag{1}$$

where s_x and s_q are learnable parameters that automatically weigh the translation and rotation errors. This learnable loss is critical for stabilizing training when removing visual features via blurring.

4 Results

4.1 Localization Accuracy Metrics

We trained models on a dataset of 400 videos (approx. 300,000 frames) collected across four floors of a university research facility using standard smartphones. Each video lasts 2–4 min, and the recordings span December 2023 to June 2024. The dataset includes four smartphone models, both portrait and landscape orientations, handheld and gimbal-stabilized capture, and lighting conditions ranging from sunrise to evening. To assess generalization across dynamic indoor environments, we used a time-separated split, with images captured before April 15 for training and images captured after May 1 for testing. To validate the "privacy-by-design" approach across different model capacities, we conducted experiments using both the ResNet-34 and MobileNet-V3 backbones. Table 1 summarizes the performance.

Across nearly all evaluated scenarios, applying face blurring improves localization performance, and the effect is not limited to translation error: orientation estimates also improve in many cases. These gains are consistent with a regularization effect in which blurring suppresses dynamic, high-frequency facial cues and encourages the model to rely on stable spatial features instead. Although a few settings show only marginal changes, the overall trend remains that anonymization preserves or improves utility rather than degrading it.

A notable finding is the performance gain in the Privacy-First setting. For example, on Level 1 using ResNet-34 (Learnable Loss), the mean error dropped from 0.70 m (Non-Blurring) to 0.56 m (Blurring), and orientation error improved from 4.30° to 2.89°.

Table 1. Mean and median errors of model variants across four floors. The table is split into two sections for readability: Basement/Lower Level (top) and Level 1/Level 2 (bottom). Blurring consistently matches or improves upon non-blurring performance.

Model	Face Privacy	Basement		Lower Level	
		Mean	Median	Mean	Median
MobileNet-V3	Non-Blurring	0.42 m, 3.90°	0.34 m, 2.81°	0.78 m, 3.20°	0.53 m, 3.14°
	Blurring	0.41 m, 3.76°	0.30 m, 3.29°	0.77 m, **3.11°**	0.55 m, **2.73°**
ResNet-34	Non-Blurring	0.39 m, 3.41°	0.33 m, 2.19°	0.76 m, 3.24°	0.50 m, 3.19°
	Blurring	**0.34 m, 3.39°**	**0.27 m, 2.02°**	**0.72 m**, 3.68°	**0.50 m**, 4.24°
Model	Face Privacy	Level 1		Level 2	
		Mean	Median	Mean	Median
MobileNet-V3	Non-Blurring	0.75 m, 4.76°	0.47 m, 3.90°	0.91 m, 4.74°	0.46 m, 3.82°
	Blurring	0.69 m, 3.89°	0.44 m, 3.71°	0.88 m, 4.51°	0.46 m, 3.53°
ResNet-34	Non-Blurring	0.70 m, 4.30°	0.46 m, 3.84°	0.87 m, **3.90°**	0.49 m, **2.41°**
	Blurring	**0.56 m, 2.89°**	**0.39 m, 2.31°**	**0.82 m**, 4.01°	**0.44 m**, 2.92°

This pattern appears across all four floors, including spaces with greater visual variability, where blurring generally yields either improved accuracy or near-parity rather than degradation. Orientation error often improves alongside translation, although a few settings show only minor changes instead of large gains.

We attribute this to the regularization effect of anonymization. In the Baseline setting, the model likely overfits to specific people or crowds present in the training set. When these "human landmarks" move or disappear in the test set, error increases. Blurring effectively masks these unreliable features, forcing the model to learn robust features from the static architecture. This suggests that datasets should be anonymized not just for ethics, but for performance.

4.2 Attention Analysis

To examine why anonymization can improve performance, we visualize model attention using Grad-CAM [21]. The resulting heatmaps (Fig. 3) consistently highlight structural features such as walls, beams, doors, ceiling lights, and floor

Fig. 3. Grad-CAM visualizations from 16 randomly selected samples across four floors show that the model relies on stable architectural cues rather than transient human content for localization.

boundaries, while de-emphasizing people and other transient objects. This observation supports the interpretation that face blurring removes task-irrelevant visual noise without disrupting the spatial evidence needed for localization.

5 Discussion

This study validates face anonymization as a viable strategy for privacy-aware indoor navigation. However, face blurring remains a minimum standard; in sparse environments, gait and clothing may still identify bystanders. While APR models benefit from this regularization, future work should evaluate geometric approaches, which may respond differently to obfuscation. Face blurring should therefore be treated as a minimum privacy standard rather than a complete solution, since identifiability may also persist through clothing, gait, screens, documents, or location metadata. Future work should compare anonymization strategies and strengths, including pixelation, masking, and different blur radii, and report explicit privacy-utility trade-offs rather than a single operating point. Pairing anonymization with interpretable diagnostics can further strengthen trust by showing that localization remains grounded in stable scene structure rather than transient human content. Nevertheless, our results provide a blueprint for a "Privacy-First" standard in assistive technology: privacy need not be a retrospective patch applied to an invasive system. By treating anonymization as a fundamental data-quality filter during training, we can build systems that are robust to visual distractions and socially responsible by design.

6 Conclusion

This study shows that face anonymization can be integrated into vision-based indoor navigation without compromising localization accuracy and can even improve it under realistic conditions. Together with the attention-analysis evidence, the results support privacy-by-design as a principled path toward assistive navigation systems that are both technically robust and socially acceptable.

References

1. Alharbi, R., Tolba, M., Petito, L.C., Hester, J., Alshurafa, N.: To mask or not to mask? balancing privacy with visual confirmation utility in activity-oriented wearable cameras. In: Proceedings of the ACM on Interactive, Mobile, Wearable and Ubiquitous Technologies, vol. 3, no. 3, pp. 1–29 (2019)
2. Auxier, B., Rainie, L., Anderson, M., Perrin, A., Kumar, M., Turner, E.: Americans and privacy: concerned, confused and feeling lack of control over their personal information (2019)
3. Beugin, Y., et al.: Building a privacy-preserving smart camera system. arXiv preprint arXiv:2201.09338 (2022)
4. Cheraghi, S.A., Namboodiri, V., Walker, L.: Guidebeacon: beacon-based indoor wayfinding for the blind, visually impaired, and disoriented. In: IEEE PerCom, pp. 121–130. IEEE (2017)
5. Dong, J., Noreikis, M., Xiao, Y., Ylä-Jääski, A.: Vinav: a vision-based indoor navigation system for smartphones. IEEE Trans. Mob. Comput. **18**(6), 1461–1475 (2018)
6. Fakeyede, O.G., Okeleke, P.A., Hassan, A., Iwuanyanwu, U., Adaramodu, O.R., Oyewole, O.O.: Navigating data privacy through it audits: GDPR, CCPA, and beyond. Int. J. Res. Eng. Sci. **11**(11) (2023)
7. Geppert, M., Larsson, V., Speciale, P., Schonberger, J.L., Pollefeys, M.: Privacy preserving localization and mapping from uncalibrated cameras. In: Proceedings of the IEEE/CVF Conference on Computer Vision and Pattern Recognition, pp. 1809–1819 (2021)
8. He, K., Zhang, X., Ren, S., Sun, J.: Deep residual learning for image recognition. In: Proceedings of the IEEE Conference on CVPR, pp. 770–778 (2016)
9. Howard, A., et al.: Searching for mobilenetv3. In: Proceedings of the IEEE/CVF ICCV, pp. 1314–1324 (2019)
10. Huang, H., Gartner, G.: A Survey of Mobile Indoor Navigation Systems. Springer, Heidelberg (2010)
11. Kendall, A., Gal, Y., Cipolla, R.: Multi-task learning using uncertainty to weigh losses for scene geometry and semantics. In: Proceedings of the IEEE Conference on CVPR, pp. 7482–7491 (2018)
12. Kendall, A., Grimes, M., Cipolla, R.: Posenet: a convolutional network for real-time 6-dof camera relocalization. In: Proceedings of the IEEE ICCV, pp. 2938–2946 (2015)
13. Khan, D., Cheng, Z., Uchiyama, H., Ali, S., Asshad, M., Kiyokawa, K.: Recent advances in vision-based indoor navigation: a systematic literature review. Comput. Graph. **104**, 24–45 (2022)
14. Lan, B.: Clew maps: crowdsourcing routes for indoor navigation (2020)

15. Lopez, J., Hinojosa, C., Arguello, H., Ghanem, B.: Privacy-preserving optics for enhancing protection in face de-identification. In: Proceedings of the IEEE/CVF Conference on Computer Vision and Pattern Recognition, pp. 12120–12129 (2024)
16. Manjari, K., Verma, M., Singal, G.: A survey on assistive technology for visually impaired. Internet Things **11**, 100188 (2020)
17. Morar, A., et al.: A comprehensive survey of indoor localization methods based on computer vision. Sensors **20**(9), 2641 (2020)
18. Nair, V., Budhai, M., Olmschenk, G., Seiple, W.H., Zhu, Z.: Assist: personalized indoor navigation via multimodal sensors and high-level semantic information. In: Proceedings of the European Conference on Computer Vision (ECCV) Workshops (2018)
19. Sato, D., Oh, U., Naito, K., Takagi, H., Kitani, K., Asakawa, C.: Navcog3: an evaluation of a smartphone-based blind indoor navigation assistant with semantic features in a large-scale environment. In: Proceedings of the 19th International ACM ASSETS, ASSETS '17, pp. 270–279. (2017)
20. Schonberger, J.L., Frahm, J.M.: Structure-from-motion revisited. In: Proceedings of the IEEE CVPR, pp. 4104–4113 (2016)
21. Selvaraju, R.R., Cogswell, M., Das, A., Vedantam, R., Parikh, D., Batra, D.: Grad-cam: visual explanations from deep networks via gradient-based localization. In: Proceedings of the IEEE ICCV, pp. 618–626 (2017)
22. Xu, Y., Yan, W., Yang, G., Luo, J., Li, T., He, J.: Centerface: joint face detection and alignment using face as point. Sci. Program. **2020**(1), 7845384 (2020)
23. Yang, A., et al.: UNAV: an infrastructure-independent vision-based navigation system for people with blindness and low vision. Sensors **22**(22), 8894 (2022)
24. Yu, J., Yang, Y., Namboodiri, V.: Navip: a low-cost, infrastructure-free indoor navigation solution for visually impaired persons. In: Proceedings of the ICCV Workshops on Assistive Computer Vision and Robotics, Honolulu, USA (2025)
25. Yu, J., Zhang, Y., Aila, B., Namboodiri, V.: Navip: an image-centric indoor navigation solution for visually impaired people. arXiv preprint arXiv:2410.18109 (2024)

Beyond Turn-by-Turn: Wall-Trailing Indoor Navigation for Blind Users

Ajay Abraham(✉) and Vinod Namboodiri

Lehigh University, Bethlehem, PA 18015, USA
{aja724,vin423}@lehigh.edu

Abstract. Most existing indoor navigation systems for corridor-based environments rely on prebuilt digital maps with predefined walkpath networks (centered along corridors) to calculate shortest paths and deliver turn-by-turn instructions to users. However, due to inconsistencies in the underlying positioning technologies, these apps often mistime turn cues, resulting in missed turns, disorientation, and reduced confidence among blind and visually impaired (BVI) users. In this work, we extend conventional indoor navigation approaches by introducing wall-trailing routes designed specifically for BVI white cane users. Wall-trailing navigation aligns with established Orientation and Mobility (O&M) techniques and enables BVI users to follow physical boundaries, such as walls, to better understand and internalize the spatial layout of an environment. Once the system determines the user's starting position and identifies nearby walls, it computes the wall-trailing routes. From that point onward, continuous user positioning is no longer provided. Instead, navigation guidance is delivered step by step: after reaching each wall corner, the user manually prompts the system for the next instruction. This interaction model encourages active engagement, positioning the user as an active participant rather than a passive recipient of directions. We evaluated this approach with five BVI white cane users. Our findings suggest that wall-trailing navigation is a valuable method to include in indoor navigation systems, in addition to turn-by-turn guidance.

Keywords: Indoor Navigation · Blind and Visually Impaired

1 Introduction

A growing body of research focuses on indoor navigation technologies that provide turn-by-turn instructions based on prebuilt digital maps. Many such systems for corridor-based environments prioritize efficiency by computing shortest-path routes on these maps, typically following corridor centerlines. These systems guide users through verbal turn instructions that assume accurate localization and precise timing. However, in real-world deployments, localization errors, sensor noise, and latency can result in turn cues not being delivered at the right time. For BVI users, especially those relying on non-visual feedback, such timing

K. Miesenberger et al. (Eds.): ICCHP 2026, LNCS 16867, pp. 256–263, 2027.
https://doi.org/10.1007/978-3-032-31308-9_31

inaccuracies can lead to missed turns, confusion, loss of orientation, and reduced trust in the system. Furthermore, shortest-path navigation does not always align with how BVI individuals naturally explore and learn indoor spaces. Orientation and Mobility (O&M) training emphasizes the use of environmental features, such as walls and tactile landmarks, to build a mental model of space and support independent travel. For white cane users in particular, wall-trailing is a well-established technique that provides continuous tactile feedback and helps maintain orientation along a route. Despite this, current indoor navigation systems rarely support routes that explicitly leverage wall-following strategies.

In this paper, we propose wall-trailing routes as a complementary form of indoor navigation for BVI white cane users. Instead of optimizing solely for distance or travel time, wall-trailing routes prioritize physical boundary following, enabling users to remain in consistent contact with walls while navigating corridors. This approach supports both immediate navigation and long-term layout learning by aligning system guidance with O&M practices already familiar to many BVI travelers. We present the design and implementation of wall-trailing routes within an indoor navigation framework and report findings from an initial user evaluation with BVI white cane users. Our results indicate that when time efficiency is not the primary concern, users strongly prefer wall-trailing routes for learning and familiarizing themselves with new environments.

The novelty of this work lies in the algorithmic generation of wall-trailing navigation routes directly from structured indoor map data (GeoJSON), enabling a navigation paradigm that aligns with how white cane users naturally navigate indoor spaces. While prior indoor navigation systems predominantly rely on turn-by-turn instructions optimized for shortest paths, they largely overlook wall-trailing strategies that are commonly used by BVI individuals for maintaining orientation and safety. Our approach transforms geometric map representations into navigable paths that explicitly follow continuous wall boundaries. This requires identifying traversable wall segments, resolving discontinuities (e.g., doorways, corners, and open spaces), and generating routes that preserve physical contact cues rather than purely minimizing distance. To our knowledge, existing systems do not provide a generalizable method for deriving wall-trailing routes from standard indoor mapping formats such as GeoJSON. This work also contributes an empirical comparison between wall-trailing and turn-by-turn navigation within the same system and environment. By evaluating both methods with white cane users in a controlled study, we demonstrate not only the feasibility of automated wall-trailing route generation but also its practical implications for usability, reliability, and user preference.

2 Related Work

Indoor navigation for BVI users has primarily focused on optimizing routes for efficiency and safety. The most common approach is shortest-path routing, with a large number of studies relying solely on travel distance [1,2], while others combine distance with real-time obstacle avoidance [3,4]. Although efficient, distance-based methods often neglect usability challenges in complex indoor spaces.

Several studies incorporate environmental constraints such as obstacles, hazards, and turning complexity into route planning. In these approaches, routes are optimized to minimize difficult features, including the number of turns [5,6] and the presence of hazards [7]. Two main strategies are used: assigning penalties to difficult segments [8] or avoiding them entirely [9]. Some approaches further enhance safety by maintaining buffer distances from obstacles [10].

Safety-oriented routing has been explicitly addressed in several studies. Approaches prioritize less crowded and more accessible paths, avoiding features such as escalators or revolving doors. In some cases, safe routes are defined simply as obstacle-free paths [10], while others consider broader accessibility constraints [11]. Landmarks have also been explored to improve navigation confidence and spatial awareness [6].

Notably, relatively few works support O&M techniques such as wall-following [6,12,13]. These approaches account for user behavior by favoring routes along walls or corridor edges. While effective and aligned with white cane navigation, such routes are often manually defined and may not suit all users, as preferences can vary. Some systems even rely on predefined accessible paths that incorporate tactile floor markers.

In general, prior work has evolved from purely distance-based routing toward more user-aware strategies that integrate safety, environmental constraints, and navigation behavior. However, to the best of our knowledge, no existing research directly compares wall-trailing and turn-by-turn navigation within a unified smartphone-based system, thereby motivating the approach presented in this work.

3 Methodology

3.1 Generating Wall-Trailing Routes

One of the most commonly practiced techniques for white cane users is wall-trailing, in which the user follows walls or other physical boundaries to maintain orientation and travel efficiently. Despite its prevalence in real-world mobility, existing indoor navigation apps, to the best of our knowledge, do not explicitly account for this reliance on natural environmental features. In this work, we leverage available shoreline information to generate fine-grained routing instructions that closely align with established O&M training practices.

Our prebuilt digital floor plan is represented as a GeoJSON file. The indoor walkable path network, which follows the centerlines of corridor spaces, is encoded as a GeoJSON FeatureCollection of LineString features. Using this representation, the routing module constructs a routable graph that supports efficient shortest-path computation from the user's current location to a specified destination.

To generate wall-trailing routes, we first construct a k-d tree over the endpoints of all corridor wall segments in the map. Starting from the centerline-based

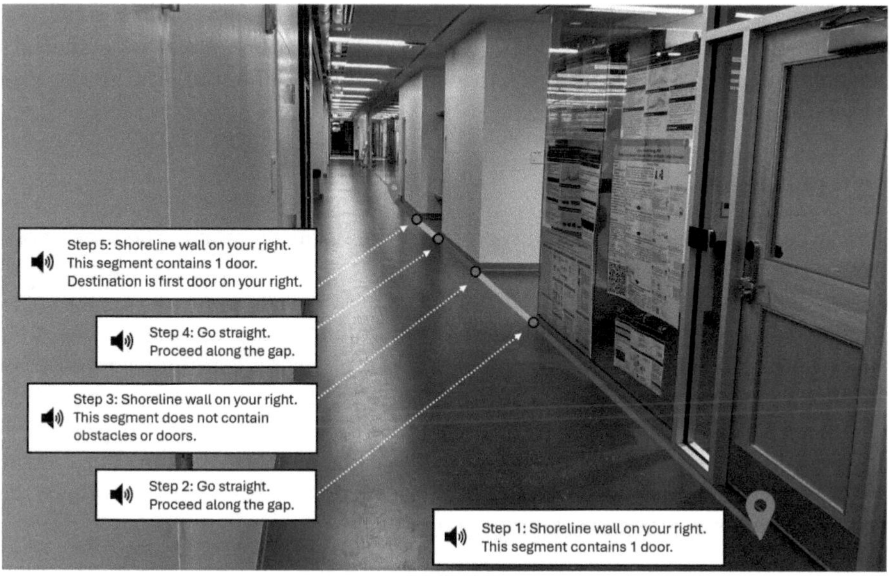

Fig. 1. Wall-trailing route.

route produced by the initial shortest-path search, we identify the nearest wall segments on both sides of each route segment. These wall segments are then connected using a modified shortest-path algorithm that links adjacent walls and bridges discontinuities, resulting in a wall-trailing path.

Since each wall is annotated with contextual information, including obstacles (e.g., furniture), hazards (objects that may not be detectable by a white cane and could pose a risk to the user), and points of interest (e.g., room entrances), the wall-trailing routes generated include this information as well. In most cases, two candidate wall-trailing routes are generated: one following the inner corridor wall and another following the outer corridor wall. The final route selection prioritizes minimizing hazards, reducing wall trailing discontinuities, particularly transitions between walls across corridor gaps, and limiting obstacles. These criteria are considered more important than simply minimizing route length.

For the selected wall-trailing route, detailed information is extracted for each wall segment, including segment length, relative direction, whether the segment follows a wall or crosses a corridor gap, and the presence and locations of points of interest, hazards, and obstacles. This enriched representation supports the generation of fine-grained audio instructions and contextual announcements for the user during navigation. The audio instructions are stored as steps for the current wall-trailing session and operate independently of the underlying localization system. When the user reaches a wall corner, they can manually prompt the app for the next instruction. Figure 1 shows a wall-trailing route where the blue markers indicate the starting and ending locations, the red line segments represent wall segments, the green circles identify the wall corners, and the orange line segments mark gaps between walls. It also shows the first audio instruction, which is automatically announced at the start of the route, along with the subsequent instructions that the user must manually prompt the app at the wall corners.

3.2 Localization

Both wall-trailing navigation and turn-by-turn navigation require the user's position on the prebuilt GeoJSON map before a route to the destination can be generated. This position is obtained through a camera-based approach (camera pose regression). However, the two approaches differ in how they use positioning after the route is created. Turn-by-turn navigation depends on continuous updates of the user's position to provide accurate, real-time directions. In contrast, wall-trailing navigation only requires the initial position. Once the route is generated, the user follows the wall and manually requests the next instruction (via a swipe gesture) when reaching each corner. Because movement is constrained along the wall, continuous position tracking is unnecessary.

3.3 User Study

Five participants (4 male, 1 female), all white cane users with light perception, were recruited for the study. A within-subjects user study was conducted to compare two indoor navigation methods implemented in an iOS mobile application: a wall-trailing method and a standard turn-by-turn method. Each participant completed navigation tasks using both methods across multiple routes, enabling direct comparison while controlling for inter-participant variability. The study was conducted across two floors of a university building, with two predefined routes per floor, resulting in a total of four routes. The system was deployed on an iPhone 13 Pro.

Participants were instructed to navigate from a fixed start point to a specified destination along each route using the mobile application while using their white cane as they normally would. For every route, participants completed the task using both navigation methods (wall-trailing and turn-by-turn), resulting in eight trials per participant. To control for learning and order effects, we employed a counterbalanced design in which both route order and method order were varied across participants. After completing a route with one method, participants proceeded to a different route before returning to the original route to complete it with the remaining method. This approach was used to minimize the chance that familiarity with a route would bias performance toward any particular method. In addition, when participants repeated a route using a different method, they were not informed that they were evaluating a previously traversed route.

Each testing session began with a brief introduction and an overview of the task instructions. Participants were then given time to try both methods on a trial route. Afterward, they completed all navigation tasks under researcher observation. No assistance was provided unless a participant deviated from the route and could not return without guidance. Upon completion of all tasks, participants provided subjective ratings and participated in a semi-structured interview to report their experiences.

We collected both quantitative and qualitative measures. Quantitative metrics included task completion rate (whether the participant successfully reached the destination), task completion time (measured from task start to arrival at destination), and error rate, defined as the number of navigation errors such as wrong turns, missed turns, or deviations from the prescribed route. Subjective measures were collected using 7-point Likert-scale ratings assessing perceived ease of use, confidence, and overall experience. Qualitative data were obtained from post-study interviews and observational notes recorded during task execution.

The study protocol was approved by the Institutional Review Board (IRB), and all participants provided informed consent prior to participation.

4 Results

The goal of the evaluation was to understand user preferences, perceived usefulness, and confidence when navigating unfamiliar indoor environments using wall-trailing routes compared to conventional shortest-path, centerline-based routes.

4.1 Quantitative Findings

All participants successfully reached their destinations in all eight navigation tasks. However, three participants veered off the intended path in a few instances and required assistance to return. In the wall-trailing condition, this occurred when transitioning between wall corners that were not aligned in a straight path or when there were large gaps between walls. In the turn-by-turn condition, deviations occurred when users either did not execute a turn immediately after it was announced or when the system prompted a turn slightly too early.

Across participants ($n = 5$), turn-by-turn navigation generally resulted in faster task completion times compared to wall-following. However, variability in completion time was higher in the turn-by-turn condition, suggesting that performance is more sensitive to instruction timing and user interpretation. Wall-following produced more consistent, though typically longer, navigation times. This method also resulted in fewer critical navigation errors (e.g., missing a turn), likely because it relies on continuous tactile feedback rather than discrete instructions. In contrast, turn-by-turn guidance showed a higher frequency of missed turns or hesitation at decision points, especially when instructions were delayed or ambiguous.

Error rates further reflected this pattern: while turn-by-turn navigation enabled more direct routes when successful, it was more sensitive to system inaccuracies. Wall-following, though less efficient, demonstrated robustness in maintaining orientation and ensuring eventual arrival at the destination.

4.2 Qualitative Findings

Participant feedback revealed distinct experiential differences between the two approaches. Turn-by-turn navigation was often described as "mentally demanding" due to the need to interpret and trust auditory instructions without continuous environmental confirmation. Users reported increased cognitive load, particularly when instructions did not align precisely with perceived surroundings. In contrast, wall-following was perceived as more intuitive and reliable. Participants expressed greater confidence in this method because it leverages familiar cane techniques and provides continuous physical reference points. However, 2 participants noted that it can feel inefficient or frustrating in environments with very long corridors or irregular layouts.

Trust emerged as a key theme. Participants were more likely to trust wall-following because it is grounded in their existing mobility skills, whereas trust in turn-by-turn navigation depended strongly on the perceived accuracy and timing of instructions. Breakdowns in guidance, such as late or unclear prompts, quickly reduced confidence in the system.

4.3 Design Implications

The results suggest a fundamental trade-off between efficiency and reliability. Turn-by-turn navigation offers speed and directness but requires high system precision and imposes greater cognitive demands. Wall-following, while slower, provides a stable and user-controlled navigation strategy with lower reliance on system accuracy. These findings point toward the potential value of hybrid approaches. For example, combining continuous environmental anchoring (e.g., wall or landmark following) with intermittent high-level guidance could balance efficiency with user confidence. Additionally, improving the timing, granularity, and contextual awareness of turn-by-turn instructions may reduce cognitive load and error rates.

5 Conclusions

While turn-by-turn navigation can improve efficiency and reduce travel time, wall-following remains a trusted, reliable, and widely preferred strategy among users. Taken together, these findings highlight the importance of supporting multiple navigation approaches within indoor navigation systems. Rather than treating these methods as competing solutions, future designs should consider integrating their complementary strengths by leveraging the efficiency of turn-by-turn guidance alongside the robustness and user trust associated with wall-trailing. Providing flexible navigation options allows users to select strategies that best align with their immediate goals, personal preferences, and the demands of specific environments.

Acknowledgments. This material is based upon work supported by the National Science Foundation under Award No. 2345057.

References

1. Bakouri, M., et al.: Sound-based localization using LSTM networks for visually impaired navigation. Sensors (Basel, Switzerland) **23**, 4033 (2023). https://doi.org/10.3390/s23084033.
2. Yang, A., et al.: UNav: an infrastructure-independent vision-based navigation system for people with blindness and low vision. Sensors (Basel, Switzerland) **22**, 8894 (2022). https://doi.org/10.3390/s22228894.
3. Yu, X., Saniie, J.: Visual impairment spatial awareness system for indoor navigation and daily activities. J. Imaging. **11**, 9 (2025). https://doi.org/10.3390/jimaging11010009
4. Bai, J., Lian, S., Liu, Z., Wang, K., Liu, D.: Virtual-blind-road following-based wearable navigation device for blind people. IEEE Trans. Consum. Electron. **64**, 136–143 (2018). https://doi.org/10.1109/tce.2018.2812498
5. Abu Doush, I., Alshatnawi, S., Al-Tamimi, A.-K., Alhasan, B., Hamasha, S.: ISAB: integrated indoor navigation system for the blind. Interact. Comput. **29** (2016). https://doi.org/10.1093/iwc/iww016
6. Ivanov, R.: An approach for developing indoor navigation systems for visually impaired people using Building Information Modeling. J. Ambient Intell. Smart Environ. **9**, 449–467 (2017). https://doi.org/10.3233/ais-170441
7. Ran, L., Helal, S., Moore, S.: Drishti: an integrated indoor/outdoor blind navigation system and service. In: 2nd IEEE Annual Conference on Pervasive Computing and Communications, Orlando, pp. 23–30 (2004). https://doi.org/10.1109/PERCOM.2004.1276842
8. Yang, Z., Ganz, A.: A sensing framework for indoor spatial awareness for blind and visually impaired users. IEEE Access **7**, 10343–10352 (2019). https://doi.org/10.1109/access.2018.2886308
9. Islam, M.I., Raj, M.M.H., Nath, S., Rahman, M.F., Hossen, S., Imam, M.H.: An indoor navigation system for visually impaired people using a path finding algorithm and a wearable cap. In: 3rd International Conference for Convergence in Technology (2018). https://doi.org/10.1109/i2ct.2018.8529757
10. Mekhalfi, M.L., Melgani, F., Zeggada, A., De Natale, F.G.B., Salem, M.A.-M., Khamis, A.: Recovering the sight to blind people in indoor environments with smart technologies. Expert Syst. Appl. **46**, 129–138 (2015). https://doi.org/10.1016/j.eswa.2015.09.054
11. Arvai, L.: Mobile phone based indoor navigation system for blind and visually impaired people: VUK - Visionless supporting frameworK. In: 19th International Carpathian Control Conference (ICCC), pp. 383–388. IEEE (2018). https://doi.org/10.1109/carpathiancc.2018.8399660
12. Ivanov, R.: An approach for microscopic path finding and obstacle avoidance for blind and visually impaired people. In: Proceedings of the 17th International Conference on Computer Systems and Technologies, pp. 285–292 (2016). https://doi.org/10.1145/2983468.2983482
13. Dong, H., Ganz, A.: Automatic generation of indoor navigation instructions for blind users using a user-centric graph. In: 36th Annual International Conference of the IEEE Engineering in Medicine and Biology Society, pp. 902–905. IEEE (2014). https://doi.org/10.1109/embc.2014.6943737

Design Requirements for Accessible Indoor Wayfinding Technologies Supporting People with Mobility Disabilities

Siny Joseph[1(✉)] and Nils A. Hakansson[2]

[1] Department of Integrated Studies, Kansas State University, Kansas, USA
siny@ksu.edu

[2] Department of Biomedical Engineering, Wichita State University, Kansas, USA
nils.hakansson@wichita.edu

Abstract. Indoor wayfinding remains a significant barrier for people with mobility impairments (MI), affecting autonomy, employment, and social participation. This study presents findings from a large-scale online survey (N = 198 valid responses) examining the indoor navigation experiences, technology use, and design preferences of MI individuals, including wheelchair users, cane and walker users, and those with balance or endurance limitations. Despite near-universal smartphone ownership, only 34% of respondents had used any indoor navigation application, revealing a critical gap between technological access and MI-specific tool availability. Participants expressed strong interest in the MABLE (Mapping for Accessible Built Environments) concept, particularly for unfamiliar venues such as airports, conference centers, and shopping malls. Key design priorities included real-time elevator status, accessible route planning, and multimodal interaction support. Findings further reveal that inaccessible indoor environments contribute to employment barriers, with employment rates dropping from 83% to 42% following disability onset. Design implications for MI-centered assistive wayfinding technologies are discussed.

Keyword: Indoor Wayfinding · Accessible Technologies · Mobility Impairments

1 Introduction

Indoor mobility remains a persistent challenge for people with mobility impairments (MI), influencing autonomy, access to services, safety, and long-term socioeconomic participation [1, 2]. While numerous navigation and environmental-awareness tools have emerged for blind and visually impaired (BVI) communities [3], indoor wayfinding solutions that address the specific needs of MI groups, such as wheelchair users, cane or walker users, and persons with balance or endurance limitations, remain underexplored [4, 5]. Limited accessibility information, inconsistent signage, lack of awareness about elevators and ramps, and difficulty planning barrier-free routes often result in stress, delayed travel, and avoidance of new or complex spaces [4, 5]. Furthermore, as noted by Karimi et al., even when the wayfinding preferences and requirements for a particular

K. Miesenberger et al. (Eds.): ICCHP 2026, LNCS 16867, pp. 264–270, 2027.
https://doi.org/10.1007/978-3-032-31308-9_32

group, for example, wheelchair users, is incorporated in wayfinding solutions, the solutions may not meet specific needs and requirements of an individual within that group [6].

To better understand the challenges encountered by MI individuals, we conducted a large-scale online survey (N $\approx$ 314) examining mobility aids used, current access to digital navigation tools, preferences for indoor landmark information, and perceptions of a prototype indoor wayfinding solution called Mapping for Accessible Built Environments (MABLE). Respondents represented diverse mobility disabilities across age groups, education levels, and employment contexts. Following [7] which provided a comparative study of features desired by BVI and MI communities in an indoor wayfinding system, this study focusses on MI community's perspective and needs. The objectives of this work are, a) Identify MI user-desired features, interaction modalities, and environmental information needs that define ideal indoor navigation experiences; and b) Evaluate MI user perceptions of MABLE concept as a prospective indoor navigation solution, including its alignment with diverse user expectations and its potential impact on independent travel, especially for MI individuals.

2 Methodology

2.1 Data Collection

This study is approved by Kansas State University IRB protocol# 10616. The survey was developed by a team of four researchers, two with MI, and distributed from January through April 2025 to the MI community using Qualtrics. Participants were recruited from listservs of organizations such as the Cerebral Palsy Foundation, FSHD Society, American Institute of Chemical Engineers (AIChE), Easterseals and the Emerging Researchers National (ERN) Conference Students in STEM with Disabilities Working Group. Of the 314 participants who consented, we considered 198 responses after accounting for duplicated responses and excluding detected bot responses. The sample included users of a wide variety of assistive mobility devices, including wheelchairs, walkers, canes, prosthetics, and people with multiple concurrent disabilities (e.g., low vision, chronic pain, orthopedic conditions).

2.2 Design of Survey

The accessible online questionnaire included 37 questions capturing demographics, mobility characteristics, technology use, indoor wayfinding needs, employment-related barriers, and responses to the MABLE concept prototype. The survey was organized by questions about survey respondents' experiences with indoor navigation and currently available apps. Based on gaps they identified in the current landscape of solutions for indoor navigation, participants were then asked to assess and weigh in on the proposed MABLE concept (a video and description was provided) about its functionality and usefulness.

The survey included likert scales, multiple-choice check-all-that-apply options, and open-ended qualitative responses. The survey flow incorporated skip logic to bypass questions irrelevant to certain respondents. Results were aggregated descriptively to reveal broad patterns in indoor wayfinding challenges and expectations for assistive technologies.

Video conceptualization of MABLE. The "Welcome to MABLE!" video explains it is available as a **web browser** and a **mobile app** and will provide digital accessibility maps of indoor environments with interfaces for assessing, planning, and navigating within these environments based on the affordances and capabilities of the user. The **technology stack** behind MABLE is explained to leverage crowdsourcing, artificial intelligence, and robotics to automate indoor mapping and provide dynamic updates. The system is demonstrated through a **prototype walkthrough** and explained as being developed using a **user-centered design** approach by people with lived experiences and informed by feedback from the persons with disabilities (PWD) community. Information provided is currently being tested in various public and educational venues to support real-world use cases such as conferences, airports, and university campuses. The project's broader **community impact** is also emphasized, with support from the National Science Foundation's Convergence Accelerator Program and collaborations across research, accessibility, and disability advocacy groups. Lastly, the video emphasizes MABLE is being developed by PWDs, with the help of PWD organizations, for PWDs.

3 Results

3.1 Participant Characteristics

Participants represented a diverse mobility-impaired (MI) population with varying onset and duration of disability. Respondents used a broad range of mobility supports: 49% used ambulatory aids such as canes, walkers, or crutches; 14% used manual wheelchairs; and 42% used power wheelchairs or scooters. Additionally, 22% relied on custom orthotics, prosthetics, or exoskeletons, 18% used human personal assistants, and 1% reported having support animals. Cross-functional accessibility needs also emerged, with 5% using text-to-speech or speech-to-text software.

Smartphone usage was nearly universal. Most participants (75%) reported visually reading their phone screen while moving, while 4% relied on haptic feedback, and another 4% who primarily used the speaker. Importantly, 25% did not use their phone at all during navigation due to safety, cognitive load, or difficulty manipulating the device while moving. iPhone and Android users were both well represented.

Despite high smartphone adoption, only 34% of respondents had downloaded any indoor navigation or environmental-awareness application. Among these users (n = 62), GoodMaps was the most widely used (32%), with smaller uptake of AccessNow (6%), AroundMe (5%), iAccess Life (5%), Wheelmap (5%), and Lazarillo (2%). The low overall adoption rate highlights limited awareness or perceived value of existing MI-oriented wayfinding tools.

3.2 Indoor Wayfinding Needs and Expectations

Participants expressed strong interest in the MABLE indoor wayfinding concept. For regularly visited buildings (n = 198), 38% were very likely and 31% somewhat likely to use the tool, with only 7% reporting they were very unlikely to use it. Interest increased substantially for unfamiliar buildings (n = 197), with 65% very likely and 21% somewhat likely to use the tool.

Participants indicated high likelihood of using an indoor wayfinding tool across complex environments such as airports-57% (n = 108 "very likely"), conference centers (51%), shopping malls (54%), office buildings (50%), and hotels (46%). These preferences reflected needs in large, multi-level spaces with long distances and critical accessibility infrastructure.

When asked about essential landmarks (n = 189), elevators were identified by 95% of respondents, followed closely by restrooms (92%), accessible entrances and exits (84%), ramps (85%), emergency exits, resting areas, and information desks. Participants emphasized the need for both accessibility-critical features and comfort-based amenities such as benches and charging stations.

3.3 User Interface

Tool input preferences varied considerably. Some participants preferred voice interaction due to limited ability to manipulate a device (26%), while others preferred typing because of speech impairments or privacy concerns (45%). Many requested multimodal support combining visual, voice, and hands-free options (22%). Associated with typing input on a smartphone app, participants noted the importance of keyboard accessibility including the ability to alter keypad size, availability of audible and haptic keystroke feedback, interaction clarity, and adequate visual contrast.

3.4 Alignment Between MABLE and Ideal Solutions

Among respondents evaluating MABLE (n = 184), the majority rated it as completely (29%), mostly (48%), or somewhat aligned (21%) with their ideal indoor wayfinding solution. Concerns about misalignment centered on the need for up-to-date accessibility data, uncertainty about business participation, elevator reliability, and the inclusion of parking or accessible drop-off points.

3.5 Broader Impacts on Work and Participation

Indoor mobility barriers were reported as a direct employment barrier by 26% of respondents. While 83% were employed before disability onset, only 42% remained employed afterward. Around 44% stated they would be more likely to seek or change employment if workplaces were fully accessible. Although only 11% directly selected indoor maps as influencing employment likelihood, qualitative comments revealed broader recognition of their potential value.

Additional qualitative themes highlighted the importance of pre-visit planning, concerns about venue adoption, and cost sensitivity. Many respondents preferred the app to be free or publicly funded and expressed unwillingness to pay unless coverage was reliable and extensive.

Figure 1 provides a visual representation of the results related to most valued landmark types, impact of disability on employment, familiarity with navigation apps, participant's mobility support, MABLE evaluation-likelihood of use and alignment to ideal solution, and phone access method during navigation.

4 Discussion

The findings reveal strong evidence of unmet needs in indoor wayfinding for mobility-impaired individuals and highlight significant design opportunities for MI-centered wayfinding systems. Although most participants owned and actively used smartphones, navigation-specific technology adoption was strikingly low, with only 34% having installed any indoor navigation or accessibility application. This discrepancy suggests that technological capability is not the barrier; rather, existing tools fail to offer MI-specific value, lack visibility, or do not provide sufficiently reliable or actionable accessibility information. Unlike many blind or visually impaired (BVI) navigation tools, which emphasize semantic descriptions or nonvisual routing, MI users require precise and timely infrastructure-linked information that reflects their physical movement constraints and dependence on elevators, ramps, accessible entrances, and resting points.

The survey underscores a central distinction in MI navigation patterns: **uncertainty is a stronger barrier than the act of wayfinding itself**. Participants showed notably higher interest in using indoor wayfinding tools in unfamiliar environments (65% very likely) than in familiar ones (38% very likely). This contrast highlights the psychological and physical costs of navigating unknown spaces, where MI users may unexpectedly encounter broken elevators, unexpected stairs, inaccessible entrances, steep inclines, or long distances without resting points. The prominence of pre-visit planning in qualitative responses reinforces that MI mobility involves significant anticipatory effort. Many respondents described scouting routes, examining maps, or contacting venues before arrival for timely infrastructure-linked information to avoid physically risky or fatiguing situations. Therefore, indoor wayfinding tools must support two interconnected use cases: real-time routing and comprehensive accessible offline assessment.

Participants' prioritization of elevators, restrooms, accessible entrances/exits, and ramps reveals a direct link between navigation and bodily capacity. Landmarks such as restrooms and benches perform not only functional roles but also enable energy management during movement, which is especially critical for individuals with fatigue, chronic pain, or limited endurance. The overwhelming request for elevator information, both location and operational status, reflects a pervasive vulnerability: elevator failures can render entire buildings inaccessible. Thus, MI-focused routing must include dynamic data about elevator functionality, detours, congestion, and alternative accessible paths. Traditional static indoor maps are insufficient; accurate MI navigation requires infrastructure-aware, condition-aware, and context-adaptive representations.

Interaction preferences further underscore the heterogeneity of MI users. While many preferred voice interaction due to reduced ability to manipulate a device while moving, others preferred text input due to speech impairments or privacy concerns. A substantial portion avoided phone use while navigating altogether. These findings indicate that no single modality can adequately support all MI users; instead, systems must offer personalizable, flexible, multimodal interaction, integrating voice, touch, haptic cues, and hands-free modes such as wearable activation or auto-advance instructions. The need for low-effort navigation support is particularly salient given that many MI users must coordinate wheelchairs, walkers, prosthetics, or personal assistants while moving.

The results also reveal the broader socioeconomic implications of inaccessible indoor environments. A notable 26% of respondents identified indoor mobility barriers as a direct contributor to employment challenges. Employment dropped from 83% before disability onset to 42% after, and many respondents indicated they would be more likely to seek or change employment if workplaces were fully accessible. These findings demonstrate that inaccessible indoor layouts restrict not only movement but also participation in professional environments, limiting autonomy, advancement, and economic opportunity. Indoor navigation tools that mitigate wayfinding uncertainty and improve accessibility could therefore support not just mobility but also workplace inclusion and long-term employment outcomes.

Perceptions of the MABLE concept reflect both enthusiasm and caution. While most respondents viewed MABLE as aligned with their ideal solution, concerns about data accuracy, venue participation, and update frequency highlight the importance of building a robust, trustworthy data ecosystem. MI users expressed low tolerance for outdated or incomplete information, particularly regarding elevators, accessible entrances, and route blockages. Their trust hinges on comprehensive venue coverage and ongoing data verification. Therefore, successful deployment requires broad institutional partnerships particularly with airports, malls, office complexes, universities, and conference centers and may require incentives or regulatory frameworks to ensure that accessibility data remains current. Cost sensitivity also emerged as a barrier, suggesting that equitable access will require public funding, healthcare subsidies, or venue-supported models rather than individual user fees.

Overall, the findings indicate that the MABLE concept is well positioned to address critical gaps in MI indoor wayfinding. To be effective, such a system must go beyond traditional turn-by-turn routing and incorporate MI-specific constraints, dynamic accessibility information, multimodal interaction, and accessible offline assessment capabilities. Equally important, its success will depend on ecosystem-level coordination among venues, facilities managers, accessibility teams, and end users. When implemented at scale, MI-centered indoor wayfinding tools have the potential to reduce mobility anxiety, expand participation in professional and social environments, and materially improve the autonomy and quality of life of mobility-impaired individuals.

5 Conclusion/Implications for the aT Field

This large-scale survey provides one of the most comprehensive datasets to date on indoor wayfinding needs among mobility-impaired individuals. Findings demonstrate a strong interest in an indoor wayfinding tool that provides accurate, accessibility-specific routing and reliable landmark information, particularly in large, complex, or unfamiliar spaces. The data highlight clear design priorities for development of tools such as MABLE, and underscore the importance of accurate mapping, multimodal interaction, up-to-date, reliable infrastructure information, and broad venue participation.

Indoor wayfinding is not a niche accessibility concern; it affects independence, comfort, workplace participation, and equitable access to public life. The survey results reinforce the urgent need for robust indoor wayfinding infrastructure tailored to the lived experiences of mobility-impaired individuals.

Acknowledgements. The authors would like to acknowledge support for this work by NSF # 2345057.

Disclosure of Interests. The authors have no competing interests to declare that are relevant to the content of this article.

References

1. Kaye, H.S., Kang, T., LaPlante, M.P.: Mobility device use in the United States. disability statistics report (14). U.S. Department of Education, National Institute on Disability and Rehabilitation Research, Washington, D.C (2000)
2. Nie, Q., Rice, L.A., Sosnoff, J.J., Shen, S., Rogers, W.A.: Understanding wheelchair use in older adults from the national health and aging trends study. Arch. Phys. Med. Rehabil. **105**(3), 514–524 (2024)
3. Plikynas, D., Žvironas, A., Budrionis, A., Gudauskis, M.: Indoor navigation systems for visually impaired persons: mapping the features of existing technologies to user needs. Sensors **20**(3), 636 (2020)
4. Torkia, C., et al.: Power wheelchair driving challenges in the community: a users' perspective. Disabil. Rehabil.: Assistive Technolnology **10**(3), 211–215 (2014)
5. Müller, K., et al.: Traveling more independently: a study on the diverse needs and challenges of people with visual or mobility impairments in unfamiliar indoor environments. ACM Trans. Accessible Comput. **15**(2), 13, 37 (2022)
6. Karimi, H.A., Hashemi, M.: Accessible wayfinding testbed: infrastructure and components. Proceedings of the 10th EAI International Conference on Testbeds and Research Infrastructures for the Development of Networks & Communities. 1(2), p. 8 (2015)
7. Joseph, S., Heydarian, C., Baguhn, S.J, Silverman, A.M., Chung H.P.: Analysis of indoor wayfinding accessible-assistive technologies for mobility, and blind and visually impaired individuals. Technology for Inclusion and Participation for All: Recent Achievements and Future Directions, 18th International Conference, AAATE 2025, Nicosia, Cyprus, September 10–12, 2025. Proceedings, Part I. Edited by Mavrou, K., Encarnação, P. (eds.), Springer Nature, Chapter 15, pp. 115–124 (2025). https://doi.org/10.1007/978-3-032-01628-7_15

Innovation, Accessibility, and Artificial Intelligence: Towards an Inclusive Technological Future

Older Adults and Generative AI: Exploring Use, Perceptions, and Challenges

Theebthan Jeyakumaran and Weiqin Chen(✉)

Oslo Metropolitan University, P.O. Box 4, St. Olavs plass, 0130 Oslo, Norway
weiqin.chen@oslomet.no

Abstract. Generative artificial intelligence (GenAI) tools are becoming increasingly integrated into everyday life, yet little is known about how older adults experience and use these systems. This qualitative study explores the perceptions, practices, and learning needs of older adults in relation to GenAI. Data were collected through semi-structured interviews with 20 participants and supplemented with chatlogs from 11 of them. Findings show that participants primarily viewed GenAI as a practical support tool rather than a novelty. Perceived advantages included efficiency, assistance with writing and language, clarification of complex information (e.g., medical or technical content), and increased independence in everyday tasks. At the same time, participants expressed concerns regarding inaccuracy, misinformation, privacy, and overreliance, which reflects a pragmatic and critical approach to use. Analysis of chatlogs revealed variation in prompting skills. Many participants expressed motivation to improve prompting, response evaluation, and to explore new application areas, while also emphasized the need for guided learning and accessible design.

Keywords: Older Adults · Generative AI · ChatGPT · Chatbot

1 Introduction

Despite the widespread adoption of GenAI tools across diverse populations, older adults remain significantly underrepresented among users. Existing research suggests that GenAI tools have strong potential to support older adults. Studies indicate that conversational AI systems can help reduce social isolation and loneliness, particularly among older adults with mild cognitive impairment (MCI), by enabling personalized interaction, providing emotional support, and facilitating communication [7]. In addition, GenAI applications can assist with everyday activities such as information seeking, healthcare management, reminders, and problem-solving, thereby enhancing accessibility and autonomy. As cognitive, sensory, and functional abilities may decline with age, GenAI-based tools have the potential to act as supportive companions that help older adults maintain independence and improve overall quality of life.

While a few studies have explored the role of GenAI in supporting older adults, particularly in healthcare and assistive contexts [5], there remains a clear

K. Miesenberger et al. (Eds.): ICCHP 2026, LNCS 16867, pp. 273–280, 2027.
https://doi.org/10.1007/978-3-032-31308-9_33

gap in research focusing specifically on older adults' everyday experiences with generative AI tools. Existing work also emphasizes usage rates [10] rather than examining how older individuals perceive, interpret, and engage with GenAI systems in practice.

This study aims to explore and investigate older adults' everyday experiences with Generative AI. The guiding research question for this study is *How do older adults experience and interact with generative AI tools such as ChatGPT in everyday contexts?* By highlighting the voices of older users, this research seeks to contribute to a more inclusive understanding of GenAI adoption and to inform the design of age-friendly AI systems that support well-being and digital participation in later life.

2 Related Work

Recent survey data suggest that older populations are not yet widely using GenAI tools compared to younger age groups. According to a 2025 U.S. survey [10], only 22.7% of adults aged 60 and above reported having used ChatGPT, compared to 84% of those aged 18–29. While just 8% of younger adults (18–29) reported never having used ChatGPT, the proportion was substantially higher among older adults, with 59.1% of those aged 60+ reporting no prior use.

As GenAI tools become more widespread, research has begun to explore their relevance for older adults [1]. However, existing research on GenAI and older adults has tended to focus on specific application areas, particularly mental health and emotional support, such as in Mazroui and Alzyoudi [2], rather than broader everyday experiences. Usability studies of Large Language Model (LLM)-based chatbots designed for mindfulness practice and emotional support among older adults highlight design considerations such as voice, interactivity, and ease of use [5]. Research on older adults' attitudes toward AI-powered conversational agents indicates that perceived social interaction quality, sociability, and empathy influence intent to use such tools [8]. The study by Peng et al. [6] shows that older adults identify trust, autonomy, and misinformation management as key concerns. In addition, evaluation studies comparing large language model responses to questions posed by older adults reveal variability in accuracy and comprehensibility across tasks, which highlights practical challenges in reliability and trustworthiness [3].

While there is a growing body of research on GenAI and aging, comprehensive investigations into older adults' general experiences with GenAI, remain limited [4]. Particularly, few studies examine how older people perceive, interact with, and integrate tools into their daily lives.

3 Method

This study employed a qualitative approach to explore older adults' experiences with GenAI, combining semi-structured interviews with practical interaction tasks to capture both perceptions and actual use.

Interviews addressed several thematic areas: demographics and general experiences, knowledge of GenAI, usage patterns, ethical considerations, advantages and disadvantages, potential use among older adults, learning goals, and accessibility. The interview guide was pilot-tested with four individuals, two adults over 60 and two younger students, to assess clarity and relevance. Feedback led to minor revisions. To complement interviews, participants completed practical tasks using GenAI. Chatlogs were collected for analysis of prompt formulation, follow-up strategies, and satisfaction with responses.

Participants aged 60+ with prior experience or interest in GenAI were recruited through two senior organizations and the researcher's personal network. Interviews were conducted in-person or online, and participants provided written or verbal consent after receiving study information. All interviews were transcribed verbatim and analysed using thematic analysis to identify patterns and themes related to knowledge, experiences, benefits, challenges, learning goals, and accessibility.

The study was reviewed and approved by the Norwegian Agency for Shared Services in Education and Research (Sikt). All participants were provided with detailed information about the project and informed of their rights to access their data and withdraw their consent at any time. All data were handled and stored securely according to approved procedures.

4 Results

4.1 Participants

Twenty older adults participated in the study, evenly divided by gender (10 males, 10 females), with ages ranging from 60 to 88 years (mean = 72.5). Participants had diverse educational and professional backgrounds, including retirees and those still employed, with varying levels of digital literacy. Several had technical or analytical professions, such as IT, engineering, and business intelligence, while others had limited professional exposure but strong personal motivation to engage with technology. Many were active in digital learning communities such as non-profit organizations promoting digital inclusion among seniors or participated in informal peer learning.

4.2 Findings from Interviews

Knowledge and Experience with GenAI. Participants demonstrated a broad range of knowledge and experience with generative AI tools, including ChatGPT, Gemini and Copilot, spanning from passive awareness to active, frequent use. Many first encountered these tools through media coverage, social networks, or recommendations from friends and family, while others engaged in self-directed learning through books, courses, or independent experimentation. For example, P10 described learning from a friend and reading about AI: "*I have a buddy... who's still quite sharp. A programmer. We have conversations about it.*"

Several participants showed a functional understanding of these tools and recognized their potential for information retrieval, task completion, and content creation, while also reported limitations and ethical considerations. P5 expressed cautious engagement, saying: "*I get very good answers. But then the disadvantage comes in. I don't know if it's true.*" Some participants had limited hands-on experience but expressed curiosity and motivation to learn, such as P8: "*I haven't tried it out, but I've had it demonstrated to me. And I think it's very exciting and really want to learn more.*"

Practical use varied across everyday tasks, creative exploration, and personalized interactions. Participants reported using GenAI for problem-solving, writing assistance, and hobby-related inquiries. P16 described professional use across multiple tools: "*So at the same time, I also use Copilot, and then work along and write in Norwegian and several other things.*" Many integrated these tools into daily routines, accessing them on multiple devices and sharing insights with peers.

Perceived Advantages, Disadvantages, and Potential of GenAI. A central advantage was efficiency and convenience. Many participants emphasized GenAI's ability to provide fast, context-aware responses that reduced time spent searching for information. As P1 noted, "*It is better than previous search systems... it can put together different knowledge into something new.*" This efficiency supported everyday tasks, professional activities, and information seeking. Participants also highlighted support for communication and understanding, particularly assistance with writing, grammar, translation, and clarification of complex concepts. P7 remarked that ChatGPT was "*much better at formulating responses than I am,*" while others valued GenAI's ability to explain unfamiliar terms and medical information in accessible language. Several participants described a sense of increased independence and reduced reliance on family members or peers for help.

Despite these benefits, participants raised concerns about inaccuracy and misinformation and emphasized the need for critical evaluation. As P1 cautioned, "*You have to use it wisely and not trust it blindly.*" Additional concerns included trust, overreliance, and social impact, with some participants worrying that frequent use might reduce critical thinking or social interaction. Technical limitations and occasional errors further underscored the need for cautious use.

Looking beyond their own experiences, participants perceived potential for GenAI to support other older adults, particularly if introduced in an accessible and supportive way. ChatGPT's conversational interface and low technical threshold were seen as well suited to older users when framed as a help function rather than a system requiring mastery. As P4 emphasized, "*You don't need any special skills. It's a conversation.*" Peer influence was viewed as an important enabler of adoption, as curiosity and use often spread through social networks. However, participants also highlighted barriers such as low digital literacy, limited motivation, and individual differences in prior experience and curiosity.

Ethical Considerations. Participants expressed diverse perspectives on the ethical and privacy implications of using GenAI, reflecting varying levels of concern, trust, and awareness. Many highlighted data privacy issues, particularly concerning how personal information is handled and stored. P1 stated: "*One thing is that it's an American program. It collects personal data... technically, it's not allowed to transfer personal data out of Norway.*" Similarly, P13 acknowledged potential monitoring risks but questioned their significance: "*Does it really matter that they know where I am, or what I say?*" Participants with professional experience in security, such as P12 and P11, emphasized the importance of adhering to legal and ethical boundaries.

Trust and caution emerged as another recurring topic. Participants reflected on the reliability of GenAI's outputs and the responsibility of users. P5 explained: "*It's not to be fully trusted, but it is to be trusted,*" while P15 noted: "*I've understood that there are built-in safeguards, so there are certain things one can't do.*" Participants like P2 and P7 described practical strategies to mitigate risks, such as avoiding sharing sensitive information and respecting privacy when using GenAI tools for personal tasks.

A few participants adopted a pragmatic stance and focused on utility over potential risks. P3 remarked: "*Even if not everything is 100% accurate, it's good enough for my purposes,*" and P10 observed: "*It's up to you – the person using this tool.*"

Learning Goals and Future Development. Participants expressed diverse intentions regarding further learning and skill development with generative AI tools. While some were satisfied with their current level of use, others identified clear goals for improving and expanding their engagement.

A common learning objective involved refining interaction skills, particularly improving prompt formulation and evaluating responses more critically. Several participants viewed effective prompting as essential for obtaining useful outputs. As P1 noted, "*I want to learn more about how I can write better prompts. I think that's where the key lies.*" Others emphasized the importance of assessing accuracy and understanding limitations, especially when using the tool for academic or professional purposes. P5 reflected this concern by stating, "*Sometimes I just trust it, but I know I shouldn't.*"

Some participants also expressed interest in broadening application areas, including creative use, professional tasks, translation, and advanced features. These participants viewed GenAI as a tool with potential that could support both work-related and personal activities.

In addition, several participants highlighted the need for guided support and structured learning, such as tutorials or onboarding features, and modules tailored to older users. P12 remarked that "*some sort of onboarding for new users*" would make the tool less overwhelming.

Accessibility and User Experience. Participants generally described GenAI as accessible and easy to use but identified several areas where the user experience could be better tailored to older adults. A recurring theme was the need for simplicity in interface design, particularly to accommodate age-related changes in vision, attention, and memory. Participants suggested larger text, clearer buttons, fewer on-screen options, and reduced visual clutter. As P1 explained, "*The interface could be even more simplified. Maybe larger text and fewer options.*" Several participants proposed a dedicated "senior mode" to support these needs.

Another key theme concerned cognitive and sensory accessibility. Participants highlighted the potential value of features such as read-aloud functions, voice input, visual aids, or slower interaction pacing. Although some of these features already existed, participants reported difficulty locating or activating them, which indicates the challenge lies in discoverability rather than availability.

Finally, participants pointed to inconsistencies across devices, particularly between mobile and desktop versions, which could cause confusion. As P17 noted, "*Make sure it's accessible on mobile. That's what most people use.*"

4.3 Findings from Chatlogs

Eleven of the twenty participants shared chatlogs, all of which documented interactions with ChatGPT. The analysis focused on participants' prompting practices, use of follow-up questions, and expressions of satisfaction, rather than on assessing the quality of ChatGPT's responses.

Overall, most participants formulated clear and detailed prompts that enabled effective interaction. For example, P2 wrote: "*The project is about training retirees in the use of computers and software... Create a step-by-step plan for a knowledge survey using Google Forms and spreadsheets.*" This prompt provides context, purpose, and specific instructions, demonstrating strong prompting skills.

Some participants, such as P1 and P9, introduced additional context through follow-up prompts. P1 initially asked, "*Do you have any tips for reupholstering an old rocking chair?*" and then clarified, "*The chair was stuffed with grass. What do you suggest I do?*"

Seven of the eleven participants used follow-up questions to refine or extend responses. For instance, P9 initially asked: "*How do I print reports in Excel? I'm trying to print a report that has 122 rows, but when I press "Ctrl + P", Excel only prints the first 70 rows or so. Why is that?*". ChatGPT provided several possible reasons, including Print Area and Page Setup. After resolving the Print Area issue, P9 followed up with: "*Point 1* [Print Area] *worked! Thanks! But now everything is very small. Where can I enlarge the contents a bit?*"

Participants showed different interaction styles. Some preferred step-by-step dialogue, while others provided all relevant information upfront. Satisfaction was expressed in different ways. Some participants, like P7 and P9, offered direct feedback in the chat (e.g. "*Point 1 worked! Thanks!*"). Others, such as P2, P5, and P6, reported that they were satisfied with the responses from ChatGPT in their emails.

5 Discussion

This study shows that older adults engage with generative AI in active, reflective, and highly practical ways, extending beyond the therapeutic or companionship focus often emphasized in earlier research [2]. While prior studies have highlighted AI chatbots as tools for reducing loneliness or supporting emotional well-being, the participants here primarily used GenAI as a general-purpose assistant for everyday problem-solving, writing support, concept clarification, translation, and understanding complex information such as medical results. At the same time, their accounts reflect broader AI literature on trust, privacy, and misinformation [6]. Participants demonstrated a pragmatic approach. They valued efficiency and convenience but remained cautious, emphasizing the need to verify information and limit personal data sharing. These findings contribute to existing research by grounding common AI-related concerns in older adults' everyday practices.

The results point to the importance of structured support, including guided onboarding and the development of skills related to prompting and critical evaluation of responses. They also highlight the potential of GenAI in supporting everyday activities such as health communication, writing, and multilingual interaction. In terms of accessibility and user experience, the findings are closely related to the principles of the Web Content Accessibility Guidelines (WCAG) [9], particularly those related to clarity, simplicity and ease of navigation. However, the reported difficulty in locating and activating existing accessibility features suggests that compliance with standards alone is not sufficient. Accessibility features must also be easily discoverable and intuitive to use. These findings suggest that applying WCAG more explicitly in the design of generative AI interfaces could enhance usability for older adults, particularly when combined with age-sensitive adaptations such as a dedicated "senior mode."

This study has several limitations. 20 older adults participated in the study, many of whom had relatively high digital competence and professional or academic backgrounds, which makes the group unrepresentative of the broader older population, particularly those with low digital literacy or limited access to technology. As participants who volunteered to participate in the study may be more curious, motivated, and positively inclined toward technology than their peers. Furthermore, although the study addresses GenAI, most findings are based on experiences with ChatGPT, as only a few participants had used Copilot. Thus, the results primarily reflect one system and cannot be generalized to all GenAI tools. In addition, only eleven participants shared chatlogs, which limited the amount of behavioral data and the conclusions made about prompting and interaction patterns based on this data.

6 Conclusion and Future Work

This study explored how older adults experience and use generative AI tools, primarily ChatGPT, in everyday contexts. The findings show that participants engaged with GenAI in diverse and practical ways, including information seeking, writing support, concept clarification, translation, creative activities, and understanding medical or technical information. Many participants emphasized efficiency, speed, and convenience as major advantages. At the same time, concerns about inaccuracy, trust, privacy, and overreliance were evident. Participants demonstrated varying levels of prompting skills and interaction strategies.

Future studies should include more diverse groups of older adults, particularly those with low digital literacy or limited access to technology. Comparative research across different GenAI systems would help determine how tool design influences user experience. Longitudinal studies could explore how use, trust, and skills develop over time. Finally, more research is needed on how GenAI affects social relationships, independence, and participation in later life.

Acknowledgments. The authors would like to sincerely thank all the participants for sharing their insights and experiences. We are also grateful to the anonymous reviewers for their valuable and constructive feedback, which greatly helped improve this paper.

References

1. Abadir, P., Chellappa, R.: Artificial Intelligence in geriatrics: riding the inevitable tide of promise, challenges, and considerations (2024)
2. Al Mazroui, K., Alzyoudi, M.: The role of ChatGPT in mitigating loneliness among older adults: an exploratory study. Online J. Commun. Media Technol. **14**(4), e202444 (2024)
3. Dawadi, R., et al.: Large language models and questions from older adults: a human and machine-based evaluation study. Disc. Artif. Intell. **5**(1), 42 (2025)
4. Enam, M.A., Murmu, C., Dixon, E.: "Artificial Intelligence-carrying us into the future": a study of older adults' perceptions of LLM-based chatbots. Int. J. Hum.-Comput. Interact. **41**(21), 13747–13770 (2025)
5. McCarren, L., Kuoppamäki, S.: A LLM-based chatbot for mindfulness practice with older adults: a development and usability study. In: Intelligent Health Systems–From Technology to Data and Knowledge, pp. 888–889. IOS Press (2025)
6. Peng, W., Lee, H.R., Lim, S.: Leveraging chatbots to combat health misinformation for older adults: participatory design study. JMIR Format. Res. **8**(1), e60712 (2024)
7. Qi, X., Wu, B.: ChatGPT: a promising tool to combat social isolation and loneliness in older adults with mild cognitive impairment. Neurol. Live **6**(3) (2023)
8. Sou, K.L., Yuan Lau, M.Z., Ouyang, F., Yow, W.Q.: Older adults' attitude towards and intent to use of AI-powered conversational agents for social support. Innov. Aging **9**(Supplement_2), igaf122–1329 (2025)
9. Stanley, J., Brink, R., Valiton, A., Bostic, T., Scollan, B.: Chatbot accessibility guidance: a review and way forward. In: Yang, X.-S., Sherratt, S., Dey, N., Joshi, A. (eds.) Proceedings of Sixth International Congress on Information and Communication Technology. LNNS, vol. 216, pp. 919–942. Springer, Singapore (2022). https://doi.org/10.1007/978-981-16-1781-2_80
10. Winston, A.R.: How people use & trust ChatGPT in 2025: AI study results (2025). https://expresslegalfunding.com/chatgpt-study/

Effectiveness of Gen AI Tools on Identification and Fixation of Accessibility Issues in Productivity Documents

Chuqiao Yan[1,2](✉) and Alireza Darvishy[3]

[1] Department of Computational Linguistic, University of Zurich, Zurich, Switzerland
chuqiao.yan@uzh.ch

[2] Digital Society Initiative, University of Zurich, Zurich, Switzerland

[3] University of Zurich, Zurich, Switzerland

Abstract. Manually remediating accessibility issues in Microsoft productivity documents is time-consuming. Recent Generative AI (Gen AI) tools have shown promise in improving efficiency in this process, but their capabilities and reliabilities remain unknown. In this study, we investigated the effectiveness of Gen AI tools on identifying and fixing accessibility issues in productivity documents. Three commonly used Gen AI tools were evaluated across documents from three Microsoft software products (Word, Excel, and PowerPoint) based on the built-in Microsoft Accessibility Assistant. Our results indicate that these Gen AI tools are able to identify accessibility issues to some extent, but they exhibit limited effectiveness in automatically fixing these issues and low reliability with respect to what they claim they can perform. These results suggest that, at the current stage, Gen AI tools are more suited as accessibility aids instead of autonomous remediation solutions for productivity documents. This study highlights open challenges and directions for future research on Gen AI and accessibility.

Keywords: Gen AI · Accessibility · Productivity Documents

1 Introduction

Productivity applications are commonly used in the workspace to create and share documents. A survey reported that 95% of persons with blindness or low vision use productivity applications during a typical workweek [12]. Thus, it is essential to ensure the resulting documents are accessible for supporting diverse users [8]. However, making productivity documents accessible remains a challenge, and prior studies have shown an overall lack of awareness to make documents accessible [3,9]. Traditionally, this process relied on step-by-step manual checking by authors, which is time-consuming. Generative AI (Gen AI) tools have shown potentials to improve effectiveness and efficiency in this process. Thus, there is a need to understand how these Gen AI tools handle accessibility issues in productivity documents.

K. Miesenberger et al. (Eds.): ICCHP 2026, LNCS 16867, pp. 281–288, 2027.
https://doi.org/10.1007/978-3-032-31308-9_34

Table 1. Accessibility issue categories and types across document formats.

Category	Issue Type	Word	Excel	PowerPoint
Color & Contrast	Hard-to-read text contrast	✓	✓	✓
	Avoid red formatting		✓	
Media & Illustrations	Missing alt text	✓	✓	✓
	Missing subtitles			✓
Tables	Missing table header	✓	✓	✓
	Use of merged/split cells	✓	✓	✓
Document Structure	No headings in document	✓		
	Default sheet name		✓	
	Missing slide title			✓
	Duplicate slide title			✓
	Reading order			✓
	Default section name			✓
	Duplicate section name			✓
Document Access	Restricted access	✓	✓	✓

Microsoft has a built-in Accessibility Assistant function within its productivity applications, it provides a practical and widely used definition for accessibility issues in the productivity documents. In this paper, we examine the effectiveness of Gen AI tools in detecting and fixing accessibility issues according to the Microsoft built-in Accessibility Assistance across productivity documents from three Microsoft products (Word, Excel, and PowerPoint). Two research questions will be addressed:

1. How accurately can Gen AI tools identify accessibility issues from productivity documents?
2. To what extent can Gen AI tools fix accessibility issues they identified?

2 Related Work

The Microsoft Accessibility Assistant categorizes potential accessibility issues into five major categories, including "Color and Contrast", "Media and Illustrations", "Tables", "Document Structure" and "Document Access" [5] (see Table 1). This rule-based function provides guidance and suggestions for authors to identify and remediate accessibility issues step-by-step during document creation.

Recent advancements in Gen AI tools have demonstrated their potential to address accessibility issues that extend beyond the capabilities of rule-based functions, which can improve efficiency and productivity. For example, this has been applied to tasks such as mathematical formula detection [10], automatic chart understanding [4,7,13], intelligent document understanding [14], and PDF remediation [11]. Additionally, a survey by Perera et *al.* [8] identified five expectations and needs from screen reader users regarding Gen-AI-enabled productivity tools, one of which is transforming inaccessible content to accessible formats.

Meanwhile, Microsoft has integrated Copilot into their software to support creation and improve productivity since 2025 [6].

As the growing adoption of these Gen AI tools in productivity workflows, many researchers have examined these Gen AI tools for accessibility [1,2]. To our knowledge, no prior work has examined the capability of these Gen AI tools on identifying and fixing accessibility issues within productivity applications.

3 Method

We prepared nine documents for evaluation: three Word documents downloaded online, three Excel documents from the Microsoft template library, and three PowerPoint documents obtained from our lecture materials. Each of these nine documents contained different numbers of accessibility issues according to the built-in Microsoft Accessibility Assistant (see Table 2). Three widely used Gen AI tools were chosen for evaluation: ChatGPT 5.2; Gemini 3, and Copilot (smart mode).

To address the first research question, each of the nine documents was uploaded to all three Gen AI tools using the same prompt: *I have uploaded this file. Can you check and list the number of accessibility issues in this file according to the Microsoft accessibility checker built-in?* We recorded the identified issues and their categories to evaluate the performance from two perspectives: 1) **Detection Accuracy**: the percentage of issues correctly identified relative to the ground-truth issues; and 2) **Category Alignment**: the percentage of issue categories that overlap between the ground truth and identified results.

Following the first step, the same prompt was used to address the second research question: *Can you fix the accessibility issues according to the Microsoft accessibility checker built-in, and return me a revised file?* We recorded the number of issues each tool claimed to fix, and re evaluated the returned documents using the Microsoft Accessibility Assistant. Two metrics were used in this evaluation: (1) **Claimed Fix Rate**: the percentage of issues claimed to fix relative to the identified issues; and (2) **True Fix Rate**: the percentage of issues successfully fixed relative to the ground-truth issues.

4 Results

Table 2 summarizes the ground-truth issues in each document identified by the Microsoft Accessibility Assistant. Among these nine documents, the PowerPoint documents contain the highest number of issues overall. In terms of issue categories, Word documents show a higher prevalence of issues in the "Hard-to-read text contrast" category. Excel documents exhibit more issues in the "Color & Contrast" and the "Tables" categories. PowerPoint documents show more issues in the "Document Structure" category. Issues in the "Media & Illustration" category is shared commonly by all documents, primarily due to missing alternative text (alt text).

Table 2. Number of ground truth accessibility issues identified by the Microsoft Accessibility Assistant for each document.

Category Document	Word			Excel			PowerPoint		
	W1	W2	W3	E1	E2	E3	P1	P2	P3
Color & Contrast	2	4	4	13	2	7	0	0	2
Media & Illustrations	2	1	1	1	0	2	25	4	5
Tables	2	0	2	5	1	2	0	1	1
Document Structure	0	1	0	0	0	0	10	5	12
Document Access	0	0	0	2	3	0	0	0	0
Total	**6**	**6**	**7**	**21**	**6**	**11**	**35**	**10**	**20**

4.1 Accessibility Issues Identification

Table 3 summarizes the average detection performance of issues identified by three tools across nine documents. All tools achieve the highest detection accuracy on Word documents, and the lowest detection accuracy on Excel documents, while performance varies on PowerPoint documents. ChatGPT and Copilot demonstrate relatively strong detection performance overall; however, Copilot tends to generate more additional issues that are not defined by Microsoft Accessibility Assistant. In contrast, Gemini shows lower detection accuracy overall.

Across all three tools, category alignment remains moderate, ranging from 28.92% to 55.55%. All tools exhibit a gap between the categories of detected issues and those defined by Microsoft Accessibility Assistant. Gemini and Copilot demonstrate comparable performance in category alignment across nine documents.

Overall, these results indicate that while these tools are capable of identifying accessibility issues, higher detection accuracy does not correspond to higher category alignment with the Microsoft Accessibility Assistant. Additionally, all tools tend to report extra issues that are out of the categories defined by Microsoft Accessibility Assistant.

4.2 Accessibility Issues Fixation

The results of fixation performance across the three tools are shown in Table 4. All three tools tend to over-claim their capabilities to fix identified accessibility issues in documents. Both ChatGPT and Copilot claimed extra corrections beyond the issues they detected in the previous step, and exhibited large discrepancies between the Claimed Fix Rate and the True Fix Rate. As for Gemini, it claimed near-perfect fixing rate; however, it returned non-downloadable documents, and its True Fix Rate remains unknown.

Based on the evaluation of revised documents, ChatGPT demonstrated more conservative fixing behavior, it was able to preserve the format and content of the

Table 3. Average accessibility issue detection performance across three tools. Values in parentheses indicate the average number of additional issues detected beyond the ground-truth accessibility categories.

Tool	Document	Detection Accuracy	Category Alignment
ChatGPT	Word	84.92% (+2)	50.00%
	Excel	45.74% (+10)	41.27%
	PowerPoint	36.45%	28.92%
Gemini	Word	62.70% (+1)	44.44%
	Excel	44.72% (+9)	54.77%
	PowerPoint	57.92%	54.80%
Copilot	Word	78.57% (+6)	55.55%
	Excel	48.24% (+10)	47.62%
	PowerPoint	71.08% (+7)	54.80%

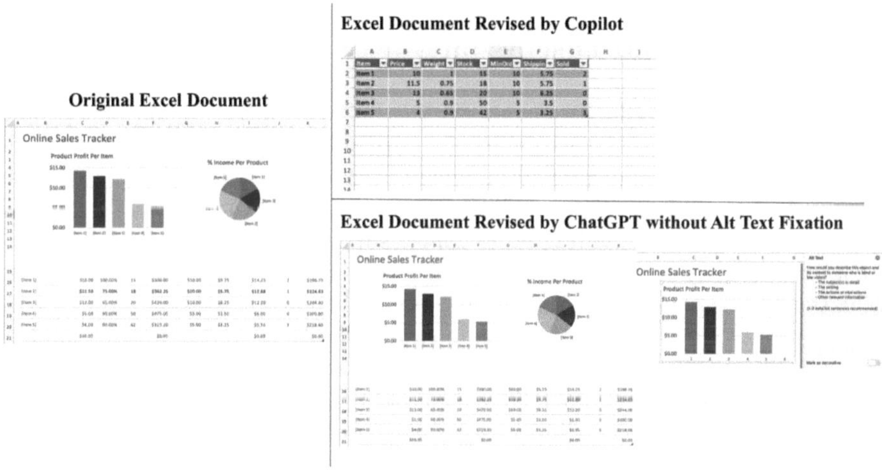

Fig. 1. A comparison of Copilot and ChatGPT on a revised document example. Given the same original document, Copilot returned the document with modified structure and content, whereas ChatGPT preserved the original content but showed poorer performance in addressing accessibility issues, particularly in missing alt text.

original document, albeit poor quality fixes. In contrast, Copilot returned over-corrected documents with aggressive modification in both content and format compared to the original documents. Examples are shown in Fig. 1.

Although all three tools attempt to remediate accessibility issues in documents, they all exhibit low claim reliability and limited fixation capabilities. These findings further indicate that these tools are not yet suitable for automatically remediating accessible documents.

Table 4. Average accessibility issues fixation performance across three tools. Values in parentheses indicate the average number of additional fixes applied beyond the ground-truth accessibility categories.

Tool	Document	Claimed Fix Rate	True Fix Rate
ChatGPT	Word	71.72% (+1)	25.40%
	Excel	100.00%	34.32%
	PowerPoint	85.19% (+1)	18.18%
Gemini	Word	93.33%	Unknown
	Excel	100.00%	Unknown
	PowerPoint	100.00%	Unknown
Copilot	Word	88.89% (+3)	45.71%
	Excel	80.70%	73.48%
	PowerPoint	93.33%	18.18%

5 Conclusion and Discussion

Gen AI has been increasingly integrated into software applications that people rely on daily in the workplace. With its capabilities in advancing tasks such as context awareness and natural language interaction, it has the potential to assist authors and reduce required efforts to detect and fix accessibility issues in documents. However, providing accessibility support requires these AI systems to comprehensively understand document structure and content. Based on our evaluation, these capabilities remain limited at the current stage.

Our results have shown that the investigated Gen AI tools have moderate capabilities in identifying accessibility issues across productivity documents (Word, Excel, and PowerPoint). This suggests that these tools can serve as initial screening tools for accessibility issues. However, none of the three tools were able to detect the same accessibility issues as the built-in Microsoft Accessibility Assistant. In terms of fixing these issues they identified, the tools demonstrated limited effectiveness. All three tools showed higher Claim Fix Rate and substantially lower True Fix Rate. Notably, there was also inconsistent behavior regarding document revision. Copilot tended to over modify the content and format from the original documents, while Gemini was unable to return downloadable documents. Overall, these tools have shown capabilities in assisting identifying accessibility issues rather than fixing the documents, human validation is still needed to ensure the documents are fully accessible.

5.1 Limitation and Future Work

This study has three limitations. First, only nine documents were evaluated, resulting in a relatively small sample size that may affect the generalizability of the findings. Second, the ground-truth issues were defined based on the built-in Microsoft Accessibility Assistant. Although it is commonly used in practice and provides a useful baseline, it may not capture all existing accessibility issues and may differ from those identified through human inspection, leading to inconsistencies in the evaluation results. Lastly, no human participants were involved at this stage; therefore, this study lacks the user-centered perspective.

Future research could involve a larger sample size and incorporate human evaluations, particularly involving people who would benefit from accessible documents. It could also focus on advancing Gen AI tools' capabilities in document structure understanding, improving issue detection accuracy, and enabling context-aware correction. In addition, accessibility assessment is often subjective and depends on users' specific needs. Therefore, this study highlights the need for further investigation into the extend to which AI should assist accessibility assessment in productivity documents.

Disclosure of Interests. The authors have no competing interests to declare that are relevant to the content of this article.

References

1. Alshaigy, B., Grande, V.: Forgotten again: addressing accessibility challenges of generative ai tools for people with disabilities. In: Adjunct Proceedings of the 2024 Nordic Conference on Human-Computer Interaction, pp. 1–6 (2024). https://doi.org/10.1145/3677045.3685493
2. Cha, Y., Jackson, V., Shu, L., Branham, S., van der Hoek, A.: "game changer" or "overenthusiastic drunk acquaintance"? Generative ai use by blind and low vision software professionals in the workplace. arXiv preprint arXiv:2512.24462 (2025). https://doi.org/10.48550/arXiv.2512.24462
3. Darvishy, A., Sethe, R., Engler, I., Pierrès, O., Manning, J.: The state of scientific pdf accessibility in repositories: a survey in Switzerland. Learned Publ. **36**(4), 577–584 (2023). https://doi.org/10.1002/leap.1581
4. Farahani, A.M., Adibi, P., Ehsani, M.S., Hutter, H.P., Darvishy, A.: Automatic chart understanding: a review. IEEE Access **11**, 76202–76221 (2023). https://doi.org/10.1109/ACCESS.2023.3298050
5. Microsoft: Improve accessibility in your documents with the accessibility assistant. https://support.microsoft.com/en-us/topic/improve-accessibility-in-your-documents-with-the-accessibility-assistant-f01562ca-0119-40ad-8dd6-f6223df50bef. Accessed 23 Jan 2026
6. Microsoft: Introducing microsoft 365 copilot – your copilot for work. https://blogs.microsoft.com/blog/2023/03/16/introducing-microsoft-365-copilot-your-copilot-for-work/. Accessed 23 Jan 2026
7. Moured, O., et al.: Alt4blind: a user interface to simplify charts alt-text creation. In: International Conference on Computers Helping People with Special Needs, pp. 291–298. Springer, Heidelberg (2024). https://doi.org/10.1007/978-3-031-62846-7_35
8. Perera, M., Ananthanarayan, S., Goncu, C., Marriott, K.: The sky is the limit: understanding how generative AI can enhance screen reader users' experience with productivity applications. In: Proceedings of the 2025 CHI Conference on Human Factors in Computing Systems, pp. 1–17 (2025). https://doi.org/10.1145/3706598.3713634

9. Pierrès, O., Schmitt-Koopmann, F., Darvishy, A.: Pdf accessibility in international academic publishers. In: International Conference on Computers Helping People with Special Needs, pp. 38–46. Springer, Heidelberg (2024). https://doi.org/10.1007/978-3-031-62846-7_5
10. Schmitt-Koopmann, F.M., Huang, E.M., Hutter, H.P., Stadelmann, T., Darvishy, A.: Mathnet: a data-centric approach for printed mathematical expression recognition. IEEE Access **12**, 76963–76974 (2024). https://doi.org/10.1109/ACCESS.2024.3404834
11. Schmitt-Koopmann, F.M., Huang, E.M., Hutter, H.P., Darvishy, A.: Towards more accessible scientific pdfs for people with visual impairments: step-by-step pdf remediation to improve tag accuracy. In: Proceedings of the 2025 CHI Conference on Human Factors in Computing Systems, pp. 1–16 (2025). https://doi.org/10.1145/3706598.3713084
12. Silverman, A.M., Rosenblum, L.P., Bolander, E.C., Rhoads, C.R., Bleach, K.: Technology and accommodations: Employment experiences of U.S. adults who are blind, have low vision, or are deafblind. Technical report, American Foundation for the Blind (2022). Accessed 23 Jan 2026
13. Song, Y., Jeong, S., Cho, W., Lim, S.B., Park, J.H.: A real-time chart explanation system for visually impaired individuals. In: International Conference on Computers Helping People with Special Needs, pp. 306–312. Springer, Heidelberg (2024). https://doi.org/10.1007/978-3-031-62846-7_37
14. Wang, W., Hu, H., Zhang, Z., Li, Z., Shao, H., Dahlmeier, D.: Document intelligence in the era of large language models: a survey. arXiv preprint arXiv:2510.13366 (2025). https://doi.org/10.48550/arXiv.2510.13366

Design and Preliminary Evaluation of an AI Dialogic Reading System for Children with Developmental Delays: Parents' Perceptions

Hui-Shan Lo[1(✉)], Hsin-Ping Tseng[2], Hsu-Kai Chang[3], and Tien-Chi Huang[4]

[1] Department of Special Education, National Pingtung University, 4-18, Minsheng Rd., Pingtung City, Pingtung County 900391, Taiwan
sunnylo519@mail.nptu.edu.tw

[2] Doctoral Program of Intelligent Engineering, National Taichung University of Science and Technology, 129, Section 3, Sanmin RD, North District, Taichung, Taiwan
s1f11336002@nutc.edu.tw

[3] Graduate Institute of Rehabilitation Counseling and Gerontological Wellbeing, National Taiwan Normal University, 162, Sec. 1 Heping East Road, Taipei, Taiwan
akai@ntnu.edu.tw

[4] Department of Information Management, National Taichung University of Science and Technology, 129, Section 3, Sanmin RD, North District, Taichung, Taiwan
tchuang@nutc.edu.tw

Abstract. This study designed an AI Dialogic Reading Companion System for young children with developmental delays, and explored parents' perceptions of its use in shared reading contexts. Grounded in dialogic reading principles, the system integrates speech recognition, large language model–based prompting, and process-level learning analytics to provide real-time guided reading support. Three parents used the system with their children and then participated in semi-structured interviews. The interview data were analyzed using thematic analysis. Findings showed that parents generally perceived the system positively. They reported that the AI-generated prompts effectively guided children's reading and responses, promoted a certain degree of independent participation, and reduced the need for constant parental prompting during shared reading. Parents also valued the system's assessment and logging functions, which allowed them to observe children's progress in language expression and response performance. At the same time, parents expressed concerns regarding usage control, content safety, and system flexibility. They emphasized the need for features such as time limits, customizable reading materials, and safeguards to ensure that AI-generated questions remain appropriate for young children. Overall, the findings suggest that AI-supported dialogic reading systems have potential to support reading engagement and reduce caregiver burden in families of children with developmental delays. However, effective implementation requires careful attention to parental oversight, safety, and the preservation of meaningful parent–child interaction.

Keyword: Generative Artificial Intelligence · Dialogic Reading · Developmental Delays

K. Miesenberger et al. (Eds.): ICCHP 2026, LNCS 16867, pp. 289–296, 2027.
https://doi.org/10.1007/978-3-032-31308-9_35

1 Introduction

In recent years, the rapid development of generative artificial intelligence (GenAI) has introduced new possibilities for interactive learning environments, particularly through large language models (LLMs) capable of generating adaptive dialogue and feedback [1]. These advancements have opened opportunities for designing systems that support language learning and engagement in early childhood contexts [2].

In early childhood education, meaningful interaction and responsive scaffolding are essential, as young children's learning is strongly influenced by dialogue-based experiences. Dialogic reading, which emphasizes open-ended questioning and active child participation, has been widely recognized as an effective approach to support language development and early literacy skills [3, 4].

For children with developmental delays, dialogic reading is especially important but often requires sustained caregiver involvement and continuous prompting [5, 6]. This creates practical challenges for families, particularly in maintaining consistent and high-quality interaction during shared reading. In this context, AI-supported dialogic reading systems may provide an alternative form of real-time scaffolding that supports children's participation while reducing caregiver burden.

2 Literature Review

2.1 Generative AI in Early Childhood

Recent advances in GenAI have created new opportunities for interaction and instructional support in early childhood education. AI technologies are increasingly used in learning activities for children aged 3 to 8, particularly through interactive agents, educational robots, and voice-based dialog systems that support language learning, problem solving, and contextual understanding [7].

In storytelling contexts, Han and Cai (2023) developed AI Story, a GenAI system that integrates text and image generation to support young children in creating personalized visual stories. Their findings indicated that such systems can enhance children's language expression, narrative development, and creativity [8]. More recently, research has extended beyond content generation to dialogic reading support. For example, AI story agents capable of posing open-ended questions and responding contingently to children's input have been found to promote story comprehension, perspective-taking, and richer language output [9, 10].

Overall, GenAI in early childhood education is shifting from one-way content generation toward interactive systems that support dialogic reading, narrative scaffolding, and process-oriented engagement, providing a strong foundation for AI-supported reading companion systems [7–10].

2.2 Dialogic Reading in Early Childhood

Dialogic reading is an interactive shared reading approach proposed by Whitehurst and colleagues that emphasizes active verbal exchanges between adults and children during storybook reading [3]. Unlike traditional read-aloud practices, it encourages adults to use open-ended questions, feedback, and scaffolding to promote children's active participation in discussing and narrating story content. Through repeated question–answer interactions, children are supported in developing language expression, comprehension, and broader cognitive skills. To guide systematic implementation, dialogic reading is commonly structured through the PEER cycle and the CROWD prompting framework, which help adults extend children's responses and encourage richer language use. Extensive evidence has demonstrated its effectiveness in improving young children's receptive and expressive vocabulary, narrative skills, emergent literacy, and reading motivation [4]. Importantly, dialogic reading has also shown positive effects for children with developmental delays, including those with autism and language impairments, by enhancing verbal participation, expressive language, and vocabulary development [11, 12].

3 Method

3.1 Tools

AI Dialogic Reading System (AI DiRe System)
The AI Dialogic Reading System (AI DiRe System) developed in this study is designed to support young children's reading interactions through an automated guided-reading process, thereby reducing the manpower demands associated with real-time adult-mediated shared reading. In addition to providing instructional scaffolding, the system leverages process-level log data to quantify children's behavioral performance, including oral language output and interaction fluency, and to support data-informed instructional feedback.

The system adopts a four-layer architecture consisting of the User Layer, Application Service Layer, Intelligent Processing Layer, and Data Layer (Fig. 1). The User Layer comprises a student interface and a teacher interface. The student interface supports participant identification, picture-book selection, and switching between guided and assessment modes, allowing children to interact with the system via speech or text while automatically recording response content and response time (Fig. 1). The teacher interface supports system administration and instructional configuration, including account management, picture-book and item-bank editing, participant data management, and review of statistical reports on learners' interaction processes and performance (Fig. 1).

The Application Service Layer functions as the core control module, integrating user operations with outputs generated by the intelligent processing components. Its responsibilities include tracking reading progress, enforcing item-skipping rules, generating questions and evaluating response correctness, and dynamically selecting subsequent scaffolding strategies based on children's performance. This layer also manages access control, instructional material administration, and statistical report generation.

The Intelligent Processing Layer embeds an AI engine that integrates multiple AI modules to enable real-time inter-active guidance and process-level analytics. Children's spoken responses are first converted into text through a speech-to-text module. An LLM-based guidance module (Gemini-2.5-Flash), working in conjunction with a question generation module, dynamically adjusts the direction and level of prompts based on children's real-time responses, the reading context, and accumulated interaction history.

To ensure pedagogical relevance and content safety, all AI-generated prompts are strictly grounded in teacher-authored, page-level instructional materials, including image-based situational descriptions and corresponding narration audio files. Cross-page constraints and de-duplication rules are applied to minimize the risk of irrelevant or extraneous content generation.

On the teacher side, the system provides quantitative indicators including the total number of responses, total corpus size, mean utterance length, and average response time, which serve as proxies for children's oral output volume, sentence elaboration, and response fluency (Fig. 1). Total corpus size is calculated as the sum of word counts across all transcribed responses, while mean utterance length is computed as the average number of words per response.

Through this integrated design, the system generates developmentally appropriate guiding utterances and follow-up questions that promote deeper thinking, inference, and emotional expression, preventing interactions from remaining at a single or closed-response level and enabling a cyclical, intelligent human–AI guided reading process.

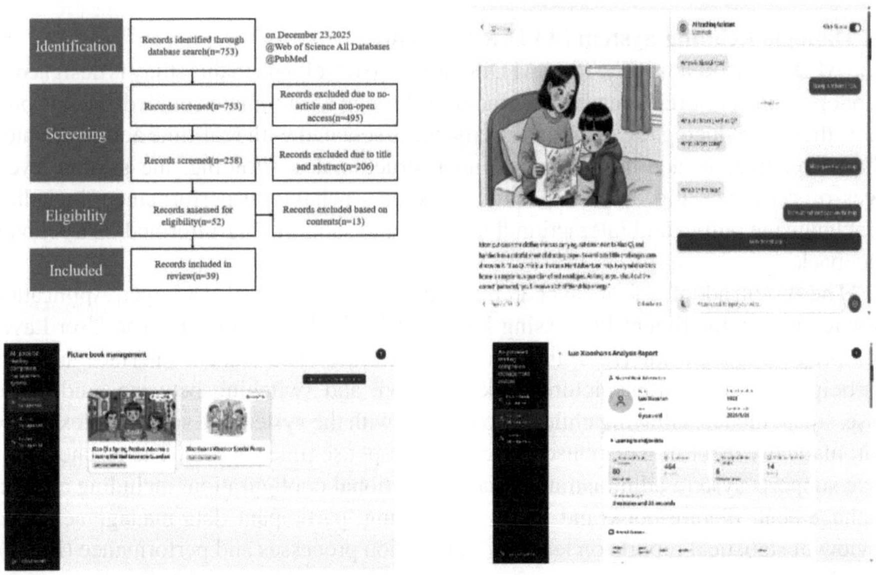

Fig. 1. Four-layer architecture of the AI DiRe System (TL); The children interact with the system (TR); Teacher interface of the AI DiRe System (DL); The AI DiRe System provides quantitative indicators (DR)

Parent Interview Guide for the AI Dialogic Reading System

A semi-structured interview guide was used in this study. The interview guide consisted of open-ended questions covering two main areas: (1) parents' overall impressions of the AI reading companion, and (2) parents' perceived benefits, challenges, and suggestions for system improvement. All questions were open-ended, and probing questions were used flexibly to encourage elaboration and clarification based on participants' responses.

3.2 Participants

Participants were three parents of young children with developmental delays. Prior to the interview phase, all three participating parents were invited to experience the AI Dialogic Reading Companion System designed by the researchers. Parents used the system with their children in a natural shared reading context, allowing them to gain firsthand experience of the AI-supported dialogic reading process. Following the system usage period, semi-structured interviews were conducted to explore parents' perceptions, experiences, and reflections regarding the use of the AI dialogic reading companion.

3.3 Data Analysis

This study employed thematic analysis as outlined by Braun and Clarke (2006) [13]. All interview recordings were transcribed verbatim, and the transcripts were read repeatedly to achieve familiarity with the data. Initial codes were then generated to identify meaningful units related to parents' experiences, perceptions, and reflections on using the AI dialogic reading companion system. Codes with conceptual similarity were subsequently grouped into broader categories, from which overarching themes were developed.

The coding and theme development were conducted by the first author, and analytic memos were maintained throughout the process to document coding decisions and enhance transparency. Given the exploratory nature of this preliminary study and the small sample size, formal inter-coder agreement was not calculated; however, to enhance the credibility of the analysis, the coding process involved iterative review, constant comparison across participants' accounts, and repeated refinement of themes.

4 Results

The thematic analysis yielded three major themes: (1) AI-guided prompting supported children's participation and reduced parental prompting burden, (2) assessment and process-logging functions enhanced parents' awareness of children's learning progress, and (3) parents emphasized the need for safety, controllability, and flexibility.

4.1 AI-Guided Prompting Supported Children's Participation and Reduced Parental Prompting Burden

Parents generally perceived the AI-guided prompting mechanism as helpful in supporting children's participation during shared reading. They reported that the system's contextual questions and follow-up prompts encouraged children to respond, elaborate, and remain engaged with the story. In addition, parents indicated that the system enabled children to participate with a certain degree of independence, thereby reducing the need for continuous real-time prompting from adults. From the parents' perspective, this feature lessened the burden typically associated with dialogic reading, especially when sustained adult scaffolding would otherwise be required throughout the activity.

4.2 Assessment and Process Logging Functions Enhanced Parents' Awareness of Children's Learning Progress

A second theme concerned the value of the system's built-in assessment and process-logging functions. Parents noted that the recorded interaction data and performance indicators provided information beyond their immediate impressions during shared reading. These records helped them observe changes in their children's responses, such as increased completeness of utterances or improvements in verbal expression. In this sense, the system was perceived not only as an interactive reading tool but also as a source of learning-related information that could support parents' understanding of their children's progress over time.

4.3 Parents Emphasized the Need for Safety, Controllability, and Flexibility

Despite these positive perceptions, parents also raised several concerns regarding practical implementation in family contexts. One major issue involved usage control, including whether the system should include time limits to prevent excessive dependence on technology. Parents also emphasized the importance of content safety, particularly whether AI-generated prompts would always remain appropriate for young children. In addition, they expressed a desire for greater system flexibility, such as the ability to upload children's preferred picture books or customize reading materials. Taken together, these concerns suggest that, for parents, the value of the system depends not only on its interactive capabilities but also on the extent to which it remains safe, controllable, and adaptable to family needs (Table 1).

Table 1. Summary of Themes Identified from Parent Interviews

Theme	Description
Theme 1 AI-guided prompting supported participation and reduced parental burden	Parents perceived that the system's prompts helped children engage in reading and reduced the need for constant adult prompting
Theme 2 Assessment and process-logging functions supported parental monitoring	Parents valued the system's records and indicators as a way to observe children's language responses and learning progress
Theme 3 Safety, controllability, and flexibility remained important concerns	Parents expressed concerns about screen-time limits, appropriateness of AI-generated prompts, and the need for customizable reading materials

5 Conclusion and Discussion

This study explored parents' perceptions of an AI dialogic reading companion system designed for children with developmental delays. The findings suggest that parents generally viewed the system as a useful tool for supporting children's participation in shared reading through contextual prompting and follow-up guidance [8.10]. Parents also perceived that the system reduced the need for constant adult prompting and provided useful learning-related information through its assessment and process-logging functions.

At the same time, the findings indicate that the adoption of AI-supported dialogic reading in family contexts requires careful attention to parental oversight, content safety, and system flexibility. In particular, parents highlighted the importance of features that allow adults to regulate children's usage time, ensure the appropriateness of AI-generated content, and adapt reading materials to children's interests and needs. These findings align with prior work suggesting that AI-based educational tools are most effective when they function as scaffolds for interaction rather than as replacements for meaningful human relationships [8].

Overall, the study provides initial evidence that AI-supported dialogic reading systems may offer practical support for families of children with developmental delays. More broadly, it highlights the importance of balancing generative interactivity with pedagogical control and family-centered design considerations.

6 Limitations and Future Research

Several limitations should be considered when interpreting the findings of this study. First, this was a preliminary qualitative study involving only three parents; therefore, the findings are intended to provide in-depth insight into user perceptions rather than to support broad generalization. Second, the study relied on parents' retrospective self-reports following system use and did not incorporate additional data sources such as direct observations, log-based behavioral analyses, or child outcome measures. Third, because the study focused on short-term use, it does not provide evidence regarding sustained engagement or longer-term developmental effects.

Future research should include larger and more diverse samples, incorporate multiple data sources for triangulation, and examine the longer-term use and effectiveness of AI-supported dialogic reading systems across home and educational settings.

Acknowledgments. The authors would like to thank the National Science and Technology Council the Republic of China for financially supporting this research under Grant No. NSTC 114-2410-H-153-028

Disclosure of Interests. The authors declare that they have no competing interests.

References

1. Education: Artificial Intelligence **3**, 100049
2. Su, J., Zhong, Y.: Artificial Intelligence (AI) in early childhood education: curriculum design and future directions. Comput. Educ.: Artif. Intell. **3**, 100072 (2022)
3. Whitehurst, G.J., et al.: Accelerating language development through picture book reading. Dev. Psychol. **24**(4), 552–559 (1988)
4. Pillinger, C., Vardy, E.J.: The story so far: a systematic review of the dialogic reading literature. J. Res. Read. **45**(4), 533–548 (2022)

5. Fleury, V.P., Schwartz, I.S.: A modified dialogic reading intervention for preschool children with autism spectrum disorder. Top. Early Child. Spec. Educ. **37**(1), 16–28 (2017)
6. Towson, J.A., Gallagher, P.A., Bingham, G.E.: Dialogic reading: language and preliteracy outcomes for young children with disabilities. J. Early Interv. **38**(4), 230–246 (2016)
7. Su, J., Yang, W.: Artificial intelligence in early childhood education: a scoping review. Comput. Educ.: Artif. Intell. **3**, 100049 (2022)
8. Han, A., Cai, Z.: Design implications of generative AI systems for visual storytelling for young learners. In: Proceedings of the 22nd Annual ACM Interaction Design and Children Conference (pp. 470–474) (2023)
9. Zhou, H., Nikolova, A., An, P.: 'My lollipop dropped'–Probing design opportunities for SEL agents through children's peer co-creation of social-emotional stories. In: Extended Abstracts of the CHI Conference on Human Factors in Computing Systems (pp. 1–8) (2024)
10. Shen, J., Chen, J.K., Findlater, L., Smith, G.D.: eaSEL: promoting social-emotional learning and parent-child interaction through AI-Mediated content consumption (2025). arXiv preprint arXiv, 2501.17819
11. Desmarais, C., Nadeau, L., Trudeau, N., Filiatrault-Veilleux, P., Maxès-Fournier, C.: Intervention for improving comprehension in 4–6 year old children with specific language impairment: practicing inferencing is a good thing. Clin. Linguist. Phon. **27**(6–7), 540–552 (2013)
12. Rahn, N.L., Coogle, C.G., Storie, S.: Preschool children's use of thematic vocabulary during dialogic reading and activity-based intervention. J. Spec. Educ. **50**(2), 98–108 (2016)
13. Braun, V., Clarke, V.: Using thematic analysis in psychology. Qual. Res. Psychol. **3**(2), 77–101 (2006)

CAAI: Cognitive Accessibility Analyzer for AI-Generated Images

Jinat Ara[1](✉) and Cecilia Sik-Lanyi[2]

[1] Department of Electrical Engineering and Information Systems, University of Pannonia, Egyetem U. 10, Veszprem 8200, Hungary
ara.jinat@mik.uni-pannon.hu

[2] Hungarian Research Network, Piarista U. 4, Budapest 1052, Hungary

Abstract. Nowadays, AI-generated images are increasingly used in education, public communication, and assistive contexts. Therefore, identification of cognitive accessibility issues in AI-generated images is crucial for their safe and effective use in accessibility-sensitive contexts. In this paper, we present a web application that automatically analyzes AI-generated images using interpretable, non-learning metrics to estimate cognitive accessibility issues. The developed CAAI tool estimates an overall accessibility score with sub-scores for six evaluated attributes (clutter, clarity, contrast, brightness, focus, and text quality) and provides improvement suggestions. To support transparency, it generates two explainable visualizations: (i) a visual-complexity overlay highlighting edge-dense regions, and (ii) a saliency heatmap indicating attention-attracting regions. The system supports batch and incremental uploads, session-level comparison dashboards, per-image details, and exportable JSON/CSV reports. This work introduces a practical evaluation workflow that enables rapid screening and accessibility-aware refinement of AI-generated images intended for cognitively accessible content.

Keywords: Cognitive Accessibility · AI-Generated Images · Visual Clutter · Saliency Heatmap · OCR Readability · Explainable Evaluation · Streamlit

1 Introduction

AI-generated images are increasingly integrated into educational materials, public information systems, and assistive technologies. Although these images often exhibit high visual realism, they may introduce cognitive accessibility barriers [1], such as excessive visual clutter, weak figure-ground separation, insufficient clarity, suboptimal brightness, competing focal regions, or distorted embedded text. These factors can increase cognitive load and reduce comprehension, particularly for users with cognitive or attentional impairments [2]. Nowadays, different accessibility-by-design principles have been initiated [3], but practical tools for assessing the cognitive accessibility of AI-generated images remain limited. Most current evaluation approaches for AI-generated images primarily focus on realism, fidelity, or aesthetic quality, often relying on subjective human studies or opaque learning-based metrics [4]. These approaches are costly, difficult to

K. Miesenberger et al. (Eds.): ICCHP 2026, LNCS 16867, pp. 297–304, 2027.
https://doi.org/10.1007/978-3-032-31308-9_36

reproduce, and rarely provide actionable design feedback [5]. Besides, accessibility considerations are mostly addressed in the later phase of the design pipeline [6]. Therefore, there is a need for a standard automated application/tool that can evaluate AI-generated images, identify potential cognitive accessibility risks, support comparison across multiple generated images, and guide iterative improvement. Therefore, in this paper, we present a web-based application for assessing the cognitive accessibility of AI-generated images. The key contribution of the proposed application is:

- Compute an overall accessibility score (0–100) and six interpretable sub-scores for clutter, clarity, contrast, brightness, focus, and text quality attributes derived from classical, explainable image analysis metrics.
- Produces visual explanations, including a complexity overlay highlighting texture and edge-dense regions and a saliency heatmap indicating attention-attracting areas.
- Generates actionable, rule-based suggestions to support accessibility-oriented image refinement.
- Supports batch analysis, comparative visualization, and evaluation report export (CSV/JSON) to facilitate reproducibility and documentation.

The system is intended as a screening and decision-support tool, complementing human evaluation rather than replacing it, and enabling accessibility-aware selection and refinement of AI-generated images in real-world applications. This paper is structured as follows: Sect. 2 explains the existing literature. Section 3 describes the methodological aspects of the developed tool, explaining the development structure and its functional properties. Section 4 discusses experimental results and a comparative analysis with existing similar studies. Finally, Sect. 5 concludes the paper.

2 State of the Art

Cognitive accessibility is relatively influenced by perceptual factors such as visual complexity, clarity, luminance balance, and competition for visual attention [2]. Existing work in human-centered evaluation and accessibility research emphasizes that generative visual content should be assessed not only for visual realism or aesthetic quality, but also for usability, interpretability, and accessibility [1]. As AI-generated imagery becomes increasingly popular, it is increasingly important that accessibility-oriented evaluation extends beyond traditional image quality metrics. In computational vision and perceptual modeling, several well-established, interpretable visual signals have been proposed to address accessibility-relevant risks. For example, high edge and texture density mostly rely on visual clutter, which can increase perceptual load and make images harder to interpret [7]. For measuring sharpness and blur, Laplacian variance is widely used to estimate image clarity and legibility. Besides, Luminance statistics and brightness distributions help to determine visual comfort and identify images that are inaccessible due to over- or under-exposure. In addition, global intensity entropy determines overall visual complexity by capturing the structural variation within an image. Beyond these global measures, saliency-based models are widely used to estimate visual attention distributions across an image [8]. However, these models identify the image focal points or fragmented attention across multiple competing regions, which can negatively impact image comprehension.

Some recent studies in accessibility-aware image analysis and human-AI interaction have highlighted the importance of combining such perceptual indicators with explainable evaluation mechanisms [9, 10]. They suggested that, rather than relying on end-to-end predictive models, it is important to consider transparent metrics to understand the facts of image inaccessibility and the actionable improvement suggestions. This need is particularly crucial for AI-generated images because of artifacts such as excessive texture, unintended visual complexity, and distorted text. Although learning-based image quality assessment (IQA) and aesthetic prediction models have demonstrated strong performance on benchmark datasets, they are often optimized for photographic realism rather than accessibility considerations [4, 5]. Furthermore, such models typically provide limited actionable feedback, making them less suitable for iterative design workflows. Therefore, in this work, we proposed an approach addressing classical visual features, attention modeling, and text quality checks with clear visual explanations and rule-based suggestions for well-known perceptual factors affecting cognitive accessibility. The proposed system is simple, interpretable, and provides practical and understandable feedback. However, the proposed system promotes human-centered evaluation tools that enable accessibility-by-design practices for AI-generated visual content.

3 Methodology

This section presents the overall methodology of the developed system. Figure 1 illustrates a detailed workflow for analyzing AI-generated images using interpretable visual and textual metrics to evaluate cognitive accessibility risks. All the development strategies are described as follows.

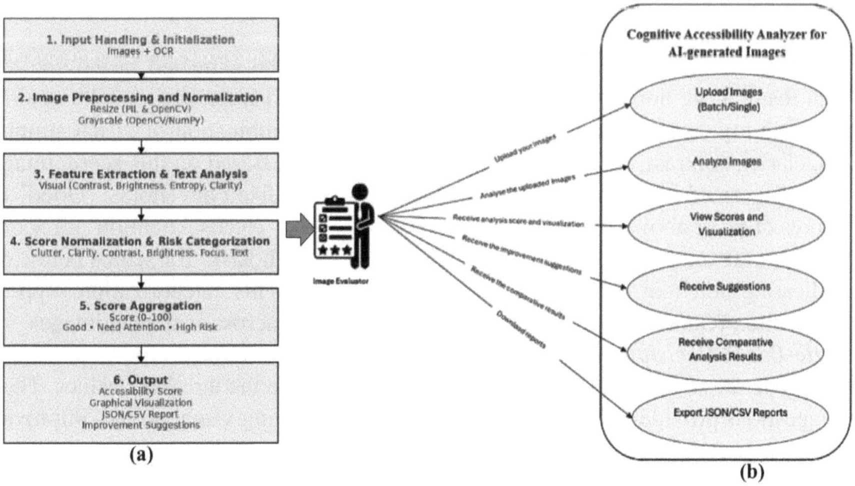

Fig. 1. Overview of the developed cognitive accessibility analysis workflow (a) for AI-generated images, demonstrated by the Use case diagram (b).

a) ***Input Handling and System Initialization:*** For application initialization, the execution environment first configures the required image processing and text analysis components. We used OpenCV for efficient visual analysis, and Tesseract OCR for the detection and confidence-based evaluation of embedded text. User input is collected through an interactive interface that allows both batch image uploads and incremental accumulation. All images are accepted in PNG or JPEG formats and normalized into a unified internal representation to ensure consistent downstream processing.
b) ***Image Preprocessing and Data Normalization:*** Each uploaded image is decoded into an RGB representation and assigned a unique identifier (using MD5 hashing) to prevent duplicate entries and consistent session tracking. Then, before analysis, images are resized to memory-safe dimensions and downscaled for a preview visualization. Then, the processed images are converted to NumPy arrays and converted to grayscale using OpenCV for final analysis.
c) ***Visual and Textual Feature Extraction:*** From the pre-processed images, the system extracts different visual and textual features that serve as indicators of cognitive accessibility. Visual features include contrast, brightness, entropy, and clarity, computed from grayscale representations using standard statistical and gradient-based measures. Besides, textual quality is assessed using OCR, combining average text recognition confidence with a simple rule-based measure that estimates the presence of distorted or nonsensical text, which is commonly observed in AI-generated images.
d) ***Explainable Overlay Generation and Saliency-Based Attention Analysis:*** To enhance system interpretability, we generate a visual-complexity overlay by estimating edge and texture density using Laplacian-based filtering. The generated visual-complexity overlay then blends with the original image. In parallel, visual attention is analyzed using a spectral residual saliency method, and focus indicators are computed based on the concentration and dispersion of attention across the image. The generated saliency heatmaps and overlays are presented alongside the original images to support visual inspection.
e) ***Score Normalization, and Risk Categorization:*** All the extracted visual and textual features are normalized into sub-scores on a 0–100 scale. An overall cognitive accessibility score is then computed as a weighted combination of visual simplicity, clarity, contrast, brightness, focus, and text quality. Based on this score, images are categorized into three qualitative risk levels using fixed thresholds: 'Good' for scores of 80 or above, indicating low accessibility risk; 'Needs Attention' for scores between 60 and 79, indicating moderate risk; and 'High Risk' for scores below 60, indicating potential cognitive accessibility concerns. This categorization supports rapid interpretation, comparison, and decision-making across evaluated images.
f) ***Rule-Based Decision Support:*** To support accessibility-oriented reporting, the system generates rule-based recommendations according to the threshold values. These suggestions provide actionable guidance, such as reducing visual clutter, improving contrast or clarity, strengthening focal regions, or replacing distorted text.
g) ***Visualization, Reporting, and Export:*** The application provides interactive dashboards for each image inspection, comparative analysis across multiple images, and transparent access to raw metrics. Results can be exported as structured JSON or CSV files at both image and session levels. Session history management prevents duplicate entries and supports reproducible analysis.

The developed application is intended to support multiple stakeholders (e.g., designers, researchers, educators) who generate AI-based visual content for accessibility-sensitive contexts such as education, public information, or assistive materials. According to the application use case diagram (as shown in Fig. 1(b)), stakeholders can analyze their AI-generated images by simply uploading them to the proposed system (either separately or together). After that, the system will automatically analyze each image and compute cognitive accessibility scores. The system ranks the uploaded images based on their overall accessibility scores and presents visual explanations, including complexity overlays and saliency heatmaps, with structured sub-scores and recommendations. From these analyses, images that receive lower scores can be further adjusted using the system's actionable suggestions, such as simplifying backgrounds, improving contrast, strengthening focal points, or correcting distorted embedded text. Finally, the analysis results can be exported in structured JSON or CSV formats, providing traceable evidence of an accessibility-oriented design and evaluation process. However, the proposed system supports an accessibility-by-design approach, allowing early detection of potential cognitive accessibility issues and facilitating iterative refinement [4]. The exported reports further support reproducibility, documentation, and evaluation reporting in the research and development approach.

4 Experimental Results and Application Validation

To validate the effectiveness of the developed system, we incorporated 30 users who independently rated 150 AI-generated images using a five-point Likert scale (1 = difficult to understand, 5 = easy to understand), reflecting perceived ease of image understanding. All the users were second and third-year bachelor's students from the Computer Science faculty at the University of Pannonia, Hungary. The selected 150 images were obtained from the "[1]DeepfakeArt Challenge benchmark dataset", a large-scale dataset specifically designed for generative AI art forgery and data poisoning detection. This dataset has 32,000 images generated through diverse AI-based manipulation techniques: inpainting, style transfer, adversarial data poisoning, and CutMix. This dataset is openly accessible by the GenAI4Good initiative for research purposes. To ensure human ratings are consistent with the system's output, we categorized human ratings across three qualitative risk categories: High Risk (Likert ≤ 2), Needs Attention (Likert > 2 to ≤ 4), and Good (Likert > 4). Similarly, to ensure system output consistency with the human rating, we categorized system output for each image into three risk categories: High Risk (Overall Score ≤ 40), Needs Attention (Overall Score > 40 to ≤ 80), and Good (Overall Score > 80). The results demonstrated in Fig. 2 (bar plots [a, b]) indicate the distribution of samples across risk categories based on human ratings and overall scores computed by the CAAI tool. It can be observed that the majority of samples are categorized as 'Needs Attention' in both cases, with only a limited number of samples classified as 'Good' and very few as 'High Risk'. The similarity in distribution between human ratings and system-generated scores demonstrates strong alignment between subjective perception and the evaluation tool, thereby validating the system's effectiveness. Furthermore, Fig. 2 (box plots [c, d]) shows the distribution of human ratings and overall scores

[1] https://www.kaggle.com/datasets/danielmao2019/deepfakeart.

across the defined three categories. A clear separation between categories is observed, where samples classified as 'High Risk' exhibit lower score ranges, while 'Good' samples consistently show higher values. The 'Needs Attention' category demonstrates a wider spread in both human ratings and overall scores, indicating increased variability in intermediate-quality samples. Importantly, similar distribution patterns are observed for both human and system-generated scores, suggesting a strong alignment between subjective evaluation and the proposed scoring mechanism.

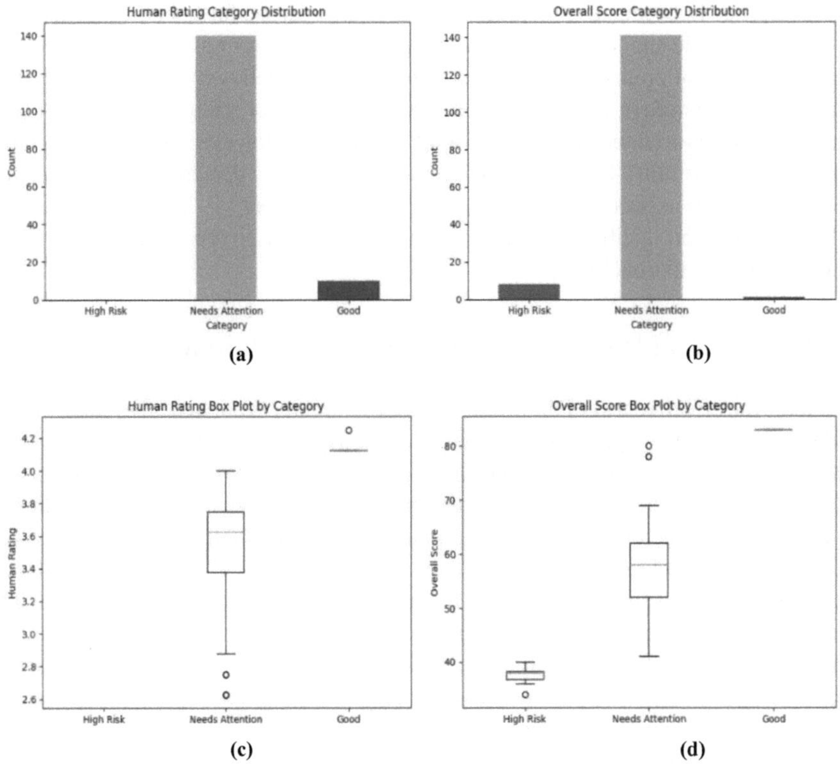

Fig. 2. Category-wise distribution and comparison of human perception (b) and aggregated overall scores by the CAAI tool (b) across three categories.

To further validate the effectiveness of our development, the application functionalities of the developed CAAI tool are compared with existing accessibility analysis tools that provide AI-based image analysis and accessibility support (as shown in Table 1). Table 1 demonstrates that while current solutions primarily focus on compliance checking, image description, or basic accessibility evaluation, they lack integrated cognitive scoring, explainable visual overlays, and structured recommendations. It indicates that the proposed system uniquely combines these aspects, providing a comprehensive and interpretable framework for evaluating the cognitive accessibility of AI-generated images. From this observation, we can state that the developed CAAI tool captures meaningful accessibility features and functions of AI-generated images and acts as a decision-support tool. However, in some cases, differences between human judgments and system outputs are observed, as human observers consider semantic and contextual aspects of image understanding, and the proposed system focuses on perceptual and structural indicators of cognitive accessibility. As a result, images that are semantically clear but visually complex, or visually simple but semantically ambiguous, may be rated differently by humans and the system.

Table 1. Comparative assessment results from existing tools.

References	Assessment Functionalities					
Feature	CAAI Tool (Proposed)	[a]Accessibility Analysis	[b]FrescAI	[c]Nexus Inclusion	[d]WAVE	[e]Seeing AI
Image-based analysis	✓(Yes)	✓(Yes)	✓(Yes)	✓(Yes)	✗ (No)	✓(Yes)
Cognitive accessibility focus	✓(Yes)	✗ (No)	✗ (No)	✗ (No)	✗ (No)	✗ (No)
Multi-metric scoring	✓(Yes)	✗ (No)	✗ (No)	✗ (No)	✗ (No)	✗ (No)
Explainable overlays	✓(Yes)	✗ (No)	✗ (No)	✗ (No)	✓(Yes)	✗ (No)
Suggestions/recommendations	✓(Yes)	✓(Yes)	✗ (No)	✓(Yes)	✓(Yes)	✗ (No)
Real-time analysis	✓(Yes)	✓(Yes)	✓(Yes)	✓(Yes)	✓(Yes)	✓(Yes)
Designed for evaluation	✓(Yes)	✓(Yes)	✓(Yes)	✓(Yes)	✓(Yes)	✗ (No)

[a]https://justbuildthings.com/ai-image-analysis/accessibility-check?utm_source=chatgpt.com.
[b]https://frescai.com/accessibility-analyzer?utm_source=chatgpt.com.
[c]https://www.nexusinclusion.com/products/image-analysis/?utm_source=chatgpt.com.
[d]https://wave.webaim.org/?utm_source=chatgpt.com.
[e]https://www.seeingai.com/?utm_source=chatgpt.com.

5 Conclusion and Future Work

In this work, we presented an explainable web-based application for evaluating AI-generated images to determine the potential cognitive accessibility risks. The system integrates interpretable, indicator-based metrics that capture key visual and textual characteristics related to cognitive load, including visual simplicity, clarity, contrast, brightness, attention concentration, and text readability. These metrics allow users to understand how individual image properties contribute to overall accessibility assessments. The key contribution of the proposed system is its explainability and decision-support functionality, including visual complexity overlays, saliency heatmaps, and rule-based recommendations for image refinement. However, the system relies on interpretable computational indicators and is not intended to replace human evaluation. Measures such as entropy and saliency provide approximate representations of visual complexity and attention and may not fully capture semantic relevance. In addition, OCR-based text quality assessment depends on the underlying OCR engine and configuration, which may affect consistency across deployment environments. Therefore, in our future work, we will validate the proposed system against a large sample of human judgments through preference-based evaluations and multi-scale user studies. Also, we plan to extend our work using typography-aware and color-accessibility metrics and reporting for research-oriented analysis across larger datasets.

Acknowledgments. The authors would like to thank the support of the National Research Development and Innovation Office, project no. 2021-1.2.4-TÉT-2021-00007.

Disclosure of Interests. There is no conflict of interest.

References

1. Caramiaux, B., Fdili Alaoui, S.: Human-centered evaluation of generative systems. ACM Trans. Comput.-Hum. Interact. **29**(6), 1–37 (2022). https://doi.org/10.1145/3558445
2. Sweller, J., Ayres, P., Kalyuga, S.: Cognitive load theory. Springer (2011). https://doi.org/10.1007/978-1-4419-8126-4
3. World Wide Web Consortium (W3C). Web Content Accessibility Guidelines (WCAG) **2**, 2 (2023). https://www.w3.org/TR/WCAG22/
4. Talebi, H., Milanfar, P.: NIMA: neural image assessment. IEEE Trans. Image Process. **27**(8), 3998–4011 (2018). https://doi.org/10.1109/TIP.2018.2831899
5. Doshi-Velez, F., Kim, B.: Towards a rigorous science of interpretable machine learning (2017). arXiv preprint arXiv:1702.08608. https://arxiv.org/abs/1702.08608
6. Lazar, J., Goldstein, D.F., Taylor, A.: Ensuring digital accessibility through process and policy. Morgan Kaufmann (2017). https://doi.org/10.1016/C2015-0-06114-0
7. Rosenholtz, R., Li, Y., Mansfield, J., Jin, Z.: Feature congestion: a measure of display clutter. Proceedings of the SIGCHI Conference on Human Factors in Computing Systems, pp. 761–770 (2005). https://doi.org/10.1145/1054972.1055076
8. Hou, X., Zhang, L.: Saliency detection: a spectral residual approach. Proceedings of CVPR, pp. 1–8 (2007). https://doi.org/10.1109/CVPR.2007.383267
9. Xu, W., Dainoff, M.J., Mark, L.S., Deane, P.: Accessibility evaluation of visual content: toward explainable and human-centered metrics. Univ. Access Inf. Soc. **18**, 877–889 (2019). https://doi.org/10.1007/s10209-018-0631-9
10. ISO 9241-210. Ergonomics of human-system interaction—Part 210: human-centred design for interactive systems. International Organization for Standardization (2019)

Assisting the Last Mile with Smart Glasses: Towards User-Centric LLM Prompt Engineering for Visually Impaired People

Sima Sommer(✉) and Timo Götzelmann

Nuremberg Institute of Technology, Kesslerplatz 12, 90489 Nuremberg, Germany
{Sima.Sommer,Timo.Goetzelmann}@th-nuernberg.de

Abstract. The independent mobility of visually impaired people remains limited, particularly on the so-called *last mile*. Obstacles, a lack of guidance systems, and the absence of visual information make it difficult to navigate public spaces. Existing aids such as white canes or guide dogs provide support but often cannot replace a sighted companion. This work investigates how modern AI-based systems can bridge this gap. We focus on the use of smart glasses in combination with large language models (LLMs) that analyze camera images and generate verbal descriptions from them. The goal is to provide situation-specific and easily understandable navigation and orientation information. Based on literature on orientation and mobility, a user-centered approach is being developed. In doing so, factors like context, culture, and personal preferences are considered and included within the framework of a structured prompt concept which can control the LLM's output. The key focus of this approach is concise and clear information. A prototype system was implemented for evaluation. It consists of smart glasses, a smartphone, and a server for model inference. Initial tests demonstrate the basic feasibility of the concept and allow for the comparison of different implementations. The findings show the possibility that LLM could be used to assist with navigation purposes. Our results also show that there is inconsistency and lack of determinism. Further research will thus concentrate on validating the system based on user experience, real-world test scenarios, and improving system reliability.

Keywords: Assistive Navigation · Visually Impaired · Blind · Smart Glasses · Large Language Models · VLM · Prompting · User-Centered Design

1 Introduction

Public transport is becoming increasingly accessible for people with visual impairments. However, the so-called *last mile*, i.e., the distance between home and the bus stop or from the bus stop to the actual destination in urban areas, remains a key challenge. In this regard, the independent and safe mobility of visually impaired people is still limited.

There are many reasons for this. For example, tactile guidance systems are often not available, interrupted, or blocked by obstacles. In addition, structural deficiencies such as damaged curbs, uneven sidewalk surfaces, or vegetation protruding into the path

K. Miesenberger et al. (Eds.): ICCHP 2026, LNCS 16867, pp. 305–312, 2027.
https://doi.org/10.1007/978-3-032-31308-9_37

make orientation and movement difficult. Relevant environmental information, such as the arrival of bus or tram lines, is also predominantly provided visually and is hardly accessible without assistance [1].

These barriers mean that visually impaired people often have to rely on sighted people for help, which is seen as limiting their independence and can make them avoid certain routes [2]. Traditional aids such as white canes, guide dogs, or tactile maps offer support, but cannot completely replace an accompanying person as a sighted assistant. However, technical systems can increasingly offer solutions to this problem. With the advent of large language models (LLMs) capable of analyzing camera images, verbal descriptions can be generated that are similar to comments made by assistants. In addition, so-called smart glasses offer the possibility of discreetly capturing camera images of objects in the field of vision.

2 State of the Art

The question of how environmental information can be captured and reproduced for people with visual impairments is not new (e.g., [3]). There are a variety of approaches to this problem that use sensors to capture the environment and convey it through visual, acoustic, or haptic signals.

Voice-based environmental descriptions have become increasingly important with the use of machine learning methods. Pre-trained deep learning models such as YOLO, SDD Mobilenet, Faster R-CNN, or DETR are often used, which are trained on large data sets and adapted for specific applications (e.g., [4, 5]). These models recognize numerous object classes in real time, thus supporting navigation and object recognition, for example for obstacles and traffic lights. The recognition results are communicated to the target group visually, auditorily, or haptically.

Voice interfaces for blind and visually impaired people enable verbal interaction and increasingly use large language models with image recognition to analyze camera images. These systems generate, for example, dynamic directions (e.g., [6]), warnings about obstacles (e.g., [7]), and contextual information about objects (e.g., [8]). They can interpret situations more flexibly and explain them in natural language than traditional rule-based approaches. Their outputs are thus similar to the support provided by sighted companions and allow intuitive interaction with queries. Accordingly, commercial assistance systems now also integrate such models to provide image descriptions for blind people (e.g., [9–11]). Notable examples include the *OrCam MyEye* and *Envision Glasses*, which provide real-time audio feedback for tasks such as text reading, object recognition, and face recognition [12]. Multi-modal AI-enabled smart glasses, such as the *Ray-Ban Meta Smart Glasses*, show strong potential for improving visual accessibility, but their proprietary design limits user-centered and extensible solutions [13].

Previous approaches have delivered technical implementations for creating generative outputs. However, none of these approaches address cultural, country-specific, or even user-specific characteristics in detail. This paper addresses these differences and proposes a user-centered approach. At the same time, the paper addresses a weakness of prompting using generative models: it discusses strategies for generating more consistent outputs, i.e., orientation and navigation descriptions.

3 Research Concept

Our approach is based on multiple sources related to navigation and orientation for visually impaired individuals. From these findings, we derive a formal concept for defining user-specific LLM prompts in Sect. 4. We also address technical characteristics of LLM and adapt them to our context.

3.1 Context- and User-Dependent Design Considerations for Assistive Navigation

There is a **context-dependent distinction** between orientation and navigation. Precise, environment-related information is particularly helpful for orientation (e.g., "a building at 9 o'clock, 10 feet away"), as it aids in understanding the current position and creating a mental map. For navigation instructions, on the other hand, more general, action-related statements are preferred (e.g., "walk to the end of the block and turn right"), as they simplify movement and are less cognitively demanding. Information from the immediate environment plays a central role, especially when traveling on unfamiliar routes [14].

The design of **user-dependent direction information** is culturally influenced, for example by clock directions in the United Kingdom or cardinal directions in the United States [15]. However, Scheuerman et al. (2017) show that simple egocentric directions such as "left" or "right" are easiest to understand, while abstract directions can lead to confusion. This highlights the importance of configurable direction formats.

Similarly, there is no global standard for **conveying distance information** for pedestrian navigation, but there are some recurring patterns. Some of the differences are unit-specific (meters, feet, yards, miles). Others relate to the way distance is communicated (absolute distance vs. minutes of walking). These differences, as well as individual preferences, emphasize the need for context-and user-dependent assistance systems [16].

Relevant Objects for Orientation for blind people are primarily clearly recognizable landmarks such as streets, intersections, and familiar buildings [16]. Descriptions of an object's location, size, or shape are considered particularly valuable, while purely visual characteristics are less relevant. Since many common obstacles can be reliably detected with a white cane, an assistance system should specifically report obstacles that are difficult to detect tactilely [14], such as objects at head height or fallen e-scooters.

A reduced Amount of Information is crucial for the orientation of blind people, as environmental sounds play an important role and verbal cues should therefore be limited to the essentials. Often, simple object recognition is sufficient, while detailed descriptions offer no additional benefit [14]. The presented system is therefore primarily not designed as a dialogue-based system.

Structured Spatial Cues for safe navigation play a central role, which is why paths, spaces, and objects are preferably described in terms of their geometric shape, as this supports the construction of mental maps [16]. This motivates the use of prompt-based control mechanisms to ensure consistent and interpretable spatial descriptions.

3.2 LLM Prompting for Blind Peoples Navigation

Need for Consistent Output. Consistent output is essential for verbal descriptions for navigation [17]. The literature shows that structured, reduced, and consistent representations of the environment (e.g., tactile maps) support mental maps [18]. The transfer of this principle to verbal LLM outputs is a design consequence of this work. In addition, visually impaired individuals can better memorize new routes when distractions are reduced [15].

Measures for Consistent Quality. This can be supported by strict prompt specifications with fixed formats. Instructive prompts help to clearly define the task scope, making responses more consistent. A negative prompt helps to avoid unwanted outputs. Building on this, the system uses a controlled vocabulary and fixed text templates [19].

Seed and Sampling Control. Seed and sampling play a central role in determinism. A fixed seed ensures reproducible outputs for the same input, while a low temperature close to zero and narrow top-k or top-p values minimize creative variations [20]. In safety-critical scenarios such as road navigation, this is essential, even if complete determinism remains limited [21].

3.3 Hardware Architecture

The basic hardware architecture consists of several components that ensure the following workflows:

- Image description: Receiving a request for information (e.g., via voice command or pressing a button), taking a photo of the user's field of vision, formulating the request to the LLM, inference, receiving the generated response, and voice output via the speakers.
- Follow-up questions: Receiving a information request, expanding the request, inference, receiving the generated response, and voice output via the speakers.

Various implementations are conceivable. Ideally, both workflows can be completely integrated into inconspicuous, lightweight glasses with a long battery life. However, this is not possible to this day. Therefore, it is conceivable to split the workflows across several devices, e.g., in a configuration with smart glasses for input and output, a smartphone as a communication interface, and a server for LLM inference.

4 Results

We conducted a basic feasibility study and implemented an experimental system. This enabled us to develop initial results and evaluate the various implementation alternatives.

4.1 Experimental Setup

For the experimental setup, we used a Smart Glass XREAL One [22] with the corresponding accessory camera as the input and output device. This device was chosen because the camera is positioned centrally between the eyes and it has an open SDK. The glasses were connected via USB cable to a Samsung S24 smartphone, which was used as a communication interface with the LLM server via a mobile data network connection. This smartphone could remain in the pocket during operation, allowing the white cane to be used (see Fig. 1).

Fig. 1. Blind User navigating with the system

The most important feature of the server for LLM inference was four Nvidia RTX2080 graphics cards. It had a dedicated IP address and provided various chat interfaces for the LLM via the Ollama library [23] (see Fig. 2).

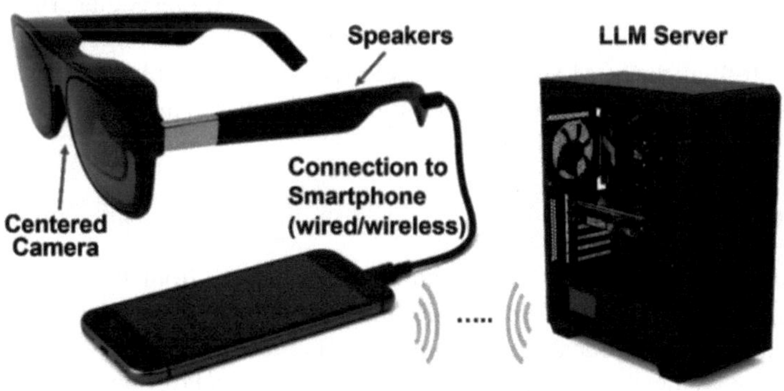

Fig. 2. Photomontage of our system setup

4.2 User-Specific Definition of LLM Prompt

The system formalizes context-dependent verbal assistance guidelines (see Sec. 3.1) as prompt components $P_1, \ldots, P_6$, each with a finite set of variants derived from the text:

P_1 = {"orientation","navigation"}: purpose.
P_2 = {"clock directions","cardinal directions", "egocentric direction"}: orientation.
P_3 = {"meters","feet", "yards", "miles", "minutes of walking", "number of blocks", ...}: distance
P_4 = {"streets", "intersections",...}: navigation_anchor.
P_5 = {"location", "shape", "size"}: description.
P_5^- = {"color", "material", "visual appearance", ...}: exemplary negative prompt.
P_6 = {"tactile-detectable", "tactile-hard-to-detect"}: obstacles.
Formally, a full prompt tuple becomes

$$x = \left(\left(p_{1j_1}, p_{1k_1}^-\right), \ldots, \left(p_{6j_6}, p_{6k_6}^-\right)\right) \in \left(P_1 \times P_1^-\right) \times \cdots \times \left(P_6 \times P_6^-\right), \tag{1}$$

concatenated pairwise as:

$$\text{concat}(x) = \sum_{i=1}^{6} \left(p_{ik_i}^- \| p_{ij_i}\right). \tag{2}$$

This generates tailored LLM instructions, e.g., combining precise orientation with egocentric directions for low-vision navigation. Please note: Rather than storing individual variants within $P_1, \ldots, P_6$, , the system holds complete, self-contained prompt sentences for each component, which already integrate both the desired instruction and its corresponding negative guidance (e.g., "Avoid coarse navigation instructions. Use precise environmental info for orientation such as 'building at 9 o'clock, 10 ft away'.").

5 Conclusion

This paper presented an approach for electronic assistants that utilize LLM and smart glasses to help blind people achieve greater independence. In addition, various user-specific differences from the literature were transferred to prompt engineering. This was done by incorporating strategies to eliminate known weaknesses of generative models. Despite controlling the LLM-specific parameters, however, it is only possible to a limited extent to make the generated outputs deterministic. To address this, our future work will therefore focus on fine-tuning LLM.

6 Future Work

In our future work, we evaluate if the requirements generated from literature are suitable for the target group's needs. This includes the consultation of people who have visual impairments and professionals from orientation and mobility instructors. Specifically, features of the system that would permit personalization will be evaluated. Additionally, a pilot trial on the use of the system will be conducted on one individual suffering from low vision. The effectiveness of the system's personalization, its suitability for the target group, and its performance in realistic settings will be determined through this evaluation.

Disclosure of Interests. The authors have no competing interests to declare that are relevant to the content of this article.

References

1. Park, J., Bamford, J., Byun, H., Chowdhury, S.: Journey by visually impaired public transport users: barriers and consequences. In: Proc. 37th Australasian Transport Research Forum, Auckland, New Zealand (2017)
2. Golledge, R.G., Marston, J.R., Costanzo, C.M.: Attitudes of visually impaired persons toward the use of public transportation. J. Vis. Impairment Blindness **91**, 446–459 (1997). https://doi.org/10.1177/0145482X9709100505
3. Meijer, P.B.L.: An experimental system for auditory image representations. IEEE Trans. Biomed. Eng. **39**, 112–121 (1992). https://doi.org/10.1109/10.121642
4. Erdaw, H.B., Taye, Y.G., Lemma, D.T.: A real-time obstacle detection and classification system for assisting blind and visually impaired people based on yolo model. In: 2023 International Conference on Information and Communication Technology for Development for Africa (ICT4DA). pp. 79–84 (2023) https://doi.org/10.1109/ICT4DA59526.2023.10302240.
5. Yee, L.R., Kamaludin, H., Safar, N.Z.M., Wahid, N., Abdullah, N., Meidelfi, D.: Intelligence eye for blinds and visually impaired by using region-based convolutional neural network (R-CNN). JOIV : Int. J. Inform. Visualization. **5**, 409 (2021). https://doi.org/10.30630/joiv.5.4.735
6. Kaniwa, Y., et al.: ChitChatGuide: conversational interaction using large language models for assisting people with visual impairments to explore a shopping mall. Proc. ACM Hum.-Comput. Interact. **8**, 1–25 (2024). https://doi.org/10.1145/3676492
7. Zhou, G., Hong, Y., Wu, Q.: NavGPT: explicit reasoning in vision-and-language navigation with large language models. http://arxiv.org/abs/2305.16986, (2023). https://doi.org/10.48550/arXiv.2305.16986
8. Seo, J., Kamath, S.S., Zeidieh, A., Venkatesh, S., McCurry, S.: MAIDR Meets AI: exploring multimodal LLM-Based Data visualization interpretation by and with blind and low-vision users. In: The 26th International ACM SIGACCESS Conference on Computers and Accessibility. pp. 1–31. ACM, St. John's NL Canada (2024). https://doi.org/10.1145/3663548.3675660
9. AI Smart Glasses for Accessibility: Ally Solos & Envision. https://www.ally.me/glasses. Last accessed 17 Dec 2025
10. Be My AI. https://www.bemyeyes.com/bme-ai/. Last accessed 17 Dec 2025
11. Envision-Assistive Technology for Blind and Low Vision. https://www.letsenvision.com. Last accessed 17 Dec 2025
12. Naayini, P., Myakala, P.K., Bura, C., Jonnalagadda, A.K., Kamatala, S.: AI-Powered assistive technologies for visual impairment (2025). http://arxiv.org/abs/2503.15494. https://doi.org/10.48550/arXiv.2503.15494
13. Zaman, N., Potluri, V., Biggs, B., Coughlan, J.M.: WhatsAI: Transforming Meta Ray-Bans into an Extensible Generative AI Platform for Accessibility (2025). http://arxiv.org/abs/2505.09823. https://doi.org/10.48550/arXiv.2505.09823
14. Hoogsteen, K.M.P., Szpiro, S., Kreiman, G., Peli, E.: Beyond the Cane: describing urban scenes to blind people for mobility tasks. ACM Trans. Access. Comput. **15**, 20:1–20:29 (2022). https://doi.org/10.1145/3522757
15. Wayfindr: Open Standard for Audio-based Wayfinding. https://www.wayfindr.net/wp-content/uploads/2017/12/Wayfindr-Open-Standard-Rec-1.1.pdf. Last accessed 06 Feb 2026

16. Scheuerman, M.K., Easley, W., Abdolrahmani, A., Hurst, A., Branham, S.: Learning the language: the importance of studying written directions in designing navigational technologies for the blind. In: Proceedings of the 2017 CHI Conference Extended Abstracts on Human Factors in Computing Systems. pp. 2922–2928. ACM, Denver Colorado USA (2017). https://doi.org/10.1145/3027063.3053260
17. Giudice, N.A.: Wayfinding without vision: learning real and virtual environments using dynamically-updated verbal descriptions. Presented at the Conference and Workshop on Assistive Technologies for Vision and Hearing Impairment (2006)
18. Ottink, L.: Mental maps with and without vision: Forming cognitive maps of space based on the visual and haptic senses (2022). https://repository.ubn.ru.nl/bitstream/handle/2066/285023/285023.pdf
19. Son, G., Kim, M.: Multi-level prompting: enhancing model performance through hierarchical instruction integration. Knowl.-Based Syst. **320**, 113545 (2025). https://doi.org/10.1016/j.knosys.2025.113545
20. Element Labs, Inc.: LM Studio Docs. https://lmstudio.ai/docs/typescript/api-reference/llm-prediction-config-input. Last accessed 07 Feb 2026
21. Klishevich, E., Denisov-Blanch, Y., Obstbaum, S., Ciobanu, I., Kosinski, M.: Measuring determinism in large language models for software code review (2025). http://arxiv.org/abs/2502.20747. https://doi.org/10.48550/arXiv.2502.20747
22. XREAL Ltd. https://www.xreal.com/. Last accessed 06 Feb 2026
23. Ollama. https://ollama.com. Last accessed 06 Feb 2026

"It Was Frustrating to See These LLMs Glitch": Evaluating Their Workflows and Products for Accessible User Experiences by Novice BLV Users

Sushil K. Oswal[1](✉) and Hitender K. Oswal[2]

[1] University of Washington, Seattle, WA, USA
oswal@uw.edu

[2] Paul G. Allen School of Computer Science and Engineering, University of Washington, Seattle, WA, USA

Abstract. This study contributes an evaluation of LLM-driven web development for novice blind and low vision (BLV) users, highlighting a critical gap where visual aesthetics are prioritized over accessibility and cultural context. Traditional web design tools remain largely inaccessible for BLV users, positioning LLMs as potential virtual assistants for independent web development. This paper presents a two-phase expert study evaluating the workflows and outputs of GPT-4o, GPT-5.2, and Gemini 3 Pro. Using JAWS-for-Windows and WAVE, we assessed the LLMs' capacity to generate a website for a vegetarian Indian restaurant. Findings reveal that despite model iterations, these LLMs remain insufficient for independent BLV use. Critical barriers include inaccessible file-management requirements, a regression in standard accessibility features like skip links, and significant cultural glitches. The study concludes that substantial improvements in accessibility specific training and dataset curation are needed for these tools to be fully useful for BLV creators.

Keywords: LLM Generated Websites · Cultural Accuracy in LLM Generated Content · Accessibility Standards & LLM Training · Generative AI and Web Content Design · Assistive Web Development with LLMs

1 Introduction

Despite significant research on the accessibility of websites for blind and low vision users (BLV), web design tools continue to present many accessibility barriers due to their reliance on drag-and-drop and other inaccessible features [1,2]. On the other hand, the emergence of large language models (LLM) has made it possible for novice users to generate their websites without web development knowledge. These LLMs also have the potential of supporting novice BLV users

K. Miesenberger et al. (Eds.): ICCHP 2026, LNCS 16867, pp. 313–320, 2027.
https://doi.org/10.1007/978-3-032-31308-9_38

in web development by eliminating the reliance on inaccessible web development tools. This paper presents results from a preliminary study that collected data on the process of creating business websites for our test case, India Café, with the help of three different LLMs. We wanted to examine their overall accessibility for generating websites by novice BLV users with little or no web development experience. We address the research question: Are LLMs reliable virtual assistants to BLV users for developing Web Content Accessibility Guidelines (WCAG) compliant websites independently? We also wanted to learn if these LLMs were aware of accessibility compliance requirements in creating websites because a novice user—BLV or not—would not have the knowledge of accessibility standards. The findings contribute to the emerging research on LLMs as virtual assistants for BLV website makers. After a brief literature review, we highlight our methodological steps and then present the data from our expert testing of the workflow and web products of GPT-4o, GPT-5.2, and Gemini 3 Pro [3–5].

2 State of the Art

Recent human computer interaction design (HCI) work has focused on accessible computing tools for supporting BLV users in designing websites independently and enjoying accessible user experiences [6]. This research ranges from accessible templates for developing websites with limited knowledge of web design to building websites using LLM affordances without any knowledge of web development [7–10]. None of these studies generated a website with the help of an LLM which is the focus of our paper. Several studies have examined dedicated website builders employing LLM APIs for creating websites without web expertise for their accessibility to BLV website makers [11,12]. Invariably, these studies point out major usability problems in these AI-driven builder tools for this population in constructing websites without sighted help [13,14]. A small number of papers have discussed LLM assistance for writing code by BLV [15].

3 Methodology

This study was conducted in two phases: June 2024 (evaluating GPT-4o) and December 2025 (evaluating GPT-5.2 and Gemini 3 Pro). We assessed the generated webpages for structure, layout, and navigation using JAWS-for-Windows 2026 with Chrome 143 to determine accessibility for BLV screen reader users. Subsequently, we performed WAVE testing to identify residual issues [16]. The screen reader was also used while generating the websites to gauge these LLMs' value as assistive tools. The evaluation was done by one of the authors who is an expert screen reader user and has conducted several BLV studies. No external participants were involved, and IRB review was not required. Both authors contributed to study design, data collection, manual analysis of HTML code of the generated webpages, and writing. Data collection used the detailed prompt below; follow-up prompts are detailed in the results. We expected the LLMs to automatically address WCAG standards since they have been trained on web accessibility standards. Therefore, our prompt did not stress accessibility.

"Imagine that you are a web developer. You are creating a new website for a business called India Cafe. This cafe has these features: 1. It has student friendly prices, 2. It has a seven-day schedule with early brunch, buffet, and late-night offerings, 3. It offers only vegetarian dishes from India. 4. It also offers popular snacks from India, 5. Its cuisine is a mix of south Indian and north Indian cooking. 6. After creating the website, also create a full menu."

4 Results

This section presents the results from our expert testing of the workflow and products of GPT-4o (June 2024), followed by GPT-5.2 and Gemini 3 Pro (late 2025). Note that we did not do Gemini testing in the 2024 phase. For each model, we report findings using the same prompt across three consistent dimensions: Page Structure and Layout, Content Creation, and Accessibility for Screen Readers. We compare the performance of the three LLMs below (Table 1).

Table 1. Performance Comparison

Dimension	GPT-4o	GPT-5.2	Gemini 3 Pro
Structure & Layout	H1-H3 hierarchy; critical black-on-black contrast error	H1-H4 with jump links; basic HTML layout	Broken hierarchy (skipped H2); rounded modular grid UI
Content Creation	North Indian bias; inaccurate image generation	Misclassified Chaat; missed South Indian items	Culturally insensitive; e.g. used meat images and burrito emojis for veg items
Media Handling	Individual files; required manual renaming/placement	Single 12-image collage; required manual cropping	Section-grouped images; some missing items
Screen Reader Accessibility	Functional skip links; detailed alt-text; 1 WAVE error	Smooth navigation; basic alt-text; 0 WAVE errors	No skip links; 24 WAVE errors; heading alerts
BLV User Effort	Manual file/directory management required.	Assumed user could crop collages and edit code.	Manual file/directory management required.

4.1 Results for GPT-4o

Page Structure and Layout. The webpage had reasonable structure with cafe title coded as heading level 1, section headings as heading level 2, and menu categories as heading level 3. However, the cafe title was invisible–black text on black background–and the text was only visible when selected.

Content Creation. The model generated a single page website targeted at students with reasonable food prices under 5 categories: Brunch, Buffet, Late-night Offerings, Snacks, and Beverages. The food menu was reasonable for a café however culturally it was biased toward North Indian dishes and snacks. Only 1 dish and 1 snack was specific to South India. Originally, GPT-4o did not include a logo or other images in the webpage. When prompted to add a logo and images with alt text to the menu items, it created a logo and individual images for menu items with alt text. However, there were some discrepancies. Some items did not have any images and/or related alt text generated. Additionally, the mango lassi image depicted a glass of mango yogurt shake garnished with a large mango slice as if it were a glass of water with a lemon slice. The image of the samosas–a savory pastry of triangular shape—had an open window to look inside, which is an inaccurate description of the pastry (Fig. 1).

(a) **(b)**

Fig. 1. (a) Mango lassi is never garnished with a mango wedge. (b) The window in the samosa is a hallucination.

Accessibility for Screen Readers. The model created a skip link which moved the JAWS cursor to the main content: "Welcome to India Café". The alt text described the images in detail in line with the appearance of the food item in the image and with a bit more detail than the menu item description on the page. More importantly, it expected the model user to manually place the images in the webpage's local directory and rename the randomly generated filenames. WAVE identified 1 contrast error recorded by us above. WAVE also questioned the length of alt text for the images.

4.2 Results for GPT-5.2

In response to the prompt for generating a vegetarian Indian cafe website with a food menu, the model generated basic HTML and CSS code for a single page.

Page Structure and Layout. This model created a reasonable page structure with the website title coded as heading level 1, major sections as heading level 2, food menu sections as heading level 3, and individual menu items as heading level 4 with descriptions following. The page also had a brief web menu with links for jumping down to the individual 4 sections. When we prompted the model to create images for each of the menu items, it created a collage of 12 of the 13 menu items and recommended cropping these images into individual files to place in the local webpage directory. The website has a basic HTML layout with most sections laid out like a print page with only rich text formatting. The schedule is a table and looks like one seen in Microsoft Word. It uses bright red and yellow backgrounds with both white and black text.

Content Creation. The model generated a reasonable menu for a vegetarian Indian cafe. The item descriptions were relevant for the vegetarian dishes throughout and were classified accurately under "Early Brunch", "Snacks & Chaat", "North Indian Curries", and "Desserts & Drinks". Interestingly, it did not create a separate section for South Indian meal items and placed them under the "Early Brunch". The section, "Snacks & Chaat", did not have a single chaat menu item.

Accessibility for Screen Readers. The navigation of the links and headings was smooth with the screen reader however the page did not have a skip link. It used universal emojis for location, phone number, and email which were read correctly by JAWS. When prompted to add descriptions to menu items, the model generated new code only for the menu section and recommended replacing the old section manually which might be a challenge to a BLV user without any web development experience. When prompted to generate alt text descriptions for each of the menu items shown in the collage, the model again created basic descriptions with some additional details from the images, e.g., served on a plate with bowls. Descriptions were not expressive enough to give a BLV consumer a good idea of what the dish might exactly look like. The model's recommendation about cropping the collage of images into individual image files ignored the needs of BLV users who might not have resources to get the images cropped. Considering the diminutive size of this website–a single page with 4 headings, WAVE did not identify any accessibility problems.

4.3 Results for Gemini 3 Pro

The same prompt generated a single HTML file with integrated CSS for a single page.

Page Structure and Layout. Gemini 3 Pro failed to create a proper hierarchy of headings in two places–jumping from heading level 1 to 3 and having two heading level 1 s. It did create proper hierarchy between heading level 3 for menu subheadings and heading level 4 for individual menu items. Gemini also created a brief web menu for dropping down to the 4 sections below. When prompted to add images and alt text for menu items, the model generated one combined image for each of the 5 sections. 3 of these images had all the items depicted but the other two left out some items. Alt text for images was basic without cultural inflections. The Gemini-generated website had a more visually appealing layout with background images pulled from the free image website, Unsplash, modular grids for menu items, rounded borders for style, and emojis. It used black and white backgrounds with black, white, orange, and green text.

Content Creation. In general, menu item descriptions were comparable to the ones by GPT-5.2 however Gemini 3 drastically failed in differentiating between vegetarian and animal food images while causing cultural violence. The main content paragraph had a background image of chicken biryani and the statement promoting North Indian food had the image of chicken tikka masala in the background. When choosing an emoji for street eats and Indian chaats, it used a Mexican burrito, again incurring cultural erasure.

Accessibility for Screen Readers. Gemini 3 Pro webpage also had smooth navigation when using a screen reader but also lacked skip link. When prompted to add images and alt text for menu items, the model expected the user to place the generated images into the website directory and rename them to match the code, a task we deem difficult for a BLV user without web development experience. WAVE reported 24 color contrast errors due to orange and green text on white backgrounds and white text on orange background. WAVE also alerted about the two heading level issues discussed above.

5 Discussion

This paper contributes the findings from the first two phases of a long-term evaluation study of the workflows and output quality of GPT-4o, GPT-5.2, and Gemini 3 Pro to determine their viability as independent web development assistants for BLV users. The findings indicate that despite the temporal progression from 2024 to 2025, these LLMs remain insufficient for independent use by novice BLV creators.

A critical barrier identified across all models is the inaccessibility of the workflow [17]. We observed a distinct regression in image handling: while GPT-4o (2024) successfully generated individual images with detailed alt text, GPT-5.2 (2025) provided a single collage. This demanded manual file management and cropping outside the chat interface, limiting usefulness for screen reader users lacking web development expertise and sighted assistance.

Regarding the generated web products, we noted a regression in standard accessibility features. While GPT-4o correctly implemented skip links in line with WCAG 2.1 advice, both 2025 models failed to include them [18]. Notably, WAVE did not report this lack of skip links or accessibility statement links, a limitation consistent with earlier evaluations of automatic web accessibility metrics [19]. Furthermore, Gemini 3 Pro's reliance on visual appeal resulted in illogical heading hierarchies and significant color contrast failures.

Finally, the models exhibited severe "cultural glitches" and hallucinations. These ranged from illogical visual fabrications—such as GPT-4o's "windowed" samosas–to offensive content mismatches [20]. Gemini 3 Pro wrought epistemic violence by including images of meat dishes in a strictly vegetarian website [21,22]. These errors suggest that despite newer models generally performing better in website development, they prioritize visual coherence over technical accessibility and context, ensuring that independent website development by BLV users is still in the future. Future research needs to look at how dataset curation and model training can be improved to handle complicated contexts involving accessibility for BLV users and cultural complexity of content. In this regard, these LLMs can improve their performance through careful curation of accessibility specific and well-articulated cultural datasets. Subject matter experts could also be instrumental in improving this performance if the companies would share more documentation about these LLMs' training. A key limitation is the focus on only three LLMs and one website generation prompt, which we will expand on in future work. The present study depended on the expert screen reader user's evaluation but we will include BLV participants in the next phase.

References

1. Ferrari, C., Hurst, A.: Accessible web development: opportunities to improve the education and practice of web development with a screen reader. ACM Trans. Accessible Comput. **14**(2), 1–32 (2021)
2. Oswal, S.K., Palmer, Z.B.: Compliance, commitment, and web accessibility: findings of an organizational study engaging accessibility experts at twenty US universities. In: Proceedings of the 42nd ACM International Conference on Design of Communication, pp. 17–25. Association for Computing Machinery, New York (2024)
3. OpenAI: GPT-4o System Card (2024). https://cdn.openai.com/gpt-4o-system-card.pdf
4. OpenAI: Update to GPT-5 System Card: GPT-5.2 (2025). https://cdn.openai.com/pdf/3a4153c8-c748-4b71-8e31-aecbde944f8d/oai_5_2_system-card.pdf
5. Google: Gemini 3 Pro Model Card (2025). https://deepmind.google/models/model-cards/gemini-3-pro/
6. Oswal, S.K.: Breaking the exclusionary boundary between user experience and access: steps toward making UX inclusive of users with disabilities. In: Proceedings of the 37th ACM International Conference on the Design of Communication, pp. 1–8. Association for Computing Machinery, New York (2019). https://doi.org/10.1145/3328020.3353957
7. Pillai, A., Shinohara, K., Tigwell, G.W.: Website builders still contribute to inaccessible web design. In: Proceedings of the 24th International ACM SIGACCESS Conference on Computers and Accessibility, pp. 1–4. Association for Computing Machinery, New York (2022). https://doi.org/10.1145/3517428.3550368
8. Campoverde-Molina, M., Lujan-Mora, S.: Artificial intelligence in web accessibility: a systematic mapping study. Comput. Stand. Interfaces **96** (2025). https://doi.org/10.1016/j.csi.2025.104055

9. Oswal, S.K., Oswal, H.K.: Conversational AI for accessible website design: integrating LLM assistants in website builders. In: Cambridge Workshop on Universal Access and Assistive Technology, pp. 251–261. Springer Nature, Cham, Switzerland (2025). https://doi.org/10.1007/978-3-031-84681-6_22
10. Acosta-Vargas, P., Salvador-Acosta, B., Novillo-Villegas, S., Sarantis, D., Salvador-Ullauri, L.: Generative artificial intelligence and web accessibility: towards an inclusive and sustainable future. Emerg. Sci. J. **8**(4), 1602–1621 (2024). https://doi.org/10.28991/ESJ-2024-08-04-021
11. Oswal, S.K., Oswal, H.K.: Examining the accessibility of generative AI website builder tools for blind and low vision users: 21 best practices for designers and developers. In: Proceedings of the 2024 IEEE International Professional Communication Conference, pp. 121–128. IEEE, New York (2024). https://doi.org/10.1109/ProComm61427.2024.00030
12. Delnevo, G., Andruccioli, M., Mirri, S.: On the interaction with large language models for web accessibility: implications and challenges. In: 2024 IEEE Consumer Communications & Networking Conference Workshops, pp. 1–6. IEEE, New York (2024). https://doi.org/10.1109/CCNC51664.2024.10454680
13. Leedy, K., Preston, M., Feng, J., Rezwana, J.: Accessibility in the age of generative AI web based builders: evaluating web design tools for inclusive practices. In: Proceedings of the 28th International Academic Mindtrek Conference, pp. 304–314. Association for Computing Machinery, New York (2025). https://doi.org/10.1145/3757980.3757989
14. Palmer, Z.B., Oswal, S.K.: Constructing websites with generative AI tools: the accessibility of their workflows and products for users with disabilities. J. Bus. Tech. Commun. **39**(1), 93–114 (2025). https://doi.org/10.1177/10506519241280644
15. Flores-Saviaga, C., Hanrahan, B.V., Imteyaz, K., Clarke, S., Savage, S.: The impact of generative AI coding assistants on developers who are visually impaired. In: Proceedings of the 2025 CHI Conference on Human Factors in Computing Systems, pp. 1–17. Association for Computing Machinery, New York (2025). https://doi.org/10.1145/3706598.3714008
16. WebAIM: Web Accessibility Evaluation Tool (WAVE) (2025). https://wave.webaim.org/
17. Aljedaani, W., Habib, A., Aljohani, A., Eler, M., Feng, Y.: Does ChatGPT generate accessible code? investigating accessibility challenges in LLM-generated source code. In: Proceedings of the 21st International Web for All Conference, pp. 165–176. Association for Computing Machinery, New York (2024). https://doi.org/10.1145/3677846.3677854
18. W3C: Web Content Accessibility Guidelines (WCAG) 2.1 (2025). https://www.w3.org/TR/WCAG21/
19. Vigo, M., Brajnik, G.: Automatic web accessibility metrics: where we are and where we can go. Interact. Comput. **23**(2), 137–155 (2011). https://doi.org/10.1016/j.intcom.2011.01.001
20. Bayramli, Z., et al.: Diffusion models through a global lens: are they culturally inclusive? arXiv:2502.08914 (2025)
21. Kay, J., Kasirzadeh, A., Mohamed, S.: Epistemic injustice in generative AI. In: Proceedings of the 2024 AAAI/ACM Conference on AI, Ethics, and Society, pp. 684–697. AAAI Press (2025)
22. Spivak, G.C.: Can the subaltern speak? In: Cain, P.H., Harrison, M. (eds.) Imperialism: Critical Concepts in Historical Studies, vol. III, pp. 171–219. Routledge, London (2023)

Rescuing History: Evaluating AI's Ability to Track Sign Language Across Decades of Archival Video

Jose Merino, Austin Baker, Christian Vogler, and Raja Kushalnagar(✉)

Gallaudet University, 800 Florida Ave NE, Washington, DC, USA
{joe.merino,austin.baker,christian.vogler,
raja.kushalnagar}@gallaudet.edu

Abstract. Sign language recognition (SLR) systems depend on reliable pose estimation, yet most evaluations rely on controlled, high-quality recordings that do not reflect real-world video variability. This study evaluates MediaPipe Holistic's landmark tracking accuracy and stability across heterogeneous American Sign Language (ASL) video conditions. We analyzed over 200 clips drawn from two sources: modern high-definition university recordings (2018–2025) and archival Deaf-produced broadcast footage (1985–1995). Using a curated subset of 85 keypoints spanning the face, upper-body pose, and both hands, we computed per-frame detection rates, frame-level stability, and modality-specific grades. MediaPipe Holistic achieved 96.7% average detection accuracy on modern footage but dropped to 54.7% on archival footage, with hand tracking showing the greatest degradation (45–54% archival versus 78–87% modern); face and pose landmarks remained robust across both datasets. These findings indicate that MediaPipe Holistic can serve as a lightweight preprocessing tool for identifying sign-active intervals, but researchers must account for video quality when using archival material in downstream SLR pipelines.

Keywords: Sign Language Recognition · American Sign Language · Pose Estimation · MediaPipe Holistic · Archival Video · Keypoint Detection · Accessibility. Introduction

1 Introduction

Sign language recognition (SLR) systems detect and interpret sign language from video input through pose estimation and action recognition and are a prerequisite for many accessibility applications for Deaf and hard-of-hearing users. Despite technical advances, SLR systems remain difficult to deploy on the kinds of heterogeneous video found outside controlled recording conditions. Sign languages such as American Sign Language (ASL) rely on the simultaneous articulation of hand shape, movement, facial expression, and body posture [1], and any recognition pipeline must contend with spatiotemporal dynamics, occlusion, inter-signer variability, and for archival material, compression artifacts, low resolution, and burned-in captions.

K. Miesenberger et al. (Eds.): ICCHP 2026, LNCS 16867, pp. 321–328, 2027.
https://doi.org/10.1007/978-3-032-31308-9_39

An underexplored question in SLR research is whether modern real-time pose estimators remain reliable preprocessing tools when applied to archival Deaf-produced footage. Such footage is a critical but fragile record of ASL use from decades for which few alternative video sources exist, and automated preprocessing is a prerequisite for any large-scale analysis or preservation pipeline. In this paper we evaluate MediaPipe Holistic [9]—a widely used real-time estimator that jointly produces pose, face, and hand landmarks—across a paired corpus of modern high-definition ASL recordings (2018–2025) collected at an institution of higher education with a substantial sign-language presence, and archival Deaf-produced broadcast footage (1985–1995). We deliberately frame our primary metric as a per-frame keypoint presence rate rather than tracking accuracy: without ground-truth landmark positions we can report only whether MediaPipe emitted a confident keypoint, not whether that keypoint was correctly placed. We return to this construct in the Methods and Limitations sections.

We frame our investigation around a research question:

- RQ: To what extent does MediaPipe Holistic produce stable keypoint detection across modern and archival ASL video content, and which landmark groups: face, pose, or hands, are most vulnerable to archival-era quality degradation?

Across a curated set of more than 200 video clips drawn from the two corpora, we find a large gap between conditions: MediaPipe Holistic emits confident keypoints on 96.7% of the 85 tracked landmarks per frame on modern recordings, but only 54.7% on archival footage. Hand landmarks degrade most sharply, while face and pose landmarks remain comparatively robust. We interpret these findings cautiously: the paired corpora differ on many dimensions beyond quality, so we present the results as a characterization rather than a causal attribution, and we outline in the Limitations section what further experiments would be required to attribute the gap to specific quality factors.

2 Related Work

Two lines of prior work motivate the present study. The first, surveyed by Cheok et al. [2], concerns tracking and feature-extraction for sign language recognition from skin-color segmentation and Kalman filtering through to skeletal tracking on elbow, shoulder, and wrist joints. The second asks not what is signed but when. Moryossef et al. [3] classify each frame as signing or non-signing using OpenPose keypoints fed to a unidirectional LSTM, achieving approximately 91% accuracy at real-time speeds on controlled recordings; Jui et al. [4] address the same segmentation question using Inflated 3D ConvNets to distinguish signing from gesticulation.

Several recent studies evaluate MediaPipe on sign-recognition tasks. Tayade and Halder [5], Bora et al. [6], and Sundar and Bagyammal [7] report about 99% accuracy for recognizing isolated signs when MediaPipe keypoints are combined with downstream machine learning, but each operates on controlled, high-quality video. Moryossef et al. [8] use optical-flow features to segment sign-active intervals on modern videos.

This work demonstrates that skeletal estimators such as MediaPipe can support both isolated-sign recognition and sign-activity segmentation on clean, modern footage. This paper analyzes how this estimator behaves on low-resolution, caption-obscured video that constitutes much of the archival ASL record. We report per-frame keypoint presence and frame-level stability for face, pose, and hand landmarks across both modern and archival ASL video.

3 Methods

We evaluate MediaPipe Holistic [9] on a paired corpus of modern and archival ASL video using a four-stage pipeline: clip segmentation, landmark extraction, metric calculation, and visualization. We describe each stage in turn and then make explicit the construct our primary metric measures.

Fig. 1. MediaPipe Holistic tracking comparison across video quality conditions. (Left) Archival broadcast footage (1985–1995). (Right) Modern high-resolution studio recording (2018–2025). Red dots indicate detected landmarks; white lines show pose skeleton connections

Clip Segmentation and Preprocessing.
We drew source material from two corpora. The modern corpus consists of ASL recordings produced between 2018 and 2025 at an institution of higher education with a substantial Deaf and signing presence; recordings were made in studio-style conditions (even lighting, plain background, camera-facing signer, 1080p or higher). The archival corpus consists of Deaf-produced broadcast material from 1985–1995; these recordings were distributed on tape and have been archived digitally. They have lower resolution, variable lighting, and in many cases burned-in open captions. Recordings in both corpora were segmented into discrete clips guided by manually annotated sign-active timestamps, and each clip was reviewed against a shared quality-control checklist: a single visible signer, no major occlusion of the hands or upper body, and the signer roughly facing the camera (Fig. 1). Clips that failed any criterion were excluded. The full set was more than 200 across both corpora.

Landmark Detection Pipeline.
Each vetted clip was processed using MediaPipe Holistic [9], which emits 543 landmarks per frame: 33 pose, 468 face, and 21 per hand. For tractable reporting we selected a curated subset of 85 keypoints closely tied to ASL articulators: 37 facial landmarks

covering the eyebrows, eyes, and mouth (the regions most implicated in non-manual grammatical markers); 6 upper-body pose landmarks at the shoulders, elbows, and wrists (the joints involved in sign movement in signing space); and all 42 hand landmarks (21 per hand), which carry hand shape, orientation, and location (Fig. 2). The face-mesh is down sampled from 468 to 37 because the dense mesh oversamples regions, such as the jawline and nose ridge, that are not grammatically significant in ASL; the pose set is down sampled from 33 to 6 because lower-body landmarks are not used in seated signing and are frequently clipped by the frame. The selection extends prior MediaPipe-based SLR work [5–7] but is not empirically optimized; we treat it as a fixed a priori choice. Each frame produced one row in a CSV output containing the frame index, timestamp, list of absent landmarks, detected-keypoint count, and x/y coordinates.

Fig. 2. Comparison of MediaPipe Holistic landmark detection strategies. (Left) All 543 landmarks including dense facial mesh (468 points), full body pose skeleton (33 points), and hand landmarks (42 points). (Right) Curated subset of 85 ASL-relevant keypoints: 37 facial landmarks focusing on expression-critical regions, 6 upper-body pose landmarks (shoulders, elbows, wrists), and all 42 hand landmarks. This approach reduces computational overhead while preserving sign-language-relevant features.

Metric Calculation.

Our primary metric is the per-frame keypoint presence rate: for each frame we record the proportion of the 85 tracked landmarks that MediaPipe Holistic emitted with visibility above its default confidence threshold, and we average this rate across the frames of a clip to obtain a mean presence rate. We deliberately use "presence" rather than "accuracy" because we do not have ground-truth landmark coordinates; the metric characterizes MediaPipe's willingness to commit to a confident keypoint, not the geometric correctness of the keypoint it commits to. A second, complementary metric captures stability: we compute the standard deviation of frame-level presence across the duration of each clip. A larger standard deviation indicates that MediaPipe's willingness to emit confident keypoints fluctuates rapidly from frame to frame, which is typically the result of landmarks flickering in and out. We adopt a threshold of 15 percentage points as a simple stability flag; this threshold is an ad hoc operational cutoff chosen for its interpretability on our data, not a value derived from an underlying distribution, and we note this choice explicitly in the Limitations.

We compute these metrics both in aggregate across all 85 keypoints and separately for each landmark groups: hands, face, and pose, so that differential sensitivity of body regions to video quality can be observed. For ease of reference, we group mean presence rates into four qualitative bands: high (80–100%), moderate (60–79%), low (40–59%), and poor (0–39%). These bands are descriptive, not evaluative, and their thresholds are chosen for readability; all quantitative comparisons in the Results are drawn on the underlying continuous percentages rather than on the band assignments.

4 Results

Across more than 200 trimmed clips, we observe a large and systematic gap in MediaPipe Holistic's keypoint presence between the modern and archival corpora, together with substantial differences across landmark groups. We report aggregate presence, per-landmark-group presence, and stability, and then note where the presentation is descriptive rather than inferential.

Overall Tracking Performance.
Aggregated across all 85 keypoints, the mean per-frame presence rate was 96.7% for modern high-definition recordings and 54.7% for archival broadcast footage, which is a gap of about 42 percentage points. Modern clips were predominantly in the high band (80–100%) with low frame-level standard deviation, indicating steady keypoint emission across the clip. Archival clips were more often in the low (40–59%) or poor (0–39%) bands and frequently exceeded the stability threshold of 15 percentage points, indicating that the estimator's confidence fluctuated across frames. Qualitatively, these fluctuations co-occurred with burned-in caption overlays, reduced lighting, motion blur, and partial occlusion.

Body Part Comparison.
The archival-vs-modern gap was highly uneven across landmark groups. Hand landmarks suffered the steepest drop: mean presence for the non-dominant hand fell from 78% in modern clips to 45% in archival clips, and for the dominant hand from 87% to 54%. Face landmarks were affected much less (above 91% in both corpora), and pose landmarks remained near ceiling (approximately 98% in both corpora). The robustness of the pose group likely reflects that our 6-point upper-body pose subset captures large, high-contrast joints that MediaPipe's pose model detects even in degraded video; by contrast, hand landmarks require resolving fine-scale finger articulation that is particularly susceptible to compression artifacts and low resolution.

Stability and Noise.
Stability followed the same pattern as mean presence. Modern clips showed low frame-level variance across all four landmark groups; archival clips repeatedly crossed the 15-point stability threshold, most often in the hand groups. The instability manifested as short-duration dropouts in hand landmarks during fingerspelling and fast co-articulated transitions, which are moments when the hand moves quickly and changes shape, and when the estimator's emitted confidence appears most likely to fall below threshold. Face and pose groups were stable in both corpora.

5 Discussion

Our findings address two concerns: the reliability of off-the-shelf real-time pose estimation as ASL preprocessing, and the practical consequences for researchers considering archival Deaf-produced video as training or evaluation data.

First, the modality-differential pattern: pose near ceiling, face high, hands low, is consistent with the geometric properties of each landmark group: large joints are easier to localize than fine finger articulation, and the gap widens where the linguistic signal is densest. Even on modern footage, this pattern recommends MediaPipe Holistic for coarse signer localization and sign-active-interval identification but discourages its unverified use for fine-grained hand analysis without additional post-processing or validation against ground-truth annotation.

Second, the presence gap between modern and archival footage is large enough that archival ASL video cannot be treated as a drop-in replacement for modern footage in training pipelines without accounting for the induced bias or removing burned-in captions through interpolation. The hand-landmark dropouts we observe on archival clips would systematically under-represent fingerspelling and fast hand articulation in any downstream model that consumes MediaPipe keypoints uncritically and would concentrate that bias in content that is linguistically informative.

These observations are descriptive. Our paired corpora differ on many dimensions: resolution, codec, lighting, framing, signer identity, and recording era. So, this reports what MediaPipe does across two real-world bodies of video rather than isolating which factor most drives the gap.

6 Limitations

Several limitations are important to state explicitly. Our mean per-frame presence rate numbers for modern recordings (96.7%) versus archival videos (54.7%) reflect the proportion of landmarks for which MediaPipe Holistic emitted keypoints above its internal visibility threshold, not the geometric accuracy of those keypoints against ground-truth positions. Without manually annotated ground-truth landmarks we cannot report accuracy in the stricter sense, and we therefore describe the metric throughout as per-frame keypoint presence.

The modern and archival corpora differ simultaneously in resolution, lighting, codec, framing, signer identity, and recording era. As a result, we characterize the performance gap but do not attribute it to any single factor. A controlled resolution, bitrate, and caption-overlay degradation applied to the modern corpus would be required to isolate the contribution of individual quality dimensions.

While the study draws on more than 200 clips in total, we do not report confidence intervals, per-signer variance decomposition, or formal significance tests on the reported numbers; point estimates should be read as descriptive rather than inferential. The 15-point standard-deviation cutoff used to flag clip-level instability is an operational readability choice rather than a value derived from an underlying distribution.

We evaluate MediaPipe Holistic only. Direct comparison against OpenPose (as used in Moryossef et al. [3]) or against more recent pose estimators on the same clips would strengthen external validity. Finally, the findings are specific to ASL and to two corpora; generalizability to other sign languages, and to other pose estimators remains an open empirical question.

7 Ethics Statement

This study uses video material from two sources: modern recordings produced at an institution of higher education with a substantial Deaf and signing presence, and archival Deaf-produced broadcast footage. The modern corpus was recorded for university communications. The archival corpus was produced for public broadcast by Deaf community members; our use of it for research is guided by a principle of respect for the communities whose labor produced this footage. No personal or demographic inferences are drawn about individual signers, and the visualizations in this paper show generic landmark overlays rather than identifying biometric analyses.

8 Conclusion and Future Work

We evaluated MediaPipe Holistic's per-frame keypoint presence on ASL video drawn from modern high-definition studio recordings (2018–2025) and archival Deaf-produced broadcast footage (1985–1995). On modern footage, the estimator emitted confident keypoints on 96.7% of the 85 tracked landmarks per frame, with low frame-to-frame variance across all four landmark groups. On archival footage, mean presence fell to 54.7%, with hand landmarks showing the steepest drop and pose landmarks remaining near ceiling. These results position MediaPipe Holistic as a viable coarse preprocessing tool for identifying sign-active intervals in modern video, and as an unreliable tool for fine-grained hand analysis on archival video without additional post-processing or ground-truth validation.

Four directions would strengthen and extend this work. First, a controlled resolution, bitrate, and caption-overlay ablation on the modern corpus would decompose the observed archival-vs-modern video gap into its contributing factors. Second, a parallel evaluation of OpenPose and of one or more recent pose estimators on the same clips would establish whether the observed degradation is MediaPipe-specific or generic to skeletal estimators. Third, manually annotating ground-truth landmark positions on a subset of clips would let keypoint presence be validated against keypoint correctness, converting the descriptive findings reported here into inferential ones. Fourth, operationalizing the keypoints into an end-to-end sign-active segmentation system, with corresponding metrics, such as latency, and throughput on test video, would address the downstream applicability question that motivated this work but that the present study does not answer.

Acknowledgments. In the US, the study was co-funded by grants from the National Science Foundation: 2425713, 2429900 and 2440601. The contents of this paper were in part supported by funding from the National Institute on Disability and Rehabilitation Research, U.S. Department of Education, grant number H133E090001 (RERC on Telecommunications Access) and a grant from the National Institute on Disability, Independent Living, and Rehabilitation Research (NIDILRR grant number 90REGE0013). NIDILRR is a Center within the Administration for Community Living (ACL), Department of Health and Human Services (HHS). This paper's contents do not necessarily represent the policy of NIDILRR, ACL, HHS, and you should not assume Federal Government endorsement.

References

1. Bragg, D., et al.: Sign language recognition, generation, and translation: an interdisciplinary perspective. In: Proceedings of the 21st International ACM SIGACCESS Conference on Computers and Accessibility (pp. 16–31). Association for Computing Machinery (2019). https://doi.org/10.1145/3308561.3353774
2. Cheok, M.J., Omar, Z., Jaward, M.H.: A review of hand gesture and sign language recognition techniques. Int. J. Mach. Learn. Cybern. **10**(1), 131–153 (2019). https://doi.org/10.1007/s13042-017-0705-5
3. Moryossef, A., Tsochantaridis, I., Aharoni, R., Ebling, S., Narayanan, S.: Real-time sign language detection using human pose estimation. In: Bartoli, A., Fusiello, A. (eds.), Computer Vision–ECCV 2020 Workshops (pp. 237–248). Springer (2020). https://doi.org/10.1007/978-3-030-66096-3_17
4. Jui, T.D., Bejarano, G., Rivas, P.: A machine learning-based segmentation approach for measuring similarity between sign languages. In: Proceedings of the LREC2022 10th Workshop on the Representation and Processing of Sign Languages: Multilingual Sign Language Resources (pp. 94–101). European Language Resources Association (2022)
5. Tayade, A., Halder, A.: Real-time vernacular sign language recognition using MediaPipe and machine learning. Int. J. Res. Publ. Rev. **2**(5), 9–17 (2021). https://doi.org/10.13140/RG.2.2.32364.03203
6. Bora, J., Dehingia, S., Boruah, A., Chetia, A.A., Gogoi, D.: Real-time assamese sign language recognition using MediaPipe and deep learning. Procedia Comput. Sci. **218**, 1384–1393 (2023). https://doi.org/10.1016/j.procs.2023.01.117
7. Sundar, B., Bagyammal, T.: American sign language recognition for alphabets using MediaPipe and LSTM. Procedia Comput. Sci. **215**, 642–651 (2022). https://doi.org/10.1016/j.procs.2022.12.066
8. Moryossef, A., Jiang, Z., Müller, M., Ebling, S., Goldberg, Y.: Linguistically motivated sign language segmentation. In: Findings of the Association for Computational Linguistics: EMNLP 2023 (pp. 12703–12724). Association for Computational Linguistics (2023). https://doi.org/10.18653/v1/2023.findings-emnlp.846
9. Lugaresi, C., et al.: MediaPipe: a framework for building perception pipelines (2019). arXiv preprint arXiv:1906.08172. https://doi.org/10.48550/arXiv.1906.08172

Special Education Teachers' Intention to Use Generative AI to Support Students with Special Needs: A Preliminary TPACK-Based Investigation

Ting-Fang Wu[1], Hui-Shan Lo[2](✉), and Hsu-Kai Chang[1]

[1] Graduate Institute of Rehabilitation Counseling and Gerontological Wellbeing, National Taiwan Normal University, 162, Sec. 1 Heping East Rd., Taipei, Taiwan
{tfwu,akai}@ntnu.edu.tw

[2] Department of Special Education, National Pingtung University, 4-18, Minsheng Rd., Pingtung City, Pingtung County, Taiwan
sunnylo519@mail.nptu.edu.tw

Abstract. This preliminary study examined special education teachers' intention to use generative artificial intelligence (GenAI) to support students with special needs through the lens of the Technological Pedagogical Content Knowledge (TPACK) framework. A total of 30 special education teachers participated in the study, and data were collected using an AI-TPACK questionnaire developed by the research team. Descriptive statistics, Pearson correlation, and stepwise regression analyses were conducted to explore the relationships among AI-related teaching knowledge, intention, and actual use. The findings revealed that teachers generally held positive attitudes toward GenAI and reported high levels of intention to adopt it in their instructional practice. However, their actual use of AI remained only moderate, indicating a noticeable gap between intention and implementation. Further analyses showed that integrated AI teaching knowledge, particularly AI-TPACK, was the strongest predictor of teachers' intention to use GenAI. In contrast, AI technological knowledge (AI-TK) emerged as the most significant predictor of actual use. These results suggest that while teachers' willingness to adopt AI is closely associated with their ability to integrate AI meaningfully into pedagogical and content-specific contexts, the translation of intention into practice depends more heavily on foundational technological competence. The study highlights the importance of strengthening both pedagogical integration knowledge and hands-on technical skills in teacher professional development. Overall, the findings provide preliminary empirical evidence for understanding AI adoption among special education teachers and offer practical implications for future AI-enhanced teacher training programs in special education.

Keyword: Generative Artificial intelligence · Special Education Teachers · Technological Pedagogical Content Knowledge Intention

K. Miesenberger et al. (Eds.): ICCHP 2026, LNCS 16867, pp. 329–336, 2027.
https://doi.org/10.1007/978-3-032-31308-9_40

1 Introduction

With the rapid advancement of generative artificial intelligence (GenAI), increasing scholarly attention has been directed toward its potential applications in special education. Research indicates that AI not only supports individualized instruction, skill development, and adaptive assessment, but has also moved beyond the role of traditional assistive technology to become a key resource shaping instructional decision-making and learning processes [1, 2]. In particular, GenAI has been recognized as a powerful tool for supporting students with disabilities by reducing cognitive load, enhancing expressive abilities, and expanding opportunities for learning participation [1–3]. Nevertheless, scholars emphasize that alongside the adoption of such technologies, careful consideration must be given to ethical concerns, including data privacy, algorithmic bias, and developmental appropriateness-issues that are especially critical in special education contexts [3].

These developments underscore the growing importance of teachers' professional competence in integrating GenAI into instructional practice. For special education teachers, effective AI integration requires more than basic operational skills; it involves the ability to make informed pedagogical judgments regarding when, how, and for whom AI should be used to support learning [2]. Without adequate theoretical grounding and professional preparation, the use of GenAI may risk being superficial or misaligned with instructional goals, potentially limiting its educational value for students with special needs.

Accordingly, this study aims to preliminarily examine special education teachers' intention to use GenAI to support students with special needs through the lens of the Technological Pedagogical Content Knowledge (TPACK) framework. By exploring teachers' AI-related teaching knowledge and their intention and behavior related to AI integration, this study seeks to contribute empirical evidence to the emerging literature on GenAI in special education and to inform teacher preparation and professional development for AI-enhanced instructional practices.

2 Literature Review

2.1 Artificial Intelligence in Special Education

Recent literature has documented a wide range of applications of AI in special education, spanning assessment, diagnosis, instructional intervention, and assistive technology. A comprehensive review synthesizes over two decades of research and highlights how AI-based systems have been employed to support learners with special educational needs through intelligent diagnostic tools, adaptive tutoring systems, and technology-enhanced intervention programs [4]. The review further emphasizes the growing role of AI as an assistive technology, noting that recent advances, and particularly large language models, have expanded the capacity of AI to provide personalized learning support, communication assistance, and adaptive feedback for students with disabilities [3]. Despite these promising developments, the review also points out persistent challenges, including limited availability of intervention tools, the absence of standardized frameworks for AI-based practices, and contextual constraints related to resources and professional training. These findings suggest that while AI technologies in special education have advanced rapidly, their effective implementation remains closely tied to educators' professional competence and their ability to integrate AI meaningfully into instructional practice.

2.2 Technological Pedagogical Content Knowledge (TPACK) of Special Education Teacher

The TPACK framework [4] conceptualizes effective technology integration as the dynamic interaction of technological, pedagogical, and content knowledge, emphasizing instructional meaning rather than tool operation alone. Research in special education contexts has shown that teachers often demonstrate strong pedagogical and content knowledge but comparatively weaker competence in integrating emerging technologies into instructional practice, particularly when translating technological affordances into pedagogically meaningful applications [5, 6]. The rapid emergence of GenAI has further intensified these challenges and prompted renewed examination of the TPACK framework, as AI increasingly functions as a core instructional resource that permeates pedagogical and content decision-making rather than merely a technological add-on. Prior studies suggest that developing integrated AI-TPACK knowledge is essential for enabling special education teachers to make informed pedagogical judgments about AI use, ensuring that AI serves as a supportive instructional resource rather than a substitute for students' active learning and interpersonal interaction [5, 6].

2.3 The Teachers' Intention in AI

Teachers' behavioral intention to use AI is widely regarded as a key predictor of actual AI adoption in educational contexts. Recent studies adopting a multi-level perspective suggest that teachers' intention to use AI is primarily shaped by teacher-level factors, including perceived usefulness, ease of use, digital skills, and pedagogical readiness, while school-level conditions tend to influence intention indirectly through these individual factors [7]. In special education settings, teachers' intention formation involves not only attitudes toward AI but also professional judgment regarding its pedagogical value, ethical implications, and developmental appropriateness. Accordingly, examining teachers' intention to use AI requires attention to their integrated professional knowledge and capacity to meaningfully incorporate AI into instructional practice.

3 Method

3.1 Participants

A total of 30 special education teachers participated in this study, including two males and 28 females. Participants ranged in age from 31 to 51 years and had between 1 and 16 years of teaching experience. Of the total sample, 20 participants were elementary school special education teachers, while the remaining 10 were junior high school special education teachers.

3.2 AI-TPACK Questionnaire

To obtain a preliminary understanding of preschool teachers' knowledge related to GenAI and their perceptions of applying AI in instructional contexts, the research team developed the AI-Integrated Teaching Knowledge Questionnaire for Educators based on the TPACK framework. The questionnaire items were adapted and revised in accordance with the variables of the present study and were subsequently reviewed by three experts in relevant fields to ensure content validity.

The finalized instrument consisted of nine constructs: AI Technological Knowledge (AI-TK), AI Technological Pedagogical Knowledge (AI-TPK), AI Techno-logical Content Knowledge (AI-TCK), AI Technological Pedagogical Content Knowledge (AI-TPACK), AI Pedagogical Knowledge (AI-PK), AI Content Knowledge (AI-CK), AI Pedagogical Content Knowledge (AI-PCK), Intention, and Behavior. Each construct consisted of five items, resulting in a total of 45 items. All items were measured using a 5-point Likert scale, with higher scores indicating stronger levels of intention and engagement in using AI for instructional purposes.

Partial Least Squares (PLS) was used to perform confirmatory factor analysis to evaluate the reliability and validity of the questionnaire. The results indicated that the Cronbach's α coefficients for the nine constructs ranged from .79 to .94, demonstrating satisfactory internal consistency. In addition, factor loadings for all items across the constructs ranged from .73 to .96, supporting adequate convergent validity. Taken together, these findings confirm that the questionnaire possesses acceptable reliability and validity for measuring special education teachers' AI-integrated teaching knowledge as well as their intention and behavior related to the use of AI in educational contexts.

3.3 Procedure

At the beginning of the study, participating special education teachers were informed of the study purpose, procedures, estimated completion time, and voluntary nature of participation. They were assured that all responses would remain anonymous and be used solely for research purposes, and informed consent was obtained prior to data collection.

After consent, participants completed an online self-administered questionnaire assessing their AI-integrated teaching knowledge and intention to use GenAI in special education. The questionnaire could be completed at a convenient time and location without a time limit. Data collection was concluded upon questionnaire submission.

3.4 Data Analysis

Data were analyzed using IBM SPSS Statistics 27.0. Descriptive statistics were computed for AI-TPACK questionnaire. Pearson correlation analyses were conducted to investigate the associations among variables, and regression analyses were performed to examine the extent to which acceptance-related constructs were associated with behavioral intentions toward system use.

4 Results

4.1 The AI-TPACK Scores of Special Education Teachers

Descriptive statistics were computed to examine participants' levels of AI-related teaching knowledge and behavioral outcomes. Among the core knowledge components, AI-CK demonstrated the highest mean score (3.97 ± 0.71), indicating that participants perceived themselves as being relatively confident in understanding how AI can be applied within subject-matter contexts. This was followed by AI-TCK (3.83 ± 0.54) and AI-TPK (3.72 ± 0.53), suggesting a moderate level of competence in integrating AI technologies with content and pedagogical strategies.

In contrast, AI-PK showed the lowest mean score (3.45 ± 0.71), reflecting comparatively lower confidence in pedagogical applications of AI. AI-TK (3.63 ± 0.79) and AI-PCK (3.58 ± 0.74) also fell within a moderate range, indicating that participants' AI-related teaching knowledge was generally above the scale midpoint but unevenly distributed across dimensions.

Regarding behavioral outcomes, participants reported a relatively high level of intention (4.15 ± 0.78), suggesting strong willingness to adopt AI in instructional practice. However, the mean score for actual use was notably lower (3.48 ± 0.98), indicating a gap between intention and real-world implementation of AI-related practices.

Overall, the descriptive results suggest that while participants demonstrated positive attitudes and intentions toward AI integration, their practical enactment of AI-supported teaching remained comparatively limited.

4.2 The Related Factor of Intention and Actual Use

To examine the factors associated with special education teachers' intention to use GenAI and their actual use of AI, Pearson correlation analyses and step-wise regression analyses were conducted (Table 1). The correlation results revealed that the AI-related knowledge constructs were generally positively associated with one another, with particularly strong relationships observed among the integrated knowledge components. AI-TPACK showed significant positive correlations with intention and actual use. Similarly, AI-PCK was positively correlated with intention and actual use. In contrast, correlations between intention and more basic AI knowledge components were relatively weaker. Actual use of AI demonstrated a strong positive association with intention to use AI, indicating a close relationship between teachers' willingness to use AI and their reported usage behavior.

To further identify the most influential predictors of intention and actual use, stepwise regression analyses were conducted. For intention to use AI, the analysis indicated that AI-TPACK was the only significant predictor. The resulting model explained 27% of the variance in intention, with AI-TPACK showing a significant positive effect. This result suggests that teachers' integrated AI teaching knowledge played a key role in shaping their intention to use GenAI (Table 2).

For actual use of AI, the stepwise regression analysis identified AI-TK as the sole significant predictor. This model accounted for 42% of the variance in actual use. AI-TK exerted a strong positive effect on actual use, indicating that teachers' foundational technological knowledge of AI was a critical factor influencing their reported use of AI in instructional practice.

Overall, the combined results from correlation and regression analyses indicate a differentiated pattern in which integrated AI-TPACK knowledge is more closely associated with teachers' intention to use AI, whereas basic AI technological knowledge plays a more prominent role in predicting teachers' actual use of AI (Table 3).

Table 1. Correlations Among TPACK, Intention and actual use

	AI-TK	AI-CK	AI-PK	AI-TPK	AI-TCK	AI-PCK	AI-TPACK	Intention
AI-TK	1							
AI-CK	0.34	1						
AI-PK	0.47	0.66**	1					
AI-TPK	0.36	0.74**	0.56*	1				
AI-TCK	0.51*	0.81**	0.73**	0.87**	1			
AI-PCK	0.69**	0.66**	0.74**	0.54*	0.78**	1		
AI-TPACK	0.52*	0.72**	0.71**	0.85**	0.84**	0.74**	1	
Intention	0.43	0.35	0.14	0.43	0.36	0.45	0.57*	1
Actual Use	0.68**	0.33	0.41	0.38	0.44	0.68**	0.64**	0.83**

* $p < .05$, ** $p < .01$

Table 2. Stepwise Regression Analysis Predicting Intention

	B	R^2	Adj R^2	R^2 Chang	*P*
(constant)	1.76	0.32	0.27		
AI-TPACK	0.68			0.32	0.022

Table 3. Stepwise Regression Analysis Predicting Actual Use

	B	R^2	Adj R^2	R^2 Chang	*P*
(constant)	0.40	0.46	0.42		
AI-TK	0.85			0.46	0.004

5 Conclusion and Discussion

This preliminary study examined special education teachers' intention to use GenAI and their actual use of AI through a TPACK-based framework. The findings indicate that while teachers reported strong intentions to adopt GenAI, their actual use of AI in instructional practice remained moderate, revealing a noticeable gap between intention and implementation.

The results demonstrate a differentiated pattern in the factors associated with intention and actual use. Integrated AI-related teaching knowledge, particularly AI-TPACK, was most strongly associated with teachers' intention to use GenAI, suggesting that intention formation is closely linked to teachers' understanding of how AI can be meaningfully integrated into pedagogical and content-specific contexts. In contrast, actual use of AI was more strongly predicted by AI technological knowledge, indicating that foundational technical competence plays a critical role in enabling teachers to translate intention into practice.

Although AI-TPACK emerged as a significant predictor of intention, the proportion of explained variance in intention remained modest. This finding suggests that teachers' intention to use GenAI may be shaped not only by knowledge-related factors, but also by additional individual and contextual influences. Prior research suggested that teachers' intention to use AI is shaped by an interplay of individual, organizational, and social factors rather than by knowledge or attitudes alone. Specifically, teacher-level factors such as perceived usefulness, perceived ease of use, digital competence, and pedagogical readiness play a direct role in intention formation, while organizational conditions, including technological infrastructure, institutional support, and professional development opportunities, tend to exert indirect influences by shaping teachers' perceptions and instructional practices [7]. In special education contexts, intention formation may be further complicated by teachers' heightened professional sensitivity to ethical and developmental considerations, such as data privacy, algorithmic bias, and the appropriateness of AI-supported instruction for students with special needs. As a result, even teachers who possess adequate AI-integrated teaching knowledge may adopt a more cautious stance toward AI use in instructional practice [7].

These findings extend TPACK-based research by demonstrating that different dimensions of AI-related teaching knowledge play distinct roles at different stages of AI adoption among special education teachers. From a practical perspective, the results suggest that professional development initiatives should address both pedagogical integration and hands-on technological skills, while also attending to teachers' concerns and contextual constraints, in order to support more effective and sustained use of GenAI in special education settings.

6 Limitation and Future Research

Despite its contributions, this study has several limitations that should be acknowledged. The findings were based on self-reported questionnaire data, which may be influenced by social desirability and may not fully capture teachers' actual instructional practices. Future studies may benefit from incorporating objective measures, such as classroom observations, system usage records, or performance-based assessments, to provide a more comprehensive representation of teachers' engagement with GenAI.

The sample size in the present study was relatively limited, and participants were drawn from a specific educational context, which may constrain the generalizability of the results. Expanding the sample to include special education teachers from diverse regions, school levels, and institutional settings would help strengthen external validity and enhance the robustness of future findings.

In addition, the cross-sectional nature of this study restricts the ability to examine changes in teachers' AI-related knowledge, intention, and actual use over time. Longitudinal or mixed-methods approaches could offer deeper insights into how teachers' intentions develop and are translated into sustained instructional practices. Further research may also consider contextual and organizational factors, such as institutional support, professional development opportunities, and policy frameworks, that could shape the adoption and implementation of GenAI in special education settings.

A further limitation is that the present study focused exclusively on teachers' perspectives and did not incorporate the voices or learning experiences of students with disabilities, who are the ultimate end users of AI-supported instructional practices. In special education, the effectiveness and appropriateness of generative AI tools may vary substantially depending on students' disability characteristics, communication needs, and levels of support required. Future studies should therefore adopt a more user-centred approach by examining students' experiences, learning outcomes, and interaction patterns with specific AI tools used in inclusive and special education settings.

Acknowledgments. The authors would like to thank the National Science and Technology Council the Republic of China for financially supporting this research under Grant No. NSTC 114-2410-H-153-028.

Disclosure of Interest. The authors declare that they have no competing interests.

References

1. Hopcan, S., Polat, E., Ozturk, M.E., Ozturk, L.: Artificial intelligence in special education: a systematic review. Interact. Learn. Environ. **31**(10), 7335–7353 (2023)
2. Marino, M.T., Vasquez, E., Dieker, L., Basham, J., Blackorby, J.: The future of artificial intelligence in special education technology. J. Spec. Educ. Technol. **38**(3), 404–416 (2023)
3. Aliu, T.V.: Artificial intelligence in special education: a literature review. Syst. Anal. **2**(2), 188–199 (2024)
4. Mishra, P., Koehler, M.J.: Technological pedagogical content knowledge: a framework for integrating technology in teacher knowledge. Teach. Coll. Rec. **108**(6), 1017–1054 (2006)
5. Huang, K.Y., Chen, Y.H., Jang, S.J.: TPACK in special education schools for SVI: a comparative study between Taiwanese and Chinese in-service teachers. Int. J. Disabil. Dev. Educ. **69**(2), 435–450 (2022)
6. Goldman, S.R., Carreon, A., Smith, S.J.: Exploring the integration of artificial intelligence into special education teacher preparation through the TPACK framework. J. Spec. Educ. Prep. **4**(2), 52–64 (2024)
7. Wu, D., Zhang, X., Wang, K., Wu, L., Yang, W.: A multi-level factors model affecting teachers' behavioral intention in AI-enabled education ecosystem. Educ. Tech. Res. Dev. **73**(1), 135–167 (2025)

AI Research and Disabled, Neurodivergent, Deaf Researchers and Other Professionals

Marion Hersh[1(✉)], Nima Ali[2], and Mata Ayoub[3]

[1] Biomedical Engineering, University of Glasgow, Glasgow, Scotland
marion.hersh@glasgow.ac.uk
[2] Heriot Watt University, Edinburgh, Scotland
[3] Kingston University, Kingston, England

Abstract. The paper presents the preliminary results of what is probably the first study of the experiences of disabled, eurodivergent and Deaf researchers in AI research. It uses a mixed methods survey to investigate their motivation, the types of research they do and any challenges, barriers and enablers. The results show that they do indeed participate in AI research across a wide range of research topics and in different roles including team leader or principal investigator. However, they are motivated more by the environmental, societal and other risks associated with AI than its potential benefits. While some of them had experienced support and respect from colleagues, barriers were more common and few had received all the reasonable adjustments they needed. They also highlighted the importance of involving disabled, neurodivergent and Deaf people as researchers and engaging with their communities and the difficulties of doing this when lack of inclusion and discrimination were seen as 'tick-box ... done'.

1 Introduction

Artificial intelligence (AI), including generative chat tools such as ChatGPT and Dalle, is increasingly being used in a wide range of different applications and contexts. Its estimated market size was 293.8 billion euros in 2024 with a growth rate of 13.5% [1]. It has potential applications in technologies to support disabled people and accessibility [2, 3], amongst other areas. However, serious concerns have been expressed about human rights, ethical and privacy issues, bias and discrimination [4]. AI algorithm bias is considered to be common and can lead to discriminatory predictions for women and members of minority groups [4]. While this bias reflects existing bias in society, AI enables it to be programmed in and the results of AI decision making can be difficult to challenge [5]. AI use is also affected by institutional discrimination and power dynamics or interactions between individuals, groups, organisations and nations which are affected by differences in power, for instance due to gender, race and disability. Power imbalances can contribute to ethical violations and the devaluation of the less powerful [6]. Concerns have been expressed about anti-democratic features of AI, including 'prioritise efficiency over accountability; and they enable absolute control coupled with unaccountable power' [7].

K. Miesenberger et al. (Eds.): ICCHP 2026, LNCS 16867, pp. 337–344, 2027.
https://doi.org/10.1007/978-3-032-31308-9_41

There has been some research on equity, diversity and inclusion (EDI) in AI and the use of AI for EDI. However, the focus has been gender with minimal research on disability. For instance, in a review of 48 studies only four mentioned disability and one neurodivergence [8]. A recent review of disabled researchers in AI [9] failed to identify any literature on the topic, though it did find at least two papers with some disabled authors [10, 11]. However, there is considerable literature on the use of AI to support disabled, neurodivergent and Deaf people who may still be seen purely as AI users, but not researchers and developers. There is clearly a gap in the literature with regard to disabled researchers in AI. This gap has motivated the current study which aims to answer the following two-part research question: (1) What types of research are disabled, neurodivergent and Deaf researchers and other professionals in AI doing (2) What are their experiences, including of barriers and enablers?

2 Methodology

The work is situated within disability studies and inclusive research methodologies, particularly emancipatory and participatory approaches [12, 13] in which lived experiences are foregrounded as a form of expertise that shapes research design, interpretation and ethical orientation. This makes the involvement of disabled, neurodivergent and Deaf researchers integral to the study's methodological and conceptual positioning. Two of the authors are disabled and neurodivergent, but none of them are Deaf. They have some experience of researching the potential impacts of AI and supervising students using AI in technologies to support disabled people.

The research also engages with ongoing debates in AI ethics and fairness in relation to bias, exclusion, and power. A growing body of work has demonstrated that AI systems can reproduce and amplify existing social inequalities, including those related to disability, through the interaction of biased data, design assumptions, and institutional structures [14, 15]. While diversity and inclusion are becoming more visible in AI research, disability remains comparatively underrepresented in terms of both research focus and the participation of disabled researchers [8, 9]. Positioning this study within these intersecting fields enables a more critical understanding of how structural inequalities are reproduced in AI research and practice. It also highlights the importance of participatory and inclusive approaches in shaping more equitable AI systems, particularly through the direct involvement of disabled, neurodivergent and Deaf researchers and engagement with their communities.

The mixed methods study used a single questionnaire with a combination of open and closed questions to obtain both qualitative and quantitative data from disabled, neurodivergent and Deaf people. The Ethics Committee of the College of Science and Engineering at the University of Glasgow provided ethical approval. The questionnaire was made available on the JISC online surveys website, as this is reasonably accessible, including to screen reader users, and meets privacy and data protection requirements. The first page of the questionnaire contained the information sheet with a compulsory four-part consent question which had to be agreed before gaining access to the survey. Signatures were not required to preserve anonymity. The questionnaire has four parts, covering personal information (for statistical purposes); research background; experiences of artificial intelligence (AI) research; and disclosure of disability, neurodivergence or Deafness and inclusion. Responses were submitted anonymously and the raw data was only visible to the three researchers, and quotations were anonymised if necessary. Only the consent question and two questions on disability and neurodivergence were compulsory. The questionnaire was piloted with two people, including a screen reader user, who found it very accessible. No changes were suggested. The questionnaire was publicised and participants recruited through information put on a number of JISC emails, professional organisations and institutions sending details to their members, organisations of disabled, neurodivergent and Deaf people, social media and our contacts. Due to space limitations the analysis was based only on triangulation, to investigate the relationship between the quantitative and qualitative data and provide deeper insights.

3 Results

32 responses were received, with 26 usable and the other participants not disabled, neurodivergent or Deaf. 54% (7) were disabled and neurodivergent, 15% (2) disabled and 31% (4) neurodivergent, with three of them undiagnosed. 60% (15/25) were female, 24% (6) male and 16% (4) non-binary. 4% (1) were aged 16–24, 35% (9) each aged 25–34 and 35–44 and 27% (7) aged 45–64. The overwhelming majority, 77% (20) were from the UK, with one each from Belgium, Brazil, Netherlandsand Polandand two (8%) from the USA. 78% (18/23) were white, 9% (2) Asian and 13% (3) mixed race. As might be expected with a questionnaire focusing on research, the participants were all highly educated, with 77% (20/23) having a PhD or equivalent (20/23, 77%) and the others a bachelor's or master's degree. The overwhelming majority (85%, 22/24) of participants were university based. 38% (9/24) had academic teaching and research roles e.g. lecturer or professor and 42% (10) had research roles e.g. senior researcher or PhD researcher. 52% (13/25) had 11–20 years research experience and 40% (3) 3–10 years. Nearly half (11/23) spent over half their time on research and 44% (10) 10–40% of their time.

Nearly 60% (15/25) did AI search, just over a quarter (7) did not and 12% (3) were unsure. Their research topics included issues related to sign language and education. Sign language research included using machine learning and computer vision to analyse phonetic patterns in American Sign Language, AI adoption by sign language interpreters and the ethics of sign language AI. AI in education included AI and assessment and teaching practice and higher education and generative AI. Other topics included more energy and cost efficient machine learning systems, agent based modelling and AI and inclusion, particularly accessible solutions for Deaf, disabled and neurodivergent people. 43% (9/23) had experience of being team lead or principal investigator (PI) on an AI project. Just over a half (11/20) had worked in AI research for up to two years, a quarter (5) for 3–5 years and 15% (3) for 6–10 years. They had got involved in various ways, including through their job, internship, PhD project, postdoc or grant proposal, being labelled an 'expert' after writing a blog on AI and then starting research to investigate the subject. Others had written modules about AI, 'constantly … asked to use it' or been attracted by the potential of accessibility solutions, for instance for deaf people.

Similar numbers of participants had experienced barriers (62%,13/21) and enablers (60%, 12/20). However, more participants commented on barriers which included institutional, ethical, and accessibility issues, as well as colleagues' attitudes. Institutional barriers included the department being anti-AI, their work being poorly understood due to working in another department than their speciality, and doing research in their own time rather than as part of paid employment. Ethics barriers included departments or universities promoting AI while ignoring ethical issues and providing insufficient resources, ignoring disability and accessibility barriers and their own values. Accessibility barriers included 'so much of the field being led by hearing, non-signing researchers, audism, ableism, male dominant space', getting overwhelmed, the high cost of assistive technology, 'the lack of accessible resources and limited inclusion in academic and professional environments'. For instance, 'my CS AI class banned us from talking about the ethics of AI' and 'They refused to clarify what they wanted me to do … an endless cycle of me guessing and them telling me off for focusing on the wrong things. They also pushed me to start earlier, so I did my onboarding during my finals week.' Attitudinal barriers included being made to feel unwelcome. For instance, 'the team I am writing the modules for would probably rather not have me participate … I keep muttering about things that are missing from the programme. The dean … is an AI specialist but hasn't engaged with me at all … despite the agreed process saying he would. … I don't think he likes me at all.'

Enablers included supportive colleagues, funding, accessibility, PhD supervision of interesting projects, interesting conferences and the potential to achieve positive change. Supportive colleagues included female mentors with technical skills, a very supportive internship, supervisor and colleagues and 'encouragement … from more senior managers who have identified the good work being done by individuals and celebrated this'. For instance, 'My supervisor was very supportive, and I really felt he listened to me. … I accidentally left it [walking stick] at a meeting, and a teammate returned it to me with a joke. They encourage me to take more holidays, are supportive of me taking time off because my brain isn't functioning, and drag me along to 3 h "team meetings" where we drink tea and don't talk about work'. Accessibility included 'deaf spaces to talk about technology' and advances in assistive technology. The potential to achieve positive change included 'support[ing] all my disabled and neurodivergent researchers to make "sensible" use of AI'; 'commitment to fostering social inclusion, expanding access to knowledge' and a positive impact on disabled people and collaborative projects.

Access to reasonable adjustments was not very satisfactory with only slightly less than a quarter (6) receiving adequate adjustments, 35% (9) none and 11 (42%) some, but insufficient. Reasonable adjustments included an office move to 'a more accessible space', equipment e.g. a laptop with a screen reader, and Dragon direct, training e.g. on Microsoft 365 and autism awareness training for colleagues, and furniture e.g. a standing desk and a footstool, sign language interpreters, Access to Work Funded personal assistance, and 'recovery time' after fieldwork. Several participants mentioned their need for flexible working and working from home, but experiences were varied. For instance 'my department has sometimes been able to support my ask for certain times when I teach; however, they have refused to accommodate when I am unwell and may need to teach virtually', whereas another participant was 'allowed to work from home 100% of my working time … allowed to compress my contracted hours into 4 days per week'.

Concern about the potential negative impacts of AI was more common than being motivated by its potential positive impacts. Nearly all participants were either very concerned (17, 74%) or concerned (5, 22%), whereas only 13% (3/23) were highly motivated by AI's potential and 22% (5) motivated, with 39% (9) not motivated. The comments also reflected this. For instance, 'I'm more motivated by the idea of the harm that AI can do if it isn't looked at in a critical way and ... I can at least draft modules that include ethics, bias and sustainability' and 'I code because I want positive change, but I don't think AI is necessarily the vehicle for a lot of that.' Specific concerns included 'negative environmental and other societal impacts', including job losses, deskilling, increasing inequalities and discrimination, for instance 'AI ... is trained on biased data and then perpetuates that bias with no hope for actual change'. Negative impacts on disabled people included 'it is yet another "innovation" that does not consider disabled people's perspectives' and 'lack of choice for disabled users'. Negative environmental impacts included 'data management centres are hurting our ability to become carbon neutral'. Job loss concerns included 'AI is taking jobs away from young people throughout the UK ... and virtually no plans will be in place to cope with the resulting mass unemployment.' And 'I have lost 95% of my work to AI, and am very concerned about its continued impact on the job market.' Concerns were also expressed about 'unethical use and development', poor quality technologies and students using AI tools rather than learning critical and analytical skills. Other than 'free people from mundane data driven tasks ... to do things only humans can do', most of the positive comments related to accessibility and inclusion. They included using AI to 'speed up ... writing', particularly for disabled people; increasing access, autonomy, choice and opportunities for deaf people', 'visibility of sign language'; and 'open up scholarship and knowledge ... otherwise ... gatekept by ableist institutions'.

Average overall satisfaction with AI research was moderate (3.2/5), highest for treatment by colleagues (3.8), followed by ability to choose projects (3.5) and lowest for support in applying for research grants (3) and treatment by managers (3.3). However response rates were low. Factors leading to satisfaction included liking labs, interesting projects, research with 'humans ... driving the questions and the answers are meant to benefit humans', and 'the potential of artificial intelligence to promote inclusion and accessibility'. Factors leading to dissatisfaction included poor quality work, high environmental impacts, lack of support, ethics and clarity. Poor quality work with high energy impacts included 'many hours of carbon heavy GPU time' to get results for a paper 'that mean very little' and low quality applications research with limited discussion of ethics. Lack of support included departmental colleagues ... occasionally outright abusive about my choice of research area'; not knowing what they are allowed to research, opposition to research that could produce negative results on AI and lack of support for research in their role. Other causes of dissatisfaction were concerns about AI 'replacing humans ... without any support for what ... they do instead'.

Participants were also negative about both the value in AI research given to their lived experience as disabled, neurodivergent and Deaf people and consideration of the needs of these groups. A third (7/21) considered this experience was not valued, a third were unsure and only 19% (4) that it was generally valued and 14% (3) sometimes valued. 68% (15/22) considered that sufficient attention was not given to the needs of these groups, 23% (5) were unsure and only 18% (2) that it generally was. Comments indicated the lack of attention to lived experiences and needs. For instance, 'never have I heard anyone in AI talk about disabled, neurodivergent or Deaf people', and 'my thesis topic wasn't approved because I wanted to interview disabled people ... and I was told that "interviews aren't Computer Science". My thesis could either be about disabled people without talking to them, or I wouldn't be able to do it at all.' There was a suggestion that AI research had 'the potential to be of great benefit to disabled/Deaf/neurodivergent individuals' but to achieve this 'the AI research community must include more disabled, Deaf, neurodivergent people in their work ... both through direct involvement of researchers with these conditions and engagement with communities of such individuals outside of academic/corporate circles' and 'until these fields see working with marginalised groups as a necessity, they cannot hope to design ethical tools.' However, there were concerns that discussion of lack of inclusion, bias and discrimination in AI was often not taken seriously. For instance, 'it's almost like a tick-box of "see we have acknowledged it, done", rather than actually meaningfully addressing it in any tangible way'. Positive comments included requests to involve disabled people, for instance to determine game accessibility and awareness of Deafness facilitating communication and collaboration on developing educational tools in Brazilian sign language. One participant considered that 'it is largely neurodivergent people leading the research in AI', whereas another considered that 'what exists is not intended for deaf people'. Lack of understanding was also noted, for instance generic university statements prohibiting AI use not recognising that some students and colleagues require 'AI-driven tools to help their reading'. Participants also noted that large language models respond differently based on the language used and it is 'well established that neurodivergent people use language differently'.

4 Discussion and Conclusions

The results show that disabled, neurodivergent and Deaf researchers are working in AI research, including as team leaders and principal investigators (PIs) and on a wide range of different research topics. They have frequently been motivated by concerns about the environmental and social impacts of AI rather than its potential benefits and considered that AI is not disability friendly. While some of them have received support from colleagues and some reasonable adjustments, barriers, including being made to feel personally unwelcome, are more common and reasonable adjustments generally insufficient to meet their needs. Participants highlighted both the importance of involving disabled, neurodivergent and Deaf researchers and talking to their communities and the difficulties in doing this with lack of 'inclusion or bias or discrimination in AI' seen as a 'tick box'.

A key strength of the work is giving direct expression to the voices of disabled, neurodivergent and Deaf researchers and other professionals in AI research, where they are significantly underrepresented. A further strength is the diversity of perspectives in terms of participants' varied roles, research topics, experiences of and attitudes to AI research. This reflects both the broader ecosystem in which AI is developed, applied, and critically examined and enables a more nuanced understanding of the barriers, enablers, and experiences associated with AI research. Another contribution is the combination of qualitative insights and descriptive quantitative patterns, with particular emphasis on the depth and significance of participants' experiences.

The main limitation is the relatively low number of participants, though there are indications of saturation in the qualitative data. However, as an exploratory study, the approach aligns with established practices of using smaller samples to identify patterns, generate insight, and inform future, larger-scale studies [16, 17]. The sample is currently weighted towards the UK and has relatively low numbers of ethnic minority and male participants. Further data collection could be used to increase participant diversity and extend geographical reach, including by translating the questionnaire into other languages. Thus, the study provides an initial, evidence-informed account of the experiences of disabled, neurodivergent and Deaf researchers and professionals in AI, while laying the groundwork for future research to build on and extend its findings.

The study findings highlight both the presence of disabled, neurodivergent and Deaf researchers within AI and the structural conditions that continue to shape their involvement. Participants' accounts of barriers, insufficient adjustments, and experiences of exclusion point to ongoing challenges in creating genuinely inclusive research environments. These findings resonate with wider critiques of institutional approaches to EDI, where inclusion is often treated as procedural or symbolic rather than embedded in practice [18]. Participants emphasised the importance of involving disabled, neurodivergent and Deaf people as technology researchers and contributors to its design and development not just as beneficiaries. This aligns with disability justice perspectives and participatory approaches, which argue that ethical and effective research must be grounded in the knowledge of those most affected [19, 20].

However, the findings raise important questions about how inclusion is currently understood and enacted within AI research. Its perception as a 'tick-box' exercise, alongside limited engagement with ethical concerns suggests a gap between stated commitments to inclusion and lived realities. This reflects broader concerns within AI ethics about the concentration of power, the marginalisation of certain voices, and the need for more accountable and inclusive forms of knowledge production [21, 22]. Thus, the study advances the emerging body of work calling for rethinking the conduct of AI research, who is involved, and whose knowledge is valued. By centring the experiences of disabled, neurodivergent and Deaf researchers, it highlights the importance of moving beyond representational inclusion towards more substantive, participatory, and ethically grounded practices in AI research.

Acknowledgements. We are very grateful to all our research participants for sharing their experiences with us and to Dr Saduf Naqvi for producing a BSL version and helping us recruit Deaf participants.

References

1. Özbilgin, M.F., Erbil, C., Gundogdu, N.: Developing Artificial Intelligence (AI) with Equality, Diversity, and Inclusion (EDI): Towards interdisciplinary co-design with scholars and practitioners of EDI and AI. In: AI and Diversity in a Datafied World of Work, pp. 249–265 Emerald Publishing Limited (2025)

2. Almufareh, M.F., Kausar, S., Humayun, M., Tehsin, S.: A conceptual model for inclusive technology: advancing disability inclusion through artificial intelligence. J. Disab. Res. **3**(1), 20230060 (2024)
3. Shuford, J.: Contribution of artificial intelligence in improving accessibility for individuals with disabilities. J. Knowl. Learn. Sci. Tech. **2**(2), 421–433 (2023)
4. de Hond, A.A., van Buchem, M.M., Hernandez-Boussard, T.: Picture a data scientist: a call to action for increasing diversity, equity, and inclusion in the age of AI. J. American Med. Info. Assoc. **29**(12), 2178–81 (2022)
5. Shulner-Tal, A., Kuflik, T., Kliger, D.: Enhancing fairness perception–towards human-centred AI and personalized explanations understanding the factors influencing laypeople's fairness perceptions of algorithmic decisions. Int. J. Human-Comp. Interact. **39**(7), 1455–1482 (2023)
6. Zacharias, K., Hersh, M., Brightman, A.O., Beever, J.: Individual and collective dimensions of ethical decision-making in engineering. The Routledge International Handbook of Engineering Ethics Education, 60 (2024)
7. Neff, G.: Can democracy survive AI? Sociologica **18**(3), 137–146 (2024)
8. Shams, R.A., Zowghi, D., Bano, M.: AI and the quest for diversity and inclusion: A systematic literature review. AI and Ethics **13**, 1–28 (2023)
9. Hersh, M.: AI research: where are the disabled researchers and the voices of disabled people. In: Int. Conf. of Assoc. for the Advancement of Assistive Technology in Europe, pp. 209–216. Springer Nature, Cham (2025)
10. Chapko, D., et al.: Supporting remote survey data analysis by co-researchers with learning disabilities through inclusive and creative practices. In: Proc. ACM Designing Interactive Sys. Conf. pp. 1668–1681 (2021)
11. Newman-Griffis, D., Swenor, B., Valdez, R., Mason, G.: Disability data futures: Achievable imaginaries for AI and disability data justice (2024). arXiv preprint arXiv:2411.03885
12. Barnes, C.: What a difference a decade makes: reflections on doing 'emancipator\y' disability research. Disability and Society **18**(1), 3–17 (2003)
13. Oliver, M.: Changing the social relations of research production? Disability, Handicap and Society **7**(2), 101–114 (1992)
14. Benjamin, R.: Race After Technology: Abolitionist Tools for the New Jim Code. Polity Press, Cambridge (2019)
15. Noble, S.U.: Algorithms of Oppression: How Search Engines Reinforce Racism. NYU Press, New York (2018)
16. Braun, V., Clarke, V.: Using thematic analysis in psychology. Qual. Res. Psychol. **3**(2), 77–101 (2006)
17. Creswell, J.W., Plano Clark, V.L.: Designing and Conducting Mixed Methods Research, 3rd edn. Sage, London (2018)
18. Ahmed, S.: On Being Included: Racism and Diversity in Institutional Life. Duke University Press, Durham (2012)
19. Costanza-Chock, S.: Design Justice: Community-Led Practices to Build the Worlds We Need. MIT Press, Cambridge, MA (2020)
20. Sins Invalid: Skin, Tooth, and Bone: The Basis of Movement is Our People, 2nd ed. (2016)
21. Birhane, A.: Algorithmic injustice: relational ethics approach. Patterns 2 (2021)
22. Selbst, A.D., Boyd, D., Friedler, S.A. Venkatasubramanian, S., Vertesi, J.: Fairness and abstraction in sociotechnical systems. Proceedings of the Conference on Fairness, Accountability, and Transparency (FAT*), pp. 59–68 (2019)

Interacting with Data for Understanding and Analysis of Complex Information

Interacting with Data for Understanding and Analysis of Complex Information Introduction to the Special Thematic Session

Gerhard Weber[1(✉)], Anna Bramwell-Dicks[2], and Helen Petrie[2]

[1] University of Technology Dresden, Dresden, Germany
gerhard.weber@tu-dresden.de
[2] University of York, York, UK
{anna.bramwell-dicks,helen.petrie}@york.ac.uk

Abstract. To better understand complex information, we often combine internal mental processing with external artifacts through a process of external cognition. These artifacts typically rely on visual formats to help users interpret, manipulate, and control data by distributing information across multiple views. While this approach allows for deep data interrogation, it remains primarily visual. Current non-visual support is often limited to static text descriptions, restricting the user to a pre-authored perspective. Although this provides some access, it lacks the flexibility required for real-time or in-depth exploration of the data. This special thematic session focuses on alternative approaches to facilitate external cognition of complex information. We specifically examine haptification and sonification, while also considering how emerging technologies might overcome the limitations of current visual-centric models.

Keywords: Multi-Modal Interaction · Haptification · Sonification · Understanding Complex Information · Analysing Complex Information

1 Introduction and Background

The inherent complexity of information limits our ability to think by exceeding our internal cognitive capacity. To compensate, internal mental processes and the perception of external objects become interwoven through external cognition, which is the process of offloading mental tasks onto an external environment [1]. This concept can be illustrated by the performance disparity between mental and assisted arithmetic. Research illustrates this disparity [2]: multiplying two-digit numbers mentally took five times as long as performing the same task with the support of pencil and paper. In this example, the use of pencil and paper acted as a cognitive artifact to better support external cognition.

Information visualization provides the methods to develop such artifacts by mapping abstract numeric, relational or textual data into expressive layouts that help to improve our thinking by using features including drawings, layouts combined with text, highlighted color, perspective, spatial orientation and many more features. [2] identifies this as a

K. Miesenberger et al. (Eds.): ICCHP 2026, LNCS 16867, pp. 347–353, 2027.
https://doi.org/10.1007/978-3-032-31308-9_42

pipeline where data are transformed into data tables, which are then mapped into visual structures and rendered as views, a process shown in Fig. 1. People who use these views to analyze such data, interact with the data, and can often control the transformations until finally "seeing" the product of the two numbers [2], achieving that moment of cognitive understanding of the complex information.

However, a clear accessibility gap persists where the mechanisms used to support external cognition primarily involve visual structures through information visualizations. To achieve accessibility for images in general, and information visualizations specifically, pre-authored text descriptions are often used to communicate the content [3]. Yet, the expressiveness of alternative text and image descriptions is frequently limited when compared to the cognitive advantages provided by visual mappings of visual structures.

As information visualizations are built upon underlying data, text descriptions of the data tables do improve accessibility by providing content in an alternative, non-visual, format. However, although tabular alternative text provides an objective description of the information visualization, it does not easily support the fluid and flexible process of supporting external cognition, by allowing the users to interact with the data. The alternative text descriptions that are embedded in web pages and PDF documents are usually unstructured and do not support complex tabular layouts. Often the authors of more complex table data will need to link to images with long text descriptions on separate web or PDF pages, fragmenting the user experience. When data tables are provided, they possess inherent limitations in supporting the identification of complex relationships.

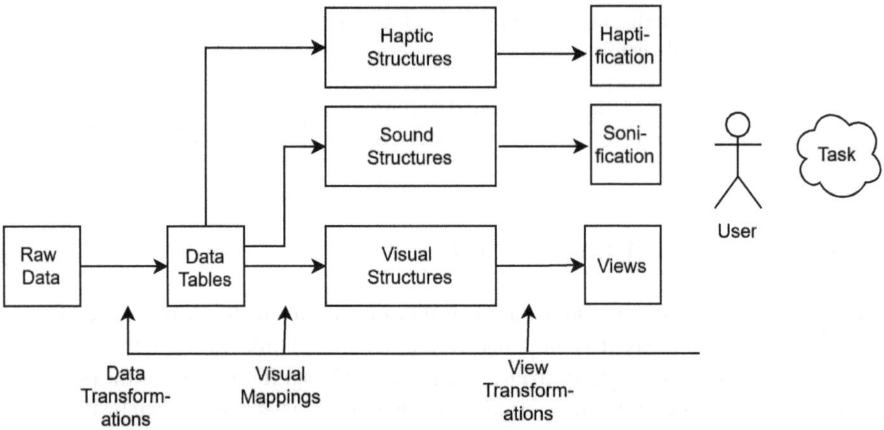

Fig. 1. A mapping process for access to complex information for sense making

This Special Thematic Session focusses on haptification and sonification of data to provide access to complex information. We present research where transformations into haptic or sound structures, specifically through user-controlled haptifications or sonifications, can enable users to access and analyze the same information through alternative sensory modalities, overcoming some of the limitations of textual descriptions. For example, a good haptification can guide the user's fingers while exploring the haptic structures, such as the rows and columns in a spreadsheet, and a sonification can sweep across the structure inherent to the data, allowing for detection of relationships by transforming them into rhythm, pitch and volume. Mapping of data tables, 2D and 3D images, into non-visual structures leads to transformations suitable for people dependent on an alternative to information visualizations. The session includes multimodal interaction with the data, control of the mappings and transformations, as well as verbalization of the information to perform the same tasks.

2 Challenges in Accessibility of Complex Information

While various frameworks govern the accessibility of visual information, the Web Content Accessibility Guidelines (WCAG) serve as the primary standard in the field [3]. For example, Guideline 1.4.1 requires that information is not solely encoded by color acknowledging that *"not everyone sees colors or sees them the same way"* [4]. This requirement is highly relevant to approaches to access information visualizations, where color is often used as a primary visual presentation mechanism. To meet this guideline, developers often include additional objects, e.g., text annotations, or modifying colored lines by applying distinct line textures or different stroke weights. These visual elements, including text, textures and stroke weights, can then be transformed into alternative sensory modalities. For example, they may be spoken, sonified according to a pre-defined metaphor, or haptified through braille or tactile textures. In these cases, sonification and haptification serve *either* as a direct translation of the visual structure into a non-visual representation *or* as a transcoding of the underlying information, which is then rendered into a different format. The transcoding approach is often necessary because the optimal mapping from data and information to most appropriate representation changes across the different sensory modalities; this requires choosing an appropriate haptic or auditory parameter, such as pitch or vibration intensity, to represent the specific data attribute effectively.

While the topic of access to visual information has been a research focus for decades, several significant challenges remain. At the core of these challenges, is the prevalence of static, inflexible data representations that present a single view of the information, as interpreted by the content creator or developer. Traditional accessibility approaches, including static tactile graphics or fixed alternative text descriptions, are limited by their pre-determined nature. The filtering, abstraction and spatial layout of the data are determined by the designer prior to the user's interaction, which means the user is only able to explore only a pre-digested view of the information. This approach restricts the user's ability to perform independent hypothesis testing, or the re-query the data, the image, or complex visual information, from a different perspective. This lack of flexibility ultimately creates a sematic bottleneck, where the richness of the raw data and information is compressed into a single, unchangeable non-visual equivalent. This leads to several specific hurdles:

2.1 Challenge 1: Scalability and Linearity

As shown in [2], transforming visual structures into accessible views is only the final step in preparing an information visualization. Accessibility must be considered much earlier, starting with the development of data tables and continuing through each subsequent step of the pipeline to create non-visual views. In addition, maintaining coherence between representations [5] ensures that readers and listeners can effectively share the knowledge gained from their respective views. This coherence can be achieved by analyzing the specific mappings used in the visual representation and determining which haptic or auditory mappings will best serve the same data-driven purpose. For example, breaking a single large data table into smaller units can allow users to navigate the tables individually, which can address the challenge of limited scalability. In a visual context, a partial view acts like a lens, by adding detail to the overall visualization.

In contrast, the time required to listen to sequential sonification or to explore sequential haptification often exceeds the capacity of working memory to re-create a similar haptic or sonic "lens" effect. While smaller data tables facilitate navigation and provide opportunities for deep focus on specific areas, a data transformation relying on smaller data table units makes it difficult for users to integrate those details into a cohesive "big picture" through haptic or sonic modalities alone, or in combination.

2.2 Challenge 2: Matching Visual and Non-Visual Structures

When haptic or sonic structures are created from complex visual information, sighted designers often find it difficult to understand the user experience, as they naturally prioritize visual structures. This reliance on a "visual-first" mindset can be misleading as sighted designers may fail to consider how a non-visual interface is explored when it lacks the explicit structural cues that were used to organize the information into a visual format. While users often develop sophisticated internal mental models to navigate data, those mental models are built differently when they have been developed solely based on information that is presented haptically or sonically. For accessibility to be truly effective, these non-visual structures must be highly independent. The haptic and sonic structures should be designed as the primary interfaces that allow the user to analyze data, understand the information, and to perform tasks directly, rather than functioning as secondary representations that force the user to mentally reconcile the information with a layout that was initially designed for visual consumption.

Challenge 3: Complexity

Data and data tables can be represented in various ways to support spatial cognition. For example, researchers may use choropleth maps (i.e., thematic maps that represent statistical data through distinct shading or patterning within geographic areas) to combine geographic information with data. More complex datasets can be displayed in 3D views, such as hyperbolic browsers and immersive data landscapes that allow for the exploration of multi-layered information [6]. However, these 3D structures significantly increase the complexity of the view, making it challenging to generate the appropriate haptic feedback through force feedback devices, or to represent these spaces effectively through spatial sound. The accessibility of 3D views is not yet well understood, and while some guidelines exist for designing 3D prints, these currently focus more on architectural features [7] rather than data representation.

2.3 Challenge 4: Practicalities—Time, Cost, Durability and Storage

Although there are many diverse approaches to providing access to visual information in non-visual formats, they often face practical limitations that prevent regular use. These include, the high time-cost of production, the expense of specialized hardware, and the physical challenges of storing or maintaining the durability of tactile materials. Further, historically, alternative text descriptions have had to be manually encoded by the developer or creator of the complex information, which in itself can be a meta-access barrier if the developer or creator is unable to translate the information into an appropriate text-based description.

3 Contributions

This Special Thematic Session integrates several aspects of visualisation, haptification and sonification, which use novel approaches to addresses the challenges described above, moving towards a more performative and interactive model of accessibility.

Scalability and Linearity: When using a keyboard with a screenreader or speaking magnifier software, exploring cells within a spreadsheet typically provides feedback for only a single cell at a time. To address this issue, [8] reports on a novel camera-based approach that monitors finger movement when exploring a tactile grid to provide spoken feedback. In this system, rows and columns are explored systematically to analyze the layout of the data. This approach utilizes multi-modal outputs by integrating different vibration patterns to categorize cell types, such as empty cells, or those containing text, numbers, or equations. This further enhances the information density by integrating kinesthetic feedback and active force sensations.

[9] utilizes a similar camera-based approach to recognize gestural input from fingers but also supports more complex tasks such as finding maximum values through voice input. The authors report on a multi-modal approach that fuses spoken input and finger pointing. This allows users to speak about specific cells they are pointing at and through co-references, such as saying the word "here". By allowing the users to receive localized feedback, these systems transform static spreadsheets into interactive, spatially-referenced environments. This approach supports external cognition by allowing the user to anchor data points to discrete physical co-ordinates, which facilities the retention of spatial relationships within working memory.

Sonification is addressed by [10] in their SoundCeption app. SoundCeption maps depth information in images to specific sound parameters, controlled by a finger placed on a touch screen. The authors report success in allowing blind users to detect the shape of various 2D maps and 3D objects.

Recognizing text in images is highly relevant for developing accessible textural content. [11] reports on an image processing system designed to detect dates, achieving an accuracy rate of more than 95%.

Matching visual and non-visual structures: Arithmetic operations rely heavily on the horizontal and vertical layout of digits. [12] describes a system that monitors finger movement and braille-labeled digits, or tangibles. Users place these digits according to specific arithmetic tasks, and spoken feedback informs them if their operations are correct or incorrect.

Complexity: Understanding the features of 3D renderings within game engines is explored by [13] through the analysis of documentation using a Large Language Model (LLM). The results highlight several meta-accessibility gaps in the Unreal and Unity game engines. The authors conclude that their novel approach will help developers create better accessibility support and more comprehensive documentation. Consequently, not only will the games themselves be more accessible, the environments used to create them will become more accessible as well.

Practicalities: New and emerging technologies provide exciting opportunities to address practical barriers to providing equitable access to complex visual information. This can be achieved using LLMs [13] and Convolutional Neural Networks (CNN) integrated with Spatial Transformer Networks (STN) [11]. Additionally, the approach taken in [10] has potential to exploit real-time analysis to translate visual information into sound. By using these emerging technologies to produce text-based descriptions of complex information, or to transform complex information and data to be accessed via one or more alternative sensory modalities, cheaper, faster, more robust approaches to access complex visual information in non-visual formats is now within reach.

Overall, this Special Thematic Session, contributes an original perspective on the transition from static data representations to dynamic, user-led exploratory agency. By integrating advances in computer vision, large language models, and the potential for real-time multi-modal feedback, the research presented in this session offers an approach to support external cognition through diverse sensory channels. The significance of these contributions lies in the ability to bridge the gap between abstract data structures and complex visual information, with the human action-perception loop. Collectively, the research demonstrates that equitable access to complex information, requires engineering interactive, spatial, tactile, sonic environments that allow users to generate independent, high-level insights into complex information.

Disclosure of Interests. The authors have no competing interests to declare that are relevant to the content of this article.

References

1. Vera, A.H., Simon, H.A.: Situated action: A symbolic interpretation. Cogn. Sci. **17**(1), 7–48 (1993)
2. Card, S.K., Mackinlay, J., Shneiderman, B. (eds.): Readings in information visualization: using vision to think. Morgan Kaufmann (1999)
3. Caldwell, B., et al.: Web content accessibility guidelines (WCAG) 2.0. WWW Consortium (W3C) **290**(1–34), 5–12 (2008)
4. W3C (World Wide Web Consortium): Understanding Success Criterion 1.4.1: Use of Color. modified September 16 (2023). https://www.w3.org/WAI/WCAG21/Understanding/use-of-color.html
5. Mynatt, E.D., Weber, G.: Nonvisual presentation of graphical user interfaces: contrasting two approaches. In: Proceedings of the SIGCHI conference on Human factors in computing systems, pp. 166–172. ACM (1994)
6. Lamping, J., Rao, R.: The hyperbolic browser: A focus+ context technique for visualizing large hierarchies. J. Vis. Lang. Comput. **7**(1), 33–55 (1996)

7. Leporini, B., Rossetti, V., Furfari, F., Pelagatti, S., Quarta, A.: Design guidelines for an interactive 3D model as a supporting tool for exploring a cultural site by visually impaired and sighted people. ACM Trans. Access. Comput. (TACCESS) **13**(3), 1–39 (2020)
8. Usabaev, B., Bührich, N., Taş, T.C., Ballin, P., Weber, G.: Integrating Tactons and Tangibles for Haptification of Spreadsheets, in this proceedings
9. Usabaev, B., Kwataganti Prakash, S.G., Weber, G.: Hands-On Interaction with Spreadsheets, in this proceedings
10. Bramwell-Dicks, A., Petrie, H.: Multi-modal Sensory Substitution for Visually Disabled Users: Initial Design and Evaluation of the SoundCeption App, in this proceedings
11. Takeuchi, Y., Suzuki, K.: Expiration Date Recognition System using YOLO and STN for the Visually Impaired
12. Lai, J., Usabaev, B., Weber, G.: Drag & Speak: A Multimodal Audio-haptic Approach for Arithmetic Operations for Screenreader Users, in this proceedings
13. Namrouti, H., Sik-Lanyi, C., Guzsvinecz, T.: Using Machine Learning to Analyze Accessibility Support in Game Engine Documentation, in this proceedings

Using Machine Learning to Analyze Accessibility Support in Game Engine Documentation

Hanan Namrouti[1(✉)], Cecilia Sik-Lanyi[1,2], and Tibor Guzsvinecz[2,3]

[1] Department of Electrical Engineering and Information Systems, Faculty of Information Technology, University of Pannonia, Egyetem U. 10, 8200 Veszprem, Hungary
hanan.namrouti@phd.mik.uni-pannon.hu
[2] Hungarian Research Network, Piarista U. 4. 1052, Budapest, Hungary
[3] Department of Information Technology and Its Applications, Faculty of Information Technology, University of Pannonia, Gasparich M. Utca 18/A, 8900 Zalaegerszeg, Hungary

Abstract. This paper proposes a machine-learning-based approach to systematically analyze game engine documentation to (1) extract and categorize documented accessibility features, (2) map these features to recognized accessibility standards such as WCAG 2.1 and EN 301 549, and (3) identify gaps where accessibility requirements are insufficiently addressed or entirely missing. By applying natural language processing (NLP) techniques to Unity and Unreal Engine documentation, this study provides a structured comparison of the accessibility support offered and highlights areas where further tooling, guidance, or documentation is needed to better support developers and users with disabilities.

Keywords: Game Engine Accessibility · Inclusive Game Development · Machine Learning · Standards Compliance · Upstream Accessibility · Documentation Analysis

1 Background and Motivation

1.1 The Meta-Accessibility Problem

Accessibility in games has gained increasing attention from researchers, practitioners, and advocacy groups (Westin et al., 2018; Game Accessibility Guidelines, 2012). However, most prior research focuses on evaluating the accessibility of games themselves, with comparatively little attention paid to the tools and engines used to create those games and the accessibility guidance provided to developers through official documentation. This creates what we call a meta-accessibility problem: the accessibility documentation itself becomes a barrier to accessible game development. Even motivated developers cannot implement accessible features if those features are poorly documented, scattered across multiple resources, or misaligned with recognized standards. Prior work (Bødker and Kaur, 2019; Östlund et al., 2019) has addressed developer practices and game evaluation, but none have systematically analyzed engine-level accessibility support through the lens of international standards.

K. Miesenberger et al. (Eds.): ICCHP 2026, LNCS 16867, pp. 354–360, 2027.
https://doi.org/10.1007/978-3-032-31308-9_43

1.2 Why This Matters: Upstream Accessibility

By analyzing platform-level accessibility (game engines, tools, standards documentation), we address accessibility upstream, before individual games reach users. Rather than auditing millions of shipped games for accessibility violations, improving the tools and documentation that developers use enables systemic improvement at the source. This approach is scalable, measurable, and actionable for engine developers.

1.3 State of the Art

Game accessibility research has largely focused on evaluating finished games and developing design guidelines rather than analyzing the underlying tools and engines. Prior work, such as the Game Accessibility Guidelines and the gap analysis between these guidelines and WCAG 2.0 by Westin et al., has highlighted that games often provide uneven support across disability categories and that general web standards do not fully capture game-specific needs. Petri et al.'s systematic review further shows that most studies concentrate on specific titles, genres, or interaction techniques, with comparatively little attention paid to how engines and middleware shape are practically achievable for developers.

At the same time, accessibility research in the web domain has begun to explore automated and semi-automated checking of WCAG conformance, as well as the use of machine learning and large language models to classify or explain accessibility issues. However, to our knowledge, there is no systematic analysis of engine-level documentation and its alignment with WCAG 2.1 and EN 301 549, nor any work that applies NLP and machine learning to game engine documentation to surface upstream accessibility gaps. This paper addresses this gap by focusing on Unity and Unreal Engine as representative, widely used platforms.

2 Research Objectives and Questions

This study addresses three interrelated problems:

- Visibility: Documentation about accessibility features is scattered and difficult to discover across manuals, tutorials, API references, and course materials.
- Standards Alignment: There is no systematic understanding of how game engine accessibility features align with established standards (WCAG 2.1, EN 301 549), creating ambiguity about conformance.
- Gap Identification: It is unclear which accessibility requirements are either unsupported by the engines or inadequately documented to enable developer implementation.

Research Questions

- RQ1: What accessibility-related features are explicitly documented by Unity and Unreal Engine?
- RQ2: How do these documented features map to recognized accessibility standards (WCAG 2.1, EN 301 549, and Game Accessibility Guidelines)?

- RQ3: Which accessibility requirements are insufficiently covered or entirely missing from the documentation?
- RQ4: How can machine learning-based analysis support continuous, scalable evaluation of accessibility support in game engine documentation?

These four research questions correspond directly to the stages of our pipeline (Fig. 1), from feature extraction (RQ1) through standards mapping and gap analysis (RQ2–RQ4).

3 Methodology: ML-Based Documentation Analysis

3.1 Four-Stage Pipeline Architecture

Rather than manual review, we propose that natural language processing and machine learning can systematically extract, categorize, and map accessibility content from game engine documentation. This approach offers several advantages: scalability (processes large corpuses quickly), objectivity (reduces subjective interpretation), reproducibility (applicable to other engines/standards), and precedent (demonstrates ML for upstream accessibility). The pipeline consists of four sequential stages:

Fig. 1. The pipeline consists of four sequential stages for ML-Based Documentation Analysis

The proposed analysis follows a four-stage computational pipeline designed to transform unstructured engine documentation into structured compliance insights. In Stage 1 (Feature Extraction), a BERT-based binary classifier, augmented by a curated accessibility vocabulary, identifies relevant segments with a target F1 score of 0.85. These segments move to Stage 2 (Feature Categorization & Attribute Extraction), where a fine-tuned BERT model paired with a Conditional Random Field (CRF) performs multi-label classification across six disability categories (Motor, Vision, Hearing, Cognitive, Speech, and General) while simultaneously extracting entities such as APIs and WCAG criteria. Stage 3 (Standards Mapping) utilizes a manual reference database for baseline linking to WCAG 2.1 and EN 301 549, using LLM-assisted prompt-based reasoning to resolve uncertain or nuanced mappings. Finally, Stage 4 (Gap Analysis) compares these features against standard requirements to classify gaps ranging from Complete to Documentation gaps and generates automated recommendations based on impact scoring and implementation feasibility. Concretely, we use a BERT-base model that is fine-tuned on a small, manually labelled subset of engine documentation, and we select hyper-parameters to maximise validation F1. The later expert review (Sect. 3.2) then verifies and corrects these automatic predictions.

3.2 Validation and Quality Assurance

A critical step to ensure accuracy is expert validation. We implemented a 7-point validation checklist verified by a panel of 3 experts (accessibility researcher, game engine engineer, game developer) reviewing 20–30% extracted features, stratified by engine, disability category, and confidence score. This mixed-methods approach balances ML efficiency with human expertise. For readers unfamiliar with machine-learning metrics, precision measures how many of the segments we flag as accessibility-related are correct, recall measures how many of the true accessibility segments we find, and F1 is the harmonic mean of precision and recall. While end-users are not directly involved at this stage, their needs are represented via the standards we target and the expertise of the review panel.

4 Expected Results and Contributions

4.1 Findings: Engine Comparison and Documentation

The preliminary analysis suggests a divide in how major engines approach accessibility. While technical foundations exist, the documentation often fails to bridge the gap between API existence and standards compliance. The study reveals that while both engines provide significant foundations for accessibility, there is a distinct lack of "Standard-aware" documentation. For each disability category, we defined a small set of concrete accessibility features (e.g., colour contrast, text size, alternative input options) based on WCAG 2.1, EN 301 549, and the Game Accessibility Guidelines, and then checked whether Unity and Unreal documentation explicitly described each feature.

Table 1 reports, for each disability category, (i) how many distinct features we considered, (ii) the percentage of those features that are explicitly documented in Unity and Unreal documentation, and (iii) the share of features that are not documented in either engine (Gap). The Gap column is computed as 100% minus the higher of the two coverage values; for example, in the Vision category, we consider 8 features and find that Unity documents 75% of them while Unreal documents 87.5%, leaving a 12.5% gap where neither engine currently documents the remaining feature.

Table 1. Documented feature coverage by disability category across Unity and Unreal Engine documentation.

Disability Category	Features Analyzed	Unity Documented	Unreal Documented	Total Coverage Gap
Vision	8	75%	87.5%	12.5%
Motor	6	67%	83%	17%
Hearing	3	33%	67%	33%
Cognitive	2	0%	50%	50%
Speech	2	0%	0%	100%
General	5	100%	100%	0%

4.2 Outcomes by Standards

The following table summarizes the observed coverage of WCAG 2.1 and EN 301 549 in the analyzed documentation, as well as the primary gaps and strategic opportunities we identified.

Table 2. Summary of observed accessibility standard coverage and implementation gaps in the analyzed documentation.

Standard	Observed Coverage	Primary Gaps	Strategic Opportunity
WCAG 2.1	~ 55% (16/29 criteria)	1.4.11 (Contrast), 2.5.4 (Motion), 4.1.3 (Status)	Transitioning from "hardcoded" UI to dynamic, user-adjustable layers
EN 301 549	~ 70% (10/14 clauses)	Clause 12 (Doc Accessibility), 11.2.4 (Foresighted Info)	Low-hanging fruit: Improving the accessibility of the manuals themselves
GAG (Game Guidelines)	Variable	Speech (0%), Cognitive (0–50%), Hearing (Minimal)	Engines require 3rd-party plugins for these specialized domains

Observed coverage is defined as the proportion of relevant success criteria or clauses for which at least one supporting feature is described in either Unity or Unreal documentation. For the Game Accessibility Guidelines, we do not compute a single scalar coverage value; instead, we summarize coverage by disability category in Table 1, which explains the "Variable" entry in Table 2.

These qualitative examples suggest concrete improvements to engine documentation: explicitly tagging accessibility-relevant features with disability categories and standards references, centralizing them in accessibility overview sections, and providing short implementation recipes that link APIs to user-facing outcomes.

4.3 Qualitative Findings and Implications

Qualitative inspection of the extracted segments reveals recurring patterns behind the quantitative gaps. For Hearing, audio events are often documented without guidance on visual or haptic alternatives, which helps explain the high gap despite partial support in Unreal. For Cognitive, we observe complex configuration and UI flows with little advice on simplifying interaction, chunking information, or providing difficulty presets. For Speech, neither engine documents native speech input or output workflows, which is consistent with the 0% coverage in Table 1 and the need for third-party solutions noted in Table 2.

These qualitative examples suggest concrete improvements to engine documentation: explicitly tagging accessibility-relevant features with disability categories and standards references, centralising them in accessibility overview sections, and providing short implementation recipes that link APIs to user-facing outcomes.

5 Limitations and Considerations

This work has inherent limitations:

- Terminology Variability: Documentation uses inconsistent accessibility terminology; synonymy resolution required
- Implicit Information: Some features are documented implicitly without explicit accessibility framing; over-reliance on keywords risks missing such content
- Version & Update Lag: Documentation may reference older versions or planned features not yet implemented

User Studies: Our evaluation focuses on documentation and expert judgement; we do not yet include empirical studies with game developers or players with disabilities to assess how improved documentation affects real-world workflows.

Model Generalization: The models are trained specifically in Unity and Unreal documentation and may not generalize to other engines or older documentation versions without adaptation and re-training.

6 Conclusion

This paper introduces a systematic, scalable approach to analyzing accessibility documentation upstream at the game engine level. By combining machine learning with expert validation, we extract accessibility features from game engine documentation and map them to WCAG 2.1, EN 301 549, and Game Accessibility Guidelines. We expect to identify significant gaps in both engine accessibility support and, more critically, in the documentation of that support. The methodology and findings (1) provided actionable recommendations for engine developers, (2) informed game developers about available accessibility features, (3) demonstrated how ML can support accessibility at the platform level, and (4) established precedent for continuous, scalable evaluation of tool and platform accessibility. Rather than asking, are games accessible? This work asks a more foundational question: are game engines accessible? And can we systematically measure and improve accessibility at the source?

References

BBC and Community Contributors: Game Accessibility Guidelines

Westin, T., Kvedalen, J.I., Hagen, K., Steensgaard, C.: Game accessibility guidelines and WCAG 2.0—A gap analysis. In: Miesenberger, K., Bühler, C., Penaz, P. (eds.) ICCHP 2018, LNCS, vol. 10896, pp. 61–69. Springer, Heidelberg (2018)

Bødker, M., Kaur, K.: Game design documents as accessibility instruments. In: Proceedings of the 2019 on Designing Interactive Systems Conference, pp. 297–310. ACM, New York (2019)

Östlund, B., Östlund, S., Holm, K.: Blind gamers' experience of digital game accessibility. Games and Culture **14**(6), 631–649 (2019)

Petri, G., von Gillessen, S., Müller, W.: Accessibility in games: a systematic literature review. Entertainment Computing **44**, 100524 (2023)

World Wide Web Consortium: Web Content Accessibility Guidelines (WCAG) 2.1. W3C CEN/CLC/ETSI: EN 301 549 V3.2.1: Accessibility requirements for ICT products and services. European Standard. European Committee for Standardization, Brussels (2021)
Devlin, J., Chang, M.W., Lee, K., Toutanova, K.: BERT: Pre-training of deep bidirectional transformers for language understanding. arXiv preprint arXiv:1810.04805 (2019)
Unity Technologies: Accessibility for Unity applications. Official Documentation. Epic Games: Designing UI for Accessibility in Unreal Engine. Official Documentation

Drag & Speak: A Multimodal Audio-Haptic Approach for Arithmetic Operations for Screenreader Users

Jinsong Lai, Bela Usabaev, and Gerhard Weber(✉)

Technische Universität Dresden, Dresden, Germany
{jinsong.lai,bela.usabaev,gerhard.weber}@tu-dresden.de

Abstract. Drag & Speak assists people who are blind or have low vision in learning and performing basic arithmetic calculations. It supports tactile exploration of digits and monitors an index finger. The setup consists of a camera and a cut out wooden plate for tactile support when placing digits into the plate's grooves. Each digit is a small tangible brick-like object consisting of an ArUco marker and Braille label. A user can speak to a voice assistant and receive support when navigating to a cell in the grid by sonification and also for simple one digit arithmetic calculations. A user study in a within-subjects design with three experimental conditions for 8 participants shows good SUS values and acceptable TLX scores.

Keywords: Multimodal · Tangible · Arithmetic

1 Introduction

Many STEM (Science, Technology, Engineering and Mathematics) disciplines are dependent on non-linear notations, as characters and symbols are combined with graphics to write formulae and develop diagrams. Already basic arithmetic operations can be challenging to learn for students who are blind or have low vision. Addition, subtraction, multiplication, and division require placing digits and numbers both horizontally and vertically aligned to each other when reading and writing calculations.

Although screenreaders can indicate digits verbally, it is cumbersome to explore numbers spatially by text-to- speech output, in particular as empty space is neglected by screenreaders. As an alternative, mathematical braille and braille displays are suitable to write and read the terms needed including spaces. Still, braille displays are not presenting a two-dimensional layout. If students fail to learn how to explore digits horizontally and vertically, their success in mastering STEM subjects can be limited.

Other non-visual approaches are needed to combine both visual and non-visual design of interactive systems for learning how mathematical tasks can be solved. We present a novel multimodal approach to basic arithmetic operations

K. Miesenberger et al. (Eds.): ICCHP 2026, LNCS 16867, pp. 361–369, 2027.
https://doi.org/10.1007/978-3-032-31308-9_44

in a tabular layout by integrating voice input with placement of tangibles and providing feedback to the student with text-to-speech output as well as sonification. Such an approach may be extended to more complex notations and diagramming techniques.

2 Related Work

Both tactile as well as acoustic modalities can contain information about two-dimensional layout. Spatial sound can present spoken text in a horizontal layout if Header Related Transfer Functions (HRTFs) are implemented [4] but vertical resolution is rather limited and depends on individual preferences. Large pin array displays [11] can hold only a few lines with only some characters. The Hyperbraille display shows 12 lines with 40 characters each but is not easily affordable. [10] have developed one of the first eLearning systems to teach geometrical concepts on a tactile display with 7200 pins.

Low-cost physical bricks can carry braille labels and allow for tactile interaction, if accidental movements can be avoided. The Brannan Cubarithm Kit Slate 100 Cubes [8] allows placement of the braille labeled cubes in a tabular rubber-based frame.

Breiter et al. suggest also grooves in a plate to stabilize the position of wooden blocks [3]. In this work the concept of tangible objects is applied to allow digitalisation of the editing process. The Tangible Grid [7] consists of a tactile grid layout to design web pages by placing physical objects.

In a digital system individual feedback can be generated to support learners. Ali et al. have developed a system guiding students who are blind or have low vision through structural information in a graphical user interface and a screen-reader for solving mathematical tasks [1]. They show an increase of efficiency but do not focus on effectiveness and learning.

The Tactonom [6] is built around affordable components: tactile feedback from microcapsule paper, a camera mounted above and a casing with a small computer generating text-to-speech output for regions identified through a finger. Similar audiohaptic devices are Talking Tactile Tablet and IVEO, but these rely on more expensive touch input sensing devices.

In this work, we extend the concept of a Tactonom by introducing tangible objects and real-time hand tracking as described below, implement sonification for guiding fingers [9] and evaluate the system with students who are blind or have low vision.

3 Methodology

3.1 System Implementation

To achieve a low-cost, replicable, and portable solution, our prototype is built around a Raspberry Pi 4 as a standalone computational unit. As shown in Fig. 1(a), the setup includes a custom height-adjustable wooden stand with a top-down Arducam camera to keep the tactile grid within the camera's field of view. The system further includes a speaker, microphone, tactile grid, and tangibles.

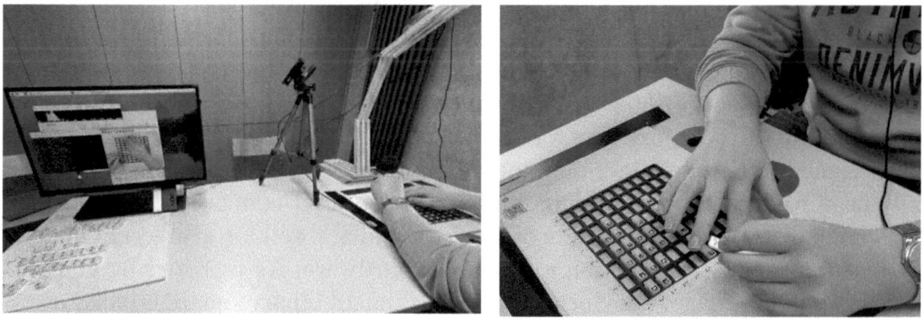

(a) Setup of the prototype

(b) Close-up view of the tactile grid and tangibles

Fig. 1. System overview. (a) Prototype setup with the custom wooden camera stand and the experimenter's monitor showing real-time object detection and hand tracking. (b) Close-up view of a user exploring the tactile grid and placing 3D-printed tangibles.

The software architecture is implemented in Python. The vision module uses OpenCV to detect the grid structure and multiple ArUco markers [5] in real time, including their IDs and positions. Concurrently, the MediaPipe framework is integrated for Hand Landmark Detection, fingertip tracking for deictic interaction, and recognition of the hand region boundary. This allows the system to identify the pointed grid cell and distinguish temporary palm occlusion from deliberate object removal. The recognition feedback is visualized in real time in the monitor view shown in Fig. 1(a).

For voice interaction, we combine online Automatic Speech Recognition (ASR) with a local offline Text-to-Speech (TTS) engine to balance accuracy and latency. Early tests with local ASR solutions (Whisper and Vosk) on the Raspberry Pi 4 did not provide sufficient real-time performance or recognition accuracy. We therefore used AssemblyAI for streaming ASR, local command parsing, and Piper for offline TTS. We also shortened prompts and feedback based on pilot testing to reduce waiting time and improve interaction fluency.

3.2 Tangible and Grid Design

The physical layer underwent several design iterations to optimize the haptic experience and recognition efficiency.

Tangibles. We replaced off-the-shelf solutions (e.g., Lego or wooden blocks) with custom 3D-printed tangibles. This approach reduced weight and allowed for precise sizing to match the ArUco markers. Because the camera must capture the whole grid from above, marker size and image resolution must be balanced against available cell space and processing load: larger markers reduce usable cell space, while higher resolution increases computation on the Raspberry Pi.

In early design stages, we tested several QR-based options, including standard QR codes with different error-correction levels and Micro QR codes. In practice, they were either too slow for real-time multi-object detection at small sizes or unsuitable for integrating Braille information. Based on these tests, we finally adopted ArUco markers for tangible recognition. Unlike QR codes, which are designed to encode larger amounts of information, the markers in our system only need to distinguish between different objects. ArUco markers are thus better aligned with the requirements of our task and are well integrated in OpenCV for fast multi-marker detection on low-cost hardware. As reported by Garrido-Jurado et al. [5], ArUco provides robust detection of binary square fiducial markers and is suitable for real-time applications. To support tactile identification, each tangible uses a split top surface: one part contains the ArUco marker for camera recognition, and the other contains 8-dot Computer Braille printed on transparent foil. Compared with traditional 6-dot Braille, the 8-dot format allows a more compact encoding of single digits and operators.

Grid. Early prototypes using microcapsule paper and magnetic tangibles caused issues with unintended magnetic attraction and repulsion, as well as accidental displacement. Consequently, the final design uses a laser-cut thin wooden board. Each cell is a cutout with a diameter slightly larger than the base of the tangible, creating passive haptic constraints. This physical slotting mechanism stabilizes the tangibles without magnets while facilitating easy removal. Users can perceive the grid structure by touching the cutouts (see Fig. 1(b)) and identify the row and column coordinates via Braille labels on the edges of the board.

3.3 Interaction and Voice Assistance

The core interaction follows a "Prompt-Action-Feedback" loop. The system guides the user by providing a task prompt to set the context (e.g., "Set up the operands"), followed by specific action instructions (e.g., "Place number 2 at position B2"). The user then places a tangible, and the system verifies the position (Row, Col) and ID via computer vision. This allows for real-time error correction or confirmation.

To reduce cognitive load, a voice assistant is integrated, activated by the wake word "Hello Assistant". It supports four intent categories:

- Task Prompting: "What is the next step?"
- Action Instruction: "What is the next action"
- Contextual Deictic Query: Users point to a tangible and ask, "What is this?", and the system identifies the digit and its place-value context.
- Calculation Support: Queries such as "What is 5 times 9?" serve to reduce the mental arithmetic load.

The system is designed for robust interruptibility. User queries can interrupt TTS output at any time. Once the Q&A is completed, the system automatically resumes the previous state to ensure continuity. Similarly, if a navigation task is interrupted, it is automatically restarted.

Table 1. Participant demographics. G: Gender (M=male, F=female), Age: in years, Hand: Handedness (R=Right, L=Left, B=Both), VA: Visual Acuity (TB = totally blind, LB = legally blind, VI = visually impaired), VL: Vision Loss (Congenital, Baby (≤ 3), Child (4–13), Adolescent (≥ 14)), BRP: Braille Reading Proficiency, Calculation Method: Daily calculation habits

P	Age	G	Hand	VA	VL	BRP	Calculation Method
P1	2004	M	B	TB	Congenital	Advanced	Mental/Braille/App
P2	1995	F	R	VI	Congenital	None	Mental
P3	2000	M	B	VI	Adolescent	Basic	Mental/Braille
P4	2008	F	R	TB	Child	Advanced	Calculator/App
P5	2007	F	B	TB	Congenital	Advanced	Calculator/App
P6	1998	F	R	TB	Congenital	Advanced	App
P7	2005	F	L	TB	Congenital	Advanced	Calculator/App
P8	2007	M	R	TB	Child	Advanced	Audio/App

4 User Study

We conducted a user study at the Educational Centre for the Blind and Visually Impaired (BBS Nürnberg) with eight participants who are blind or have low vision. Participant demographics, including their visual acuity and preferred calculation methods, are detailed in Table 1. The experimental task consisted of standard written arithmetic operations (e.g., 23×45), performed using the tangible grid layout. We used a within-subjects design with three experimental conditions:

- V1 (Baseline): The system provided step-by-step task prompts, action instructions, and verification feedback. Users relied solely on tactile exploration for spatial orientation on the grid.

- V2 (Voice Assistant): V1 plus voice-based Q&A, but without active finger navigation.
- V3 (Full Support): V2 plus finger navigation. Before each action, the system guided the user's finger to the target cell using clock-face directional cues (e.g., "9 o'clock") and sonification, where the pitch frequency increased as the finger approached the target.

We collected both quantitative and qualitative data, including demographic questionnaires and post-task evaluations. Subjective workload was measured using the NASA-TLX, and usability was assessed via the System Usability Scale (SUS). Additionally, custom 5-point Likert scales were used to evaluate the perceived effectiveness of the guidance and feedback mechanisms.

5 Results

The overall usability of the system was evaluated using the System Usability Scale (SUS). As shown in Fig. 2, individual scores ranged from 57.5 to 95.0 with a mean score of 75.9 (SD=13.8). According to Bangor et al. [2], this falls into the "Good" range (Grade B).

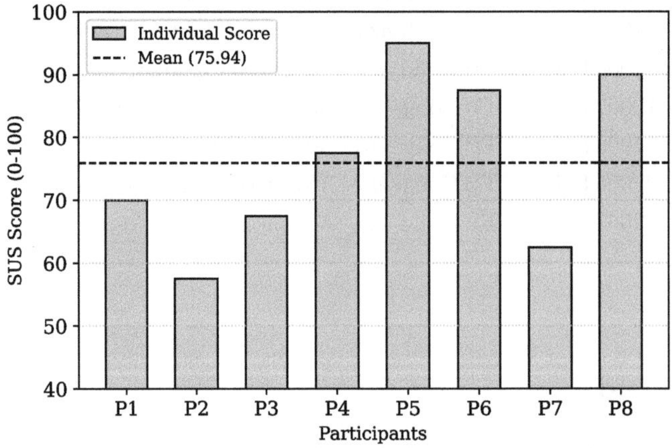

Fig. 2. Individual System Usability Scale (SUS) scores for the eight participants. The dashed line represents the mean score.

Because SUS reflects overall usability rather than mathematics learning outcomes, we complemented it with custom Likert ratings and qualitative feedback on the physical layer. Participants rated the grid structure as easy to understand (4.50) and the cell boundaries as distinguishable (4.63). This interpretation is supported by qualitative feedback: P7 noted that the laser-cut holes were more stable than magnets, and P1 reported that placing one or two tangibles was enough to understand the basic interaction.

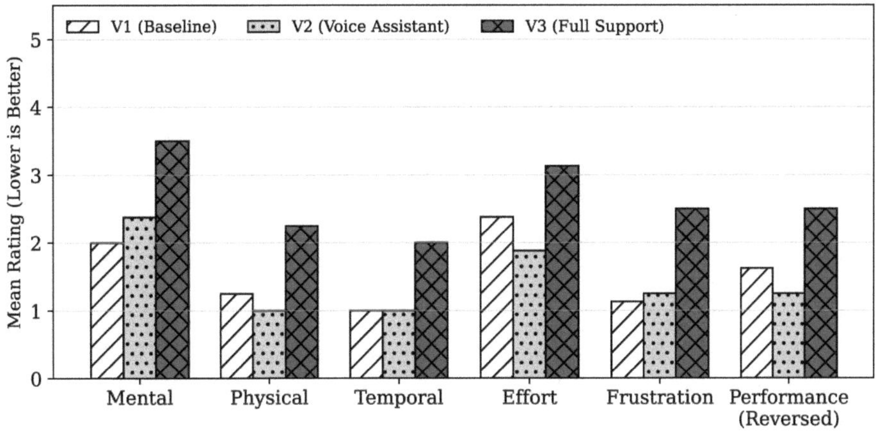

Fig. 3. Mean NASA-TLX scores across six dimensions for the three conditions: V1 (Baseline), V2 (Voice Assistant), and V3 (Full Support). Note: The "Performance" scale is inverted, so that for all dimensions, a lower bar indicates a better user experience.

At the same time, although "the intuitiveness of the tangibles" (4.13) and "ease of manipulation" (4.38) were also rated positively, our observations showed that users still relied strongly on the Braille labels at the grid edges for row and column orientation. Once their fingers moved into the middle area, some participants became more likely to lose orientation because continuous physical reference points were missing. In addition, a few participants, such as P7 who preferred the left hand, showed some difficulty with a navigation approach that mainly designed for right-hand use.

Subjective workload was analyzed using the NASA-TLX (see Fig. 3). V1 (Baseline) and V2 (Voice Assistant) showed similar workload levels across most dimensions, with V2 yielding slightly more favorable scores in Mental Demand (M=2.38) and Performance (inverted score M=1.25). This suggests that the voice assistant provided some support.

By contrast, V3 (Full Support) showed higher workload ratings across all dimensions, especially in Temporal Demand (M = 2.00), Effort (M = 3.13), and Frustration (M = 2.50). Qualitative feedback indicates that system latency was the main cause of this additional burden. P1 explained that, despite the navigation cues, it was still difficult to confirm the correct position. The finger often overshot the target and then circled around it, for example receiving "9 o'clock," then "6 o'clock," and then "3 o'clock," because the audio feedback lagged behind the hand movement. P3 likewise described the continuous beeping as "annoying" because of the delay. At the same time, several participants reported that they gradually adapted to the latency after a few attempts. When they deliberately slowed down their finger movements, the navigation function became usable. This suggests that the main issue in V3 may have been hardware-related latency rather than the interaction concept itself.

The higher Mental Demand in V3 (M=3.50) was also related to spatial cue interpretation. Three congenitally blind participants reported that clock-face directions were not an intuitive reference and first had to be translated into left/right directions, adding cognitive effort.

6 Discussion and Outlook

Standard arithmetic tasks are typically represented and calculated through a two-dimensional spatial layout, while non-visual access is often sequential, for example through screen readers. Drag & Speak addresses this gap by providing a tangible grid as a stable physical anchor and by translating spatial arithmetic into a structured sequence of tactile and auditory cues. This enables users to explore rows and columns step by step and supports access to spatial relations in a more manageable way.

Limitations have been detected in automatically starting to guide the user automatically. Controllability of the interaction can be enhanced in future versions.

Future work will focus on adapting the system for use in primary school education and connecting it more closely to early mathematics teaching. In particular, future versions could support foundational concepts such as place value and carrying, which can be difficult to access in non-visual learning contexts. In this way, Drag & Speak may develop into not only an assistive system, but also a pedagogical tool for inclusive mathematics education.

References

1. Ali, A., Khusro, S., Algamdi, S.A.: Accessible interactive learning of missing-digit arithmetic problems for students with visual disabilities. Sci. Rep. **15**(1), 17804 (2025). https://doi.org/10.1038/s41598-025-01473-6
2. Bangor, A., Kortum, P., Miller, J.: An empirical evaluation of the system usability scale. Int. J. Hum.-Comput. Interact. **24**(6), 574–594 (2008). https://doi.org/10.1080/10447310802205776
3. Breiter, Y., Karshmer, A., Karshmer, J.: AutOMathic blocks usability testing phase one. In: International Conference on Computers for Handicapped Persons, pp. 191–195. Springer Berlin Heidelberg, Berlin, Heidelberg (2012). https://doi.org/10.1007/978-3-642-31522-0_29
4. Crispien, K., Würz, W., Weber, G.: Using spatial audio for the enhanced presentation of synthesised speech within screen-readers for blind computer users. In: International Conference on Computers for Handicapped Persons, pp. 144–153. Springer Berlin Heidelberg, Berlin, Heidelberg (2012). https://doi.org/10.1007/3-540-58476-5_117
5. Garrido-Jurado, S., Muñoz-Salinas, R., Madrid-Cuevas, F.J., Marín-Jiménez, M.J.: Automatic generation and detection of highly reliable fiducial markers under occlusion. Pattern Recogn. **47**(6), 2280–2292 (2014). https://doi.org/10.1016/j.patcog.2014.01.005
6. Inventivio: Tactonom (2026). https://www.tactonom.com

7. Li, J., Yan, Z., Jarjue, E., Shetty, A., Peng, H.: TangibleGrid: tangible web layout design for blind users. In: Proceedings of the 35th Annual ACM Symposium on User Interface Software and Technology, pp. 1–12 (2022). https://doi.org/10.1145/3526113.3545618
8. MaxiAids: Brannan cubarithm kit slate 100 cubes (2025). https://www.maxiaids.com/product/brannan-cubarithm-kit-slate-100-cubes
9. Ramôa, G., Schmidt, V., Schwarz, T., Stiefelhagen, R., König, P.: Sonoice! a sonar-voice dynamic user interface for assisting individuals with blindness and visual impairment in pinpointing elements in 2d tactile readers. Front. Rehabil. Sci. **5**, 1368983 (2024)
10. Schweikhardt, W., Fehrle, T.: A computer-based drawing station for the blind (ein rechner unterstützter zeichenplatz für blinde, in german). In: Proceedings of 5th International Workshop Computerized Braille Production, 30 October-1 November 1985, Winterthur, Switzerland, pp. 251–261 (1986)
11. Zeng, L., Weber, G.: Advancements in Pin-Array Tactile Displays: Designing Multimodal User Interfaces for Braille and Graphics. Springer (2025). https://doi.org/10.1007/978-3-032-03151-8

Multi-modal Sensory Substitution for Visually Disabled Users: Initial Design and Evaluation of the SoundCeption App

Anna Bramwell-Dicks[1](✉) and Helen Petrie[2]

[1] School of Arts and Creative Technologies, University of York, York YO10 5DD, UK
anna.bramwell-dicks@york.ac.uk
[2] Department of Computer Science, University of York, York YO10 5DD, UK
helen.petrie@york.ac.uk

Abstract. Sensory substitution devices for visually disabled people have traditionally required expensive, specialist equipment and only converted visual information into one other modality, usually either touch or sound. Advances in digital technologies, particularly smartphones and tablets, provide opportunities for developing app based and multi-modal solutions. This paper reports on the user-centred design process to create a prototype for a multi-modal sensory substitution app - SoundCeption - to enable visually disabled people to interpret 2D and 3D images using a combination of their senses of hearing and proprioception. Two iterations of development and evaluation with a small group of blind users are reported. These revealed a number of interesting features to support multi-modal interaction with images and showed that the users could gain an understanding of the contents and perception of depth in the images.

Keywords: Sensory Substitution · Multi-Modal · Depth Perception · Visually Disabled People

1 Introduction

The question of how best to present visual information, including images, graphs, and maps, to visually disabled people in a manner which they can usefully interpret is an area that has been researched for many years. Different methods for producing tactile images have been developed [2, 6] including images on refreshable displays [e.g. 13], as well as audio-tactile images [9]. A more technologically sophisticated solution comes in the form of sensory substitution devices (SSDs) [1] which convert visual information into a format that is suitable for interpretation through other senses (e.g. touch or hearing). Until very recently, SSDs required expensive and often intrusive equipment, but developments in small personal devices with touchscreens (i.e. smartphones and tablet computers) and digital cameras means a new generation of SSDs is emerging, the best known of which is probably Microsoft's Soundscape research system which translates visual map information into 3D sound to support visually disabled people in understanding and navigating their environments [11].

K. Miesenberger et al. (Eds.): ICCHP 2026, LNCS 16867, pp. 370–379, 2027.
https://doi.org/10.1007/978-3-032-31308-9_45

In this paper, we present the initial design and evaluation of a prototype sensory substitution app – SoundCeption - which was created following a user-centred design approach working closely with a small group of blind people. SoundCeption exploits existing technology that many users may already own (e.g. a tablet computer) or could inexpensively acquire, and was developed as a sensory substitution *app* rather than a sensory substitution *device*, so is therefore more readily available. In this research, we aimed to establish if it was possible to combine users' sense of hearing with proprioception, the awareness of the position and movement of the body, to interpret the content of 2D and 3D images.

2 Background

An SSD typically takes visual information and converts it to an alternative modality, allowing blind and visually impaired people to receive information using another sense. The alternative modality is often audition or haptics, which predominantly uses the sense of touch, but also includes proprioception. In Bach-y-Rita's original demonstration of this principle, visual information was converted into a tactile display on the blind person's back [1]. The vOICe system [10] is an early example of an SSD that converted visual information into sound. Bach-y-Rita's work used state-of-the-art technology at the time, but it was not practical for everyday use. Since then, many researchers have used technological advances to improve SSD. Bach-y-Rita himself helped develop BrainPort, which converts visual information into a tactile display on the user's tongue [3], a product which has been commercialized. Caraiman et al. [4] developed a research prototype of a system to provide blind users with a 3D representation of their environment in sound. Von Erp et al. pioneered the idea of using a belt around the torso to convey visual information about the environment to blind pedestrians [7]. As an alternative to the belt, Kilian et al. [8] developed a glove to provide the tactile information.

Historically, SSDs have mainly used a one-to-one mapping with visual information converted into a single alternate modality. But, with the development of inexpensive touchscreen technology, SSDs can now convert visual information into a combination of both haptics and sound information, marking a shift towards multi-modal sensory substitution. For example, Chundury et al. [5] use an iPad to present visual graphics to blind people using sound and their sense of proprioception based on the position of their fingers on the screen.

SoundCeption builds on this line of research by investigating the possibility of visually disabled people interacting with both 2D and 3D images using proprioception and sound, particularly focusing on whether they can gain an understanding of how depth is depicted in 2D visual images of 3D objects.

3 SoundCeption Version 1.0

Our primary aim for the SoundCeption App was to facilitate image presentation in a format that allows visually disabled people to use their senses of hearing and proprioception together, to understand both 2D and 3D images. This approach adopts a one-to-two multi-modal mapping, converting visual information into a presentation format that can be explored through both hearing and with gestures. While the delivery mechanism is multi-modal, the access mechanism is distributed across auditory and proprioceptive senses. These channels are functionally interdependent, relying on cross-modal integration, as neither sense alone is sufficient to access the full image content.

The early design of the SoundCeption App began with knowledge derived from our previous experiences working with visually disabled people. As the core concepts underpinning a multi-modal sensory substitution app are difficult to convey in the abstract, we thought it was essential to begin by providing a tangible demonstration of the concept to facilitate meaningful discussion with blind people about the potential and opportunities for the app. We created a set of materials to showcase potential functionality and design features to blind users. However, to avoid prejudicing responses and to allow participants to critique our initial ideas and add their own, we intentionally used a low-fidelity prototype and framed it as an early-stage development. This approach aimed to encourage open, creative and critical participant feedback [12].

SoundCeption version 1.0 included a single 3D depth-map image of a sphere (Fig. 1) that was encoded with sounds that mapped to specific features of the image. The user interacted with the image by tapping the tips of their fingers on the screen which triggered the associated sound for that area of the image. We hoped that users would be able to interpret the content of the image based on their knowledge of both their fingers' position (i.e. using their sense of proprioception) and their understanding of the meaning of the sounds that were generated and played back to them.

Our initial exploration of the SoundCeption App concept focused on two different situational contexts, one where SoundCeption was used at home and the other when it is used as a real-time navigation aid. Our initial design ideas related to:

- how the SoundCeption App interface would be presented on an iPad, and its integration with VoiceOver,
- the range of audio parameters that could be manipulated to convey information to the user: including pitch, volume, timbre and stereo pan,
- different options for the audio hardware (e.g. headphones, bone conducting headsets) that could be used with SoundCeption.

Fig. 1. The 3D depth map image of a sphere used in SoundCeption v1.0

The SoundCeption v1.0 prototype used a monochrome 3D depth map image of a sphere (Fig. 1). In a depth map image of a 3D object, pixel intensity (i.e. brightness) corresponds to proximity to the camera (i.e. depth data); specifically brighter, higher intensity pixels, represent the areas that are closest to the camera. SoundCeption was programmed to map an audible sine wave tone to the pixel intensity value, which was triggered when the user's finger made contact with any pixel value higher than zero. In this mapping, pixels in the image that have less depth (i.e. were closer to the camera) had a higher intensity, and were mapped to a sine wave with a higher pitch. As a result, the pitch is highest at the centre of the image, where the surface of the sphere is nearest to the camera. As the user moves their finger away from the centre of the image to trace the surface of the sphere in any direction, the pitch decreased accordingly. The auditory feedback was delivered by the iPad either using the device's built-in speakers, connected headphones or bonephones.

SoundCeption v1.0 was evaluated in semi-structured interviews with 4 totally blind participants. All participants were male, with ages ranging from 36 to 65 years. Two participants have been blind since birth and two lost their sight as adults. All participants were competent to expert users of iPads with VoiceOver.

All the participants were able to trace the surface of the sphere with their fingers and identify the surface point closest to the camera using a combination of hearing and proprioception. However, as sounds were only generated when the image pixel had an intensity value higher than zero, the black areas of the image, where there was no intensity, were silent. This lack of feedback was problematic, as when tapping these "empty" areas, no sound was generated, and the participants were unsure if the app was broken or if they had just tapped incorrectly. To address this, a distinct background sound is needed for areas of the image where there is no intensity, to indicate an empty area of the image.

Further, we identified a need for a dedicated boundary sound. Since the boundaries of the image do not necessarily align with the physical edge of the screen (Fig. 2), users need auditory cues to distinguish whether their finger has reached the limit of the image area, or the boundary of the app window. Participants also requested a distinct sound to mark the "edge" of the sphere itself. While the sphere image technically has a smooth surface and no sharp geometric edge, users felt a definitive marker sound was necessary to indicate the change from the object's surface to the background. This concept is known as a silhouette edge, which is the outer boundary when an object meets its background from the viewer's perspective. Such cues may be necessary for more complex shapes and objects such as cuboids or cylinders (see Fig. 3). In these cases, a distinction must be made between the object's physical sharp geometric edges and the silhouette edges created by perspective. As the SoundCeption app has potential to teach blind people about shape and perspective, incorporating distinctive boundary, geometric edge and silhouette edge sounds, would be useful. Participants also felt that depth map images of more complex 3D objects would need additional verbal descriptions to aid interpretation.

The participants felt it was important that the user could generate sounds by scrolling with their finger (i.e. through continuous contact with the screen) rather than repetitive tapping to allow them to retain contextual information better via proprioception. Further, all participants wanted to be able to use both hands, and multiple fingers, to scan the image and generate sounds. Therefore, SoundCeption should ultimately support poly- rather than mono-phonic sound generation.

The participants also found it difficult to use SoundCeption unless the iPad was in a fixed position. In this evaluation, the device was placed flat on a table and we held it in place, so that the participant could tap the screen without the device moving. If the device moved even slightly it became difficult for the user to retain contextual information and interpret the content of the image.

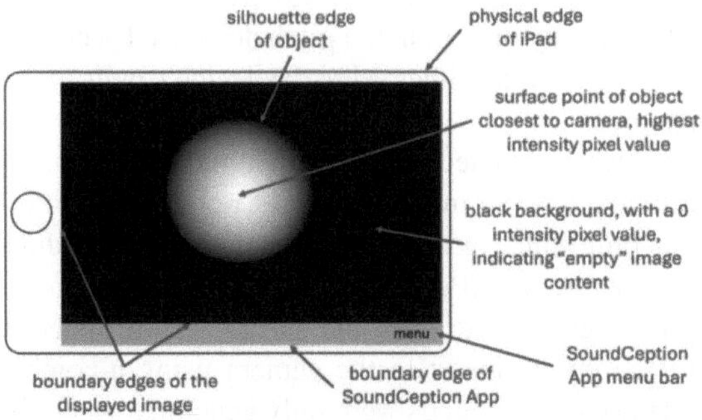

Fig. 2. Key features of the interface and image that need to be distinguished

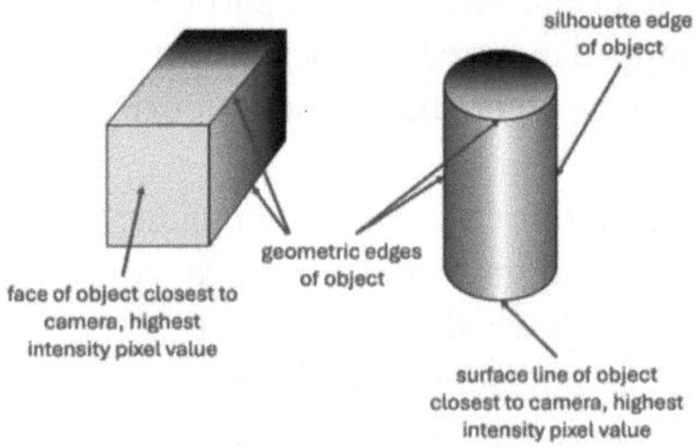

Fig. 3. Examples of image features that need distinctive sounds in 3D geometric shapes

4 SoundCeption Version 2.0

Following the evaluation of v1.0, the SoundCeption concept was further developed to include a broader range of visual content. SoundCeption v2.0 included two more 3D depth map images of a Buddha figurine (Fig. 4a) and a horse figurine (Fig. 4b). SoundCeption v2.0 also included a 2D map of part of the University of York campus (Fig. 4c).

4.1 Method

SoundCeption v2.0 included a few different approaches to mapping audio parameters to image features. For the 3D depth map images, three different mappings of audio parameter to pixel intensity were implemented:

- **3D Mapping 1 – pitch manipulation**: the pitch of the sine wave increased as the pixel intensity increased, i.e. as the pixel was closer to the camera;

- **3D Mapping 2 – amplitude manipulation:** the amplitude (i.e. the loudness) of the sine wave increased as pixel intensity increased;
- **3D Mapping 3:** a fusion sound combining pitch and amplitude manipulation, so that the highest intensity pixels (i.e. the areas of the image that are closest to the camera and have the shortest depth) were both at a higher pitch and louder.

A distinct high pitched edge sound was included to indicate when the user had reached the boundary edge of the image with their finger. We also included a distinct sound which highlighted when the user was touching an empty area of the image that did not contain any pixel intensity information. As we were taking an iterative approach to the design and development of SoundCeption, we did not yet include a specific silhouette edge sound in the 3D image mappings, nor did we incorporate polyphonic sounds or support multiple fingers generating sounds together.

For the 2D campus map, we used the same three approaches to mapping intensity of the image pixel to audio parameter as with the 3D images. However, in the 2D context, the meaning of the sounds differs as there is no depth to convey from a 2D image:

- **2D Mapping 1 – pitch manipulation**: the footpaths (white lines, with highest intensity) have a constant high pitch. The darkest area on the map is the campus lake, which was mapped to a low pitch due to the low pixel intensity. Dark grey medium thickness lines indicate roads, while the dark grey shapes were buildings. However, these features have similar pixel intensities, and we did not want to use a pitch that was close to that which was mapped to the lake. The roads and buildings features also needed to be distinct from each other, despite having a similar colour in the 2D image. So, a mid-range tone was used for the roads and a slightly deeper tone was used for the buildings. The light grey indicates grass parkland areas of the campus in the map, which were assigned a higher pitch than the roads or buildings, but lower than the footpath sounds.
- **2D Mapping 2 – amplitude manipulation:** the amplitude (i.e. the volume) of the sine wave was manipulated, so the higher intensity pixels (e.g. the footpaths) were louder than other areas with lower intensity pixels (e.g. the lake).
- **2D Mapping 3:** a fusion sound that combined both the pitch and amplitude manipulation approaches.

The 2D image did not require use of the "empty" sound, as the 2D campus map did not include any areas with no image information.

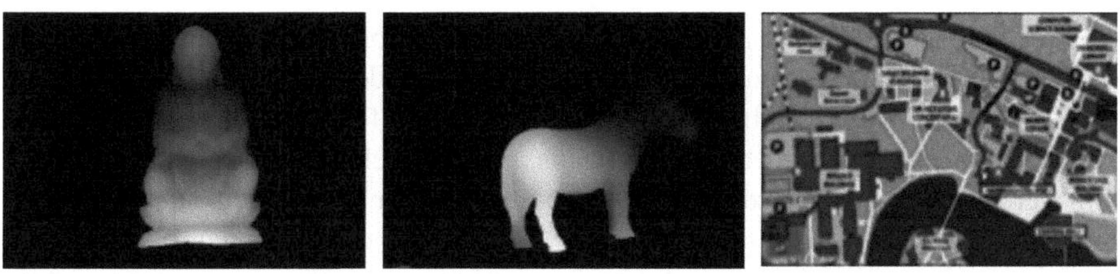

Fig. 4. The images used in the SoundCeption version 2.0 app: (a) The sitting Buddha figurine image; (b) The horse figurine image; (c) The campus map image

Finally, v2.0 allowed the users to interact with the image via continuous scanning rather than using the tapping gesture required in v1.0.

4.2 User Evaluation

Version 2.0 was evaluated by the same four participants as v1.0, and focused on the following questions:

1. How much training do blind people need to be comfortable using SoundCeption to interact with 2D and 3D images?
2. What features of 2D maps and 3D images can blind people identify using the multimodal SoundCeption approach combining their senses of hearing and proprioception?
3. Which mappings of image feature to audio parameter are most effective?
4. What contextual information does the SoundCeption app need to include to better support blind users to interact with the images?

The evaluations took place in a quiet office space with a desk and comfortable chair using SoundCeption v2.0 on an iPad. The participants were asked to interact with the set of images using the different audio mapping approaches and were asked set questions after interacting with each mapping for all the images.

The first image presented was the sphere image (Fig. 1). This image was used to illustrate the new features of the system – the edge sound, the background sound and the three sound mappings (loudness change only, pitch change only, fusion of loudness and pitch change). Participants were then asked to identify the image and to trace the (silhouette) edge of the sphere and find the point closest to them. The same procedure was then used with the other 3D images (Fig. 4a and b).

The final image used in the evaluation was the 2D map of the University of York campus (Fig. 4c). Participants were introduced to the different sounds for the footpaths, roads, buildings and lake. For the map, text descriptions and labels had not been implemented as sounds, so the researcher provided a Wizard of Oz audio description of building names and important features. Participants were asked to follow the footpath along the lake and explore the layout of the university campus.

Finally, participants were asked for their views about how the system might be developed further and their overall opinion of the SoundCeption App.

4.3 Results

For the 3D images, all the participants preferred the fusion mapping (mapping 3) over the other mappings. Three participants found it easier to detect auditory changes in the fusion sound compared to the other two mappings; the fourth participant noted little difference in detectability between the fusion and the pitch-only mapping, but felt that both were preferable to the volume-only mapping. Further, one participant reported that the fusion mapping was *"aesthetically more pleasing"* than the other approaches.

All participants liked the use of a background sound for the empty image content, particularly for the fusion mapping where the difference between the empty space and image features was more pronounced. Two participants commented that it was effective in telling them that they were on the display, without being distracting. All participants liked the inclusion of a boundary edge sound, although two participants found the particular tone used too intrusive and wanted something more subtle. The participants were also very pleased they could now scan the screen with their fingertips and hear the sounds continuously. This specific improvement meant their need to have the device held in a fixed position was greatly reduced because in v2.0 any slight movements of the device had less impact because their fingers were maintaining constant contact with the image.

All participants found it easy to trace the surface of the sphere, to find the silhouette boundary of the shape in the image (even though no specific silhouette edge sound was included), and to find the point of the sphere that was closest to the viewer. The two participants who lost their sight as adults had no difficulty understanding the shape. However, the two participants who were blind since birth were less confident about the shape of the object, as the pitch/volume change of the curvature of the sphere was confusing. This finding was not surprising, given previously they would have only had access to tactile diagrams with very limited height differentials. Some training with real objects and their equivalent SoundCeption images would be very useful for congenitally blind people to explain these concepts, as well as concepts of depth perception and 2D rendering of perspective.

For the Buddha image, all the participants found it easy to trace the surface via the silhouette edge and immediately recognized the base of the statue was closest to the camera. When informed it was a Buddha figurine, two participants (one adult blind, one congenitally blind) were able to work out the basic anatomy, with one participant identifying features in some detail. One congenitally blind participant thought that the lower pitch/volume head was *"less detailed, not so in focus"* as the higher intensity foreground areas, suggesting a misalignment of the mapping to the visual perspective, where distance was represented by reduced intensity. Further training in the app, specifically in translating the depth-map mapping to real-world perspective, could potentially remedy this issue.

The participants found the mapping approach for the 2D campus map particularly interesting, identifying that encoding different map elements with different types of sounds was highly effective. For example, the lake sound was a deep pitch which was described as *"a bit like a swimming pool"*. Although, this specific auditory quality was not an intentional design choice, the participants felt it an appropriate choice to represent water. In addition, the footpaths were mapped to a high-pitched sound, which participants found was appropriate as it was easy to follow and sounded *"thinner"* than the roads. However, they felt the roads required a more striking sound or urgent sound, as roads represent a potential danger point for blind pedestrians and they felt the mid-range pitch was not distinctive enough. This feedback highlights that designing the sounds to afford an understanding of specific features must be closely aligned with priorities of the target users.

Overall, the participants thought that using SoundCeption v2.0 to explore the campus map demonstrated significant potential. They thought that visually disabled students and visitors could use SoundCeption to study the layout before visiting the campus, allowing them to construct an overview mental model. Participants suggested that students could also use the map to find routes to places that they did not visit regularly. Two participants said they would take the map out with them, particularly if the device would fit in their pocket, so that they could consult it using headphones.

Ultimately, the participants thought SoundCeption has a lot of potential to present image information to blind people, for both 2D and 3D images. They see the applications particularly in the educational, cultural and personal navigation areas. One participant also suggested that the approach could have a very useful application in the music education of visually disabled children, who need to understand the visual notation of music, which they thought could be presented using SoundCeption.

5 Discussion

This initial design and development of SoundCeption shows that the concept of using proprioception and hearing has potential for visually disabled users to explore and understand different features of both 2D and 3D images. The research identified several key user requirements for such a system and demonstrates the importance of adopting a user-centred design approach from early in the design-cycle when developing sensory substitution apps and devices. Changing the interaction from tapping to scanning and adding additional image boundary sounds were all easy to incorporate at the early stage of development.

This research also indicates that minimal training is needed for blind people to be able interpret the content of 2D and 3D images using multi-modal sensory substitution, particularly the depiction of depth in 2D visual representations of 3D objects. Although the SoundCeption concept is more complex for visually disabled people to interpret than a traditional tactile image, due to the multi-modal nature of the app, it was clear that it did not require extensive training. Our evaluations have shown that some training would be needed and useful, but it would not need to be excessive.

Finally, the study shows that with current general-purpose technologies (which are equipped with assistive features such as a screenreader for visually disabled users) it is possible to provide multi-modal sensory substitution functionality a relatively low cost. While full design and development of the SoundCeption app would require investment of time and money, it should be feasible to provide this to users at a reasonable cost. By leveraging contemporary mobile devices, we have transitioned from the era of Bach-y-Rita's pioneering but somewhat cumbersome "dental chair" device, which required room-sized equipment to facilitate tactile vision, to an approach where sensory substitution can be achieved via small, portable devices. This approach offers significant potential for applications in various areas, including educating visually disabled children and young people, and navigational support for both children and adults.

References

1. Bach-y-Rita, P., Collins, C.C., Saunders, F.A., White, B., Scadden, L.: Vision substitution by tactile image projection. Nature **221**, 963–964 (1969). https://doi.org/10.1038/221963a0
2. Bentzen, B.L.: Tangible graphic displays in the education of the blind persons. In: Schiff, W., Foulke, E. (eds.) Tactual perception: a sourcebook. Cambridge University Press (1982)

3. BrainPort Technologies Wicab inc. BrainPort Vision Pro. (2022) https://www.wicab.com/brainport-vision-pro
4. Caraiman, S., Morar, A., Owczarek, M., et al.: Computer vision for the visually impaired: the sound of vision system. Proceedings of the IEEE International Conference on Computer Vision Workshops, pp. 1480–1489 (2017)
5. Chundury, P., Reyazuddin, Y., Jordan, J.B., Lazar, J., Elmqvist, N.: TactualPlot: Spatializing Data as Sound Using Sensory Substitution for Touchscreen Accessibility. IEEE Trans. Visual Comput. Graphics **30**(1), 836–846 (2024). https://doi.org/10.1109/TVCG.2023.3326937
6. Edman, P.K.: Tactile graphics. American Foundation for the Blind, New York (1992)
7. Erp, J.B.V., Veen, H.A.V., Jansen, C., Dobbins, T.: Waypoint navigation with a vibrotactile waist belt. ACM Trans. Appl. Percept. (TAP) **2**(2), 106–117 (2005)
8. Kilian, J., Neugebauer, A., Scherffig, L., Wahl, S.: The unfolding space glove: A wearable spatio-visual to haptic sensory substitution device for blind people. Sensors **22**(5), 1859 (2022)
9. Maćkowski, M., Brzoza, P., Kawulok, M., Meisel, R., Spinczyk, D.: Multimodal presentation of interactive audio-tactile graphics supporting the perception of visual information by blind people. ACM Trans. Multimed. Comput. Commun. Appl. **19**(5s), 1–22 (2023)
10. Meijer, P.B.L.: An experimental system for auditory image representations. IEEE Trans. Biomed. Eng. **39**(2), 112–121 (1992)
11. Microsoft.: Microsoft soundscape. https://www.microsoft.com/en-us/research/product/soundscape/
12. Petrie, H., Bevan, N.: The evaluation of accessibility, usability and user experience. In: Stephanidis, C. (ed.) The Universal Access Handbook. Taylor and Francis, London (2009)
13. Völkel, T., Weber, G., Baumann, U.: Tactile graphics revised: the novel brailledis 9000 pin-matrix device with multitouch input. In: International conference on computers for handicapped persons, pp. 835–842. Springer Berlin Heidelberg, Berlin, Heidelberg (2008)

Integrating Tactons and Tangibles for Haptification of Spreadsheets

Bela Usabaev[1], Nicola Bührich[2](✉), Tutku Can Taş[2], Philipp Ballin[1], and Gerhard Weber[1]

[1] Faculty of Computer Science, Chair of Human-Computer-Interaction, Technische Universität Dresden, 01062 Dresden, Germany
{bela.usabaev,philipp.ballin,gerhard.weber}@tu-dresden.de

[2] BBS Nürnberg - Educational Center for the Blind and Visually Impaired, 90471 Nuremberg, Germany
{Nicola.Buehrich,TutkuCan.Tas}@bbs-nuernberg.de

Abstract. We present a camera-based setup enabling blind or visually impaired users to explore the spatial layout of tabular data with index finger movements on a tactile grid. In a study with 8 participants, three different output modes (vibrating wristband, vibrating plate, speech synthesis) and two levels of complexity in data layouts are compared. Self-reported workload, duration, and errors in placing tangibles corresponding to a vibration pattern or a spoken label show errors increase with layout complexity. Spoken feedback is often faster than the other output modes, though this advantage may be due to a learning effect.

Keywords: haptification · tables · vibration

1 Introduction

Screenreaders provide access to spreadsheet applications, but the spatial layout of tabular data requires a good understanding of the contents and relationships among cells making up a spreadsheet. Empty or merged cells, unspecified labels, and missing headers make it difficult for people who are blind or have low vision to gain an overview, perform common tasks such as finding trends and maxima, or detect irregularities by inspecting a single cell via text-to-speech output. Even if multiple cells can be read on a braille display with 40/80 braille characters, vertical relationships remain to be explored. We present a study in the context of the development of the haptification of spreadsheets to support the hands with palm and all fingers in grasping more information about the horizontal and vertical distribution of information by tactile feedback from microcapsule paper and vibration. [8] have shown in a Wizard-of-Oz study, hands-on interaction in a voice user interface without keyboard operation but voice input can be beneficial to improve non-visual interaction, if voice output can also refer to the position of hands and fingers. In that study, participants explored spreadsheets using magnets as orientation aids, while two team members acting as wizards simulated two

K. Miesenberger et al. (Eds.): ICCHP 2026, LNCS 16867, pp. 380–387, 2027.
https://doi.org/10.1007/978-3-032-31308-9_46

speech assistants for voice-based table navigation. The study aimed to identify preferred input modes voice and gesture as a basis for subsequent assistive technology development. Vibrotactile feedback as a complementary output modality was not yet considered, a gap the present work addresses. Our research questions (RQ) are RQ 1) "How does vibrotactile feedback contribute to the mental model of people who are blind or have low vision about tabular information explored by hands and fingers?" and RQ 2) "Is placement of the vibration on the wrist preferred over a vibrating surface while exploring tabular data by the hand and fingers?". We design several vibration patterns (tactons) and analyze placement of vibration feedback on the user's body for efficient and effective tactile/haptic interaction with cells containing different types of information, resembling numbers, text or formulae.

2 Related Work

Tactile/haptic interaction is well known to people who are blind or have low vision since braille displays were developed in the late 1970s and dynamic changes as well as gestural input have since become possible [4]. Resolution and outline of individual tactile dots have been utilized also for presenting tactile graphics through embossers with thousands of braille dots [7] at a resolution of 2.5 mm typically. Microcapsule paper provides a much finer resolution than embossers achieve. Audiohaptic interaction utilizes such fine textures to convey for example grids and textured tactile graphics as well as verbal content thereby supporting a better spatial understanding [6]. Dynamic tactile feedback is also possible by vibrotactile output. Tactons are an effective tactile method for structured messages conveyed by vibration [1]. A functional line width supporting vibrotactile information detection should be 4 mm and the minimal line width can be just 1 mm [2]. A size of spreadsheet cells of more than 10 mm therefore can be easily detected by a fingertip. Commonly, off-the-shelf devices integrate tactile graphics with spoken feedback and track a single or multiple fingers through touch by projected capacitive sensing technology. While this technology cannot identify the finger used, camera-based approaches allow for reconstructing the skeleton of the hands and support recognizing fingers [9]. The index finger's moving position can be tracked and vibratory feedback can be sensed while fingers are not moving. For people who are blind or have low vision, verbalizing a mental map developed from tactile feedback can be challenging, as verbalization may follow different strategies [3]. In this study, we therefore expect participants to replicate the spatial layout of information [5] using cylindrical tangibles, without requiring verbalization.

3 Methodology

We developed a vibrotactile user interface supporting tracking of an index finger, see Fig. 1, and evaluated it with 8 people who are blind or have low vision using three output modes (two methods of sensing vibration and speech synthesis for a control condition) and with two increasing levels of layout complexity. The setup is based on a camera approx. 75 cm above an A3 sheet of microcapsule paper placed on a thin wooden plate with circular cutouts, displaying a spreadsheet with row and column addresses in braille. In the following we describe the components in more detail.

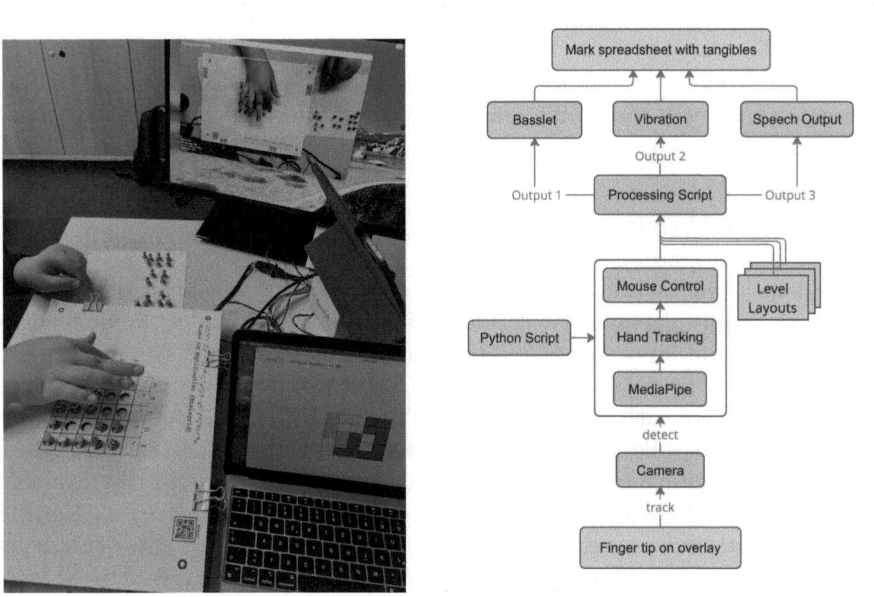

Fig. 1. a) Magnetic tangibles on microcapsule paper grid, camera view on extra screen, and colorized tacton layout at level 2 on laptop. b) Processing of finger tip position for three types of output. (Color figure online)

Tactons for Microcapsule Paper. The prototype consists of a flat wooden support plate with a thickness of approximately 4 mm and an A3 footprint, designed to hold microcapsule paper sheets. To ensure mechanical decoupling from the supporting surface and to improve vibrational isolation, the plate is mounted on leg supports made of soft polymer material, cast from silicone rubber (MoldStar 20T) and function as supports and vibration-damping elements. Four vibrotactile actuators (Lofelt L5-101) are mounted on the underside of the plate in each corner. Each motor is encased in a 3D-printed custom-designed enclosure to ensure precise positioning and mechanical stability. The actuators are driven via an external sound card connected to a four-channel amplifier module. Three distinct vibrotactile patterns (tactons) generated at a fixed frequency of 100 Hz are used to encode cell types, each mapped to a specific tangible with a unique tactile texture and a corresponding speech label:

1) Fast pulse ("number"):Rapid rhythmic vibration sections with equal on/off intervals (vibration:pause ratio 1:1; 200 ms on, 200 ms pause; 150 bpm), represented in blue and assigned to the sandpaper magnet.
2) Medium pulse ("text"):Longer rhythmic vibration sections with very short pauses (vibration:pause ratio 5:1; 500 ms on, 100 ms pause; 100 bpm), represented in red and assigned to the foam rubber magnet.
3) Slow pulse ("formula"):Short rhythmic vibration sections with longer pauses (vibration:pause ratio 2:5; 200 ms on, 500 ms pause; nearly 86 bpm), represented in green and assigned to the smooth magnet.

Initially a fourth tacton was considered to explicitly mark empty cells. This idea was abandoned in favor of a more consistent mapping: the absence of a tangible and the absence of a tacton together represent the concept of an empty cell. The option of a boundary-signalling tacton was ultimately not pursued.

Wrist-Worn Haptic Feedback. As an alternative output modality, vibrotactile feedback is delivered via the Basslet, a bracelet equipped with a Lofelt L5-101 vibration motor. The device can be worn on either hand.

Screenreader Feedback. As a third output modality, speech synthesis provides speech feedback, replacing the vibrotactile signal with the corresponding speech label. In all conditions, output was triggered while touching the circular cutout of a cell with the tracked index finger.

Tracking Fingers and Hands. Input from hands and fingers is detected by a camera with a frequency of 120 fps and controls output signals. Hands are separated from the background (microcapsule paper). A Python script tracks the position of either the left or right index finger using MediaPipe as preferred by the user. Prior to execution, the orientation of microcapsule paper and the position of the user interface window are calibrated, the result is indicated by a green border (see Fig. 1). Based on the tracked finger position, the script controls the system mouse cursor. A control program is implemented in Processing to generate and output vibrotactile signals from mouse hover events. Fig 1a) shows the specification of coloured cells, each color corresponding to one of the three different tactons as described above. The Processing script provides a user interface to adjust relevant output parameters. The control program drives output for both the table-based actuator system and the Basslet.

Tangibles. A central focus of the pilot study was the iterative refinement of the tactile markers (tangibles) and the table layout. The final design featured an additional 4 mm wooden plate on top of the microcapsule paper, with precisely cut circular recesses (∅ 13 mm, depth 4 mm) to accommodate conical metal magnets (base ∅ 12 mm, height 16 mm, graspable portion ∅ 8 mm) that snapped into place like game pieces. To enable haptic differentiation of the three cell types, one third of the magnet tops remained smooth, while the others were fitted with sandpaper and foam rubber, respectively. This final configuration formed the basis for the main study.

Complexity of Information. We designed a set of progressively structured tasks to test whether vibrational feedback could improve participants' spatial understanding of the relationships between cells. As a warm-up, participants detected all three tactons in a 4 × 2 and a 4 × 4 grid. The vibrating wooden plate and the Basslet were alternated as the starting device between participants to ensure randomization. Speech output was always presented last. In each device condition, participants identified the tacton of each cell and marked it by placing the corresponding tangible on top of it. All three test conditions used the same 5 × 5 grid with cells measuring 26 mm × 21.93 mm and consisted of different layouts with two levels of complexity: Level 1 with block-wise (region-based) tacton arrangements and Level 2 with more randomly distributed tacton patterns (see Fig 1).

Table 1. Demographic information with details for each participant: gender (M=male, F=female), visual acuity (TB = totally blind, LB = legally blind, VI = visually impaired), onset of visual impairment and Braille reading skills

part.	birth year	gender	visual acuity	onset	Braille reading
P1	2007	M	LB < 2%	Childhood (4–13)	experienced
P2	2004	M	TB < 2%	Congenital	experienced
P3	2000	M	VI < 30%	Adolescence (14–17)	beginner
P4	2007	M	LB < 2%	Childhood (4–13)	experienced
P5	1992	M	LB < 2%	Congenital	experienced
P6	1995	F	LB < 2%	Childhood (4–13)	none
P7	2005	F	TB < 2%	Congenital	experienced
P8	2005	F	LB < 2%	Childhood (4–13)	experienced

Participants. The eight participants were born between 1992 and 2007 (see Table 1). Five participants identified as male, three as female. Seven classified themselves as blind (visual acuity < 2%), one as visually impaired (visual acuity < 30%). Visual impairment was congenital, occured during childhood, or adolescence. Six participants were right-handed, two left-handed. Two participants reported rare use of vibration as an assistive tool, three reported occasional use, and three frequent use. Regarding smartwatch familiarity, five participants had no prior experience, one used them occasionally, and two regularly. Seven participants were familiar with the matching game Memory, one was not. Experience with computer games involving navigation, spatial orientation, or object placement in virtual environments varied: three participants had no experience, four occasional, and one frequent. Only six were experienced Braille readers.

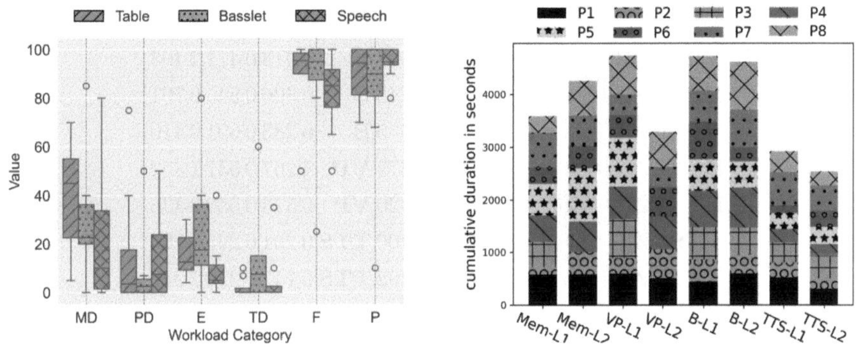

Fig. 2. Box plots for TLX-based scores (left), time needed for each test condition (right).

4 Measurements

We collected subjective workload measurements using a slightly adapted version of the NASA TLX scale measuring mental and physical demand (MD, PD), general effort (E), temporal demand (TD), level of fun (F) - replacing the frustration subscale - and perceived performance (P) in solving the tasks. We further collected the time needed to complete both levels of each condition. The success rate in replicating the spatial arrangement of vibration patterns via three types of tangible magnets was determined by two of the authors independently. No cases of discrepancy were observed.

Workload. Figure 2 (left) shows the user responses for each device: vibrating plate, Basslet and speech. A two-sample t-test for each of the workload categories was not significant across the three devices ($p > 0.17$).

Duration and Error Rate. The time for completing each level condition was limited to 10–12 min. Only after this period, participants were asked to proceed to the next device. Two participants skipped Level 2 (Memory L2) of the warm-up and one participant skipped Level 2 of the VP condition in favor of attempting all devices of the study. The duration of each task across all participants is shown in Fig. 2 (right) (Table 2).

Based on the collected data, performance differed across modalities in both error count and completion time. TTS shows the lowest mean number of errors

Table 2. Error rate (ER) and duration in seconds (d) (ER—d) for each participant for every level and output device, M = modalities, P = participant, VP = vibration plate, B = Basslet, TTS = speech synthesis, TC = task cancelled

M	P1		P3		P5		P7		P8		M	P2		P4		P6	
VP	0	342	1	721	0	315	0	290	0	385	**B**	3	162	0	251	1	212
VP	1	324	TC		13	900	0	468	0	637	**B**	0	313	0	471	2	403
VP	1	492	1	609	7	596	0	314	1	748	**B**	0	306	0	545	0	701
VP	0	458	TC		TC		1	287	0	685	**B**	0	283	0	691	9	410
B	0	397	0	446	1	569	0	439	1	679	**VP**	4	267	0	537	1	352
B	0	238	0	386	2	413	0	428	1	620	**VP**	0	373	0	550	2	438
TTS	0	246	2	358	2	199	0	402	0	400	**TTS**	0	201	0	225	1	186
TTS	0	240	1	317	0	262	0	364	0	292	**TTS**	0	147	0	220	2	240

(0.50 (sd=0.82)) and the shortest mean completion time (269 s (sd=79 s)). The B condition shows intermediate performance in both error count (0.91 (sd=2.00)) and completion time (426 s (sd=157 s)). The VP condition produces the highest mean number of errors (1.50 (sd=3.05)) and the longest mean completion time (479 s (sd=178 s)). Median values show the same general pattern, with error rate median [min-max]: VP = 0.5 [0–13], B = 0 [0–9], TTS = 0 [0–2], and duration median [min-max]: VP = 448 s [267 s-900 s], B = 412 s [162 s-701 s], TTS = 243 s [147 s-402 s]. The larger standard deviation and wider duration range in the VP condition suggest greater variability and less consistent performance across trials. In addition, all three TC cases occur in the VP condition. These findings should be interpreted with caution, because the TTS condition was always performed last and practice or order effects therefore cannot be ruled out.

Qualitative Feedback. Qualitative feedback indicated that participants generally perceived language output as the clearest and most intuitive modality. Vibration-based feedback was often described as noticeable and effective, but some participants reported that it could be distracting or difficult to interpret consistently. Task cancellations were mainly associated with uncertainty about signal meaning or confusion caused by denser layouts.

5 Discussion and Outlook

Placing tangibles into a grid was successfully supported by the improved setup, enabling stable placement for all participants and resulting in high perceived performance and high levels of enjoyment across modalities. Ratings indicate low to moderate mental demand without clear differences between output conditions. In other words, vibration alone can replace screenreader output to allow users to reconstruct the spatial layout of spreadsheets across both complexity levels (RQ 1).

Placement of the vibration actuators does not appear to be crucial (RQ 2), as both the Basslet and the vibrating plate yield comparable task durations and (low) error rates. Vibration-based interaction required more time than spoken feedback, likely due to learning effects rather than modality differences.

We conclude that the effective and efficient use of spoken feedback (the state of the art for screen reader users) is not always error-free, and that vibration offers a comparable alternative. Text-to-speech feedback may benefit from the placement of tangibles. Future work will need to examine learning effects in more detail across varying spreadsheet layouts, while also investigating the impact of higher layout complexity to address potential ceiling effects.

Acknowledgments. The work is funded by the German Federal Ministry of Education and Research (BMBF) under the grant number 16SV9289. Thank you to all the participants for their valuable contributions.

Disclosure of Interests. The authors have no competing interests to declare that are relevant to the content of this article.

References

1. Brown, L.M., Brewster, S.A., Purchase, H.C.: A first investigation into the effectiveness of Tactons. In: First Joint Eurohaptics Conference and Symposium on Haptic Interfaces for Virtual Environment and Teleoperator Systems. World Haptics Conference, pp. 167–176. IEEE (2005)
2. Gorlewicz, J.L., et al.: Design guidelines and recommendations for multimodal, touchscreen-based graphics. ACM Trans. Accessible Comput. (TACCESS) **13**(3), 1–30 (2020)
3. Kim, G., Kim, J., Kim, Y.S.: "explain what a TreeMap is": exploratory investigation of strategies for explaining unfamiliar chart to blind and low vision users. In: Proceedings of the 2023 CHI Conference on Human Factors in Computing Systems, pp. 1–13 (2023)
4. Kipke, S.: Sensitive braille displays with ATC technology (active tactile control) as a tool for learning braille. In: International Conference on Computers for Handicapped Persons, pp. 843–850. Springer (2008)
5. Miao, M., Zeng, L., Weber, G.: Externalizing cognitive maps via map reconstruction and verbal description. Univ. Access Inf. Soc. **16**(3), 667–680 (2017)
6. Parkes, D.: Audio tactile systems for designing and learning complex environments as a vision impaired person: static and dynamic spatial information access. Learn. Environ. Technol.: Sel. Pap. LETA **94**, 219–223 (1994)
7. Schweikhardt, W.: Interaktives erkunden tastbarer grafiken durch blinde. In: Teubner, B.G. (ed.) Software-Erqonomie '85: Mensch-Computer-lnteraktion, pp. 366–375 (1985)
8. Usabaev, B., Bührich, N., Taş, T.C., Weber, G., Ondrusek, P.: Integrating touch, gestures and speech for multi-modal conversations with an audio-tactile graphics reader. In: IFIP Conference on Human-Computer Interaction, pp. 323–332. Springer (2025)
9. Zhang, F., et al.: MediaPipe hands: on-device real-time hand tracking. arXiv preprint: arXiv:2006.10214 (2020)

Hands-On Interaction with Spreadsheets

Bela Usabaev(✉), Sai Gokul Kwataganti Prakash, and Gerhard Weber

Faculty of Computer Science, Chair of Human-Computer-Interaction, Technische Universität Dresden, 01062 Dresden, Germany
{bela.usabaev,gerhard.weber}@tu-dresden.de,
sai_gokul.kwataganti_prakash@mailbox.tu-dresden.de

Abstract. We present a study to propose a multimodal interaction system that allows blind and low-vision users to operate spreadsheet applications using speech and hand gestures on a tactile spreadsheet printed on raised microcapsule paper with braille coordinates without relying on a keyboard. The system combines a voice assistant integrating LLM-backed natural language understanding, gesture recognition via a camera and a spreadsheet application with screenreader function to allow interaction via speech and gesture input. The system is evaluated in a study with 10 blind and low vision participants demonstrating entering numbers, text and formulas and constructing a table in the spreadsheet application via multimodal and synergistic interaction.

Keywords: Multimodal · Gesture · Voice User Interface

1 Introduction

Spreadsheets are a common tool at work and in education for people who are blind or have low vision since screenreaders provide access to these applications. Visual inspection of spreadsheet data is fast in finding anomalies, trends, or in comparing values, for example. In contrast, screenreader users rely on listening to a verbalisation of single cells. Visually simple tasks are not well supported by screenreaders, particularly if spreadsheets contain labelled cells, merged cells, empty cell sets, unlabelled columns and rows of data. For example, it is challenging for students to edit an invoice as a spreadsheet. In Germany as part of vocational training, a typical exam task provides spreadsheet data and formatting instructions as a list and asks to fill a spreadsheet with a title, items, their price and quantity to calculate sum, tax and grand total. For students who are blind or have low vision such a task is challenging as the tax label must be placed properly and the title spans multiple columns. Alternative approaches to gain access to data have been developed, but scalability is still an issue even if alternative text or tactile graphics are produced. Alternative text of charts containing normalized data can be tabular again to provide the basis for performing some data analysis by people who are blind or have low vision. Data can be represented by tactile graphics, and some analytical tasks are supported sufficiently

K. Miesenberger et al. (Eds.): ICCHP 2026, LNCS 16867, pp. 388–396, 2027.
https://doi.org/10.1007/978-3-032-31308-9_47

if they are presented spatially [2,3]. In this work we aim at a better understanding of how gestures and voice input are used with a screenreader to manipulate spreadsheets without a keyboard. Specifically, we want to understand a) if users who are blind or have low vision can edit spreadsheets via gestures and voice input but without a keyboard and b) if multimodal, uni-modal or synergistic approaches are applied.

2 Related Work

Screenreaders extend graphical user interfaces and turn them into a multimodal user interface. Blind users operate applications via keyboard and listen to speech output or read braille output. Sighted users also may use the keyboard or a pointing device and observe the screen [4]. The design space for multimodal systems consists also of a temporal component [5] as input can be multimodal sequentially or in parallel. Screenreaders provide a kind of parallel multimodality but with alternative inputs. [5] refers also to parallel but synergistic multimodality when users utilize for example touch and speech input as in the "Put that there" study [1]. Touchscreens are an absolute pointing device supporting movement of fingers to the target in one step. [7] has shown gestural input on such a touch input device can be fused with speech input to support a more effective form of synergistic interaction. [1] reports on gestures such as circling an area of interest with a single finger for reference by a verbal expression ("here"). Touch and speech input is supported also by screen readers of mobile phones, but only accessible to people who are blind or have low vision if expressed sequentially and without any synergistic fusion. Synergistic multimodal user interfaces can provide access to complex information such as charts using a refreshable large pin array display and speech input [9]. In a Wizard-of-Oz study the concept of an audio-haptic user interface with microcapsule paper and speech as well as gesture input was evaluated successfully [10]. Synergistic multimodality can occur in these studies, but is by no means to be expected all the time by users [6]. While sequential input is slower, sighted users speak differently as remarked already by [6]. It is unclear how blind people express deictic input using gestures and speech when referring verbally to some region of interest. Many gestures are available to control a graphical user interface on a mobile phone such as point, tap, or swipe with one or more fingers. A "rotator" gesture is expressed by a partial circular movement with thumb and forefinger and commonly used to trigger a menu. None of these gestures have a spatial component other than a single point. This is in contrast to two-handed reading of braille and tactile graphics [8]. In the following we present a study with people who are blind or have low vision supporting synergistic multimodal input to control a spreadsheet application using gestures and speech input.

3 Methodology

The system, shown in Fig. 1, supports the users in navigating on the tactile spreadsheet via gestures and speech feedback and input number, text and formula values in the spreadsheet application read out by the screen reader. We use a tactile graphic to connect user's gestures across the haptic spreadsheet coordinates with the system via gesture recognition and spoken input coordinates. The haptic spreadsheet is printed on microcapsule paper in A3 format with the individual cells represented by raised squares of 6×6 mm, approximately the size of a fingertip. Coordinates (letter, number) appear as row and column headers in braille, see Fig. 2 for an example.

3.1 Apparatus/System Overview

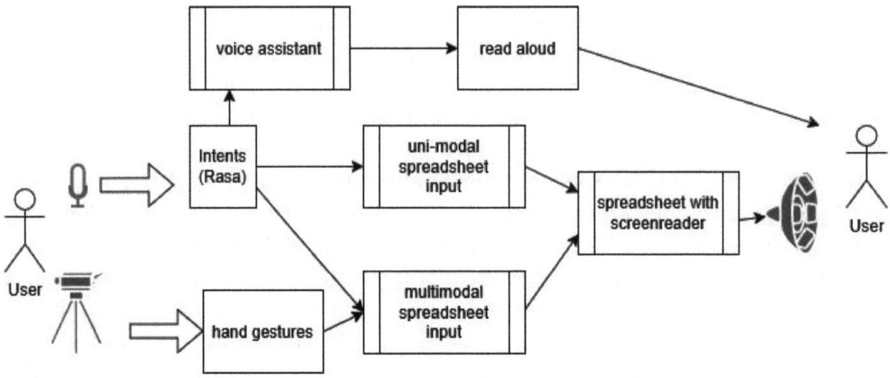

Fig. 1. Multimodal processing of gestures and voice input.

Speech Processing and Natural Language Understanding. The voice assistant uses the Rasa framework[1] as a backend for natural language understanding (NLU) and the modelling of the dialogue between the screen reader user and the system. The intents to input a number, a text or a formula and the cell are encoded as individual dialogue flows or a sequence of speech turns between the user and the system in the rasa dialogue system, extracting the relevant slots in the user's utterance containing the relevant speech inputs: number, cell, text and formula. Processing of the dialogue takes place in a restricted rule-based manner according to the automatically recognized flow to be used, while the transcript or user's utterance is being processed by a large language model (LLM), as part of the Rasa CALM system[2]. This way the user can utter their intents unrestricted using more free, subjective and colloquial speech patterns. The voice assistant is further comprised of a speech processing and slot fusion unit. The speech is processed via a laptop microphone using the assemblyAI[3]

[1] https://rasa.com/platform.
[2] https://www.rasa.com/docs/learn/concepts/calm.
[3] https://www.assemblyai.com/research/universal-1.

speech processing library, which works with a minimal delay to produce robust ASR recognition, outputting the transcript in an incremental manner. The voice assistant communicates via a websocket with the local Rasa server and is running the ASR component as the main process, processing the responses from the server. The collected data slots and the response from Rasa are returned back to the voice assistant (process) and are used to manipulate the concurrently running spreadsheet server application, to enter the spoken and selected values into the spreadsheet via a websocket connection. The screen reader of the spreadsheet application registers and returns the spreadsheet inputs to the user via speech feedback[4]. The Rasa LLM response is kept for further interaction, but is not utilized in the current study. The following intents are encoded as flows in the Rasa system:

- input [number — text — formula] @ cell
- input [number — text — formula] “here”

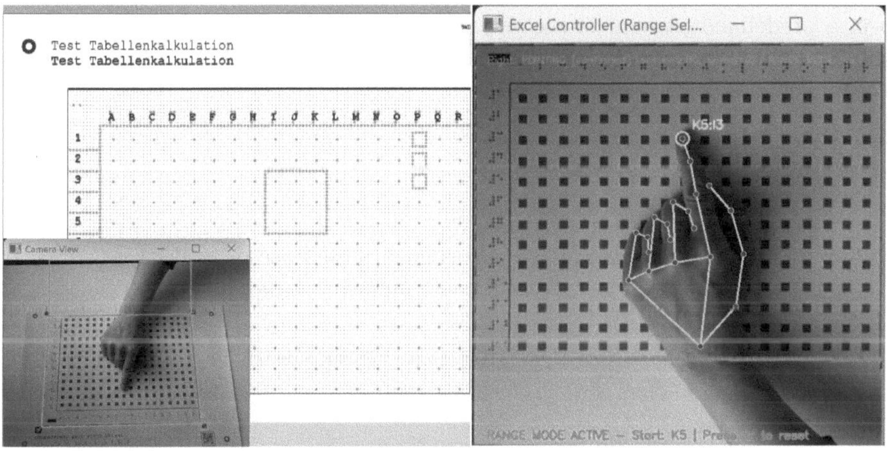

Fig. 2. Controlling a spreadsheet application by hand gestures.

Gesture Recognition Module. The voice assistant further communicates with the gesture recognition module via a websocket connection. The gesture recognition module is implemented using MediaPipe[5] and is following the hand movements on the haptic spreadsheet via a webcam camera, tracking whether the currently tracked finger, e.g. the index finger, is over a cell of the spreadsheet, sending data when a point gesture is recognized. The current cell is being sent as a cell select command to the spreadsheet application to be registered by the

[4] https://www.tactonom.com/.

[5] https://ai.google.dev/edge/mediapipe.

screen reader and is being tracked in the voice assistant system as context. The module also supports a span mode for selecting a range of cells. The user activates span mode through a voice command. Once in span mode, the user performs point gestures over the start cell to mark it. After that, as the user drags their finger across the spreadsheet, the range from the start cell to the current cell is continuously updated in the spreadsheet application via a websocket connection dynamically reading out the selected range, similar to how range selection in spreadsheets works by touch on mobile devices. When the user exits span mode, the last selected range stays highlighted in the spreadsheet. The span mode is shown in Fig. 2

Multimodal Processing of Inputs. The processing of multimodal inputs is based on resolving deictic pronouns in the spoken inputs. The voice assistant is registering when a deictic input such as "this" or "here" has been made and is checking the currently tracked cell. In this way the system can take into account cell inputs made via point gesture as well as via speech. Only inputs within the range of 20–60 s are taken into account, i.e. if the current cell is not updated for over a predefined amount of seconds, it will not be associated with the current speech input (see Table 1).

4 Participants

Table 1. Demographic data of the participants, visual acuity is given according to German legislation regulations. Screen reader abbreviated as SR., gen = gender.

part.	birth year	gen.	visual acuity	onset	gesture usage on mobile SR	Siri/Alexa usage	Excel usage	Braille skills
P1	2005	F	<2%	cong.	often	often	often	exp.
P2	2007	F	<5%	cong.	often	often	often	exp.
P3	2004	M	<2%	infant	often	often	often	exp.
P4	2004	M	<5%	child	rarely	occ.	occ.	beg.
P5	2000	F	<2%	infant	often	occ.	occ.	exp.
P6	2007	M	<2%	cong.	often	rarely	occ.	exp.
P7	1992	M	<2%	child	often	often	occ.	beg.
P8	1995	F	<30%	cong.	no	no	no	no
P9	1987	F	<30%	adult	no	no	no	beg.
P10	2006	M	>30%	teenager	no	no	occ.	no

We recruited 10 participants, 5 male and 5 female with birth year ranging from 1987 to 2007 (sd=7.02) from a vocational education center for blind and visually impaired students. 4 congenitally blind, 2 with onset of visual impairment as an infant, 2 as a child, 1 as an adult and 1 as teenager. We asked to self-report given the blindness identification according to German legislation, i.e. legally blind: visual acuity (VA) <2%, severely visually impaired: VA <5%, visually impaired: VA <30% and partially sighted: VA > 30%. 7 reported as right-handed, 1 left-handed, and 2 both left and right-handed. 6 reported to be in vocational training for massage and physiotherapy course, 2 in vocational training for office professions, and 2 in the preparatory vocational course. We further asked to report usage of screen readers (VoiceOver or Talkback) along with gestures on smartphones, and voice assistant usage, such as Siri or Alexa, as well as experience with spreadsheet applications. Braille reading skills varied between no usage, beginner and experienced.

	A	B	C	O	P	Q	R
1	Abteilung	Kosten			A1:Abteilung		
2	Reinigung	120			B2: Summe der Kosten		
3	Wäschedienst	140			A5: Gesamt		
4	Massage	360					
5	Gesamt	620					
6							

Fig. 3. Example of a finished task 2 and the task instructions in column P on the right.

5 Study Setup and Procedure

We conducted the study with 10 blind and low vision participants in 10 consecutive sessions of 1.5 h each, where the participants were asked to solve 5 tasks using the system. Each session started with collecting demographic data, reading and signing a privacy declaration. We then asked the participants to listen to screen reader feedback and system sounds via headphones and use a clip-on microphone for voice inputs, introducing the haptic spreadsheet and span and speech mode. The tasks were structured as follows: a) initial exploration (try out spoken mode commands, try out touch gestures and screenreader, get familiar with system sonification), b) test span mode, c) input random values in random locations in empty spreadsheet using speech mode, 1) input a set of given values from a list in a given location (3 number, text and formula values each with an associated cell address listed in columns O, P and Q), 2) construct a table from a partial set of given values (3 headings for a 2 by 5 table listed in column P, given column headings and their locations, fill table with own values, make a final calculation summing up own values for the result cell), see task and example of a finished table in Fig. 3. No time limit was set to solve the tasks. The tasks were moderated and introduced gradually with every new xlsx spreadsheet template opened in the spreadsheet application. System responses were read aloud to the participants after the screenreader ended.

6 Analysis and Measurements

The sessions were screen and video recorded and transcribed using MAXQDA[6]. The transcripts were used as subtitles for the session video recordings to mark the occurrences of the voice input intents and point and hold gestures using DaVinci Resolve[7].

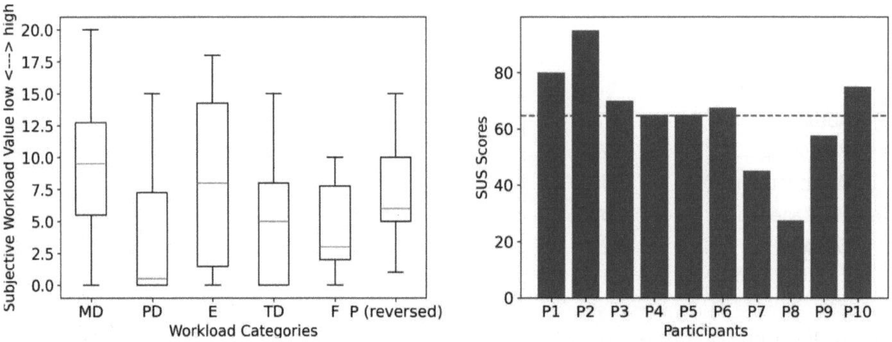

Fig. 4. TLX and SUS scores for the system (mean SUS score = 64,75).

Participants demonstrated both unimodal and synergistic use of voice as well as gestural input. Typical utterances for uni-modal voice input were: "Input in cell K5 the number 3" (Trage in die Zelle K5 die Zahl 3 ein) (P1), "Enter 350 in K4" (Trage 350 in K4 ein) (P2), synergistic point gesture and voice input: "Enter here the value 10" (Trage hier die Zahl 10 ein), "Calculate here the sum from B2 to B4" (Bilde hier die Summe von B2 bis B4), "Enter here the text sum of the costs" (Trage hier den Text Summe der Kosten ein) (P1), "Enter here the sum from D6 to D3" (Trage hier die Summe von D6 bis D3 ein) (P2). Some participants preferred synergistic use of pointing to a cell to enter numbers, text and formulas, e.g. entering text synergistically pointing to a cell 17 times (P1), while other participants preferred the uni-modal speech mode, e.g. entering text by speaking the cell address 16 times (P2), and 4 times using "here" (P2). Some participants used a multimodal but not synergistic mode of interaction, e.g. navigating to the relevant cell address, holding or pointing to it and speaking the cell value and address (P3). Modifier words specifying the value type, e.g. "number" for numerical values, "text", "word" or "phrase" for text values, "formula" for sum formulas and "cell" for addresses consistently led to better intent recognition, e.g. (enter) "number" [number] in "cell" [cell] or (enter) "text" [text] "here". We collected TLX workload and SUS scores, shown in Fig. 4, after completing task 2 and asked for free feedback. The mean SUS score is 64,75 ranging slightly below 68, the standard usability value, indicating that

[6] https://www.maxqda.com.

[7] https://www.blackmagicdesign.com/de/products/davinciresolve.

improvements should be made. The TLX scores show a higher mental demand (MD), ranging widely across participants, a lower physical demand, a widely ranged effort similar to MD, lower frustration and a less widely ranging good to intermediate subjective performance. Nearly all participants finished task 1 and 2, one participant had persisting difficulties to make inputs via speech.

7 Discussion

Figure 4 shows the TLX and SUS scores for the system. The system created a mental workload as participants had to memorize the tasks while navigating to the relevant locations in the spreadsheet to make the inputs. As gesture detection is affected by noise, the location of the index finger on cells sometimes had to be readjusted. The LLM-backed intent classification of the Rasa CALM system can lead to semantically connected, but wrong intents, such as understanding costs or total to stand for formulas and not text labels for cells. Speaking modifier words before cell values solved this problem during interaction. The higher SUS scores indicate that the possibility to access and manipulate the spreadsheet application via a haptic interface and speech is effective, however speech and intent recognition was lacking for non-native speakers and the uncommon task presentation led to low SUS score for some participants.

8 Limitations

The users are required to make inputs using a single input utterance. The possibility of a short dialogue consisting of several dialogue turns would make the process of entering values and the system more flexible. Storing the task instruction list inside the spreadsheet might create more mental workload overhead than printing the list out in Braille or in a separate text file accessible via a braille display. The spreadsheet design was ambiguous for some users, e.g. grooves perceived as cells. We evaluated the system only using German, while the speech processing model is universal. Persons with speech impediment need a possibility to adapt the system further.

Acknowledgments. The work is funded by the German Federal Ministry of Education and Research (BMBF) under the grant number 16SV9289. Thank you to all the participants for their valuable contributions.

Disclosure of Interests. The authors have no competing interests to declare that are relevant to the content of this article.

References

1. Bolt, R.A.: "put-that-there": voice and gesture at the graphics interface. SIGGRAPH Comput. Graph. **14**(3), 262–270 (1980). https://doi.org/10.1145/965105.807503

2. Chen, M.K., Pedraza Pineros, I., Satyanarayan, A., Zong, J.: Tactile Vega-lite: rapidly prototyping tactile charts with smart defaults. In: Proceedings of the 2025 CHI Conference on Human Factors in Computing Systems. CHI '25. Association for Computing Machinery, New York (2025). https://doi.org/10.1145/3706598.3714132
3. Engel, C., Weber, G.: Improve the accessibility of tactile charts. In: Bernhaupt, R., Dalvi, G., Joshi, A., K. Balkrishan, D., O'Neill, J., Winckler, M. (eds.) Human-Computer Interaction - INTERACT 2017, pp. 187–195. Springer International Publishing, Cham (2017)
4. Mynatt, E.D., Weber, G.: Nonvisual presentation of graphical user interfaces: contrasting two approaches. In: Proceedings of the SIGCHI Conference on Human Factors in Computing Systems, CHI '94, pp. 166–172. Association for Computing Machinery, New York (1994). https://doi.org/10.1145/191666.191732
5. Nigay, L., Coutaz, J.: A design space for multimodal systems: concurrent processing and data fusion. In: Proceedings of the INTERACT '93 and CHI '93 Conference on Human Factors in Computing Systems, CHI '93, pp. 172–178. Association for Computing Machinery, New York (1993). https://doi.org/10.1145/169059.169143
6. Oviatt, S.: Ten myths of multimodal interaction. Commun. ACM **42**(11), 74–81 (1999). https://doi.org/10.1145/319382.319398
7. Oviatt, S.: Multimodal interfaces. In: Sears, A., Jacko, J., Jacko, J. (eds.) The Human-Computer Interaction Handbook: Fundamentals, Evolving Technologies and Emerging Applications, chap. 21, pp. 439–458. CRC Press, Boca Raton, 2 edn. (2007). https://doi.org/10.1201/9781410615862
8. Prescher, D., Bornschein, J., Köhlmann, W., Weber, G.: Touching graphical applications: bimanual tactile interaction on the HyperBraille pin-matrix display. Univers. Access Inf. Soc. **17**, 391–409 (2018). https://doi.org/10.1007/s10209-017-0538-8
9. Reinders, S., Butler, M., Zukerman, I., Lee, B., Qu, L., Marriott, K.: When refreshable tactile displays meet conversational agents: investigating accessible data presentation and analysis with touch and speech. IEEE Trans. Visual Comput. Graphics **31**(1), 864–874 (2025). https://doi.org/10.1109/tvcg.2024.3456358
10. Usabaev, B., Bührich, N., Taş, T.C., Weber, G., Ondrusek, P.: Integrating touch, gestures and speech for multi-modal conversations with an audio-tactile graphics reader. In: Human-Computer Interaction – INTERACT 2025: 20th IFIP TC 13 International Conference, Belo Horizonte, Brazil, 8–12 September 2025, Proceedings, Part III, pp. 323–332. Springer-Verlag, Berlin (2025). https://doi.org/10.1007/978-3-032-05005-2_17

Expiration Date Recognition System Using YOLO and STN for the Visually Impaired

Yoshinori Takeuchi(✉) and Kengo Suzuki

Daido University, 10-3 Takiharu-cho Minami-ku, Nagoya, Japan
ytake@daido-it.ac.jp

Abstract. Visually impaired individuals face significant challenges in daily activities such as shopping because they struggle to access essential product details like expiration dates. To address this, we propose an automatic expiration date recognition system that utilizes a two-stage neural network pipeline. The first stage employs the YOLOv12n architecture for high-precision detection within complex backgrounds. This model was evaluated using a dataset of 1,775 images collected from real supermarket environments. In inference experiments using 178 test images, the detection stage achieved a 100% success rate in accurately identifying the bounding box of the expiration date. The second stage utilizes a Convolutional Neural Network (CNN) integrated with a Spatial Transformer Network (STN) for numeric recognition. To prepare this stage, 90,000 synthesized images featuring random rotations and translations were used for training to ensure robustness against camera distortions common when visually impaired users capture images. The system consists of six STN-CNN units, where the STNs automatically correct the alignment of each digit for the CNNs to process. In a comprehensive evaluation using 1,054 test images, the system achieved a recognition accuracy of 95.64%, demonstrating high reliability for practical assistive use.

Keywords: Character recognition · Expiration Date · You Look Only Once · Spatial Transformer Network

1 Introduction

Visually impaired individuals often face significant challenges in daily activities such as shopping, which relies heavily on visual information. While many can navigate to product shelves independently by memorizing store layouts [1], they frequently struggle to access essential details, including product names, prices, and expiration dates. To address this, we propose a system designed to provide such information, thereby empowering them to shop more independently.

Previous literature has explored various methodologies for expiration date recognition. Seker et al. developed a comprehensive dataset of 1,767 images

K. Miesenberger et al. (Eds.): ICCHP 2026, LNCS 16867, pp. 397–404, 2027.
https://doi.org/10.1007/978-3-032-31308-9_48

featuring 12,000 date samples to train models on 13 different display formats, achieving a recognition rate of 97.74% [2]. Zheng et al. proposed a character detection algorithm using DBNet (a segmentation-based text detection method) as the base network, combined with the Convolutional Block Attention Module to improve its feature extraction of characters in complex contexts, reaching 97.9% accuracy on a Jetson Nano implementation [3]. Takeuchi and Suzuki proposed a combination of Region-based Convolutional Neural Networks (CNNs) and Spatial Transformer Networks (STNs) [4] to handle dot-matrix characters, achieving 98.44% accuracy [5]. Mobile-centric approaches have also emerged, such as Hao et al.'s lightweight Android application using a Convolutional Recurrent Neural Network [6] and Dospinescu et al.'s household food management system which integrates Google's Firebase ML Kit with CNN-based classification [7].

Most existing systems utilize a two-stage pipeline: first, detecting the expiration date region within a cluttered background, and second, recognizing the numeric characters within that region. While state-of-the-art Vision Language Models (VLMs) like ChatGPT or Gemini show impressive performance, they often require significant computational resources and stable internet connectivity, leading to unacceptable latency for real-time assistive applications. In contrast, our proposed system employs the lightweight You Look Only Once (YOLO)v12n [8], optimized for edge devices to provide instantaneous feedback. Furthermore, unlike general-purpose OCR applications that struggle with dot-matrix fonts common on food packaging, our specialized pipeline is specifically trained on these challenging formats.

2 Expiration Date Recognition System

2.1 Overview

The proposed system is designed to recognize the expiration dates of products and output the information via audio to assist visually impaired users. As illustrated in Fig. 1, the process consists of two primary neural network stages: a detection stage and a recognition stage.

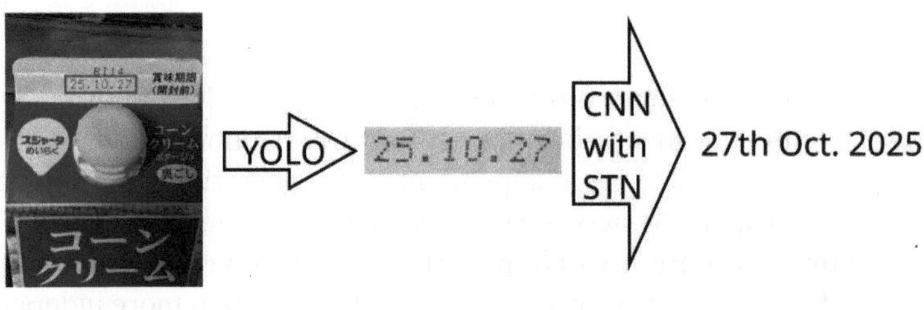

Fig. 1. Process of expiration date recognition.

2.2 Detection Stage Using YOLOv12

In the first stage, the system identifies the bounding box containing the expiration date from the input image. We utilize YOLOv12n, which represents the latest advancement in real-time object detection architecture. This model is particularly effective at focusing on relevant features within noisy environments, ensuring that the target date is accurately isolated before being passed to the recognition stage.

2.3 Recognition Stage Using CNN and STN

The second stage processes the cropped image to recognize the numeric characters. We employ a Convolutional Neural Network (CNN) integrated with a Spatial Transformer Network (STN). The STN plays a vital role in this system by providing automatic distortion correction for skews and rotations, which frequently occur when visually impaired users capture images at suboptimal angles.

2.4 Contribution of the Proposed System

The design and implementation of the proposed system lead to several significant contributions, which are summarized below:

1. high-precision detection with YOLOv12: By integrating the state-of-the-art YOLOv12 architecture, the system leverages advanced attention mechanisms to distinguish expiration dates from noisy backgrounds. This enables the system to achieve high-precision detection, resulting in a 100% success rate in our inference experiments.
2. optimized for real-time use: Unlike VLMs such as ChatGPT or Gemini, which require substantial computational resources and introduce latency, our system utilizes lightweight models (YOLOv12n and CNN-STN). This ensures that the recognition can be performed efficiently, making it suitable for future integration into mobile applications.
3. robustness in assistive technology: The combination of precise detection and STN-based distortion correction addresses the practical challenges faced by visually impaired users. By ensuring that even imperfectly captured images can be processed reliably, this research provides a robust foundation for independent shopping assistance.

3 Experimental Results

3.1 Training

Detection Stage. For the detection stage, we captured 1,775 images of the various products featuring expiration date. These images were manually collected using a smartphone camera within a real-world supermarket environment; this was done to ensure the model could account for diverse lighting conditions, varying angles, and complex shelf backgrounds.

To reduce computational overhead and ensure consistent input dimensions, all images were resized to 300×400 pixels. The dataset was randomly partitioned into a training set of 1,420 images (80%), a validation set of 177 images (10%), and a test set of 178 images (10%). We adopted a simple hold-out validation approach.

Regarding the model architecture, we utilized the YOLOv12n variant and conducted the training process over a duration of 100 epochs. All other hyper-parameters were maintained at the default values specified in the official YOLOv12n configuration.

Recognition Stage. For the recognition stage, we first prepared a preliminary dataset by cropping 100 images for each digit from 0 to 9. These images were used to pre-train the CNN component. Table 1 provides the detailed architecture of the recognition CNN. For pre-training, the dataset was split into 80 images for training, 10 for validation, and 10 for testing. The batch size was 100 and trained the model for 10,000 epochs. The categorical cross-entropy loss function was minimized using the Adadelta optimizer.

Table 1. Detailed implementation of the recognition CNN

layer	no. of filters/units	kernel size	activation
Conv2D	32	3×3	relu
Conv2D	32	3×3	relu
BatchNormalization			
MaxPooling		2×2	
DropOut			
Conv2D	32	3×3	relu
Conv2D	32	3×3	relu
BatchNormalization			
MaxPooling		2×2	
DropOut			
Flatten			
Dense	255		relu
Dense	10		softmax

We synthesized the date images to increase the number of training images and to improve the recognition of future dates. We applied random translations and rotations to simulate real-world distortions, such as skewed, misaligned, or partially missing characters. We synthesized 90,000 images for training and 10,000 images for validation. Examples of the synthesized images are shown in Fig. 2. These images were used to train the date recognition network.

The complete date recognition neural network consists of six STNs, each followed by an dedicated CNN. All six STNs are identical except for the output

Fig. 2. example of synthesized training images. The images are translated and rotated randomly.

bias, which are initialized to focus on corresponding segment of the expiration date image. Each STN outputs the rectified digit image with a resolution of 16×32 pixels, which is subsequently processed by the CNN for classification. The detailed implementation of the localization network within each STN is summarized in Table 2. The output of this network is the probability of the corresponding number. Combine the outputs of the six CNNs to obtain the final expiration date.

Table 2. Detailed implementation of the localisation network

layer	no. of filters/units	kernel size	activation
Conv2D	8	7×7	relu
MaxPooling		2×2	
Conv2D	10	5×5	relu
MaxPooling		2×2	
Dense	32		relu
Dense	6		linear

During the final training phase, the batch size was set to 100, and training was conducted for up to 100 epochs. To prevent overfitting, an early stopping mechanism was employed, terminating the process if the validation loss failed to improve for five consecutive epochs. The total loss function was defined as the sum of the six categorical cross-entropy losses, and the Adam optimizer was used for parameter updates.

3.2 Results and Discussion

Detection Stage. The training metrics for the detection part are presented in Fig. 3. Starting from the top left, the charts illustrate the transition of box loss, classification loss, and DFL (Distribution Focal Loss) during training, followed by precision and recall. From the bottom left, the charts show the validation results for box loss, classification loss, and DF loss, as well as the mean Average Precision at an IoU threshold of 50% (mAP50) and the mean Average Precision across IoU thresholds from 50% to 95% (mAP50-95).

Regarding the training loss, the values exhibit a steady decline, indicating that the learning process is proceeding effectively. The initial low validation loss is likely an artifact of the early training phase and does not represent true convergence. Subsequently, the loss increases temporarily before converging to a lower value starting from approximately the 45th epoch. Similarly, the precision,

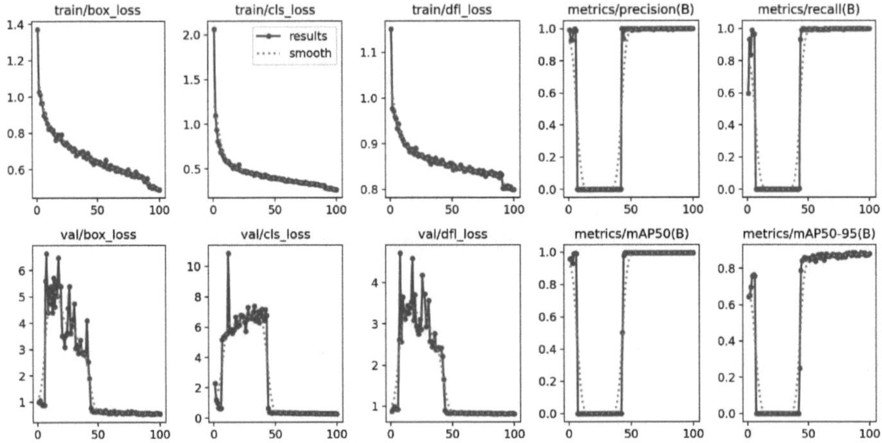

Fig. 3. Training and validation metrics over epochs. The plots include box loss, classification loss, and DF loss for both training and validation sets, along with precision, recall, mAP50, and mAP50–95.

recall, and mAP values initially showed high results by chance, followed by a temporary decrease, and have been improving again since around the 45th epoch.

We conducted an inference experiment by using the test set of 178 images. A detection is considered correct if only the date is identified within the image. If multiple dates are detected, the result is counted as a correct answer provided that at least one detection accurately identifies only the date. Conversely, cases where no date is detected or where the detection bounding box contains non-date elements are classified as incorrect. As a result, inference was successful for all 178 images, achieving a precision of 100%. Figure 4 shows examples of detection results.

Fig. 4. examples of detection results. The text "date" represents the object label, followed by the confidence score.

Recognition Stage. Figure 5 shows the accuracy and loss curves for the recognition stage. Due to the use of pre-training, the training process was remarkably rapid, reaching the early stopping criteria in only six epochs.

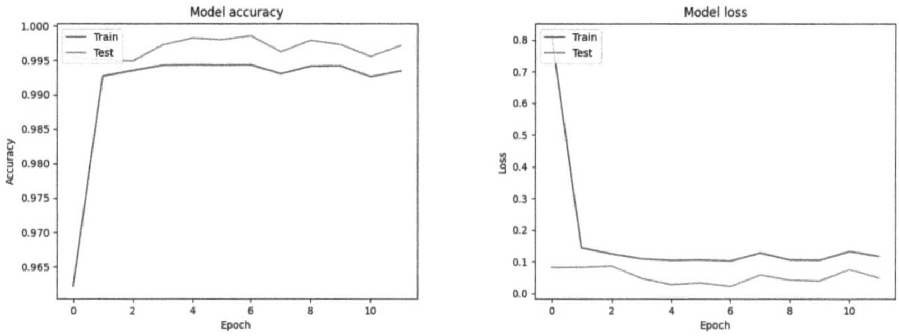

Fig. 5. Training loss and accuracy for date recognition network.

Inference was conducted on 1,054 images that were not included in the training dataset. A trial is considered successful only if all six digits are correctly identified; otherwise, it is classified as an incorrect result. Consequently, 1,008 images were successfully recognized, achieving an accuracy of 95.64%. Table 3 presents examples of images and their recognition result.

Table 3. Recognition examples of expiration date

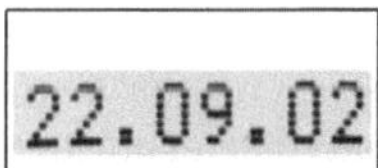	220902	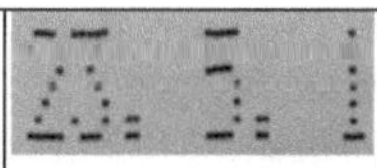	230501	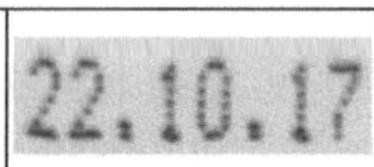	221017
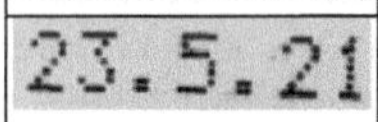	235521	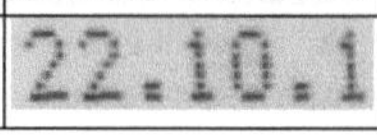	220101	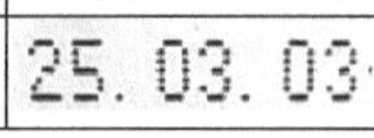	250308

The results demonstrate a high recognition rate for date identification. The errors were characterized by the confusion of similar-looking numerals (e.g., recognizing "3" as "8") and digit-level misidentifications. It is anticipated that these errors can be mitigated by increasing the volume and diversity of the training data.

Regarding the user interface, the high-speed inference of our model serves as a foundation for a future smartphone application. This app will incorporate real-time audio guidance, such as 'Take a photo of the opposite side' or 'Move the camera slightly to the right,' based on the detection result provided by the YOLO stage."

4 Conclusion

In this paper, we proposed an expiration date recognition system using YOLO and STN to assist visually impaired individuals in shopping independently. The system consists of two main stages: a detection stage that identifies the date region from complex backgrounds using YOLOv12n, and a recognition stage that employs STN for distortion correction followed by a CNN for character recognition. The experimental results demonstrated the effectiveness of the proposed approach, achieving a high detection rate of 100% and a recognition accuracy of 95.64%. The use of YOLOv12n is quite useful for the detection of the expiration date.

For future work, we plan to implement an audio feedback interface to convey the recognized information to users. Furthermore, we aim to develop a smartphone-based application and conduct usability evaluations with visually impaired participants to verify the system's effectiveness and practical utility in real-world shopping environments.

References

1. Tanaka, N., Doi, Y., Matsumoto, T., Takeuchi, Y., Kudo, H., Ohnishi, N.: A system helping the blind to get merchandise information. In: Miesenberger, K., Karshmer, A., Penaz, P., Zagler, W. (eds.) ICCHP 2012. LNCS, vol. 7383, pp.596–598. Springer, Cham (2012). https://doi.org/10.1007/978-3-642-31534-3_87
2. Seker, A.C., Ahn, C.A.: A generalized framework for recognition of expiration on product packages using fully convolutional networks. Expert Syst. Appl. **203**, 117310 (2022). https://doi.org/10.1016/j.eswa.2022.117310
3. Zheng, J., Li, J., Ding, Z., Kong, L., Chen, Q.: Recognition of expiry data on food packages based on improved DBNet. Connect. Sci. **35**(1), 1–16 (2023). https://doi.org/10.1080/09540091.2023.2202363
4. Jaderberg, M., Simonyan, K., Zisserman, A., Koray, K.: Spatial transformer networks. In: Cortes, C., Lawrence, N.D., Lee, D.D., Sugiyama, M., and Garnett, R. (eds.) Advances in Neural Information Processing Systems 28, pp. 2017–2025. Curran Associates, Inc. (2015)
5. Takeuchi, Y., Suzuki, K.: Expiration date recognition system using spatial transformer network for visually impaired. In: Miesenberger, K., Peňáz, P., Kobayashi, M. (eds.) ICCHP 2024. LNCS, vol. 14750, pp. 517–524. Springer, Heidelberg (2024). https://doi.org/10.1007/978-3-031-62846-7_61
6. Peng, H., Bayon, J., Recas, J., Guijarro, M.: Efficient expiration date recognition in food packages for mobile applications. Algorithms **18**(5) (2025). https://doi.org/10.3390/a18050286
7. Dospinescu, O., Grigorcea, G.-L., Lefter, B.-I.: A mobile approach to food expiration date determination using OCR and on-cloud image classification. Appl. Syst. Innov. **8**(176) (2025). https://doi.org/10.3390/asi8060176
8. Tian, Y., Ye, Q., Doermann, D.: YOLOv12: attention-centric real-time object detectors. arXiv:2502.12524

Interaction Techniques for Motor Disabled Users

Text Entry Using a Scanning Keyboard and Squeezable Bulb

I. Scott MacKenzie(✉) and Sarika Patel

Department of Electrical Engineering and Computer Science, York University, Toronto, Canada
mack@yorku.ca, sarikap@my.yorku.ca

Abstract. A squeezable bulb as an input device for controlling an ABC scanning keyboard was evaluated. The keyboard included word completion with six candidates words offered for early selection. Twelve participants entered five text phrases per session, over five sessions. To promote learning, the scanning interval decreased over the five sessions, beginning at 900 ms in session 1 and finishing at 500 ms in session 5. Entry speed increased by 50%, from 3.01 wpm in the first session to 4.51 wpm in the last session. Error rates were extremely low at 0.2% overall. Efficiency was modest at 79.4% indicating participants missed opportunities to enter predicted words at the earliest opportunity. Further practice is expected to improve efficiency and increase entry speed.

Keywords: Accessible technologies · scanning keyboard · text input · single-switch input · squeezable bulb input device · rubber bulb input device

1 Introduction

Single-switch scanning on a virtual keyboard is a common method for accessible text entry. Keys are highlighted in sequence ("scanned") and selected with an input switch when the key bearing the desired character is highlighted. Common techniques to speed-up entry include (a) using a two-tier scanning pattern with row scanning followed by column scanning to reach the desired letter and (b) offering a list of candidate words as input proceeds letter-by-letter [5, pp. 103–107]. Another technique to speed-up entry is to organize the layout with high-frequency letters (e.g., *e*, *a*, or *t*, for English) near the beginning of the scanning sequence [2,3,7,10,11]. Such "optimized" layouts reduce the number of scan steps to reach letters. One downside is the unfamiliar letter arrangement. This adds visual search to the interaction for novice users. The research described herein avoids this by using an alphabetic arrangement (described below).

As technology evolves, there comes the need to make advancements accessible to all users. Many technologies require novel input methods due to motor limitations in the user's hands or arms. Our work tests a novel input method that requires just one hand grasping and squeezing a rubber bulb.

K. Miesenberger et al. (Eds.): ICCHP 2026, LNCS 16867, pp. 407–418, 2027.
https://doi.org/10.1007/978-3-032-31308-9_49

2 Input Using a Squeezable Bulb

A proof-of-concept implementation or our squeezable bulb apparatus is shown in Fig. 1. The device was used in an earlier study by Chen Liu et al. [1]. Their study compared four input sensors: a button, an accelerometer, a flex sensor, and a squeezable bulb connected to a pressure sensor [1]. The task was text entry, using a Qwerty layout keyboard and without word prediction. Results indicated that among the four types of sensors, the button had the fastest entry speed and was the most efficient. Based on user feedback, it was also the most preferred among participants, as it was the most liked, least fatiguing, and considered comfortable. Although the button performed the best overall, the study presented herein focuses on the pressure sensor as it is a viable and adaptable option for people with motor impairments. The other sensors in the earlier study required more refined motor dexterity.

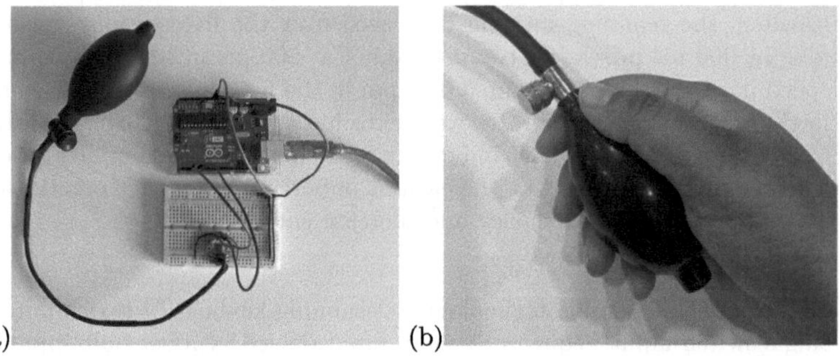

(a) (b)

Fig. 1. Squeezable bulb pressure-sensing apparatus. (a) Via a rubber hose, the bulb attaches to an HX710 pressure sensor and an Arduino UNO board. Squeezing the bulb passes on a "click" event to the host computer. (b) A participant gripping the squeezable bulb.

The research described herein extended the work of Chen Liu et al. [1] in several ways. Rather than a Qwerty keyboard, we used a soft keyboard with an alphabetic layout having letters arranged on just two rows, A-M along the top row and N-Z along the second row. Below the letters a row of candidate words appeared and below that command keys for correcting mistakes and ENTER. See Fig. 2. The candidate words in the figure are the six most common words in English. This list appears before entry of a word, but is updated as letters are added while forming a word.

2.1 SPC as an Analytic Metric

Scansteps per character (SPC) is a useful metric for scanning keyboards [4]. There are two uses for SPC. The first, presented here, treats SPC as an analytic metric. The calculation is done a priori, without user testing, and is done for

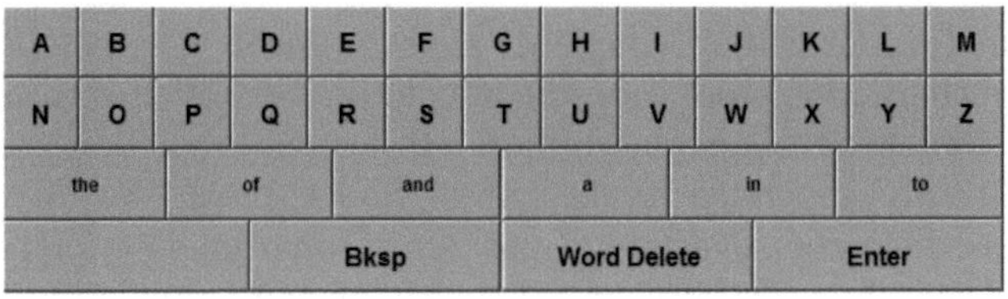

Fig. 2. Scanning keyboard layout.

words, phrases, or as a overall average for a language, such as English. The calculation can proceed for different layouts and scanning patterns, and with or without word prediction. Using SPC, alternative scanning keyboards can be compared to inform design decisions [4, p. 427]. Figure 3 shows the scansteps and SPC for an example phrase from a standardized set of 500 phrases [6]. Entry uses two-tier scanning with the layout in Fig. 2. There are two illustrations, one without word prediction and another with word prediction. Bear in mind that SPC, as described here, is a characteristic measure; it reflects potential usage, not actual usage.

```
    Phrase: you should visit a doctor (324 of 500)

    Not using Word Prediction
     33   you          .▌...........y.▌.o.▌.......u...▌_
     54   should       .▌.....s▌.......h.▌.o.▌.......u▌...........l▌...d...▌_
     53   visit        .▌........v▌........i.▌.....s▌........i.▌......t...▌_
      7   a            ▌a...▌_
     38   doctor       ▌...d.▌.o▌..c.▌......t.▌.o.▌....r...▌_
(a) 185 scansteps total (SPC = 7.12)

    Using Word Prediction
     18   you          .▌...........y..▌W
     16   should       .▌.....s..▌....W
     27   visit        .▌........v▌........i..▌..W
      7   a            ..▌...W
     17   doctor       ▌...d.▌.o▌..c..▌W
(b)  85 scansteps total (SPC = 3.27)

    Notes:
    . = passive scanstep
    ▌ = row select
    W = word select
```

Fig. 3. Scansteps and scansteps per character (SPC) for an example phrase (a) without word prediction, and (b) with word prediction.

The calculation for SPC is simple: It is the number of scansteps divided by the number of characters produced, which include a SPACE after each word. Note in the figure that SPACE is explicitly notated if word prediction is not used ( ) or is automatically appended if word prediction is used (**W**). SPC is a more stable measure than the scansteps count, since it normalizes for the length of the phrase. The values are SPC = 7.12 without word prediction and SPC = 3.27 with word prediction (see figure). These will vary slightly according to the linguistic make-up of the phrase.

The most dramatic observation in Fig. 3 is the benefit of word prediction. The phrase is entered in 185 scansteps without word prediction or less than half that at 85 scansteps with word prediction. Of course, the calculation using word prediction is influenced by numerous issues, including the dictionary. The analyses herein use a dictionary with 9197 words from the British National Corpus [8].

SPC can also be calculated as a weighted average over the full dictionary. For the layout in Fig. 2 and the just-noted dictionary, SPC = 6.73 without word prediction or SPC = 3.19 with word prediction. These values are an overall average: the number of scansteps per character to enter text in a given language for a given keyboard layout and scanning pattern. Thus, as an overall average, using word prediction reduces SPC by 54% for the keyboard layout in Fig. 2.

The analytic metric for SPC combined with the scanning interval yields an approximate upper limit for text entry speed, under the assumption that users proceed optimally at a pace set by the scanning interval. As an example, the layout in Fig. 2 with SPC = 3.19 and a scanning interval of 1 s (1000 ms) constrains entry speed to an upper limit of approximately 3.76 words per minute. The rate is faster for shorter scanning intervals or slower for longer scanning intervals. Determining the actual entry speed requires user testing.

The second use of SPC is in measuring the performance of users while entering text. This will be explored in the user study described next.

3 Method

An empirical evaluation of a pressure sensor with a squeezable bulb as an input method for a scanning keyboard was conducted. The study measured text entry speed, error rate, efficiency, and improvement over time.

3.1 Participants

Twelve participants were recruited on a voluntary basis from the local university and community. Participants ranged from 18 to 30 years with an even split of males and females. The participants had no motor impairments, adequate computer skills, but little to no experience using a scanning keyboard.

3.2 Apparatus

The study evaluated a squeezable bulb connected to a pressure sensor as an input for a scanning keyboard. The interface consists of an HX710 pressure sensor connected to a Arduino UNO R3 microcontroller. See Fig. 1. The Arduino program converted sensor signals to serial data for processing on a Windows 11 computer running a Python program that interpreted keyboard inputs.

The computer ran the ScanningKeyboardExperiment[1] experiment application, configured to use the ABC layout with word prediction, as shown in Fig. 2. Five phrases per session were randomly selected from a standardized phrase set [6]. The scanning interval was set to 900 ms for the first session and was decreased by 100 ms in each subsequent session, finishing at 500 ms in the last session. Scanning is shown in Fig. 4, with row scanning in Fig. 4a and column scanning in Fig. 4b. Note in Fig. 4b that the user is entering the second word in the phrase, *laser*. The first two letters (*la*) are entered, but *laser* does not yet appear as a candidate (3rd row). The user is about to enter the third letter (*s*). Perhaps *laser* will then appear, allowing early selection.

(a)

(b)

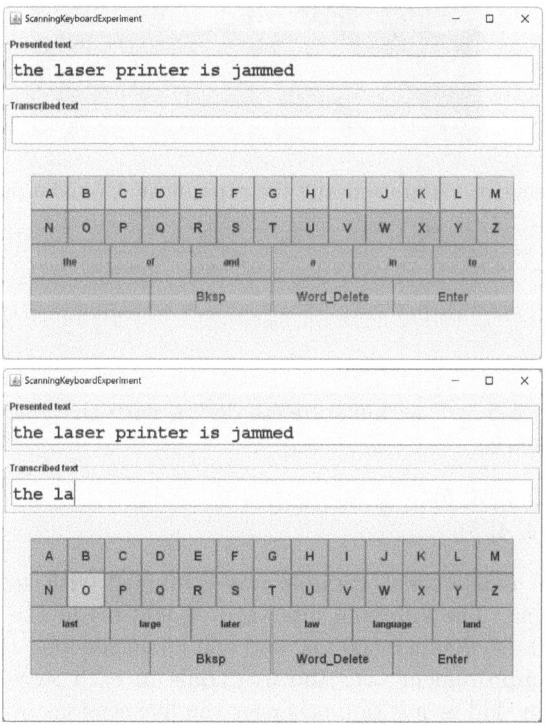

Fig. 4. Scanning with the ABC keyboard and word completion: (a) row scanning, and (b) column scanning. See text for discussion.

[1] https://www.yorku.ca/mack/ExperimentSoftware.

Each selection was followed with an additional scan delay of 500 ms to give participants extra time to react to the change induced by the selection. The scanning keyboard software recorded numerous performance measures, including entry speed, error rate, and efficiency.

3.3 Procedure

Participants received a brief introduction to the scanning keyboard software and its functionality. Prior to testing, participants entered a practice phrases. Figure 5 shows a participant and the apparatus.

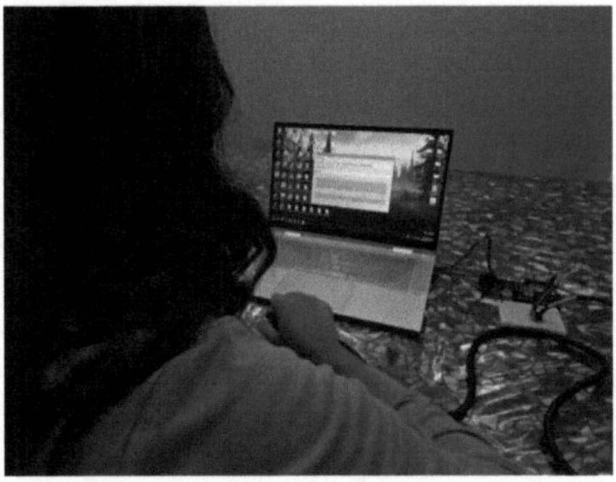

Fig. 5. Experiment procedure showing the experiment UI and a participant using the squeezable bulb.

3.4 Design

The study was a 5 × 5 within-subjects design with the following independent variables and levels:

- Session (1, 2, 3, 4, 5)
- Trial (1, 2, 3, 4, 5)

The session independent variable was combined with scanning interval to promote learning. The scanning interval was 900 ms in the first session with intervals of 800 ms, 700 ms, 600 ms, and 500 ms in sessions 2 to 5, respectively.

Although improvement over the five trials in each session was likely, our main interest in skill acquisition was over the five sessions of input. Trials were included to give participants more practice and to stabilize results within each session. Thus, analyses of the results "by trial" were not pursued.

The following dependent variables were used:

- Entry Speed (wpm)

- Error Rate (%)
- Efficiency (%)

Efficiency was computed for each phrase as the minimum number of scansteps divided by the actual number of scansteps, reported as a percent. This is discussed in further detail below.

The total number of trials was 300 (= 12 participants × 5 sessions × 5 phrases/session).

4 Results and Discussion

Of the 300 total phrases, one was deemed an outlier due to a participant forgetting to select ENTER at the end of the phrase. This highly inflated the time to enter the phrase. Thus, one phrase was omitted. The analyses below are for 299 phrases.

4.1 Entry Speed

The grand mean for entry speed was 3.85 wpm. There was a consistent improvement with practice over the five sessions with means of 3.01 wpm in session 1 to 4.51 wpm in session 5, representing an improvement of 49.8%. See Fig. 6. The differences were statistically significant ($F_{4,44} = 24.9$, $p < .0001$). While learning is the obvious explanation for the increases in entry speed in Fig. 6, this must be tempered with knowledge that the scanning interval decreased session-to-session. This, in itself, supports an increase in entry over the five sessions.

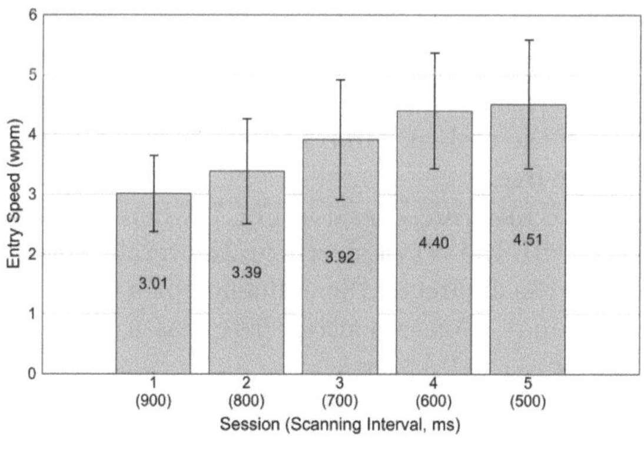

Fig. 6. Entry speed (wpm) by session. Error bars shows ±1 *SD*. Scanning interval was decreased by 100 ms in each session to promote and assist participants in learning to use the scanning keyboard.

It was noted earlier that the scanning interval brings forth an upper limit for text entry speed. So, it is worth investigating not only participants' improvement in entry speed, but also how their actual entry speed compared, session by session, with the system's upper limit for entry speed. This is shown in Table 1. Participants entered text at just over 70% of the maximum speed over sessions 1 to 4. However, for session 5, where the scanning interval (500 ms) provided an upper limit potential of 7.52 wpm, participants only achieved a text entry rate of 4.51 wpm or 59.9% of the upper limit. Although participants were gaining proficiency in using the scanning keyboard, the quick half-second duration for each scanning step likely challenged their ability to perceive and react to changes in the system state.

Table 1. Progression over the five sessions of testing for scanning interval, the upper limit for entry speed, and the observed entry speed. Upper-limit calculations assume SPC = 3.19.

Session	1	2	3	4	5
Scanning Interval (ms)	900	800	700	600	500
Entry Speed (wpm) – upper limit	4.18	4.70	5.37	6.27	7.52
Entry Speed (wpm) – observed	3.01	3.39	3.92	4.40	4.51
Observed/upper limit	72.0%	72.1%	72.8%	70.2%	59.9%

4.2 Error Rate

Errors were measured at the character-level using the minimum-string distance (MSD) between the presented text phrase and the transcribed text phrase. MSD articulates the minimum number of primitive operations (deletion, insertion, substitution) to turn either phrase into the other [9]. The grand mean for error rate was 0.19%. This is remarkably low and indicates that participants conscientiously proceeded with the task at hand. In fact, of the 299 phrases for analysis, 289 (96.6%) were error-free.

By session, the error rates are shown in Fig. 7, where considerable variability is evident. Combined with the very low error rate overall, we attribute the wide-ranging variability in the figure to the influence of a small number of errors on mostly error-free input. Consequently, there was a non-significant effect of session on error rate ($F_{4,44} = 0.78$, ns).

Although there were 289 phrases where the transcribed text was correct (see above), 143 of these phrases were entered with errors that were corrected. That is, of the 289 error-free phrases, 143 included some activity with either BKSP or WORD_DELETE to correct mistakes along the way. This behaviour is reflected in "efficiency" as a dependent variable.

4.3 Efficiency

Full or 100% efficiency implies the participant entered the phrase without any mistakes and selected words from the candidate list at the earliest opportunity.

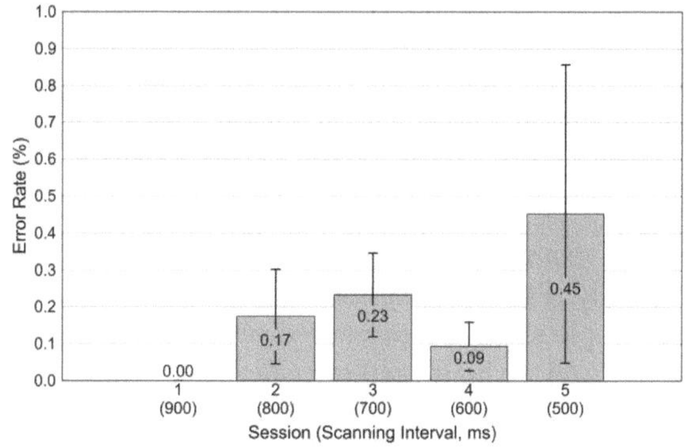

Fig. 7. Error rate (%) by session. Error bars shows ±1 *SD*. See text for discussion.

Values below 100% reflect additional "keystrokes" (i.e., scansteps) due to participants correcting errors or missing opportunities to select the desired word in the candidate list.

The grand mean for efficiency was 79.4%. See Fig. 8. Is evident in the figure that efficiency was relatively flat over the five sessions. Consequently, the effect of session on efficiency was not statistically significant ($F_{4,44} = 1.59$, $p > .05$). Efficiency was expected to rise with practice, as participants anticipate words in the candidate list, but this effect is not apparent in Fig. 8. Our sense is that the current user study provided insufficient practice for such behaviour to emerge.

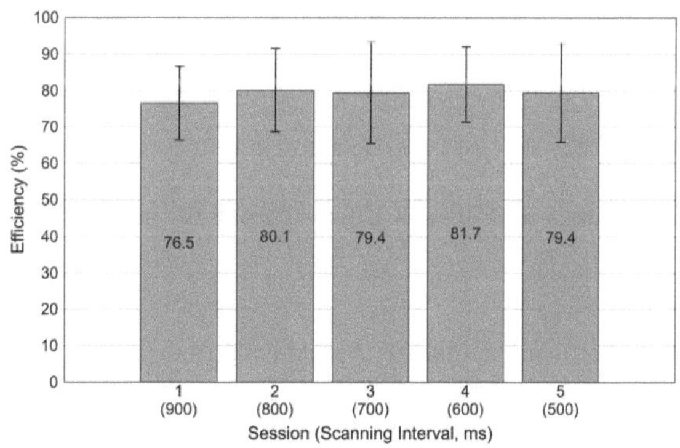

Fig. 8. Efficiency (%) by session. Error bars shows ±1 *SD*. See text for discussion.

4.4 SPC as a Performance Metric

The scansteps illustrated earlier in Fig. 3 reflect ideal behaviour: participants entering text without errors and selecting words at the earliest opportunity (if word prediction is used). In practice, users make mistakes, sometimes correct them, and sometime miss opportunities to enter an intended word when it first appears in the candidate list. These behaviours are reflected in the scansteps and in the SPC calculation using the data collected. The actual SPC is particularly useful if considered alongside the analytic or optimal SPC. This was presented above using "efficiency" as a dependent variable.

Figure 9 shows an example of actual scansteps for a participant entering a phrase in the user study. The scansteps are illustrate word by word in the phrase. The interaction is simple since the presented phrase (*my bare face in the wind*) was entered error-free and without corrective actions. The six words were entered in 101 scansteps. With 25 characters in the phrase (including SPACE after each word), SPC = 101 / 25 = 4.04 (see figure).

```
Phrase 11 of 300 (Participant: P01, Session: S03, Phrase: 1)

Presented:   my bare face in the wind
Transcribed: my bare face in the wind

 18  my       ▌............m..▌W

 18  bare     ▌.b▌a.▌....r..▌..W

 18  face     ▌.....f▌a▌..c..▌.W

 12  in       ..▌........W

  4  the      ..▌W

 31  wind     .▌.........w▌........i.▌n..▌..W
─────
101 scansteps total (SPC = 4.04)

Notes:
. = passive scanstep
▌ = row select
W = word select
```

Fig. 9. Example from the user study of the scansteps for a phrase. See text for discussion.

However, the minimum scansteps for the phrase is 94, not 101. Thus, the analytic SPC = 94 / 25 = 3.76. So, entry of the phrase was not optimal. The additional scansteps (7) were due to "missed opportunities"—not selecting the intended word when it first appeared in the candidate list. For this example, the user selected *face* after entering *f*, *a*, and *c* (see figure); however *face* was in the candidate list after entering *f* and *a*. The user probably didn't notice.

Scanstep examples involving corrections are in Fig. 10. Bear in mind that the keys for correcting errors are on the soft keyboard (see Fig. 2), not on the system's keyboard. In Fig. 10a, the user enters *hao*, realizes the mistake, enters BKSP to delete *o*, enters *i*, then selects the intended word *hair* from the candidate list. In Fig. 10b, the user intends to enter *as*, but selects *and* from candidate list after entering *a*. Realizing the error, the user enters WORD_DELETE followed by *a* and *s* to achieve the desired result.

Fig. 10. Illustration of scanning sequences with corrections: (a) correcting a letter error using BKSP and (b) correcting a word error using WORD_DELETE.

4.5 Additional User Feedback

As no interaction methods were compared in this user study, participants were not given a post-testing questionnaire. Overall, participants felt entering text with the scanning keyboard and squeezable bulb was simple yet tiring. The bulb was considered comfortable and easy to use overall, but some participants had difficulty finding the correct squeezing pressure to trigger the input switch.

5 Conclusion

This user study tested a squeezable rubber bulb as an input switch with a scanning keyboard for text entry. Text phrases were entered over five sessions, with five phrases per session. The scanning interval started at 900 ms in the first session and was reduced by 100 ms in subsequent sessions, ending at 500 ms in the fifth session. Entry speed was 3.85 wpm overall with rates rising from 3.01 wpm in session 1 to 4.51 wpm in session 5. Users operated at about 80% efficiency overall, indicating room for improvement with additional practice.

References

1. Chen Liu, H.A., Patel, S., Verma, A., Ramesh, K., MacKenzie, I.S.: A comparison of four sensor-based input methods for scanning keyboards. In: Proceedings of the 15th International Conference on Human Interaction & Emerging Technologies – IHIET 2025, pp. 377–387. AFHE Open Access, USA (2025). https://doi.org/10.54941/ahfe1006730
2. Koester, H.H., Levine, S.P.: Modeling the speed of text entry with a word prediction interface. IEEE Trans. Rehabil. Eng. **2**(3), 177–187 (1994). https://doi.org/10.1109/86.331567
3. Lesher, G., Moulton, B., Higginbotham, D.J.: Techniques for augmenting scanning communication. Augment. Altern. Commun. (AAC) **14**(2), 81–101 (1998). https://doi.org/10.1080/07434619812331278236

4. MacKenzie, I.S.: Modeling text input for single-switch scanning. In: Miesenberger, K., Karshmer, A., Penaz, P., Zagler, W. (eds.) ICCHP 2012. LNCS, vol. 7383, pp. 423–430. Springer, Heidelberg (2012). https://doi.org/10.1007/978-3-642-31534-3_63
5. MacKenzie, I.S.: Human-Computer Interaction: An Empirical Research Perspective, 2nd edn. Morgan Kaufmann (an imprint of Elsevier), Cambridge (2024). https://doi.org/10.1016/C2022-0-02755-0, https://www.yorku.ca/mack/HCIbook2e/
6. MacKenzie, I.S., Soukoreff, R.W.: Phrase sets for evaluating text entry techniques. In: Extended Abstracts of the ACM SIGCHI Conference on Human Factors in Computing Systems – CHI 2003, pp. 754–755. ACM, New York (2003).https://doi.org/10.1145/765891.765971
7. Mankowski, R.E.: Predicting communication rates: efficacy of a scanning model. MSc thesis, Univerisity of Pittsburgh, Pittsburgh, PA (2009). https://d-scholarship.pitt.edu/8619/
8. Silfverberg, M., MacKenzie, I.S., Korhonen, P.: Predicting text entry speed on mobile phones. In: Proceedings of the ACM SIGCHI Conference on Human Factors in Computing Systems – CHI 2000, pp. 9–16. ACM, New York (2000).https://doi.org/10.1145/332040.332044
9. Soukoreff, R.W., MacKenzie, I.S.: Measuring errors in text entry tasks: an application of the Levenshtein string distance statistic. In: Extended Abstracts of the ACM SIGCHI Conference on Human Factors in Computing Systems – CHI 2001, pp. 319–320. ACM, New York (2001). https://doi.org/10.1145/634067.634256
10. Steriadis, C.E., Constantinou, P.: Designing human-computer interfaces for quadriplegic people. ACM Trans. Comput.-Hum. Interact. (TOCHI) **10**(2), 87–118 (2003). https://doi.org/10.1145/772047.772049
11. Szeto, A.Y.J., Allen, E.J., Littrell, M.C.: Comparison of speed and accuracy for selected electronic communication devices and input methods. Augment. Altern. Commun. **9**(4), 229–242 (1993). https://doi.org/10.1080/07434619312331276651

Analysis of Conversations in a Robot Café Customer Service Utilizing a Gesture Interface

Ikushi Yoda[1(✉)] and Michie Kawashima[2]

[1] National Institute of Advanced Industrial Science and Technology (AIST), Tsukuba 305-8560, Japan
i-yoda@aist.go.jp
[2] Kyoto Sangyo University, Kyoto 603-8555, Japan

Abstract. This study investigated robot–human interactions in an **Avatar Robot Café** service encounter. The robots were remotely operated by individuals with severe physical disabilities using the **augmentative and alternative gesture interface (AAGI)**, which translates subtle gestures into robotic actions. Through **conversation analysis** of interactions from 2023–2025, this study examined how the precise timing of robotic gestures contributes to social bonding. Three primary interactional functions were identified: (1) establishing **affiliative relationships** through synchronized nodding during small talk, (2) generating **shared laughter** using gestures to confirm positive assessments, and (3) facilitating **smooth transitions** from social talk to task-oriented service via multi-channel gestural coordination. Intuitive gesture control enhanced the telepresence of operators and fostered mutual engagement, bridging the gap between remote pilots and physical customers.

Keywords: Service Robot · Gesture Interface · Assistive Technology · Severe Motor Dysfunction

1 Introduction

This study examined robot–human interactions in a service environment. The robots are remotely manipulated by people with severe motor disabilities who are housebound. The augmentative and alternative gesture interface (AAGI) enables the intuitive management of robot movement. The robot café server takes orders and chats with customers. When the robot is controlled remotely, interactional contingencies occur. This study examined robot–human interaction management in the actual service environment.

The structure of the remaining paper is as follows. Section 2 consists of the background of this study and related literature. Section 3 comprises the data and methods used in the study. Section 4 deals with the analysis of the methods. Section 5 is composed of the conclusions following the study.

K. Miesenberger et al. (Eds.): ICCHP 2026, LNCS 16867, pp. 419–426, 2027.
https://doi.org/10.1007/978-3-032-31308-9_50

2 Background and Literature

Individuals with severe motor dysfunction are unable to use existing computer interfaces due to disabilities including spasticity and involuntary movements. These individuals are limited to using customized switch interfaces, making it difficult to easily operate a computer. To solve this problem, a switch gesture interface was developed that utilizes commercially available 3D (RGB-D) and USB video class (UVC) cameras. The AAGI consists of seven recognition modules based on body parts (head, around eyes, mouth/tongue, shoulders, finger, knees, and feet) and two recognition modules independent of body parts (front object and slight movements) [1–6]. A key feature of AAGI is that, within the same field of view, multiple modules can be combined to create multiple switches. Additionally, a combination of one depth camera and one standard RGB camera is available. A combination of one RGB-D camera and one UVC camera is currently available for use [7]. This is effective for body parts that cannot be captured by a single camera, such as the upper and lower body. Using two cameras to create multiple switches based on the upper and lower body is also possible. Users first select the body part they want to use the module for and perform the gesture about 10 times; the system then learns the movement and converts it into the specified key operations.

This study described an application involving a pilot operating a robot DAWN Avatar Robot Café. The user, who has myelopathic muscular atrophy, operated a Windows PC using a trackball and single ultra-light switch. Being able to fully operate the PC enabled the user to become an active user and engage in activities. The Avatar Robot Café is a permanent experimental cafe operated by OryLab Inc. People who have difficulty leaving their homes can remotely operate OriHime avatar robots to provide café services [8]. The user worked as a customer service representative at this café by remotely operating a robot from his home PC (Fig. 1).

In remotely operated robots, telepresence and co-presence are crucial aspects. Almeida et al. [9] provided a comprehensive review of how embodiment influences the sense of involvement of participants and perception of interpersonal relationships, regardless of mobility or physical complexity, along with evaluation metrics. Kim et al. [10] experimentally compared three conditions (telepresence robots, video conferencing, and face-to-face interaction) and quantitatively evaluated co-presence, social presence, and learning outcomes. They demonstrated that telepresence robots generate higher levels of co-presence and user engagement than video conferencing systems. Hasegawa and Nakauchi [11] addressed the enhancement of telepresence and co-presence through embodied manipulation by exaggerating robotic gestures as an implementation strategy.

Building on these studies, this study qualitatively evaluated, through conversation analysis, how individuals with motor impairments influenced communication by intuitively controlling robot gestures using their own bodily gestures.

3 Data and Methods

The user provided customer service while operating an OriHime robot. This user controlled the camera-equipped head of the robot to maintain visual attention toward customer faces. The built-in microphone and speaker of the robot enabled continuous verbal interaction similar to online video conferencing. The robot gestures were controlled via a gesture interface. The robot could perform six types of gestures by clicking on on-screen buttons (the rightmost column of Fig. 1) (Fig. 2).

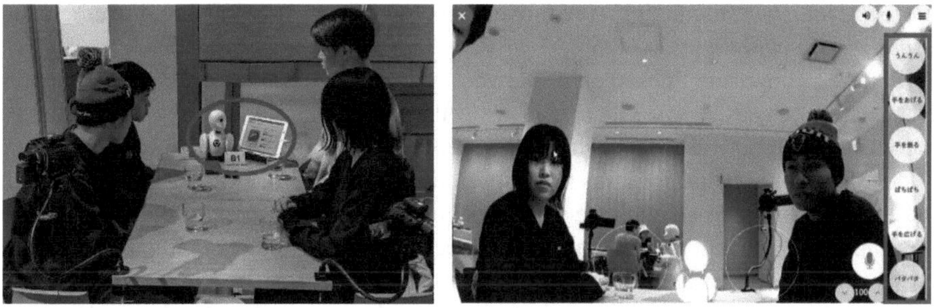

Fig. 1. Robot Café (OriHime robot and menu monitor) (left), Interface window (six gesture buttons positioned on the right side) (right)

Fig. 2. Third session: controlling three robotic gestures using three bodily gestures

Figure 1 shows the on-screen operation interface. It was designed under the assumption that gestures are selected and triggered via mouse cursor clicks on a PC. However, such manipulation was not straightforward. As the pilot had a motor impairment, rapidly moving the mouse cursor to select and click a gesture was difficult. Moreover, even for able-bodied users, producing well-timed robotic gestures while engaging in conversation is not trivial. Coordinating multiple gestures with appropriate timing further increases the difficulty.

To address this issue, OryLab Inc. Was requested to assign keyboard bindings to all gesture commands. This modification enabled the pilot to control the robot gestures through their own bodily gestures. The most frequently used robot gestures are *nodding*, *raising the right hand*, and *clapping with both hands*. Three experimental sessions involving real-world use were conducted and video recorded. In the first two sessions (Kyoto 2023 and Tokyo 2024), **movements of the mouth** were mapped to the *nodding* gesture. In the most recent session (Tokyo 2025), movements of three body parts (nose, right toe, and left toe) were utilized. Specifically, **nose** movements were mapped to *raising the right hand*, **right-toe** movements to *nodding*, and **left-toe** movements to *clapping with both hands.*

Figure 1 shows the PC screen as viewed by the pilot during operation. The upper-left panel displays the live video feed from the robot along with the gesture control interface. The upper-right panel shows the feed from the first camera capturing the face of the pilot; when the pilot moves their nose, the robot performs *raising the right hand*. The lower-right panel shows video feeds of the right and left toes of the pilot, where movements of the right and left toes are mapped to *nodding* and *clapping*, respectively.

We used conversation analysis to evaluate the effectiveness of AAGI used in actual service encounter. Conversation analysis is a sociological method to clarify details of social interaction, which enabled us to capture the nuances of the natural course of interaction of participants [12]. This method was based on ethnomethodological understanding of human–robot interaction [13–15]. Identifying the interactional resources that created smooth communication or hindered its development was also possible. Mondada has developed a transcribing system for the multimodal aspects of social interaction [16], which was applied to create transcripts in this article. As this method enabled to capture the precise timing of gesture and talk, it could assess affiliative/dis-affiliative moments of social interaction.

4 Analysis

Pilots are responsible for the quality of service at the café. Fulfilling customer needs is important for them. Customers come to the robot café for a unique experience with robots. A key challenge faced by the pilot is entertaining customers in a relatively short time while a robot introduces the menu and customers decide what to order. The analysis demonstrated three main methods through which pilots form affiliative interaction through coordination of balancing gestures and talking in robot-human interaction.

First, small talk in opening interactions often involved the frequent mutual engagement through synchronized nodding. Second, nodding at specific times could generate laughter among participants. Third, robots could use multiple channels for nodding and hand movements to initiate topic changes during task-oriented interactions.

4.1 Establishing Affiliation in Small Talk

Opening interactions are a crucial phase as they define relationships among participants. Small talk occurs in the opening interaction while participants are establishing the basis of their robot–human interaction. During the opening, robots nod when affiliation is due among participants. As nodding can be controlled by the AAGI, the timing can be precisely managed. When a robot nods, its recipients also nod. Through mutual engagement, smooth robot–human interaction can be achieved.

【Ex.120231223-1500】 C1(Customer1) C2（Customer 2）RB（Robot）＊transcription conventions (|=overlapping gesture, (1.3)=length of silence []= overlapping talk, ---=duration of gesture ::=stretch of sound $=smiling tone hhh=laughter)

(2:08~)
01 RB: |upward hand movement|
02 RB: |Yes |(.)|Welcom to::::.Robot café! |yes:::|
03 RB:→ |-----Look at C2--------------|nodding------|
04 C2: |Ye:s|
05 C2:→ |nodding|
06 (1.3)
07 RB: My name is (.)(NAME). I am your waiter today.
08 C2: Nice |to mee[t you.|]
09 RB: |---Look at C1---|
10 RB: [Nice to] meet you.

In this example, two points exist where a robot used nodding strategically to achieve mutual engagement with its recipient. At line 3, the robot welcomed its customer and nodded toward the end of the turn. Turn ends could indicate a transition among participants. By nodding at the turn end, the robot elicited a reaction from its recipient. At line 4, customer 2 nodded and responded "Yes" to the welcoming turn of the robot.

4.2 Laughter Generating Nodding

Mutual laughter can indicate heightened affiliation and social bonding [17]. The analysis found that such moments were initiated by the robot nodding. In the following example, the robot nodded multiple times in response to a positive assessment from the customer, which generated mutual laughter.

【Ex.2 20231223-1504】 C1(Customer1) C2（Customer 2）RB（Robot）
11 C1: |Nice meeting you.|=
12 RB: |--Lifting right arm-|
13 C2: Wow<Cute(.) lifting |hand!::[hhhhhhhhh.|
14 RB: [Thank you very much:.|
15 RB:→ |- noddings----|-------|
16 C2:→ |nodding--|
17 RB: |$for saying cute!$|
18 RB: |facing middle and nodding-|
19 C1: [hhhhhhhhh
20 C2: [hhhhhhhhh
21 RB: $Very|often people say| that$.
22 RB: |--moving both hands--|
23 C1: Often[( ).
24 C2: [$people say that often$haha:::

At line 13, customer 2 offered a positive evaluation of the hand raising gesture of the robot. The pilot expressed gratitude toward the compliment and nodded twice at line 14. This gesture confirmed the positive evaluation of the customer. Considering that a positive evaluation from another individual is normatively downgraded, this extra confirmation is often taken as a "joke". At lines 19 and 20, the customers started laughing. This mutual laughter had important implications for continuing interaction as it further defined their positive relationship.

4.3 Smooth Transition to Task-Oriented Talk

In contrast to the previous two examples, in which only one channel of the AAGI was available and designated for nodding, the following example is from the most recent development (2025 version), where a pilot could use three different channels for different gestures. With the smooth coordination of nodding and hand movements, the pilot enhanced affiliative mutual engagement among participants. The **synchronization of** gestures among participants was observed.

```
【Ex.3 20250217-1504】
C1(Customer1)  C2 (Customer 2) C3(Customer3)  C4 (Customer 4) RB (Robot)
01 RB:   okay everyone, (.)|Welcome! Thank you for |coming:::!|
02 RB:→                    |-----hand clapping--------------------|
03 C2:   hhehe  cut|e : [ : .
04 C1:              [cute :   :
05 C3: →              |---hand cr|apping---|
06 C2: →                         |--hand carping--|
07 RB:  oh::Th|ank($) you::|.  People often say that[::.  ]
08 RB:         |---nodding---|
09 C2:                                            [hhaah]hhh[hhh
10 C1:                                            [Oh, do you($)get that often? hh
11 C3:                                            [hhhhhh
12 C4:                                            [hhhhhh
13 C1 :   O|h, I see.
14 RB:→   |-raising |right hand-|---|
15 C2:              |next、      |
16 C2:→             |raising right hand|
17 RB:  hhahh haha hahaha.
18 RB:  Okay、 so firstly | I am going to explain about menu.|
19 RB:                   |------------hand crapping ------------|
20 C2:  Oh please.
```

Two points existed where the hand movements of the robot caused synchronization. At line 1, the pilot welcomed customers with clapping hands. It received positive assessment from customers at lines 3 and 4. Customers 2 and 3 clapped their hands simultaneously at lines 5 and 6. This synchronization of gestures formed affiliative strata for future interactions among participants.

In addition, after the pilot offered a joke about being described as "cute" by other customers, the robot moved its right hand up at line 14. Customer 2 responded to this movement by saying "next" at line 15. This showed their understanding that the hand movement of the robot at the end of the previous sequence was a sign to move forward. Customer 2 also exhibited synchronized hand movement at line 16. This was a gestural precursor for the movement of the pilot toward task-oriented talk from the previous small talk. It also occurred with perfect timing at the tail end of the previous utterance of the customer, which closed the previous sequence at line 13.

5 Conclusion

This study has qualitatively analyzed how the use of the AAGI by pilots with motor impairments influenced communication in a robot-mediated service setting. The analysis demonstrated that the ability to control robot gestures through intuitive bodily movements was not merely a functional tool for task execution but a vital resource for **social interactional work**.

When robot nodding was synchronized with customer speech, it fostered a sense of "being heard" and built immediate affiliation. Furthermore, the 2025 version of the interface, allowing simultaneous control with multiple body parts, showed that sophisticated coordination between gestures could effectively signal topic shifts and manage the flow of service. By enabling pilots to project their physical presence through timed robotic movements, the AAGI reduced the interactional contingencies often found in remote operation.

In future research, by increasing the number of detailed analyses, we aim to further clarify the essence of what contributes to nuanced, embodied communication, rather than relying solely on case studies of individuals with disabilities. Ultimately, this research seeks to demonstrate how assistive technologies can contribute to providing employment opportunities through subtle, embodied communication. We also aim to uncover insights that deeply enrich the quality of social inclusion for people with disabilities and disseminate these findings throughout society.

Acknowledgments. This work was supported by Council for Science, Technology and Innovation (CSTI), Cross-ministerial Strategic Innovation Promotion Program (SIP), the 3rd period of SIP "Creation of new ways of learning and working in a post-COVID-19 era" Grant Number JPJ012347 (Funding agency: JST).

Disclosure of Interests. The authors have no competing interests to declare that are relevant to the content of this article.

References

1. Yoda, I., Itoh, K., Nakayama, T.: Collection and Classification of Gestures from People with Severe Motor Dysfunction for Developing Modular Gesture Interface. In: Antona, M., Stephanidis, C. (eds.) International Conference on Universal Access in Human-Computer Interaction, pp. 58–68. Springer (2015)
2. Yoda, I., Itoh, K., Nakayama, T.: Long-Term Evaluation of a Modular Gesture Interface at Home for Persons with Sever Motor Dysfunction. In: International Conference on Universal Access in Human-Computer Interaction, pp. 102–116. Springer (2016)
3. Yoda, I., Itoh, K., Nakayama, T.: Modular Gesture Interface for People with Severe Motor Dysfunction: Foot Recognition. Proceedings of AAATE 2017, (Harnessing the Power of Technology to Improve Lives), pp. 725–732. IOS Press (2017)
4. Yoda, I., Nakayama, T., Itoh, K., Nishida, D., Mizuno, K.: Application of Gesture Interface to Transcription for People with Motor Dysfunction. Computers Helping People with Special Needs, Lecture Note in Computer Science, pp. 343–347. Springer LNCS 12377 (2020)

5. Yoda, I., Itoh, K., Nakayama, Y.: Head Gesture Interface for Mouse Stick Users by AAGI. In: Archambault, D., Kouroupetroglou, G. (eds.) Assistive Technology: Shaping a Sustainable and Inclusive World, pp. 481–486. IOS Press (2023)
6. Yoda, I., Itoh, K., Nakayama, T.: Gesture Interface for Providing Interaction to a Child with Cerebral Palsy. Technology for Inclusion and Participation for All: Recent Achievements and Future Directions. pp. 177–182. AAATE 2025 Part II (2025)
7. AAGI Homepage, http://gestureinterface.jp/en/. Last accessed 16 April 2026
8. Takeuchi, K., Yamazaki, Y., Yoshifuji, K.: Avatar work: Telework for disabled people unable to go outside by using avatar robots "OriHime-D" and its verification. In: Proceedings of the 2020 ACM/IEEE International Conference on Human-Robot Interaction, pp. 53–60 (2020)
9. Almeida, L., Menezes, P., Dias, J., Santos, V.: Telepresence social robotics towards co-presence: a review. Appl. Sci. **12**(11), 5557 (2022)
10. Kim, M.J., Shaw, T., Kim, B., Phillips, E.: Does presence and embodiment matter? Investigating telepresence robots as a superior educational modality to videoconferencing. Int. J. Soc. Robot. **17**(8), 1425–1436 (2025)
11. Hasegawa, K., Nakauchi, Y.: Facilitation of telepresence robot turn-takings by gesture exaggeration. In: Proceedings of the 2014 IEEE/SICE International Symposium on System Integration (SII2014), pp. 650–654. IEEE (2014)
12. Sacks, H., Schegloff, E., Jefferson, G.: A simplest systematics for the organization of turn taking in conversation. Language **50**(4), 696–735 (1974)
13. Arend, B., Sunnen, P.: Coping with turn-taking: Investigating breakdowns in human-robot interaction from a conversation analysis (CA) perspective. In: Proceedings of the 8th International Conference on Society and Information Technologies, pp. 149–154 (2017)
14. Greatbatch, D., Heath, C., Luff, P., Campion, P.: Conversation analysis: Human-computer interaction and the general practice consultation. In: Monk, A.F., Gilbert, N.G. (eds.) Perspectives on HCI: Diverse Approaches, pp. 199–222. Academic Press, New York (1995)
15. Kuzuoka, H., Suzuki, Y., Yamashita, J., Yamazaki, K.: Reconfiguring spatial formation arrangement by robot body orientation. In: Proceedings of the 5th ACM/IEEE International Conference on Human-Robot Interaction (HRI '10), pp. 285–292 (2010)
16. Mondada, L.: Multiple temporalities of language and body in interaction: Challenges for transcribing multimodality. Res. Lang. Soc. Interact. **51**(1), 85–106 (2018)
17. Jefferson, G.: A Technique for Inviting Laughter and Its Subsequent Acceptance/Declination. In: Psathas, G. (ed.) Everyday Language: Studies in Ethnomethodology, pp. 79–96 (1979)

Assessing Sequential Scrolling Strategies in Virtual Reality

Noémie Kempa[1,2(✉)], Isabelle Barbet[2], Clémence Drogoul[2], and Jérôme Dupire[2]

[1] Laboratoire Paragraphe, Université Paris 8, 93 200 Saint-Denis, France
noemie.kempa@lecnam.net
[2] Laboratoire Cédric, Conservatoire national des arts et métiers, 75 003 Paris, France

Abstract. This study aims to adapt the sequential scrolling interaction technique to virtual reality (VR) interactions to provide an alternative interaction method to the use of controllers, particularly for users with motor impairments. Proven in 2D environments, this technique has the advantage of requiring limited motor skills and being configurable in terms of both positioning and type of actuators. To optimize its integration into VR, we compared two scrolling strategies (object-by-object scanning vs. cluster scanning) and two control modes (manual vs. automatic) as part of an object selection task. The evaluation was conducted with 20 participants divided into two groups: a group of users with bilateral motor impairments of the upper limbs and a control group. Performance data were collected. The results highlight the solution's usability for a variety of user profiles, although a disparity in performance between the "control" group and the "target users" group was observed. Furthermore, a phenomenon of learning the method was also noted. While the results appear encouraging, at this stage, the adaptation of this interaction method remains limited to the task of object selection. It appears necessary to expand the range of actions within the virtual environment, as well as to evaluate this method in specific usage contexts, in order to identify avenues for improvement.

Keywords: Virtual reality · interaction · motor disorders · sequential scrolling

1 Introduction

Virtual reality (VR) involves creating computer-generated 3D environments or objects that users can interact with in an immersive and realistic way [1]. Its goal is to enable sensorimotor and cognitive interaction within a digital world, whether fictional, symbolic, or based on aspects of the real world [2].

VR can be experienced through a variety of systems and combinations of devices, including output peripherals (display technologies, haptic devices, auditory systems, and multisensory interfaces) and input peripherals (controllers,

K. Miesenberger et al. (Eds.): ICCHP 2026, LNCS 16867, pp. 427–434, 2027.
https://doi.org/10.1007/978-3-032-31308-9_51

navigation devices, or body-tracking systems) [3]. VR systems offer different levels of immersion, from non-immersive to fully immersive experiences [4]. Head-mounted displays (HMDs) with handheld controllers are the most common immersive devices today, largely due to recent cost reductions that have made them widely accessible [5]. Interacting with 3D objects in VR requires manipulating them along three axes [6]. Standard HMD controllers enable this through sensors and input surfaces but demand significant upper-limb and fine motor skills [7] [8]. This complexity can limit accessibility, leading to alternative solutions such as gesture-based interaction or eye tracking. However, the diversity of user profiles and needs calls for the development of alternative solutions to broaden the range of available interaction methods.

The scanning interaction technique, or sequential scrolling, provides a way to interact with two-dimensional environments while requiring minimal motor abilities. This interaction technique is based on the sequential highlighting of each object arranged in a grid. When the target object is highlighted, the user activates a switch to interact with it [9]. Switches are binary input devices, typically activated by a press. They come in various forms, differing in characteristics such as weight, shape, size, or the force required for activation. These devices can be operated through multiple modalities, including hand, head, foot, or finger presses, as well as breath activation [10].

Two types of scrolling are commonly used: automatic scrolling and manual scrolling. In automatic scrolling, the focus moves automatically across the various objects in the scene according to a user-defined scroll delay. The user then activates a switch to select the object when the focus is on the item of interest. In manual scrolling, the user controls the movement of the focus through switch activations and performs the selection by pressing a separate switch.

Several 2D scanning strategies also exist, such as object-by-object selection, row/column selection, or diagonal scanning [11]. The ability to choose both the scrolling mode and strategy, as well as the type and placement of switches, makes this interaction technique adaptable to a wide range of users with varying motor abilities. Furthermore, this method requires minimal equipment, making it a low-cost and easily accessible solution [12].

Building on these findings, we adapted this interaction method to three-dimensional settings, particularly in the context of VR headsets.

2 Method

2.1 Apparatus and Virtual Environment

The experiment was conducted using a test platform developed with the Unreal Engine game engine. The virtual environment was designed to display a variable number of 3D objects differing in shape, color, and surface patterns. Several interface parameters could be adjusted, including focus color, focus thickness, and focus movement speed in automatic mode.

Interaction with the environment was performed through switches connected to a Meta Quest 2 virtual reality headset via an Xbox Adaptive Controller. The number, configuration, and placement of the switches were customized according to each participant's physical abilities and preferred input modality.

2.2 Participants

The study was conducted with 20 participants divided into two groups: Target users group (participants with limitations affecting both upper limbs, including reduced range of motion, strength, dexterity, motor control, and/or increased fatigability) and the control group (participants without any upper-limb limitations).

Exclusion criteria for both groups were: Inability to perceive the scene and/or the highlighting around the object even after adjusting focus color and width and inability to understand the test instructions.

The participants' mean age was 33.1 years (SD = 8.9). The sample included 10 men, 9 women, and 1 non-binary individual. Half of the participants had never used a VR headset, and most of those with prior VR experience reported only occasional use.

2.3 Task

The objective of the test was to select a target object indicated on a screen prior to the selection task. Participants were then immersed in the test scene and asked to select the specified object using sequential scrolling. A panel displaying the target object was positioned in the upper-right corner of the test scene to serve as a constant visual reference.

2.4 Design and Procedure

Participants were assigned to different experimental conditions. Three independent variables, each with two levels, were manipulated:

- Scrolling type: automatic vs user-controlled
- Scrolling strategy: cluster-based or object-by-object
- Order of test phases: A – B vs B-A

In the cluster-based scrolling strategy, the focus moves across groups of objects organized by spatial proximity. Three clusters were defined: objects on the left side of the scene, objects in the center, and objects on the right side (figure to be added). In the object-by-object scrolling strategy, the focus moves sequentially over all objects in the scene from left to right (Fig. 1).

The test was divided into two phases that differed in scene complexity. In Phase A, participants were required to select 10 target objects from a scene containing 10 objects. In Phase B, they were required to select 10 target objects from a scene containing 20 objects. The order of phases was counterbalanced: half of the participants completed the phases in the A–B order, and the other half in the B–A order.

The dependent variables were performance-based and included:

Fig. 1. Screenshots of the left and middle clusters

- Task completion time
- Number of errors
- Number of loops completed (a loop being defined as a full traversal of all objects in the scene without making a selection).

Experimental conditions were assigned using a minimization procedure to reduce imbalances between the participant groups (Fig. 2).

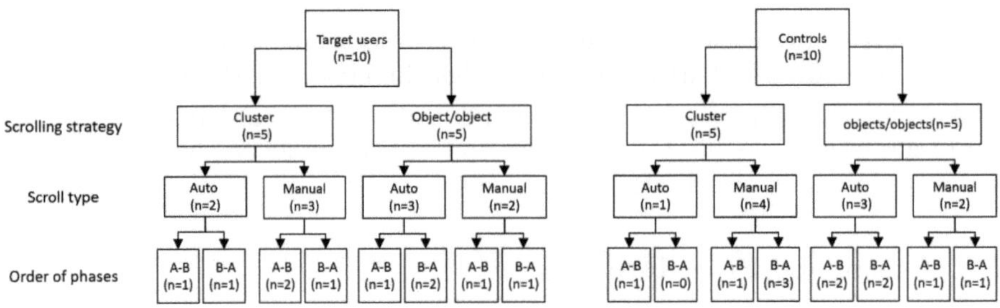

Fig. 2. Distribution of conditions assigned to participants

The factors considered in this procedure were user group (control vs. target), gender and age.

After reading the information sheet and providing informed consent, participants were enrolled in the study. Following a detailed explanation of the instructions, preliminary trials were conducted to determine the most suitable switch configuration for each participant. Once finalized, they donned the VR headset and performed practice trials in a training scene similar to the test environment. During this familiarization, settings could be adjusted to optimize comfort and usability. After these adjustments, participants began the test at their own pace.

3 Results

Switch configurations were adapted to participants' abilities and preferences. Control group participants used one or two switches positionned on the desk in front of them, depending on the scrolling condition. In contrast, target users employed more individualized setups based on motor capacity and fatigue. In the automatic condition, most participants used a single switch positioned on the knee ipsilateral to the active limb, while one participant with tetraplegia used a head-based activation. Switches requiring frequent activation were consistently positioned on the side with the greatest motor ability, lowest fatigability, and according to user preference.

Thus, during test administration, it was observed that despite the heterogeneity of participants' motor abilities, the sequential scrolling interaction method in VR could be used by all participants. This approach provided adaptable options tailored to each user's abilities and preferences. Inferential statistical analyses were conducted to identify potential significant differences in performance according to the dependent variables studied, namely scrolling strategy (cluster vs. object), scrolling mode (manual vs. automatic), test phase (A or B), and participant group (target users vs. controls).

Comparisons between independent groups were performed using non-parametric Wilcoxon– Mann–Whitney tests, with a significance level set at 0.05 ($p < 0.05$). These analyses revealed a significant difference in the number of errors between the control group and the target users group across both test phases. In Phase A, participants in the target users group made more errors on average ($M = 2.2$; $SD = 2.23$) than control participants ($M = 0.4$; $SD = 0.92$; $p = 0.004$). A similar pattern was observed in Phase B ($p = 0.005$), with target users producing a higher average number of errors ($M = 1.8$; $SD = 1.4$) compared to controls ($M = 0.1$; $SD = 0.3$). No significant differences were found in performance data when comparing scrolling strategies (clusters vs. object-by-object) or scrolling modes (manual vs. automatic).

Wilcoxon signed-rank test were conducted to examine differences in completion times between the two test phases, with a significance threshold set at 0.05 ($p < 0.05$). These analyses revealed a significant difference in task durations between phases ($p = 0.048$). On average, participants completed Phase B more quickly ($M = 177$ s; $SD = 151$) than Phase A ($M = 217$ s; $SD = 141$). A significant difference was also observed in the number of errors between the two phases ($p = 0.044$). Participants made fewer errors on average during Phase B ($M = 0.8$; $SD = 1.28$) compared to Phase A ($M = 1.45$; $SD = 2.06$).

Participants were also asked to rate the likelihood of using this interaction method in future VR applications using 5-point Likert scales. On average, participants in the target users group reported a higher likelihood of adopting this method ($M = 4.2$; $SD = 0.42$) than participants in the control group ($M = 2.9$; $SD = 1.37$; $p = 0.018$).

4 Discussion

This study aimed to evaluate the adaptation of sequential scrolling to an immersive virtual reality environment and to analyze its usability and performance among users with and without upper-limb motor impairments.

The results show that all participants, including those with significant motor limitations, were able to use this interaction technique. These findings confirm the feasibility of implementing sequential scrolling in immersive environments and highlight its potential as an alternative to traditional controllers for accessing virtual reality.

However, although all participants were able to use this interaction technique, disparities were observed in performance across the different test phases, particularly in terms of completion times and error rates. These differences are especially evident when comparing participants from the "control" group with those from the "target user" group. This gap may be partly explained by the presence of associated impairments within the target user group. Indeed, some participants presented cognitive impairments, particularly affecting memory, attention, and executive functions (planning, execution, etc.). We can therefore hypothesize that cognitive impairments may impact the use of the sequential scrolling interaction method.

Our second hypothesis is that, although all participants were able to use this interaction technique, they did not exhibit the same execution speed in their movements, which may have affected the time required to complete the task.

These hypotheses are consistent with the observations of Fager and colleagues, who emphasize that the use of this interaction method in 2D environments involves attentional demands as well as motor planning skills [13].

Differences were also observed in participants' performance across the two test phases. Indeed, an improvement in performance (in terms of completion time and error rate) was noted between the first and second phases for both groups. These results suggest a gradual learning effect for the interaction method, in line with the observations of Koester and Simpson, who showed that users' performance improved over time through their optimization method for single-switch scanning parameter settings [14].

It also appears that task completion time increases with scene complexity. The greater the number of objects present in the scene, the longer it takes to select the target object.

The absence of a significant difference between the performances observed for the two scanning strategies ("clusters" and "object-by-object") may be explained by user heterogeneity. It is difficult to determine which method yields better overall performance due to variability in users' abilities and preferences. The different possibilities for adapting the method (scrolling mode, strategy, switch setup, adjustment of the scanning delay, etc.) make it possible to tailor it to the specific needs of each user.

Moreover, the tests were conducted in a specific context in which users were only required to select a single object. It is likely that the usage context and the nature of the task to be performed have an impact on the relevance of the scanning strategy.

All participants in the "target user' group mentioned the possibility of using this interaction method, unlike those in the "control" group.

It should be noted that within the "target user" group, only two participants had prior experience with virtual reality: one in a contemplative, non-interactive context, and the other with usability difficulties, particularly in handling controllers.

These findings suggest that this technique addresses a specific need for users who experience difficulties with traditional controllers and confirm its potential as an accessibility solution in virtual reality.

The results of this study highlight several implications for the design of interfaces based on sequential scrolling in virtual reality.

First, the ability to adapt both the positioning and the type of switches appears essential to enable the use of this technique by users with diverse motor profiles. Hardware flexibility therefore constitutes a key element in the design of accessible systems.

Second, scene complexity—particularly the number of interactive objects—must be taken into account in order to limit selection times. Spatial structuring strategies, such as grouping objects or dynamically adapting the scrolling process, could help optimize performance.

Third, the presence of a learning effect highlights the importance of incorporating training phases or assistance mechanisms that allow users to gradually become familiar with this interaction technique.

Finally, the observed inter-individual variability in configurations and performance underscores the need to provide configurable interfaces, enabling interaction parameters to be adapted to the specific needs of each user.

5 Conclusion

This study investigated the adaptation of the sequential scanning interaction technique in virtual reality among two populations: a "control" group and a "target user" group with upper-limb motor impairments. Different scanning strategies were tested—"cluster" and "object-by-object"—as well as different scrolling methods: "manual" and "automatic". Data collected during the tests indicate that scrolling methods and strategies do not have a significant effect on user performance, whereas participants' motor and/or cognitive abilities are likely to influence it. However, although performance may vary, all participants were able to use this interaction technique, which offers multiple adaptation possibilities, allowing users to employ the movements of their choice (movements of one or both upper limbs, head movements, etc.). Scene complexity, particularly the number of objects present, also affects the speed of task completion. In addition, a learning effect was observed, resulting in improved participant performance over the course of the test.

This work contributes to the exploration of interaction techniques as alternatives to traditional controllers and opens new avenues for designing more inclusive virtual reality interfaces. Future work will aim to extend this approach to more complex interactions and evaluate its usability in real-world contexts.

Acknowledgments. We would like to thank Vassily Bérard for developing the test platform during his internship at the Cédric laboratory. This work was supported by the ANR under the MALIN project ANR-21-CE38-0014

Ethics Review Board. Approval No. 25-1171, dated January 14, 2025, issued by CEEI/IRB0000388.

References

1. Dionisio, D.N., Iii, W.G.B., Gilbert, R.: 3D virtual worlds and the metaverse: current status and future possibilities. ACM Comput. Surv. (CSUR) **45**(3), 1–38 (2013)
2. Fuchs, P.: Le traité de la réalité virtuelle. Presses des MINES, vol. 2 (2006)
3. Anthes, C., García-Hernández, R.J., Wiedemann, M., Kranzlmüller, D.: State of the art of virtual reality technology. In: 2016 IEEE Aerospace Conference, pp. 1–19. IEEE (2016)
4. Salatino, A., et al.: Virtual reality rehabilitation for unilateral spatial neglect: a systematic review of immersive, semi-immersive and non-immersive techniques. Neurosci. Biobehav. Rev. **152**, 105248 (2023)
5. Combe, T., Chardonnet, J.-R., Merienne, F., Ovtcharova, J.: Cave and HMD: distance perception comparative study. Virtual Reality **27**(3), 2003–2013 (2023)
6. Mendes, D., Caputo, F.M., Giachetti, A., Ferreira, A., Jorge, J.: A survey on 3D virtual object manipulation: from the desktop to immersive virtual environments. In: Computer Graphics Forum, vol. 38, no. 1, pp. 21–45. Wiley Online Library (2019)
7. Luong, T., Cheng, Y.F., Möbus, M., Fender, A., Holz, C.: Controllers or bare hands? A controlled evaluation of input techniques on interaction performance and exertion in virtual reality. IEEE Trans. Visual Comput. Graphics **29**(11), 4633–4643 (2023)
8. Dube, T.J., Arif, A.S.: Free-hand input and interaction in virtual reality using a custom force-based digital thimble. Appl. Sci. **14**(23), 11018 (2024)
9. Scherer, R., et al.: Thought-based row-column scanning communication board for individuals with cerebral palsy. Ann. Phys. Rehabil. Med. **58**(1), 14–22 (2015)
10. Ntoa, S., Margetis, G., Antona, M., Stephanidis, C.: Scanning- based interaction techniques for motor impaired users. In: Assistive Technologies and Computer Access for Motor Disabilities, pp. 57–89. IGI Global (2014)
11. MacKenzie, I.S., Ashtiani, B.: BlinkWrite: efficient text entry using eye blinks. Univ. Access Inf. Soc. **10**(1), 69–80 (2011)
12. Elsahar, Y., Hu, S., Bouazza-Marouf, K., Kerr, D., Mansor, A.: Augmentative and alternative communication (AAC) advances: a review of configurations for individuals with a speech disability. Sensors **19**(8), 1911 (2019)
13. Fager, S., Bardach, L., Russell, S., Higginbotham, J.: Access to augmentative and alternative communication: new technologies and clinical decision-making. J. Pediatr. Rehabil. Med. **5**(1), 53–61 (2012)
14. Koester, H.H., Simpson, R.C.: Method for enhancing text entry rate with single-switch scanning. J. Rehabil. Res. Dev. **51**(6), 995 (2014)

Mouth Bytes: Prototyping Electronic Musical Instruments Through Embodied, Mouth-Based Interactions

Luke Franzke[1(✉)], Gerhard Nussbaum[2], and Martin Kaltenbrunner[3]

[1] Zurich University of the Arts, Zurich, Switzerland
luke.franzke@zhdk.ch

[2] Competence Network Information Technology to support the Integration of People With Disabilities (KI-I), Linz, Austria
gn@ki-i.at

[3] University of Arts Linz, Linz, Austria
martin.kaltenbrunner@kunstuni-linz.at

Abstract. The mouth is the most primal musical instrument and a central interface for wind performance, yet it remains largely overlooked in the design of contemporary electronic instruments. Given its exceptional sensory acuity and fine motor control, this neglect represents a loss of expressive potential and a hindrance to musicians with motor disabilities. This paper documents a participatory workshop on electronic mouth-only instruments, co-led by an expert with tetraplegia. Grounded in Tangible Musical Interface design, our approach emphasises sensorimotor interactions to reconnect digital sound creation with embodied experience. To support the playful exploration of this design space, we developed a modular toolset combining electronic input and feedback modalities for the mouth, along with methods for custom-built accessibility devices.

Keywords: Musical Instruments · Accessible User Interfaces · Inclusive Design Methods · Education · HCI

1 Introduction

The mouth has diverse sensory faculties paired with precise, fatigue-resistant motor control. Most mouth function is supported by cranial nerves, which are typically unharmed in spinal cord injuries and resilient to some neuromuscular disorders, making the mouth an essential means of operating accessibility devices. However, the mouth remains relatively unexplored as a means of interfacing with digital instruments. In this paper, we describe a three-day workshop that invites participants to explore new possibilities for accessible musical interfaces while emphasising embodied interaction. The context for this workshop was the Master's programme in Postdigital Lutherie at the Tangible Music Lab, where students work at the intersections of design, technology, composition, and musical performance. During this practical workshop, the students were introduced to a toolset of technologies and methods for quickly prototyping their ideas.

K. Miesenberger et al. (Eds.): ICCHP 2026, LNCS 16867, pp. 435–442, 2027.
https://doi.org/10.1007/978-3-032-31308-9_52

2 State of the Art

2.1 The Mouth and Human-Computer-Interaction (HCI)

For vocalisation, tasting, mastication, and swallowing, the mouth has evolved high degrees of dexterity and tactile and chemical sensitivity. The mouth's environment serves as a wet lab for sensory measurements, providing us with rich sensory information. For example, the tongue has the most sensitive touch receptors of any part of the body [1, 2]. These observations have motivated explorations of mouth- and intraoral computer interfaces in HCI. Two of the most famous examples are accessibility aids, with the Sip-and-puff device [3] and the Tongue Display Unit [4]. Further examples exist for a broad range of use cases, such as discreet interaction, hands-free operation, and silent speech [5–8], some of which have been repurposed for AT [9]. Extensive exploration also exists in HCI research for sensory modalities of the mouth, such as electrotactile [10], vibrotactile [11], acoustic bone conduction [12], and electronic taste simulation [13, 14]. Frameworks are also emerging for mouth-based gestures and interactions [15].

2.2 Enactivism and Tangibility in Musical Instruments

Tangible Musical Interfaces use physical devices that afford the creation of sound through direct, "hands-on" interaction. Such interfaces reduce cognitive load by leveraging our innate spatial and embodied cognitive processes [16]. They are inherently multimodal, integrating touch, proprioception, and action with auditory feedback, so that physical gestures are closely coupled to perceived musical outcomes. These interfaces are also inherently enactive, in that they mediate experience through real-time sensorimotor coupling. In other words, actions drive experience, making them more accessible than conventional digital interfaces [17]. Designing tangible interfaces for the mouth introduces distinct, largely unexplored challenges but also unique opportunities: the oral cavity is a highly sensitive, dexterous, and multimodal region of the body, offering new possibilities for expanding embodied experiences of music making. Mouth interaction is central to wind instruments, but it also offers a compelling foundation for hands-free, accessible instrument design [18].

2.3 Related Work

Musical instruments have historically been underrepresented in the field of Assistive Technology (AT). However, in recent years, some solutions have been developed to close this gap, particularly those suitable for people with tetraplegia. Examples like *The Magic Flute* demonstrate breath-controlled interfaces for hands-free performance [29]. *Skoog* is a tactile, multi-sensory and customisable electronic musical instrument designed to be inclusive and accessible [19]. The *Clarion* is a digital instrument that can be played with any part of the body, including head movements or eye tracking [20]. *Soundbeam* takes a similar approach, allowing any physical movement to be translated into MIDI data [21]. There are also several examples of playful mouth-based musical interfaces that are not explicitly designed for people with disabilities but are inherently accessible by addressing modalities beyond hand-based interactions [22, 23]. However, few systems integrate both input and feedback modalities within the oral cavity, limiting opportunities for tightly coupled interaction.

3 Methodology

3.1 Awareness Raising and Participatory Approach

The workshop was designed using a participatory approach, ensuring the target user group remained central to the process. To facilitate this, the author Gerhard Nussbaum, who has high-level tetraplegia, was present throughout the workshop, providing feedback and lived-experience expertise to the students. He has extensive experience in accessible technology and design, but is not a professional musician. The workshop had six master's students who are burgeoning experts in the design and technology of digital instrument-making. The students had some prior exposure to accessibility topics, and the workshop was an assessed part of their curriculum. The students developed three functional prototypes over three days of inputs, ideation and experimentation.

Sensitisation and Demonstration. The session commenced with a dedicated awareness-raising phase. The expert demonstrated a variety of mouth-operated AT solutions and specialised techniques used in his daily life, including a mouth-stick for keyboard and mouse use, writing, and handicrafts such as macramé and weaving (via video). There was also a live demonstration of an RC helicopter controlled via a specialised mouth-operated joystick.

Hands-on (Mouth-on) Experience. Following the demonstration, a practical "learning-by-doing" approach was implemented to deepen the students' empathy and technical understanding. Students were tasked with constructing their own functional mouth sticks and using them to perform specific tasks, such as typing on a computer keyboard and completing cursive writing and drawing exercises. This transition from observation to active participation enabled students to directly experience the ergonomic challenges and motor-skill demands of mouth-controlled interfaces, fostering a more nuanced perspective on inclusive design [24].

3.2 Design Brief

The students were instructed to create a musical object or instrument that can be used via a novel mouth interface, without the need for hands. They were instructed to consider enactive aspects of the interaction and the sensory qualities of the user experience. There will always be both sensory and motor aspects to any user interaction, but students were explicitly instructed to consider how the design can incorporate additional layers of information and feedback to enhance the interaction experience. Additionally, the students were asked to maintain hygiene and to consider how components that contact the mouth can be sterilised or replaced. To conclude the initial session, a 'Spaeed Dating' [29] was conducted to facilitate the rapid idea development.

3.3 Introduction to the Toolset and Technology

A toolset was introduced to allow the participants to rapidly develop interactive prototypes. The selection supported ergonomic design and diverse input and output modalities. All tools were provided with instructions and examples of their usage in accessibility aids. The students were already familiar with CircuitPython, the ESP32 microcontroller and had experience with programming and various software tools for musical synthesis. All students opted to use Ableton Live with the Max for Live plugin for visual coding for audio synthesis. The toolset consisted of the following items (Fig. 1):

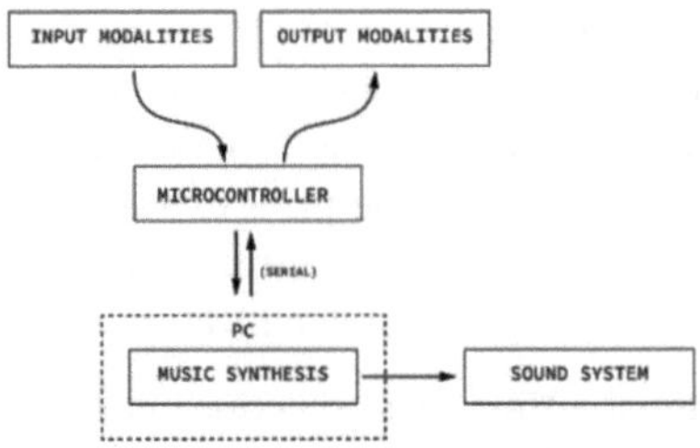

Fig. 1. A high-level system overview of the technology setup.

- **Mouthpieces:** 3D-Printed Mouthpieces made from FDA-compliant XPETG [25], designed and printed by the author Gerhard Nussbaum with high-level tetraplegia.
- **Pressure Sensors:** The ST LPS35HW sensor was provided for building Sip'n'puff-style interfaces, with a convenient nozzle for attaching silicone tubing.
- **Force Sensors:** Flexible force sensors, like those produced by Tekscan, can capture pressure from the tongue, lips or cheeks, or biting with the teeth.
- **TDU Pop (Tongue Display Unit):** We developed a custom TDU device with a 5×5 electrode grid that can be easily integrated into a prototypical interface. The hardware design is open source [26] and based on Kaczmarek's work [10].
- **Bone Transducers and Haptics:** We provided the 1 W Bone Transducer from Adafruit, and the DRV2605L haptic driver together with a selection of ERM and LRA haptic engines. These provide in-mouth tactile and auditory feedback.

The toolset's electronic components were provided with CircuitPython example code to facilitate rapid experimentation [27].

3.4 Fabrication Methods

We have to take care when designing oral interfaces so that they are both safe for the user and that the electronics are protected from saliva. Recent developments in digital fabrication methods for orthodontics have allowed many possibilities for fabricating intraoral computer interfaces [28]. There are a number of resins and filaments available for both SLA and FDM that are certified for prolonged contact with the mouth, such as FDA-compliant PLA or PETG.

4 Results

4.1 Prototypes

Mouth Hocketing. A tongue- and bite-controlled mouth interface designed for duo performance. One performer's bite gestures enable sound generation, while tongue gestures control parameters and provide electrotactile feedback to the other performer's tongue, creating an interdependent, distributed instrument. The design draws on the medieval hocket technique, in which a melody is shared through alternating voices (Fig. 2).

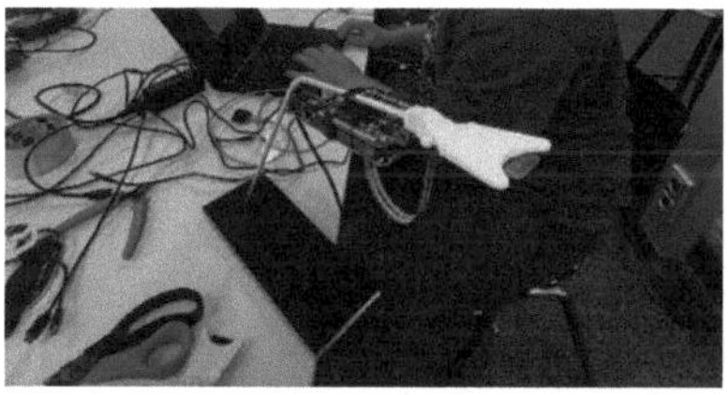

Fig. 2. The Mouth Hocketing device, showing the integration of TDU, mouthpiece and force sensors. Further workshop images are omitted to preserve anonymity during review.

Bitwise Operator. A bite- and touch-controlled mouth interface for a drum sampler and looper with integrated haptic feedback. Drum samples are selected via a mouth held stylus. Sounds are then triggered or looped through bite duration, enabling layered rhythmic composition. Vibro-acoustic feedback to the teeth confirms triggering and recording actions.

Smoking Hot. This instrument is integrated into a cigarette holder, with inhalation translated into melody, which is heard through the mouthpiece itself via bone conduction at the jaw, resulting in a private musical augmentation to the smoking ritual. This prototype is an artistic exploration and was not intended to promote tobacco use.

4.2 User Tests

During the final hour of the workshop, Gerhard Nussbaum tested and evaluated all three prototypes. Following a brief introduction by the students, he successfully interacted with each device, generating musical outputs in accordance with the students' original design concepts and specifications.

Mouth Hocketing. The participant successfully selected and generated tones using tongue interactions on the Tongue Display Unit (TDU). He noted that while precise tone selection is achievable with practice, the initial interaction had interesting qualities more akin to experimental sound art than a traditional musical instrument.

Bitwise Operator. This prototype allowed him to immediately generate drum rhythms. He successfully selected different beats, seamlessly adding them to and removing them from the loop. The vibroacoustic feedback transmitted through the teeth supported intuitive operation of the looper (Fig. 3).

Fig. 3. Students debugging their instrument with assistance from Gerhard Nussbaum.

Smoking Hot. Sound production was successfully achieved during testing with the prototype, but controlling the tone required practice. He categorised the experience as a sonification of the act of smoking.

Beyond the technological evaluation, the author highlighted the group's creative dynamics as a significant qualitative outcome. The students demonstrated a remarkable ability to navigate the complex intersection of alternative input methods, AT, and musical instrument design. The most significant outcome was the high level of student engagement with AT and enthusiasm for building accessible musical instruments.

5 Discussion

This work was not designed with systematic usability evaluation in mind, but rather as an exploratory, practice-based workshop. Further development of individual outcomes is beyond the scope of this paper, but could include evaluations with a broader range of individuals to assess usability and expressive potential. It also remains unclear how our approaches would translate to professional musical contexts, where questions of virtuosity, reliability, and integration into existing performance practices become critical. Finally, the prototypes raise important ergonomic considerations; further iterations should address long-term comfort and fatigue, and develop more refined, custom-fitted, and durable mouth interfaces suitable for extended use.

In the workshop, we deliberately spent little time discussing best practices for inclusive design. While this belongs in the curricula across all disciplines in design education, no set of guidelines can account for the diversity of lived experience. What is more fundamental is the ability to engage people with disabilities as experts within the design process. The workshop methodology presented here empowers students to collaborate directly with users and develop situated, practice-based approaches to inclusive design. Such collaboration is essential not only for creating accessible technologies but for cultivating a lasting, embodied understanding of inclusion. Future work should explore how this approach can be adapted and applied across different design disciplines.

6 Conclusion

This work demonstrates that mouth-based musical interfaces can expand both accessibility and performative expression by emphasising embodied interaction and tangibility. The workshop shows how participatory and embodied design methods, supported by a prototyping toolset, enable rapid exploration of inclusive electronic instruments within an educational context. While technologically grounded, this approach prioritises playful exploration, collaboration, and exchange with people with motor disabilities, rather than a problem-solving model typical of engineering-led design frameworks. Framing accessibility as a possibility for playful experimentation benefited both participants with and without disabilities, revealing mouth-based interaction not as compensatory but as a potential for expressive and sensorily rich musical performance.

The authors highly recommend implementing such interdisciplinary participatory workshops in design education. Directly engaging users with disabilities alongside students is crucial for designing accessible musical interfaces or AT in a broader sense and serves as an invaluable tool for cultivating a lasting awareness of inclusive design.

Acknowledgments. We would like to thank the students for their contributions: *Mouth Hocketing* by Gorka Egino and Ricardo Pastor; *Bitewise Operator* by Boris Shershenkov, Mobina Vatandoost, and Omid Zolfaghari; *Smoking Hot* by Saumil Bhandari.

References

1. Aktar, T., Chen, J., Ettelaie, R., Holmes, M.: Tactile sensitivity and capability of soft-solid texture discrimination. J. Texture Stud. **46**, 429–439 (2015)
2. Won, S.-Y., Kim, H.-K., Kim, M.-E., Kim, K.-S.: Two-point discrimination values vary depending on test site, sex and test modality in the orofacial region: a preliminary study. J. Appl. Oral Sci. **25**, 427–435 (2017)
3. Maling, R.G., Clarkson, D.C.: Electronic controls for the tetraplegic (possum) (patient operated selector mechanisms—P.O. S.M.) (1963). https://doi.org/10.1038/sc.1963.15
4. Bach-y-Rita, P., Kaczmarek, K.A., Tyler, M.E., Garcia-Lara, J.: Form perception with a 49-point electrotactile stimulus array on the tongue. J. Rehabil. Res. Dev. **35**, 427–430 (1998)
5. Vaidyanathan, R., et al.: Tongue-movement communication and control concept for hands-free human–machine interfaces. IEEE Trans. Syst. Man Cybern. A Syst. Hum. **37**, 533–546 (2007)
6. Maag, B., Zhou, Z., Saukh, O., Thiele, L.: BARTON: Low power tongue movement sensing with in-ear barometers. In: 2017 IEEE 23rd International Conference on Parallel and Distributed Systems (ICPADS), pp. 9–16. IEEE (2017)
7. Sun, R., et al.: EchoNose: Sensing mouth, breathing and tongue gestures inside oral cavity using a non-contact nose interface. ACM ISWC23 (2023)
8. Zhang, Q., Gollakota, S., Taskar, B., Rao, R.P.N.: Non-intrusive tongue machine interface. In: Proceedings of the SIGCHI Conference on Human Factors in Computing Systems. ACM, New York, NY, USA (2014)
9. Jain, P., Salter, C.L.: "Can I use my mouth to navigate in VR?": Integrating Mouth Gestures in XR with (and for) Disabled Artists through Criptastic Hacking. ACM CHI (2025)
10. Kaczmarek, K.A.: The tongue display unit (TDU) for electrotactile spatiotemporal pattern presentation. Sci. Iran D Comput. Sci. Eng. Electr. Eng. **18**, 1476–1485 (2011)
11. Jiang, Y., et al.: MouthIO: Customizable oral user interfaces with integrated sensing and actuation. ACM SCF24 (2024)
12. Popelka, G.: SoundBite hearing system by sonitus medical: A new approach to single-sided deafness. Semin. Hear. **31**, 393–409 (2010)

13. Ranasinghe, N., Nakatsu, R., Nii, H., Gopalakrishnakone, P.: Tongue mounted interface for digitally actuating the sense of taste. In: 2012 16th International Symposium on Wearable Computers, pp. 80–87. IEEE (2012)
14. Miyashita, H.: Norimaki Synthesizer: Taste Display Using Ion Electrophoresis in Five Gels. ACM CHI 20 (2020)
15. Chen, V., et al.: Understanding the Design Space of Mouth Microgestures. ACM DIS21 (2021)
16. Ishii, H., Ullmer, B.: Tangible bits. In: Proceedings of the ACM SIGCHI Conference on Human factors in computing systems, pp. 234–241. ACM, New York, NY, USA (1997)
17. Vetter, J., Kaltenbrunner, M., Schmid, E.: Sonic interactions - towards accessible digital music-making. In: Lecture Notes in Computer Science, pp. 489–496. Springer Nature Switzerland, Cham (2024)
18. Davanzo, N., Avanzini, F.: Hands-free accessible digital musical instruments: Conceptual framework, challenges, and perspectives. IEEE Access. **8**, 163975–163995 (2020)
19. Rinta, T.: A casestudy on the use of an innovative, technical, musical instrument, Skoog, in a special needs education setting with a child with autism and its effects on social skills. J. Music Technol. Educ. **12**, 179–200 (2019)
20. The Clarion, https://theclarion.uk/. Last accessed 06 February 2026
21. Soundbeam, https://www.soundbeam.co.uk/. Last accessed 06 February 2026
22. Wang, Y., Li, Z., Jarvis, R., Khot, R.A., Mueller, F.: The singing carrot: Designing playful experiences with food sounds. CHI PLAY18 (2018)
23. LICKESTRA, https://emiliebaltz.com/experiments/lickestra/. Last accessed 04 February 2026
24. Ernst, W., Nussbaum, G., Berger V.M., Major, Z.: Mouthsticks – A Participatory Approach. In: Studies in Health Technology and Informatics. IOS Press (2017)
25. XPETG MATT, https://extrudr.com/en/at/products/xpetg-matt/. Last accessed 06 February 2026
26. Franzke, L.: TDU_Pop, https://github.com/pixeloxx/TDU_Pop. Last accessed 08 April 2026
27. Nussbaum, G., Franzke, L.: accessibility_design_linz_25, https://github.com/pixeloxx/accessibility_design_linz_25. Last accessed 08 April 2026
28. Franzke, L., Gartmann, J., Bachmann, D., Töpper, T., Franinović, K.: TOFI: Designing Intraoral Computer Interfaces for Gamified Myofunctional Therapy. ACM CHI 23 (2023)
29. Davidoff, S., Lee, M.K., Dey, A.K., Zimmerman, J.: Rapidly exploring application design through speed dating. In: UbiComp 2007: Ubiquitous Computing, pp. 429–446. Springer Berlin Heidelberg, Berlin, Heidelberg (2007)

Tactile Graphics and 3D Models for Blind People and Shape Recognition by Touch

Tactile Graphics and 3D Models for Blind People and Shape Recognition by Touch Introduction to the Special Thematic Session

Tetsuya Watanabe[1](✉), Yoshinori Teshima[2], and Kazunori Minatani[3]

[1] Faculty of Engineering, Niigata University, Ikarashi 2-8050, Nishi-Ku, Niigata 950-2181, Japan
t2.nabe@eng.niigata-u.ac.jp

[2] Faculty of Engineering, Chiba Institute of Technology, Tsudanuma 2-17-1, Narashino-Shi, Chiba 275-0016, Japan
yoshinori.teshima@chibatech.ac.jp

[3] National Center for University Entrance Examinations, Komaba 2-19-23, Meguro-Ku, Tokyo 153-8501, Japan
minatani@dnc.ac.jp

Abstract. This Special Thematic Session highlights recent advances in tactile graphics and 3D models for people who are blind or visually impaired. The session covers eight papers addressing 3D-printed educational models, tactile maps, audio-haptic games, and spatial guidance systems. A particular focus is placed on how emerging fabrication and interaction technologies improve accessibility, spatial understanding, and educational support compared with conventional tactile graphics and audio-based methods. These studies collectively demonstrate the growing role of 3D tactile media in assistive technology and inclusive education.

Keywords: Tactile Graphics · 3D Models · People who are Blind or Visually impaired · Shape Recognition

1 Introduction: Importance of 3D Models

The English word photography, that refers to images captured by a camera, was coined in 1839 by the British scientist John Herschel, combining the Greek words phos ("light") and graphein ("to draw"), a term that aptly describes the method itself. In Japanese, on the other hand, pictures taken by a camera is called "shashin," where "sha" means draw or capture and "shin" means truth. So, the combination of these two words literally means "a true copy of what is seen" or "a faithful representation of reality." When this technology was introduced to Japan from the Netherlands around 1840–1860, it appears that the pre-existing word "shashin" was adopted for this new technology, as its meaning matched the concept of faithfully capturing reality.

For sighted people, the term "shashin" is highly appropriate, as it literally means capturing what is seen. However, for people with visual impairments, understanding tactile graphics that represent objects in two dimensions is not always straightforward,

K. Miesenberger et al. (Eds.): ICCHP 2026, LNCS 16867, pp. 445–450, 2027.
https://doi.org/10.1007/978-3-032-31308-9_53

and such representations can hardly be considered equivalent to a "true copy." In contrast, understanding through touching 3D objects is much easier. In this sense, it can be said that 3D-printed models *are* the "shashin" (true copy) for people with visual impairments.

This is vividly illustrated by the reactions of people with visual impairments when they touch 3D models. Over the past five years (2020—2024), we provided a service in which we created and delivered 3D models requested by visually impaired clients [1]. Many recipients commented that the shapes they perceived through touch differed substantially from those they had imagined from written descriptions in books or documents. Others reported that they understood the shapes of famous buildings for the first time when they touch the models although they knew their names.

As part of the above project, we organized a series of online symposia on 3D models twice a year. A distinctive feature of these symposia is that the 3D models discussed during the event were sent to the audience with visual impairments in advance, allowing them to touch the models themselves while listening to the panelists' speech [2]. A questionnaire survey conducted among symposium participants in the middle of 2020 revealed that 14 of the 28 respondents who answered questions about tactile exploration of models stated that they liked touching objects or were strongly interested in doing so [1]. One respondent commented, "It is not simply that I like it; it is instinctive. Instead of seeing with the eyes, I observe with my hands and fingers." Other comments reflected a strong desire for tactile experiences: "At schools for the blind, we learned by touching real objects and models, but after entering university, opportunities to touch things drastically decreased"; "I always buy models, if any, at tourist sites"; and "If there is even one object that are allowed to touch in a museum, I feel the visit was worthwhile." Some respondents with low vision also emphasized advantages of tactile exploration over visual observation, stating that "touching allows understanding of the whole structure as well as the details better than viewing a photograph or the actual object from a single viewpoint," and "after touching the model and then looking at photographs, I realized the model had accurately represented the object," implying that important spatial features had not been noticed through vision alone.

In the same survey, 20 respondents commented on the differences between tactile graphics and 3D models. Most stated that tactile graphics were difficult to use for understanding the shapes of 3D objects, whereas 3D models were easier to comprehend. Three respondents further noted that touching 3D models improved memory for object shapes. One suggestion was that, for complex objects, understanding the 3D model becomes easier by examining a simplified tactile graphic before touching the model. Some respondents remarked that training is necessary to accurately translate between 2D tactile graphics and 3D objects, while others—particularly congenitally blind participants—reported that they were unable to imagine 3D shapes from tactile graphics alone. On the other hand, tactile graphics were considered well suited for understanding information that is inherently 2D, such as maps and graphs. On the other hand, a scale model of a university campus was highly appreciated because it enabled users to understand spatial relationships more clearly than with a 2D map (made of capsule paper).

2 Evolution of Research and Practice Involving 3D Models

As mentioned in the first section, the advantages of 3D models over tactile graphics are clearly reflected in the words of individuals with visual impairments. In addition to such subjective reports, scientifically validated findings obtained through experimental studies would further strengthen the argument. Research and practice involving 3D models began to increase, including ours, notably from around the mid-2010s, when 3D printers became affordable enough for individual purchase. In the early stage of introducing a new technology, simply applying it to a target field—in our case, assistive technology—was itself considered novel. However, after several years, this type of novelty gradually diminished. Instead, the focus has shifted toward evaluating how much 3D models improve education and quality of life compared with previous methods. In the field of support for people with visual impairments, the main question is whether the use of 3D models, either instead of or in combination with tactile graphics and audio, can improve communication and understanding. This session also includes several studies of this kind.

3 Papers in this Session

This Special Thematic Session was initiated in 2010, several years before 3D printers became widely accessible, and the 2026 edition marks its ninth installment. This years session involves eight papers, of which five address 3D printing, three focus on tactile maps, and two deal with haptic games, with some overlap across categories.

Both "Effectiveness of tactile diagrams and 3D models in yoga instructions for people who are blind or visually impaired" and "Development of models for anatomical learning for the visually impaired: Skull model, ventricle and brainstem model, eyeball model" address the development and evaluation of 3D tactile educational models of the human body [3, 4]. The former study evaluates how accurately participants can reproduce human body postures using their own bodies. The latter has been developing 3D educational materials based on requests from teachers in the therapeutic education department of schools for the blind, providing them to the schools, receiving feedback, and continuously refining them through an iterative cycle."Using 3D pens for creating personalized tactile learning models for students with visual impairments" also deals with tactile learning materials; however, its primary focus is on the methodology for creating such materials [5]. In situations where the introduction and operation of 3D printers are difficult, the paper proposes the use of 3D pens as an alternative and demonstrates the creation of 3D geometry learning materials. "Development of spatial haptic-guidance presentation system for visually impaired individuals and evaluation of 3D tactile perception and ball-game situation transmission" used 3D-printed models as educational materials for visually impaired users, and a spatial haptic-guidance presentation system was developed to effectively support the understanding of 3D structures and dynamic ball-game situations through combined haptic and auditory presentation [6].

3D printers are also being applied to the creation of indoor tactile maps. "3D building model with interactive tactile maps for older adults with vision impairments" focuses on their usability for older adults with visual impairments, examining the comprehensibility of the 3D-printed models [7]. Two more papers deal with tactile maps and tactile graphics. The key novelty of "An end-to-end pipeline to generate augmented tactile maps from floor plans" lies in the seamless integration of automatic tactile map generation from architectural floor plans and hotspot-based speech augmentation [8]. " Cognitive maps and audio-haptic game performance in individuals with visual impairments: A correlational study" investigates the relationship between performance in an audio-haptic navigation game and the quality of cognitive maps constructed by individuals with visual impairments [9].

The final paper "Smooth, structured, and strategic: Hand movement proficiency of visually impaired players in tactile puzzle game Tactris" also deals with games, but its particular focus is on whether hand movements during tactile game play differ between expert players and beginners [10]. Both the research focus and the methodology of this study could also be extended to the analysis of tactile exploration behaviors in the use of tactile graphics and 3D models in general.

4 Future Research Directions

Research themes involving 3D models extend far beyond simply evaluating their effectiveness. As 3D fabrication technologies mature and become integrated with new materials, AI, and generative design, new research directions are rapidly emerging in both assistive technology and mainstream engineering fields.

One important topic concerns the representation of dynamic body movements. Previous studies have proposed presenting motion through tactile animations using a refreshable tactile display (RTD) [11]. Because RTDs are refreshable by nature, they are suitable for expressing temporal changes and sequential motion. Nevertheless, the fundamental difficulty of comprehending tactile graphics remains. In contrast, 3D models are generally easier to understand tactilely, but conventional 3D-printed objects are static. Even when movable models are introduced, the posture intended by the designer may unintentionally change while being touched by the user. Furthermore, highly flexible motions of the human body are difficult to reproduce faithfully using mechanical joints alone. At present, a practical approach may be to identify and present a limited number of characteristic or informative postures using 3D models. Future research is therefore expected to investigate which postures are most effective for conveying movement, motor intention, or spatial relationships, and how sequences of tactile poses can support the understanding of dynamic actions.

Another promising direction involves soft materials to realize movable models. One paper in this session focuses on anatomical learning models [4]. Traditionally, tactile anatomy education has relied mainly on rigid bone models or detachable anatomical parts. However, understanding anatomy also requires comprehension of joint movement, muscle attachment, and biomechanical interaction. Recent advances in flexible filaments, silicone casting, and multi-material 3D printing suggest the possibility of constructing hybrid tactile models in which soft muscle structures can be attached to rigid skeletal components while preserving joint mobility. Such models could enable visually impaired students to understand not only static structures but also functional movement and mechanical relationships within the body. Similar approaches are already emerging in medical simulation, indicating strong potential for future applications in education for visually impaired students.

A third emerging topic is 3D modeling by visually impaired people themselves. In the past, tactile model creation required advanced CAD skills or programming knowledge. Some blind users with strong technical backgrounds have successfully created models using script-based systems such as OpenSCAD, in which 3D structures are defined through textual commands [12]. However, such approaches remain inaccessible to many users. Recent developments in generative AI, text-to-3D systems, and conversational modeling interfaces may dramatically lower this barrier. In the near future, visually impaired users may be able to obtain printable 3D data simply by describing an object verbally, for example, "Create a simplified printable model of a traditional Japanese castle" or "Generate the approximate shape of a dolphin." Similar needs are currently driving rapid progress in AI-assisted 3D modeling for animation, gaming, and virtual reality. Monitoring these broader technological trends may therefore reveal highly transferable technologies for assistive applications.

More generally, 3D technologies are highly versatile and are advancing rapidly across a wide range of disciplines, including manufacturing, medicine, robotics, digital fabrication, entertainment, and human-computer interaction. The future development of assistive technology will likely depend not only on research conducted specifically for disability support, but also on the active incorporation of innovations emerging from mainstream technological fields.

References

1. Watanabe, T., Minatani, K., Iwamura, M.: 3D model supplying service for blind people—Analysis of service usage and questionnaire responses. IEICE Technical Report **120**(279), 45–49 (2020)
2. Minatani, K., Watanabe, T.: Online symposium with touch: An attempt to organise an online 3D model tactile symposium for the visually impaired. In: Proceedings of the 16th International Conference on PErvasive Technologies Related to Assistive Environments (PETRA 2023), Corfu, Greece, July 5–7, pp. 1–5. ACM, New York (2023). https://doi.org/10.1145/3594806.3594830
3. Oyanagi, K., Watanabe, T., Kunishima, K.: Effectiveness of tactile diagrams and 3D models in yoga instructions for people who are blind or visually impaired. In: Miesenberger, K., Petrie, H., Penaz, P. (eds.) ICCHP 2026, Computers Helping People with Special Needs, 20th International Conference; Linz, Austria, Proceedings. Springer (2026)
4. Teshima, Y.: Development of models for anatomical learning for the visually impaired: skull model, ventricle and brainstem model, eyeball model. In: Petz, A., Miesenberger, K. (eds.) ICCHP Open Access Compendium "Future Perspectives on Accessibility, AT and eInclusion"; Linz, Austria, Proceedings. Johannes Kepler University Linz (2026)
5. Pokorná, B., Bátorová, M.: Using 3D pens for creating personalized tactile learning models for students with visual impairments. In: Miesenberger, K., Petrie, H., Penaz, P. (eds.) ICCHP 2026, Computers Helping People with Special Needs, 20th International Conference; Linz, Austria, Proceedings. Springer (2026)
6. Sakai, T., et al.: Development of spatial haptic-guidance presentation system for visually impaired individuals and evaluation of 3D tactile perception and ball-game situation transmission. In: Miesenberger, K., Petrie, H., Penaz, P. (eds.) ICCHP 2026, Computers Helping People with Special Needs, 20th International Conference; Linz, Austria, Proceedings. Springer (2026)

7. Macík, M., Šebestová, K., Míkovec, Z.: 3D building model with interactive tactile maps for older adults with vision impairments. In: Miesenberger, K., Petrie, H., Penaz, P. (eds.) ICCHP 2026, Computers Helping People with Special Needs, 20th International Conference; Linz, Austria, Proceedings. Springer (2026)
8. Quach, M., .: An end-to-end pipeline to generate augmented tactile maps from floor plans. In: Miesenberger, K., Petrie, H., Penaz, P. (eds.) ICCHP 2026, Computers Helping People with Special Needs, 20th International Conference; Linz, Austria, Proceedings. Springer (2026)
9. Koustriava, E., Chronopoulou, E., Fountouki, C., Michailidou, S., Papadopoulos, K.: Cognitive maps and audio-haptic game performance in individuals with visual impairments: A correlational study. In: Miesenberger, K., Petrie, H., Penaz, P. (eds.) ICCHP 2026, Computers Helping People with Special Needs, 20th International Conference; Linz, Austria, Proceedings. Springer (2026)
10. Matsuo, M., et al.: Smooth, structured, and strategic: Hand movement proficiency of visually impaired players in tactile puzzle game Tactris. In: Miesenberger, K., Petrie, H., Penaz, P. (eds.) ICCHP 2026, Computers Helping People with Special Needs, 20th International Conference; Linz, Austria, Proceedings. Springer (2026)
11. De Silva, M., Goodwin, S., Holloway, L., Butler, M.: Understanding challenges and opportunities in body movement education of people who are blind or have low vision. In: Proc. of the 25th International ACM SIGACCESS Conference on Computers and Accessibility (ASSETS '23), 1–12. ACM, New York (2023)
12. Minatani, K.: Finding 3D CAD Data Production Methods that Work for People with Visual Impairments. In: Stephanidis, C. (ed.) HCI International 2017 – Posters' Extended Abstracts. CCIS, 713, pp. 397–403. Springer (2017)

3D Building Model with Interactive Tactile Maps for Older Adults with Vision Impairments

Miroslav Macík[1(✉)], Kateřina Šebestová[2], and Zdeněk Míkovec[1]

[1] FEE, Czech Technical University in Prague, Prague, Czech Republic
macikmir@fel.cvut.cz
[2] University College London, London, UK

Abstract. A tactile model of a building with integrated interactive tactile maps was evaluated with eight older adults with vision impairment (mean age = 81 years). The results show that the audio feedback triggered by the buttons facilitates spatial learning. Combining audio feedback with tactile symbols may further support this process, but symbol interpretation is strongly influenced by personal experience.

Keywords: Tactile Maps · Vision Impairment · Older Adults

1 Introduction

People with severe vision impairment (according to WHO classification [10]) appear mainly among older adults. According to Bourne et al. [3], 86.3 % of blind people are older than 50 years and 52.8 % older than 70 years, and this trend prevails in subsequent studies [2]. However, the group of older adults with vision impairments (*VIOA*) is underrepresented in the current research [12,14]. We present a qualitative exploratory evaluation of a 3D building model with integrated interactive tactile maps as depicted in Fig. 1.

2 Related Work

Independent orientation and mobility in spatial environments is one of the most essential preconditions for *VIOA* well-being [1]. Efficient orientation and route-finding require creation and maintenance of a *Cognitive Map* – an internal mental representation of the environment [15]. It comprises multiple parallel representations of an environment, including allocentric (object-to-object) and egocentric (subject-to-object) representations [5], typically categorized as locations and landmarks, layout, routes, and distances/directions between locations [11].

Natural acquisition of *Cognitive Maps* during navigation in spatial environments is often supplemented by scaled environment projections – (tactile) maps. Reading a tactile map is a cognitively more intensive task than reading a visual

K. Miesenberger et al. (Eds.): ICCHP 2026, LNCS 16867, pp. 451–458, 2027.
https://doi.org/10.1007/978-3-032-31308-9_54

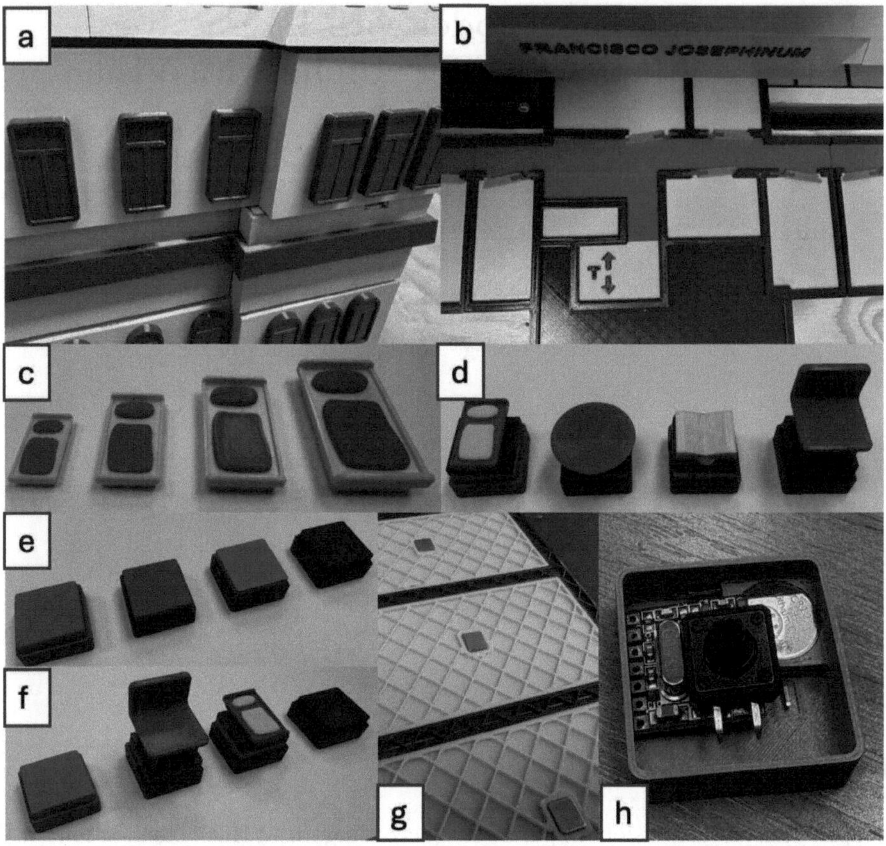

Fig. 1. 3D building model with integrated interactive tactile maps. Exterior tactile symbols (a), interactive tactile maps in drawers (b), different scale of symbols (c), magnetic symbols used for experiment (d), magnetic wireless buttons to trigger output (e), magnetic symbols can be attached to buttons (f), magnets embedded 3D-printed into tactile map (g), implementation of wireless buttons using RF433 (h).

map due to the need for constant referencing and orientation via touch [6]. Digital tactile maps can reduce cognitive load by incorporating high-fidelity media output such as audio information [4,7] and may also encourage exploration [17].

Cole in [6] proposed a research agenda for tactile cartography in the digital age, highlighting the absence of research on the usage of tactile maps. Tactile maps can be useful not only before visiting a real environment but also during or after the visit to supplement/improve the spatial knowledge. For example, a blind participant in the study [16] expressed her desire to use a tactile map after visiting a place in person to better integrate the knowledge gained.

The introduction of multi-story buildings has recently attracted the attention of the research community. Nagassa et al. [9] show that overlapping multi-story tactile maps of buildings are preferred over separate floor plans. They tested sliding and rotating arrangements. Sargsyan et al. [13] propose a 3D interactive model allowing representation of complex multi-story spatial environments with skeuomorphic features. To our knowledge, there is no research on tactile models that combines tactile representations of building exteriors and interactive tactile plans of interiors.

3 Experiment

3.1 The Model

The exterior of the building is represented as a 3D model with tactile symbols indicating key architectural features. Interior spaces are presented through tactile floor plans stored in drawers integrated into the model (Fig. 1). Each 3D-printed floor plan contains embedded magnets that allow flexible placement of interactive elements. The map encodes spatial structure through raised walls, corridors, and rooms, with high-contrast surfaces. The door segments on tactile floor plans are attached using flexible material to allow natural movement (side, direction) similar to real doors (see Fig. 1 b). Interactive wireless buttons (depicted in Fig. 1 h) allow sending a signal to a computer-connected base station using the RF433 radio. This solution, similar to wireless doorbells, provides a cheap, reliable, and battery-efficient way to implement interactive symbols without additional wiring.

3.2 Experiment Design

The experiment was carried out in a *VIOA* residential care facility using an interactive tactile model of the building with interchangeable floor plans. The model included magnetic points for placing interactive elements: 3D tactile symbols (bed, book, chair, plate) printed in four sizes (see Fig. 1 c), and interactive buttons providing audio feedback via a double-press mechanism (see Fig. 1 d), whereby the room name was followed by additional orientation information. Tactile symbols could be combined with the interactive buttons using magnets. Qualitative data were collected through audio and video recordings, observation, and explicit feedback, focusing on exploration strategies, symbol recognition errors, and signs of cognitive overload. Quantitative data were obtained using a post-test 5-point Likert scale System Usability Scale (SUS) [8].

3.3 Participants

A total of eight participants participated in the study (5 females, 3 males), representing residents of a long-term care facility, see Table 1. They were recruited in collaboration with the institution to evenly represent groups according to their length of stay in the care facility. Each participant received compensation. One participant withdrew. The age range of the sample was 71 to 90 years (M = 80.6, SD = 6.3). Visual impairment according to WHO IDC-11 categories ranged from 3 (severe vision impairment) to 6 (blindness) [10], with a duration

Table 1. Participant characteristics.

Participant	Gender	Age	Imp. Cat.	Imp Duration (yrs)	In Care Inst. (yrs)	SUS
P1	F	73	3–4	65	2	85
P2	M	86	3–4	1	0.3	70
P3	F	82	3	13	4	70
P4	M	81	3	5	3	92.5
P5	F	83	3	80	3	65
P6	M	71	5	5	0.75	95
P7	F	79	4	5	1	DNF
P8	F	90	3	10	2	22.5

of impairment ranging from 1 to 80 years (M = 23, SD = 31.0). They had been living in residential care for 0.3 to 4 years (M = 2.0, SD = 1.3).

The participants were divided into three groups according to their length of stay in the care facility, corresponding to their familiarity with the building. New residents (n = 2) had lived in the facility for less than a year, established residents (n = 3) for one to two years, and experienced residents (n = 3) for more than two years.

3.4 Procedure

An informed consent about the experiment procedure and data collection (including recording) was read to the participants, and the research team answered all related questions. Then, they were introduced to the experiment and instructed to follow the think-aloud protocol. The first phase began with familiarization with the model, including exploration of the exterior (Task 1) and the third-floor tactile map (Task 2), identifying key points (entrance, room, door). In Task 3, participants evaluated four tactile symbols in four sizes based on recognition accuracy, room association, and preferred size.

The next phase (Task 4) focused on comparing the effectiveness of interactive elements. Participants explored a map with audio-feedback buttons. The intuitiveness of the double-press mechanism and the usefulness of the messages were assessed. The participants then compared symbols and buttons and evaluated a combined solution integrating both.

In the final phase, the participants' ability to apply the knowledge acquired was tested. The participants first located key points on the map (Task 5). Task 6 assessed allocentric navigation through route pointing and egocentric navigation through verbal route descriptions. Perspective transfer and narrative complexity (route vs. spatial knowledge) were recorded, followed by a System Usability Scale (SUS) questionnaire. After the experiment ended, the participants were debriefed and given the opportunity to provide any additional feedback.

3.5 Analysis

Session recordings were rewatched and annotated by the researcher, producing structured observation notes that captured behavioural patterns, participant quotes, and emerging interpretations. These notes were then organised into thematic clusters (e.g., symbol recognition, exploration strategies, audio feedback reactions, ego/allocentric confusion).

3.6 Results

Reactions to audio feedback were consistently positive across participants. A particularly notable outcome emerged among participants who had lived in the facility for years yet held inaccurate spatial models of the building. P6, who is fully blind, described how the exterior model revealed that his room was positioned differently than he had always assumed: 'I thought, almost always, that my window from the room faces the other side.' This illustrates the potential of tactile building models to build new cognitive maps and revise misconceptions about familiar environments.

The double-press mechanism was typically intuitive only after brief explanation (P1, P3, P4, P5, P7, P8), while P6 found it non-intuitive and expected the full message after the first press. A recurring issue was perseverance, where the participants kept pressing despite completed output (P1, P5, P7). Combining non-interactive symbols with interactive buttons led to confusion (P3).

Exploration typically began slowly and cautiously, with participants starting near familiar anchor points such as their own room before gradually extending outward (P1,P3. P1 expressed concern about handling the model itself: 'I'm afraid I'll rip it out.' Over time, participants grew more confident and began connecting newly discovered locations to personal memories and routines: 'Oh, that's the dining room I go to…' (P3), indicating active, experience-driven spatial learning rather than reliance on simple left/right directions. Confusion with ego- and allocentric left/right orientation cues occurred in several participants (P5, P7, P8).

The tactile symbols varied in level of recognition: the chair was usually quickly identified (P1, P4), while the bed and plate were frequently misinterpreted. Overall, participants preferred larger symbols. Symbol interpretation was heavily based on experience, as participants mapped items to familiar places rather than abstract categories. Recognition often improved after providing hints. For instance, the book symbol was consistently associated with a library, despite no library existing in the facility. Recognition often improved after providing hints: P1 noted that even smaller ones became recognisable once learned: 'Now that I know, even the smaller ones are recognisable'

The average SUS score was 71.4 (MIN = 22.5, MAX = 95, $STDEV$ = 24.6). One session had to be ended early without completing the SUS form. One participant showed values indicative of a potential outlier (SUS score 22.5). The SUS score excluding this participant was 79.6 (MIN = 65, MAX = 95, $STDEV$ = 12.9) indicating good usability.

4 Discussion and Conclusion

Participants consistently associated symbols with real-world experiences, reflecting their own experiences rather than abstract categories. Even seemingly obvious objects (e.g., a bed) were prone to misinterpretation, suggesting that tactile maps for older users should first consider the context of familiar objects. Participants demonstrated active and iterative exploration. They often revisited familiar rooms and used them as landmarks for further orientation. They also tended to instantly connect the places they discovered on the map with their own experiences, often mentioning activities or other residents.

When participants felt uncertain or appeared lost on the map, they relied heavily on auditory cues provided by interactive buttons. This may indicate the importance of multimodal feedback in supporting the spatial perception of *VIOA*. This is in line with the results of Götzelmann [7] or Brock [4]. In contrast, tactile symbols alone did not appear to be as supportive.

The general trend was that multi-stage feedback made the exploration and learning easier. However, some participants had difficulty understanding the double-click mechanism, which led to repeated button presses without waiting for the audio output to finish. In these cases, provision of ongoing instructions and guidance was necessary, suggesting that independent exploration may not be realistic in this context. Introducing a tactile map as part of structured training or supervised learning sessions could be an effective way to maximize its positive impact. Overall, users were able to successfully transform allocentric map information into egocentric routes, suggesting the advantages of using tactile maps in combination with interactive elements.

In conclusion, our findings suggest that audio feedback is central to spatial learning and cognitive mapping for *VIOA*, whereas tactile symbols offer more variable, context-dependent support.

Based on the nature and extent of the research presented in this paper, we identified the following limitations. First, the evaluation was limited to a sample of seven participants (one participant left the session earlier). The experiment was also limited to a single session in one residential care institution. Therefore, a broad generalization is not supported by the data nor intended in this phase od research. We identified an outlier (P8) with a clear negative attitude toward the concept.

Future work should address the limitations by conducting a long-term study involving a larger sample of *VIOA* representatives. To allow a broader generalization, another type of building should be investigated. The future study should also cover the broader context of adaptation and usage, focusing on practical impact on spatial orientation confidence and efficiency. Furthermore, participants with a negative attitude to the concept observed in our study (P7, P8) suggest that the proposed concept may not be equally suited to all users within the target population. Future work should therefore aim to characterize subgroups for whom the interaction model shows inappropriate, or to investigate personalization and adaptive strategies to allow broader acceptance.

Acknowledgments. This research was supported by research project New interaction methods in virtual reality (SGS25/149/OHK3/3T/13) supported by the Czech Technical University in Prague.

References

1. Bleau, M., Kafle, K., Wang, M., Kabore, S.S., Cueva-Vargas, J.L., Nemargut, J.P.: International prevalence of tactile map usage and its impact on navigational independence and well-being of people with visual impairments. Sci. Rep. **15**(1), 27245 (2025)
2. Bourne, R., et al.: Trends in prevalence of blindness and distance and near vision impairment over 30 years: an analysis for the global burden of disease study. Lancet Glob. Health **9**(2), e130–e143 (2021)
3. Bourne, R.R., et al.: Magnitude, temporal trends, and projections of the global prevalence of blindness and distance and near vision impairment: a systematic review and meta-analysis. Lancet Glob. Health **5**(9), e888–e897 (2017)
4. Brock, A.M., Truillet, P., Oriola, B., Picard, D., Jouffrais, C.: Interactivity improves usability of geographic maps for visually impaired people. Hum. Comput. Interact. **30**(2), 156–194 (2015)
5. Burgess, N.: Spatial cognition and the brain. Ann. N. Y. Acad. Sci. **1124**(1), 77–97 (2008)
6. Cole, H.: Tactile cartography in the digital age: a review and research agenda. Prog. Hum. Geogr. **45**(4), 834–854 (2021)
7. Götzelmann, T.: Visually augmented audio-tactile graphics for visually impaired people. ACM Trans. Accessible Comput. (TACCESS) **11**(2), 1–31 (2018)
8. Lewis, J.R.: The system usability scale: past, present, and future. Int. J. Hum. Comput. Interact. **34**(7), 577–590 (2018)
9. Nagassa, R.G., Butler, M., Holloway, L., Goncu, C., Marriott, K.: 3d building plans: supporting navigation by people who are blind or have low vision in multi-storey buildings. In: Proceedings of the 2023 CHI Conference on Human Factors in Computing Systems, pp. 1–19 (2023)
10. Organization, W.H.: International classification of diseases 11 - vision impairment including blindness (2018). https://icd.who.int/browse11/l-m/en#/, http://id.who.int/icd/entity/1103667651
11. Ottink, L., Buimer, H., van Raalte, B., Doeller, C.F., van der Geest, T.M., van Wezel, R.J.: Cognitive map formation supported by auditory, haptic, and multimodal information in persons with blindness. Neurosci. Biobehav. Rev. **140**, 104797 (2022)
12. Palivcová, D., Macík, M., Míkovec, Z.: Interactive tactile map as a tool for building spatial knowledge of visually impaired older adults. In: Extended abstracts of the 2020 CHI conference on human factors in computing systems, pp. 1–9 (2020)
13. Sargsyan, E., Oriola, B., Macé, M.J., Serrano, M., Jouffrais, C.: 3d printed interactive multi-storey model for people with visual impairments. In: Proceedings of the 2023 CHI Conference on Human Factors in Computing Systems, pp. 1–15 (2023)
14. Thomas, J., Almidani, L., Swenor, B.K., Varadaraj, V.: Digital technology use among older adults with vision impairment. JAMA Ophthalmol. **142**(5), 445–452 (2024)
15. Tolman, E.C.: Cognitive maps in rats and men. Psychol. Rev. **55**(4), 189 (1948)

16. Trinh, V., Manduchi, R.: Feeling your way around: assessing the perceived utility of multi-scale indoor tactile maps. In: Extended Abstracts of the 2020 CHI Conference on Human Factors in Computing Systems, pp. 1–8 (2020)
17. Zeng, L., Weber, G.: Exploration of location-aware you-are-here maps on a pin-matrix display. IEEE Trans. Hum. Mach. Syst. **46**(1), 88–100 (2015)

Effectiveness of Tactile Diagrams and 3D Models in Yoga Instruction for People Who Are Blind or Visually Impaired

Kohei Oyanagi[1], Tetsuya Watanabe[2(✉)], and Kaori Kunishima[3]

[1] Graduate School of Science and Technology, Niigata University, Ikarashi 2-8050, Nishi-Ku, Niigata 950-2181, Japan

[2] Faculty of Engineering, Niigata University, Ikarashi 2-8050, Nishi-Ku, Niigata 950-2181, Japan
t2.nabe@eng.niigata-u.ac.jp

[3] Incorporated Association Challenged Yoga—Yoga for People with Visual Impairments, Tokorozawa, Japan
christinkaoru@gmail.com

Abstract. Yoga is widely used as a suitable form of physical exercise for people with visual impairments; however, understanding and performing yoga poses remains challenging due to the lack of visual information. This study examines the effectiveness of tactile diagrams and three-dimensional (3D) models as instructional supports for yoga lessons. Nine adults with visual impairments participated in an experiment comparing three instructional conditions: audio-only instruction, tactile diagrams with audio, and 3D models with audio. Participants reproduced yoga poses following six verbal instructions per pose. Comprehension time, reproduction time, pose quality evaluated by a yoga instructor, and subjective preferences were measured. Although tactile materials required longer comprehension and reproduction times than audio-only instruction, pose quality was comparable across conditions. Subjective evaluations showed a strong preference for the 3D model condition, suggesting that tactile materials, particularly 3D models, enhance perceived understanding and provide a useful alternative to physical contact in yoga instruction.

Keywords: Tactile Diagram · 3D Models · Yoga Instruction · People who are Blind or Visually Impaired

1 Introduction

People with visual impairments are at increased risk of physical inactivity, and various physical activity interventions have been proposed to address this issue. Among these, yoga has been widely adopted because yoga consists primarily of slow movements and the maintenance of static postures, without requiring vigorous physical exertion [1]. Despite its suitability, understanding and accurately performing yoga postures remains a significant challenge for individuals with visual impairments, as yoga instruction often relies heavily on visual demonstration [2].

K. Miesenberger et al. (Eds.): ICCHP 2026, LNCS 16867, pp. 459–466, 2027.
https://doi.org/10.1007/978-3-032-31308-9_55

Conveying body posture and movement is a well-known challenge not only in yoga instruction but also across a wide range of sports and physical education activities for individuals with visual impairments. In practice, posture is commonly conveyed through verbal explanation, often supplemented by direct physical contact between the instructor and learner [3]. However, verbal instructions alone may be insufficient to convey precise body configurations, while physical contact may be uncomfortable or unacceptable for some learners and therefore requires careful consideration of personal preferences and consent [4]. To address these limitations, alternative tactile approaches have been proposed, including tactile diagrams, refreshable tactile displays (RTDs), and 3D models. These methods have shown promise in supporting the understanding of body configuration or movements among learners with visual impairments [5–7]. In this study, we investigate whether learning yoga poses using tactile diagrams and 3D models can facilitate pose comprehension for people with visual impairments, thereby reducing reliance on verbal explanation and physical contact.

2 State of the Art

To convey body posture and movement to individuals with visual impairment, the use of tactile materials—such as tactile diagrams, RTDs, and 3D models—have been proposed. Among these, tactile diagrams have long been used to convey shape and spatial structure to people with visual impairments [5]. They can be produced using dedicated techniques such as braille embossers and swell paper, as well as low-tech cut-and-paste methods based on readily available materials.

In contrast to tactile diagrams, RTDs and 3D models represent more recent approaches. RTDs are particularly well suited not only for presenting static graphics but also for conveying motion. For example, Holloway et al. represented Tai Chi poses using tactile graphics and an RTD and compared preferences among people with visual impairments, finding that the RTD was preferred [6].

3D printers have increasingly been used to convey human body postures. Sakashita et al. recorded dance movements with a camera, analyzed the joint positions, and generated a series of 3D human body models [8]. Sucharitakul et al. demonstrated that teaching Thai dance to students with visual impairments using 3D models, in combination with audio instruction, led to greater improvements than audio-only instruction [7]. De Silva et al. reported that commercially available flexible human body models are used in practice for body movement education for blind and low-vision learners [5].

Focusing on yoga instruction for people with visual impairments, Rector et al. developed an exergame that uses depth cameras to track body posture and provide non-visual feedback, and showed that such feedback enables the participants who were blind or low vision to perform and correct yoga poses [2]. Islam et al. demonstrated that vibrotactile feedback effectively improved yoga pose correction performance and user preference in both sighted and visually impaired participants [9]. Mohanty et al. taught yoga to 41 students with visual impairments using five instructional methods and conducted a questionnaire survey on preferred learning methods [10]. Their results indicated that instruction involving direct physical contact was most preferred (79%), followed by tactile diagrams (52%). Mohanty et al. employed tactile diagrams; however, 3D models have been suggested to be more understandable than tactile diagrams. In addition, while Mohanty et al. relied solely on subjective evaluations, we considered it important to objectively assess learners' understanding. Thus, our research purpose is to objectively investigate the effectiveness of tactile diagrams and 3D models for teaching yoga postures to people with visual impairments.

3 Methodology

3.1 Participants

Nine participants with visual impairments, aged between 61 and 80 years (mean age = 70.6 years, SD = 6.6) took part in the study. All nine participants were women; four had congenital visual impairments and five had acquired visual impairments. Seven participants had prior experience with yoga, while two had no such experience.

This experiment was reviewed by the "Ethical Review Committee for Research Involving Human Subjects" of Niigata University in accordance with the guidelines of the Declaration of Helsinki for research involving human subjects and conducted with the permission of the President of Niigata University (Approval No. 2025–0058). Written informed consent was obtained from all participants, with the forms completed by a third party independent of the experimenter.

3.2 Materials

We selected four beginner-level yoga poses that can be achieved through six verbal instructions: Gate, Crescent Lunge, Triangle, and Upward Facing Dog Poses. The first one was used for learning of experimental procedure and the other three for the actual experiment.

An example of verbal instructions for Crescent Lunge Pose is as follows: (1) Step one foot forward. (2) Bend the knee of the forward leg. (3) Lower the knee of the opposite leg to the floor. (4) Bring your palms together and extend both arms overhead. (5) Lift your face and look toward your fingertips. (6) Gently arch your back. These instructional sentences were read aloud using a text-to-speech system (CoeFont).

For the production of the 3D models, an upright human figure was downloaded and modified into yoga poses using the 3D CAD software Fusion 360 (Autodesk). For printing, the model was scaled to a height of 165 mm in an upright posture. This size is close to the one (18 cm) that was most preferred and yielded the highest level of comprehension in an experiment comparing three different model sizes [11]. The models were printed using a 3D printer (Ultimaker S3) and white PLA filament. In total, 24 pose models were created (four yoga poses times six (five intermediate and one final) postures) (Fig. 1). Apart from the experiment, the 3D models of the final poses were displayed at an exhibition for people with visual impairments, where they were well received by visitors.

The above-created 3D data were saved as images and imported into a web-based tactile map drawing application [12]. When drawing tactile posture diagrams, the views were selected so that the most diagnostically important joint angles and limb relationships for each pose are maximally distinguishable. The outlines of the images were manually traced, and the resulting image files were converted to PNG format and printed on A4-sized swell paper (Matsumoto Yushi-Seiyaku) using a laser printer (Canon, LBP9510C). The printed capsule paper was then processed using a swell-form machine (American Thermoform) (Fig. 1).

Fig. 1. Tactile diagrams and 3D models for three yoga poses. From the left, Crescent Lunge, Triangle, and Upward Facing Dog Poses.

3.3 Procedure

Participants were instructed to perform the yoga poses following three different instructional methods: Audio-only instruction, tactile diagram and audio (hereafter referred to as tactile diagram) instruction, and 3D model and audio (hereafter referred to as 3D model) instruction.

The experiment consisted of three sessions. In each session, participants were instructed to complete two kinds of yoga poses using one of the three instructional methods. The first pose, Gate, was used for familiarization with the experimental procedure, and the second pose was used for measurement. Performing a yoga pose consisted of six steps that coincided with the six verbal instructions. At the beginning of each step, the audio instruction was played back; in the tactile diagram and 3D model conditions, the participants also began exploring the tactile materials at this time. Under all the conditions, the participants were allowed to listen to the audio instructions repeatedly, and in the tactile diagram and 3D models conditions, they were allowed to explore the tactile materials until they felt that they had understood the indicated pose. After understanding the pose, participants were asked to reproduce it using their own bodies. From the second instructional sentence onward, the pose indicated by the next instruction was added to the pose formed by the preceding instruction(s). The pose comprehension and reproduction time was measured by a stopwatch. This procedure was repeated until the sixth step was completed. The final pose was photographed. After performing the yoga poses under all three conditions, participants were asked to rank the three conditions by preference. Three different presentation orders of the three conditions were assigned to groups of three participants each. The combinations of the conditions and yoga poses were also varied across the participants.

After the experiment, the third author, a certified yoga instructor with experience teaching people with visual impairments, observed the photos of the final poses online and evaluated their quality on a five-point scale.

4 Results

4.1 Comprehension Time

The average pose comprehension time for the audio condition was the shortest, 8.3 s, followed by 3D model, 16.9 s, and tactile diagram, 23.4 s (Fig. 2). Compared to the audio condition, tactile diagram took approximately three times as long, and 3D model, twice as long. A one-way analysis of variance (ANOVA) revealed a significant difference among the three presentation conditions ($F(2,16) = 18.45, p < 0.001$). Post hoc multiple comparisons using the Bonferroni method showed that the tactile diagram condition ($p = 0.0037$) and the 3D model condition ($p = 0.0017$) both resulted in significantly longer posture comprehension times than the audio condition. This increase in comprehension time with tactile materials is due to the tactile exploration time, and the tactile diagrams needed more time than the 3D models.

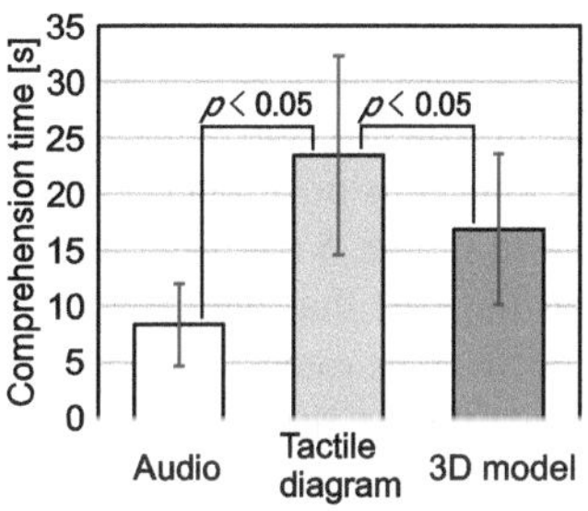

Fig. 2. Comprehension time.

4.2 Pose Reproduction Time

The average pose reproduction time for the audio condition was the shortest, 8.0 s, followed by 3D model, 11.8 s, and tactile diagram, 15.6 s (Fig. 3). Compared to the audio condition, tactile diagram took approximately twice as long, and 3D model, 1.5 times as long. A Friedman test revealed a significant difference among the three presentation conditions ($\chi^2(2) = 8.00$, $p = 0.018$). Post hoc multiple comparisons using Wilcoxon signed-rank tests with Bonferroni correction showed that the pose reproduction time was significantly longer in the tactile diagram condition than in the audio condition ($p = 0.023$). Under the audio condition, many participants maintained the immediately preceding pose while listening to the audio instruction. In contrast, under the tactile diagram and 3D model conditions, many participants sat down to explore the tactile materials while listening to the instructions and then began reproducing the pose sequentially from the first step. This difference in actions led to the longer pose reproduction times in the tactile material conditions.

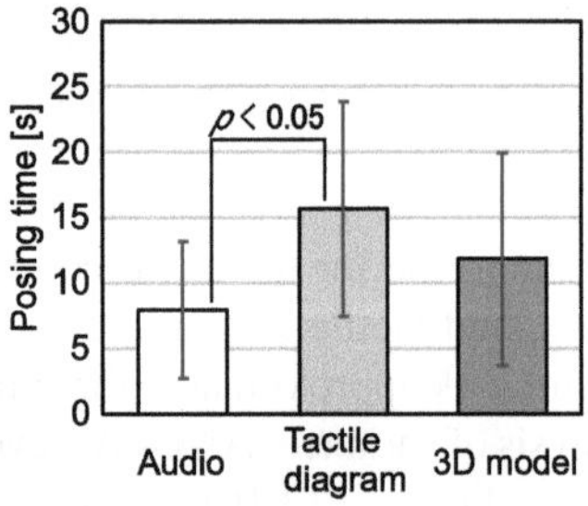

Fig. 3. Reproduction time.

4.3 Pose Quality Evaluation

The mean scores of pose quality evaluation, in descending order, were 3.89 for the 3D model condition, 3.56 for tactile diagram, and 3.44 for audio; the scores were generally comparable across conditions (Fig. 4). A Friedman test revealed no significant difference among the three presentation conditions ($\chi^2(2) = 1.52$, $p = 0.47$). Figure 5 presents examples of the poses that did not receive full scores. The pose in Fig. 5 (a) was rated three points because the front knee was positioned ahead of the ankle and the rear leg was not fully extended. The pose in Fig. 5 (b) was rated three points due to the narrow distance between the feet and the fact that the arm extended toward the ceiling was not straight. The pose in Fig. 5 (c) was rated four points because the elbows were not fully extended. These examples indicate that while participants were generally able to perform the actions explicitly described in the instructional sentences, the third author as a yoga instructor evaluated the poses based on criteria that were not fully captured by the verbal instructions, such as precise body alignment and safe joint angles.

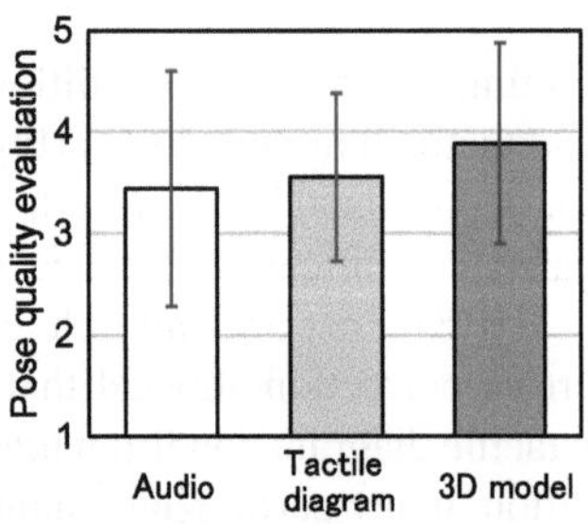

Fig. 4. Pose quality evaluation.

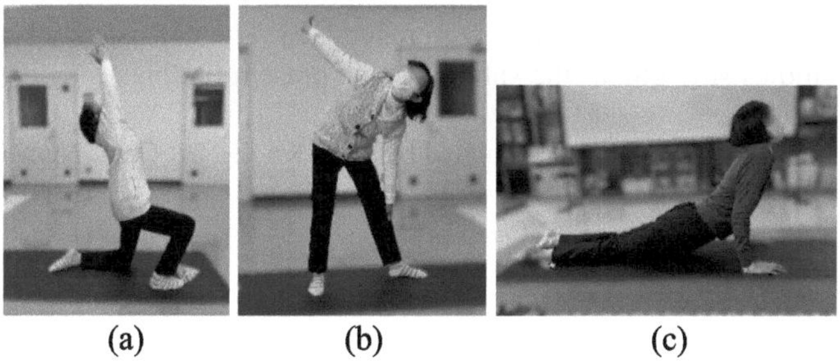

Fig. 5. Examples of pose reproductions that did not receive full scores.

4.4 Preferance

Seven out of the nine participants preferred the 3D model condition the most (Fig. 6).

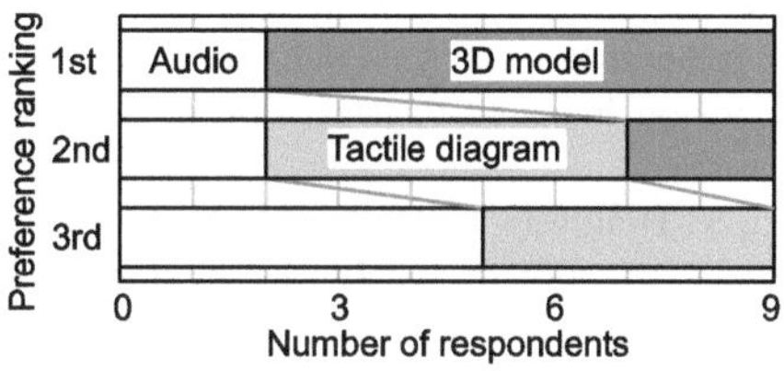

Fig. 6. Preferences of each condition.

5 Discussion and Conclusion

Considering the instructor's evaluations and the physical benefits that yoga poses provide, verbal instructions alone are insufficient for accurately reproducing desirable postures. Information such as joint angles, the orientation and position of the arms and legs, and the degree of back arching was not adequately conveyed by the audio instructions, which likely contributed to the participants' inability to accurately reproduce the pose. Likewise, these features were also difficult to infer from the tactile diagrams and the 3D models. For sighted learners, the gap between the instructed pose and their own body alignment can be compared visually; however, for learners with visual impairments, this gap must be addressed through physical contact or the use of tactile instructional materials.

Although the use of tactile materials required longer comprehension and reproduction times than audio alone, participants' preferences—particularly for the 3D model condition—indicated that these materials fostered a stronger sense of understanding of the poses. From this perspective, incorporating tactile instructional materials, especially easily explorable 3D models, appears to be meaningful in yoga instruction. In particular, for learners who are reluctant to engage in physical contact, the use of 3D models can be considered a desirable alternative.

Interestingly, similar findings have recently been reported in other studies on non-visual body movement instruction, where 3D tactile models were found to improve learners' perceived understanding and preference [13]. The consistency between these independent studies strengthens the validity of the present findings.

Acknowledgements. This work was supported by JSPS KAKENHI Grant Number 20H01705 and 24H00162.

References

1. Jeter, P.E., Dagnelie, G., Khalsa, S.B.S., Haaz, S., Bittner, A.K.: Yoga for persons with severe visual impairment: a feasibility study. Altern. Med. Stud. **2**, e5 (2012)
2. Rector, K., Bennett, C.L., Kientz, J.A.: Eyes-free yoga: an exergame using depth cameras for blind and low vision exercise. In: Proceedings of the 15th International ACM SIGACCESS Conference on Computers and Accessibility (ASSETS 2013), pp. 1–8. ACM, Washington (2013)
3. Lieberman, L.J., Lepore, M., Lepore-Stevens, M., Ball, L.: Physical education for children with visual impairment or blindness. J. Phys. Educ. Recreation Dance **90**(1), 30–38 (2019)
4. Vision Sports Ireland: Vision Impaired Physical Education Guide. Vision Sports Ireland, Dublin (2023)
5. De Silva, M., Goodwin, S., Holloway, L., Butler, M.: Understanding challenges and opportunities in body movement education of people who are blind or have low vision. In: Proc. of the 25th International ACM SIGACCESS Conference on Computers and Accessibility (ASSETS '23), pp. 1–19. ACM, New York (2023). https://dl.acm.org/doi/10.1145/3597638.3608409
6. Holloway, L., et al.: Animations at your fingertips: using a refreshable tactile display to convey motion graphics for people who are blind or have low vision. In: Proc. of the 24th International ACM SIGACCESS Conference on Computers and Accessibility (ASSETS '22), pp. 1–16. ACM, New York (2022). https://doi.org/10.1145/3517428.3544797
7. Sucharitakul, S., Phuengngern, C., Ketaiam, K., Hongyeesibed, S.: Educational tool kits for basic traditional Thai dancing for learners with visual impairment. Cogent Arts Hum. **10**, 2281234 (2023). https://doi.org/10.1080/23311983.2023.2283948
8. Sakashita, M., Suzuki, K., Kawahara, K., Takazawa, K., Ochiai, Y.: Materialization of motions: tangible representation of dance movements for learning and archiving. In: Proc. of ACM SIGGRAPH '17, Article 7, ACM, New York (2017)
9. Islam, M.S., Lee, S.W., Harden, S.M., Lim, S.: Effects of vibrotactile feedback on yoga practice. Front. Sports Active Liv. **4**, 1023456 (2022). https://doi.org/10.3389/fspor.2022.1005003
10. Mohanty, S., Hankey, A., Pradhan, B., Ranjita, R.: Yoga-teaching protocol adapted for children with visual impairment. Int. J. Yoga **9**(2), 114–120 (2016)
11. Watanabe, T., Sato, K.: Suitable size of 3D printing architecture models for tactile exploration. J. Technol. Persons Disabil. **7**, 45–53 (2019). http://hdl.handle.net/10211.3/210389
12. Mori, Y., Watanabe, T.: Development of a web application for supporting the creation of tactile maps on swell paper. IEICE Techn. Rep. **119**(322), 119–124 (2019)
13. Tanaka, K., Wang, X., Takagi, H., Ochiai, Y., Asakawa, C.: Touching movement: 3D tactile poses for supporting blind people in learning body movements. In: Proceedings of the Twentieth International Conference on Tangible, Embedded, and Embodied Interaction (TEI 2026), Article 29, pp. 1–19. ACM, New York, NY (2026). https://doi.org/10.1145/3731459.3773325

Using 3D Pens for Creating Personalized Tactile Learning Models for Students with Visual Impairments

Barbora Pokorná(✉) and Martina Bátorová

Faculty of Mathematics, Physics and Informatics, Comenius University in Bratislava, Mlynská dolina, 842 48 Bratislava, Slovakia
{barbora.pokorna,martina.batorova}@fmph.uniba.sk
https://fmph.uniba.sk/en/departments/department-of-algebra-and-geometry/

Abstract. Access to tactile learning materials is essential for students with visual impairments; however, such materials are often costly, inflexible, or require advanced technical skills to produce. This paper explores the use of 3D pens as an innovative, low-cost, and teacher-friendly assistive tools for creating personalized tactile learning models in educational settings, and their preliminary evaluation in the context of education of visually impaired pupils. The proposed approach emphasizes accessibility, rapid customization, and minimal digital skill requirements.

Keywords: Tactile Learning · Inclusive Education · Geometry Learning · Visual Impairment · 3D Pen

1 Introduction and Motivation

Inclusive education is an important objective of modern educational systems, aiming to ensure equal access to quality education for all students, including those with disabilities. Students with visual impairments require specific teaching approaches, adapted materials, and appropriate compensatory aids in order to fully participate in the educational process. Although Slovak legislation formally guarantees this right under Act No. 245/2008 on Education [7], practical barriers persist, particularly in non-specialized schools. Limited financial resources, insufficient teacher training, and restricted access to assistive educational aids often create a gap between inclusive policy and classroom reality.

In Slovakia, the Slovak blind and partially sighted union [3] connects many organizations supporting people with visual impairments. However, only two specialized primary schools focus on students with visual impairments [1,2], while no dedicated non-vocational secondary school exists. Consequently, many students continue their education in mainstream secondary schools, where adequate support is not always available. These challenges are especially evident in mathematics education. While some subjects can be adapted relatively easily, e. g. by transcribing textbooks into Braille, geometry requires carefully designed

K. Miesenberger et al. (Eds.): ICCHP 2026, LNCS 16867, pp. 467–475, 2027.
https://doi.org/10.1007/978-3-032-31308-9_56

tactile representations. This need becomes even more pronounced in solid geometry, where learners rely heavily on physical models to construct accurate mental representations of spatial relationships.

The practical relevance of this challenge became evident through collaboration with a specialized school for students with visual impairments [1], which requested the development of tactile teaching aids to support the instruction of solid geometry at the seventh-grade level. At this stage, the curriculum covers topics such as the volume and surface area of basic solids (e.g. cubes, prisms, and pyramids) as well as spatial elements including body diagonals. The school emphasized the need for solutions that are affordable, easily producible, and adaptable to students' learning needs.

Currently available models in Slovak schools are usually designed either as solid objects or as wireframe structures without filled faces, see Fig. 1 (left). While solid models allow students to form a general mental representation of the shape, they do not enable exploration of internal geometric relationships. In contrast, wireframe models often hinder the formation of a complete mental image and may lack important elements, such as the height of the solid, body diagonals, or face diagonals. As a result, visually impaired students may experience reduced engagement and fewer opportunities for active participation.

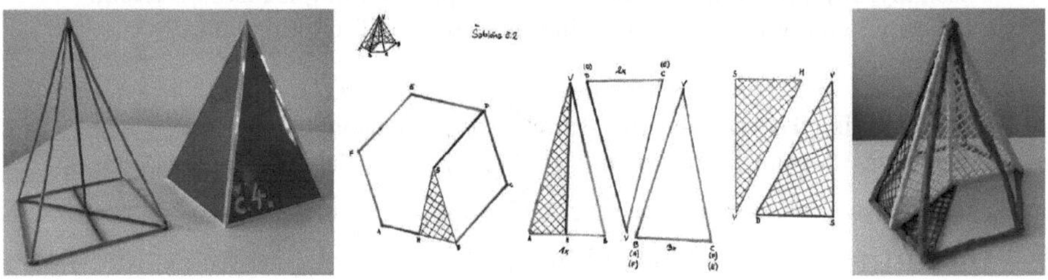

Fig. 1. The models typically available in schools in Slovakia (left). Hand-drawn template used for constructing the tactile model (center) and the corresponding completed geometric solid (right).

2 Related Work

During our initial exploration, we identified primarily open-source repositories of 3D-printable models as available resources for teaching spatial geometry. However, these solutions typically require access to 3D printing technology and digital modeling skills, limiting their practical usability in everyday classroom settings.

Although several repositories providing ready-to-print 3D models for geometry teaching are available (e.g., [16]), prior research suggests that the creation, adaptation, and practical classroom use of such materials remain challenging for educators. According to [12], teachers often prefer real objects and physical three-dimensional models because they provide a more natural learning experience for students; however, such materials are frequently difficult to obtain and can be costly. In contrast, many advanced technologies (e.g. 3D printing) remain underutilized, as they are often perceived as expensive, complex, and not always well aligned with specific instructional goals. Research [4] indicates that tactile graphics can be challenging for students with visual impairments when they are overly complex or poorly designed, underscoring the need for materials that align with principles of tactile perception and usability.

Research on the use of 3D pens in geometry instruction has primarily advanced through a five-year program led by Ng and colleagues [11]. Early work demonstrated that students developed concepts such as tangent lines and solids of revolution through the physical manipulation of mathematical representations, which improved spatial visualization [10]. Subsequent studies introduced lesson designs for teaching the properties of prisms, pyramids, and cross-sections [8] and compared learning outcomes between students using 3D pens and those working with dynamic geometry environments [9].

Collectively, this body of work highlights the role of embodied interaction in mathematics learning, suggesting that 3D pens support visualization, investigation, and retention of geometric relationships.

While existing research demonstrates the educational potential of 3D pens among sighted learners, their capacity to support tactile learning for students with visual impairments remains underexplored. This gap is especially evident in the Slovak secondary education context. Research on effective methods and teaching strategies for spatial geometry instruction for visually impaired students is still limited, despite the recognized importance of inclusive mathematics education. This highlights the need for further investigation to support accessible learning and ensure equal educational opportunities for all.

3 Methodology

An important consideration for implementing assistive technologies in educational settings is their accessibility and usability for teachers themselves, who are key facilitators of learning. In many school systems, including Slovakia, the average age of teachers exceeds 45 years [17], suggesting a predominantly experienced but potentially less technology-oriented workforce. Therefore, approaches that minimize the need for advanced digital skills are particularly valuable, as integrating complex software or design tools for creating instructional materials can present a significant barrier to adoption by education professionals.

Also, as Slovakia lacks specialized non-vocational secondary schools for certain student populations, those intending to pursue higher education are typically integrated into mainstream secondary schools. The proposed approach enables sighted students to support their integrated peers by creating customized physical models using 3D pens. Such practices facilitate the understanding of spatial concepts and promote inclusion, integration, and the reduction of barriers between typically developing and integrated students. Furthermore, this approach contributes to raising awareness and fostering sensitivity within the broader public toward the needs of visually impaired students.

To address these objectives, we selected a 3D printing pen as the primary fabrication tool. It is a handheld fabrication device that enables the creation of three-dimensional objects through the controlled extrusion of heated thermoplastic filament, the specifics on its usage can be found in [13,14]. Functionally similar to desktop 3D printers, the pen melts plastic material and deposits it layer by layer. A 3D pen requires minimal technical setup and can be used almost immediately after activation. Another important advantage is its cost accessibility, positioning it as a feasible option even for resource-constrained schools.

Based on the needs of the partner school [1], our main objective was to design templates for creating tactile models of geometric solids using a 3D pen that can be used in solving tasks focused on the application of the Pythagorean theorem. During the initial consultation with a special education teacher from this school, a key limitation of existing wireframe models (Fig. 1, left) was identified. Specifically, students are unable to correctly recognize right triangles, as the available models represent only the edges without filled surfaces. As a result, students cannot perceive the complete triangular shape through touch and often become disoriented among the individual edges, making it difficult for them to understand the relationships between geometric elements.

Therefore, we designed wireframe models of solids in which all relevant right triangles are made accessible by touch, including their filled interior surfaces, as shown in Fig. 1 (right) and Fig. 3 (left). The models were intended to facilitate a task in which the students were required to determine the height of the solid based on the known lengths of its edges, as well as to solve similar tasks. By physically exploring the structure, the students could locate the relevant right triangles and apply the Pythagorean relationship to calculate the unknown variable.

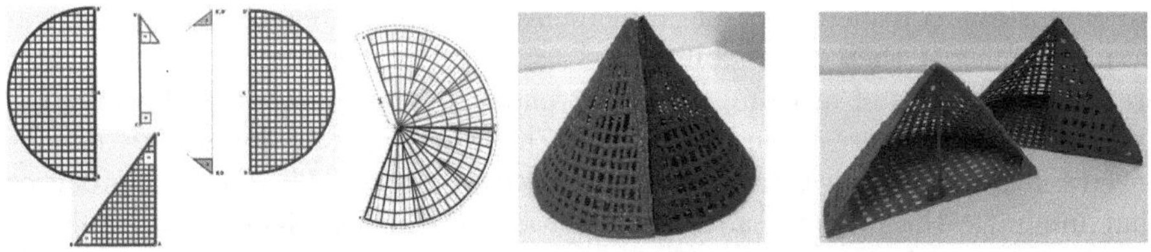

Fig. 2. Cone model enabling exploration of both its internal structure (Pythagorean triangle) and its overall shape thanks to the possibility of separating it into two parts.

Although the wireframe model proved highly beneficial for students, the absence of filled surfaces (faces) did not provide students with sufficient sensory feedback for a comprehensive understanding of the shape; the individual faces had to be mentally inferred, requiring a level of spatial abstraction that can be particularly demanding for learners with congenital blindness. We filled the faces and added magnets so that the interior of the models was accessible, and the modified models were tested again, see Fig. 2.

The models with filled faces were subsequently presented to a special education teacher with over 30 years of professional experience and were tested by two students from [1]. The teacher evaluated the tested model as the most suitable among all the proposed designs, lending strong credibility to this assessment despite the small sample size of student testing.

4 Practical Validation and Educational Workshops

The ability of in-service teachers without previous experience with the 3D pen was tested during practical workshops in Bratislava (09/2025, [14]) and Prague (02/2026, [15]). After a brief instruction, they were able to create geometric models within 70 min, see Fig. 3 (center). Around 50 participants reported a high level of satisfaction with the clarity, practicality, and immediate applicability of the activity in classroom settings. We also received several invitations from various schools and universities in Slovakia to organize a similar workshop for students and pre-service teachers during the academic year 2025/26.

Fig. 3. Wireframe model of a cube (left) with an internal triangle illustrating the computation of the space diagonal using two applications of the Pythagorean theorem. Tactile models of planar cross-sections of solids created during workshops (center) and created by pre-service mathematics teachers (right).

In addition to teacher workshops, the approach was also tested directly with sighted students in classroom settings [13] where students collaboratively created models as part of mathematics lessons. These activities elicited strong engagement, and students aged 12–13 were able to use the 3D pen without significant difficulty.

We also decided to incorporate this approach into the training of pre-service mathematics teachers. Several examples of the students' work can be seen in Fig. 3 (right); further details are provided in [6]. This phase was closely coordinated with the Support centre for students with special needs at the Comenius University in Bratislava [5].

5 Contribution and Discussion

In this paper, we identified the broad potential for the application of 3D pens in the education of visually impaired students. In particular, we highlight the rapid prototyping and testing of solutions directly in teaching practice and their fast, cost-effective implementation and reevaluation with a rapid feedback loop.

While open-access repositories provide 3D printable models for mathematics instruction, modifying these resources typically requires proficiency in CAD or similar software, which may exceed the technical comfort level of many in-service teachers. In contrast, 3D pens allow for direct creation and customization of tactile models without specialized software, thereby lowering technical and cognitive barriers. Templates for constructing the models may be produced either manually or with the support of graphical software, depending on the educator's skills and preferences. The manually created template in Fig. 1 (center) was produced by a 13-year-old student, highlighting the low technical barrier of the approach.

Additionally, the material and equipment costs associated with 3D pens are considerably lower than those of traditional 3D printing setups, making them a cost-effective option for producing personalized learning aids. Beyond financial considerations, 3D printing may be less suitable for models involving suspended or diagonal structures, as these often require support elements that must be manually removed. Production time presents another limitation: printing a single model may take several hours, particularly when a larger size is necessary for meaningful haptic exploration. By comparison, 3D pens support faster fabrication of appropriately scaled models while maintaining low material costs.

The 3D pens also support step-by-step constructions since some spatial geometry constructions require a series of complex steps, e. g. using auxiliary planes and/or lines. Educators or assistants can guide visually impaired students through each stage of the construction in real-time (see Fig. 4). This process-oriented approach supports deeper understanding by linking the formation of the model with the underlying geometric reasoning.

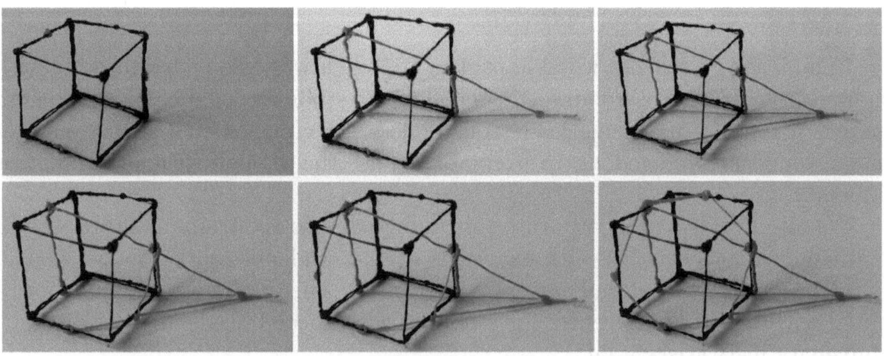

Fig. 4. Step-by-step construction of a planar cross-section of a cube.

An additional advantage of our approach lies in its potential for home use. Due to the relatively low cost and ease of operation of 3D pens, parents may acquire the device and actively support their children's learning outside the classroom, supporting their individual learning needs.

Despite their advantages, 3D pens also present several limitations that should be considered in educational contexts. Models produced with 3D pens tend to be more fragile than those fabricated through conventional 3D printing, which may affect their long-term durability under frequent classroom use. However, their ease and speed of fabrication make them particularly suitable for rapid prototyping of geometric configurations or instructional tasks. Once a model has proven to be pedagogically effective and sufficiently illustrative, teachers may consider producing a more durable version using 3D printing. In addition, the geometric precision of hand-fabricated models can vary depending on the maker's skill level, potentially leading to minor irregularities in shape or proportion.

Also, as a relatively recent technology, the quality of commercially available 3D pens is not yet fully standardized. Lower-cost devices may exhibit technical shortcomings, such as overheating power adapters, highlighting the importance of careful product selection to ensure safe and reliable operation in school environments.

6 Conclusion

This paper presents 3D pens as an accessible tool for creating tactile models to support geometry teaching for students with visual impairments. The approach addresses practical limitations of traditional fabrication methods by offering a low-cost, flexible, and teacher-friendly solution for producing personalized learning materials. Classroom use shows that these tactile models can support spatial reasoning and problem-solving, especially in tasks involving geometric relationships in three-dimensional structures. Their adaptability to individual learning needs further emphasizes their pedagogical value.

So far, our research has focused on a proof of concept, demonstrating the feasibility of using 3D pens in educational settings across different age groups and levels, including teachers, mainstream students, and integrated students. The research involved exploratory probes, case studies, and small-scale collaboration events at schools. Although feedback was largely informal, it was consistently positive, supporting further investigation. Future work will involve systematically designed, rigorous pedagogical research to obtain reliable, measurable, and actionable results.

Acknowledgements. The authors would like to thank Mrs. Zuzana Kucharová for producing the model and photographs used in Fig. 1 (left) and Fig. 2; to Ms. Paulína Pokorná for producing the models and template used in Fig. 1 (center, right) and Fig. 3 (left); and to the partner school [1] for their cooperation and the opportunity to validate the proposed educational aids in practice.

This research was supported by the KEGA grants 038UK-4/2024 and 070UK-4/2026 (both from Comenius University in Bratislava).

Disclosure of Interests. The authors have no competing interests to declare that are relevant to the content of this article.

References

1. Primary boarding school for blind and visually impaired children in Bratislava (Spojená škola internátna pre žiakov so zrakovým postihnutím, Svrčia, Bratislava, Slovakia). https://svrcia.edupage.org/. Accessed 10 Apr 2026
2. Primary boarding school for blind and visually impaired children in Levoča (Spojená škola internátna, Levoča, Slovakia). https://www.skola.nevidiaci.sk/index.php/english. Accessed 10 Apr 2026
3. Slovak blind and partially sighted union. https://unss.sk/slovak-blind-and-partially-sighted-union/. Accessed 10 Apr 2026
4. Aldrich, F.K., Sheppard, L.: Tactile graphics in school education: perspectives from pupils. Br. J. Vis. Impair. **19**(2), 69–73 (2001). https://doi.org/10.1177/026461960101900204
5. Comenius University in Bratislava: Support center for students with special needs. https://uniba.sk/en/about/rektorat-uk/support-center-for-students-with-special-needs/. Accessed 11 Apr 2026
6. Makovník, M., Pokorná, B.: 3D pens in geometry education: a tool for pre-service mathematics teachers. In: Proceedings of the 22nd Internation Conference on Geometry and Graphics (2026). (accepted for publication)
7. National Council of the Slovak Republic: Act No. 245/2008 Coll. on Education (School Act) and on Amendments to Certain Acts (2008). https://www.slov-lex.sk/ezbierky/pravne-predpisy/SK/ZZ/2008/245/. Accessed 10 Apr 2026
8. Ng, O.L., Ferrara, F.: Towards a materialist vision of "learning as making": the case of 3D printing pens in school mathematics. Int. J. Sci. Math. Educ. **18**, 925–944 (2020). https://doi.org/10.1007/s10763-019-10000-9
9. Ng, O.L., Shi, L., Ting, F.: Exploring differences in primary students' geometry learning outcomes in two technology-enhanced environments: dynamic geometry and 3D printing. Int. J. STEM Educ. (2020)
10. Ng, O.L., Sinclair, N.: Drawing in space: doing mathematics with 3D pens. In: Uses of Technology in Primary and Secondary Mathematics Education. ICME-13 Monographs, Springer, Cham (2018)
11. Ng, O.L., Ye, H.: Doing mathematics with 3D pens: five years of research on 3D printing integration in mathematics classrooms. In: Learning Mathematics in the Context of 3D Printing, pp. 143–162. Springer, Germany (2022)
12. Phutane, M., et al.: Tactile materials in practice: understanding the experiences of teachers of the visually impaired. ACM Trans. Accessible Comput. (2022)
13. Pokorná, B.: 3D pen-supported geometry learning in secondary schools. In: Proceedings of the 11th Slovak-Czech Conference on Geometry and Graphics, pp. 141–148. Vydavateľstvo SCHK (2025)
14. Pokorná, B.: Teaching spatial geometry using a 3D pen (in Slovak: Výučba stereometrie pomocou 3D pera). In: Dva dni s didaktikou matematiky 2025, p. 79 (2025). https://fmph.uniba.sk/fileadmin/fmfi/microsites/kdmfi/odm/zbornik2025.pdf
15. Pokorná, B., Bátorová, M.: Innovative teaching of stereometry using a 3D pen (in Slovak, Inovatívne vyučovanie stereometrie s využitím 3D pera). In: Dva dny s didaktikou matematiky 2026 (Sborník příspěvků) (2026). https://www.suma.jcmf.cz/materialy-pro-ucitele/sborniky-z-konferenci/. (accepted for publication)

16. Prusa Research: Printables Education: 3D Models for Educational Use. https://www.printables.com/education?subject=11. Accessed 10 Apr 2026
17. SITA (Slovak information and print agency): Slovak teachers are aging, their average age has increased significantly in recent years (in Slovak) (2025). https://sita.sk/vskolstve/slovenski-ucitelia-starnu-ich-priemerny-vek-za-posledne-roky-vyrazne-vzrastol/. Accessed 04 Feb 2026

Development of Spatial Haptic-Guidance Presentation System for Visually Impaired Individuals and Evaluation of 3D Tactile Perception and Ball-Game Situation Transmission

Tadahiro Sakai[1](✉), Junji Onishi[1], Masatsugu Sakajiri[1], Masaki Matsuo[1], Masamitsu Misono[1], and Takahiro Miura[2]

[1] Tsukuba University of Technology, Tsukuba, Japan
sakai@somlab.org

[2] National Institute of Advanced Industrial Science and Technology, Tsukuba, Japan

Abstract. This study develops a spatial haptic-guidance presentation system that enables visually impaired individuals to rapidly comprehend three-dimensional (3D) information, such as educational models, and to perceive the trajectories of moving objects, such as sports balls. The system integrates standard free exploration with haptic guidance, conveying spatial information through proprioception by pulling the user's fingers. This paper presents an overview of the developed system and reports on two evaluation experiments examining its effectiveness in supporting 3D object understanding and its capability to convey ballgame situations. In the first experiment, we compared the ease of understanding of 3D objects using free exploration versus haptic guidance. Subjective evaluations and introspective reports confirmed that comprehension significantly improved when haptic guidance was used either alone or in combination with free exploration, compared to free exploration alone. Furthermore, a stepwise combination of both methods yielded synergistic effects, further deepening user comprehension. Next, we evaluated the system's ability to convey ballgame situations, focusing on goalball and volleyball. Three presentation conditions were tested: audio only, haptic guidance only, and their combination. The response variables were grasp of the ball's position and trajectory, understand the game situation, and the impact on emotion. Results indicated that audio contributed to immersion, and the inclusion of commentary improved both situational understanding and enjoyment. While haptic guidance was highly effective for grasping spatial positions and the combination of audio information produced enhanced complementary and synergistic effects. Further introspective reports suggested that the multimodal approach offers visually impaired individuals an immersive spectator experience characterized by presence and enjoyment.

Keywords: Visually Impaired Individuals · Spatial Haptic Guidance · 3D Information · Sports Balls · Spatial Movement Trajectory

K. Miesenberger et al. (Eds.): ICCHP 2026, LNCS 16867, pp. 476–484, 2027.
https://doi.org/10.1007/978-3-032-31308-9_57

1 Introduction

Visually impaired individuals who can touch and understand artworks such as paintings and sculptures in museums are highly demanded [1]. In the education field, visual or three-dimensional (3D) content is learned using tactile diagrams and 3D objects. Active tactile perception through free exploration is fundamental for understanding 3D objects [2, 3]; however, it is not easy to understand the shape and content solely through tactile exploration. For example, when learning about the structure of the heart using a model, an individual may require a certain amount of time to understand the relationships between multiple organs; additionally, understanding aspects such as blood flow can be difficult. Research on effective methods for conveying 3D information from this perspective remains limited. Although systems such as I3M (Interactive 3D-printed Models) can interactively present information about explored positions through audio and vibration [4], they still rely heavily on the user's active exploration, which poses challenges for self-learning. Recent studies have explored machine learning approaches to automatically generate guidance for tactile exploration [5]; however, applying these techniques to complex shapes remains highly challenging.

Meanwhile, interest in sports for visually impaired individuals has increased in recent years. In ball games, there are limitations to conveying game rules and match situations using audio commentary alone. Methods suggested for addressing this situation include extracting the soccer ball's position and projecting it on a tactile display with a protruding indication [6], conveying the ball's movement by touching a cursor that follows the ball's movement via magnetic coupling [7], or using tactile impacts to convey the timing of actions in tennis or volleyball [8]. However, these methods involve passive recognition through the sense of touch, thus rendering it difficult to perceive the ball's position and trajectory in real time, and spatial movement cannot be transmitted.

Consequently, effective engineering solutions for presenting 3D spatial information and dynamic movement trajectories to visually impaired individuals have not yet been fully established. To address these challenges and support individuals with visual impairments in understanding the content of 3D objects, as well as conveying the position and dynamic trajectory of balls in ball games, we have been developing a spatial haptic-guided presentation system that convey spatial information using proprioceptive feedback by guiding the fingers, in addition to active tactile cognition through conventional free exploration[9]. Haptic guidance typically involves an assistant guiding a visually impaired individual's finger to teach the structure and functions of 3D objects.

This article provides an overview of the system and presents the evaluation experiments conducted to determine the effects of haptic guidance on 3D tactile perception and ball sports comprehension, as well as to identify appropriate presentation methods using the developed system.

2 Overview of Spatial Haptic-Guidance Presentation System

Figure 1 illustrates the concept of the spatial haptic-guidance method. The system features a function known as haptic guidance in addition free exploration, which mechanically guides the finger along a predefined trajectory to convey the overall structure, key points, and pathways of 3D objects to understand the 3D object created by 3D printers. Information regarding areas touched during free exploration or important regions highlighted by haptic guidance is provided through synchronized audio output. Additionally, the system can convey the real-time position and movement of objects, such as balls, moving through space.

In this system, audio language information as well as haptic-guidance trajectory data, are recorded in XML (eXtensible Markup Language) format with text-to-speech output and guidance trajectory tags, respectively, to provide the desired responses. The trajectory of moving objects such as balls in sports is created by sampling spatial coordinates at regular time intervals corresponding to finger movements in space by the trajectory creator, thereby allowing the continuous creation of guidance trajectory data along the time axis. The haptic device used for the presentation system is the Touch device (made by 3D systems), which allows the user to freely explore the 3D object with both hands while maintaining six degrees of freedom for active tactile exploration.

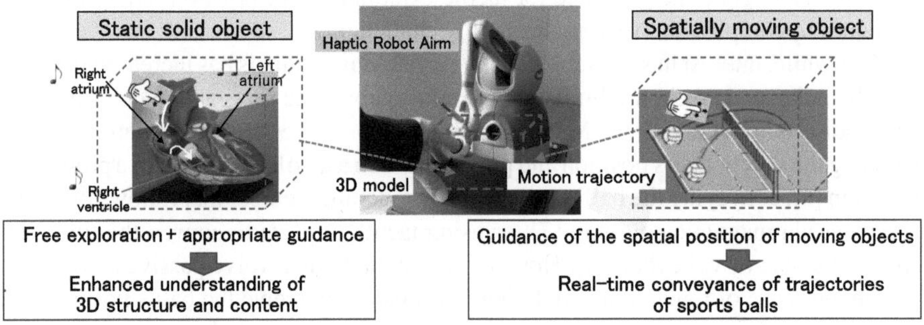

Fig. 1. Concept of spatial haptic-guidance presentation system.

3 Evaluation Experiments

3.1 Evaluation of 3D Tactile Perception

Evaluation Purpose and Experiment Design

The purpose of the evaluation is to clarify the effects and impact of using the spatial haptic-guidance presentation system on shape recognition and content understanding, and to determine the most appropriate presentation method. In designing the experiment, the factors and levels were set as shown in Table 1.

Table 1. Evaluation factors and levels.

Factors	Levels
Presentation method	A. Free exploration B. Haptic guidance C. Combination of A and B

Three types of 3D objects with varying complexities and comprehension difficulties were used for the evaluation (Fig. 2). Eight participants, either completely Blind or with low vision, participated in the experiment. A within-subject experimental design was used.

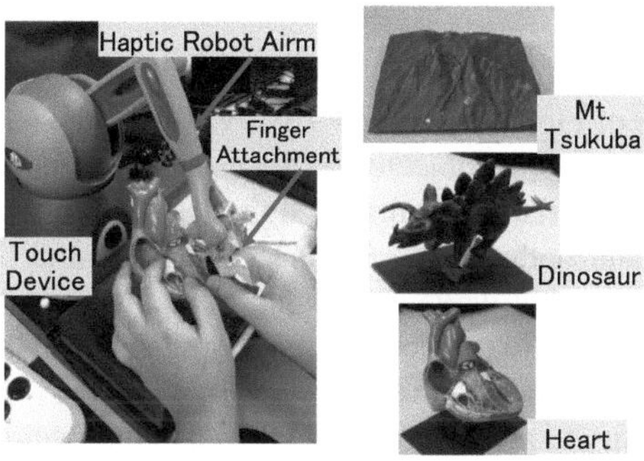

Fig. 2. Experimental setup and 3D objects

The evaluation method is as shown in a–c, and each 3D object was evaluated after free exploration and haptic guidance.

a. Ease of understanding shape and content (5-point subjective evaluation).
b. Content understanding (response in percentage).
c. Subjective evaluation and understanding when using both free exploration and haptic guidance

In haptic guidance, two aspects were presented for each 3D object:

- the overall structure and major areas, and.
- functional explanations such as climbing routes, dinosaur-head details, or heart blood flow.

Procedure

Evaluation was performed as follows for each 3D object:

Listen to the explanation regarding shape and content → ② Explore object freely for 5 min and understand the shape and content → ③ After exploration, provide subjective evaluation and understanding → ④ After listening to haptic-guidance content, conduct two types of guidance twice → ⑤ After completing guidance, provide responses regarding subjective evaluation and understanding, including for presentation method C.

Results and Discussion

Figure 3 shows the average subjective evaluation scores and content understanding for the three types of 3D objects as evaluated by eight participants and result of a two-way ANOVA with 3D object type and presentation method as factors. The results indicate the following relationships between the presentation method and evaluation scores.

For the subjective evaluation scores and understanding,

1. haptic guidance provided higher scores for all 3D objects compared with free exploration.
2. combining both free exploration and haptic guidance resulted in considerable improvements, particularly for complex objects such as the heart, which require specialized knowledge.

As shown in Table of Fig. 3, a two-way ANOVA indicated a significant main effect of presentation method on both subjective evaluation scores and comprehension levels ($p < 0.01$). Multiple comparisons confirmed significant differences ($p < 0.05$) between free exploration (A) and both haptic guidance alone (B) and the combined method (C). These results suggest that while free exploration allows participants to explore at their own pace, it often leads to overlooking important details, which negatively affects overall comprehension. In contrast, the improvement in scores with haptic guidance can be attributed to the ability to achieve reliable understanding within a defined range.

Based on introspective reports, free exploration allowed the participants to explore at their own pace and understand all three 3D objects completely; however, some points were overlooked. By contrast, haptic guidance allowed the participants to determine the positions of important areas without overlooking any points. However, perceiving the surrounding information during haptic guidance is challenging, thus highlighting the complementary effects of combining both methods. Regarding the presentation method, almost all participants reported that the process of ① overall explanation → ② free exploration (overview) → ③ haptic guidance (detailed complement) → ④ second free exploration (confirmation and consolidation) was effective for deepening understanding.

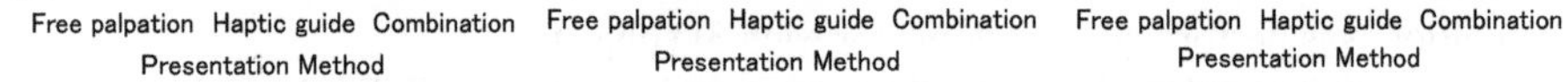

Factors	Subjective evaluation value	Understanding
Type of 3D model	F(2.14)=2.33 p=0.13	F(2.14)=1.60 p=0.24
Presentation method	F(2.14)=8.39 p=0.004	F(2.14)=17.66 p<0.001

Fig. 3. Evaluation results of the ease of grasping and understanding 3D objects and result of a two-way ANOVA.

3.2 Evaluation of Ball-Game Sports Understanding

Evaluation Purpose and Experiment Design

The evaluation purpose is to clarify the effects of the spatial haptic-guidance presentation system on one's understanding of the situation in ball games and the role of venue sounds and commentary. The evaluation focused on two types of ball games, namely goalball, which features almost flat trajectories, and volleyball, which features many aerial movements (Fig. 4).

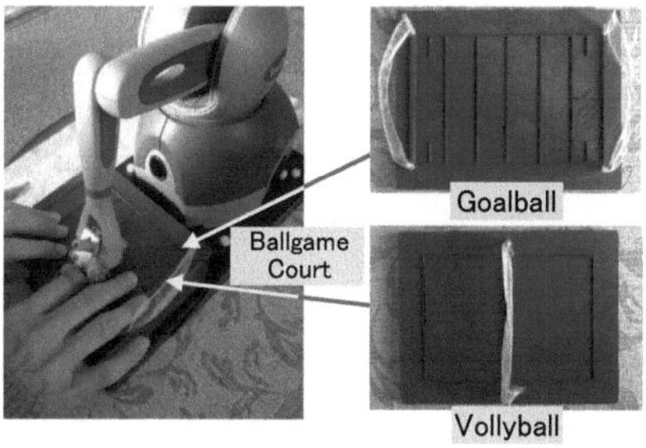

Fig. 4. Experimental setup and scene.

The evaluation items were set as follows: a. ball position, b. movement trajectory, c. understanding of the game situation, d. sense of presence (immersion), and e. fun/enjoyment. Five-point subjective evaluations based on ease of understanding and feelings experienced were used for a–c and d–e, respectively. The factors in the evaluation are presented as shown in Table 2, and three presentation condition types were compared. The experiment was participated by 10 individuals who were either completely blind or had low vision.

Table 2. Factors and levels.

Factors	Levels
Presentation method	A. Audio only (with/without venue sounds and commentary) B. Haptic guidance only (without venue sounds and commentary) C. Audio + haptic guidance (with/without venue sounds and commentary)

Evaluation Materials

The evaluation materials were created based on actual video footage of goalball and volleyball. Presentation method A (audio only) included two variations, i.e., with and without commentary, whereas presentation method C combined haptic guidance with ball movement to method A. Presentation method B is essentially presentation method C with the audio muted. The scenes differed between commentary and non-commentary conditions. The ball's movement trajectory via haptic guidance was created using the method described in Sect. 2. The timing for the sports, such as when the ball was stopped in goalball or when the ball was received or spiked in volleyball, was created such that the subject would experience the impact.

Procedure

Evaluation was conducted following the procedure below:

① Experience of ball's movement in both sports using haptic guidance → ② Explanation of rules of goalball using haptic guidance → ③ Sequential presentation of six combinations of presentation method and commentary availability → ④ Subjective evaluation for each item after completing one presentation condition → ⑤ Provision of Introspective reports after completing all six presentation conditions → ⑥ Repeat steps ①–⑤ for volleyball.

Results and Discussion

Figure 5 presents the subjective evaluation scores for each item based on a comparison of the three presentation methods (A, B, and C). The figure shows the results under the presence or absence of commentary. The subjective evaluation scores were the averages score of the 10 participants. In addition, the table in Fig. 5 summarizes the results of multiple comparisons, showing significant differences between the presentation meth od levels, as well as presenting the results of a two-way ANOVA that included the presence or absence of commentary as an additional factor for Presentation Method A (audio only) and Presentation Method C (audio + haptic guidance).

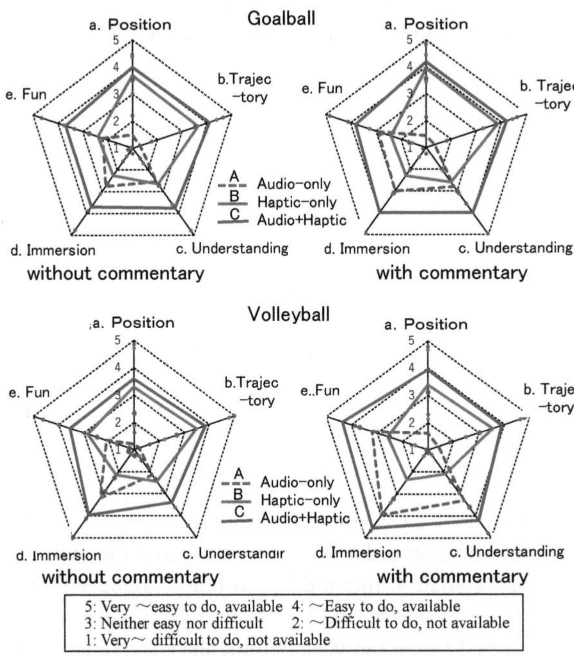

Presentation method. (Goalball)

	Pos.	Tra.	Und.	Imm.	Fun
A⇔B	***	***	—	—	—
A⇔C	***	***	**	*	***
C⇔B	—	*	**	**	**

Presentation method × commentary.

		Pos.	Tra.	Und.	Imm.	Fun
A	Y⇔N	—	—	—	—	*
C	Y⇔N	—	—	—	—	—
Y	A⇔C	***	***	**	**	**
N	A⇔C	***	***	*	**	**

Presentation method. (Volleyball)

	Pos.	Tra.	Und.	Imm.	Fun
A⇔B	**	***	—	**	—
A⇔C	***	***	**	**	***
C⇔B	—	*	**	***	**

Presentation method × commentary.

		Pos.	Tra.	Und.	Imm.	Fun
A	Y⇔N	*	—	***	**	**
C	Y⇔N	—	—	**	*	*
Y	A⇔C	***	***	**	**	***
N	A⇔C	***	***	**	*	***

A,B,C: Presentation method A,B,C
Y: commentary N: No commentary

p-value in ANOVA
***: p<0.001 **: p<0.01
*: p<0.05 —: n.s.

Fig. 5. Chart of subjective evaluation scores for each evaluation criterion, and significant differences between levels by multiple comparisons.

The results from Fig. 5 indicate the following relationships between the presentation method and subjective evaluation scores:

The subjective evaluation scores for both goalball and volleyball.

1. were considerably higher under presentation method C (audio + guidance) than under presentation method A (audio only) across all items.
2. When comparing presentation method A (audio only) and presentation method B (guidance only), haptic guidance was more effective in determining the ball's position and trajectory but scored lower in terms of the sense of presence and fun. Audio alone could not convey the ball's position and trajectory but improved the sense of presence, thus highlighting the trade-off between the two methods.
3. When comparing presentation method B (guidance only) and presentation method C (audio + guidance), no significant difference in determining the ball's position and trajectory was indicated; however, the addition of audio improved one's understanding of the situation, sense of presence, and enjoyment.
4. In the audio presentation, commentary contributed to understanding the situation, sense of presence, and enjoyment. The contribution of commentary was greater for volleyball than for goalball.

The results of variance analysis showed that for both games, the presentation method was the significant factor for all evaluation items ($p < 0.001$). Multiple comparisons confirmed the statistical significance of points 1–4. The effect of haptic guidance was synergistic; it contributed not only to the conveyance of the ball's position and trajectory but also enhanced the understanding of the sport, sense of presence, and enjoyment when integrated with audio commentary.

The Introspective reports and script analysis yielded the following results:

1. In presentation method A (audio only), linguistic and symbolic understanding was possible; however, spatial and motion understanding was lacking, and spatial representation could not be formed.
2. In presentation method B (guidance only), spatial information was excellent, and the ball's position and trajectory were clear; however, understanding of the game's meaning and flow as well as emotional stimulation were insufficient.
3. Presentation method C (audio + guidance) provided the most complete and complementary viewing experience by integrating spatial understanding and game-meaning comprehension as well as by incorporating emotional stimuli.

In the introspective reports, expressions such as "feeling like I'm watching" and "feeling like I'm playing together" were indicated, thus suggesting that haptic guidance allowed for the participants to physically relive the ball's movement.

The subjective evaluations and introspective reports clearly showed that, compared with audio-only, haptic guidance alone exerted a certain effect on conveying the situation. The fusion of audio, particularly commentary, and haptic guidance considerably enhanced not only spatial information but also emotional aspects such as understanding the game and experiencing the sense of presence and enjoyment. The multimodal presentation method combining audio and haptic guidance does not merely increase the information volume; rather, different modalities mutually complement each other in spatial and meaningful understanding, it can be said to enhance immersion and enjoyment that goes beyond conventional audio-based comprehension. This suggests that the haptic-guidance method utilizing proprioception may fundamentally alter the structure of how visually impaired individuals understand ball game spectators.

4 Summary and Future Challenges

This study presented an overview of the spatial haptic-guidance presentation system and demonstrated through evaluation experiments that adding haptic guidance to conventional audio presentation and free exploration effectively significantly improves support for 3D spatial understanding and ball-game situation transmission.

Future research should address the following issues:

- Investigating appropriate presentation methods that account for differences among visually impaired users (e.g., degree of visual impairment, prior experience with 3D tactile exploration and knowledge of ball sports).
- Developing effective methods for creating accessible 3D presentation content suitable for educational applications.
- Exploring techniques for acquiring spatial coordinates of balls during actual sports events and evaluating their applicability to live haptic guidance for spectators.

Future work will aim to address these challenges and achieve practical implementation.

Acknowledgments. This work was partially supported by JSPS KAKENHI Grant Numbers JP 23K25246 and JP22H03992, JP 23K25693 and JP23H00996.

References

1. Hirose, T.: Deepening and application of hands-on tactile exhibitions. Minpaku Tsushin **145**, 18–19 (2014)
2. Gibson, J.J.: Observations on active touch. Psychobiol. Handl Rev. **69**(6), 477–491 (1962)
3. Lederman, S.J., Klatzky, R.L.: The hand as a perceptual. The psychology, pp16–35 (1998)
4. Reinders,S., et al.: It Brought the Model to Life: Exploring the Embodiment of Multimodal I3Ms for People who are Blind or have Low Vision. In: CHI '25 (2025)
5. Smith, E.J., e al.: Active 3D shape reconstruction from vision and touch (2021). arXiv:2107.09584v2
6. Kobayashi, M., Fukunaga, Y., Shimada, S.: Basic study of blind football play-by-play system for visually impaired spectators using quasi-zenith satellites system. In: ICCHP, pp.23–27 (2018)
7. Touch2see: Revolutionising sports tracking for blind and partially sighted people. European Blind Union. Accessed 25 Jan 2026
8. Handa, T., Makiko, M., Shimizu, T., Kondoh, S.: A ball-type haptic interface to enjoy sports games. In: Proceedings of the 23rd Annual Conference of the VRSJ, 21A-5 (2018)
9. Sakai,T., Ohnishi,J., Sakajiri,M., Miura,T.: Proposal and development of spatial haptic guidance presentation system for visually impaired people. In: IEICE Technical Report, WIT-2023-4, pp18–23 (2023)

An End-to-End Pipeline to Generate Augmented Tactile Maps from Floor Plans

Michelle Quach[1], James M. Coughlan[2(✉)], Dragan Ahmetovic[3], Matteo Manzoni[3], Sergio Mascetti[3], and Roberto Manduchi[1]

[1] Department of Computer Science and Engineering, UC Santa Cruz, Santa Cruz, CA 95064, USA
{mitquach,manduchi}@ucsc.edu
[2] Smith-Kettlewell Eye Research Institute, San Francisco, CA, USA
coughlan@ski.org
[3] Department of Computer Science, Università degli Studi di Milano, Milan, Italy
{dragan.ahmetovic,matteo.manzoni,sergio.mascetti}@unimi.it

Abstract. This paper presents an end-to-end pipeline for transforming indoor floor plans into accessible tactile maps enriched with audio annotations. The approach integrates SIM (Semantic Interior Mapology), which allows authors to trace floor plans and assign semantic labels to relevant spatial features (e.g., rooms, corridors, restrooms, and stairs), with CamIO, a camera-based web application that delivers spoken feedback when users point to interactive regions (hotspots) on a tactile graphic. A pilot study with two blind participants and a follow-up study with five additional participants showed that users could successfully complete room-finding and route-tracing tasks and appreciated the system's support for spatial understanding. Usability evaluation yielded a mean SUS score of 77, indicating good usability, while NASA-TLX results showed a relatively low perceived workload, supporting the effectiveness of the proposed solution. Results also highlighted areas for improvement, including lower latency and clearer interaction around doors and small hotspots.

Keywords: Tactile Maps · Audio Augmentation · Indoor Accessibility · Floor Plans

1 Introduction

Tactile Maps (TMs) are often used by people who are Blind or have Low Vision (BLV) to access information about an environment and to orient themselves within it [2]. However, TMs need to be specifically designed to properly convey the environment layout tactually. This can be time-consuming and requires unique expertise. Additionally, TMs can contain only a limited amount of information due to the low spatial resolution of tactile sensing. Braille can supplement tactile elements with textual information, but space limitations typically restrict labels to short abbreviations, and many BLV people cannot read braille [15].

K. Miesenberger et al. (Eds.): ICCHP 2026, LNCS 16867, pp. 485–492, 2027.
https://doi.org/10.1007/978-3-032-31308-9_58

Several semi-automated TM creation systems have been proposed. For example, TMAP [11] is an online tool that allows to specify a urban area (*e.g.*, a city block), and generate a TM using OpenStreetMaps data. SIM (Semantic Interior Mapology) [13] similarly allows one to create indoor environment TMs from floor plans. Various techniques exist to augment tactile exploration with additional information provided through various feedback modalities, and in particular speech [4,10,12,17]. For example, CamIO [1] is a web app that identifies touch interactions on a TM using a video camera and produces verbal feedback based on text annotations associated with the touched map location.

In this work, we propose a new end-to-end pipeline to generate SIM TMs and the associated CamIO map annotations, which can then be used to augment the produced TMs. Specifically, while authoring SIM maps, users assign names and attributes to spaces such as rooms, corridors, and hallways, which are then used to automatically generate CamIO annotations.

We conducted a pilot study with two blind participants who explored two TMs produced with SIM and augmented through CamIO. A follow-up study was then conducted with an additional five participants who received training on one TM and explored three additional TMs. The studies show that participants were able to complete the proposed tasks and found the system useful for understanding the spatial layout of the rooms, while also providing insights for further improvements to the system.

2 State of the Art

Tactile graphics and TMs can serve as spatial learning tools across a wide range of applications, including learning basic geometric primitives, exploring the shapes of stylized objects, examining geographic maps, and becoming familiar with the layout of a building prior to visiting it. Traditionally, TMs are created individually by expert designers [5]. In order to reduce the authoring cost and expand the availability of TMs, various mechanisms for automatic map production have been proposed. For outdoor maps, spatial information can be sourced from geographical information systems (GIS) such as OpenStreetMap [6,11,14]. For indoor spaces, existing floor plans can be converted to a format that is amenable to printing on swell paper or embossing [9]. For example, SIM[1] [13] is a web app that allows one to quickly trace an existing floor plan image (Fig. 2a), generating a TM image which can then be printed (Fig. 2c).

Various approaches have been proposed for augmenting tactile graphics and TMs to provide additional feedback based on where the user is touching [4,10,12,17]. For instance, the T3 Tactile Tablet[2] is a proprietary tablet device that allows users to place a tactile graphic on its surface. The tablet's touchscreen detects where the user is touching, and the system plays audio feedback corresponding to that location. Other approaches, based on computer vision, detect where the user is pointing using webcams [12] or a smartphone camera [4,17]. For

[1] SIM is publicly available at: https://sim.acad.ucsc.edu.
[2] https://www.touchgraphics.com/store/p/t3-tactile-tablet.

example, CamIO[3] [1] is a web-based application that runs on most desktop and mobile devices equipped with a web browser and a camera. It allows users to frame a previously annotated tactile graphic using their device's camera and receive verbal feedback on the elements they explore. The annotation process, supported by the CamIO-Creator web application (Fig. 1), allows interactive elements (called hotspots) to be defined, providing their names and descriptions (Fig. 1a), and the corresponding areas on the tactile graphics (Fig. 1b).

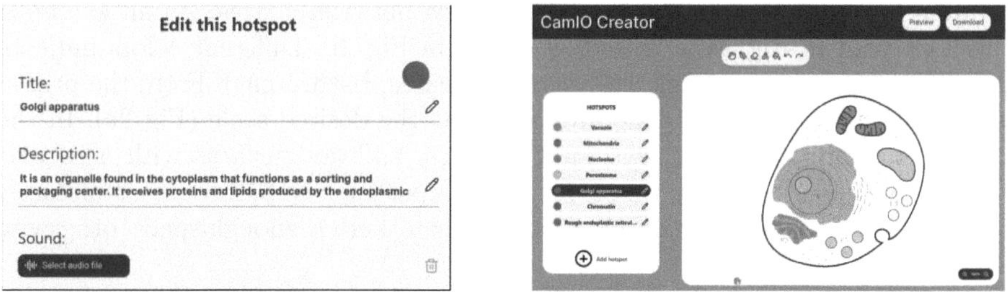

(a) Name and description of an element

(b) Hotspots of the tactile graphics

Fig. 1. Annotation of a cell figure using CamIO-Creator(See footnote 3).

In place of tactile graphics, some solutions use a Refreshable Tactile Display (RTD), representing content through an array of tactile pins that can be raised or lowered [16]. Touch-sensitive RTDs can support augmentation based on the touched location [18]. However, refreshable tactile displays are still not widespread; they are expensive and have limited resolution [18].

3 Methodology

3.1 CamIO Tactile Graphics Annotations

CamIO tactile graphics annotations, produced using CamIO-Creator (Fig. 1), are saved in a *.camio* file, which is loaded into the CamIO web app for exploration. This file comprises three components: (1) a scan of the tactile graphic, used by CamIO to identify it in the camera feed; (2) a color map in which each hotspot area is annotated with a unique color (Fig. 1b); and (3) the list of the hotspots, each with its name, description, and the color used to mark it in the color map. During exploration, CamIO continuously localizes the tactile graphic within the camera frame and detects the user's pointing gesture. Thus, the system naturally compensates for any shift in the position of the graphic, the camera, or the user's hand, without requiring explicit recalibration. When a pointing gesture is detected, CamIO determines the hotspot indicated (if any) through the color map and reads aloud the associated text. To ensure hotspots are clearly distinguishable, we empirically determined a minimum size of 1 cm.

[3] CamIO is publicly available at: https://develop.ewlab.di.unimi.it/camio.

3.2 Generating Tactile Maps and CamIO Annotations with SIM

SIM represents maps using a planar *primal* graph and its *dual* multigraph. The vertices of the planar graph represent wall junctions in the floor plans, while edges are walls. Openings (doors) are represented as attributes of the graph edges. The faces of this planar graph represent *spaces* (typically, rooms or hallways), and form the vertices of the dual multigraph, which can be annotated with space type and space ID. The edges of this multigraph are the walls separating adjacent spaces. Thus, the primal graph can be used to draw the map, while its dual is useful to create traversable routes between spaces. As an example, the floor plan in Fig. 2a is traced as shown in Fig. 2b. Different colors indicate different space types (rooms, hallways, staircases, bathrooms). From the primal graph, SIM automatically generates a TM at the desired scale (Fig. 2c). In the current version, the TM shows walls as lines, hallway surfaces with a regular texture, and uses specific symbols for space types such as bathrooms, staircases, or elevators. Doors are displayed as circles when there is enough space, otherwise as gaps in the wall.

CamIO annotations are generated using information from the dual graph (Fig. 2d). The CamIO color map is created where each space (vertex of the dual graph) represents a hotspot. Likewise, information about each hotspot (listed in a JSON file) is sourced directly from the space annotations in the dual graph. Note that doors and openings do not have an associated hotspot, as users can easily perceive their presence via the corresponding tactile symbol.

4 Results

4.1 Study Design

A pilot study was conducted with two participants (**P1** and **P2**, Table 1) to test the feasibility of integrating SIM and CamIO in a form that is usable to BLV individuals. In this study, two floor plans were created with SIM and rendered as TMs on swell paper using a ZyFuse machine. Corridors and other walkable areas were marked with a distinctive tactile dot pattern, and each door was indicated by a tactile circle whose diameter matched the door's width. Floor plans were also automatically converted to CamIO format, but with manual hotspot annotations to specify unique names for each room. The experimenter ran CamIO on a Windows laptop with an external document webcam positioned to capture a clear view of each tactile graphic, which was secured to a table using tape. Participants were first instructed how to activate hotspots by making a pointing gesture, with the index finger pointing straight and the other fingers curled into a fist (see setup and pointing gesture in Fig. 3.) The study was organized into three tasks. First, participants were given the names of 3 rooms on the map and were asked to locate them. Then, given the names of two distinct rooms on the map, they were asked to trace a walking path from the first room to the second. During this task, participants were instructed to enter and exit each room through its designated entrance or exit door. Finally, participants had to trace the border of a specific room.

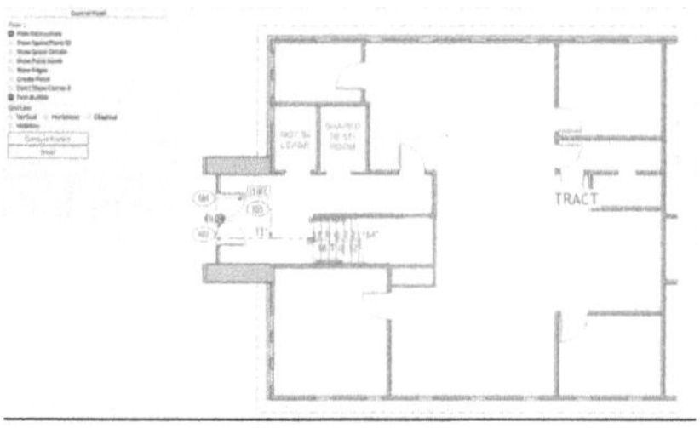

(a) A floor plan loaded in SIM

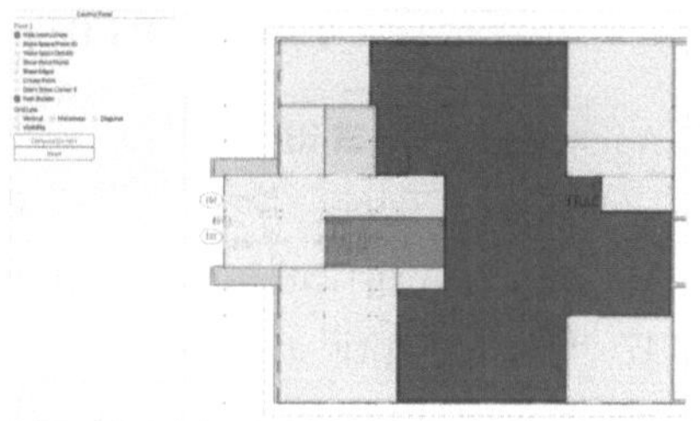

(b) Spaces obtained by tracing the floor plan

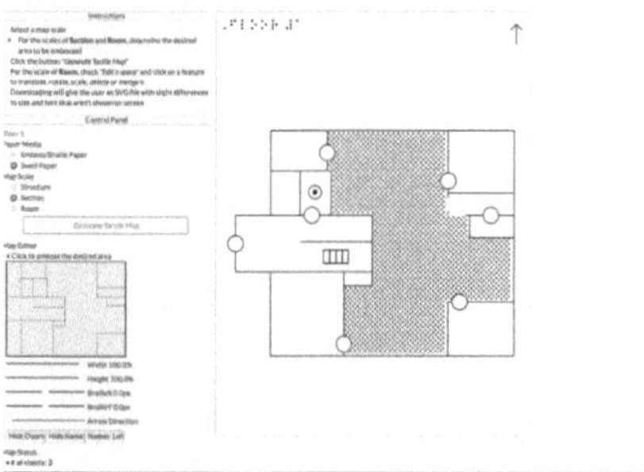

(c) Automatically generated tactile map

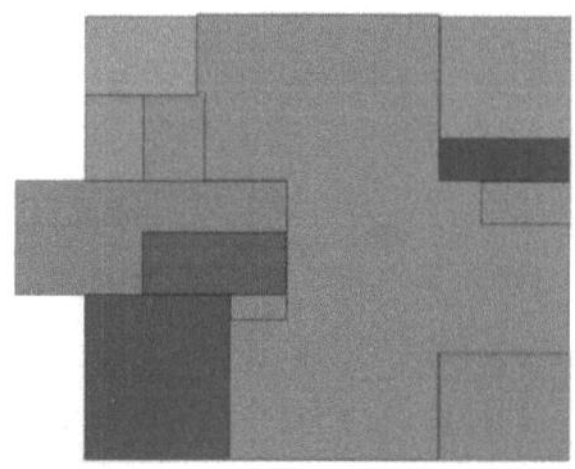

(d) Color image annotation for CamIO

Fig. 2. Creation of a TM and CamIO annotation from a floorplan using SIM(See footnote 1).

Next, a follow-up study was carried out with five participants (**P3**-**P7**, Table 1). Compared to the preliminary study, the main differences included the addition of a short training session with one TM, testing on three additional TMs, and the inclusion of SUS [3] and NASA-TLX [7] questionnaires, as well as a semi-structured interview. The testing on each TM was the same as in the pilot study, except with an additional task in which the participant was asked to find the room number corresponding to a specific name (the room number was the CamIO name of the room and the occupant name was its CamIO description).

4.2 Study Results

In the pilot study, both participants **P1** and **P2** successfully completed the first and third tasks. For the second task, participants succeeded when using the TM with larger door symbols (due to the map's larger spatial scale), but experienced difficulties locating the door symbols in the other TM.

In response to this issue, a uniform sized door symbol was used in all the maps in the follow-up study, which also included an additional map used solely for a brief training period at the beginning of the experiment. All five participants completed the tasks successfully, with one exception: **P3** was unable to find the

Table 1. Participants' demographic data.

ID	Age	Gender	Disability			Expertise	
			Type	Onset	Forms/Light	Braille	Tactile Graphics
P1	53	M	Cortical impairment	Birth	Both	None	Low
P2	47	F	Optic atrophy	Birth	Both	High	Medium
P3	40	F	ROP	Birth	No	High	High
P4	39	M	Congenital Lieber's	Birth	Light	High	Mid
P5	78	F	ROP	Birth	Forms	High	Low
P6	36	M	LHON (Leber)	14 y	Both	High	Mid
P7	24	F	Scelero cornea	Birth	Light	Mid	Mid

(a) Setup showing webcam, TM and laptop **(b)** Participant making a pointing gesture on the TM

Fig. 3. Experimental setting and interaction.

room occupied by a specified person for one map, likely because this room was significantly smaller than the others on the map, preventing the participant from triggering its hotspot.

Many positive aspects of the system were noted, including the opportunity to understand the rooms' spatial layout, the information contained in the tactile features and the usefulness of the audio feedback for interpreting the TMs without the need to read braille. Participants also highlighted several areas for improvement: (a) the need for lower latency in hotspot announcements; (b) confusion about audio feedback when the finger points directly on a wall, which can unpredictably trigger the hotspot on either side of the wall; (c) the desire to elicit feedback with a special gesture such as a double tap, to enable silent exploration with one pointing finger (since some participants primarily use their index finger to explore a tactile map); (d) the system should indicate when their fingertip was pointing outside the map; and (e) sometimes the hand tracking algorithm was confused by the presence of two hands simultaneously visible to the camera. When asked how they might use the system in real life, participants expressed interest in using it to preview grocery stores and other shopping areas, medical office buildings, sports arenas, airports and other unfamiliar areas; **P5** suggested using it to find a walking route to a desired destination in a building with many offices.

System usability was overall positive, with a mean SUS score of 77.0 ± 14.83, corresponding to a B grade (70–79th percentile) according to established benchmarks. Item-level results show generally high usability, with the highest-rated questions being **Q1** (4.0 ± 1.22), **Q4** (1.4 ± 0.89), **Q5** (4.4 ± 0.89), and **Q9** (4.8 ± 0.45), suggesting strong willingness to use the system, low need for support, good integration of functionalities, and high user confidence. Lower scores were reported for **Q6** (2.4 ± 1.34) and **Q7** (3.6 ± 1.14), suggesting and a step learning curve to use the system. Overall, results are above the average SUS benchmark and fall within the "good" usability range.

Perceived workload was overall moderate, with a mean NASA-TLX score of 25 ± 14.62. Considering benchmark values for special-needs user studies, this corresponds to a relatively low workload compared to typical accessibility-related tasks reported in the literature [8]. Among subscales, mental demand (46 ± 25.35) and effort (44 ± 34.17) were the highest contributors, followed by physical demand (21 ± 30.29). Temporal demand (13 ± 13.04), perceived performance (13 ± 5.70), and frustration (13 ± 9.08) remained low, indicating limited negative affect and a generally manageable task experience.

5 Conclusions and Future Work

This work introduced an end-to-end pipeline for generating tactile maps from indoor floor plans, enriched with audio annotations through the integration of SIM and CamIO. The proposed approach reduces the effort required to create accessible maps while enabling richer, multimodal exploration for blind and low vision users. User studies demonstrated that participants could effectively perform spatial tasks and reported good usability and low workload, highlighting the potential of the system to support spatial understanding without relying on braille. At the same time, the findings revealed areas for improvement, including reducing audio feedback latency, refining interaction near walls and doors, and improving hotspot accessibility at small scales.

Future work will focus on addressing the issues identified in this evaluation, as well as exploring the integration of a large language model to complement tactile exploration and audio feedback with natural voice interaction.

Acknowledgments. We thank Dr. Nasif Zaman for valuable suggestions about the experimental protocol and help preparing the experimental materials.

Research reported in this article was supported by the National Eye Institute of the National Institutes of Health (NIH) under awards 2R01EY025332 and R01EY035433, by the National Institute on Disability, Independent Living, and Rehabilitation Research (NIDILRR) under Grant 90REGE0018, and by The Smith-Kettlewell Eye Research Institute. The content is solely the responsibility of the authors and does not necessarily represent the official views of NIH or NIDILRR.

References

1. Ahmetovic, D., Coughlan, J., Dal Santo, G., Ezrouri, K., Manzoni, M., Mascetti, S.: Camio in the browser: a cross-platform audio label tool for tactile graphics. In: International Conference on Mobile Human-Computer Interaction (2025)
2. Bentzen, B.L.: Orientation maps for visually impaired persons. J. Vis. Impairment Blindness (1977)
3. Brooke, J.: Sus-a quick and dirty usability scale. Usability evaluation in industry (1996)
4. Coughlan, J.M., Shen, H., Biggs, B.: Towards accessible audio labeling of 3D objects. J. Technol. Persons Disabil. CSUN (2020)
5. Edman, P.: Tactile graphics. AFB (1992)
6. Götzelmann, T.: Visually augmented audio-tactile graphics for visually impaired people. ACM Trans. Accessible Comput. (2018)
7. Hart, S.G.: Nasa-task load index (nasa-tlx); 20 years later. In: Proceedings of the Human Factors and Ergonom. Society Annual Meeting, vol. 50, no. 9, pp. 904–908 (2006)
8. Hertzum, M.: Reference values and subscale patterns for the task load index (TLX): a meta-analytic review. Ergonomics **64**(7), 869–878 (2021)
9. Madugalla, A., Marriott, K., Marinai, S., Capobianco, S., Goncu, C.: Creating accessible online floor plans for visually impaired readers. ACM Trans on Accessible Comput. (2020)
10. Manzoni, M., Mascetti, S., Ahmetovic, D., Crabb, R., Coughlan, J.: Mapio: a gestural and conversational interface for tactile maps. IEEE Access (2025)
11. Miele, J.A., Landau, S., Gilden, D.: Talking tmap: automated generation of audio-tactile maps using smith-kettlewell's tmap software. Br. J. Vis. Impairment (2006)
12. Shi, L., Zhao, Y., Azenkot, S.: Markit and talkit: a low-barrier toolkit to augment 3d printed models with audio annotations. In: Annual ACM Symposium on User Interface Software and Technology (2017)
13. Trinh, V., Manduchi, R., Giudice, N.A.: Experimental evaluation of multi-scale tactile maps created with sim, a web app for indoor map authoring. ACM Trans Accessible Comput. (2023)
14. Watanabe, T., Yamaguchi, T., Koda, S., Minatani, K.: Tactile map automated creation system using OpenStreetMap. In: Miesenberger, K., Fels, D., Archambault, D., Peňáz, P., Zagler, W. (eds.) ICCHP 2014. LNCS, vol. 8548, pp. 42–49. Springer, Cham (2014). https://doi.org/10.1007/978-3-319-08599-9_7
15. Wiazowski, J.: Can braille be revived? a possible impact of high-end braille and mainstream technology on the revival of tactile literacy medium. Assistive Technol. (2014)
16. Yang, W., Huang, J., Wang, R., Zhang, W., Liu, H., Xiao, J.: A survey on tactile displays for visually impaired people. Trans. Haptics (2021)
17. Zeinullin, M., Hersh, M.: Tactile audio responsive intelligent system. IEEE Access (2022)
18. Zeng, L., Weber, G.: The overview of haptic displays. In: Advancements in Pin-Array Tactile Displays: Designing Multimodal User Interfaces for Braille and Graphics, Springer, Cham (2025)

Cognitive Maps and Audio-Haptic Game Performance in Individuals with Visual Impairments: A Correlational Study

Eleni Koustriava[1(✉)], Elena Chronopoulou[2], Christina Fountouki[1], Sofia Michailidou[1], and Konstantinos Papadopoulos[1]

[1] University of Macedonia, 156 Egnatia Str, 54636 Thessaloniki, Greece
elkous@uom.edu.gr

[2] Aristotle University of Thessaloniki, University Campus, 54124 Thessaloniki, Greece

Abstract. The aim of the study was to investigate whether potential correlations exist between the performance of individuals with visual impairments in an audio-haptic game concerning a city center and various variables related to their cognitive maps of the same areas of this city center. Eleven adults with visual impairments, 8 individuals with blindness and 3 individuals with severe visual impairments participated in the study. Nine participants were males and two females, with a mean age of 38.3 years. The experiment was conducted using a virtual audio-haptic game played with the Novint Falcon device. Participants received information through haptic stimuli and auditory feedback (i.e., street names, intersections, and distance traveled) via synthetic speech. Right after completing the game, participants were asked to create a tactile model of the area they had navigated, including as many elements as possible. Correlation analysis was conducted to examine potential statistically significant correlations between the participants' scores in the audio-haptic game and the variables related to their cognitive maps. Enhanced performance in the audio-haptic game, as indicated by reduced task completion times, was found to be associated with the presence of more detailed and comprehensive cognitive maps.

Keywords: Visual Impairments · Cognitive Maps · Audio-Haptic Game · City Center

1 Introduction

Cognitive mapping refers to the mental representation of spatial knowledge, involving the acquisition, storage, recall, and interpretation of information about environmental locations and attributes [3, 10]. Cognitive mapping relies heavily on visual input [16], making it more challenging for individuals with visual impairments, depending on the degree of vision loss. On the other hand, it has been demonstrated that when spatial information provided through non-visual senses is sufficient, individuals with blindness are capable of forming cognitive maps [18]. Compensatory sensory channels play a critical role in supporting cognitive mapping [15], and understanding how individuals

K. Miesenberger et al. (Eds.): ICCHP 2026, LNCS 16867, pp. 493–500, 2027.
https://doi.org/10.1007/978-3-032-31308-9_59

with visual impairments develop cognitive maps can inform environmental planning and improve wayfinding [8]. Their cognitive maps typically include key environmental features such as streets, buildings, parks, fixed obstacles, and bus stops, shaped by the information they receive [19]. Research shows that individuals with visual impairments can form effective cognitive maps of familiar environments [2], learn unfamiliar routes through repeated travel [4, 7, 17], and demonstrate advanced spatial abilities, including orientation and distance estimation [9].

Individuals with blindness rely mainly on auditory, olfactory, and tactile cues for wayfinding. Koutsoklenis and Papadopoulos [12–14] found a mismatch between frequently used and most useful cues for navigation, environmental recognition, and hazard avoidance in urban contexts. Gardiner and Perkins [5] categorized park-related sensory information, identifying which elements should or should not be included in tactile maps and emphasized the need to map hazards.

Orientation and mobility (O&M) aids have been proven to be significant supportive tools for cognitive mapping and navigation. More specifically, tactile maps can be raised-line or three-dimensional when depicting the layout of a building or outdoor environment, or multimodal, when they include both tactile and auditory information [6]. Engagement with multimodal maps appears to promote the development of spatial skills and to support navigation among individuals with blindness [11]. Other studies have also mentioned the impact of audio-haptic maps in cognitive representations and O&M of people with visual impairments [20–25]. Abd Hamid and Edwards [1] highlighted the importance of including key landmarks and auditory cues in audio-tactile maps.

2 Study

The aim of the study was to investigate whether potential correlations exist between the performance of individuals with visual impairments in an audio-haptic game concerning a city center and various variables related to their cognitive maps of the same areas of this city center.

The study was conducted following the ethical principles of the Declaration of Helsinki and informed consent was obtained from all participants before their involvement. Before that, the research protocol had been approved by the Committee for the Research Ethics of the implementing entity.

2.1 Participants

The sample was recruited using snowball sampling, starting from the researchers' networks. Eleven adults with visual impairments, 8 individuals with blindness and 3 individuals with severe visual impairments participated in the study. Nine participants were males and two females, with a mean age of 38.3 years (SD = 5.16). The visual impairment was congenital in 7 individuals, while 4 individuals had acquired visual impairments after birth: 2 participants before the age of five and 2 participants after the age of five. Regarding their level of education, the sample consisted of 3 master's degree graduates, 5 undergraduate graduates, 2 graduates of vocational training institutes, and 1 high school graduate.

In response to a question about whether they move independently or with the help of a sighted person, 5 participants answered that they move independently, while 6 answered that they sometimes move independently and sometimes with assistance. Participants also responded to a 5-point Likert scale question regarding the frequency of their independent movement (1 = never, 2 = a few times, 3 = sometimes, 4 = most of the time, 5 = always). According to their responses, four participants move "always" independently, five participants move independently "most of the time" and two participants move "sometimes" independently.

2.2 Procedures

Audio-haptic map. The experiment began with 40 min of familiarization for participants. After describing the device and the virtual environment participants would use at the game, the researchers provided instructions on grip use and the buttons' functions. They then explained the procedure to be followed in the three phases of the experiment and the requirements of the final assessment, listing in detail the names of the streets and intersections participants would need to locate. Participants were encouraged to familiarize themselves with the game and memorize the map elements (i.e., streets and street intersections) in as much detail as possible.

After the familiarization phase, participants were asked to complete four additional tasks designed to maintain their engagement with the game and further support their learning of the area. Specifically, they were asked to: 1) navigate all the horizontal and vertical streets on the map, 2) locate and move along two streets indicated by the researchers, 3) simply locate three additional streets, and 4) identify four intersections within the area. All tasks and sub-tasks were the same for all participants. No assessment was conducted regarding participants' success in locating the points or the time required.

The final assessment for participants included three main tasks and eleven sub-tasks:

- Locating two requested streets (two sub-tasks: T1.1 & T1.2)
- Locating four requested street intersections (four sub-tasks: T2.1, T2.2, T2.3, & T2.4)
- Following a route from a designated starting point to a predetermined destination, passing through four specified street intersections (five sub-tasks: T3.1, T3.2, T3.3, T3.4, & T3.5)

For every sub-task, participants returned to the starting point, located in the upper-right corner of the map. Researchers recorded the time participants needed to complete each sub-task. There was no time restriction for completing each sub-task.

Cognitive map. Right after completing the game, participants were asked to create a tactile model of the area they had navigated, including as many elements as possible. The map was created using laces on a foam board surface (KAPA fix type). The researchers prepared the surface by covering it with two A3 sheets of paper, carefully calculating the dimensions to maintain the correct scale. They placed four laces on the top, bottom, right, and left sides to create a frame within which the participants would place the remaining roads. Participants were asked to represent the map accurately, based on their knowledge of the area and their audio-haptic experience with the game. They were instructed to preserve the correct distances, lengths, spatial relationships, and directions of the roads. After participants completed their maps, the researchers removed the materials and traced the maps with a pencil. The time required to complete the map was recorded.

2.3 Instruments

The experiment was conducted using a virtual audio-haptic game played with the Novint Falcon device. The device has also been used in a study with individuals with visual impairments to enable navigation in an imaginary virtual map and to assess participants' acquired spatial knowledge [11]. Novint Falcon was also preferred for the present study as it provides haptic feedback during movement (up, down, right, and left on the map) and supports the development of additional functions through its buttons.

Specifically, in addition to navigating the city center map, moving the grip, users could use the device's buttons to: 1) Reposition the device's grip to extend movement space. Since the device's range of motion in real space is limited, repositioning the grip without moving the cursor position in the virtual game environment was necessary. 2) Hear the names of streets, intersections, and the distance traveled. 3) Defining and returning to the starting point. These functions facilitated the experimental process by minimizing the time and effort required to navigate to the starting point. The starting point was defined by the researchers, while participants could return to it at any time or at the beginning of each task.

Participants received information through haptic stimuli (i.e., when passing from intersections) and auditory feedback. Auditory information (i.e., street names, intersections, and distance traveled) was provided via synthetic speech using the device buttons. Additional sounds were added at specific points on the map, based on recordings of the real soundscape.

Participants represented their cognitive maps by creating a tactile model of the area, using laces on a KAPA fix surface covered with A3 paper sheets (see Procedures).

2.4 Analysis

For the analysis of the quality of participants' cognitive maps, the researchers defined a set of variables corresponding to different levels of spatial representation: streets, street segments, and intersections. For each variable, a corresponding measure was calculated for every participant's cognitive map. The variables employed were as follows:

- R Found: The total number of streets included in the participant's cognitive map.
- R Position Relevant: The number of streets placed by the participant in positions that were relatively accurate with respect to the other streets in the cognitive map. A street's position was considered relatively accurate if the topological arrangement was preserved, based on the sequence in which streets appear from top to bottom and from left to right.
- S Found: The total number of street segments included by the participant in their cognitive map. "Street segments" are defined as individual sections of a street bounded by intersections with other streets.

- I Found: The total number of street intersections included by the participant in their cognitive map.

For the analysis of performance in the audio-tactile game, the time required by participants to complete each sub-task was used. Consequently, eleven variables related to the game were included in the analysis, one for each sub-task.

3 Results

Table 1 presents the results of the descriptive statistical analysis concerning the variables related to the participants' cognitive maps.

Table 1. Participants' scores and standard deviations (SD) in the variables related to their cognitive maps.

	Mean	SD
R found	21.6	7.35
S found	92.4	32.27
I found	60.3	19.64
R Position Relevant	19.3	6.97

Correlation analysis (see Table 2) was conducted to examine potential statistically significant correlations between the participants' scores in the audio-haptic game and the variables related to their cognitive maps.

The analysis revealed a statistically significant negative correlation between the participants' performance on the sub-task "T2.4" and the variables "R found" ($r = -.623$, $p < .05$), "I found" ($r = -.604$, $p < .05$), and "R Position Relevant" ($r = -.635$, $p < .05$). Moreover, the analysis revealed a statistically significant negative correlation between the participants' performance on the sub-task "T3.3" and the variables "R found" ($r = -.696$, $p < .05$), "S found" ($r = -.681$, $p < .05$), "I found" ($r = -.685$, $p < .05$), and "R Position Relevant" ($r = -.622$, $p < .05$).

Table 2. Pearson's correlation coefficient (r) between the variables concerning the participants' scores in the audio-haptic game and those related to their cognitive maps.

Sub-tasks	R Found	S Found	I Found	R Position Relevant
T1.1	−0.166	-0.150	−0.202	−0.247
T1.2	−0.004	−0.047	−0.057	−0.087
T2.1	−0.091	−0.108	−0.118	−0.171
T2.2	−0.546	−0.498	−0.547	−0.505
T2.3	0.146	0.130	0.129	−0.021
T2.4	**−0.623***	−0.542	**−0.604***	**−0.635***
T3.1	0.451	0.382	0.415	0.357
T3.2	0.248	0.189	0.195	0.024
T3.3	**−0.696***	**−0.681***	**−0.685***	**−0.622***
T3.4	−0.148	−0.189	−0.197	−0.261
T3.5	−0.498	−0.471	−0.519	−0.560

* $p < .05$

4 Discussion-Conclusions

Enhanced performance in the audio-haptic game, as indicated by reduced task completion times, was found to be associated with the presence of more detailed and comprehensive cognitive maps.

Given that the evaluation of participants' cognitive maps took place after their interaction with the audio-haptic game, it can be hypothesized that those who learned the area more effectively and achieved higher performance on game-related tasks developed richer cognitive maps than participants with lower performance. However, to draw firm conclusions, it is essential to consider that participants may have already possessed pre-existing cognitive maps of the area. Consequently, individuals with more detailed prior maps may also have performed better in the game than those with less developed ones.

A third, and perhaps most plausible, hypothesis is that both mechanisms are at play: participants possess pre-existing cognitive maps that become further enriched through interaction with the audio-haptic game. Future studies could employ an appropriate experimental design to determine which of these hypotheses is most likely to hold true.

Acknowledgments. This study was funded in the context of the research project supported by the Hellenic Foundation for Research and Innovation (H.F.R.I.) under the "2nd Call for H.F.R.I. Research Projects to support Faculty Members & Researchers" (Project Number: 4478).

Disclosure of Interests. The authors have no competing interests to declare that are relevant to the content of this article.

References

1. Abd Hamid, N.N., Edwards, A.: Facilitating route learning using interactive audio-tactile maps for blind and visually impaired people [Conference session]. CHI '13 Extended Abstracts on Human Factors in Computing Systems (CHI EA '13), Paris, France (2013). https://doi.org/10.1145/2468356.2468364
2. Casey, S.M.: Cognitive mapping by the blind. J. Vis. Impairment Blindness **72**(8), 297–301 (1978). https://doi.org/10.1177/0145482X7807200801
3. Downs, M.R., Stea, D.: Image and environment: cognitive mapping and spatial behavior. Edward Arnold, London, UK (1973)
4. Espinosa, M.A., Ungar, S., Ochaita, E., Blades, M., Spencer, C.: Comparing methods for introducing blind and visually impaired people to unfamiliar urban environments. J. Environ. Psychol. **18**(3), 277–287 (1998). https://doi.org/10.1006/jevp.1998.0097
5. Gardiner, A., Perkins, C.: "It's a sort of echo ...": sensory perception of the environment as an aid to tactile map design. Br. J. Vis. Impair. **23**(2), 84–91 (2005). https://doi.org/10.1177/0264619605054780
6. Giudice, N.A., Guenther, B.A., Jensen, N.A., Haase, K.N.: Cognitive mapping without vision: Comparing wayfinding performance after learning from digital touchscreen-based multimodal maps vs. embossed tactile overlays. Front. Hum. Neurosci. **14**(87) (2020). https://doi.org/10.3389/fnhum.2020.00087
7. Golledge, R., Jacobson, R.D., Kitchin, R., Blades, M.: Cognitive maps, spatial abilities, and human wayfinding. Geograph. Rev. Jpn. Ser. B **73**, 93–104 (2000). https://doi.org/10.4157/grj1984b.73.93
8. Jacobson, R.D., Kitchin, R.M.: Assessing the configurational knowledge of people with visual impairments or blindness. Swansea Geogr. **32**, 14–24 (1995)
9. Jacobson, R., Lippa, Y., Golledge, R., Kitchin, R., Blades, M.: Rapid development of cognitive maps in people with visual impairments when exploring novel geographic spaces. Bull. People-Environ. Stud. **18**, 3–6 (2001)
10. Kitchin, R.M.: Cognitive maps: what are they and why study them? J. Environ. Psychol. **14**, 1–19 (1994). https://doi.org/10.1016/S0272-4944(05)80194-X
11. Koukourikos, P., Papadopoulos, K.: Development of cognitive maps by individuals with blindness using a multisensory application. Procedia Comput. Sci. **67**, 213–222 (2015). https://doi.org/10.1016/j.procs.2015.09.265
12. Koutsoklenis, A., Papadopoulos, K.: Auditory cues used for wayfinding in urban environments by individuals with visual impairments. J. Vis. Impairment Blindness **105**, 703–714 (2011). https://doi.org/10.1177/0145482X1110501016
13. Koutsoklenis, A., Papadopoulos, K.: Olfactory cues used for wayfinding in urban environments by individuals with visual impairments. J. Vis. Impairment Blindness **105**, 692–702 (2011). https://doi.org/10.1177/0145482X1110501015
14. Koutsoklenis, A., Papadopoulos, K.: Haptic cues used for outdoor wayfinding by individuals with visual impairments. J. Vis. Impairment Blindness **108**, 43–53 (2014). https://doi.org/10.1177/0145482X1410800105
15. Lahav, O., Mioduser, D.: Haptic-feedback support for cognitive mapping of unknown spaces by people who are blind. Int. J. Hum Comput Stud. **66**, 23–35 (2008). https://doi.org/10.1016/j.ijhcs.2007.08.001
16. Loomis, M.J., Klatzky, L.R., Golledge, G.R., Cicinelli, G.J., Pellegrino, W.J., Fry, A.P.: Nonvisual navigation by blind and sighted: Assessment of path integration ability. J. Exp. Psychol.: Gen. **122**, 73–91 (1993). https://doi.org/10.1037/0096-3445.122.1.73
17. Ochaita, E., Huertas, J.A.: Spatial representation by persons who are blind: a study of the effects of learning and development. J. Vis. Impairment Blindness **87**(2), 37–41 (1993). https://doi.org/10.1177/0145482X9308700201

18. Ottink, L., Buimer, H., van Raalte, B., Doeller, C.F., van der Geest, T.M., van Wezel, R.J.: Cognitive map formation supported by auditory, haptic, and multimodal information in persons with blindness. Neurosci. Biobehav. Rev. **140**, 104797 (2022). https://doi.org/10.1016/j.neubiorev.2022.104797
19. Papadopoulos, K.S.: A school programme contributes to the environmental knowledge of blind people. Br. J. Vis. Impair. **22**(3), 101–104 (2004). https://doi.org/10.1177/0264619604050046
20. Papadopoulos, K., Barouti, M.: The contribution of audio-tactile maps to spatial knowledge of individuals with visual impairments. In: International Conference on Enabling Access for Persons with Visual Impairment (ICEAPVI), pp. 141–146 (2015)
21. Papadopoulos, K., Koukourikos, P., Koustriava, E., Misiou, M., Varveris, A., Valari, E.: Audio-haptic map: an orientation and mobility aid for individuals with blindness. Procedia Comput. Sci. **67**, 223–230 (2015). https://doi.org/10.1016/j.procs.2015.09.266
22. Papadopoulos, K., Koustriava, E., Barouti, M.: Cognitive maps of individuals with blindness for familiar and unfamiliar spaces: construction through audio-tactile maps and walked experience. Comput. Hum. Behav. **75**, 376–384 (2017). https://doi.org/10.1016/j.chb.2017.04.057
23. Papadopoulos, K., Koustriava, E., Koukourikos, P., Kartasidou, L., Barouti, M., Varveris, A., et al.: Comparison of three orientation and mobility aids for individuals with blindness: verbal description, audio-tactile map and audio-haptic map. Assist. Technol. **29**(1), 1–7 (2017). https://doi.org/10.1080/10400435.2016.1171809
24. Papadopoulos, K., Koustriava, E., Koukourikos, P.: Orientation and mobility aids for individuals with blindness: verbal description vs. audio-tactile map. Assistive Technol. **30**(4), 191–200 (2018). https://doi.org/10.1080/10400435.2017.1307879
25. Papadopoulos, K., Barouti, M., Koustriava, E.: Differences in spatial knowledge of individuals with blindness when using audiotactile maps, using tactile maps, and walking. Except. Child. **84**(3), 330–343 (2018). https://doi.org/10.1177/0014402918764300

Smooth, Structured, and Strategic: Hand Movement Proficiency of Visually Impaired Players in Tactile Puzzle Game *Tactris*

Masaki Matsuo[1], Delgerbayar Erdenesambuu[1], Masatsugu Sakajiri[1], Junji Onishi[1], Tadahiro Sakai[1], and Takahiro Miura[1,2](✉)

[1] Tsukuba University of Technology, 4-12-7 Kasuga, Tsukuba 305-0821, Japan
{matsuo,sakajiri,onishi,sakai}@cs.k.tsukuba-tech.ac.jp
[2] National Institute of Advanced Industrial Science and Technology (AIST), 6-2-3 Kashiwanoha, Kashiwa, Chiba 277-0882, Japan
miura-t@aist.go.jp

Abstract. This study presents a markerless, MediaPipe-based analysis pipeline for quantitatively assessing hand movement proficiency during tactile display exploration in the inclusive falling-block puzzle game *Tactris*. Video recordings from above captured the finger movements of one expert and six novices. From these, 20 kinematic, coordination, and strategic parameters were extracted. All spatial metrics were normalized by palm length to ensure body-size-invariant comparisons. One-sample t-tests showed that the distinction between expert and novice was most clearly demonstrated by bimanual coordination flexibility (conjoint ratio, $d = 2.45$), direction reversal rate ($d = 1.37$), exploration time ($d = 1.29$), strategy stability ($d = 1.09$), and Hurst exponent ($d = -0.93$). These results indicate that tactile exploration proficiency primarily depends on movement quality, being efficient, smooth, and strategic, rather than hand posture or procedure selection.

Keywords: Tactile display · Hand movement analysis · MediaPipe · Visual impairment · Game accessibility

1 Introduction

Esports has seen a notable rise in popularity in recent years. Novel accessibility features have recently been introduced to enable visually impaired gamers to play mainstream titles such as *Forza Motorsport* (Turn 10 Studios) and *Street Fighter 6* (CAPCOM) [11,17,18]. At the same time, efforts are underway to develop games that are accessible to and inclusive of both visually impaired and sighted players. For example, an accessible action role-playing game has been developed that relies solely on sound and touch feedback [14–16]. Subsequently, the game *Tactris*, a falling-block puzzle game that utilizes audio cues and tactile diagrams displayed on a specialized device, was introduced [13]. In Tactris, players are

K. Miesenberger et al. (Eds.): ICCHP 2026, LNCS 16867, pp. 501–509, 2027.
https://doi.org/10.1007/978-3-032-31308-9_60

instructed to feel the shapes of falling blocks through touch, develop strategies, and respond quickly.

Over time, we observed that visually impaired players who continued to play Tactris improved their ability to read tactile maps. By analyzing their gameplay, they identified hand movements that distinguish experts in using tactile displays from beginners. Most existing research has relied on manual video review or sensor tracking to study this [4,19]. However, these methods are not suitable for large-scale studies or practical, real-world applications.

In this study, we aim to compare the finger movement patterns of expert and beginner Tactris players. We recorded their finger movements from above, performed markerless hand landmark detection using MediaPipe [24], and analyzed parameters including movement speed, smoothness, angular stability, bimanual coordination, exploration strategy, exploratory procedure (EP) distribution [12], and temporal structure. To the best of our knowledge, this is the first application of computer vision-based hand tracking for the quantitative assessment of tactile display exploration proficiency.

2 Method

2.1 Data Acquisition

Participants interacted with a refreshable tactile pin-array display while playing Tactris (Fig. 1). An RGB camera recorded their hand movements from an overhead perspective at 30 fps. The camera was positioned directly above the display to capture both hands. No sensors or markers were attached to participants' hands, ensuring that their natural exploration behavior was preserved.

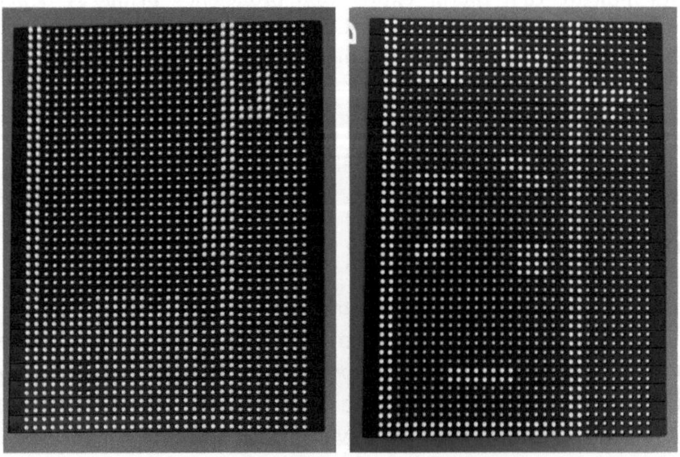

Fig. 1. Screenshots of the Tactris.

2.2 Analysis

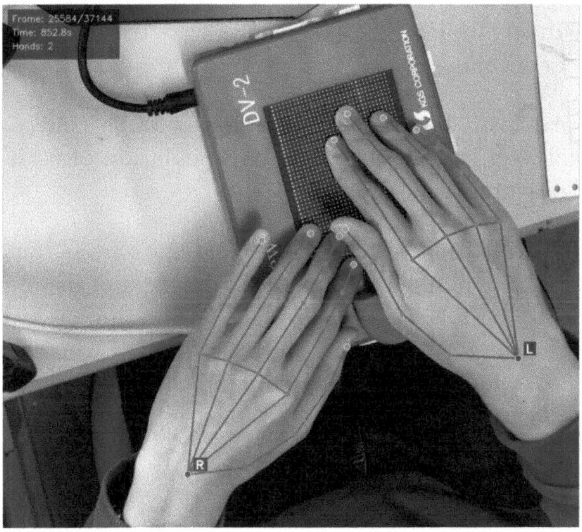

Fig. 2. Hand recognition using MediaPipe. Although the L (left) and R (right) labels on the hands are incorrect, they are not an issue because the analysis is not performed on the left or right hand individually.

Hand Landmark Extraction. Hand pose estimation was performed using MediaPipe Hands [24]. The system detected 21 three-dimensional landmarks for each hand from RGB video, as shown in Fig. 2. Both hands were tracked simultaneously. Frames with detection confidence levels below 0.5 were not considered. Short gaps of up to 5 frames were filled through interpolation. Ferraris et al. [6] validated MediaPipe by comparing it with optical motion capture, and found that MediaPipe provides acceptable accuracy for finger kinematic analysis.

Hand-Size Normalization. Since MediaPipe provides coordinates scaled to frame resolution, raw pixel velocities cannot be directly compared across different setups. Following Hof [9], who suggested dividing kinematic variables by a characteristic body-segment length, we normalized all spatial quantities by the Euclidean distance between the wrist (landmark #0) and the middle-finger MCP (landmark #9). This palm-length measure is commonly used in MediaPipe hand analysis [7] because it is reliably detected and remains stable across finger postures. The distances for each frame were summarized using the session median. After normalization, velocities are expressed in palm-lengths per second (PL/s).

Kinematic Parameters. Positional data from the tip of the dominant-hand index finger (landmark #8) were smoothed using a second-order Butterworth low-pass filter with a 6 Hz cutoff frequency [22]. Instantaneous velocity was calculated through central differences. To assess movement smoothness, three metrics were used: the number of acceleration zero-crossings, which indicate movement intermittency [10,19]; the number of direction reversals, reflecting hesitation [5]; and the root-mean-square jerk [2]. The counts were divided by exploration time to derive rates per second.

Angular Orientation. The roll, pitch, and yaw of the index finger were calculated from joint vectors [19]. The standard deviation of each angle was used as a measure of postural stability.

Bimanual Coordination Each frame was categorized as bimanual, left-only, right-only, or none. For bimanual frames, the inter-hand distance (measured in PL) and the velocity correlation, which is the cosine similarity of hand centroid velocities, were measured. A correlation above 0.5 was considered indicative of conjoint movement, while a value below -0.5 indicated disjoint movement, based on prior research [3,23].

Exploration Strategy and Exploratory Procedure (EP) Classification. Trajectories were segmented into 5-second windows and classified into gridline, cyclic, back-and-forth, or random/local strategies [1,21]. A sliding-window classifier identified EPs (static contact, lateral motion, contour following, and enclosure) based on speed, inter-finger distance, and direction consistency [12,22].

Detrended Fluctuation Analysis (DFA). The DFA [20] was used on the speed time series to determine the Hurst exponent (H), which measures long-range temporal correlations. A higher H reflects more structured, anticipatory dynamics, indicating greater proficiency [19].

3 Results and Discussion

One-sample t-tests compared the novice group ($n = 6$) with the expert's reference values across 20 parameters divided into six categories (Tables 1, 2, 3, 4, 5 and 6). Effect sizes were measured using Cohen's d. Velocity, jerk, and inter-hand distance were analyzed after normalizing for hand size in palm lengths.

3.1 Speed and Exploration Efficiency

After normalizing for hand size, the expert showed higher mean fingertip velocities than novices, who needed significantly longer exploration times (Table 1). The finding that the expert scans more quickly and complete tasks sooner aligns with Gori et al. [8], who observed increased haptic velocity in congenitally blind individuals, indicating that tactile expertise improves high-speed information extraction. Velocity variability and jerk RMS showed no significant differences after normalization, suggesting that earlier observed differences were mainly due to resolution-dependent scaling.

Table 1. Speed and exploration efficiency

Parameter	t	p	Signif.	d	Magnitude
Mean velocity (normalized)	−2.99	0.0153	*	−0.94	large
SD of velocity (normalized)	0.76	0.4658		0.24	small
RMS jerk (normalized)	1.37	0.2049		0.43	small
Exploration time	4.09	0.0027	**	1.29	large

Table 2. Movement smoothness

Parameter	t	p	Signif.	d	Magnitude
Acceleration zero-crossings	3.40	0.0078	**	1.08	large
Acceleration zero-crossings per second	1.18	0.2693		0.37	small
Direction reversals	2.33	0.0450	*	0.74	medium
Direction reversals per second	4.35	0.0019	**	1.37	large

3.2 Movement Smoothness

Novices showed significantly higher raw acceleration zero-crossing counts, though the per-second rate was not significant (Table 2). This indicates that the higher counts partly result from longer exploration times. Direction reversals were significant in both raw counts and per-second rates, confirming that novices hesitate more frequently per unit time [5, 10]. Therefore, the direction reversal rate appears to be a more reliable indicator of proficiency, as it is unaffected by spatial scale and exploration duration.

Table 3. Angular stability of finger posture

Parameter	t	p	Signif.	d	Magnitude
SD of roll	2.03	0.0728	+	0.64	medium
SD of pitch	−1.51	0.1662		−0.48	small
SD of yaw	2.10	0.0649	+	0.66	medium

3.3 Angular Stability

Roll and yaw showed slight trends, with novices displaying more angular variability (Table 3). Although these effects were not statistically significant, their medium effect sizes suggest finger postural control may influence tactile display proficiency, meriting further study with larger samples. Pitch variability showed no difference.

Table 4. Bimanual coordination

Parameter	t	p	Signif.	d	Magnitude
Mean inter-hand distance (normalized)	−0.25	0.8079		−0.08	negligible
Bimanual ratio	1.19	0.2633		0.38	small
Conjoint ratio	7.75	<0.001	***	2.45	large

3.4 Bimanual Coordination

The inter-hand distance and bimanual ratio did not differ, suggesting that both groups used two hands with similar frequency and spatial separation (Table 4). However, novices had a significantly higher conjoint ratio, by the largest margin in the dataset ($d = 2.45$), indicating more rigid, same-direction bimanual movement. The expert alternated flexibly between conjoint scanning for global surveying and disjoint movement for split-field exploration [3,23].

Table 5. Temporal structure and exploration strategy

Parameter	t	p	Signif.	d	Magnitude
Hurst exponent	−2.94	0.0164	*	−0.93	large
Strategy transitions	3.45	0.0072	**	1.09	large

3.5 Temporal Structure and Exploration Strategy

The Hurst exponent was significantly lower in novices (Table 5), indicating weaker long-range temporal correlations in their velocity time series. The higher H value in experts suggests more structured, anticipatory dynamics, where their current scanning pace is influenced by previous exploration [19]. Strategy changes occurred more frequently among novices, showing less stable, more shifting exploration patterns rather than a consistent, systematic scanning plan.

Table 6. Distribution of exploratory procedures

Parameter	t	p	Signif.	d	Magnitude
Lateral motion ratio	0.29	0.7799		0.09	negligible
Contour following ratio	1.00	0.3434		0.32	small
Static contact ratio	−1.93	0.0857	+	−0.61	medium
Enclosure ratio	−1.04	0.3269		−0.33	small

3.6 Distribution of Exploratory Procedures

The static contact ratio slightly increased, suggesting that the expert tend to pause more often for tactile feature integration, as shown in Table 6. The other EP ratios did not differ significantly, indicating similar types of EPs used across groups.

3.7 Limitations

This study has several limitations. First, only one expert served as the reference point, and six novices were compared to this individual's values using one-sample t-tests. This approach does not account for variability among experts and limits the applicability of the reference profile. Second, the analysis only examined the dominant hand's index fingertip (landmark #8), even though MediaPipe detects all 21 landmarks per hand. As a result, multi-finger coordination and per-digit spatial strategies were not assessed. Third, the thresholds for EP classification were based on pilot observations rather than data-driven methods. Using machine learning classifiers trained on expert-annotated data could improve accuracy and reproducibility. Fourth, the analysis is cross-sectional. Long-term tracking across multiple Tactris sessions is needed to understand skill development and if the identified kinematic markers predict sustained tactile proficiency.

4 Conclusion: Future Work

This study employed a MediaPipe-based, markerless hand tracking system to compare finger movement patterns between an expert and six novices in the inclusive tactile puzzle game *Tactris*. As a result, clear differences between expert and novice were most evident in the conjoint ratio ($d = 2.45$), direction reversal rate ($d = 1.37$), exploration time ($d = 1.29$), strategy transitions ($d = 1.09$), acceleration zero-crossings ($d = 1.08$), normalized velocity ($d = -0.94$), and Hurst exponent ($d = -0.93$). Proficiency involves efficient, rapid scanning, smooth and confident movements, structured temporal dynamics, and flexible bimanual coordination. These features reflect the expert's ability to extract tactile information quickly and systematically. Future research will include more experts, a larger group of novices, analysis of multi-finger trajectories, and longitudinal studies of skill development.

Acknowledgments. This work was supported by JSPS KAKENHI Grant Numbers JP23K16919, JP23K25693, and JP24K21471, and by JST FOREST Grant Number JPMJFR234Y.

References

1. Sadia, B., Sadic, A., Ayyildiz, M., Basdogan, C.: Exploration strategies for tactile graphics displayed by electrovibration on a touchscreen. Int. J. Hum Comput Stud. **160**, 102760 (2022). https://doi.org/10.1016/j.ijhcs.2021.102760
2. Balasubramanian, S., Melendez-Calderon, A., Roby-Brami, A., Burdet, E.: On the analysis of movement smoothness. J. Neuroeng. Rehabil. **12**, 112 (2015). https://doi.org/10.1186/s12984-015-0090-9
3. Bertelson, P., Mousty, P., D'Alimonte, G.: A study of braille reading: 2. Patterns of hand activity in one-handed and two-handed reading. Q. J. Exp. Psychol. Sect. A **37**(2), 235–256 (1985). https://doi.org/10.1080/14640748508400932
4. Breidegard, B., Eriksson, Y., Fellenius, K., Jönsson, B.: Computer-based automatic finger- and speech-tracking system. Behav. Res. Methods **40**(1), 185–195 (2008). https://doi.org/10.3758/BF03192975
5. Davidson, P.W., Appelle, S., Haber, R.N.: Haptic scanning of braille cells by low- and high-proficiency blind readers. Res. Dev. Disabil. **13**(2), 99–111 (1992). https://doi.org/10.1016/0891-4222(92)90018-2
6. Amprimo, G., Masi, G., Pettiti, G., Olmo, G., Priano, L., Ferraris, C.: Hand tracking for clinical applications: validation of the Google MediaPipe Hand (GMH) and the Depth-Enhanced GMH-D frameworks. Biomed. Signal Process. Control **96**, 106508 (2024). https://doi.org/10.1016/j.bspc.2024.106508
7. Gil-Martín, M., Marini, M., Martín-Fernández, I., Esteban-Romero, S., Cinque, L.: Hand gesture recognition using MediaPipe landmarks and deep learning networks. In: Proceedings of the 17th International Conference on Agents and Artificial Intelligence (ICAART 2025), pp. 24–30. SciTePress (2025). https://doi.org/10.5220/0013053500003890
8. Leo, F., Gori, M., Sciutti, A.: Early blindness modulates haptic object recognition. Front. Hum. Neurosci. **16**, 941593 (2022). https://doi.org/10.3389/fnhum.2022.941593
9. Hof, A.L.: Scaling gait data to body size. Gait Posture **4**(3), 222–223 (1996). https://doi.org/10.1016/0966-6362(95)01057-2
10. Hughes, B.: Movement kinematics of the braille-reading finger. J. Vis. Impairment Blindness **105**(6), 370–381 (2011). https://doi.org/10.1177/0145482X1110500608
11. Ifukube, T.: Sound-Based Assistive Technology. Springer (2017). https://doi.org/10.1007/978-3-319-47997-2
12. Lederman, S.J., Klatzky, R.L.: Hand movements: a window into haptic object recognition. Cogn. Psychol. **19**(3), 342–368 (1987). https://doi.org/10.1016/0010-0285(87)90008-9
13. Matsuo, M., Erdenesambuu, D., Sakajiri, M., Onishi, J., Miura, T.: Tactris: inclusive falling block puzzle game with audio-tactile effects for visually impaired people. In: Lecture Notes in Computer Science, vol. 14750, pp. 128–136 (2024). https://doi.org/10.1007/978-3-031-62846-7_16
14. Matsuo, M., Hasegawa, A., Miura, T., Onishi, J., Sakajiri, M.: Mixed-ability game development via disabled-led inclusive action research: building the accessible action role-playing game (RPG) planet saga. J. Technol. Pers. Disabil. **14**, 66–83 (2026). https://hdl.handle.net/20.500.12680/794087292
15. Matsuo, M., Miura, T., Onishi, J., Sakajiri, M., Ono, T.: Experience report of blind gamer to develop the accessible action RPG. J. Technol. Pers. Disabil. **5**, 172–191 (2017). https://hdl.handle.net/10211.3/190211

16. Matsuo, M., Miura, T., Yabu, K., Katagiri, A., Sakajiri, M., Onishi, J., Kurata, T., Ifukube, T. Inclusive action game presenting real-time multimodal presentations for sighted and blind persons. In: Proceedings of the ICMI 2021, pp. 62–70. ACM, New York (2021). https://doi.org/10.1145/3462244.3479912
17. Miura, T., Yabu, K.: Narrative review of assistive technologies and sensory substitution in people with visual and hearing impairment. Psychologia **65**(1), 70–99 (2023). https://doi.org/10.2117/psysoc.2022-B031
18. Miura, T., Tanaka, T.: Assisting visually impaired people: sports and eSports. In: Tanaka, T. (eds.) Inclusive and Barrier-Free Designs for Rehabilitation Engineering, pp. 161–186. Springer, Singapore (2026). https://doi.org/10.1007/978-981-95-5783-7_10
19. Nonaka, T., Ito, K., Stoffregen, T.A.: Structure of variability in scanning movement predicts braille reading performance in children. Sci. Rep. **11**, 7182 (2021). https://doi.org/10.1038/s41598-021-86674-5
20. Peng, C.-K., Havlin, S., Stanley, H.E., Goldberger, A.L.: Quantification of scaling exponents and crossover phenomena in nonstationary heartbeat time series. Chaos **5**(1), 82–87 (1995). https://doi.org/10.1063/1.166141
21. Ungar, S., Blades, M., Spencer, C.: Strategies for knowledge acquisition from cartographic maps by blind and visually impaired adults. Cartogr. J. **34**(2), 93–110 (1997). https://doi.org/10.1179/caj.1997.34.2.93
22. Jansen, S.E., Bergmann Tiest, W.M., Kappers, A.M.L.: Haptic exploratory behavior during object discrimination: a novel automatic annotation method. PLoS ONE **10**(2), e0117017 (2015). https://doi.org/10.1371/journal.pone.0117017
23. Wright, T., Wormsley, D.P., Kamei-Hannan, C.: Hand movements and braille reading efficiency: data from the alphabetic braille and contracted braille study. J. Vis. Impairment Blindness **103**(10), 649–661 (2009). https://doi.org/10.1177/0145482X0910301008
24. Zhang, F., et al.: MediaPipe hands: on-device real-time hand tracking. arXiv preprint arXiv:2006.10214 (2020). https://doi.org/10.48550/arXiv.2006.10214

Digital Accessibility – From Inclusive Design and UX to Implementation and Evaluation

Digital Accessibility-from Inclusive Design and UX to Implementation and Evaluation Introduction to the Special Thematic Session

Nataša Rajh[1(✉)], Matjaž Debevc[2], Klaus Höckner[3], Reinhard Koutny[1], and Klaus Miesenberger[1]

[1] Institut Integriert Studieren, Johannes Kepler University, Linz, Austria
Natasa.Rajh@partner.jku.at, {Reinhard.Koutny, Klaus.Miesenberger}@jku.at
[2] Institute of Media Communications, Faculty of Electrical Engineering and Computer, Science, University of Maribor, Maribor, Slovenia
matjaz.debevc@guest.um.si
[3] Hilfsgemeinschaft der Blinden Und Sehschwachen Österreichs, Vienna, Austria
hoeckner@hilfsgemeinschaft.at

Abstract. This session continues ICCHP's long-standing series of presenting research and development in web, software, and digital accessibility, following the most recent session chaired by our group [2]. For nearly forty years, ever since the beginnings of ICCHP, digital accessibility has remained one of its core themes. Although specific research priorities have evolved over time and topics have varied from year to year, the field's presence within academic research has remained strong. This year is no exception, featuring twelve papers that explore diverse facets of the discipline, including inclusive design methodologies, user experience, and the practical implementation and evaluation of accessible digital environments. The papers presented reflect varying levels of research maturity, with some offering conceptual frameworks, others reporting direct practical studies or solutions, and others identifying areas that require further investigation and development.

Keywords: Digital Accessibility · Inclusive Design · Participatory Design

1 Introduction

With the European Accessibility Act (EAA) [1] getting fully enforced from June 2025 and the Shift Left approach borrowed from DevOps methodologies, we expect that accessibility will move from a simple compliance topic toward proactive integration. This is in line with comparable movements around the globe, driven by the US ADA [2] and Sect. 508 [3] legislation.

The focus on user-centric topics like participatory design, user experience, and inclusive design, strongly presented in this thematic session, gives the impression that we are

https://www.jku.at/institut-integriert-studieren/

K. Miesenberger et al. (Eds.): ICCHP 2026, LNCS 16867, pp. 513–521, 2027.
https://doi.org/10.1007/978-3-032-31308-9_61

on the right path of including accessibility long before developers even open their IDEs and start coding. However, is this the current reality? Is it true already, or are we still primarily discussing ideals while the industry continues to catch up to these standards in practice?

The latest WebAIM study [4], which evaluated the home pages of the top one million websites, highlights a concerning reality: an average of 56.1 errors were detected per page, with 95.9% of home pages failing to meet WCAG standards. This represents an increase of 1.1 percentage points from 2025, when failures were detected on 94.8% of pages. This huge number clearly underlines that there is still a strong need for R&D impacting on better inclusion and integration of Accessibility into the design and development processes, paving the way towards inclusive UX. The contributions to this session highlight recent developments in this domain of growing importance.

When looking at previous ICCHP proceedings [5, 6, 8], we find a substantial number of studies on web accessibility, or broader digital accessibility, spread across dedicated and related STSs, as this field has been a core topic throughout the years. While many sessions are relevant, if we select just a few, certain ones stand out due to their direct links to this year's session.

The most recent one [5], organized by the same group of chairs, focused on specific subdomains of digital accessibility, namely Software Accessibility, Web Accessibility, and Document Accessibility. While the sessions share substantial similarities in scope and thematic orientation, document accessibility is not explicitly addressed in this year's edition. In addition, the previous session did not place a specific emphasis on user involvement or user experience.

If we look at ICCHP 2022 [6], the Digital Accessibility session was dedicated to readability and understandability. The topics ranged from authentication methods and alternative content descriptions (such as alt text and audio descriptions for videos) to overlays, which are also a strongly discussed topic in this year's STS. Overlay tools as a method for making websites accessible are a controversial topic, as they are frequently used but have limited evidence of effectiveness in fully addressing accessibility issues [7].

In alignment with the high volume of papers addressing user-centered design this year, in 2020 [8] the conference hosted a specific STS session on User Centred Design and User Participation in Inclusive R&D, highlighting the growing prominence and prioritization of inclusivity in technical development.

2 Overview of the Contributions

The collection of contributions presented in this STS provides a wide-ranging perspective on both the current state and evolving directions of digital accessibility research and practice. Consisting of twelve papers, the contributions are grouped into three thematic areas that collectively cover a broad spectrum of subtopics within digital accessibility. This structure enables a more targeted discussion of each thematic group while also pointing out how broad the field actually is.

The first thematic group, and also the most prominently represented, focuses on inclusive design, participatory design, and user experience, reflecting the central role of users in accessibility research and practice [9–13]. This session sees users not as passive recipients, but as active participants in the development process. Furthermore, it explores the role of UX designers, who are often referred to as user advocates, and examines how they handle the challenge of including accessibility in modern design workflows. The last paper in this group presents a real-time accessibility web application for Deaf/hard of hearing and blind/low vision users at live events, introducing a reciprocal model in which users are both contributors and consumers.

The second thematic group, "Evaluation methods & accessibility standards", examines monitoring and testing frameworks, the European Accessibility Act, and cybersecurity protocols [14–17]. The first paper in this group highlights the need for more usable standards, emphasizing the role of HCI researchers in actively engaging with their development. Next, there are two papers covering evaluation tools and techniques, the first one comparing the effectiveness of three governmentally used automated evaluation tools, and the second evaluating three procedures for testing mobile apps. Last paper in this group addresses accessible and usable cybersecurity.

The final thematic group, "Overlays and Browsers", features two studies on overlay technologies and a paper dedicated to improving table accessibility for magnifier users [18–20].

2.1 Inclusive Design, Participatory Design, User Experience

With their paper "Inclusive Design Capability Maturity Framework", Velleman et al. [9] provide a great start into this year's STS, highlighting a strong focus on user-centric approaches. The paper frames inclusive design capability as an organizational rather than individual competence, proposing a reflective, non-linear maturity approach that emphasizes learning and adaptation while avoiding reduction to compliance, benchmarking, or optimization. Organizations often recognize the importance of inclusion but are uncertain about how to address it, as reflected by the wide range of stakeholders participating in the study. The stakeholders used the Participatory Action Research (PAR) approach, consisting of desk research, a Learning Community (LC), surveys, in-depth interviews, and visualizations. The framework presented in the study moves away from predefined maturity levels and benchmarking, instead offering a cyclical, reflective model based on four quadrants—strategy, culture, process, and results—that help organizations map and understand their inclusive design capabilities in context. It supports ongoing reflection and tailored, non-prescriptive improvement of inclusive design practices.

The second paper, "Defining Accessibility as Experiences in Technology Mediated Meaningful Activities" by Power [10], highlights that accessibility in human-computer interaction (HCI) is shaped by two complementary traditions: one focused on technological solutions to enable perception and operation for disabled users, and another focused on optimizing interfaces to ensure users can effectively complete tasks. While the paper does not claim that both traditions are not valuable, it argues that accessibility should be reoriented around experiential outcomes; otherwise, an important question of whether valued experiences are truly achievable even when technical and interaction barriers are removed is left unanswered. Current accessibility research misses barriers that lie beyond the system. The author proposes that "accessibility needs to be defined as barrier-free access to meaningful activities mediated by technology that yield experiences that disabled people value." Activity theory is presented as a framework for this definition and illustrates its strengths and limitations using examples from digital games.

Conventional human-centered methods may not fully capture the complexities of disability contexts, underscoring the need for participatory design approaches that remain insufficiently explored in assistive technology and ICT. To address this research gap, Moro et al. [11] conducted a literature review on participatory design in this domain, examining which disabilities are addressed, the roles participants assume in the design process, and how their involvement influences outcomes. Participation was mapped across the design lifecycle using the Double Diamond framework to enable comparison. The final sample comprised 39 papers that involved people with disabilities as active participants, applied participatory or co-creative approaches, and focused on welfare-related assistive technologies. The main finding is that participatory design in this field is most often limited to gathering input and feedback, while substantial shared decision-making and more meaningful co-creation are much less frequent. Participation was most consistently reported in the Discover and Develop phases.

While all previous papers described either inclusive design or participatory design, the paper from Rajh et al. [12] addresses the practices of those highly responsible for these approaches—designers. It seems like the design community is well informed about accessibility by now, but the most commonly detected issue persists to be insufficient color contrast [4] - without doubt a designer´s responsibility. For that reason, the authors explore designers´ accessibility practices and highlight the need for workflow support and accessibility features in design tools. What Velleman et al. [9] already pointed out, designers encountering barriers throughout the design process, is what Rajh et al. [12] explore further. With the help of an extensive review of existing quantitative and qualitative studies involving designers, and with their own survey, the authors explore how accessibility is currently integrated into UX design practices, and how it should be, for designers to receive the help they might require. As of April 2026, the survey was still accepting responses, so the results presented are preliminary.

Again, widening the scope of our STS's emphasis on improving user involvement and participation through accessible tools, Shiraishi et al.'s [13] paper "Reciprocal Support for Accessible Live Events (Real-Time Timeline Web App for DHH/BLV Participants" presents field evaluation of a browser-based, zero-install real-time timeline web application designed for deaf/hard of hearing (DHH) and blind/low vision (BLV) spectators at live events. The system, on the edge between assistive technology and mainstream accessibility, enables a reciprocal accessibility model, where participants alternate between contributing and consuming accessibility-relevant information—such as live commentary, scores, and LLM-generated media descriptions—rather than relying solely on one-way professional services. Building on earlier pilot studies that identified learnability issues, the updated system incorporates stakeholder-driven improvements, including simplified onboarding, multimodal LLM augmentation, and personalised filtering panels. Field deployment at Deaflympics 2025 (N = 21) yielded a mean SUS score of 72.1 and an overall experience rating of 4.67/5. A supplementary exposition study (N = 35 general visitors) returned even higher acceptance scores. The results provide concrete, in-situ evidence that crowd-mediated, role-switching participation can complement professional accessibility services in time-critical event environments. For our topic and session, the paper demonstrates a transferable approach towards integrating AI and user-driven activities for accessibility.

2.2 Evaluation Methods & Accessibility Standards

In her work "Making Accessibility Work in Practice: European ICT Accessibility Standards under the European Accessibility Act (EAA)", Sawicka [14] highlights the potential of the EAA as an important opportunity to improve accessibility; however, she argues that this is not guaranteed but depends on the quality and coherence of the underlying technical standards. This contribution provides a strong introduction to the thematic area of evaluation methods and accessibility standards. The author further argues that HCI researchers should engage more with accessibility standardization and policy processes to make them more robust and usable, drawing on their expertise in user-centered design, usability, and accessibility evaluation. Accessibility standardization can be understood as a form of design activity that shapes systems before they are even built. Sawicka states that: "Accessibility standards function as a translation gearbox between inclusive design values, accessibility legislation and real-world ICT systems and users."

Next in this thematic area are two papers focusing on the evaluation phase. The first one, by de Andrade et al. [15], is a study on tools for monitoring digital accessibility adopted by governmental initiatives in different countries. The paper examines the calculation models used by three automated evaluation tools employed by governmental institutions in Brazil (Ases Web), Italy (Mauve++), and Portugal (AccessMonitor). A sample of reference websites provided by the W3C was tested with each tool, and the results were compared with previously conducted manual expert audits. The findings revealed significant discrepancies among the tools, prompting the authors to emphasize the need for standardization and for validation methods that go beyond reliance on automated evaluations, particularly in the context of governmental accessibility monitoring.

Steininger et al. [16] compare manual accessibility testing procedures for mobile apps. Their study examines three procedures used in Germany: the certification-oriented BIK BITV Test and BIT inklusiv App Test, alongside the simplified Easy App Check designed for non-experts. The study investigates how these procedures compare in terms of structural characteristics and practical performance when used by non-experts. It combines an analytical comparison based on a structured criteria catalog with an empirical user study. For the empirical component, 23 novice evaluators assessed two apps using the procedures. Preliminary results indicate that while the BIT inclusive procedure achieved the highest usability ratings, all methods posed challenges in tasks such as contrast verification, highlighting trade-offs between procedural depth and usability, and the need for improved guidance.

The last paper of this group, "A Proposed Accessible Cyber Security Support (AcCeSS) Framework", by Binsedeeq, et al. [17], extends the scope of the session towards accessible and usable cyber security by introducing the AcCeSS (Accessible Cyber Security Support) framework, a structured decision-support tool aimed at bridging the persistent gap between cybersecurity design and the needs of users with disabilities. The framework guides stakeholders—designers, developers, deployers, and standards advisors—through nine accessibility dimensions (e.g., cognitive complexity, visual demand, time sensitivity) using predefined criteria groups and automatically generated, actionable recommendations. A three-level prioritization scheme helps practitioners address the most impactful barriers first. The framework is designed to be applicable across diverse disability groups and technology contexts. Validation through structured stakeholder sessions with pre-and post-surveys completes the paper. The work directly supports the session's focus on user-centred, inclusive web and software accessibility practices.

2.3 Overlays and Browsers

The first paper in this group points out how the web has evolved into dynamic, distributed systems where third-party services can inject content via JavaScript. Simultaneously, browsers have transformed into powerful Chromium-based platforms that allow the reshaping of the browsing experience by modifying site behavior via extensions or browser-integrated functionalities. Accessibility governance, however, remains source-centered, creating a mismatch with modern post-source approaches such as overlays and browser-based tools. As these do not reliably meet WCAG criteria, Wolberger [18] highlights the need to examine why such accessibility functions are not integrated into browsers directly, and evaluates how Chrome supports post-source accessibility under controlled conditions. The study shows what browsers can and cannot do for accessibility after a page loads.

While the first paper in this thematic group essentially asks whether browsers themselves can perform the types of accessibility remediations that overlays claim to provide, Sajka [19] extends this discussion by proposing a systematic examination of where and why post-source solutions (at the browser, proxy, or edge layer) may outperform traditional in-source development, offering a structured framework for combining both approaches to accessibility. The three areas identified where post-source remediation is functionally superior include Radical Personalization, Third-Party and Legacy Content, and Cross-Site Consistency. The author is comparing three known claims and premises, namely the critique about overlays, the view that WCAG remains the same regardless of when they are applied, and lastly, the idea previously discussed by Wolberger [18] that browsers should play a role in addressing accessibility issues. To properly assess these claims, the author evaluates a set of "high-impact" edge capabilities, such as color contrast adjustment for in-source compliance and post-source (edge) remediation. The author highlights recognizing the user agent's role in enabling accessibility by empowering users at the edge to create more flexible and personalized digital experiences.

The last paper in this thematic area, authored by Sandnes and MacKenzie [20], moves away from overlays and proposes a solution for improving the usability of web tables for magnifier users through the use of annotations, crumbs, and snippets. While the authors highlight the usefulness of web tables as a way of providing detailed real-time information, they also note the challenges that large tables present, not only cognitively but especially for users with reduced vision. Magnifier users are typically unable to view an entire table at once, seeing only a small portion of it. When accessing tables through a reduced, narrow viewport with panning, the authors identified several usability issues and proposed three possible solutions: adding annotations, crumbs, or snippets. The authors evaluated these approaches in a controlled experiment.

3 Conclusions

The session demonstrates and underlines the ongoing need for R&D in the domain of digital accessibility. We see a clear shift towards more automated and tool-supported approaches, in particular including AI. But at the same time, as underlined over the last 30 years in the ICCHP sessions on digital accessibility, more evidence is provided that accessibility is the foundation of and has to be embedded into usability (ISO 9241 processes)—a concept coined as "usable accessibility" [18]. This clearly underlines the demand for personalization and personal adaptation, with a strong need to integrate accessibility into the individual user experience, and thereby into care and support infrastructures.

This session confirms that digital accessibility is no longer adequately framed as a narrow issue of technical compliance. Across the twelve contributions, accessibility emerges instead as a design, evaluation, and governance challenge that must be addressed throughout the whole lifecycle of digital systems. The papers collectively show a clear movement towards earlier and more meaningful integration of accessibility into design processes, with particular emphasis on inclusive design capability, participatory methods, and the role of user experience professionals in shaping accessible outcomes. At the same time, the session makes equally clear that this shift is still incomplete: persistent accessibility failures in practice indicate that the field remains far from achieving systematic mainstream adoption.

A second important contribution of this session lies in showing that progress depends not only on better design methods, but also on more usable standards, more reliable evaluation procedures, and a more critical understanding of tool-supported accessibility. The papers on monitoring, mobile testing, cybersecurity, overlays, browser-based remediation, and table accessibility demonstrate that automated or post-source solutions may complement accessibility work, but they do not remove the need for sound design decisions, human judgment, and context-sensitive evaluation.

In conclusion, together, the session reinforces a long-standing ICCHP message: accessibility must be embedded into usability and personalization as a core principle shaping the lived experience of persons with disabilities.

References

1. European Parliament and Council of the European Union: Directive (EU) 2019/882 on the accessibility requirements for products and services (European Accessibility Act). Official J. Eur. Union (2019)
2. United States: Americans with Disabilities Act of 1990, Pub. L. pp. 101–336 (1990)
3. United States: Rehabilitation Act of 1973, Section 508, as amended by the Workforce Investment Act of 1998 (1998)
4. WebAIM: The WebAIM Million: The 2026 report on the accessibility of the top 1,000,000 home pages. https://webaim.org/projects/million. Accessed 12 Apr 2026
5. Rajh, N., Debevc, M., Höckner, K., Koutny, R., Miesenberger, K.: Software, Web and Document Accessibility: introduction to the Special Thematic Session. In: International Conference on Computers Helping People with Special Needs (ICCHP), pp. 3–10. Springer Nature Switzerland, Cham (2024)

6. Petrie, H., Höckner, K., Rosenberger, W.: Digital accessibility: readability and understandability: introduction to the special thematic session. In: International Conference on Computers Helping People with Special Needs (ICCHP), pp. 3–5. Springer International Publishing, Cham (2022)
7. Egger, N., Zimmermann, G., Strobbe, C.: Overlay tools as a support for accessible websites – possibilities and limitations. In: International Conference on Computers Helping People with Special Needs (ICCHP), pp. 6–17. Springer International Publishing, Cham (2022)
8. Miesenberger, K., Edler, C., Dirks, S., Bühler, C., Heumader, P.: User centered design and user participation in inclusive R&D: Introduction to the special thematic session. In: International Conference on Computers Helping People with Special Needs (ICCHP), pp. 3–9. Springer International Publishing, Cham (2020)
9. Velleman, E.M., van Hooff, A.C., Havinga, J., Kemp, H., van Tuijl, E.: Inclusive design capability maturity framework. In: Miesenberger, K., Petrie, H., Peňáz, P. (eds.): ICCHP 2026–Computers Helping People with Special Needs, 20th International Conference, Linz, Austria, Proceedings. Springer (2026)
10. Power, C.: Defining accessibility as experiences in technology mediated meaningful activities. In: Miesenberger, K., Petrie, H., Peňáz, P. (eds.): ICCHP 2026–Computers Helping People with Special Needs, 20th International Conference, Linz, Austria, Proceedings. Springer (2026)
11. Moro, S., Kobashi, M., Takagi, S., Ohashi, T.: From discover to deliver: how and when people with disabilities participate and its clinical relevance across design phases. In: Petz, A.; Miesenberger, K. (eds.): ICCHP Open Access Compendium "Future Perspectives on Accessibility, AT and eInclusion", Linz, Austria, Proceedings. Johannes Kepler University Linz (2026)
12. Rajh, N., Miesenberger, K., Koutny, R.: Accessibility in UX design: the need for workflow support and accessibility features in design tools. In: Miesenberger, K., Petrie, H., Peňáz, P. (eds.), ICCHP 2026–Computers Helping People with Special Needs, 20th International Conference, Linz, Austria, Proceedings. Springer (2026)
13. Shiraishi, Y., Zhong, Y., Kobayashi, M., Wakatsuki, D., Suzuki, T., Shionome, T., Hiraga, R.: Reciprocal information support for accessible live events: field evaluation of a real-time timeline web app for DHH/BLV and all participants. In: Miesenberger, K., Petrie, H., Peňáz, P. (eds.), ICCHP 2026–Computers Helping People with Special Needs, 20th International Conference, Linz, Austria, Proceedings. Springer (2026)
14. Sawicka, A.: Making accessibility work in practice: European ICT accessibility standards under the European accessibility act (EAA), In: Petz, A., Miesenberger, K. (eds.), ICCHP Open Access Compendium "Future Perspectives on Accessibility, AT and eInclusion", Linz, Austria, Proceedings. Johannes Kepler University Linz (2026)
15. de Andrade, S.G., Ribeiro, E.A., Siqueira, M.S.S., Freire, A.P.: Monitoring digital accessibility: a study of measuring tools adopted by governmental initiatives in different countries. In: Miesenberger, K., Petrie, H., Peňáz, P. (eds.), ICCHP 2026 – Computers Helping People with Special Needs, 20th International Conference, Linz, Austria, Proceedings. Springer (2026)
16. Steininger, M., Gersbacher, P., Zimmermann, G.: Manual accessibility testing procedures for mobile apps: a comparative evaluation. In: Miesenberger, K., Petrie, H., Peňáz, P. (eds.), ICCHP 2026–Computers Helping People with Special Needs, 20th International Conference, Linz, Austria, Proceedings. Springer (2026)
17. Binsedeeq, A., Furnell, S., Carpent, X., Gervassis, N.: A proposed accessible cyber security support (AcCeSS) framework. In: Miesenberger, K., Petrie, H., Peňáz, P. (eds.), ICCHP 2026–Computers Helping People with Special Needs, 20th International Conference, Linz, Austria, Proceedings. Springer (2026)

18. Wolberger, L.: Current state of post-source implementation: the browser table—Are browsers adequately supporting accessibility needs. In: Miesenberger, K., Petrie, H., Peňáz, P. (eds.), ICCHP 2026–Computers Helping People with Special Needs, 20th International Conference, Linz, Austria, Proceedings. Springer (2026)
19. Sajka, J.: Beyond the source: evaluating the role of post-source accessibility remediation. In: Miesenberger, K., Petrie, H., Peňáz, P. (eds.), ICCHP 2026–Computers Helping People with Special Needs, 20th International Conference, Linz, Austria, Proceedings. Springer (2026)
20. Sandnes, F.E., MacKenzie, I.S.: Improving the accessibility of web tables for magnifier users with annotations, crumbs, and snippets. In, Miesenberger, K., Petrie, H., Peňáz, P. (eds.), ICCHP 2026–Computers Helping People with Special Needs, 20th International Conference, Linz, Austria, Proceedings. Springer (2026)
21. Waddell, C., et al.: Constructing accessible web sites. Apress (2003)

Inclusive Design Capability Maturity Framework

Eric Martin Velleman[1](✉), Elisa van Tuijl[1], Annoëlle van Hooff[2], Jeroen Havinga[3], and Hans Kemp[3]

[1] HAN University of Applied Sciences, Ruitenberglaan 26, 6826 CC Arnhem, The Netherlands
eric.velleman@han.nl
[2] Hogeschool Utrecht, Padualaan 99, 3584 CH Utrecht, The Netherlands
[3] Keen Design, Springweg 7, 3511 VH Utrecht, The Netherlands

Abstract. Inclusive design is not only about meeting end-user needs or improving accessibility outcomes. It also requires organizational and professional capabilities to embed inclusion and accessibility structurally into everyday design practice. This paper conceptualizes inclusive design capability as an organizational capability rather than an individual skill. It argues that inclusive design capability requires a reflective, non-normative maturity approach rather than a linear or compliance-driven one. It reframes maturity as a capability for reflection, learning, and adaptation, and presents a maturity approach that supports context sensitive development without reducing inclusive design practice to benchmarking or optimization. It assumes that accessibility compliance is a necessary but insufficient condition for inclusive design.

Keywords: Inclusive Design · Maturity Model · UX · Capability · Accessibility · Inclusion · Framework

1 Introduction

Research on inclusive design has traditionally focused on understanding the needs of end users. Designing products and services around those needs can improve usability for targeted audiences, but this does not automatically result in inclusive or accessible outcomes for all users. Many people continue to experience difficulties accessing or using digital products and services, for example because of a (physical) disability or because they lack specific (digital) skills or resources. Lawmakers recognize this challenge and increasingly require accessibility and inclusion when it comes to products and services (like the European Accessibility Act).

However, designers encounter barriers throughout the design process. This limits their ability to translate inclusive design knowledge into routine ways of working. As a result, organizations often recognize the importance of inclusion, but are not sure where they stand, what issues they face and what should be their next steps.

This paper builds on the Active Inclusive Design project [1]. The focus shifted from inclusive design as a set of methods or outcomes to inclusive design as an organizational

K. Miesenberger et al. (Eds.): ICCHP 2026, LNCS 16867, pp. 522–529, 2027.
https://doi.org/10.1007/978-3-032-31308-9_62

capability. By integrating empirical insights from this project with existing literature on inclusive design, accessibility, UX maturity, and organizational learning, the paper develops a reflective, non-linear and non-normative inclusive design capability maturity framework: *How can inclusive design capability be conceptualized, developed, and assessed within design organizations?*

2 State of the Art

Inclusive design is often positioned alongside accessibility, yet the two are not synonymous. Numerous studies in Human Computer Interaction and design research have shown that accessibility compliance does not necessarily result in inclusive or usable systems [2, 3]. Inclusive design can extend accessibility by addressing diversity in capabilities, situations, and lived experiences. The Dutch code for inclusive design (CIDO) further operationalizes this perspective by emphasizing the structural involvement of people with lived experience throughout the design process [4].

Many publications describe the importance of integrating inclusion and accessibility into the organizational lifecycle of digital products, including governance, procurement, and maintenance [5, 6]. It implies that policymakers, managers and other organizational actors influencing design processes and outcomes should recognize barriers not merely as constraints, but as meaningful drivers for reflection and change. This goes beyond simply endorsing inclusion as a value; it involves the capability and willingness to engage with uncertainty, to experiment and to critically explore inclusive design challenges as part of an ongoing learning process. Inclusive design concerns not only the resulting artefacts, but also the design process itself.

Inclusive design is closely related to other user-oriented design approaches. These include human-centered design, user-centered design, participatory design, co-design and value-sensitive design [7–9]. All of which emphasize user involvement or ethical considerations in the design process. Inclusive design is distinguished from these approaches by taking user diversity as its starting point and by integrating process and outcome perspectives. And it intersects with accessibility standards, such as the EN 301549 and universal design or design-for-all approaches, while acknowledging that a single solution may not always suffice for all users.

2.1 Organizational Capability and Maturity

Literature provides insights into measuring UX capability [10], accessibility maturity [11, 12], and other maturity models including how to assess how accessibility is governed, implemented, and maintained across organizations [13]. Norman Group [14] similarly argues that UX maturity goes beyond addressing end-user needs describing it as an organizations' desire and ability to consistently deliver user-centered design through its processes, resources, tools, and operations, as well as through sustained support from leadership, workforce, and organizational culture.

The uptake of tools and practices depends on factors including perceived usefulness, ease of use, social influence, and facilitating conditions [15]. These models provide valuable insight into why inclusive design tools and guidelines are not consistently adopted in practice. Designers may recognize the value of inclusive design but lack organizational support, incentives, or resources to apply it systematically. They also often struggle to structurally integrate the perspectives of people with lived experience into design processes. Common barriers include limited time and resources, insufficient access to users, uncertainty about appropriate methods and lack of demand from clients [16].

In many design processes, people with lived experience are primarily involved as research participants or end-users rather than as members of the design team itself. This is partly because commonly used design processes, methods and tools are often not accessible for designers with a (visual-, auditory-, motor-or other) disability. If design organizations aim to practice inclusive design consistently, they must also address accessibility and inclusion within their own professional practices, enabling designers with lived experience or temporary impairments to fully participate as professionals.

Inclusive design capability refers to designers and their organizations' knowledge, skills, and attitudes; their access to and effective use of tools, methods, and guidelines; the presence of managerial and organizational support; and the ability to draw on, reflect on and learn. It extends beyond technical design skills alone. It encompasses competencies such as leadership, vision development, mental flexibility, stakeholder management, accessibility expertise, facilitating collaboration among diverse participants, and navigating organizational and societal complexity [17, 18]. Importantly, this broader conception of capability also entails creating conditions that enable designers with disabilities to participate fully and meaningfully in professional design practice. This is missing in most other existing models.

3 Methodology

The project included includes 9 design agencies (*Keen Design, Ideate, Greenberry, Afdeling/Buitengewone Zaken, Design Innovation Group, Muzus, Netrex, theRevolution, Vrienden van Verandering*), 3 knowledge institutions (*Utrecht University of Applied Sciences, HAN University of Applied Sciences, Delft University of Technology*) and subject related organizations (*Gebruiker Centraal; CLICKNL; BNO, Visio, LFB, Iederin, Accessibility).*

They regularly met within the project's Learning Community (LC), and used the Participatory Action Research (PAR) approach [19], a form of practice-oriented research in which they collaboratively and iteratively explore issues, test interventions in their daily practice. This way, thay generate situated knowledge, and develop actionable solutions through a reflective cycle whereby participants collectively collect and analyse their actions and experiences and subsequently reflect on the effects and learnings [20]. The approach is meant to empower communities to solve their own problems by integrating lived experiences with professional practice and academic knowledge based on their real world daily work experiences.

PAR shifts the focus from studying people to working with them, producing findings that are inherently context-dependent rather than universally generalizable. The PAR approach for this paper includes deskresearch, LC, surveys, interviews and visualizations.

Data were gathered and synthesized from diverse sources, most importantly the actual experience of the design agencies within the project (they tested everything in their daily practice), literature, narratives, lived experiences, surveys, interviews, focus group outputs and quantitative inputs; themes and patterns were identified together with participants through collective sensemaking activities, such as clustering notes and discussing emerging insights; findings were interpreted, clarified, and validated in dialogue with participants, allowing experiences to be reflected upon and meanings to be jointly constructed; results were then shared in forms suited to different stakeholder audiences, including stories, reports, presentations, and visualizations; finally, insights from each cycle lead to informed decisions about subsequent actions and iterations.

4 Results

The team started with a maturity ladder but soon concluded that the ladder metaphor was experienced as comparative and normative: assigning maturity levels was perceived as benchmarking organizations against one another, whereas the intention was to support reflection and adoption of inclusive design practices within each organization's own context.

During testing within participating organizations and subsequent discussions in the LC, the participants concluded that classification or benchmarking would not sufficiently support organizations in adopting and implementing inclusive design capability. They experienced the ladder-based model as overly linear and normative, while they perceived inclusive design practices to vary strongly across organizations, contexts, and moments in time.

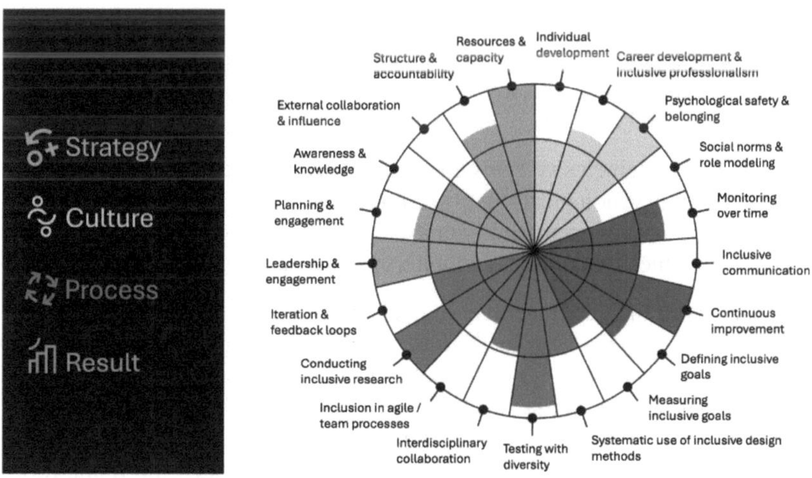

Fig. 1. Figure: the four quadrants used for visualization during the application of the framework.

The development then moved towards a framework consisting of a number of cyclic rounds using four quadrants. The participants describe the framework as *an internal, reflective design instrument that enables organizations to map their inclusive design capabilities and to identify context-specific opportunities for improvement acknowledging differences between individuals, organizational settings, context and moment.*

The four quadrants are based on the NN/g UX maturity model, but were reinterpreted to reflect inclusive design as conceptualized within this project. Rather than focusing on general UX practices, the quadrants and associated questions were reformulated to reflect inclusion and accessibility as integral aspects of design capability:

- **Strategy:** the extent to which inclusive design is embedded in an organization's vision, priorities, and decision-making structures. It addresses whether inclusion is articulated as an explicit organizational goal, how it informs strategic choices, and whether inclusive design is understood as a long-term responsibility rather than a project-specific or compliance-driven activity.
- **Culture:** the shared values, norms, and everyday behaviors that shape how inclusion is understood, discussed, and practiced within teams and across the organization including psychological safety, openness to diverse perspectives, and the extent to which inclusion-related questions, tensions, and uncertainties can be raised, explored, and learned from without fear of negative consequences.
- **Process:** the degree to which inclusive design practices are structurally embedded within design and development workflows. This includes the use of methods and tools for involving people with lived experience.
- **Results:** extent to which inclusive intentions are translated into concrete and observable outcomes including inclusion of persons with lived experience and whether insights from these evaluations are systematically fed back into organizational learning and future design decisions.

For each quadrant, the research formulated a set of dimensions that operationalize inclusive design capability in a concrete and discussable way. These dimensions capture recurring organizational patterns that influence how inclusive design is understood, enacted, and sustained in practice. Examples of such dimensions include:

- the extent to which inclusive goals are explicitly formulated and shared
- the presence of psychological safety within teams
- how user diversity is systematically embedded in design activities
- the degree to which outcomes are monitored and evaluated with stakeholders

The Framework includes a number of cyclical (sub)phases:

- > Intake - > Survey - > Visualization - > Focus setting - > In-depth interviews - > Advice and interventions - > Feedback and re-measurement - >

Organizations with a similar inclusive design capability profile may choose different priorities and interventions, depending on their organizational structure, project landscape, client demands, and available resources. In this way, the framework supports informed choice rather than compliance with an external standard. The value of the Framework lies in its ability to repeatedly structure reflection, sense-making, and decision-making in response to the changing conditions. For example, in the survey, the questions are intended to support reflection and dialogue rather than evaluation. During testing and evaluation, it became clear that many aspects of inclusive design capability cannot be meaningfully captured through purely quantitative measures. At the same time, some degree of aggregation and comparison was needed to support visualization and discussion. To address this tension, the survey was further refined by adding, removing, and reformulating questions so that responses could be partially represented statistically, while still allowing respondents to contextualize and elaborate on their answers.

The radar diagram (Fig. 1) was used to visualize the survey outcomes. This form of visualization supported a holistic view of inclusive design capability, allowing multiple dimensions to be considered simultaneously rather than reducing the outcomes to a single score or level. In practice, the radar diagram was found to:

- Make strengths and areas for development visible without implying a hierarchical or normative judgment.
- Support collective reflection and discussion, for example by asking what is recognized and what is not.
- Facilitate deliberate and targeted choices about where to focus developmental efforts.

Another form of visualization used was to take a team outside and draw the 4 quadrants on the floor. For every question or statement about inclusive design capability in their organization, the team members were asked to move physically inside the quadrants: close to the middle they agreed, further to the outside meant they disagreed. The positioning was used for discussion. During rain, we used a board and stickers.

The advice given in this framework is not prescriptive or uniform. Insights from the LC indicate that periodic reflection moments, whether through re-measurement or more regular conversations or other workforms, help to keep inclusive design on the organizational agenda. Repeating the phases supports continuity and learning, rather than closure or final assessment.

The result is an internal, reflective design instrument that enables organizations to map their inclusive design capabilities and to identify context-specific opportunities for improvement acknowledging differences between individuals, organizational settings, context and moment.

A more complete description of the framework including more information about the cyclical (sub)phases can be found on the projectwebsite [1].

5 Conclusion

The Inclusive Design Capability Maturity Framework emerged from a combination of existing UX maturity model knowledge, Participatory Action Research, and practical experience and application by 9 design organizations. Initially conceived as a step-based maturity model, it was deliberately redesigned into a framework to move away from classification, benchmarking, and linear progression, which were found insufficient to support inclusive design capability in practice.

It concentrates on how inclusion is embedded in the design of products and services. This includes the structural involvement of people with lived experience, as well as attention to the accessibility and inclusivity of design processes themselves for designers and professionals within organizations.

A maturity model for inclusive design capability can support (design) organizations and their clients in understanding how inclusive attitudes, processes, competencies and outcomes are currently configured within their practice. By linking inclusive design capability to organizational factors and observable practices, such a model can improve communication with clients, support implementation strategies, and increase the likelihood that inclusive design is embedded more sustainably in everyday work.

In this paper, the inclusive design capability maturity model is explicitly positioned as reflective, multidimensional, non-normative and non-linear. Organizations may be relatively advanced in some dimensions while still developing in others, depending on context and constraints. For example, an organization may demonstrate a high level of maturity in engaging a diverse range of users during the front-end design process of their website, yet continue to face challenges in achieving employee diversity within the in-house design team.

The core of the model is therefore not diagnostic, evaluative, or predictive, but explicitly reflective and action-oriented. Its aim is to support organizations in adopting both a reflective and reflexive stance toward their own design practices, enabling them to identify blind spots, develop shared understanding across roles and disciplines, and formulate feasible, context-sensitive strategies for becoming more inclusive over time.

Limitation and discussion. The use of PAR means that findings are inherently context-dependent, thus limiting its applicability to other contexts. Also it is based on self-reported data, reflective sessions, and qualitative inputs in the LC. This aligns with the reflective and non-normative nature of the framework, but may introduce subjectivity in how capabilities are assessed and interpreted. By avoiding standardized metrics, this model reduces comparability across organizations and over time, limiting its applicability in contexts where external evaluation or accountability is required. Finally, long-term effects on organizational change and inclusive design outcomes have not yet been systematically evaluated. Future research could focus on more and longitudal validation and explore how the framework performs across different domains and scales.

Acknowledgments. We thank the organizations that have participated in this project and in the LC. This study was funded by Regieorgaan SIA.

Disclosure of Interests. The authors have no competing interests to declare that are relevant to the content of this article.

References

1. Website of the Active Inclusive Design project. https://activeinclusivedesign.nl/. Last accessed 09 Apr 2026
2. Aizpurua, A., Harper, S., Vigo, M.: Exploring the relationship between web accessibility and user experience. Int. J. Hum. Comput. Stud. **91**, 13–23 (2016). https://doi.org/10.1016/j.ijhcs.2016.03.008
3. Petrie, H., Kheir, O.: The relationship between accessibility and usability of websites. https://doi.org/10.1145/1240624.1240688

4. van Welbergen, A., Sadée, C.: Code inclusief digitaal ontwerpen. Standaard voor het inclusief ontwerpen van digitale producten en diensten met de inzet van ervaringsdeskundigheid. {Accessibility} (2025)
5. BSI Standards Publication: BSI-2010-BSI 8878 Web accessibility–Code of practice. BSI, London (2010). https://doi.org/10.3403/30180388U
6. Velleman, E.M.: The implementation of web accessibility standards by Dutch municipalities: factors of resistance and support (2018)
7. ISO: ISO 13407:1999 Human-centred design processes for interactive systems. International Organization for Standardization, Geneva (1999)
8. Schuler, D., (ed.): N.A.: Participatory design: principles and practices (1993)
9. Friedman, B., Hendry, D.G.: Value sensitive design: shaping technology with moral imagination (2019)
10. Rukonić, L., Kervyn de Meerendré, V., Kieffer, S.: Measuring UX capability and maturity in organizations. In: Design, User Experience, and Usability. Practice and Case Studies. pp. 346–365. Springer International Publishing, Cham (2019). https://doi.org/10.1007/978-3-030-23535-2_26
11. Curtis-Davidson, B.: The Digital Accessibility Maturity Model (DAMM) enabling digital accessibility operations (2016)
12. W3C, Fazio, D., Byrne-Haber, S., Sajka, J., LaPierre, C., Jadhav, N.M.: Accessibility Maturity Model (Note). https://www.w3.org/TR/2025/NOTE-maturity-model-20251104/. Last accessed 03 Jan 2026
13. Nacheva, R.: Digital accessibility maturity models. Proceedings from 10th International Conference on (2025)
14. Pernice, K., Gibbons, S., Moran, K., Whitenton, K.: The 6 Levels of UX Maturity. https://www.nngroup.com/articles/ux-maturity-model/. Last accessed 03 Jan 2026
15. Venkatesh, V., Morris, M.G., Davis, G.B., Davis, F.D.: User acceptance of information technology: toward a unified view. Miss. Q. **27**, 425–478 (2003). https://doi.org/10.2307/30036540
16. Keates, S., Clarkson, J.: Countering design exclusion. In: Countering design exclusion. pp. 140–156. Springer London, London (2004). https://doi.org/10.1007/978-1-4471-0013-3_11
17. de Waal, J., Wolfensberger, B., Hekkert, P., Ahsmann, B., van Zoonen, L., de Randamie, K.: Kennis-en innovatieagenda voor de creatieve industrie 2020–2023. CLICKNL (2020)
18. Enninga, T.L.: Armchair travelling the innovation journey (2018)
19. Cornish, F., et al.: Participatory action research. Nat. Rev. Methods Primers. **3**, 34 (2023). https://doi.org/10.1038/s43586-023-00214-1
20. Baum, F., MacDougall, C., Smith, D.: Participatory action research. J. Epidemiol. Community Health **60**, 854–857 (2006). https://doi.org/10.1136/jech.2004.028662

How and When People with Disabilities Participate Across Design Phases in Assistive Technology and ICT

Seiya Moro[1,2](✉), Mizuki Kobashi[3], Sota Takagi[1], and Takumi Ohashi[1]

[1] Institute of Science Tokyo, Tokyo, Japan
moro.s.aa@m.titech.ac.jp
[2] Japan Society for the Promotion of Science, Tokyo, Japan
[3] Graduate School of Rehabilitation, Kobe Gakuin University, Kobe, Japan

Abstract. Participatory design (PD) is increasingly used in assistive technology (AT) and disability-related information and communication technology (ICT), yet evidence remains fragmented regarding who participates, at which design stages, and how participation relates to design outcomes. This study conducted a scoping review to clarify participation patterns in AT/ICT design involving people with disabilities. Searches of Web of Science All Databases and PubMed identified 753 records, of which 39 studies met the inclusion criteria. To enable cross-study comparison, participation activities were mapped onto the Design Council's Double Diamond framework (Discover, Define, Develop, Deliver). The review found that acquired brain injury/traumatic brain injury was the most frequently represented target group, while intellectual disability and psychosocial/mental health-related conditions were comparatively under-represented. Across studies, participation was most consistently reported in Discover and Develop activities, such as needs elicitation, prototyping, and iterative testing, whereas Define and Deliver were described less explicitly and with greater variability. Reported outcomes clustered around contextual fit and personalization, usability and accessibility, communication and social participation, and autonomy, while safety, reliability, and cost/access repeatedly emerged as constraints on uptake. These findings suggest that PD in disability-related AT/ICT is most often implemented as elicitation and feedback rather than deeper shared decision-making. The Double Diamond proved useful as an analytic lens for identifying uneven phase coverage and reporting gaps, supporting more explicit planning of who to involve, when, and for what design purpose.

Keywords: Participatory Design · Assistive Technology · Double Diamond · Disability · Scoping Review

1 Introduction

Assistive technology (AT) and information and communication technology (ICT) are increasingly important for supporting the autonomy, social participation, and quality of life of people with disabilities. This importance has been emphasized internationally

K. Miesenberger et al. (Eds.): ICCHP 2026, LNCS 16867, pp. 530–537, 2027.
https://doi.org/10.1007/978-3-032-31308-9_63

through the Convention on the Rights of Persons with Disabilities [1] and the World Health Organization's Priority Assistive Products List [2], both of which highlight the need not only for access to technology but also for solutions that are meaningful in everyday life.

While human-centered design (HCD) provides a general basis for designing around users' needs and contexts of use [3], disability-related contexts often require more direct involvement of people with disabilities in the design process. Designers may otherwise overlook embodied, sensory, cognitive, and social aspects of lived experience that are difficult to capture through conventional user-centered methods alone. For this reason, participatory design (PD) has become especially important in disability-related AT/ICT. PD is not a single method, but a methodological orientation in which users actively contribute to shaping technologies and their conditions of use [4].

Despite the growing use of PD in disability-related AT/ICT, participation is reported unevenly across studies. In many cases, participant roles, phase-specific activities, and the timing of involvement are described only briefly or indirectly rather than in a consistent and comparable form. This makes cross-study comparison difficult and limits understanding of how different forms of participation relate to reported design outcomes.

To address this gap, this study conducts a scoping review of PD in AT and disability-related ICT and maps participation onto the Double Diamond phases of Discover, Define, Develop, and Deliver. Three research questions guide the review: (1) Which disability populations are represented as target groups in participatory AT/ICT research? (2) At which design phases, and through what types of activities, are people with disabilities reported to participate? and (3) What design outcomes are reported in association with these participatory processes?

2 Related Work

2.1 PD in aT and ICT

PD has become increasingly used in disability-related AT and ICT development. Their importance is grounded not only in ethical commitments to inclusion, but also in the practical recognition that people with disabilities hold situated knowledge about everyday barriers, usability constraints, and support environments that may not be captured through conventional design processes alone. PD is therefore valued to improve the contextual relevance, accessibility, and acceptability of technologies by bringing this situated knowledge into the design process rather than treating it as an external input to interpret.

Methodologically, PD is not a single technique but a family of approaches in which users may take different roles and degrees of influence throughout the design process [4]. Prior studies have suggested that participatory approaches can improve the fitness between technologies and users' lives, particularly in contexts where designers have limited access to embodied, sensory, or cognitive experiences [5]. At the same time, participation in disability-related design is often shaped by mediation, for example through caregivers, proxies, or institutional arrangements, which may influence how directly people with disabilities are involved [6].

Although the value of PD is widely acknowledged, literature remains difficult to compare across studies. Individual papers use different vocabularies (e.g., "co-design," "participatory workshops," "inclusive design," "user involvement") and describe participatory activities at different levels of granularity, so that it is often unclear which phase of the design process a given activity belongs to. This heterogeneity in reporting limits the ability to synthesize evidence across projects and motivates the use of a shared, process-oriented lens for cross-study comparison.

2.2 Double Diamond as a Shared Process Lens for Synthesis

To compare heterogeneous reports of participatory design, a shared process-oriented lens is needed. ISO 9241-210 provides broad lifecycle principles for human-centered design [3], but it does not standardize how participatory activities are described in research reports. The Design Council's Double Diamond provides a pragmatic structure for addressing this issue [7]. By distinguishing four broad phases—Discover, Define, Develop, and Deliver—it offers a common vocabulary at a level of abstraction that is compatible with the diverse methods used across disability-related AT/ICT studies. Importantly, the Double Diamond is used here not as a prescriptive model that all included studies explicitly followed, but as an analytic lens for organizing reported design activities. Although studies use different methods and terms, many still report activities that correspond broadly to early exploration, problem framing, iterative development, or implementation and delivery, which makes it possible to examine how participation is distributed across the design lifecycle. Applying the Double Diamond in this descriptive role therefore supports cross-study comparison without requiring that all included studies follow the same design model in practice.

2.3 Resulting Research Gap and Rationale for This Study

Taken together, prior research shows that PD/co-design is valuable in disability-related technology development and that meaningful participation can contribute to better contextual fit, usability, and acceptability. What is still missing, however, is a synthesis-level account that compares studies in a structured way: specifically, how participation is distributed across the design lifecycle, which disability populations are involved at which phases, and which outcome themes are reported in association with patterns of participation.

This gap matters because, without a comparable account of participation, individual projects are difficult to interpret in relation to one another, and the field cannot easily identify where participation is well documented and where it is under-reported. A scoping review is well suited to addressing this gap, as it enables heterogeneous evidence to be mapped systematically while clarifying concepts and knowledge gaps [8, 9]. Combining scoping review methods with Double Diamond stage mapping allows this study to clarify which disability populations are represented in participatory AT/ICT research, how participation is distributed across design phases and activities, and what design outcomes are reported in association with these participatory processes. In doing so, it provides a more structured basis for future planning and reporting of participation, and for considering what forms of participation may be more appropriate across different design phases and disability-related contexts.

3 Method

3.1 Research Design

This study adopts a scoping review methodology to examine how PD is implemented in AT and disability-related ICT. Scoping reviews are appropriate for mapping heterogeneous bodies of literature, identifying key concepts, and clarifying research gaps [8, 9].

This study aims to synthesize how participation is described across studies, with a particular focus on participant roles, design phases, and reported design outcomes, rather than to compare the effectiveness of individual interventions. To enable structured comparison across studies, participation was analyzed using the Double Diamond framework as an analytic lens.

3.2 Data Sources and Search Strategy

The literature search was conducted on December 23, 2025, using Web of Science All Databases and PubMed. Web of Science included multiple indices such as the Web of Science Core Collection, BIOSIS Citation Index, MEDLINE, and other relevant databases.

The search strategy followed the PRISMA-ScR guidelines [10] and combined terms related to participatory design, disability, and assistive technology/ICT. The search query was:

TS:("participatory design" OR "co-design" OR "co creation" OR "Research through Design" OR "Action Research" OR "participatory approach" OR "inclusive design")

AND TS:("disabilit*" OR "physical disabilit*" OR "intellectual disabilit*" OR "developmental disabilit*" OR "disorder*" OR "cognitive impair*" OR "autis*" OR "ASD")AND TS:("assistive technolog*" OR "assistive device*" OR "support technolog*" OR "rehabilitation technolog*" OR "ICT")

Screening was conducted independently by two authors through title/abstract screening followed by full-text review.

3.3 Eligibility Criteria

We included peer-reviewed English journal or international conference papers that: (1) involved people with disabilities as direct participants in design/development/evaluation (not professionals only), (2) explicitly used participatory/co-creative approaches, and (3) addressed welfare-related assistive technologies (including ICT). We excluded studies without direct involvement of disabled participants, those limited to user testing only, primarily clinical/medical intervention studies, secondary research (reviews), non-peer-reviewed items, and no-access full texts.

3.4 Data Extraction and Analysis

Data were extracted from each included study focusing on three aspects:(1) target disability category, (2) participation roles of people with disabilities, and(3) reported outcomes related to design. To enable cross-study comparison, participation was mapped onto the four phases of the Double Diamond framework: Discover, Define, Develop, and Deliver. Coding was conducted based on explicit descriptions of design activities reported in each study.

- Discover was coded when studies reported activities such as needs exploration, contextual inquiry, or early-stage problem framing.
- Define was coded when studies described synthesis activities, such as requirement definition, concept framing, or decision-making processes.
- Develop was coded when participatory activities were involved in prototyping, iterative design, or refinement.
- Deliver was coded when participation extended to real-world deployment, implementation, or evaluation in use contexts.

4 Results

4.1 Literature Selection Process and Target Papers: A Scoping Review

Figure 1 shows the flowchart of the scoping review process according to the PRISMA-ScR guidelines. We initially identified 753 papers from an extensive search across the Web of Science All Databases and PubMed. These papers underwent a detailed screening process based on the inclusion and exclusion criteria. This screening narrowed the selection to 258 peer-reviewed English-language journal and conference papers. Subsequently, the first author and second author carefully reviewed the titles and abstracts of these 258 papers and selected those that met the criteria detailed in Sect. 3.3. This process further refined the selection to 52 papers. Following secondary screening based on the same criteria, a total of 39 papers were selected as subjects for this study. This comprehensive process ensured the exhaustive collection of studies sufficiently relevant for analysis.

4.2 Target Populations and Participation-Role Patterns

Table 1 shows the number of studies reporting participation activities at each Double Diamond phase across disability categories, with darker shading indicating higher counts. Across all 39 studies, participation was documented most consistently in Discover (39 studies), followed by Develop (31 studies) and Define (28 studies), while Deliver (23 studies) was reported least often. By category, acquired brain injury (ABI/TBI) studies showed the broadest coverage, reporting participation in Discover/Define/Develop in 8 studies each and in Deliver in 5 studies. Sensory impairment (vision/hearing) studies also showed relatively broad coverage, including Deliver in 5 studies (Discover 6, Define 4, Develop 5). In contrast, mobility impairment and neurodevelopmental conditions showed a drop in later phases, mobility impairment and neurodevelopmental conditions showed a drop in later phases, with Deliver reported in 2 studies in each category (mobility: Discover 6, Define 6, Develop 3; neurodevelopmental: Discover 5, Define 3, Develop 4). Neurocognitive disorders were frequently reported in Discover and Develop (5 studies each), but less often in Define (2 studies), while Deliver appeared in 4 studies. Categories with fewer included papers (e.g., intellectual disability, psychosocial/mental health, and mixed/unclear disability) showed more variable phase coverage, including no Define reporting in the mixed/unclear category. Overall, these patterns suggest that participation was more consistently documented in early and mid-stage design activities than in later-stage implementation and delivery.

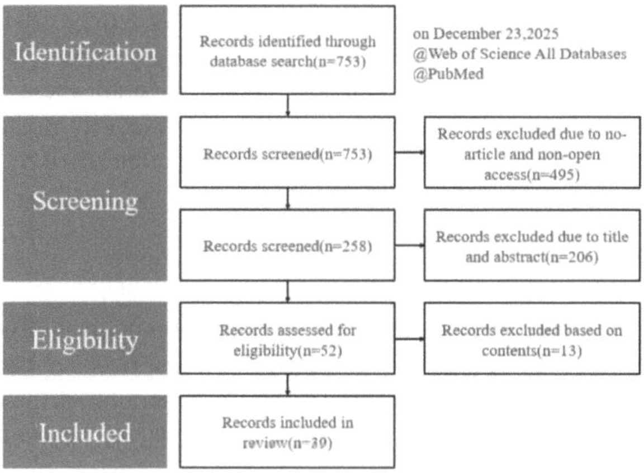

Fig. 1. PRISMA-ScR flow diagram

Table. 1. Phase coverage of reported participation across target disability categories ($n = 39$).

Disability category	Discover	Define	Develop	Deliver
Acquired brain injury (ABI/TBI)	8	8	8	5
Mobility impairment	6	6	3	2
Neurodevelopmental conditions	5	3	4	2
Neurocognitive disorders	5	2	5	4
Sensory impairment: vision / hearing	6	4	5	5
Intellectual disability	2	2	1	2
Neurological conditions: stroke / Parkinson's disease	3	2	3	1
Psychosocial disability / mental health-related conditions	1	1	1	0
Mixed / unclear disability	3	0	1	2
Total (n)	**39**	**28**	**31**	**23**

4.3 How Participation-Related Outcomes Are Reported

Across the included studies, reported design outcomes associated with participatory processes showed a relatively consistent pattern. Many studies linked participation to contextual fit and personalization (n = 18), as well as to usability and accessibility improvements (n = 17), suggesting that participatory processes were most often associated with technologies that better matched users' everyday routines, needs, and functional profiles. Beyond usability, studies also reported outcomes related to communication and social participation (n = 15) and to autonomy, empowerment, and choice/control (n = 13), indicating that participation shaped not only interface features but also the broader conditions of use and self-directed action. At the same time, safety, reliability, and accuracy concerns (n = 11), along with cost, access, and diffusion conditions (n = 10), were frequently identified as constraints on broader uptake. Overall, these findings suggest that the reported outcomes of participatory processes in disability-related AT/ICT were shaped not only by design qualities such as usability and contextual fit.

5 Discussion

This review suggests three main points. First, participation in disability-related AT/ICT is uneven across both research areas and design phases. Broader phase coverage in some areas should not be interpreted simply as a characteristic of the disability group itself, but may also reflect differences in research traditions, infrastructure, funding, and publication practices.

Second, participation is more consistently documented in exploratory and developmental activities than in convergence-oriented or implementation-oriented ones. This suggests that participatory processes in disability-related AT/ICT are more often described in relation to needs exploration and iterative refinement than to problem framing, decision-making, and sustained implementation. From this perspective, the value of the Double Diamond lies not in prescribing an ideal process, but in providing a shared analytic structure for making differences in phase coverage visible and comparable across heterogeneous studies. Limited visibility in Define and Deliver may therefore reflect not only gaps in practice but also gaps in reporting.

Third, the reported outcomes associated with participatory processes extend beyond usability alone. Alongside contextual fit, usability, and accessibility, the reviewed studies also pointed to communication, social participation, autonomy, and practical conditions affecting sustained use.

Participation in disability-related AT/ICT should therefore be understood not only in terms of interface improvement, but also in relation to the broader support contexts in which technologies are introduced, used, and maintained. At the same time, these findings should be interpreted as patterns in reported outcomes rather than as evidence of causal effectiveness.

Taken together, these findings suggest that no single form of participation is universally optimal in disability-related AT/ICT design. Appropriate participation depends on both the design phase and context: early phases may require needs elicitation and contextual understanding, development phases benefit from iterative feedback and prototype-related involvement, and later phases may require broader participation involving caregivers, support staff, and others who shape implementation and sustained use. Future work should therefore make participation choices more explicit, better justified, and more consistently reported across the lifecycle design.

6 Conclusion

This study examined participatory design in disability-related assistive technology and ICT through a scoping review of 39 studies. Mapping participation onto the Double Diamond showed that involvement was reported most consistently in Discover and Develop, while Define and Deliver were less clearly documented, with variation across disability populations. Reported outcomes clustered around contextual fit, usability and accessibility, communication and social participation, and autonomy, while safety, reliability, and cost/access recurred as constraints on uptake. Taken together, these findings suggest that participatory processes in disability-related AT/ICT are currently most visible as elicitation and iterative feedback, and that their value lies not only in improving usability but also in shaping the conditions of sustained use. Future research should report participation roles, activities, and outcome themes more explicitly across design phases to support more comparable and actionable knowledge for inclusive technology development.

References

1. United Nations General Assembly. Convention on the Rights of Persons with Disabilities (A/RES/61/106). New York (2006)
2. World Health Organization: Priority assistive products list: improving access to assistive technology for everyone, everywhere (2016)
3. International Organization for Standardization. ISO 9241-210: Ergonomics of human-system interaction-Human-centred design for interactive systems (2019)
4. Spinuzzi, C.: The methodology of participatory design. Techn. Commun. **52**(2), 163–174 (2005)
5. Sanders, E.B.-N., Stappers, P.J.: Co-creation and the new landscapes of design. CoDesign **4**(1), 5–18 (2008)
6. Brereton, M., Sitbon, L., Abdullah, M.H.L., Vanderberg, M., Koplick, S.: Design after design to bridge between people living with cognitive or sensory impairments, their friends and proxies. CoDesign **11**(1), 4–20 (2015)
7. Design Council. 11 lessons: a study of the design process (2007)
8. Arksey, H., O'Malley, L.: Scoping studies: towards a methodological framework. Int. J. Soc. Res. Methodol. **8**(1), 19–32 (2005)
9. Levac, D., Colquhoun, H., O'Brien, K.K.: Scoping studies: advancing the methodology. Implement. Sci. **5**, 69 (2010)
10. Tricco, A.C., et al.: PRISMA Extension for Scoping Reviews (PRISMA-ScR): checklist and explanation. Ann. Intern. Med. **169**(7), 467–473 (2018)

Accessibility in UX Design: The Need for Workflow Support and Accessibility Features in Design Tools

Nataša Rajh(✉), Klaus Miesenberger, and Reinhard Koutny

Institut Integriert Studieren, Johannes Kepler University, Linz, Austria
Natasa.Rajh@partner.jku.at, {Klaus.Miesenberger, Reinhard.Koutny}@jku.at

Abstract. With the European Accessibility Act (EAA) and the Web Accessibility Directive now in effect, most user experience (UX) designers should be familiar with accessibility requirements. Yet, insufficient color contrast, which is inarguably a designer's responsibility, remains the most frequent accessibility violation. This raises a key question: why do designers still struggle to design accessibly, and what practices do they follow? This paper examines designers' approaches to digital accessibility. We present the current state of research and development on accessibility, focusing specifically on UX designers and therefore extending beyond our previous systematic literature review. We argue that embedding accessibility directly into designers' normal workflows through integration into design tools is key for seamlessly achieving accessible design, as previous studies show that designers have little or no extra time to devote to accessibility. We believe such integration would allow accessibility to be addressed with minimal, if any, additional effort. Building on identified research gaps, we developed a questionnaire aimed at generating practical insights into workflows—an area that remains underexplored—and into accessibility support within design tools, which, to our knowledge, has not yet been studied. In this paper, we present the preliminary results.

Keywords: Digital Accessibility · Accessibility Tools · UX · User Experience Professionals · Design Tools

1 Introduction

The relationship between accessibility and design has evolved from an early tension to becoming a core element of modern user experience practice. Looking more than twenty years into the past [1], designers commonly viewed accessibility guidelines as constraints that resulted in dull and visually unappealing interfaces rather than opportunities for creative design. While these perceptions reflect designer attitudes at that time, later research demonstrates that accessibility and user experience are closely intertwined

https://www.jku.at/institut-integriert-studieren/

K. Miesenberger et al. (Eds.): ICCHP 2026, LNCS 16867, pp. 538–545, 2027.
https://doi.org/10.1007/978-3-032-31308-9_64

and that accessibility has measurable benefits for UX. A decade later, Aizpurua et al. [2] showed that web accessibility improves overall user experience both implicitly and explicitly. Their study proved that accessible websites are associated with better usability, positive emotions, and engaging experiences, whereas non-accessible sites often lead to frustration and negative perceptions. This evidence demonstrates that accessibility enhances overall UX.

Given their role as user advocates who center design and development on user needs [3], UX designers are automatically perceived as one of the primary stakeholders in the successful implementation of accessibility. However, they do not carry the responsibility of creating accessible products alone. Most individuals involved in website creation recognize that accessibility is a team effort and a shared responsibility. They believe that everyone, at every stage of website development and maintenance, should contribute to making a site accessible [4, 5], but all stakeholders agree that designers often play a central role [5]. This principle also applies to other digital products. UX professionals and designers were even rated as the two most knowledgeable groups among people involved in the creation of digital products in a Nordic study from 2020 [6]. Yet, despite seemingly widespread industry awareness and knowledge, data from the 2026 WebAIM Million report reveals that low contrast has been the most frequently automatically detected accessibility violation for the eighth consecutive year [7].

Inal et al. surveyed UX designers on the proportion of their working time dedicated to digital accessibility, with most respondents reporting that they spend less than 10% of their time on these activities [6]. After being asked the same question, Finnish UX designers working at a consulting company reported that they could not estimate the time spent on accessibility, as these tasks are not separated from other user experience work [8]. We agree with this statement and believe that accessibility should be integrated into daily work to such an extent that allocating specific time for it would no longer be necessary. The goal should be to integrate accessibility into everyday workflows rather than view it as an extra task. We further believe that one of the ways to achieve this is by integrating accessibility support into the tools designers already use. As our previous work [10] has stated that developers would benefit most from seamlessly integrated accessibility support in their IDEs, we perceive design tools in the same way for designers.

Previous studies [5, 6, 8, 9] indicate that limited time frequently hinders accessibility considerations, which further supports our view that embedding accessibility directly into standard design workflows and the tools designers already use is the most effective approach. Because tools and workflows play a crucial role in accessibility adoption, they have shaped our research questions.

To gain an understanding of what designers are currently doing in terms of accessibility, we defined the following research questions:

RQ1: What is the state of the art in research and development on accessibility practices in UX design?
RQ2: Do UX designers employ tools, methods, and techniques to integrate accessibility into their design workflows? If yes, which, and to what extent?

After analyzing existing research and identifying research gaps, we formulated a third research question, focusing on UX designers' desired tool support and potential workflow improvements.

RQ3: What tool- or workflow-based improvements do UX designers believe would make it easier to ensure accessibility in their work?

2 State of the Art

Our previous systematic literature review [10], published in 2024, compiled a broad set of guidelines, standards, methods, techniques, and tools supporting accessible software development. While the design phase has not been sparsely researched—on the contrary, it ranks second in several SLRs—existing work rarely focuses on designers' practices in industry contexts beyond academic settings. Moreover, prior research has predominantly focused on developers, while designers have received little involvement, even in studies addressing the design phase.

Among all papers we analyzed in our previous SLR [10], one paper [11] stood out, in relevance for UX designers, as it reported on the migration of a design system to WCAG 2.1 and detailed what should be tested and how. However, none of the methods and tools discussed in that paper were integrated into design software for designers or into IDEs for developers. To the best of our knowledge, academic research on design systems remains sparse, despite their role being seen as key enablers of accessible digital products. However, several design systems from prominent industry names—for example, IBM's Carbon Design System [12]—incorporate accessibility guidelines.

2.1 Empirical Studies on UX Designers' Accessibility Practices

Following our previous SLR [10], which had a broader scope, we decided to conduct another literature review, this time specifically targeting designers. In a structured literature review conducted between November and December 2025, we identified several studies investigating how practitioners in digital product development understand and apply accessibility practices, as well as the factors that hinder them from doing so. Our search focused on empirical studies published after 2015 that used surveys, focus groups, or interviews. Most studies encompassed multiple job roles, and their presentation of data made it impossible to isolate findings specifically for designers. We decided to include only studies that surveyed or interviewed UX professionals directly [5, 6, 8, 9, 13–15], or reported results for at least one of the questions by job profile [16, 17]. Using a snowballing approach, we also identified an earlier relevant study [18].

For each paper, we extracted individual survey questions and interview topics. These were then grouped into thematic clusters using an affinity diagramming approach. Motivations and barriers for (not) addressing accessibility are particularly well covered in the literature. These factors shape the remaining clusters, which relate to the context in which designers work (including their background and organization), accessibility practice itself, and the capabilities that support it (knowledge, skills, and education). Additionally, collaboration and responsibility, that is, who owns accessibility and how teams and experts interact, are addressed in some of the papers as well.

The question of how practitioners consider accessibility in their work was addressed in several papers, but it was not a central focus in any of them. Most studies have focused on general accessibility practices rather than on designers' workflows and detailed tool usage. While some studies inquired about accessibility tools used by designers [6, 8, 9, 14, 17], none examined the reasons for selecting them or participants' perceptions of their effectiveness. None specifically addressed the tools used for design, and their potential accessibility features. Previous research also lacked information on AI usage, likely reflecting the time periods in which the studies were conducted.

Both accessibility, particularly in relation to legislation, and UX are rapidly evolving fields, making cross-study comparisons difficult. Key factors include country and time period. For example, U.S. studies may not be comparable to European research, as the risk of costly lawsuits likely drives greater attention to accessibility.

3 Survey to Bridge the Research Gap

Existing research has provided insights relevant to our RQ1 and RQ2. However, we aimed to obtain more up-to-date perspectives on RQ2 and to address RQ3. For this purpose, we designed our own detailed survey. Data collection began in April and remains ongoing at the time of writing; therefore, only preliminary results are presented.

The survey covered the following question groups: about the respondent as a UX professional, their employer / their most recent client, UX and accessibility practices at their employer, general accessibility knowledge, personal involvement in accessibility, testing in projects, individual testing practices, tools, AI support, accessibility support in design tools, and demographics. While some of the groups primarily capture contextual and background information and do not directly provide insights into workflows and practices, they enable us to explore potential explanatory factors.

The questionnaire was iteratively refined before being pilot tested with six UX professionals deliberately selected to ensure diversity in experience (junior to UX lead), employment status, and product types. The pilot led to improvements to structure, wording, and response options, and already revealed substantial variation in experiences, opinions, and expectations regarding support in existing tools.

3.1 Methodology

Our target group consisted of people who design websites, apps, or other digital interfaces (UX, UI, product design, etc.). To reach a larger and more diverse sample, we chose an online survey over interviews, balancing wider reach with reduced qualitative depth. To retain nuance, we combined fixed-choice questions with open-ended ones.

We employed a multi-channel recruitment strategy, distributing the survey through a variety of online platforms to reach a diverse group of UX professionals. This included posting in Facebook groups and Slack communities dedicated to UX, sharing the survey on LinkedIn, and engaging with relevant Reddit communities (subreddits).

3.2 Preliminary Results

Due to page limitations, only a small subset of the survey questions and their corresponding responses are presented in this paper. Within the first week of data collection, we received 47 complete responses.

Demographics, Professional Background, and Employment Context: 32 participants were based in the European Union, while 15 were from outside the EU.

The sample is largely experienced, with 48.94% of participants having over 7 years of UX/UI experience, while only 27.7% having less than 3 years of experience.

Employed participants were asked how their employer expects them to address accessibility in their role. The expectation was most often described as a minor or occasional expectation at 36.1% or a major expectation at 33.3%, while 27.8% reported addressing it voluntarily, suggesting that accessibility is not yet consistently established as a core responsibility.

Knowledge: Although most participants reported only a basic level of overall accessibility knowledge, familiarity with WCAG was notably higher. When asked about their perceived level of knowledge regarding accessibility, assistive technologies, and how disabled people use digital products, 51.1% of participants reported a basic level and 40.4% an advanced level. In contrast, when asked about their familiarity with WCAG, 46.8% reported being very familiar and 25.5% moderately familiar, indicating higher confidence in knowing guidelines than in overall accessibility expertise.

Accessibility Involvement: Despite relatively low self-assessed knowledge and the fact that most employers do not strongly require accessibility to be a core responsibility, the results for practical application were higher than expected. Accessibility is considered regularly by most participants, with 72.3% addressing it either for complete products or most major features.

Accessibility is most commonly considered during the design phase (89.1%), followed by testing phase (58.7%) and during development (54.3%). Other stages are less frequently addressed, indicating that accessibility is often integrated later in the process rather than systematically throughout.

Accessibility testing is most commonly performed through color checks (78.7%), while fewer participants use automated (42.6%) or manual testing methods (44.7%). More advanced practices, such as manual code inspection (27.7%) and usability testing with disabled users (17.0%), are less frequent. 12.8% of participants report not conducting any accessibility testing at all.

Tools: Figma is by far the most widely used design tool among participants, with 43 out of 47 reporting its use in their work. Those who do not use Figma indicated working with Adobe XD or Sketch, while one participant reported not using any design tools due to a role focused solely on evaluating others' work.

In line with this, Figma's built-in color contrast checker emerged as the most commonly used method for assessing color contrast (14 out of 37 participants). When combined with the 7 participants who reported preferring Figma plugins, more than half of the respondents rely on solutions within the Figma ecosystem. This suggests a tendency toward integrated, workflow-native tools over external alternatives. However, given the relatively small sample size, this observation should be interpreted with caution.

Responses regarding the use of free accessibility testing tools reveal generally low adoption. Browser DevTools/Inspector (18), Lighthouse (17), WAVE (16), and Axe (15) were among the more commonly reported tools. Figma plugins such as Stark (12) and axe for Designers (10) were mentioned less frequently.

Participants also reported various limitations in existing tools, including limited coverage, false positives, inconsistencies, usability issues, and a lack of comprehensive guidance.

Accessibility Workflows: When asked how accessibility is incorporated into their work, 55.3% of participants reported that they dedicate additional time beyond standard workflows, while 38.3% indicated that accessibility is integrated into their workflows.

Among participants who dedicate additional time to accessibility, half reported spending up to 1 h per week, while 34.6% spend up to half a workday. A smaller proportion indicated spending up to a full workday (7.7%) or more than one workday (3.8%).

Among participants who reported that accessibility is integrated into their workflows, 44.4% described it as well integrated, 33.3% as partially integrated, and 16.7% as fully integrated, while a small proportion (5.6%) indicated that it is only weakly integrated.

Participants emphasized the need for stronger organizational support, better collaboration between designers and developers, and improved tools, training, and guidelines. They also stressed that accessibility should be integrated throughout the entire workflow and supported by user testing with people with disabilities.

AI-Usage: Participants were asked how often they use AI for accessibility support across several tasks, including generating alternative text for images, creating captions or transcripts, detecting accessibility issues, simplifying content, chatbot-based guidance, and preparing accessibility guidelines. The results show that AI use varies across tasks, with no single application being consistently used by a majority of participants. AI is used most frequently for simplifying content and generating alternative text. Other applications are more commonly reported as being used rarely or never.

Accessibility Support in Design Tools: We aimed to evaluate various ideas for integrated accessibility features. Proposed features received generally positive but mixed evaluations, with no option universally preferred or clearly unhelpful.

Immediate, actionable support within the design workflow was perceived as most valuable. Issue prioritization received the highest rating, with 55.3% of participants considering it very helpful, followed by suggestions for improvements (51.1%) and both real-time warnings and on-demand issue lists (48.9% each). In contrast, more informational or supportive features were rated less favorably and showed greater variability in responses. Training materials (25.5% very helpful, 19.1% not helpful), expert review (23.4% very helpful, 14.9% not helpful), and workflow recommendations (12.8% very helpful, 17.0% not helpful) received more mixed evaluations.

Responses to the open-ended question highlight a preference for practical, non-intrusive accessibility support. At the same time, there was notable resistance to real-time or intrusive features, with participants emphasizing the need for on-demand tools that do not interrupt workflow.

4 Discussion and Future Work

There has been a lot of research done on accessibility tools, methods, and other assets. However, these studies rarely focus specifically on UX designers. Many cover the design phase or some specific design tasks, but their approaches are often too generic or rigid. To genuinely support industry adoption, we need to dive deeper into what is actually happening in practice. Much of the research in the past did not manage to fully bridge the gap between academia and industry professions, which we think can be alleviated by talking directly to a large sample size of industry professionals of different profiles.

Some studies have already engaged industry professionals, but they often had limitations: very small samples, participants with overly similar backgrounds, or inclusion of roles not directly involved in design. Many also relied on interviews with participants recruited from accessibility-focused communities. While without a doubt providing informative insights, these participants usually already possess substantial accessibility knowledge, which goes far above average, so the findings may not reflect the realities of broader industry practices.

Instead of continuing to research designers' motivations or awareness, which is already well covered, future studies should focus on helping designers integrate accessibility into their workflows by providing sufficient support and practical guidance. This is especially important in a fast-changing field, where both UX practices and the tools designers use evolve rapidly.

As already mentioned, many large-scale studies survey multiple job profiles together. We believe that analyzing each role separately is important, as tasks, responsibilities, and toolsets differ. Aggregated analyses limit our ability to offer concrete recommendations or actionable support, as these require an in-depth understanding of the specific profile under consideration. However, it is important to note an observation from our own study: official job titles do not always precisely reflect the actual tasks a person performs. For example, some front-end developers are also responsible for UX work. Consequently, determining whether a participant fits into the target group is not always straightforward, especially if the survey does not include questions that allow categorizing their roles accurately.

Findings from the preliminary analysis of our ongoing survey suggest that embedding accessibility directly into designers' workflows may support more seamless accessible design, supporting our claims of this being the best approach. Participants themselves highlighted the need for integrated accessibility features within design tools, as well as supporting resources such as component libraries, guidelines, and checklists. Their emphasis on incorporating accessibility throughout the entire workflow, rather than treating it as a separate phase, aligns with the idea that accessibility should require minimal additional effort.

In future work, we will present a full analysis of the survey results. Participants were also invited to take part in follow-up interviews; to date, three individuals with diverse professional profiles have volunteered. Conducting these in-depth interviews will form the next step of the research and enrich the findings for a more comprehensive understanding of accessibility in design.

References

1. Regan, B.: Accessibility and design: a failure of the imagination. In: Proceedings of the 2004 International Cross-Disciplinary Workshop on Web Accessibility (W4A), pp. 29–37 (2004)
2. Aizpurua, A., Harper, S., Vigo, M.: Exploring the relationship between web accessibility and user experience. Int. J. Hum.-Comput. Stud. **91**, 13–23 (2016)
3. Interaction Design Foundation: User experience design-What is User Experience Design? https://www.interaction-design.org/literature/topics/ux-design. Accessed 12 Apr 2026
4. Lazar, J., Dudley-Sponaugle, A., Greenidge, K.D.: Improving web accessibility: a study of webmaster perceptions. Comput. Hum. Behav. **20**(2), 269–288 (2004)
5. Inal, Y., Rızvanoğlu, K., Yesilada, Y.: Web accessibility in Turkey: awareness, understanding and practices of user experience professionals. Univers. Access Inf. Soc. **18**(2), 387–398 (2019)
6. Inal, Y., Guribye, F., Rajanen, D., Rajanen, M., Rost, M.: Perspectives and practices of digital accessibility: A survey of user experience professionals in Nordic countries. In: Proc. 11th Nordic Conf. Human-Computer Interaction (NordiCHI), pp. 1–11 (2020)
7. WebAIM: The WebAIM Million: the 2026 report on the accessibility of the top 1,000,000 home pages. https://webaim.org/projects/million. Accessed 12 Apr 2026
8. Palm, A.: Including accessibility in the work of a UX consultant (2022)
9. Söderholm, E.: Future-proofing accessibility in UX: Swedish perspectives on the European Accessibility Act (2024)
10. Rajh, N., Miesenberger, K., Koutny, R.: Accessibility in the software engineering (SE) process and in integrated development environments (IDEs): a systematic literature review. In: Miesenberger, K., Kobayashi, M., Peňáz, P. (eds.), ICCHP 2024. LNCS, pp. 11–18. Springer, Cham (2024). https://doi.org/10.1007/978-3-031-62846-7_2
11. Shah, H.: Harnessing web accessibility tools for WCAG 2.1 migration of a design system. In: Proc. Int. Conf. Computing, Networking, Telecommunications & Engineering Sciences Applications (CoNTESA), pp. 54–60. IEEE (2023)
12. IBM: Carbon Design System–Accessibility. https://carbondesignsystem.com/guidelines/accessibility/overview/. Accessed 12 Apr 2026
13. Putnam, C., Rose, E.J., MacDonald, C.M.: "It could be better. It could be much worse": understanding accessibility in user experience practice with implications for industry and education. ACM Trans. Access. Comput. **16**(1), 1–25 (2023)
14. Vahid, C.: Towards accessible accessibility: exploring challenges and opportunities for integrating accessibility into the design process (2023)
15. Gupta, C.N., Bruce, C.: Exploring the experiences of UX professionals in accessibility. J. Technol. Pers. Disabil. **9**, 201–212 (2021)
16. Leite, M.V.R., Scatalon, L.P., Freire, A.P., Eler, M.M.: Accessibility in the mobile development industry in Brazil: awareness, knowledge, adoption, motivations and barriers. J. Syst. Softw. **177**, 110942 (2021)
17. WebAIM: Survey of Web Accessibility Practitioners #3 Results. https://webaim.org/projects/practitionersurvey3/. Accessed 12 Apr 2026
18. Putnam, C., Wozniak, K., Zefeldt, M.J., Cheng, J., Caputo, M., Duffield, C.: How do professionals who create computing technologies consider accessibility? In: Proc. 14th Int. ACM SIGACCESS Conf. Computers and Accessibility (ASSETS), pp. 87–94 (2012)

Monitoring Digital Accessibility: a Study of Measuring Tools Adopted by Governmental Initiatives in Different Countries

Saimon Gabriel de Andrade, Eduardo Augusto Ribeiro, Monique Scalco Soares Siqueira, and André Pimenta Freire(✉)

Department of Computer Science, Federal University of Lavras, Lavras, Brazil
apfreire@ufla.br

Abstract. The integration of digital accessibility into public policy requires the investigation of effective monitoring methods to ensure governmental compliance. Driven by regulatory advancements, several countries have adopted automated evaluation tools to monitor the accessibility of websites. However, there is a scarcity of studies investigating the behavior of the metrics employed by these tools and the impact on surveillance policies. This paper analyzes the calculation outcomes yielded by three official automated evaluators: Ases Web (Brazil), Mauve++ (Italy) and AccessMonitor (Portugal). The methodology comprises documentary analysis and empirical application on web pages with previous results from manual audits by experts. The findings indicate significant discrepancies among the tools, highlighting the limitations of automated metrics and underscoring the necessity for standardization and complementary validation within the context of accessibility monitoring by governmental bodies.

Keywords: Accessibility Monitoring · Automated Tools

1 Introduction

Governments across various regions have adopted digital accessibility guidelines as mandatory standards. The most widely recognized and utilized set of international guidelines is the Web Content Accessibility Guidelines (WCAG) [4], which establishes requirements and recommendations to ensure web content is accessible to persons with disabilities. In the European Union, for instance, Directive (EU) 2016/2102 [10] mandates that all public sector bodies in member states adhere to WCAG 2.1 Level AA criteria through standard EN 301 549 [11], which defines accessibility requirements for Information and Communication Technology (ICT) products and services. Similarly, in the United States, Sect. 508 of the Rehabilitation Act [24] adopts requirements derived from WCAG. In Brazil, regulation is established through the Brazilian Law for Inclusion (Law No. 13.146/2015) [3].

K. Miesenberger et al. (Eds.): ICCHP 2026, LNCS 16867, pp. 546–553, 2027.
https://doi.org/10.1007/978-3-032-31308-9_65

The existence of these standards requires that governments monitor accessibility across their websites and portals to ensure compliance with established legal and technical requirements. To conduct this monitoring, the use of metrics to measure and quantify the accessibility quality of digital products and services is fundamental. Several metrics can be adopted in this context [16], and their application is generally associated with automated evaluation tools, in which assessment is performed by software implementing one or more metrics. Such automated evaluation tools cannot fully assess the compliance of websites with technical standards, but provide a preliminary evaluation that can help in decision-making in surveillance processes.

In this context, different countries have structured institutional mechanisms to enable the continuous monitoring of digital accessibility at large scale. Among these mechanisms, accessibility observatories stand out, which are initiatives aimed at the continuous monitoring of an ecosystem, such as, for example, all the websites of a government. According to Mohamad & Velasco [18], accessibility observatories are infrastructures for holistic and large-scale evaluation, requiring high computational capacity to handle massive data. Generally, these systems operate through the automated application of evaluation tools, which enable the continuous generation of accessibility indicators and reports.

In the international scenario, one of the pioneering studies on accessibility observatories was the European Internet Accessibility Observatory (EIAO) [6, 7, 22], which aimed to create a system capable of automatically evaluating the accessibility of thousands of websites, implementing the Unified Web Evaluation Methodology (UWEM) [19]. The project ended in 2007, but its contributions were fundamental to the advancement of automated web accessibility monitoring approaches.

From these initiatives, and also with the creation of the European Directive (EU) 2016/2102 [10], several countries in the European Union created observatories to monitor the accessibility of their portals and seek compliance with the Directive. One example is the government of Spain [8, 14], which uses an automatic tool called OAW Tracker [13] to analyze the accessibility of public websites in the country. In the case of Spain, automatic accessibility reports are also generated, used as a basis for continuous monitoring [8]. Another example is Portugal, which maintains the Portuguese Web Accessibility Observatory (PWA-O) [1, 9], with an ecosystem aimed at monitoring accessibility at the national level.

The European Union has also invested in initiatives that seek to make accessibility more standardized and consistent. One example is the Web Accessibility Directive Decision Support Environment (WADcher) project [23, 25], whose objective was to develop an integrated platform to monitor and ensure that websites and mobile applications of public sector bodies comply with the accessibility requirements established by the European Union Web Accessibility Directive [26]. Although it is not an accessibility observatory, WADcher proposes a decision support environment, in which the results are contextualized and presented in a way that supports more comprehensive evaluation processes.

In the Brazilian scenario, a similar initiative is observed through the TIC Web project developed by the Center for Studies on Web Technologies, an area of NIC.br [5,20]. This project uses the Brazilian government's automatic evaluation tool, Ases Web [15], to generate accessibility reports for government portals. The study [12] presents the platform developed to verify the accessibility of websites and their pages, covering the entire process from collection and processing to the presentation of results at different levels of abstraction.

However, automated evaluation tools present significant limitations regarding accessibility analysis. A recent study [2] highlights several of these constraints, including ambiguities in guideline interpretation and limited consideration of semantic perspectives. When employed as the sole method of verification, these tools may not reflect the actual accessibility of a website. This limitation can lead to misinterpretations, creating a false impression of accessibility for a site that still presents usability barriers.

Another relevant issue is the limited knowledge regarding the properties of metrics used in practice for web accessibility monitoring. Automated evaluation tools adopt different metrics and implementation criteria within their software; this diversity often creates difficulty in understanding which parameters are effectively being considered by each tool. The study by Silva *et al.* [21] indicated that when automated tools are utilized as the sole form of evaluation, fewer than 40% of a website's accessibility issues can be detected. Despite this limitation, a study on the analysis of legal procedures of reports of inaccessibility in websites in Brazil showed that the majority of the decisions for filing the cases were taken solely based on the metrics generated by automated tools [17].

Therefore, the objective of this work is to present the results from tools used by different countries, such as Brazil, Portugal and Italy, analyzing the distinct approaches adopted in calculating the metrics employed by these tools. Furthermore, the study presents a comparison of each tool's performance considering the WCAG 2.2 criteria, using a sample of websites that were at some point compliant with Levels A, AA and AAA provided by the W3C as a reference model.

2 Method

The methodology of this study was divided into four main stages: (i) selection of automated evaluation tools; (ii) selection of the website sample to be analyzed; (iii) execution of the automated evaluation; and (iv) analysis of the results of the identified metrics.

The first stage of the study consisted of identifying the automated evaluation tools to be analyzed. Considering the context of increasing demands for digital accessibility in public portals—driven by national and international legislation and guidelines, the study investigated which tools have been officially adopted by governments of different countries to monitor the accessibility of their websites.

To achieve this objective, an exploratory web search process was conducted. Specific consultations were also carried out in institutional sources that incorporate digital accessibility laws into their standards, such as the Brazilian Federal

Government services portal and the European Union website. The goal was to locate direct references to governmental accessibility evaluation initiatives.

For each search result obtained, two verification criteria were applied. The first analyzed whether the tool was publicly accessible, even if with partial functionality, allowing any user to utilize its evaluation features. The second verified the existence of technical or institutional documentation regarding the metrics used by the tool, enabling a deeper analysis of its evaluation criteria and the model adopted for measuring accessibility.

To ensure a comparable evaluation baseline across tools, the websites listed in the WCAG 2.2 Implementation Report [27], maintained by the W3C, were utilized. This document compiles examples of pages considered references for conformance levels A, AA and AAA of WCAG 2.2, WCAG 2.1 and WCAG 2.0. The selection of these pages is justified by their previously known and validated accessibility levels, which allows for a more precise comparison between the results produced by the automated tools and the pages' actual compliance with WCAG guidelines. However, we acknowledge that these websites were not continually evaluated after the implementation report, and might not be compliant at those levels.

The first author of this paper used all four selected evaluation tools with each selected web page. The results were tabulated, and each metric obtained from the tools were then collated.

The results from the metrics obtained for each website's homepage were analysed using tables and descriptive analyses.

3 Results

The evaluation used three evaluation tools: Ases Web (Brazil)[1], Mauve++ (Italy)[2], and AccessMonitor (Portugal)[3].

The tools employed different metrics with features reported in the literature, such as calculating the proportion of violations of success criteria in relation to how many potential problems could have happened. For example, if a web page has ten images, there are potentially ten problems if those are violated. However, they employ different weighing systems to calculate a single metric across all success criteria. Table 1 presents the main results from each tool to each selected website.

Overall, the tools initially present a quantitative overview of the evaluation, including a global score, the total number of criteria analyzed, and the distribution among compliant and non-compliant criteria, as well as those requiring manual verification. In addition to this summary, detailed reports indicate the evaluated guideline, the technique applied, the corresponding compliance level (A, AA or AAA), and the location of the potential failure within the source code.

[1] http://asesweb.governoeletronico.gov.br.
[2] https://mauve.isti.cnr.it/.
[3] https://accessmonitor.acessibilidade.gov.pt/.

Table 1. Accessibility Evaluation Results

Website	WCAG Conformance Level	ASES Score (%)	AccessMonitor (0–10)	Mauve++ (%)
standardweb.it	A	76,04%	9,6	100%
mitsue.co.jp	A	93,00%	9,6	96%
nomensa.com	AA	87,13%	7,6	90%
davidmacd.com	AA	84,63%	9,6	89%
dequeuniversity.com	AA	87,73%	9,7	91%
knowbility.org	AA	79,15%	9,3	72%
a11yrules.com	AA	85,57%	8,6	98%
funka.com	AAA	94,59%	9,6	89%
lflegal.com	AAA	86,58%	9,2	97%

Among the observed results, the performance of the Nomensa website evaluated using the AccessMonitor tool is notable, as it presented the lowest overall score, as shown in Table 1. In an evaluation conducted in June 2025, the page obtained a score of 7.6 out of a total of 37 verified criteria, with the identification of 6 Level A errors and 1 Level AA error. In a subsequent evaluation conducted in September 2025, the score dropped to 6.9, accompanied by an increase in the number of Level A errors. Given that the page had previously obtained compliance at Levels A and AA, these results indicate a high variability of results based on a small subset of success criteria that can be evaluated automatically.

Regarding the ASES Web tool, a relevant methodological distinction is observed: its normative basis is the e-MAG (Electronic Government Accessibility Model), which, although grounded in WCAG 2.0, features adaptations specific to the Brazilian context. This particularity may account for variations in results when directly compared with tools that strictly apply WCAG guidelines.

The Mauve++ tool presented advanced configuration features, allowing the selection of compliance level (A, AA, or AAA), WCAG version (2.0 or 2.1), and simulation environment (device, operating system, and browser). For this study, evaluations were conducted simulating a desktop environment with the Windows operating system and Google Chrome browser, utilizing WCAG 2.0 for Level A pages and WCAG 2.1 for Level AA pages.

In one of the analyzed cases shown in Table 1, the Mitsue website presented an accessibility score of 96%, recording 4 errors, 2 warnings, 6 passed criteria, and 13 non-applicable criteria. The evaluation completeness was 95%, indicating a minimal need for complementary manual verification. However, according to the official WCAG implementation report, this page fully had previously been deemed to comply with Level A criteria.

The results of this evaluation showed how even pages with previous manual auditing, such as those indicated by the W3C in WCAG's implementation report, have substantial variation from the evaluation from different tools. This raises important concerns as to how their results are used in decision-making processes and in governmental-led initiatives, such as accessibility observatories.

4 Conclusions and Future Work

The findings of this study demonstrate that while automated tools are essential for large-scale governmental monitoring, they currently lack the standardization required to be a trustworthy source.

The analysis conducted in this paper provides insights into how accessibility metrics from automated tools can be used in the process of monitoring digital accessibility by governmental agencies. Despite serving as a first filter to help signal websites that need attention, their results cannot be used as the sole aspect to be observed, as reported in previous studies [17]. Therefore, public policy must shift from score-based compliance to holistic monitoring. This should include 'hybrid' surveillance models where automated metrics trigger, but do not replace, manual expert audits and direct testing by users with disabilities. Without this integration, there is a significant risk that digital accessibility policies will remain a 'checkbox exercise' that fails to remove actual barriers for citizens.

Further studies need to be conducted into how different stakeholders interpret such results and how to help public policies effectively integrate other methods for evaluation and monitoring of digital accessibility, including manual auditing and evaluations by users with disabilities.

Acknowledgments. This study was funded by CAPES, CNPq, FAPEMIG and FINEP. The authors used Gemini as an AI tool solely to revise the text. The authors take full responsibility for the publication's content.

Disclosure of Interests. The authors have no competing interests to declare that are relevant to the content of this article.

References

1. Agência para a Modernização Administrativa (AMA): Observatório de acessibilidade web. Portal oficial (2026). https://observatorio.acessibilidade.gov.pt/
2. Ara, J., Sik-Lanyi, C., Kelemen, A., Guzsvinecz, T.: An inclusive framework for automated web content accessibility evaluation. Univ. Access Inf. Soc. **24**(2), 1581–1607 (2025)
3. Brazil: Law no. 13,146, of July 6, 2015 - Brazilian law for the inclusion of persons with disabilities. Official Gazette of the Federal Executive (2015). http://www.planalto.gov.br/ccivil_03/_ato2015-2018/2015/lei/l13146.htm
4. Campbell, A., Adams, C., Montgomery, R.B., Cooper, M., Kirkpatrick, A.: Web content accessibility guidelines (WCAG) 2.2. W3C Recommendation (2023). https://www.w3.org/TR/WCAG22/
5. Centro de Estudos sobre Tecnologias Web (Ceweb.br): Tic web acessibilidade. Ceweb.br (2026). https://ticwebacessibilidade.ceweb.br/
6. European Commission: European internet accessibility observatory (EIAO). Interoperable Europe Portal (2007). https://interoperable-europe.ec.europa.eu/collection/einclusion/document/european-internet-accessibility-observatory-eiao
7. European Commission: European internet accessibility observatory (EIAO). CORDIS - EU Research Results (2008). https://cordis.europa.eu/project/id/004526

8. European Commission: Web accessibility observatory. Interoperable Europe Portal (2018). https://interoperable-europe.ec.europa.eu/collection/tallinn-ministerial-declaration/solution/web-accessibility-observatory. Initiative to monitor and improve the accessibility of public sector websites through periodic large-scale evaluation, automated diagnostics, and reporting services, aligned with EU accessibility directives
9. European Commission: Accessmonitor. Interoperable Europe Portal (OSOR) (2026). https://interoperable-europe.ec.europa.eu/collection/open-source-observatory-osor/accessmonitor
10. European Parliament, Council of the European Union: Directive (EU) 2016/2102 of the European parliament and of the council of 26 October 2016 on the accessibility of the websites and mobile applications of public sector bodies (2016). https://eur-lex.europa.eu/eli/dir/2016/2102/oj/eng
11. European Telecommunications Standards Institute: En 301 549 v3.2.1: Accessibility requirements for ICT products and services (2021). https://rb.gy/h0jvsj
12. Ferraz, R., Duarte, A., Bárbara, J., Pereira, A.C., Meira, W.: A platform to check website compliance with web accessibility standards. In: Proceedings of the 20th International Web for All Conference, pp. 75–78 (2023)
13. Gobierno de España: Observatorio de accesibilidad web (oaw). Centro de Transferencia de Tecnología (CTT) (2024). https://administracionelectronica.gob.es/ctt/oaw/abstract
14. Gobierno de España: Web accessibility observatory. Portal de Administración Electrónica (2024). https://shorturl.at/1tV19
15. Governo Federal do Brasil: Ases web: Avaliador e simulador de acessibilidade em sítios. Portal Governo Eletrônico (2026). https://asesweb.governoeletronico.gov.br/
16. Martins, B., Duarte, C.: Large-scale study of web accessibility metrics. Univ. Access Inf. Soc. **23**(1), 411–434 (2024)
17. Mateus, D.A., et al.: The legal handling of digital accessibility: a comparison of evaluation and policy approaches in federal-level cases in Brazil and the united states. J. Braz. Comput. Soc. **30**(1), 363–379 (2024)
18. Mohamad, Y., Velasco, C.A.: Large scale web accessibility observatories. In: Miesenberger, K., Manduchi, R., Covarrubias Rodriguez, M., Peňáz, P. (eds.) ICCHP 2020. LNCS, vol. 12376, pp. 245–249. Springer, Cham (2020). https://doi.org/10.1007/978-3-030-58796-3_29
19. Nietzio, A., Strobbe, C., Velleman, E.: The unified web evaluation methodology (UWEM) 1.2 for WCAG 1.0. In: Miesenberger, K., Klaus, J., Zagler, W., Karshmer, A. (eds.) ICCHP 2008. LNCS, vol. 5105, pp. 394–401. Springer, Heidelberg (2008). https://doi.org/10.1007/978-3-540-70540-6_57
20. Núcleo de Informação e Coordenação do Ponto BR (NIC.br): Nic.br (2026). https://nic.br/
21. Silva, C.A., de Oliveira, A.F., Mateus, D.A., Costa, H.A.X., Freire, A.P.: Types of problems encountered by automated tool accessibility assessments, expert inspections and user testing: a systematic literature mapping. In: Proceedings of the 18th Brazilian Symposium on Human Factors in Computing Systems, pp. 1–11 (2019)
22. Snaprud, M., Sawicka, A.: Large scale web accessibility evaluation - a European perspective. In: Stephanidis, C. (ed.) UAHCI 2007. LNCS, vol. 4556, pp. 150–159. Springer, Heidelberg (2007). https://doi.org/10.1007/978-3-540-73283-9_18
23. Spyrou, A., etal.: Wadcher: a unified web accessibility assessment framework. In: Proceedings of the Smart Accessibility (2019)

24. U.S. General Services Administration: Section 508 of the rehabilitation act. Section508.gov (2024). https://www.section508.gov/manage/laws-and-policies/section-508-law/
25. Velasco Nunez, C., Mohamad, Y.: Wadcher: Public final report (2021). https://zenodo.org/records/5579307
26. Vogelauer, C.: Pilot studies for evaluating a web accessibility observatory. In: Proceedings of the 9th International Conference on Software Development and Technologies for Enhancing Accessibility and Fighting Info-exclusion, pp. 29–32 (2020)
27. World Wide Web Consortium: WCAG 2.2 implementation report. W3C Web Accessibility Initiative (WAI) (2023). https://www.w3.org/WAI/WCAG22/implementation-report/. Documenting the implementation experience for the Web Content Accessibility Guidelines 2.2

Manual Accessibility Testing Procedures for Mobile Apps: A Comparative Evaluation

Mona Steininger(✉), Pirmin Gersbacher, and Gottfried Zimmermann

Competence Center for Digital Accessibility, Stuttgart Media University, Nobelstr. 10, 70569 Stuttgart, Germany

m.steininger97@gmail.com, gersbacher@hdm-stuttgart.de, gzimmermann@acm.org

Abstract. Mobile apps are essential for digital participation, yet accessibility compliance remains critically low despite legal mandates. While automated tools offer efficiency, manual testing remains indispensable for mobile apps due to technical limitations. This study compares three German manual testing procedures: the comprehensive BIK BITV Test and BIT inklusiv App Test, which enable certification, and the simplified checklist Easy App Check for non-experts. Using a dual approach, we conducted an analytical comparison of the procedures and an empirical evaluation with 23 novice evaluators assessing two real-world apps. The obtained scores from the analytical comparison reveal a structural hierarchy (BIK BITV: 0.79, BIT inklusiv: 0.61, Easy App Check: 0.20), with all three procedures failing to cover BITV 2.0-specific requirements and none providing a fully integrated testing tool. Empirically, BIT inklusiv achieved the highest F1-score for barrier detection and the highest perceived usability rating among novice evaluators.

Keywords: Mobile Accessibility · Manual Testing · Accessibility Evaluation Method · Conformance · Comparative Study

1 Introduction

Smartphones have become critical tools for independence and digital participation among people with disabilities, serving as essential hubs for communication, information access, and managing daily activities [1]. Screen reader users increasingly prefer apps over websites for tasks such as online shopping and banking [2]. With approximately 7.9 million people living with severe disabilities in Germany [3] ensuring mobile app accessibility is crucial for digital inclusion.

Despite legal mandates such as the Web Accessibility Directive (WAD), compliance remains critically low. Germany's most recent monitoring report reveals that none of the observed public sector mobile apps achieved full accessibility [4]. Mobile apps frequently lack accessible source code for automated analysis, and automated tools cannot identify all barriers [5], making manual evaluations essential.

K. Miesenberger et al. (Eds.): ICCHP 2026, LNCS 16867, pp. 554–561, 2027.
https://doi.org/10.1007/978-3-032-31308-9_66

In Germany, there are two main manual testing procedures for formal accessibility certification: The BIK BITV Test [6] and BIT inklusiv App Test [7]. In contrast, the rapid screening checklist Easy App Check [8] was explicitly designed for users without deep technical expertise and evaluates only frequently found barriers. Currently, no systematic comparison of these procedures exists. This study addresses that gap by asking: How do BIK BITV, BIT inklusiv, and the Easy App Check compare in structural characteristics and practical performance when applied by novice evaluators? We provide the first evidence-based guidance for selecting appropriate testing methods and reveal how effectively non-experts could apply procedures of varying complexity.

2 Background

2.1 Legal Aspects and Testing Approaches

Germany's accessibility requirements for apps of public sector bodies stem from the Web Accessibility Directive (WAD) [9], published in 2016 by the European Commission and transposed into German law through the BITV 2.0 [10]. Public sector bodies must conduct regular monitoring, publish accessibility statements and ensure compliance with the European norm EN 301 549 [11]. The EN defines accessibility in the EU and directly refers the de-facto global standard WCAG 2.1 [12]. The European Accessibility Act (EAA) [13], which came in effect in June 2025, extends requirements to private sector products and services.

Accessibility testing employs three main approaches: user testing with people with disabilities, automated tools and manual expert evaluations [14]. User tests are demanding to facilitate [15] but offer deeper information about the user experience than tools [14]. Even though automation promises a resource-efficient and simple approach, manual testing remains dominant across EU member states for mobile apps. For websites, manual and automated approaches are used almost equally [5]. The lack of automated tools exists because source code is often not available for reviewers [16]. Also, tools cannot identify all barriers and results still need to be verified manually [14]. These disadvantages point towards a hybrid approach where automated tools serve as an accompaniment [17].

2.2 The Selected Testing Procedures

BIK BITV App Test [6] and BIT inklusiv App Test [7] are comprehensive conformance procedures covering all mandatory EN requirements, with detailed test steps and certification pathways. Both are publicly documented and designed for expert evaluators. The Easy App Check [8] is a lightweight screening tool that was designed at Stuttgart Media University. It covers only 30 of 110 mandatory criteria across 33 checkpoints selected to represent the most frequently found barriers.

By comparing two comprehensive procedures with one simplified approach, our study captures a methodological divide: thoroughness versus usability for non-experts.

3 Methodology

3.1 Analytical Comparison

The analytical comparison builds upon systematically researched criteria for a comparison of manual testing procedures for websites [18]. We conducted a focus group with three experts to adapt the web criteria for mobile apps. The outcome was a weighted list of criteria. The metrics to measure the criteria were defined by us based on the focus group discussion. Subsequently, we assessed the three procedures systematically against the criteria and computed total analytical scores based on the criterion scores and weights.

3.2 Empirical Comparison

We recruited 23 participants from a workshop and a lecture on digital accessibility fundamentals. Novice evaluators were defined as individuals with no prior experience applying formal accessibility testing procedures. Both course contexts supported this assumption, which was confirmed through a knowledge questionnaire. Participants were randomly assigned to one of three groups: 11 to BIK BITV, 6 each to BIT inklusiv and Easy App Check. The group imbalance resulted from participant error.

Participants analyzed screens from two native apps: SSB Move [19] and the KiKA App [20], selected for their diversity of interaction patterns. Our analysis focused on 23 EN 301 549 criteria shared across all three procedures, split into two homework packages. Participants judged each criterion as fulfilled, not fulfilled, or not applicable. The work was conducted asynchronously (one week per package), alone or in groups of up to three. Group submissions were counted per participant to increase feasibility. Participants could submit each package independently, but only complete submissions were included in the analysis.

Results were compared against a reference solution created beforehand and refined iteratively through expert discussion to resolve ambiguous cases. We treated each criterion-participant pair as a binary classification decision and computed Recall, Precision, and F1-score separately for two analyses: (1) detection of non-fulfilled criteria, where a true positive is a criterion correctly rated as not fulfilled, and (2) identification of non-applicable criteria, where a true positive is a criterion correctly rated as not applicable. The two analyses were kept separate because judging inapplicable criteria reflects a distinct evaluation challenge from barrier detection.

After completing the homework, 21 participants completed an adapted version of the 10 item System Usability Scale measuring perceived usability of the testing procedure, covering the dimensions learnability, efficiency and overall satisfaction [21]. We replaced Item 5 („I found the various functions in this system were well integrated") with „I find the testing procedure is clearly structured", as the original item targets system integration, which has no direct equivalent in manual evaluation procedures. Since this adaptation goes beyond terminological substitution, we interpret the scores comparatively, not against normative SUS benchmarks. We collected qualitative feedback via forum posts and analyzed it by using thematic analysis [22].

4 Results

4.1 Analytical Comparison

The weighted criteria catalog yielded clear differences (see Table 1). BIK BITV achieved the highest overall score (0.79), followed by BIT inklusiv (0.61), while the Easy App Check scored considerably lower (0.20). Both BIK BITV and BIT inklusiv fully cover EN 301 549, WCAG 2.1 AA, and WCAG 2.2 AA (score: 1.00 each), whereas the Easy App Check covers less than half of these criteria. Notably, all three procedures scored 0.00 for BITV 2.0 coverage, as none addresses these Germany-specific public sector requirements explicitly. BIT inklusiv scored 0.00 on sampling quality due to the absence of a publicly documented sampling methodology. All three procedures scored 0.00 for integrated tool support.

Table 1. Summary of the Analytical Comparison

Criterion	Weight (%)	BIK BITV	BIT inklusiv	Easy App Check
EN 301 549 coverage	12.08	1.00	1.00	0.10
BITV 2.0 coverage	12.08	0.00	0.00	0.00
WCAG 2.1 AA coverage	10.42	1.00	1.00	0.48
Report quality	9.58	0.88	0.75	0.00
Sampling quality	7.92	1.00	0.00	0.00
WCAG 2.2 AA coverage	6.67	1.00	1.00	0.00
Quality assurance measures	6.25	1.00	1.00	0.25
Workflow tool support	5.83	0.00	0.00	0.00
Supplementary tool list	5.42	1.00	0.66	0.33
Report file formats	5.42	0.66	0.00	0.00
License transparency	5.00	1.00	1.00	1.00
Evaluator qualification	4.58	1.00	0.33	0.00
Public accessibility of procedure	4.58	1.00	1.00	1.00
Certification / badge	3.33	1.00	1.00	0.00
Covered usage constellations	0.83	1.00	1.00	0.71
Overall score		**0.79**	**0.61**	**0.20**

4.2 Empirical Comparison

Participant Performance. 19 of 23 participants submitted complete homework sets (BIK BITV: n = 9, BIT inklusiv: n = 5, Easy App Check: n = 5).

For the detection of non-fulfilled test steps (see Fig. 1), BIT inklusiv achieved the highest F1-score (M = 0.65, 95% CI [0.61, 0.69]), followed by Easy App Check (M = 0.57, CI [0.57, 0.57]) and BIK BITV (M = 0.53, CI [0.49, 0.57]). A one-way ANOVA revealed no statistically significant difference between groups ($F(2,16) = 2.07, p = 0.16$), though $\eta 2 = 0.21$ indicates a large practical effect size, suggesting that differences may become detectable with a larger sample. A closer look at the Recall/Precision trade-off reveals a distinct pattern for BIK BITV: it achieved a comparatively higher Recall (R = 0.68) but notably lower Precision (P = 0.44) than BIT inklusiv (R = 0.74, P = 0.59) and Easy App Check (R = 0.58, P = 0.57). In this context, higher Recall indicates that evaluators correctly identified a larger proportion of unfulfilled test steps, while lower Precision reflects a higher rate of test steps rated as not fulfilled that were in fact fulfilled according to the reference solution.

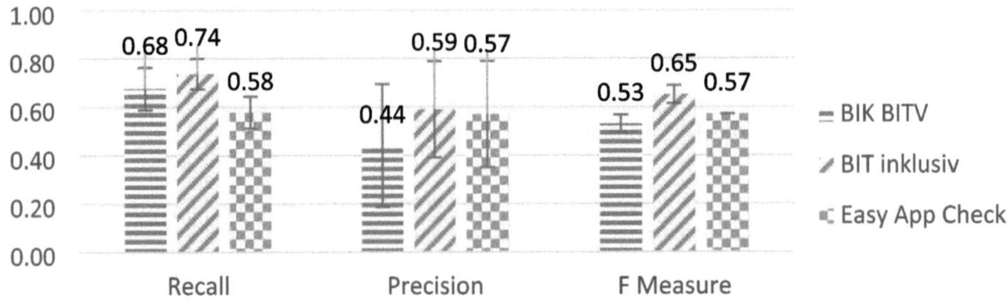

Fig. 1. Results of Analysis of non-fulfilled test steps

For the identification of non-applicable test steps (see Fig. 2), the pattern reversed: BIK BITV achieved the highest F1-score with 0.81 (CI [0.73, 0.89]), closely followed by Easy App Check with 0.78 (CI [0.67, 0.89]), while BIT inklusiv scored lowest with 0.52 (CI [-0.01, 1.05]).). The BIT inklusiv group showed high variance, suggesting that it led to inconsistent applicability decisions. A one-way ANOVA again showed no significant difference ($F(2,16) = 2.70$, $p = 0.10$, $\eta 2 = 0.25$).

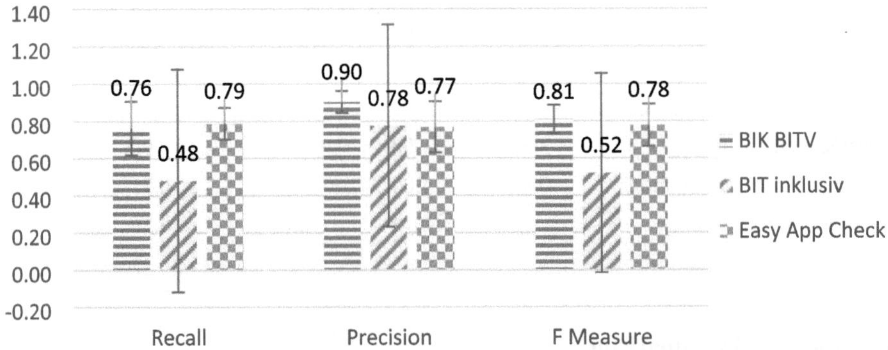

Fig. 2. Results of Analysis of non-applicable test steps

Perceived Usability. 21 participants completed the usability questionnaire (BIK BITV: n = 9, BIT inklusiv: n = 6, Easy App Check: n = 6). BIT inklusiv achieved the highest mean usability score (M = 65.83, 95% CI [54.37, 77.29]), followed by Easy App Check

(M = 57.50, 95% CI [36.91, 78.09]) and BIK BITV (M = 54.25, 95% CI [41.16, 67.34]). A one-way ANOVA revealed no statistically significant difference ($F(2,18) = 0.97$, $p = 0.40$, $\eta 2 = 0.11$). Notably, Easy App Check showed the widest confidence interval (range: 20.59 points), indicating substantial individual variation in perceived usability, while BIT inklusiv's interval was comparatively narrow (11.46 points), suggesting more consistent experiences across participants.

Qualitative Findings. Our thematic analysis of forum contributions (BIK BITV: 19 posts, BIT inklusiv and Easy App Check: 8 posts each) identified four themes. Rating uncertainty (1) was the most prominent challenge: participants across all three groups reported difficulty categorizing requirements, particularly those only partially fulfilled or requiring subjective judgement (such as deciding when input suggestion is meaningful). Regarding the procedure descriptions (2), BIT inklusiv was specifically praised for its intuitive navigation between test steps, while BIK BITV was criticised for its length and information density, despite being positively noted for its clear rationale for individual requirements. Participants mentioned several possibilities for improvement, such as short summaries for long test steps and inclusion of visual examples. Difficulties with tools (3), especially contrast verification were mentioned in both the BIK BITV and Easy App Check group, typically because contrasts cannot be tested directly on mobile devices. Procedural documentation (4) was raised primarily by a BIT inklusiv user, who described uncertainty about how to document mixed results.

5 Discussion

Our analytical comparison reveals a clear structural hierarchy among the three procedures. BIK BITV achieved the highest overall score, followed by BIT inklusiv and Easy App Check. This pattern reflects their different purposes: the first two are designed as comprehensive conformance testing procedures, while Easy App Check serves as a lightweight screening tool. The overall missing coverage of requirements from BITV 2.0 is particularly relevant for German public-sector apps. BIK BITV and BIT inklusiv achieve full normative coverage of EN 301 549 and WCAG. None of the procedures currently provides an integrated testing tool to support the testing workflow.

The Easy App Check's empirical performance warrants particular attention. Despite its considerably lower analytical score, novice evaluators achieved comparable testing performance. This may reflect the procedure's concise checklist style: rather than presenting exhaustive test steps, it provides brief, actionable prompts with links to BIK BITV steps for additional detail. For novices, this layered approach may reduce cognitive load–a factor that BIK BITV's richer but denser documentation does not optimize for. This aligns with the criticism BIK BITV received for its length and information density despite being appreciated for its explanations. Adding concise summaries to longer test steps in BIK BITV and BIT inklusiv could have meaningful impact. However, the wide confidence intervals for Easy App Check's usability scores suggest considerable individual variation that should be further investigated.

Empirically, BIT inklusiv achieved the highest F1-score for barrier detection and the highest perceived usability rating despite ranking second analytically. This demonstrates that procedural depth and practical accessibility are not mutually exclusive. BIK BITV, while analytically the strongest procedure, scored lowest in usability and showed a high recall but low precision pattern, suggesting that novice evaluators responded to its detailed prescriptions by defaulting to "not fulfilled" decisions. The differences across procedures were not statistically significant, likely due to the small sample size.

Qualitative findings corroborate the quantitative results. Participants requested visual examples, pointing to a need for illustrative guidance that helps novices verify they are on the right track. BIT inklusiv's more compact structure with easy navigation appeared to reduce cognitive load for non-experts, even though BIK BITV's richer documentation was explicitly appreciated for its explanatory quality. The gap between analytical strength and experienced usability underlines that procedural quality must be assessed along two independent dimensions.

Several limitations constrain the generalizability of our findings. The unbalanced group sizes limit the comparability of group-level estimates and reduce statistical power. However, the observed effect sizes were consistently large, suggesting that meaningful differences between procedures exist and may become statistically detectable with larger, balanced samples. We therefore consider the findings interpretable as preliminary evidence, while acknowledging that definitive conclusions require replication. Group submissions were weighted per participant, which may reduce the independence of observations within groups. Additionally, the SUS adaptation precludes comparison against normative benchmarks and usability scores should be interpreted comparatively between procedures only. Finally, the analytical comparison reflects only what is publicly prescribed and testing organizations may apply higher standards.

6 Conclusion

This study provides the first evidence-based comparison of German, manual mobile accessibility testing procedures, combining an analytical weighted-criteria evaluation with an empirical study of 23 novice evaluators assessing selected screens of two real-world apps. Our findings yield concrete guidance for procedure selection: BIK BITV is the most methodologically robust choice for formal conformance testing and regulatory contexts. BIT inklusiv offers the best balance between normative coverage and practical accessibility for less experienced evaluators. Easy App Check functions reliably within its intended scope as a rapid screening instrument, though it cannot substitute a full conformance evaluation. We recommend treating the three procedures not as alternatives but as complementary stages of a testing process – from Easy App Check as an early-stage quality indicator, to BIT inklusiv as an accessible entry point for full conformance testing, to BIK BITV for legal certification by accredited experts.

Disclosure of Interests. The authors have no competing interests to declare that are relevant to the content of this article.

References

1. Borgstedt, S., Möller-Slawinski, H.: Digitale Teilhabe von Menschen mit Behinderung (2020)

2. WebAIM: Screen Reader User Survey. webaim.org/projects/screenreadersurvey10/. Last accessed 08 Feb 2026
3. Statistisches Bundesamt: Behinderte Menschen, destatis.de. Last accessed 08 Feb 2026
4. Wahl, M., Schmidt, D., Pfingstl, A.: Bericht der BRD an die EU-Kommission: Periodische Überwachung der Barrierefreiheitsanforderungen. BFIT-Bund (2025)
5. Mateus, D.A., Silva, C.A., Eler, M.M., Freire, A.P.: Accessibility of mobile applications: evaluation by users with visual impairment and by automated tools. In: IHC '20. pp. 1–10. Association for Computing Machinery (2020). https://doi.org/10.1145/3424953.3426633
6. DIAS GmbH: Prüfschritte BITV-Test / EN 301 549 (App) | BIK BITV-Test, bitvtest.de/pruefverfahren/bitv-20-app. Last accessed 06 Feb 2026
7. BIT inklusiv: BITV-APP-Test. apptest.bit-inklusiv.de. Last accessed 06 Feb 2026
8. Gersbacher, P.: Easy App Check. barrierefreiheit.hdm-stuttgart.de/wp-content/uploads/2023/06/EasyAppCheck.Checkliste.pdf (2023)
9. Directive (EU) 2016/2102 of the European Parliament and of the Council (2016)
10. BITV 2.0-Barrierefreie Informationstechnik Verordnung
11. EN 301 549 V3.2.1: Accessibility requirements for ICT products and services (2021)
12. World Wide Web Consortium: WCAG 2.1, w3.org/TR/WCAG21/. Last accessed 08 Feb 2026
13. Directive (EU) 2019/882 of the European Parliament and of the Council (2019)
14. Matos, M., Seixas Pereira, L., Duarte, C.: Evaluation of the accessibility of mobile applications: current approaches and challenges. In: HCI International 2023, pp. 352–371. Springer, Cham (2023). https://doi.org/10.1007/978-3-031-48041-6_24
15. Brajnik, G.: A comparative test of web accessibility evaluation methods. In: Proc. ASSETS 2008. pp. 113–120. ACM, Halifax Nova Scotia Canada (2008). https://doi.org/10.1145/1414471.1414494
16. Acosta-Vargas, P., Salvador-Acosta, B., Salvador-Ullauri, L., Villegas-Ch., W., Gonzalez, M.: Accessibility in native mobile applications for users with disabilities: a scoping review. Appl Sci. **11**, 5707 (2021). https://doi.org/10.3390/app11125707
17. Seixas Pereira, L., Matos, M., Duarte, C.: Exploring mobile device accessibility: challenges, insights, and recommendations for evaluation methodologies. In: Proc. CHI 2024. pp. 1–17. ACM (2024). https://doi.org/10.1145/3613904.3642526
18. Kollotzek, G., Zimmermann, G., Ableitner, T., Nebe, A.-M.: Comparison of manual evaluation methods for assessing the accessibility of websites based on EN 301 549: In: Proc. CHIRA 2021. pp. 24–35. SCITEPRESS (2021). https://doi.org/10.5220/0010647000003060
19. SSB AG: SSB Move App-SSB, ssb-ag.de/tickets/ssb-move-app/. Last accessed 07 Feb 2026
20. KiKA: KiKA-App, kika.de/eltern/applikationen/kika-player/kika-app-134.html. Last accessed 07 Feb 2026
21. Brooke, J.: SUS: a quick and dirty usability scale. Usability Eval. Ind. **189** (1995)
22. Braun, V., Clarke, V.: Using thematic analysis in psychology. Qual. Res. Psychol. **3**, 77–101 (2006). https://doi.org/10.1191/1478088706qp063oa

Digital Accessibility as Meaningful Participation in Technology-Mediated Activities

Christopher Power(✉)

University of Prince Edward Island, Charlottetown, PE C1A 4P3, Canada
cdspower@upei.ca

Abstract. Digital accessibility research has focused the person-system dyad, producing definitions that mask the volition of disabled people, the felt experience of technology-mediated activity, and the socio-cultural conditions shaping both. This paper extends Hedvall's Activity Diamond to incorporate volition and experience, identifies six structural tensions between activity elements, and proposes three thresholds of accessibility: Technical, Action, and Participatory. On this basis, it redefines Digital Accessibility as existing when a technology-mediated activity is designed to support a disabled person's meaningful participation by enabling interaction, action, and valued experiences, sustaining volition to engage over time.

Keywords: Accessibility · Activity Theory · User Experience

1 Introduction

Digital accessibility in interactive technologies has produced essential work in two broad and complementary traditions. The first-wave [9], centred on technological innovation, resolves mismatches between a disabled person and system that interrupt the interaction loop, creating a person-interface fit [12]. The second-wave tradition centres on interface-level optimization, where success is the resolution of barriers that are present only after the interaction loop is available, where a disabled person is interrupted in progression towards the goals, tasks or outcomes afforded by an interface in a context of use, meeting some aspects of subjective usability criteria [14]. These two traditions have been, and will continue, to be foundational to the field of accessibility.

However, this paper argues that these waves and their definitions have produced a narrow concept of *digital accessibility*, framing research and practice predominantly at the person-system dyad and masking the complexity of an individual and their felt experience with a technology-mediated activity. Further, as a result of this constrained definition questions about barriers that come from the context, whether from artifactual, natural or socio-cultural sources, can be left unexamined in design processes. This paper proposes that in order to

K. Miesenberger et al. (Eds.): ICCHP 2026, LNCS 16867, pp. 562–572, 2027.
https://doi.org/10.1007/978-3-032-31308-9_67

move research and practice forward, the definition of digital accessibility must be expanded to prompt researchers and designers to ask about those unexamined barriers.

This paper first presents evidence that the field's research is concentrated at the person-system dyad, supporting the claim that current definitions contribute to practical and theoretical gaps. It then reviews the design traditions that have shaped those definitions, introduces recent innovations in differentiating accessibility, usability, and universal design. Building on these, the paper extends Hedvall's Activity Diamond [11], a model grounded in Cultural-Historical Activity Theory and proposes a new definition of digital accessibility.

2 Research Landscape of Digital Accessibility

Digital accessibility has typically found a home in the now broad field of human-computer interaction (HCI). Originally starting with the information-processor model of interaction [4], the broader field of HCI began to move beyond the interface-level concerns in the mid-1980s [1] turning to how users' goals and tasks are mediated through technology. The introduction of user experience as a research concern rose to prominence through the 2000s [10], acknowledging that technology use is shaped by and influences an individual's lived experiences. Yet despite this disciplinary shift, accessibility research has remained concentrated in the first and second waves of HCI [3]. The third wave of HCI [3,9], characterized by research questions turning toward the volition behind why people undertake activities with technology and their lived experience in doing so, has had comparatively little focus in accessibility research.

A survey by Mack et al. [19] of 506 papers published in ACM CHI and ASSETS between 1994 and 2019 demonstrated that over a third of accessibility-related papers were concerned with increasing digital access through technology innovation (36.8%), often without situating that technology in any specific context. A further near third (27.5%) focused on understanding user needs and abilities in relation to system-supported task completion. Looking across these themes, over 60% of papers followed a recognizable pipeline of building an artifact and evaluating it, a pattern in which the research contribution begins and ends with the person interacting with a system.

Mack et al. [19] also observed that fewer than 9% of papers in two of the field's most prominent venues made theoretical contributions. As a result, accessibility lacks the theoretical frameworks available to the rest of HCI for systematically describing, conceiving, and investigating barriers in design beyond the person-system dyad [20]. This theoretical deficit is both reflected in and reinforced by how accessibility itself is defined. When accessibility is understood as access to a system, then research questions will focus on system barriers, and the questions about the alignment of disabled people's experiences with their volition are systematically excluded.

3 Digital Accessibility and Design Traditions

Where theoretical commitments in accessibility have been most explicit, they have been in design traditions rather than in formal theory. The design traditions of Universal Design (UD), Inclusive Design (ID) and Design for All (DfA) have all contributed to shifting the field away from a medical model of disability and toward a social model that recognizes the role of design in creating barriers to participation. Each of them indicates in different ways that accessibility increases participation, but each stops short of the analytical tools needed to address the gaps in removing barriers from sources outside of the person-system dyad.

Mace's Universal Design definition [6] and its seven principles have been influential in that they provide a set of high level principles and operational guidelines for evaluation. While some guidelines, such as Guidelines **1b**[1] and **3b**[2] implicitly describe a relationship between an individual's volition and their experience, they are predominantly focused on accessibility of the interaction loop. There have been several refinements to UD that have defined more broadly the concept of accessibility. Iwarsson and Ståhl [14] refine UD by juxtaposing accessibility and usability, where accessibility is objective and focused on barriers between person and environment, grounded in standards and legislation. In comparison, usability is what access becomes when a person acts over an *activity* in that environment. With those definitions, UD is said to incorporate design over both of those concepts, but as accessibility in information processing was still developing, the distinction of system versus the broader context remains unclear. Steinfeld and Maisel's process-oriented definition [21] shifted the UD definition towards universal goals, and while this included aspects of socio-cultural factors of personalization to an individual and social integration and cultural appropriateness related to their communities, it does not provide a framework for describing the barriers that come from those factors. Other critiques of UD, such as Imrie [13] explicitly state that attitudes and values that shape interactions are not fully integrated into programs that are predominantly technology-led, and Lid [18] calls for grounding UD in something beyond the social model of barriers, both of which echo the argument for a clearer definition of digital accessibility.

Inclusive Design advanced accessible design in distinct but complementary traditions. The UK tradition reframed inclusion as a measurable design-management concern by introducing the concept of *design exclusion*: quantifying the capability demands a product places on users against population data across sensory, motor, and cognitive dimensions to estimate how many people a given design excludes [16]. In contrast, the Canadian tradition [23] goes further by organizing practice around three dimensions: valuing human difference as an asset rather than averaging it away; co-designing with people at the margins who frame the problem; and attending to the complex adaptive systems through which design decisions propagate. Because digital systems are not constrained to a single physical form and individuals have broad diversity, the Canadian

[1] Avoid segregating or stigmatizing any users.

[2] Be consistent with user expectations and intuition.

tradition pursues "one-size-fits-one" adaptability. However it too describes the *distribution* of needs but not the *structure* of the activity system in which those needs arise. ID makes inclusion and accessible design actionable, but its unit of analysis remains the person-product dyad: it measures which people are excluded from using a product.

The European DfA tradition provides perhaps the most explicit link between meaningful participation and the removal of barriers. The original EIDD Stockholm Declaration [7] links human diversity, social inclusion, and equality to designs that *"provide opportunities for equal opportunities to participate in every aspect of society [sic]"*. However, when operationalized in information technology, DfA has typically been framed within the same person-system dyad [22], with adaptive interfaces and user modelling standing in for the broader participatory vision the Declaration articulates. As a process and design framework, DfA names participation as the destination but leaves the specific barriers beyond the interface outside its analytical scope.

All of the above design traditions share important commitments: designing for the widest possible range of people, shifting the burden of accessibility from the individual to the designed environment, attending to human values, and rejecting the framing of accessibility as an afterthought. Yet a common pattern emerges. Each tradition provides a rich vocabulary for asking whether and how a disabled person can use technology, but none of them provides a structured analytical framework for asking a different question: once technology access is secured, does the technology-mediated activity yield experiences that a disabled person genuinely seeks and values?

Hedvall, Ståhl, and Iwarsson [12] have recently confirmed that conceptual confusion among accessibility, usability, and Universal Design persists more than two decades after Iwarsson and Ståhl's [14] original analysis. Their proposed harmonized model positions UD as a value-based vision grounded in human rights, with accessibility and usability as complementary tools for translating that vision into practice, all oriented toward the ultimate goal of participation. Most importantly for this paper, the authors [12] themselves acknowledge that achieving participation requires more than accessibility and usability can provide. They note that whether an individual participates cannot be determined by external factors alone, and that individual capacity, experiences of personal influence over one's environment, feelings of connection and relatedness, and personal volition are all at play. This paper aims to operationalize all of these factors to provide the analytical tools needed for investigating what participation means in the context of a specific technology-mediated activity.

4 Theoretical Framework: Activity Theory

Cultural-Historical Activity Theory (CHAT) provides a theoretical tradition well suited to expanding the definition of digital accessibility. Originating in the work of Vygotsky on mediated action and developed by Leont'ev into a hierarchical model of activity, CHAT distinguishes three levels of analysis: *activities*, driven by motives and oriented toward objects that carry social and personal significance; *actions*, directed by conscious goals; and *operations*, carried out automatically and shaped by the conditions at hand [8].

Engeström [8] extended this hierarchy into a systemic model in which an activity is constituted not only by a subject acting on an object through mediating tools, but also by a community, shared rules, and a division of labour. Crucially, this model situates individual action within a web of social and institutional relations, making it possible to analyze how factors entirely outside the person-system interaction shape the quality and meaning of an activity. Kaptelinin and Nardi [15] established activity theory as a productive framework within HCI, demonstrating its capacity to move interaction research beyond the person-interface dyad. They situated the experience of a user as being within the central unit of *activity* that is mediated by the interactive system. Clemmensen et al. [5] subsequently analyzed how activity theory has been applied across HCI research, confirming its analytical power in both conceptualization, as done in this paper, and for analyzing interactions in different domains for *tensions* where there is the potential for *breakdowns*, the manifestation of barriers to interaction within the activity.

5 Digital Accessibility In Technology-Mediated Activity

This paper extends Hedvall's [11] Activity Diamond which is a four-element structure representing an activity (D) comprised of: a **Subject** (S), who is the individual engaged in the activity; the **Object** (O), which is the motive-bearing focus of the activity; the **Artifactual–Natural Environment** (A), comprising the tools, technologies, standards, and physical conditions that mediate engagement between the S and O; and the **Human Environment** (H), including the people, relationships, institutions, attitudes, and cultural norms that shape participation in the activity.

In this extension of the model, S is comprised of two components that are internal to the individual. The **volition** of an individual is comprised of their *personal causation* that moves an individual to participate in relation to their own perceived capacity to act based on their prior experience, the *values* of the individual regarding what is important and meaningful, and their *interests* that lead to anticipated enjoyment or satisfaction [17].

Crucially, a person's volition is shaped by their prior experience, with negative experiences eroding confidence and personal causation, reducing interest in participation, or devaluing that experience as a future pursuit. Conversely, positive experiences strengthen personal causation as skills and capacities develop, interest grows, and the activity takes on meaning consistent with the person's values.

The **experience** is an emergent property of the technology-mediated activity felt by an individual while they engage with it. This could include satisfaction in undertaking and achieving the desired outcome of the activity, feelings of improved competence, belonging through connection and relatedness, or deeper meaning-making for that individual. Volition and experience are therefore coupled: the experiences an activity produces feed back into the volition with which a person approaches it next time.

5.1 Tensions and Accessibility Barriers

A *tension* is a structural mismatch in alignment between two related elements of an activity that have the potential to manifest as an accessibility barrier. Listed below are six possible tensions, each presented with the experiential question and the mechanism by which barriers can manifest between those two elements, and an illustrative example of a barrier from the domain of digital gaming with a player Logan who wishes to play the fictional racing game *Maple Rush* with their friends.

- $S \longleftrightarrow A$: Can the person interact with the system?
  Addressed by first-wave traditions, this tension arises from a mismatch between an a person and their ability to perceive or operate the mediating technology. When unresolved, the gateway to the activity remains closed and engagement cannot begin. *Example Barrier:* Logan is unable to use a standard controller and so they cannot drive a car with default controls.
- $S \longleftrightarrow O$: Can the person accomplish their goals?
  Addressed in part by second-wave traditions, this tension arises from a mismatch between an individual's skills and the challenges posed by the motive-bearing focus of the activity. When unresolved, the person can operate the technology but encounters a persistent mismatch between what the activity asks of them and what they can achieve. *Example Barrier:* Logan can access the game, but is unable to complete races and play with their friends as the default level of challenge is too high.
- $A \longleftrightarrow O$: Can the person engage with the authentic activity?
  This tension arises when the mediating technology presents an impoverished or reduced version of the activity's focus, restricting the range of meaningful engagement the individual can pursue. When unresolved, the person can act but only upon a diminished *Object*, undermining satisfaction and meaning making. *Example Barrier:* Logan wants to race with their friends in ranked races, but because they have different settings they can only race together in unranked races.
- $S \longleftrightarrow H$: Can the person participate without stigma?
  This tension arises when community attitudes, cultural norms, or institutional practices exclude or stigmatize the individual. When unresolved, the person participates under indifferent or hostile conditions, undermining belonging and identity affirmation. *Example Barrier:* Logan encounters derogatory language about people who use accessibility settings or slurs towards disabled people in the lobby chat.
- $H \longleftrightarrow O$: Can the person see themselves in the activity?
  This tension arises when social norms, cultural attitudes, or community practices embed harmful or absent representations within the object of the activity. When unresolved, the person's identity is erased from or distorted within

the very thing they are participating in, undermining meaning, belonging, and identity affirmation. *Example Barrier: Maple Rush* provides cheering crowds, but none of the people in the crowd have visible disabilities like Logan's.

- $A \longleftrightarrow H$: Can the person participate on equitable terms?
  This tension arises when standards or design practices label an adapted design as atypical. While participation may be possible, it is marked. Equitable experiences require not only that different paths to participation deliver comparable experiences, but that those paths do not come at the cost of social standing, undermining meaning and belonging. *Example Barrier:* When Logan finishes a race there is an asterisk (*) on the global leaderboard indicating that Logan is using an alternative controller.

5.2 Thresholds of Digital Accessibility

These tensions are not mutually exclusive, and they can interact in complex ways. For example, if Logan cannot map an alternative controller in *Maple Rush* the $S \longleftrightarrow A$ barrier remains and they cannot play. However, if Logan can remap a controller, they will encounter new barriers trying to get around the track, either due to their own skill with their alternative controller, or perhaps because the default challenge is too high for a new player. Assuming *Maple Rush* has some means of resolving those $S \longleftrightarrow O$ barriers, such as steering assist options, it is only then that Logan encounters the remaining barriers listed above along the other tensions. Even more complex is the propagation of barriers. The resolution of the $S \longleftrightarrow A$ barrier with an alternative controller and remapped controls for seems like an excellent solution; however, if in response to that option the design team adds the asterisk that calls out a player using it and Logan feels lousy about that, they have unintentionally introduced a new experiential barrier at the $A \longleftrightarrow H$ tension. Alternatively, as Logan plays more, they may wish to try new game modes, but maybe the steering assists introduced to address $S \longleftrightarrow O$ barriers reduce the parts of the game Logan and their friends can play, creating a new barrier along the $A \longleftrightarrow O$ tension.

This complexity defines three nested *thresholds* of digital accessibility, each subsuming the previous and grouping tensions by when they are likely to be encountered. **Technical Accessibility** is the focus of first-wave research and practice, resolving *exclusively* the $S \longleftrightarrow A$ barriers, such as Logan's re-mappable controls. **Action Accessibility** builds on Technical Accessibility and additionally considers whether the person can act towards their motivations and objectives in ways that meet their competencies and capacities, resolving $S \longleftrightarrow O$ barriers. This is where second-wave research and practice excels, focusing on usability attributes of the interaction.

However, as seen with Logan playing *Maple Rush*, resolving barriers that relate to those two tensions creates pathways to new barriers outside the person-system dyad. This model explicitly locates those barriers, which are discussed in research and practice [2] but are unvoiced in our accessibility definitions and theoretical frameworks. This third threshold, that of **Participatory Accessibility**, subsumes the previous two and encompasses how well the activity addresses aspects of belonging, identity, meaning making, and how well the activity aligns with an individual's perception of themselves, their values and their interests. The term Participatory Accessibility emphasizes that accessibility at this level concerns not only effective action, but legitimate, meaningful, and sustaining participation in the technology-mediated activity. The tensions between the different elements along with their threshold of accessibility are displayed in Fig. 1.

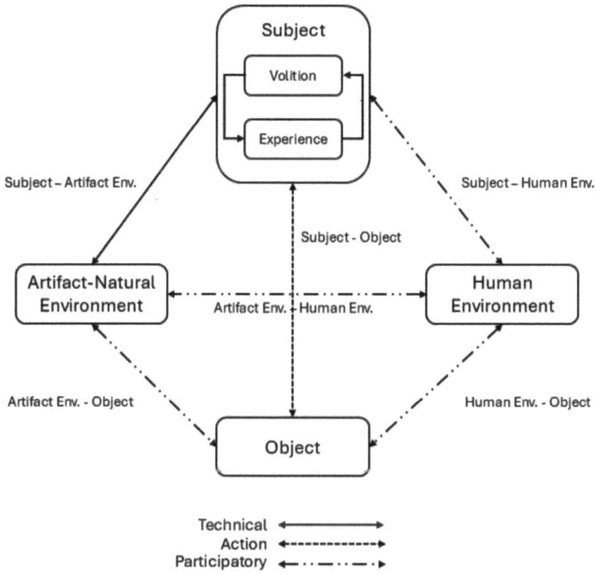

Fig. 1. Extended Activity Diamond Model of Meaningful Participation in Technology-Mediated Experiences [11] showing six structural tension relationships between elements.

5.3 Defining Digital Accessibility

This paper has argued that moving research beyond first-wave and second-wave paradigms requires a new definition capable of operationalizing participation in a technology-mediated activity. The preceding analysis structures the relevant tensions and their associated barriers so that they can be applied analytically. Technical Accessibility remains a necessary foundation for accessing interaction, and Action Accessibility a necessary condition for progress within the activity. What this model adds explicitly are the barriers to meaningful, sustainable, and socially and culturally supported engagement.

On this basis, this paper proposes that **Digital Accessibility** exists when a technology-mediated activity is designed to support a disabled person's meaningful participation by enabling interaction, action, and valued experiences, sustaining volition to engage over time.

By bringing the volition and the experience of a participating individual forward in the definition, it distinguishes digital accessibility from other HCI concepts, and situates it within recent conceptualizations of universal design [12].

6 Discussion

This paper set out to address a persistent gap in how digital accessibility is defined and studied in interactive technologies. Decades of accessibility research have substantially improved access to devices and supported effective interaction with interfaces, but these advances do not guarantee that disabled people can participate in technology-mediated activities in ways that are meaningful, sustaining, or aligned with what they seek and value. Accessibility work can succeed at enabling use while failing at enabling participation. This paper argues that this gap is not merely structural, or empirical, but definitional: how accessibility is conceptualized shapes what questions are asked, what barriers are noticed, and what design outcomes are pursued as observed in previous work [19].

To address this gap, this paper reframed digital accessibility at the level of technology-mediated activity. It examined the set of tensions between elements of an activity, extending previous contributions from cultural-historical activity theory into accessibility [11]. This examination of tensions and the potential barriers has proposed three thresholds and a new definition that describes how to resolve barriers such that disabled individuals become increasingly included in an activity.

The model developed in this paper is a theoretical contribution. Its value lies in generating productive empirical work and informing design practice. Three directions follow from the model, each corresponding to a different mode of engagement: description, translation, and method.

The six tensions and three thresholds provide a classification that can be applied to any technology-mediated activity. A natural first step is to develop empirical inventories of barriers structured within the three thresholds in specific domains such as digital gaming, web interaction, online education, social media and more. For each domain, researchers can ask: which tensions have been documented? Which have been addressed by existing designs? Which remain under-investigated?

Such inventories would first serve to test the model's descriptive adequacy in documenting barriers located at specific tensions. Cases where the mapping fails would identify where the model requires refinement. Second, they would make visible the distribution of research effort across thresholds. A barrier inventory would also support cross-domain comparison and translation of designs, such as when the asterisk design on the leaderboard has analogues in other domains like education.

Accessibility guidelines, design patterns, and heuristic evaluation frameworks are the intermediary representations through which research findings reach practice. The proposed model suggests these representations require expansion, or at the very least, re-categorization, with many being heavily focused on Technical and Action Accessibility. However, the purpose of such extensions is not necessarily to legislate Participatory Accessibility, but instead to identify if there are ways to make the tensions across that threshold visible to practitioners at different stages of design.

Perhaps the most consequential implication of the model is methodological. This definition positions digital accessibility as an analytic property of the encounter of a person with an activity through technology, rather than a design stance; UD, ID and DfA remain the complementary process-oriented concepts that aim to produce such encounters at the population level. However, if digital accessibility is defined in that way, then design and evaluation must be capable of assessing both volition and experience, not only interface conformance and usability criteria. Critique of our current methods through the lens of participation is needed to examine not only what we need to measure, but how and when to deploy measures.

Together, these extensions would move accessibility research and practice from asking *can the person use the system?* to asking *does the system mediate meaningful activity in ways that enable the experiences this person seeks and values?* This is the question that the proposed definition places at the centre of the field.

Acknowledgments. We acknowledge the support of the Natural Sciences and Engineering Research Council of Canada (NSERC), grant RGPIN-2020-05570.

References

1. Bannon, L.J.: Issues in design: some notes. In: Norman, D.A., Draper, S.W. (eds.) User Centered System Design: New Perspectives on Human-Computer Interaction, chap. 3. Lawrence Erlbaum, Hillsdale (1986)
2. Beeston, J.J.: Social experiences of people with disabilities in playing (in)accessible digital games. Ph.D. thesis, University of York, York, UK (2020)
3. Bødker, S.: When second wave HCI meets third wave challenges. In: NordiCHI 2006, pp. 1–8. ACM, New York (2006). https://doi.org/10.1145/1182475.1182476
4. Card, S.K., Moran, T.P., Newell, A.: The psychology of human-computer interaction. LEA, Hillsdale, NJ (1983)
5. Clemmensen, T., Kaptelinin, V., Nardi, B.: Making HCI theory work: an analysis of the use of activity theory in HCI research. Behav. Inf. Technol. **35**(8), 608–627 (2016). https://doi.org/10.1080/0144929X.2016.1175507
6. Connell, B.R., et al.: The principles of universal design, version 2.0. Center for Universal Design, North Carolina State University (1997)
7. EIDD – Design for All Europe: The EIDD Stockholm Declaration (2004). https://dfaeurope.eu/what-is-dfa/dfa-documents/the-eidd-stockholm-declaration-2004/

8. Engeström, Y.: Learning by Expanding: An Activity-Theoretical Approach to Developmental Research, 2nd edn. Cambridge University Press, Helsinki (1987). https://doi.org/10.1017/CBO9781139814744
9. Harrison, S., Sengers, P., Tatar, D.: Making epistemological trouble: third-paradigm HCI as successor science. Interact. Comput. **23**(5), 385–392 (2011). https://doi.org/10.1016/j.intcom.2011.03.005
10. Hassenzahl, M., Tractinsky, N.: User experience - a research agenda. Behav. Inf. Technol. **25**(2), 91–97 (2006). https://doi.org/10.1080/01449290500330331
11. Hedvall, P.O.: The activity diamond – modelling an enhanced accessibility. Ph.D. thesis, Lund University, Certec (Rehabilitation Engineering and Design), Lund, Sweden (2009)
12. Hedvall, P.O., Ståhl, A., Iwarsson, S.: Accessibility, usability and universal design – still confusing? Harmonisation of key concepts describing person-environment interaction to create conditions for participation. Disabil. Rehabil. 1–10 (2025). https://doi.org/10.1080/09638288.2025.2491831
13. Imrie, R.: Universalism, universal design and equitable access to the built environment. Disabil. Rehabil. **34**(10), 873–882 (2012). https://doi.org/10.3109/09638288.2011.624250
14. Iwarsson, S., Ståhl, A.: Accessibility, usability and universal design - positioning and definition of concepts describing person-environment relationships. Disabil. Rehabil. **25**(2), 57–66 (2003). https://doi.org/10.1080/dre.25.2.57.66
15. Kaptelinin, V., Nardi, B.A.: Activity Theory in HCI: Fundamentals and Reflections. Synthesis Lectures on Human-Centered Informatics. Morgan & Claypool, San Rafael (2012). https://doi.org/10.1007/978-3-031-02196-1
16. Keates, S., Clarkson, P.J.: Countering design exclusion through inclusive design. In: CUU 2003, pp. 69–76. ACM, New York (2003). https://doi.org/10.1145/957205.957218
17. Kielhofner, G.: Model of Human Occupation: Theory and Application, 4th edn. Lippincott Williams & Wilkins, Baltimore (2008)
18. Lid, I.M.: Developing the theoretical content in universal design. Scand. J. Disabil. Res. **15**(3), 203–215 (2013). https://doi.org/10.1080/15017419.2012.724445
19. Mack, K., McDonnell, E., Jain, D., Wang, L.L., Froehlich, J.E., Findlater, L.: What Do We Mean by "accessibility research"? A literature survey of accessibility papers in CHI and ASSETS from 1994 to 2019. In: CHI 2021. ACM, New York (2021). https://doi.org/10.1145/3411764.3445412
20. Oulasvirta, A., Hornbæk, K.: Counterfactual thinking: what theories do in design. IJHCI **38**(1), 78–92 (2022). https://doi.org/10.1080/10447318.2021.1925436
21. Steinfeld, E., Maisel, J.: Universal Design: Creating Inclusive Environments. Wiley, Hoboken (2012)
22. Stephanidis, C., Salvendy, G.: Toward an information society for all: an international research and development agenda. IJHCI **10**(2), 107–134 (1998). https://doi.org/10.1207/s15327590ijhc1002_2
23. Treviranus, J.: Inclusive design: valuing difference, recognizing complexity. In: Rioux, M.H., Buettgen, A., Zubrow, E., Viera, J. (eds.) Handbook of Disability: Critical Thought and Social Change in a Globalizing World, pp. 1–24. Springer, Cham (2021). https://doi.org/10.1007/978-981-16-1278-7_98-1

Beyond the Source: Evaluating the Role of Post-source Accessibility Remediations

Janina Sajka(✉)

Level Access, 800 Corporate Drive, Suite 301 PMB #645, Stafford, VA 22554, USA
janina.sajka@levelaccess.com

Abstract. A prevailing principle in web accessibility asserts that all remediations should be accomplished within the published HTML, CSS, ARIA, and JavaScript source code. However, various accessibility remediations are increasingly being performed in realtime, after source code has been read, but before content reaches the user. This paper examines three key bodies of literature regarding this practice: the Overlay Fact Sheet (OFS), the Accessibility Capabilities re-port of the A11yEdge Community Group, and the now largely abandoned W3C User Agent Accessibility Guidelines (UAAG). We argue that the current overemphasis on source accessibility emerged only after W3C withdrew from writing normative requirements on user agents. We find more agreement between the OFS and the Capabilities report than commonly acknowledged, while concluding that both in-source and post-source remediations have essential roles to play. We urge a return to a comprehensive pipeline-oriented approach to accessibility standards and recommend updating UAAG 2.0.

Keywords: W3C · WAI · WCAG · UAAG · Standardization · User Agent Accessibility · Browser Accessibility · Post-Source · Overlays

1 Introduction

A widely held principle of web accessibility asserts that all remediations should be accomplished within the published codebase—that is, within the HTML, CSS, ARIA, and JavaScript source code published by the authors. Yet it is also widely acknowledged that various accessibility remediations are being performed in-process as web content is delivered to end users. For some, this is problematic. Others assert that "post-source" remediation is essential if the best possible accessibility experience is to be provided.

This paper examines the conceptual framework underlying this debate. We conclude that source-only approaches became uniquely emphasized only after the W3C withdrew from publishing normative accessibility requirements on user agents, and that this withdrawal has harmed accessibility. We urge a conscious return to approaches that provide guidance across the entire web content delivery pipeline.

K. Miesenberger et al. (Eds.): ICCHP 2026, LNCS 16867, pp. 573–580, 2027.
https://doi.org/10.1007/978-3-032-31308-9_68

2 Terminology

We adopt the term "post-source" from the A11yEdge Community Group Capabilities report. "Post-source" encompasses browser modifications, overlays, and other technologies applied in the process of delivering published web content to end users—providing a taxonomic term where no other serves quite as well.

3 Data Flow Model

Figure 1 illustrates the flow of digital content and code from origin to user. Entities in the diagram are drawn as clouds, except Source and User, which appear as rectangles to represent clearly bounded entities. Post-source modifications—whether Source-Authorized (e.g., CDN assets, third-party scripts) or User-Authorized (e.g., browser extensions, assistive technologies)—merge with the main data flow along the way. The user receives the final "mashed-up" digital content on their own devices.

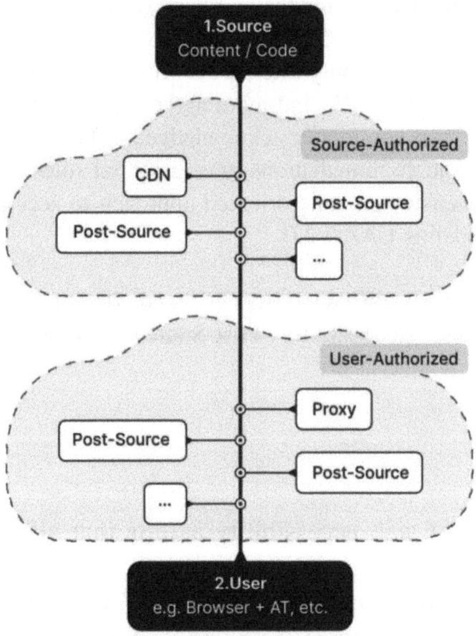

Fig. 1. Fundamental Diagram of Data Flow from Source to User, showing Source-Authorized and User-Authorized post-source modifications (A11yEdge CG). Diagram and explanatory text courtesy of Accessibilty Capabilities: Post-Source Code and Content [1]

4 Methodology

This paper examines three bodies of literature germane to the topic of post-source accessibility:

- The Overlay Fact Sheet (OFS), which has served as a prominent critic of post-source remediations, with over 1,000 signatories including well-known accessibility practitioners.

- The report "Accessibility Capabilities: Post-Source Code and Content," recently published by the Accessibility at the Edge (A11yEdge) Community Group (November 2025), which systematically evaluates post-source accessibility capabilities.
- The now largely neglected work of the W3C Web Accessibility Initiative (WAI) regarding user agent accessibility (UAAG 1.0 and UAAG 2.0).

Because our focus is conceptual frameworks, we necessarily rely on a priori reasoning. We assume that the end user should have access to all available technological tools to accomplish web content access and interaction in the manner they find most accommodating.

5 Source Document Analysis

5.1 WAI and User Agent Accessibility

It is unassailable that the W3C/WAI originally intended to publish normative recommendations regarding what we today call post-source accessibility remediation. We need look no further than the historical archive of chartered work in W3C to demonstrate this fact. W3C charters are formal directives voted by W3C membership. In December 1997 the User Agent Accessibility Guidelines Working Group was chartered [6] to accomplish the following mission:

"The working group will develop user interface guidelines that improve accessibility of WWW browsers, including improved navigation and orientation to information on WWW documents and scripting languages, and more flexible and enhanced presentation of document information to meeti the needs of specific disabilities. The goal is to develop guidelines that allow people with disabilities to have equal access to the able-bodied peers. The guidelines should support features that benefit both novice and skilled computer users with disabilities. The group will also develop technical guidelines to help WWW browser and assistive technology vendors be aware of the strategies that are available to achieve the user interface guidelines."

For its part the Web Content Accessibility Guidelines (WCAG) 1.0 (1999) explicitly contextualized itself as part of a series that includes UAAG 1.0—a full three years before UAAG 1.0 became a normative W3C recommendation in 2002 [3].

Unlike WCAG 1.0 which is now marked "superceded," UAAG 1.0 remains a normative W3C recommendation today. Its requirements remain instructive:

- Support input and output device-independence
- Ensure user access to all content
- Allow configuration to suppress content that may reduce accessibility
- Ensure user control of rendering
- Ensure user control of user interface behavior

These concerns remain central to both the Capabilities report and the OFS, 25 years later.

Work on a successor User Agent Accessibility Guidelines 2.0 was chartered [7] in December 2010. However, in a significant reorganization, UAAG 2.0 was published only as a Working Group Note in December 2015 [4] – not as a normative recommendation.

This represented a W3C retrenchment away from normative requirements on browsers. W3C stepped away entirely from developing normative accessibility recommendations on user agents.

Shortly thereafter–in the 2017–2019 time frame--the user agent industry transitioned away from primarily rendering static documents. Rather, browsers became full application platforms. While JavaScript had always been able to manipulate the DOM, browsers dramatically improved and standardized APIs that allowed large portions of the DOM to be dynamically rewritten in real time without full page reloads.

This major shift was driven by the rise of application-style web experiences like Gmail, React-based SPAs, mobile-first interfaces, and native-app expectations. Browsers optimized heavily for JavaScript execution, dynamic rendering, async updates, and stateful UI behavior through APIs such as the History API, Fetch API, MutationObserver, requestAnimationFrame, Shadow DOM, and Web Components.

Frameworks like React accelerated this shift by popularizing virtual DOM and component-driven rendering models, pushing browsers to optimize for continuous DOM mutation rather than static HTML pages.

Notably, UAAG 2.0 categorically states: "Web accessibility depends on both accessible user agents and accessible content." Yet while normative guidelines on content authoring continue to be developed, no industry effort has addressed normative guidance on user agents in over a decade, even as the toolkits capable of effecting powerful post-source accessibility transformation and personalization became the common technologies applied in serving other web use cases.

5.2 Post-Source Capabilities

Developed by leading engineers from three companies competing in post-source accessibility remediation, the Capabilities report [1] systematically explores approximately 75 atomic "capabilities"—predominantly features currently used in post-source remediation, with a handful of aspirational items. Each capability is analyzed according to a consistent schema, examining what source can do, what post-source benefits are possible, and the trade-offs between the two.

The report acknowledges that "WCAG remains the valid international consensus standard whether applied to source or post-source" accessibility evaluation. It cross-references WCAG Success Criteria extensively. Seventeen evaluated capabilities are assessed as providing no significant benefit when remediated post-source rather than in-source, yet many of these remain important for accessibility—meaning inadequate source implementations can still be corrected post-source.

The report emphasizes that modern web content is a "mashup" of multiple sources: third-party widgets, advertisements, and legacy components. A site owner cannot fix a third-party iframe's source code. Post-source "edge" layers can inject missing ARIA labels or repair keyboard focus paths across disparate sources. Among aspirational capabilities is cross-site consistency—particularly valuable for users with cognitive disabilities who benefit from consistent UI patterns across all sites they visit, as also described in UAAG 2.0 (Guidelines 1.2 and 1.4) [4].

Particularly notable is the report's argument regarding accessibility evaluation. Content providers can only estimate the end user's actual experience through limited testing scenarios. Edge technologies, by contrast, are positioned to identify, quantify, and report on accessibility challenges that end users actually encounter—at scale, and in real time. As the report notes, "only the edge knows for sure whether any particular web content experience can be called accessible."

5.3 The Overlay Fact Sheet (OFS)

The Overlay Fact Sheet styles itself as "a non-biased, community-driven, fact-based information sheet aimed at educating customers on web accessibility overlays." Its content is subject to revision without formal changelog, a point the OFS itself acknowledges in its GitHub README. Our analysis is therefore based on the OFS as published on 13 April 2026, and we do not consider positions that may have once appeared on OFS but have since been removed.

The OFS is primarily focused on injected UI elements such as pop-up control panels or "accessibility widgets." The Capabilities report explicitly does not advocate for such additional UI elements, noting that all evaluated capabilities "can be accomplished through appropriate post-source methods without recourse to pop-up control panels or accessibility widgets."

6 Analysis: Agreements and Disagreements

We find more points of agreement between the OFS and the Capabilities report than anticipated. The following itemizes key technological concerns from the OFS and assesses them against the Capabilities report and UAAG.

6.1 Strengths and Weaknesses of Overlays

The OFS prominently acknowledges that "overlays have both strengths and weaknesses," and notes that "a non-trivial array of accessibility problems can be repaired" by overlays that address the pages hosting them. This fundamental acknowledgement of benefit is often overlooked in discussions of the OFS's position.

6.2 Alternative Text

The OFS states that "automated application of text alternatives for images is not reliable." The Capabilities report agrees, noting that while source-provided alternative text is generally superior in quality, post-source methods can engage expert alt text authors and that there is "no longer any excuse for missing alt text." The report assesses alternative text as "among the most likely nodes on the accessibility tree to benefit from post-source automation" in many cases, particularly for static images. UAAG 1.0 focuses on ensuring users can discover and access alternative text, rather than on remediation of its content.

6.3 Form Controls

The OFS states that automated repair of field labels, error management, and focus control on forms is not reliable. The Capabilities report explicitly agrees: automation can detect and add missing labels by analyzing form structure, but ensuring contextually appropriate labels still requires human input. Post-source remediation may be the only viable option for third-party forms embedded in pages, where the site owner has no ability to modify source code.

6.4 Keyboard Access

The OFS states that "automated repair of keyboard access is not reliable." Again, the Capabilities report agrees, noting that comprehensive keyboard support may require significant restructuring of event handlers, and assessing this as not automatable today.

6.5 Component-Based Interfaces

The OFS raises the concern that modern JavaScript-based UI frameworks (React, Angular, Vue) may change page state independently of any overlay, rendering it unable to fix dynamically generated content. The Capabilities report agrees, noting that "automation can assist in identifying accessibility issues within components but cannot rebuild them."

6.6 Cross-Site Functionality

The OFS argues that features provided by an overlay widget are of limited use because "if those features were necessary to use the website, they'd be needed for all websites." Despite the logical limitations of this generalization, it does identify a real user need: consistent accessibility features across all sites. The Capabilities report addresses this in Sect. 6.2.1 ("Configure Once, Use Everywhere"), and UAAG 2.0 Guideline 1.7 addresses this through CSS override requirements. Importantly, it is a false dilemma to suggest a feature has no value unless it is available across the entire web.

6.7 Are Overlays Redundant?

The OFS argues that "overlay widgets are unnecessary" because end users already have necessary features available through built-in OS or assistive technology capabilities. Setting aside the logical problems with this generalization, Two considerations merit further research:

1. If post-source remediations impose unwanted changes on users, the Capabilities report supports user control in Sect. 4.8 "Reset All Personalizations", though this capability is currently aspirational.
2. A mechanism to auto-disable overlay widgets when the user already has appropriate assistive technology installed warrants investigation in W3C. Perhaps we could technologically support keeping some users from stumbling even while supporting others who might benefit.

7 Conclusions and Recommendations

Post-source accessibility remediation has a deep history beginning from the earliest days of web accessibility work. The current overemphasis on in-source remediation is not an inevitable or principled outcome—it emerged from a specific historical moment in which W3C withdrew from publishing normative guidance for user agents.

Our analysis yields the following recommendations:

- Return to the historical conceptual framework for web accessibility to again encompass the complete content delivery pipeline, from source through post-source processing to the user.
- Acknowledgement the inherent inequity in imposing mandatory regulation and standardization on content creation but not on content consumption.
- Recognize that accessibility standards applying only to content authoring and publication can leave significant accessibility gains unrealized.
- Consider updating UAAG 2.0 at W3C, even if it can only be an updated Note-track publication, to guide the application of post-source technologies in serving accessibility use cases.
- Explore additional opportunities within and outside of W3C to enhance post-source accessibility standardizations such as the Accessibility Compat Data project (8) hosted on github.
- Pursue collaborative research in W3C on quantifying the real-world benefit of post-source accessibility features, including mechanisms that intelligently defer to users' existing assistive technologies.

Source and post-source accessibility need not be adversaries. Both serve the same goal: ensuring that every user can perceive, operate, understand, and robustly interact with web content. A principled, pipeline-aware approach to accessibility standards is the most promising path toward achieving that goal.

References

1. A11yEdge Community Group: Accessibility Capabilities: Post-Source Code and Content. W3C Community Group Report (2025). https://bit.ly/a11yedge
2. W3C: Web Content Accessibility Guidelines (WCAG) 1.0. W3C Recommendation (1999). https://www.w3.org/TR/WCAG10/
3. Jacobs, I., Gunderson, J., Hansen, E. (eds.): User Agent Accessibility Guidelines (UAAG) 1.0. W3C Recommendation (2002). https://www.w3.org/TR/UAAG10/
4. Allan, J., Kirkpatrick, A., Henry, S.L. (eds.): User Agent Accessibility Guidelines (UAAG) 2.0. W3C Working Group Note (2015). https://www.w3.org/TR/UAAG20/
5. Groves, K. et al.: Overlay Fact Sheet. https://overlayfactsheet.com/. Last accessed 13 Apr 2026
6. User Agent Accessibility Guidelines Working Group Charter (1997). https://www.w3.org/WAI/UA/charter
7. User Agent Accessibility Guidelines (2.0) Working Group Charter (2010). https://www.w3.org/WAI/UA/2010/uawg_charter.html
8. Odelola, L., et al.: Accessibility Compat Data. https://github.com/lolaslab/accessibility-compat-data/tree/master

Improving the Accessibility of Web Tables for Magnifier Users with Annotations and Crumbs

Frode Eika Sandnes[1(✉)], Nusrat Akter[1], and I. Scott MacKenzie[2]

[1] Oslo Metropolitan University, 0130 Oslo, Norway
frodes@oslomet.no
[2] York University, Toronto, ON, Canada
mack@yorku.ca

Abstract. Tables on the web are difficult to access with magnification. When magnified, only a portion of the table is visible. Consequently, users must scroll (or pan) around the table to access its cells which can be disorientating. This study explores visual and interactive mechanisms for table navigation. Two table navigation support mechanisms, annotations and crumbs, were implemented and evaluated in a user study with 30 participants. Results show that visually embellished tables improved access compared to plain tables. Annotating cells with header information led to the least movement and highest preference ratings, while highlighting visited table cells using crumbs gave the highest success rate but lower ratings. Combining several mechanisms may help make tables more accessible to magnifier users.

Keywords: Magnification · Accessible Tables · Accessible Web · Fixed Headers · Low Vision

1 Introduction

Tables provide detailed reference material in documents. On the web, tables are especially useful as they can update in real-time to reflect changes and new information. Common table use-cases include airport departure information, product details, food menus, financial records, and sports results. Tables can be structured in a variety of ways. This study assumes that tables follow the common convention where each item appears on a separate row, and that the attributes or characteristics of items are provided in columns.

Accessing large tables is cognitively straining and especially challenging for individuals with reduced vision. Most discussion on table accessibility for magnifier users takes place among practitioners and is found in discussion forums and blogs. Some argue that the so-called "fixed" table header, also referred to as "sticky" table header, is a CSS accessibility feature (e.g., the IT department at Stanford University [1]), but we are unaware of any empirical research studying this. The fixed header mechanism

K. Miesenberger et al. (Eds.): ICCHP 2026, LNCS 16867, pp. 581–591, 2027.
https://doi.org/10.1007/978-3-032-31308-9_69

ensures that header rows are visible regardless of which cell is highlighted. When viewing tables without magnification, fixed table headers are useful to avoid scrolling back to view the contents of the corresponding column or row headers. However, fixed or sticky content is problematic in several web-magnification use cases [2]. Doing a simple test confirms that with magnification, fixed table headers compete with cells for visible viewport real estate. With high magnification, fixed table headers obstruct cell contents altogether. In fact, W3C [3] states that this feature should only be used if there is enough space available.

Magnification users typically have reduced vision, yet prefer visual information as opposed to audio or tactile modalities. For web interaction, many users rely on browser magnification. For example, Chrome, Edge, and Firefox currently allow 500% magnification. A survey by the Institute for Disability Research, Policy, and Practice [4] showed that about 30% of the magnification users utilized 200–400% browser magnification, 10% relied on magnifications in the range 400–600%, and 8% relied on magnification levels greater than 600%. Modern webpages are responsive, meaning that text is reflowed to fit the viewport. However, a table is two-dimensional and cannot reflow without losing structural information. While non-magnification users often view the entire table on the display, a magnifier user can only view a small rectangular window into the table, sometimes only a few cells at a time. The user must scroll through the table to access its content. This is known as the *keyhole effect*.

Our study addresses three challenges in accessing tables through a narrow viewport. First, the user does not know a cell's row or column. For example, if a cell contains "5," the users do not know to what 5 refers. Second, when seeing only a portion of a table it is difficult for the viewer to orient and navigate effectively. Third, it is hard to compare items in different parts of a table without noting down the individual values. Say, for instance, to compare a product at the top of the table with another at the bottom, the user must revisit the first one after having viewed the second.

Obviously, the ease of accessing tables depends on the display dimensions. Magnification users often need to magnify a table even on a large desktop display. A non-magnification user may experience a similar situation if viewing a complex table on a smartphone with a small form factor. In such situations, the table is too wide to fit in the viewport, requiring the user to view content by sideways scrolling or panning operations. In other words, the mechanisms explored herein are not only useful for magnification users, but are relevant for all visually oriented users.

2 Related Work

Unlike general screen magnifiers, web browsing with magnification is aided by so-called responsiveness, meaning that web content adapts to fit the viewport, thereby eliminating, or greatly reducing, horizontal scrolling. Users can therefore navigate by vertical scrolling only [5]. Web content may include cards, images, or user interface controls, but text is common and which is reflowed to fit the viewport (see for instance WCAG success criterion 1.4.10). It is also possible to reflow bitmap text in scanned documents [6] and images of text [7]. Images on the other hand, cannot be reflowed, albeit use of neural networks to identify areas of interest such as faces in a group photo have been explored [8]. However, tables pose a particular challenge as they cannot be reflowed in the same manner as text, nor is it trivial to predict which cells are of particular interest.

Several voices point out that accessible tables receive little research attention [9]. Most literature on table accessibility focuses on referencing tables with screen readers, and most screen reader products have table viewing modes to support the inspection of contents. For example, Wang et al. [10] studied how screen reader users access tabular data. Prakash et al. [11] addressed the problem screen readers experience when readers jump between related elements on a webpage. Venkatraman et al. [12] addressed the problems of reading food menus without semantic table structures with screen readers. Filepp et al. [13] described an approach of transforming tables into synthetic audio descriptions. Wang et al. [14] described an approach where table content is are accessed through transformations involving grouping of cells, marking empty cells as empty, splitting cells spanning several columns or rows, and splitting complex tables into several smaller tables. Mo et al. [15] proposed an approach for making tables rendered as images accessible. Although a diminishing practice, tables were previously often used to control page layouts. Clearly, using tables for this non-intended purpose results in several accessibility issues [16].

The accessibility of tables for magnification users has received much less attention. Proposals include space compaction [17] and Lee et al.'s web table extension [18] allowing the user to configure which columns to display, adjust the width of the columns, and configure visual properties such as text size. In this work, a different approach is taken: Instead of asking the user to configure the viewing, the information needs of the user are estimated dynamically by observing the user's exploration of the table.

Zebra stripes are often used both online and in print with the intention to simplify navigation through large tables, in which alternating rows, or row groups are given different background color shades. Zebra stripes can also work with alternating columns or column groups, or both rows and columns. Enders et al. [19] conducted a controlled experiment to evaluate zebra stripes, but were unable to observe any effects.

3 Table Embellishments

The work explored herein assumes that the user views a table with magnification. Moreover, cells viewed longer are likely of greater interest than cells viewed briefly. Two mechanisms for facilitating table referencing through small viewports are explored, namely cell annotations and table crumbs.

Cell annotation (Fig. 1) is a simple mechanism inspired by the table viewing mode in screen readers, where cell content is combined with the column and row header values, making it easier for the user to understand the content of the cell. To transfer this mechanism to the table view, the column and row header are shown around (top and right) the cell in view (beneath the cursor). It is like a fixed table header, but unlike fixed table headers that show all the headers, the annotation only shows the header for the current cell. Moreover, to minimize obstruction, the header labels are placed beside the cell and between rows.

Table crumbs (Fig. 2) are inspired by breadcrumbs and involve detecting and highlighting the rows and columns viewed by the user, that is, the corresponding cells viewed

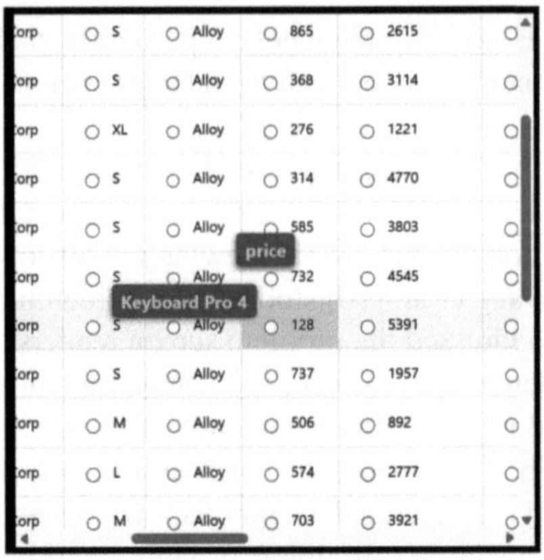

Fig. 1. Annotation

for a duration beyond a threshold. Visited columns are highlighted in red, visited rows in green, and visited cells in yellow. To be considered "visited," we used a minimum dwell time of 500 ms. To signal cell importance, highlighting intensity increases with the cell dwell time. That is, a cell viewed longer is considered more important.

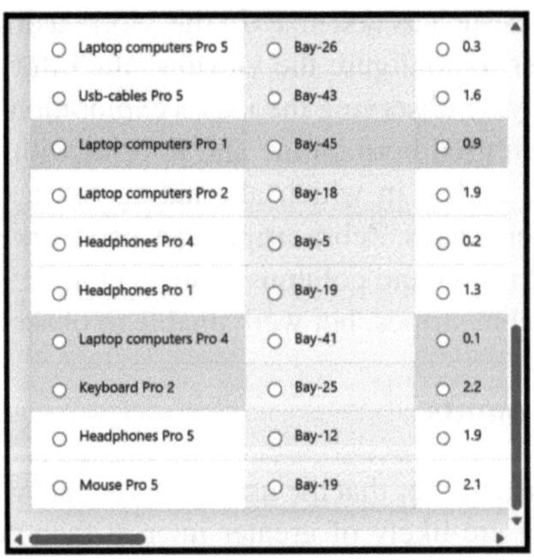

Fig. 2. Crumbs

We also explored a third concept, table snippets (Fig. 3). Table snippets are subsets of the table comprising the cells previously viewed. Table snippets appear as popups when the user rests on a cell. The snippets are generated by analyzing the history of visited cells. First, the cells were sorted in descending order on column frequency. That is, if the user most frequently views price, the price items are shown. These are shown in the original order of occurrence. Clearly, the popup grows quickly and cannot simultaneously display all items. A snippet consumes real estate in the viewport and consequently makes table access more difficult. We therefore did not explore this embellishment further.

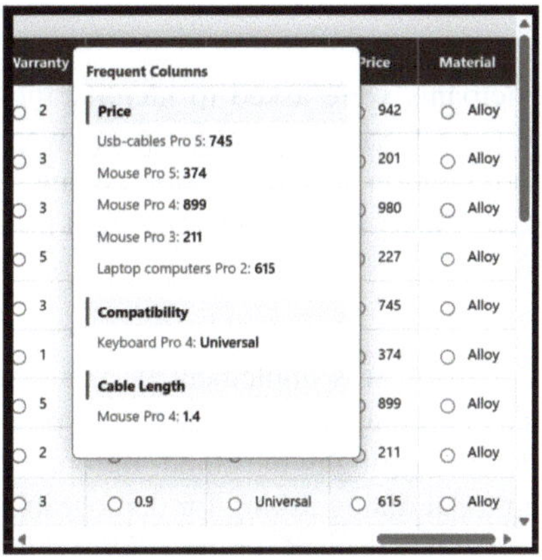

Fig. 3. Snippet

Our table embellishment prototypes were implemented in JavaScript by inspecting and modifying the DOM (document object model). We envisage two pragmatic modes of deployment. A page owner can enable the proposed mechanism by including our JavaScript library, or the user can activate the functionality through a bookmarklet. The code, bookmarklets, and a live demo is available at https://github.com/frode-sandnes/table-magnify-exp-2026.

4 Method

4.1 Participants

Thirty participants were recruited from the international student population at the local university. Of these, 14 identified as male and 16 identified as female. The age breakdown was 83.3% between 20–29 years, 10% between 30–39 years, and 6.7% between 10–19 years. None of the participants reported having reduced vision or dyscalculia. All participants were non-native English speakers.

4.2 Materials

A unique table was randomly assigned to each trial. They contained 25 computer-related products from five product categories. For each product the table listed 15 attributes including product numbers, color, price, etc. Both the products and the attributes were shuffled into random order. Moreover, the cell contents, such as prices, were randomized. All the material was presented in English. The rendered tables were approximately 1800 CSS pixels wide and 1133 CSS pixels tall. Although there were more rows than columns, the table widths became larger than the table heights because the cell contents spanned horizontally.

4.3 Task

During each trial the participants were asked to identify the product within a given product category with the lowest price. The participants were asked to indicate their answer by clicking on a radio button within the form. When satisfied with the answer, the participants were clicked "Next" to proceed to the next trial.

4.4 Equipment

A web-based experiment platform was implemented. The platform managed the trial presentation order, solicited demographic information and preference ratings, collected comments, and performed data logging in the cloud. Before the experiment started, the user was presented with a modal dialog asking for demographic information. For each trial, the table was displayed within a small iFrame (475 × 475 CSS pixels) of the main page with a Next button beside the iFrame to simulate the keyhole effect experienced by magnifier users. Preference ratings were collected using a 7-item Likert scale presented as a modal dialog after each trial in response to the prompt "How much did you like to use this table?" The tests were run with a screen resolution of 2940 × 1912 physical pixels and a virtual resolution of 1470 × 956 CSS pixels. Hence, the default zoom level was 200%.

4.5 Procedure

Participants were tested individually and in person, supervised by one of the authors. They were first briefed about the experiment, its purpose, and their rights, including the freedom to withdraw from the experiment at any time. Each participant completed the tasks using the experimenter's laptop computer to keep the experimental conditions constant. The browser zoom level was restored to the original state before each session. Comments and observations of unexpected events were noted by the experimenter during each session. At the end of each session, participants were also invited to provide verbal feedback to elaborate on their written feedback.

The experiment was anonymous and no personal or sensitive information was collected. Consequently, no data handling permissions were collected as per the authors' institutional research ethics policy.

4.6 Design

A groups experiment was designed with *embellishment* as a within-groups independent variable. Embellishment had three levels, namely *plain* (control), *annotate,* and *crumbs.* A 3 × 3 Latin square was used to counterbalance the three tasks and reduce order effects. The dependent variables included task completion time (seconds), task completion success rates (%), subjective ratings (7-item Likert scales), number of zoom operations, mouse movement distances (CSS pixels), horizontal and vertical scroll distances (CSS pixels, and counts for the horizontal and vertical scroll turns. Turn counts are the number of times a participant changes scroll direction (from left to right, or vice versa). Each task was repeated twice with the first repetition treated as training. Only the measurements of the second repetition were used in the analysis. Each participant conducted six trials, which took between 10 and 15 min to complete.

5 Results

The results showed that annotate exhibited the shortest task-completion time ($M = 35.8$, $SD = 17.4$), followed by plain ($M = 45.5$, $SD = 32.9$) and crumbs ($M = 58.5$, $SD = 44.5$) An ANOVA confirms that the task completion times are statistically different ($F(2, 54) = 4.297$, $p = .019$, $\omega 2 = 0.067$). A post hoc test shows that annotate and crumbs are significantly different. A QQ plot showed that the data are slightly skewed.

Table 1 lists the task completion success rates. Crumbs were associated with the highest success rate (70%) and plain the lowest success rate (60%). Moreover, crumbs had the highest rate of answers being in the correct column (96.7%), while plain had the lowest success rate of participants selecting the correct category. Participants made marginally more mistakes while selecting the correct row than selecting the right column.

Table 1. Task completion success rates (correct cell, category, and column).

Embellishment	Cell	Category	Column
Plain	60.0%	76.7%	93.3%
Annotate	66.7%	83.3%	93.3%
Crumbs	70.0%	83.3%	96.7%

Figure 4 shows a diverging stacked bar graph of participant responses to the question "How much did you like to use this table?". Annotate was rated the highest ($M = 4.9$, $SD = 1.8$), followed by crumbs ($M = 2.9$, $SD = 1.4$), and plain ($M = 2.6$, $SD = 1.6$) the lowest. A Friedman test showed a significant difference ($X^2(2) = 26.72$, $p < .001$, $W = 0.445$) and Conover post-hoc tests showed that annotate were different from both plain and crumbs, but plain and crumbs were not significantly different.

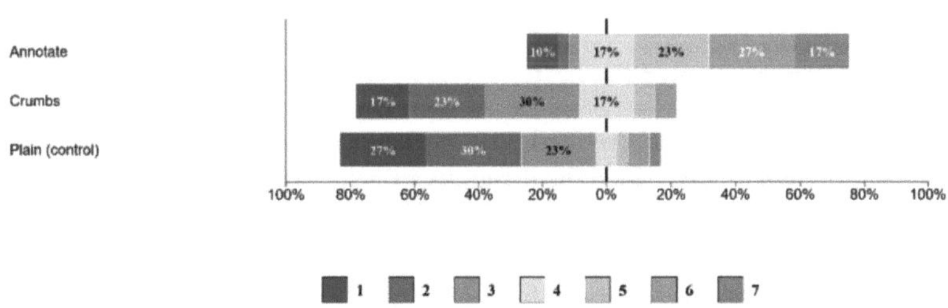

Fig. 4. Embellishment rating distributions

Annotate had the shortest total mouse movement distances and crumbs the longest.

Annotate had the shortest total mouse movement distances ($M = 5535$, $SD = 2188$), followed by plain ($M = 8397$, $SD = 6626$), and crumbs ($M = 9690$, $SD = 6566$). There was a significant difference ($F(2, 54) = 5.121$, $p = .009$, $\omega^2 = 0.072$). A post hoc test shows that annotate was different from crumbs.

Figure 5 shows the horizontal and vertical scroll distances. An ANOVA indicates a significant difference in scroll distance across embellishments ($F(2, 54) = 8.463$, $p < .001$, $\omega^2 = 0.144$), and direction ($F(1, 27) = 17.01$, $p < .001$, $\omega^2 = 0.190$); that is, vertical versus horizontal scroll. Post hoc testing showed that annotate was significantly different from both plain and crumbs, while crumbs and plain were not different. Annotate exhibited the shortest total scroll distance. Moreover, for annotate there was no difference between the vertical and horizontal scroll distance, while the horizontal scroll distances were significantly longer for both plain and crumbs.

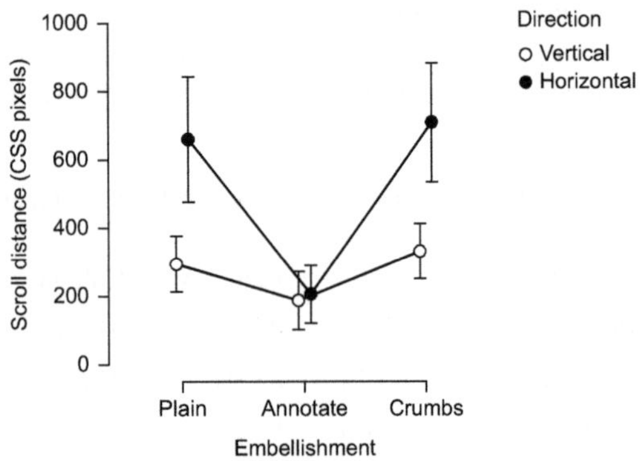

Fig. 5. Mean horizontal and vertical scrolling distances. Error bars show 95% CI.

Similar observations were made for the number of scroll turns. Scrolling turns varied significantly across both the embellishments ($F(1.644, 44.39) = 9.528$, $p < .001$, $\omega^2 = 0.165$) and direction ($F(1, 27) = 31.90$, $p < .001$, $\omega^2 = 0.218$). Note that a Greenhouse Geisser correction was used since a Mauchly test reported a deviation from sphericity. Again, annotate had the fewest turns. For plain and crumbs there were more horizontal turns than vertical turns. None of the participants used the browser zoom.

5.1 Written Comments and Participant Observations

Two thirds of the participants provided written feedback on the experiment after completing the tasks. Several described the difficulty of accessing the table through the "tiny window" and the inconvenience of scrolling back and forth to find the price. It was commented that navigation was easier when the price was closer to the product name. Several participants preferred annotate because it revealed information about the current cell. One acknowledged that annotate was probably the most efficient, yet still preferred the plain table. Several participants indicated they did not understand the purpose of crumbs and the meaning of the colors, while two expressed that they found it useful. Others commented that the changing colors were confusing. Several participants were negative to the color choices, especially the colors used with annotate (yellow text on a saturated magenta background). One participant described the colors as "jarring".

The written feedback is consistent with the verbal comments and observations of the experimenter during testing. Hence, most participants expressed a more positive impression of annotate, and the most negative impression of plain. We also observed that some participants selected the product instead of the price, or vice versa, as they were either in a hurry or did not fully understand the task.

6 Discussion

The subjective ratings, qualitative feedback and participant observations show that annotate was the preferred embellishment. Indeed, the information about the currently active cell helped participants access the table. This also manifested itself in fewer mouse movements and less scrolling across the table as the participants did not have to go back and forth to find which column and row a particular cell was connected to. Consequently, with less movement, the corresponding task completion times were shorter. Task success was only marginally higher with annotate than with crumbs and plain. Since the tables were wide, there were more horizontal movements than vertical movements.

The preference for annotating is not aligned with the success rates observed. Crumbs were associated with a higher success rate than both annotate and plain, suggesting that it is a more reliable embellishment even though users favored annotate. It would therefore have been interesting to explore if the combination of annotate and plain would reap the perceived comfort of annotate and the possible task reliability of crumbs.

Although the rating for annotate ($M = 4.9$) is on the positive side of the scale, it is well below 7, the highest rating. This suggests that there is room for improvement in realizing comfortable and accessible table access mechanisms.

The results for crumbs were varied. A small portion of the participants determined how to exploit the visual cues, while most did not. Unlike annotate, which can be used without training, crumbs may require training or experience to be fully utilized. For instance, one coping strategy could be to traverse the columns and rows, respectively, and "mark" the respective rows and columns of interest, and later scan to the intersection points. It seems that the use of dwell-times to select rows, columns, and cells may be more confusing than useful. Perhaps another strategy is to have users explicitly selects rows, columns or cells. This would indeed be consistent with the accessibility principle that interactions should not be time dependent.

The fact that no participants used the zoom functionality could indicate that they were not magnifier users, as expert magnification users tend to use zoom controls actively to switch between overviews and details [20].

6.1 Limitations

The users were given two rounds for each embellishment; subsequent rounds are likely to result in learning and development of more sophisticated coping strategies. Our setup could result in potential carryover effects, which we were unable to test for as the experimentation resulted in unbalanced distribution of presentation orders, giving unequal variances. For example, the group that started with crumbs generally took longer for all tasks compared to those who started with plain and annotate, as they had to handle both the new task and the unfamiliar embellishment. Those who started with plain, generally completed the task quicker as the participants gradually learned to handle the task, while the lowest individual task completion times (outliers) were observed for the group that started with annotate. In hindsight, six groups representing all the embellishment permutations should have been used instead of the Latin square, alternatively a between-groups design should have been used to eliminate carry-over effects.

It could also be relevant to follow participants over time to get insight into these coping strategies, as well as to recruit expert magnification users as they may have already developed table access strategies.

Several participants reacted negatively to the colors, suggesting that either more moderate colors should have been selected or explicit explanations given on the meaning of the colors.

7 Conclusions

Two mechanisms for improving access to large tables on the web with magnification were explored, namely annotate and crumbs. Results show that both mechanisms result in shorter task completion times, higher success, higher ratings, and fewer movements. The annotate embellishment shares similarities with the fixed table header mechanism mentioned in W3C technical documentation. Unlike the fixed table header mechanism, which fills the viewport with header information, the annotate mechanism only shows header information for the active table cell. To the best of our knowledge, there is no empirical knowledge in support of the fixed table header mechanism. Hence, one may argue that our results provide empirical evidence in support of fixed table headers in use-cases where there is sufficient space in the viewport to show both headers and table contents. Each mechanism was treated separately in the user study. However, in practice one may combine the two mechanisms to reap the benefits of both. Prototype bookmarklets are available on the project GitHub repository, demonstrating how the technique can be deployed on arbitrary websites.

References

1. Stanford University: Accessible table with fixed "sticky" headers (2023). Accessed 11 Apr 2026. https://uit.stanford.edu/accessibility/concepts/tables/sticky-headers
2. Sandnes, F.E.: "Consent notices are obstructing my view": viewing sticky elements on responsive websites under the magnifying glass. Displays **81**, 102579 (2024)
3. W3C (2026). Technique C34: Using media queries to un-fixing sticky headers/footers. Accessed 11 Apr 2026. https://www.w3.org/WAI/WCAG21/Techniques/css/C34
4. WebAIM: Survey of users with low vision #2. Institute for disability research, policy, and practice (2018). Accessed 11 Apr 2026. https://webaim.org/projects/lowvisionsurvey2/
5. Hallett, E.C., et al.: The usability of magnification methods: a comparative study between screen magnifiers and responsive web design. In: International Conference on Human Interface and the Management of Information, pp. 181–189. Cham: Springer (2015)
6. Sandnes, F.E.: Lost in OCR-Translation: pixel-based text reflow to the rescue: magnification of archival raster image documents in the browser without horizontal scrolling. In: Proceedings of the 15th International Conference on PErvasive Technologies Related to Assistive Environments, pp. 500–506, New York, ACM (2022)

7. Sandnes, F.E., Murad, N., Khaled, M., El Nassani, F.: A smart handheld magnifier for reflowing printed text notices in public spaces. Disabil. Rehabil. Assist. Technol. **19**(8), 3153–3165 (2024)
8. Sandnes, F.E.: Towards "Image Reflow" on the web: avoiding excessive panning of magnified images by multiplexing automatically cropped regions of interest. In: IFIP Conference on Human-Computer Interaction, pp. 315–319. Cham: Springer (2023)
9. Haider, W., Yesilada, Y.: Tables on the web accessible? Unfortunately not!. In: Proceedings of the 17th International Web for All Conference, pp. 1–5, New York, ACM (2020)
10. Wang, Y., Srinivasan, A., Kim, Y.S.: Enabling tabular data exploration for blind and low-vision users. In: Proceedings of the 2024 ACM Designing Interactive Systems Conference, pp. 1218–1233, New York, ACM (2024)
11. Prakash, Y., Nayak, A.K., Sunkara, M., Jayarathna, S., Lee, H.N., Ashok, V.: All in one place: ensuring usable access to online shopping items for blind users. Proc. ACM Hum.-Comput. Inter. **8**(EICS), 1–25 (2024)
12. Venkatraman, N., Kolgar Nayak, A., Dahal, S., Prakash, Y., Lee, H.N., Ashok, V.: Access-Menu: enhancing usability of online restaurant menus for screen reader users. In: Proceedings of the 22nd International Web for All Conference, pp. 36–47, New York, ACM (2025)
13. Filepp, R., Challenger, J., Rosu, D.: Improving the accessibility of aurally rendered html tables. In: Proceedings of the Fifth International ACM Conference on Assistive Technologies, pp. 9–16, New York, ACM (2002)
14. Wang, Y., Wang, R., Jung, C., Kim, Y.S.: What makes web data tables accessible? Insights and a tool for rendering accessible tables for people with visual impairments. In: Proceedings of the 2022 CHI Conference on Human Factors in Computing Systems, pp. 1–20, New York, ACM (2022)
15. Mo, Y., et al.: TableNarrator: making image tables accessible to blind and low vision people. In: Proceedings of the 2025 CHI Conference on Human Factors in Computing Systems, pp. 1–17, ACM (2025)
16. Johnson, M.A., Cagle, L.E.: Designing accessible tables: when technical communication competencies come into conflict. Commun. Des. Q. **13**(1), 1–14 (2025)
17. Islam, M.T., Billah, S.M.: SpaceX mag: an automatic, scalable, and rapid space compactor for optimizing smartphone app interfaces for low-vision users. Proc. ACM Interact. Mobile Wearable Ubiquitous Technol. **7**(2), 1–36 (2023)
18. Lee, H.N., Ashok, V.: Customizable tabular access to web data records for convenient low-vision screen magnifier interaction. ACM Trans. Accessible Comput. (TACCESS) **15**(2), 1–22 (2022)
19. Enders, J.: Zebra striping: does it really help? In: Proceedings of the 19th Australasian Conference on Computer-Human Interaction, pp. 319–322, (2007)
20. Sandnes, F.E.: Interactive magnification for low-vision users. In: Handbook of Human Computer Interaction, pp. 1–23, Cham, Springer (2025)

Reciprocal Support for Accessible Live Events: Field Evaluation of a Real-Time Timeline Web App for DHH/BLV and All Participants

Yuhki Shiraishi[1(✉)], Ying Zhong[1], Makoto Kobayashi[2], Daisuke Wakatsuki[1], Takuya Suzuki[1], Takeaki Shionome[3], and Rumi Hiraga[1]

[1] Faculty of Industrial Technology,Tsukuba University of Technology,Tsukuba, Ibaraki 305-8520, Japan
{yuhkis,ying,waka,suzukit,rhiraga}@a.tsukuba-tech.ac.jp

[2] Faculty of Health Sciences,Tsukuba University of Technology,Tsukuba, Ibaraki 305-8521, Japan
koba@cs.k.tsukuba-tech.ac.jp

[3] Faculty of Science and Engineering,Teikyo University,Utsunomiya, Tochigi 320-8551, Japan
shionome.takeaki.hy@teikyo-u.ac.jp
https://www.iseee.info

Abstract. Live events convey critical information through auditory announcements and rapidly changing situational cues, creating accessibility barriers for Deaf and hard of hearing (DHH) and blind or low vision (BLV) spectators. Accessibility therefore requires both alternative descriptions and selective access to key updates in high-volume streams. This selectivity reduces reading burden for DHH and can also support BLV use when text-based updates and media descriptions are available. We propose a *reciprocal accessibility* model in which any participant can alternate between contributing and benefiting from accessibility-relevant information. Building on pilot studies of a real-time timeline web application, we refined the system based on stakeholder feedback.

We evaluated the updated system in situ during Deaflympics 2025 across three team-competition days. DHH/BLV participants posted and read updates; deaf badminton players served as designated commentators, providing commentary-tagged explanations. Across all questionnaire responses ($N = 21$; DHH responses: 18; BLV responses: 3), SUS averaged 72.1 ($SD = 14.9$) and overall experience 4.67/5 ($SD = 0.66$). Supplementary surveys at a large public exposition ($N = 35$) yielded mean experience 4.83/5 ($SD = 0.45$). These deployments provide field evidence that reciprocal, role-switching information sharing can complement professional services in time-critical live events.

Keywords: Information Accessibility · Information Support · Web Application · Deaf and Hard of Hearing · Blind and Low Vision

K. Miesenberger et al. (Eds.): ICCHP 2026, LNCS 16867, pp. 592–599, 2027.
https://doi.org/10.1007/978-3-032-31308-9_70

1 Introduction

Large-scale public events (e.g., sports tournaments, ceremonies, and expositions) rely on public-address announcements and real-time situational cues. For DHH spectators, missing announcements and in-venue explanations can reduce understanding and enjoyment. For BLV spectators, a lack of accessible alternatives to visual cues can similarly constrain participation. While professional captioning and human support are effective, they are difficult to scale to all venues and ad-hoc situations. Importantly, although DHH and BLV stakeholders are primary beneficiaries and evaluators in this work, the system is intentionally designed to be useful for all spectators: people may alternate between providing and receiving support depending on momentary needs, attention, and context.

In this paper, we use *accessibility* to denote UI- and content-level barrier reduction (e.g., WCAG-oriented design and alternative descriptions [1]), *inclusion* to denote the ability for diverse participants to engage in the event experience, and *mutual support* to denote the reciprocal, role-switching nature of participation. We position *reciprocal accessibility* as a shift from one-way service delivery to participation-centric, crowd-mediated support.

To complement human services, we have developed an accessible real-time timeline web application that enables spectators and/or support staff to share event information as short posts (text and media) that are instantly delivered to participants in the same event room. The system provides tag- and filter-based access to information and supports automatic augmentation of user-generated content (e.g., speech recognition or image understanding) to improve accessibility.

In prior pilot studies of our system, DHH participants reported SUS scores in the low-70 s in a sports-viewing setting and in the mid-50 s in a museum context, highlighting learnability issues and motivating tutorial support and usability refinement [2]. Motivated by these findings, we report stakeholder-driven redesign and field evaluation at a major international event.

Research Questions. We ask whether a reciprocal real-time timeline web app can enable DHH and BLV participants to both contribute accessibility-relevant information and benefit from it in live-event settings with acceptable usability and perceived usefulness (**RQ1**), and how deployment context and lightweight role orchestration shape perceived value and remaining barriers (**RQ2**).

Contributions. We contribute:

1. **Operationalization:** a zero-install timeline web app implementing stakeholder-derived low-effort contribution, personalization, and scoped access for role-switching participation.
2. **Field evidence:** Deaflympics 2025 in-situ deployment suggests DHH/BLV spectators can both contribute and benefit, with acceptable usability and high usefulness in time-critical settings.
3. **Broader acceptance:** exposition surveys (N=35) indicate positive reception by general visitors, suggesting applicability beyond DHH/BLV-focused deployments.

2 State of the Art

Access services for DHH and BLV people in live events commonly include captioning, interpreting, assistive listening, accessible signage, staff-based guidance, and remote assistance. However, venue-wide coverage and responsiveness remain challenging under time pressure and staffing constraints. Research on captions in sports broadcasting has highlighted benefits and persistent issues such as delay and interference with core content [3]. Participatory and human-centered design practices (e.g., ISO 9241-210) are broadly recommended for assistive technology, as needs vary across communication preferences, sensory profiles, and contexts [4]. Recent reviews also argue that standards such as WCAG do not fully address DHH-specific communication needs or context-specific implementation challenges [11].

For BLV and deafblind users, communication and access barriers are often compounded by sequential access constraints and combined sensory demands. Prior reviews and intervention studies on communication and dual sensory loss emphasize individualized access strategies, environmental adaptation, and communication support [7,8]. Commercial services such as Aira Explorer and Samsung Good Vibes illustrate one-to-one remote visual interpreting or direct communication support, but not reciprocal, many-to-many participation in live-event settings [9,10].

Real-time, mobile-accessible systems can complement existing services by enabling rapid, localized information sharing. Usability is often quantified using the System Usability Scale (SUS) [5]. Building on prior work in crowdsourcing and real-time information support [6], we emphasize a *reciprocal accessibility* framing in which inclusion is achieved through mutual, role-switching participation. Field evidence for reciprocal, role-switching participation with lightweight role orchestration in large-scale live events remains limited; we address this gap through in-situ evaluation at Deaflympics 2025.

3 Methodology

3.1 System Overview

The proposed system is a browser-based web application (smartphone/PC) that provides:

- **Real-time timeline + filtering:** push-updated posts with tag/keyword filters and multi-panel views.
- **Tagged contribution:** text/media posts with tags (e.g., commentary, score, question) plus low-effort templates/emoji reactions.
- **Progressive and scoped access:** zero-install browser use; no account needed for viewing/text posts; accounts only for media uploads; *floors* (event containers) with multiple *rooms* (sessions) and URL-based access (incl. hidden floors/rooms) to manage information spread.
- **LLM-based augmentation:** optional image/video/audio/environmental-sound to text, and editable alternative descriptions.

In practice, DHH users primarily benefit from real-time text/commentary when announcements are inaccessible. BLV participants used the same browser-based system in the field deployment, and their feedback highlighted both the value of text-based updates and media descriptions and the remaining limitations of the current system (Fig. 1).

Fig. 1. Conceptual overview of the real-time timeline web app for reciprocal support in live events.

3.2 Field Deployments

Deaflympics 2025 field evaluation. We conducted in-situ deployment during Deaflympics 2025 in two contexts:

- **Badminton matches:** conducted in late November 2025 (three consecutive team-competition days); $N = 15$ questionnaire responses (DHH: $N = 12$, BLV: $N = 3$).
- **Opening/closing ceremonies:** $N = 6$ questionnaire responses (DHH: $N = 6$); the opening and closing ceremonies (mid/late Nov 2025) were evaluated while participants followed the event via an official live stream.

Questionnaires were collected separately for each event day; these counts therefore refer to responses rather than unique individuals, and repeat responses across days are possible.

Role-Based Participation (Designated Commentators). In addition to general posts by DHH/BLV participants, we invited deaf badminton players to act as designated commentators. They posted short explanations of game flow and

Table 1. Stakeholder-driven improvements implemented after the pilot studies.

Improvement theme	Implementation in the updated system
Onboarding/registration	Simplified registration via federated login and fewer first-use steps
Tutorial/learnability	Short tutorial videos and a concise manual for self-paced learning
Multimodal augmentation	Expanded LLM-based media augmentation (image/video/audio-to-text) for accessible alternative descriptions
Context awareness	Environmental sound recognition for textual descriptions of non-speech sounds (e.g., crowd reactions)
Low-effort contribution	Templates and emoji/quick reactions for fast posting under time pressure
Personalization/filtering	Advanced filtering and display settings (e.g., score- or substitution-focused panels and readability presets)
UI refinements	Incremental UI and consistency fixes based on pilot feedback

salient situations using the *commentary* tag, which readers accessed via a dedicated filtered panel. This lightweight orchestration addresses the need for structured narration in fast-paced sports timelines (Table 1).

Participants used their own devices (smartphones and one PC in badminton) via a standard web browser. The deployment covered three days of team competition in late November 2025; each day consisted of a full-day team-competition session (approx. 7–8 h including breaks, preparation, and post-session questionnaires) in a naturalistic field setting. Participants accessed the system intermittently while watching the matches, rather than engaging in continuous task-based interaction. Before the field trial, they reviewed a short manual and tutorial video, performed trial posts with tags, and tested multimodal functions by uploading sample images and videos for LLM-based text generation. During the event, DHH/BLV participants both viewed and posted content.

Exposition 2025 Supplementary Demonstration. We ran a short demonstration at a large exposition in August 2025 and analyzed brief on-site surveys (N = 35) collected on the demonstration day (predominantly general visitors). This dataset is treated as supplementary acceptance feedback rather than a controlled DHH/BLV usability evaluation.

3.3 Measures and Analysis

Questionnaires. For the Deaflympics deployments, the core questionnaire structure was shared across DHH and BLV participants and included:

- SUS (10 items, 5-point Likert) for usability [5],
- experience items (5-point Likert): enjoyment, perceived usefulness, and overall experience,
- feature preferences (multi-select), and
- open-ended feedback.

We also collected self-reported background information, including disability category, disability certificate grade in the Japanese administrative system, and, where applicable, hearing level, hearing devices, and everyday script. For the exposition deployment, we collected two 5-point Likert items (overall experience and perceived value of the project) together with open comments.

Table 2. Deaflympics 2025 outcomes (mean (SD)). N indicates questionnaire responses. Likert items: 1–5.

Context	N	SUS (0–100)	Overall exp.	Usefulness
Badminton matches	15	74.2 (15.3)	4.93 (0.26)	4.67 (0.62)
Ceremonies	6	67.1 (13.6)	4.00 (0.89)	4.33 (0.82)
All Deaflympics	21	**72.1 (14.9)**	**4.67 (0.66)**	**4.57 (0.68)**

Analysis. Because these were field deployments in naturalistic event settings and questionnaire counts refer to responses rather than unique individuals, we report descriptive statistics only. For quantitative items, we report means and standard deviations. Open-ended comments were reviewed and summarized using thematic grouping.

4 Results

4.1 Quantitative Results

Table 2 summarizes the key outcomes from the Deaflympics 2025 deployment. Across all questionnaire responses, SUS averaged 72.1 ($SD = 14.9$), with high enjoyment (4.52/5), usefulness (4.57/5), and overall experience (4.67/5). For the badminton matches, exploratory subgroup descriptives based on questionnaire responses showed SUS = 73.3 (SD = 17.0; DHH responses: N = 12) and 77.5 (SD = 4.3; BLV responses: N = 3). Given the small number of BLV responses and the response-based counts, these values are reported for transparency only.

Overall experience was lower in ceremonies ($M = 4.00$) than in matches ($M = 4.93$), although usefulness remained high ($M = 4.33$). Comments suggest that live-stream viewing introduced caption-timing inconsistencies and a dual-task load (watching while interacting), which may have reduced enjoyment.

Supplementary Exposition Feedback. In the exposition demonstration ($N = 35$), the mean overall experience was 4.83/5 ($SD = 0.45$), and the perceived value of the project was 4.77/5 ($SD = 0.43$).

4.2 Qualitative Themes

Across the Deaflympics questionnaire responses, open-ended comments emphasized three themes:

1. **Real-time situational access:** receiving score and flow information via posts reduced feelings of being left out when announcements or visual cues were inaccessible.
2. **Reciprocity beyond commentary:** lightweight reactions and spectator posts conveyed atmosphere and situational cues alongside designated commentary; ambient cues also supported co-presence and mutual support.
3. **Accessibility and remaining issues:** responses from BLV users highlighted the value of automatic media descriptions, while noting that imperfect accuracy, session stability (e.g., unintended logout), and overlapping screen-reader outputs could reduce usefulness.

5 Discussion and Limitations

The field results indicate that stakeholder-driven iteration can yield high perceived usefulness and positive experiences in dynamic event venues. The difference between badminton and ceremonies suggests that pacing, content type, and available alternative channels influence perceived value.

Several limitations should be noted. First, the deployments were conducted in context-specific field settings, and the questionnaire counts reported in this paper refer to responses rather than unique individuals; in the badminton deployment, repeat responses across days were possible. Second, the study relies primarily on self-report measures and descriptive analysis. Third, the BLV response count was small, and the exposition survey should be interpreted as acceptance-oriented y feedback rather than as a controlled DHH/BLV usability evaluation. Although the redesign was informed by prior pilot deployments, stakeholder involvement was stronger in iterative refinement than in the earliest concept-generation phase.

Future work will add log-based analyses and targeted evaluations of new features (e.g., environmental sound recognition and video analysis). As a practical next step, we plan to release a self-hostable open-source implementation to support community-run deployments and context-specific customization.

6 Conclusion

We reported stakeholder-driven improvements to an accessible real-time timeline web application and presented field evidence from Deaflympics 2025, supported by SUS, experience ratings, and qualitative feedback. The findings suggest that iterative, stakeholder-led development can translate into positive outcomes in real-world, time-critical event environments, while pointing to next-step refinements for content accuracy, session robustness, and inclusive participation.

Acknowledgments. This study was supported by internal funding from National University Corporation Tsukuba University of Technology through its management expenses grants (mission-oriented strategic funding).

Disclosure of Interests. The authors have no competing interests to declare that are relevant to the content of this article.

References

1. World Wide Web Consortium (W3C): Web Content Accessibility Guidelines (WCAG) 2.1 (2018). https://www.w3.org/TR/WCAG21/. Accessed 17 Apr 2026
2. Shiraishi, Y., et al.: Enhancing accessibility in sports and cultural live events: a web application for deaf, hard of hearing, blind, low vision, and all individuals. In: Miesenberger, K., Peňáz, P., Kobayashi, M. (eds.) ICCHP 2024. LNCS, vol. 14750, pp. 155–163. Springer, Cham (2024). https://doi.org/10.1007/978-3-031-62846-7_19
3. Butler, J.: Perspectives of deaf and hard of hearing viewers of captions. Am. Ann. Deaf **163**(5), 534–553 (2019). https://doi.org/10.1353/aad.2019.0002
4. International Organization for Standardization: ISO 9241-210:2019. Ergonomics of human-system interaction—Part 210: Human-centred design for interactive systems (2019)
5. Brooke, J.: SUS: a "quick and dirty" usability scale. In: Jordan, P.W., Thomas, B., Weerdmeester, B.A., McClelland, I.L. (eds.) Usability Evaluation in Industry, pp. 189–194. Taylor & Francis, London (1996)
6. Lasecki, W.S., Miller, C.D., Bigham, J.P.: Warping time for more effective real-time crowdsourcing. In: Proceedings of the SIGCHI Conference on Human Factors in Computing Systems (CHI 2013), pp. 2033–2036. ACM, New York (2013). https://doi.org/10.1145/2470654.2466269
7. Luckner, J.L., Bruce, S.M., Ferrell, K.A.: A summary of the communication and literacy evidence-based practices for students who are deaf or hard of hearing, visually impaired, and deafblind. Commun. Disord. Q. **37**(4), 225–241 (2016). https://doi.org/10.1177/1525740115597507
8. Vreeken, H.L., van Nispen, R.M.A., Kramer, S.E., van Rens, G.H.M.B.: 'Dual sensory loss protocol' for communication and wellbeing of older adults with vision and hearing impairment - a randomized controlled trial. Front. Psychol. **11**, 570339 (2020). https://doi.org/10.3389/fpsyg.2020.570339
9. Aira: Aira Explorer: on-demand visual interpreting for the blind and low vision community (2026). https://go.aira.io/. Accessed 17 Apr 2026
10. Samsung: Samsung Good Vibes and Relúmĭno to brighten up lives of the deafblind and vision impaired (2018). https://news.samsung.com/in/samsung-good-vibes-and-relumino-to-brighten-up-lives-of-the-deafblind-and-vision-impaired. Accessed 17 Apr 2026
11. Loaiza-Ramírez, I., González-Beltrán, B.A.: Digital accessibility guidelines for deaf and hard of hearing persons: a state-of-the-art review article. Univ. Access Inf. Soc. **25**, 4 (2026). https://doi.org/10.1007/s10209-025-01270-y

Author Index

K. Miesenberger et al. (Eds.): ICCHP 2026, LNCS 16867, pp. 601–603, 2027.
https://doi.org/10.1007/978-3-032-31308-9

MIX
Papier aus verantwortungsvollen Quellen
Paper from responsible sources
FSC® C105338

If you have any concerns about our products,
you can contact us on
ProductSafety@springernature.com

In case Publisher is established outside the EU,
the EU authorized representative is:
Springer Nature Customer Service Center GmbH
Europaplatz 3, 69115 Heidelberg, Germany

Printed by Libri Plureos GmbH
in Hamburg, Germany